TEACHING TODAY
Tasks and Challenges

J. Michael Palardy
University of Alabama

Macmillan Publishing Co., Inc.
New York

Collier Macmillan Publishers
London

Macmillan Publishing Co., Inc.
866 Third Avenue, New York, New York 10022
Collier-Macmillan Canada, Ltd.

Library of Congress Cataloging in Publication Data

Palardy, J   Michael, comp.
  Teaching today; tasks and challenges.

  Includes bibliographies.
  1. Teaching—Addresses, essays, lectures. I. Title.
LB1025.2.P34   371.1′02′08   73-19493
ISBN 0-02-390410-0

Printing: 1 2 3 4 5 6 7 8   Year: 5 6 7 8 9 0

dedicated to
ARTHUR and AUDREY PALARDY

Preface

This book of readings is intended specifically for prospective and practicing teachers at the elementary and secondary levels. It is intended generally for anyone interested in learning about one of today's most demanding professional activities—teaching.

The complexity of teaching is reflected in the book's seven parts—Part I: "An Overview of Teaching," Part II: "Planning for Teaching," Part III: "Teaching for Thinking and Feeling," Part IV: "Some Strategies of Teaching," Part V: "Motivating and Managing in Teaching," Part VI: "Understanding and Teaching the 'Different' Student," and Part VII: "Evaluating in Teaching." Articles for each part were selected on the basis of three criteria. First, they were deemed particularly capable of provoking thought and discussion at differing conceptual levels. Second, they were viewed as being highly related to the instructional concerns of both elementary and secondary educators. Third, they were seen as representing a variety of current viewpoints.

Readers need to apply the same criteria in studying the articles as the editor used in selecting them. For if they are not discussed and analyzed publicly, much of their potential impact will be wasted. If they are not viewed as relating to the instructional concerns of both elementary and secondary educators, much of the commonality inherent in teaching at any level will go unnoticed. And if they are not seen as offering divergent points of view about key educational issues and problems, much of the challenge of teaching today will remain underestimated and many of its tasks undischarged.

To the writers and publishers who kindly granted permission to reprint their materials the editor extends his sincere thanks, and to the readers of these materials he wishes the best of success.

J. M. P.

Contents

I An Overview of Teaching

In the first chapter of his book Crisis in the Classroom, *Charles Silberman makes the following statement:*

It is not possible to spend any prolonged period visiting public school classrooms without being appalled by the mutilation visible everywhere—mutilation of spontaneity, of joy in learning, of pleasure in creating, of sense of self. The public schools . . . are the kind of institution one cannot really dislike until one gets to know them well. Because adults take the schools so much for granted, they fail to appreciate what grim, joyless places most American schools are, how oppressive and petty are the rules by which they are governed, how intellectually sterile and esthetically barren the atmosphere, what an appalling lack of civility obtains on the part of teachers and principals, what contempt they unconsciously display for children as children.[1]

[1] Charles E. Silberman, *Crisis in the Classroom* (New York: Random House, Inc., 1970), p. 10.

In selection 1, Silberman elaborates on these remarks. The reader might question why his selection—as critical of education as it is—was chosen as the initial selection. The answer is twofold. First, in the opinion of many, Silberman's assessment of what schools are like is correct. The reader needs to know early that such opinions do exist. Second, it is not the intention here to sell the reader on teaching or to persuade him to enter the profession. It is, rather, to present him with the challenge of helping the schools improve. If the reader can muster the courage and master the skills needed to confront this challenge, in my opinion —regardless of how good or bad today's schools are—tomorrow's will be better.

Like Silberman, Jackson also believes some schools are failing, but he thinks their failures are generally less numerous and serious. Jackson, in article 2, points out that today's more radical critics are claiming that schools have outlived or outgrown their usefulness and that society would be better off without them. Theirs is the so-called school-is-dead argument. Jackson identifies three potential strategies opponents of this argument could use. The first is to ignore the argument; the second is to expose weaknesses in it; and the third is to learn and profit from it. It is the last of these strategies that Jackson endorses.

Broudy begins his selection (3) by noting that most critics of today's schools identify teachers as the basic obstacle to progress. Why, Broudy asks, are teachers so nonadaptive in responding to calls for educational change? The answer, Broudy suggests, is that teachers are being asked to fill roles that are beyond any reasonable set of expectations. "First, there is the over-all expectation that the teacher be an expert in teaching; second, that he represent the ideal parent; third, that he represent the community at its ideal best; fourth, that he represent the human being at his best."[2] Broudy's analysis of these expectations should help place whatever shortcomings teachers might have in proper perspective.

In selection 3, Broudy claims that research designed to identify characteristics of good teachers has been generally, if not totally, nonproductive. But Hamachek, in article 4, disagrees and makes the counterclaim that research has identified at least some of these characteristics. With all other factors being equal, Hamachek argues, effective and ineffective teachers differ in one or more of the following ways: (1) their personality styles, (2) their instructional procedures, (3) their self-perceptions, and (4) their perceptions of others. Additional research is needed, Hamachek admits, but not so much as the application of what is already known.

In article 5, Graybeal presents data showing that there is now, and probably will continue to be, an oversupply of beginning teachers. It should be noted that even in the late 1960s and early 1970s many teachers were finding positions difficult to find, particularly in certain geographic regions and in some content areas. Obviously, the prospective teacher needs to consider these data carefully before committing himself to a professional education sequence. Happily, the

[2] Harry S. Broudy, *The Real World of the Public Schools* (New York: Harcourt Brace Jovanovich, Inc., 1972), p. 54.

time is past when teaching could be considered a safe bet against the perils of an unpredictable marketplace.

Southworth, in article 6, projects an image of the classroom teacher of 1980. He will be highly prepared, well paid, and extremely competent. Among educators, at least, there is little disagreement about the need for realizing this image. But there is considerable disagreement about two of its specific features, namely competence and preparation. What constitutes competence in teaching, and which method of preparing teachers best facilitates their achieving it? As seen in earlier articles, these and related questions are not easily answered. Unless and until they are, Southworth's projection may be in jeopardy.

1 Crisis in the Classroom: Education for Docility

Charles E. Silberman

Teachers almost invariably take their pupils as they find them; they turn them, beat them, card them, comb them, drill them into certain forms, and expect them to become a finished and polished product; and if the result does not come up to their expectations (and I ask you how could it?) they are indignant, angry, and furious. And yet we are surprised that some men shrink and recoil from such a system. Far more is it a matter for surprise that any one can endure it at all.

—John Amos Comenius,
The Great Didactic, 1632

I

Our preoccupation with the urban crisis must not be permitted to blind us to the important, if less urgent, defects of public schools everywhere. In good measure, the defects and failures of the slum schools are but an exaggerated version of what's wrong with *all* schools. To be sure, the schools in middle-class neighborhoods seem to do a better job of teaching the basic skills of literacy and computation, hence their students are better equipped to earn a living. But this "success" is due far less to the schools themselves than to what has been called "the hidden curriculum of the middle-class home."

Moreover, students need to learn far more than the basic skills. For children who may still be in the labor force in the year 2030, nothing could be more wildly impractical than an education designed to prepare them for specific vocations or professions or to facilitate their adjustment to the world as it is. To be "practical," an education should prepare them for work that does not yet exist and whose nature cannot even be imagined. This can only be done by teaching them how to learn, by giving them the kind of intellectual discipline that will enable them to apply man's accumulated wisdom to new problems as they arise—the kind of wisdom that will enable them to *recognize* new problems as they arise. "The qualities essential to employability and productivity," Francis S. Chase, former dean of the Graduate School of Education of the University of

Chicago, has written, with some exaggeration, "are coming closer and closer to the characteristics that have long been attributed to the educated person."

More important, education should prepare people not just to earn a living but to live a life—a creative, humane, and sensitive life. This means that the schools must provide a liberal, humanizing education. And the purpose of liberal education must be, and indeed always has been, to educate educators —to turn out men and women who are capable of educating their families, their friends, their communities, and most importantly, themselves. "Though we cannot promise to produce educated men and women," says the catalogue of the College of the University of Chicago, whose faculty has thought harder about educational purpose than most faculties, "we do endeavour to bring each student . . . to a point beyond which he can educate himself." This must also be the purpose of the public schools.

Of what does the capacity to educate oneself consist? It means that a person has both the desire and the capacity to learn for himself, to dig out what he needs to know, as well as the capacity to judge what is worth learning. It means, too, that one can think for himself, so that he is dependent on neither the opinions nor the facts of others, and that he uses that capacity to think about his own education, which means to think about his own nature and his place in the universe—about the meaning of life and of knowledge and of the relations between them. "To refuse the effort to understand," Wayne Booth, dean of the College of the University of Chicago, argues, "is to resign from the human race." You cannot distinguish an educated man, he continues, "by whether or not he believes in God, or in UFO's. But you can tell an educated man by the way he takes hold of the question of whether God exists, or whether UFO's are from Mars."[1]

To be educated in this sense means also to know something of the experience of beauty—if not in the sense of creating it or discoursing about it, then at the very least, in the sense of being able to respond to it, to respond both to the beauty of nature and to the art made by our fellow men. "To find and appreciate beauty in the ordinary and the extraordinary is the right of every child," the Ontario, Canada Provincial Committee on Aims and Objectives of Education, has written, "for esthetic experience is a basic need of all men in their universal struggle to add meaning to life. We owe to children the freedom to explore the full range of their senses; to appreciate subtle differences; to be aware of beauty wherever it is found; to see, to touch, to smell, to hear, to taste, so that each in his own way will strive to find and express the meaning of man and human destiny."[2]

[1] Wayne C. Booth, "Is There Any Knowledge That a Man Must Have?", in Wayne C. Booth, ed., *The Knowledge Most Worth Having,* University of Chicago Press, 1967. Booth's essay and his introduction to the volume represent the best brief statement about liberal education in recent years.

[2] *Living and Learning: A Report of the Provincial Committee on Aims and Objectives of Education in the Schools of Ontario,* Ontario, Canada: Department of Education, 1968.

To be educated also means to understand something of how to make our intentions effective in the real world—of how to apply knowledge to the life one lives and the society in which one lives it. The aim of education, as Alfred North Whitehead has written, "is the acquisition of the art of the utilization of knowledge." Indeed, "a merely well-informed man is the most useless bore on God's earth."

The schools fail to achieve any of these goals. They fail in another and equally important way. Education is not only a preparation for later life; it is an aspect of life itself. The great bulk of the young now spend a minimum of twelve years in school; with kindergarten attendance, and now preschool programs, becoming more widespread, more and more of the young will have spent thirteen to fifteen years in school by the time they receive their high school diploma.

The quality of that experience must be regarded as important in its own right. A good school, as the English "Plowden Committee" insists in its magnificent report on *Children and Their Primary Schools,* "is a community in which children learn to live first and foremost as children and not as future adults."[3] The Committee is exaggerating, to be sure, when it goes on to insist that "the best preparation for being a happy and useful man and woman is to live fully as a child"—an exaggeration from which many American progressive schools of the 1920s and 1930s suffered. "Merely to let children live free, natural, childlike lives," as Carleton Washburne, one of the giants of American progressivism, warned in 1925, "may be to fail to give them the training they need to meet the problems of later life." Thus Washburne insisted on a dual focus. "Every child has the right to live fully and naturally as a child," he wrote. "Every child has the right also to be prepared adequately for later effective living as an adult."[4] In the grim, repressive, joyless places most schools now are, children are denied both those rights.

II

Every society educates its young. Until fairly recently, however, few societies saw fit to educate many of their young in schools. For most of man's history, most children have received most of their education informally and incidentally. Family and community, and in some societies, the church, were the primary educating institutions, shaping young people's attitudes, forming their behavior, endowing them with morals and manners, and teaching them the vocational and other skills needed to get along in their physical and social environments. The processes of education were informal, traditional, and

[3] Central Advisory Council for Education (England), *Children and Their Primary Schools,* London: Her Majesty's Stationery Office, 1967.

[4] *Progressive Education,* July–September 1925.

largely unconscious and unarticulated; children learned in the main by being included in adult activities.[5]

Much education is still carried on in this way. During their first years of life, children—all children—manage perhaps the most complicated bit of learning that humans do: they learn to talk, to use language. And they learn this through processes so informal, yet so complex, that we can barely describe, let alone understand, them. What we *are* beginning to understand is the enormity of the accomplishment. Learning to speak involves far more than simply absorbing, through constant repetition, the patterns of speech the child has heard around his home. On the contrary, much of what the child who has learned to talk says in the course of ordinary conversation is entirely new. His conversation is not a repetition of anything he has heard before. The same is true of what he hears: the number of sentences we are all able to understand, immediately and with no sense of strangeness, is almost infinite.[6]

Looking at the success of the informal processes of learning to talk—Paul Goodman calls it "the archetype of successful education"—and contrasting it with the widespread failures of formal schooling, a growing number of critics have begun to wonder if *all* education should not be carried on informally and incidentally.[7] These critics are part of a tradition several centuries old. "Go, my sons . . . burn your books . . . buy yourselves stout shoes, get away to the mountains, search the valleys, the deserts, the shores of the sea, and the deepest recesses of the earth . . ." Peter Severinus urged,[8] expressing sentiments that might have been lifted from any number of Paul Goodman's essays and books. The warning that "our pedantic mania for instruction is always leading us to teach children things which they would learn better of their own accord" sounds like John Holt; it was Rousseau's.

There is another tradition of criticism, however, typified by John Amos Comenius, a seventeenth-century Czech religious leader. Comenius was as harshly critical of the schools of his day—"slaughterhouses of the mind," he called them—as Rousseau was of the schools of his, but Comenius proposed to reform rather than abolish them. To Rousseau, as to Goodman and Holt, Nature made formal education unnecessary; the best education was to let Nature unfold, to permit the child to follow his own instincts and desires. Comenius, on

[5] Cf., for example, the description of education in colonial America in Bernard Bailyn, *Education in the Forming of American Society*, New York: Vintage Books, 1960.

[6] Cf. Noam Chomsky, *Language and Mind*, New York: Harcourt, Brace & World, 1968.

[7] Cf. John Holt, *How Children Fail*, New York: Pitman Publishing Corp., 1964; Paul Goodman, "The Present Moment in Education," *New York Review of Books*, April 10, 1969, and *Compulsory Mis-Education*, New York: Horizon Press, 1965; Fred M. Newmann and Donald W. Oliver, "Education and Community," *Harvard Educational Review*, Winter 1967; Edgar Z. Friedenberg, *The Dignity of Youth & Other Atavisms*, Boston: Beacon Press, 1965, and *Coming of Age in America*, New York: Random House, 1964; George Dennison, *The Lives of Children*, New York: Random House, 1969; A. S. Neill, *Summerhill*, New York: Hart Publishing Company, 1960.

[8] Thomas Woody, "Historical Sketch of Activism," in National Society for the Study of Education, 33rd Year Book, Part II, *The Activity Movement*, 1934.

the other hand, saw Nature as providing the basis for education, but not education itself. "While the seeds of knowledge, of virtue, and of piety are naturally implanted within us," he wrote, "the actual knowledge, virtue and piety are not so given. These must be acquired." Hence "all who are born to man's estate have need of instruction" if they are to fulfill their potential as men. Comenius has been succeeded by a long roster of reformers—Pestalozzi, Froebel, Herbart, Horace Mann, John Dewey—who railed against the evils of the schools and tried to reform them.

The persistence of the same kinds of criticisms of the schools over several centuries makes it clear that despite profound differences in cultures, technologies, languages, and the like, there are remarkable uniformities in the way schools are organized and run. "In a fundamental sense," as Philip W. Jackson of the University of Chicago, one of the most sensitive and subtle contemporary students of schooling, concludes, "school is school, no matter where it happens"[9] This is so because of a number of characteristics virtually all schools share in common. (Other institutions, of course, e.g., factories, offices, the armed services, share some or all of these characteristics.)

1. There is, to begin with, the element of compulsion, the fact that children are in school involuntarily. In the United States, school attendance is required by law. But even when attendance is not legally required, the decision to attend school, especially for younger children, generally is made not by the child but by his parents. Whether compulsion is by the state or by his parents is largely immaterial to the child; what matters to him is that he *must* be in school whether he wants to or not—and that there are likely to be penalties for not being there.

2. Children not only must be in school, they must be in school for long periods of time. School generally lasts five to six hours a day, five days a week, thirty to forty weeks a year, for twelve or more years.

3. School is a collective experience, since the economies of scale require a student-teacher ratio of more than one. This is crucial for the child: being in school means being in a crowd. And it is crucial for the teacher, who is always responsible for a group of students.

4. School is almost always evaluative. Going to school means living under a constant condition of having one's words and deeds evaluated by others. Given the way in which evaluation is usually handled, this in turn means a sharp demarcation of power and authority between student and teacher. The teacher not only is the one who keeps the child in school, he is also the one who evaluates him.

Most of the characteristics that make school school, no matter where it is, flow out of these four constants. Indeed, they produce patterns of behavior so uniform and constant over time and across cultures as to suggest that schools

---

[9] Philip W. Jackson, *Life in Classrooms,* New York: Holt, Rinehart & Winston, 1968. Jackson offers a devastating picture of how repressive and stultifying schools are—all the more devastating, in view of the fact that Jackson, who is principal of the University of Chicago's Nursery School as well as professor of education, essentially approves of the way schools are run, on the grounds that there is no other way.

form almost a subculture of their own. Schools differ, of course, according to the nature of the community they serve, the education of the children's parents, the school's own history and tradition, the outlook of its teachers and administrators, and so on. But the differences tend to be differences in degree, not in kind; in any case, they are relatively trivial compared to the uniformities and similarities. . . .

III

The most important characteristic schools share in common is a preoccupation with order and control. In part, this preoccupation grows out of the fact that school is a collective experience requiring, in the minds of those who run it, subordination of individual to collective or institutional desires and objectives. "It is only because teachers wish to force students to learn that any unpleasantness ever arises to mar their relationship," Willard Waller observed nearly four decades ago, in his classic *The Sociology of Teaching.* "We have defined the school as the place where people meet for the purpose of giving and receiving instruction. If this process were unforced, if students could be allowed to learn only what interested them, to learn in their own way, and to learn no more and no better than it pleased them to do, if good order were not considered a prerequisite to learning, if teachers did not have to be taskmasters, but merely helpers and friends, then life would be sweet in the school room. These, however," Waller adds, "are all conditions contrary to fact. The conditions of mass instruction and of book instruction make it necessary that learning be forced."[10] Or as Philip Jackson puts it, "If students were allowed to stick with a subject until they grew tired of it on their own, our present curriculum would have to be modified drastically. Obviously, some kinds of controls are necessary if the school goals are to be reached and social chaos averted."

One of the most important controls is the clock; as Jackson puts it, "school is a place where things often happen not because students want them to, but because it is time for them to occur." This in turn means that a major part of the teacher's role is to serve as traffic manager and timekeeper, either deciding on a schedule himself or making sure that a schedule others have made is adhered to.

Several things follow from this. Adherence to a timetable means that a great deal of time is wasted, the experiencing of delay being one of the inevitable outcomes of traffic management. No one who examines classroom life carefully can fail to be astounded by the proportion of the students' time that is taken up just in waiting. The time is rarely used productively. Hence in the elementary grades, an able student can be absent from school for an entire week and, quite literally, catch up with all he has missed in a single morning.

More important, adherence to a rigid timetable means that activities, as

[10] Willard Waller, *The Sociology of Teaching,* New York: John Wiley & Sons Science Editions, 1965.

Jackson puts it, "often begin before interest is aroused and terminate before interest disappears." Adherence to the schedule also means that lessons frequently end before the students have mastered the subject at hand. As Herbert Kohl points out, "the tightness with time that exists in the elementary school has nothing to do with the quantity that must be learned or the children's needs. It represents the teacher's fear of loss of control and is nothing but a weapon used to weaken the solidarity and opposition of the children that too many teachers unconsciously dread."[11]

It is all too easy, of course, for the outsider to criticize. Unless one has taught (as this writer and members of his staff have), or has studied classroom procedures close-up (as we have also done), it is hard to imagine the extent of the demands made on a teacher's attention. Jackson's studies of teacher-student interchange, for example, indicate that "the teacher typically changes the focus of his concern about 1,000 times daily," with many lasting only a few seconds, most less than a minute.[12] One of the hard facts of teaching (and teaching is a very hard occupation), therefore, as Professor Lee J. Cronbach of Stanford suggests, is that "there will always be some momentary distraction; habitually pursuing the spur-of-the-moment theme reduces the curriculum to a shambles." There are occasions when it is wise to depart from the lesson plan—surely the assassination of a President, a distinguished civil rights leader and Nobel Laureate, and a senator contending for the Presidency are such occasions—but there are also times when the teacher may be well advised to resist the seduction of talking about the day's headlines.

The trouble, then, is not with the schedule or the lesson plan *per se*, but with the fact that teachers too often see them as ends in themselves rather than as means to an end. As Professor Joseph C. Grannis of Teachers College puts it, the lesson plan tends to be regarded not as a convenient device for regulating classroom decisions, but as a "moral contract that a teacher is *obliged* to deliver on." (Emphasis his) Even when children are excited about something directly related to the curriculum, therefore, teachers ignore or suppress the interest if it is not on the agenda for that period.

The tyranny of the lesson plan in turn encourages an obsession with routine for the sake of routine. School is filled with countless examples of teachers and administrators confusing means with ends, thereby making it impossible to reach the end for which the means were devised.

Administrators tend to be even guiltier of this kind of mindlessness and slavish adherence to routine for the sake of routine. It is, in a sense, built into their

[11] Herbert Kohl, *36 Children*, New York: New American Library, 1967.

[12] Philip W. Jackson, "The Way Teaching Is," in Association for Supervision and Curriculum Development and the Center for the Study of Instruction, *The Way Teaching Is,* Washington, D.C.: National Education Association, 1966. Cf. also Herbert M. Kliebard, "The Observation of Classroom Behavior—Some Recent Research," in the same pamphlet.

job description and into the way in which they view their role. Most schools are organized and run to facilitate order; the principal or superintendent is considered, and considers himself, a manager whose job is to keep the organization running as efficiently as possible.[13]

    .　　.　　.

This preoccupation with efficiency, which is to say with order and control, turns the teacher into a disciplinarian as well as a timekeeper and traffic manager. In the interest of efficiency, moreover, discipline is defined in simple but rigid terms: the absence of noise and of movement. "When we ask children *not* to move, we should have excellent reasons for doing so," an English psychologist and educator, Susan Isaacs of the University of London, argued in 1932. "It is stillness we have to justify, not movement." But no justification is offered or expected. Indeed, there is no more firmly rooted school tradition than the one that holds that children must sit still at their desks without conversing at all, both during periods of waiting, when they have nothing to do, and during activities that almost demand conversation. Yet even on an assembly line, there is conversation and interaction among workers, and there are coffee breaks and work pauses as well.

    .　　.　　.

Silence is demanded, moreover, despite the fact that school children work in very close quarters. "Even factory workers are not clustered as close together as students in a standard classroom," Jackson observes. "Once we leave the classroom we seldom again are required to have contact with so many people for so long a time." Yet despite the close contact, students are required to ignore those around them. They "must try to behave as if they were in solitude, when in point of fact they are not. They must keep their eyes on their paper when human faces beckon. Indeed, in the early grades it is not uncommon to find students facing each other around a table while at the same time being required not to communicate with each other." To become successful students, they "must learn how to be alone in a crowd."

Silence is demanded even when students are moving from one class to another.

    .　　.　　.

The ban on movement extends to the entire school. Thus, students in most schools cannot leave the classroom (or the library or the study hall) without permission, even to get a drink of water or to go to the toilet, and the length of time they can spend there is rigidly prescribed. In high schools and junior highs, the corridors are usually guarded by teachers and students on patrol duty, whose principal function is to check the credentials of any student walking through. In the typical high school, no student may walk down the corridor without a form, signed by a teacher, telling where he is coming from, where he is going, and the

---

[13] Cf. Raymond E. Callahan, *Education and the Cult of Efficiency*, University of Chicago Press, 1962. This myopia is not limited to school administrators. Cf. Peter F. Drucker, *The Effective Executive*, New York: Harper & Row, 1967, on the need to distinguish between effectiveness (getting the right things done) and efficiency (getting things done right).

time, to the minute, during which the pass is valid. In many schools, the toilets are kept locked except during class breaks, so that a student not only must obtain a pass but must find the custodian and persuade him to unlock the needed facility. Indeed, the American high school's "most memorable arrangements," as Edgar Z. Friedenberg puts it, "are its corridor passes and its johns; they dominate social interaction."[14] There are schools, of course, where some of these arrangements have a rational basis—where school authorities are legitimately concerned about the intrusion of outsiders, where traffic in heroin and other narcotics is brisk. But the same regulations have obtained for as long as anyone can recall. Even during periods when students do not have a class, they must be in a study hall or some other prescribed place. It is a rare school, for example, in which students are permitted to go to the library if they have a free period; the library is open to them only if they have an assigned "library period," or if they manage to wangle a pass for that purpose from the librarian or some other person in authority.

.   .   .

These petty rules and regulations are necessary not simply because of the importance schoolmen attach to control—they like to exercise control, it would seem, over what comes out of the bladder as well as the mouth—but also because schools, and school systems, operate on the assumption of distrust. "The school board has no faith in the central administration, the central administration has no faith in the principals, the principals have no faith in the teachers, and the teachers have no faith in the students," Christopher Jencks has observed. "In such a system it seems natural not to give the principal of a school control over his budget, not to give the teachers control over their syllabus, and not to give the students control over anything. Distrust is the order of the day."

IV

But how can a group "achieve enough maturity to keep itself under control" if its members never have an opportunity to exercise control? Far from helping students to develop into mature, self-reliant, self-motivated individuals, schools seem to do everything they can to keep youngsters in a state of chronic, almost infantile, dependency. The pervasive atmosphere of distrust, together with rules covering the most minute aspects of existence, teach students every day that they are not people of worth, and certainly not individuals capable of regulating their own behavior.

.   .   .

More important, schools discourage students from developing the capacity to learn by and for themselves; they make it impossible for a youngster to take responsibility for his own education, for they are structured in such a way as to make students totally dependent upon the teachers. Whatever rhetoric they may

[14] Edgar Z. Friedenberg, *Coming of Age in America*, New York: Random House, 1965.

subscribe to, most schools in practice define education as something teachers do to or for students, not something students do to and for themselves, with a teacher's assistance. "Seated at his desk, the teacher is in a position to do something," Jackson reports. *"It is the teacher's job to declare what that something shall be."* (Empahsis added) "It is the teacher who decides who will speak and in what order," and it is the teacher who decides who will have access to the materials of learning.

. . .

The result is to destroy students' curiosity along with their ability—more serious, their desire—to think or act for themselves.

. . .

At the heart of the schoolmen's inability to turn responsibility over to the students is the fact that the teacher-student relationship in its conventional form is, as Willard Waller states, "a form of institutionalized dominance and subordination. Teacher and pupil confront each other in the school with an original conflict of desires, and however much that conflict may be reduced in amount, or however much it may be hidden, it still remains. The teacher represents the adult group, ever the enemy of the spontaneous life of groups of children. The teacher represents the formal curriculum, and his interest is in imposing that curriculum upon the children in the form of tasks; pupils are much more interested in life in their own world than in the desiccated bits of adult life which teachers have to offer. The teacher represents the established social order in the school, and his interest is in maintaining that order, whereas pupils have only a negative interest in that feudal superstructure. Teacher and pupil confront each other with attitudes from which the underlying hostility can never be altogether removed." There is a kernel of truth, in short, as well as a large element of self-pity in the young rebels' fondness for the metaphor of the "student as nigger."

A major source of the underlying hostility is the preoccupation with grades. "Tests are as indigenous to the school environment as are textbooks or pieces of chalk," Jackson observes. "But tests, though they are the classic form of educational evaluation, are not all there is to the process." Indeed, the use of tests "is insufficient to explain the distinctively evaluative atmosphere that pervades the classroom from the earliest grades onward," for almost anything and everything the student does is likely to be evaluated and graded.

The teacher, of course, is the chief source of evaluation. "He is called upon continuously to make judgments of students' work and behavior and to communicate that judgment to the students in question and to others. No one who has observed an elementary classroom for any length of time can have failed to be impressed by the vast number of times the teacher performs this function. Typically, in most classrooms students come to know when things are right or wrong, good or bad, pretty or ugly, largely as a result of what the teacher tells them."

. . .

A corollary of teacher dominance is the teacher's role in doling out privileges from which status flows. "In elementary classrooms, it is usually the teacher who assigns coveted duties, such as serving on the safety patrol, or running the movie projector, or clapping erasers, or handing out supplies," Jackson observes. "Although the delegation of these duties may not take up much of the teacher's time, it does help to give structure to the activities of the room and to fashion the quality of the total experience for many of the partici- pants."

The phenomenon is not limited to elementary schools. "The concept of privilege is important at Milgrim," Edgar Z. Friedenberg observes of one of the representative high schools he describes in *Coming of Age in America*. "Teachers go to the head of the chow line at lunch; whenever I would attempt quietly to stand in line the teacher on hall duty would remonstrate with me. He was right, probably; I was fouling up an entire informal social system by my ostentation. Students on hall patrol also, when relieved from duty, were privileged to come bouncing up to the head of the line; so did seniors. Much of the behavior Milgrim depends on to keep it going is motivated by the reward of getting a government-surplus peanut butter or tuna fish sandwich without stand- ing in line for it."

Still another by-product of teacher dominance, one that has profound consequences for children's attitudes toward learning, is the sharp but wholly artificial dichotomy between work and play which schools create and maintain. Young children make no such distinction. They learn through play, and until they have been taught to make the distinction ("Let's stop playing now, children; it's time to start our work"), they regard all activities in the same light. But the dichotomy grows out of the assumption that nothing can happen unless the teacher makes it happen. "Work entails becoming engaged in a purposeful activity that has been prescribed for us by someone else, an activity in which we would not at that moment be engaged if it were not for some system of authority relationships," Jackson explains. "The teacher, with his prescriptive dicta and his surveillance over the student's attention, provides the missing ingredient that makes work real. The teacher, although he may disclaim the title, is the student's first 'Boss.'"

V

Why are schools so bad?

To read some of the more important and influential contemporary critics of education—men like Edgar Friedenberg, Paul Goodman, John Holt, Jonathan Kozol—one might think that the schools are staffed by sadists and clods who are drawn into teaching by the lure of upward mobility and the opportunity to take out their anger—Friedenberg prefers the sociological term *ressentiment,* or "a kind of free floating ill-temper"—on the students.[15] This impression is conveyed

[15] Edgar Z. Friedenberg, "The Gifted Student and His Enemies," in Friedenberg, *The Dignity of Youth & Other Atavisms,* Boston: Beacon Press, 1965.

less by explicit statement than by nuance and tone—a kind of "aristocratic insouciance," as David Riesman calls it, which these writers affect, in turn reflecting the general snobbery of the educated upper middle class toward the white collar, lower-middle-class world of teachers, social workers, civil servants, and policemen. In recent years this snobbery has become a nasty and sometimes spiteful form of bigotry on the part of many self-made intellectuals, who seem to feel the need to demonstrate their moral and cultural superiority to the lower middle class from which they escaped. A number of critics of American culture, moreover, such as Friedenberg, who is a conscious elitist, Paul Goodman, Norman Mailer, and Leslie Fiedler seem to be particularly attracted by the virility and violence of lower-class life, which they tend to romanticize. They seem unable to show empathy for the problems of the lower-middle-class teacher, whose passivity and fear of violence they deride as effeminate and whose humanity they seem, at times, almost to deny.[16]

But teachers *are* human. To be sure, teaching—like the ministry, law, medicine, business, and government—has its share of angry, hostile, and incompetent people. Most teachers, however, are decent, honest, well-intentioned people who do their best under the most trying circumstances. If they appear otherwise, it is because the institution in which they are engulfed demands it of them. . . .

[16] Compare David Riesman, Introduction to the Grosset Universal Library edition of Reuel Denney's *The Astonished Muse.*

2 Deschooling? No!

Philip W. Jackson

The criticism of schools is a profitable pastime, as a visit to our local bookstore or a glance at a current issue of almost any of our most widely circulated magazines will quickly show. There, in volume after volume and article after article, some of our most well-schooled and well-read journalists, novelists, academicians, ex-teachers, and just plain critics describe the evils of our educational system and discuss what should be done about them. The quality of the writing and the sharpness of the criticism vary from one author to the next, but the overall tone is one of uniform dissatisfaction with things as they are.

Reprinted from *Today's Education: NEA Journal,* 61 (8): 18–22 (November 1972), by permission of author and publisher.

Despite the up-to-the-minute freshness of much of this writing, the fact that many people seem to be unhappy with current educational practices is not exactly new. Our schools have long been the target of critics from all walks of life. Moreover, it would be surprising if this were not so, given the centrality of schooling in the lives of our citizens and the complexity of the institution designed to perform this important service.

What *is* new in the current situation is a marked increase in the amount of criticism reflecting a corresponding growth in the size of the critics' audience. What is also new and even more important in the current scene is a marked radicalization of the critics' proposals for change.

Until quite recently, the desirability of schools and of compulsory attendance by the young were more or less taken for granted by friend and foe alike. The aim of both, even of those who were most unhappy with the status quo, was not to do away with schools as we now know them, but somehow to improve their operation.

Now from a growing number of writers—including such prominent critics as Ivan Illich, Everett Reimer, John Holt, and the late Paul Goodman—the message is that improving what we presently have is not enough. Today's schools, so the argument goes, have outlived or outgrown their usefulness. They are institutional dinosaurs that should either be hunted down or allowed to sink of their own dead weight into the swamps of academia.

The aggressive brashness of such a charge, with its not-so-subtle promise of a good old-fashioned free-for-all between defenders of our schools and their attackers, is bound to generate excitement and to bring out crowds of onlookers. And, clearly, the school-is-dead argument has done just that. Its proponents appear on talk shows, testify before Congressional committees, are given front-page space in Sunday magazine sections, and are even in demand as speakers at educational conventions!

For those of us who work in these allegedly dead or dying institutions, living, as it were, like parasites ecologically tied to the fate our dinosaur hosts, there is the serious question of what to do in the face of such allegations. Should we simply ignore them and get on with our work? Should we pause to reply? Might we, in a more hopeful vein, actually learn something from those who would have us go out of business and, armed with that new learning, return with even greater strength and deepened conviction to the task at hand? In my judgment, there is something to be said on behalf of each of these alternatives.

At first glance, the strategy of simply ignoring the deschoolers does seem a bit foolhardy, if not downright stupid. It brings to mind images of Nero with his legendary fiddle or of ostriches with their heads stuck in the sand.

How dare we ignore the enemy veritably clamoring at our gates? The answer, in part, depends on how serious we judge the threat to be, a judgment that requires a detailed examination of the critics' charges. If Rome is *really* burning or if the ostrich hunters are *really* nearby, then larger numbers of us had better turn from whatever we are doing and consider what should be done about the disturbance. This involves becoming critics of the critics, so to speak, an alternative about which more will be said later.

But even if the threat is real, the fact remains that we do have schools that have to be run as best we know how. No matter what the future holds, millions of students and the public at large are counting on us to perform those duties for which we are being paid. Teaching, if it is done well, and school administration, if it is done at all, are full-time jobs, requiring almost all the available time and energy of those who engage in them.

What with daily classes, preparing lessons, grading papers, attending meetings, consulting with parents, and all the other things he is expected to do, there is not much time left for the average teacher to man the barricades, even if the will and ability to do so were strong.

And most school administrators are in a similar fix. Even as I write this, during the final days of my summer vacation, I realize that it is a great luxury for me to have the time to turn my attention to what critics are saying about our schools and to compose, however sketchily, a reasoned reply. Next week, the demands of school administration will descend with a dull thud, and I will look back on this moment and this activity with a feeling akin to nostalgia.

The truth is that most of us who work in schools are (or should be!) too busy to be more than casually engaged in listening to the school- is-dead critics or in responding to what they say. Teaching is a serious undertaking, as is the job of administering a school.

If those who are engaged in these pursuits take their work seriously, they often find little time for anything else. Yet, there may be teachers and administrators who, for a variety of reasons, have energy and time to spare, or there may be teachers from other walks of life, such as university professors, who feel sufficiently incensed to take arms, as it were, against a sea of troubles.

Theirs is the strategy of countercriticism or, if you prefer, counterattack. Fortunately for those of us who are interested in preserving our school system, the writings of most critics reveal weaknesses that seriously damage the force of their argument. The most blatant of these is surely to be found in the demagogic style that characterizes so much of the school-is-dead literature. The tone throughout is strident and at times borders on hysteria.

We are told that our present schools are little more than prisons or concentration camps for the young. Teachers (*all* teachers, presumably) are depicted as mindless and inhumane, and administrators are described as pigheaded and petty tyrants whose main purpose in life seems to be to keep the halls clean and the cafeteria running smoothly. Students, poor things, are crushed by their exposure to these horrible conditions and leave school much worse off than when they entered—with psyches destroyed, spirits sagging, and minds devoid of any true knowledge. It is enough to make the blood boil, which is precisely the intended effect of the authors who write in such a style.

It does not require much analytic power to discern the emotionalism and propagandistic aims of such prose. Hopefully, even the casual reader will take these qualities into account as he judges the critics' case. What does require closer analysis is the detection of flaws in the critics' logic or the scantiness of the evidence they present. Also, more than a casual reading is required to reveal deficiencies in the historical perspective of those who criticize today's schools and in the reasonableness of the alternative proposals they put forth.

Let us consider one or two quick examples of what such an analysis might yield.

Take, for instance, the following statement by John Holt that appeared in a recent issue of *Harper's Magazine* in an article entitled, significantly enough, "The Little Red Prison."

"Thus, as more people learn in school to dislike reading, fewer buy books from bookstores and borrow them from libraries. The bookstores close and the libraries cut back their services, and so we have fewer places in which people outside of school can have ready access to books. This is just one of the ways in which too much school works against education."

A grim picture, indeed. It makes a person want to run out and buy or borrow a couple of books while they are still to be had! But we must ask: Is it true? *Are* more people learning to dislike reading in school? Is the sale of books *really* declining? Are libraries across the nation cutting back their services because of a shortage of interest in their wares? The answer, as all the statistics on publishing and library usage clearly indicate, is emphatically "No!"

Or take another instance, this one chosen almost at random from Ivan Illich's book, *Deschooling Society*. In attempting to analyze what he calls "the phenomenology of school," Illich offers his readers the following gem of syllogistic reasoning:

"School groups people according to age. This grouping rests on three unquestioned premises. Children belong in school. Children learn in school. Children can be taught only in school. I think these unexamined premises deserve serious questioning."

Indeed they do, Mr. Illich. But so does the logic by which the premises are said to lead to the conclusion: "School groups people according to age." We can begin with the assumption that Illich was referring not to the system of grades by which students customarily are grouped *within* school, but rather to the fact that children go to school and adults, for the most part, do not. School, in other words, segregates children from adults. Fair enough, but how does that fact "rest" on the premises? And, further, are the premises themselves seriously held by a significant segment of our population, including, incidentally, our professional educators? Who among us seriously believes that children can be taught only in school?

Other instances of illogic or scant evidence or unreasonable assumptions are easy to come by in the writings of the deschoolers, but these two will have to suffice as illustrations of the kind of detailed criticism that must surely come if we are to take such writings and the proposals contained within them seriously. Some of this countercriticism is already beginning to appear in print, and more is bound to be written.

The chief danger in focusing on flaws in the deschoolers' argument is that such a strategy may blind us to the strengths that are also there. In our zest to prove them wrong, in other words, we may overlook the extent to which the critics are right. And, let's face it: There *is* basis for concern about what our schools are doing and how their operation might be improved. Perhaps, contrary to what John Holt contends, more and more students are not being taught to dislike reading by their school experience, but a goodly number *are,* and we should be worried about that.

Obviously our high schools are *not* the concentration camps that some critics would have us believe, but many students within them do feel constrained and bridled by their experience, and that fact should trouble us.

Certainly the vast majority of our teachers and school administrators are *not* the mindless and unfeeling creatures depicted by some of the less responsible attackers of our schools, but too many of them *are* halfheartedly engaged in what they are about, more concerned with the benefits of their position than with the services they perform. We cannot rest easy so long as this is true.

The list could be extended, but the point is already obvious: There is serious work to be done within our schools.

This brings us to the third and last of the alternative responses educators might presumably take in the face of the deschooling argument. The first was to ignore the critics and get on with our work. The second was to expose weaknesses in the critics' argument, to counterattack, so to speak. The third is to learn from the critics, not simply by having them reinforce our awareness of our schools' shortcomings, but by seeing where their efforts fall short of perfection and by trying to avoid similar pitfalls as we go about trying to improve our schools. Two such shortcomings are worthy of mention and serve well as examples of lessons to be learned from those who would bring lessons, as such, to an end.

As I study the contemporary critics of our schools, it becomes increasingly evident to me that most of them are animated more by a sense of what is *wrong* with our present system than by a conception of what education is all about and how it might proceed. They lack, in other words, a vision of the good in educational terms. What they are *against* is more evident than what they are *for.*

This same tendency, incidentally, is also apparent within the ranks of professional educators as they impatiently work to reduce the abrasiveness of schooling without pausing to give sufficient thought to the educational purpose of the institution. I plead as guilty as the rest in yielding to the natural appeal of such a tactic. After all, it is easier to put oil on squeaky wheels than to ask about where the vehicle is headed in the first place and to ponder the necessity of a change in direction. The danger, of course, is that by so doing we may create a smoothly running machine that is moving in the wrong direction or not at all.

And this is precisely the likelihood we face if we only ask: What is wrong with our schools and how can we correct those faults? In answering such questions, we may indeed produce conditions in which students and teachers are happier and more contented than is presently true, but will those happier and more contented people still be students and teachers in the educational sense of those terms?

Our goal, in other words, cannot simply be to eliminate the discomfort of schooling, though certainly there is much that should be eliminated. Nor can it even be simply to provide environments in which students are learning things they *want* to learn—a favorite image of many of the romantic critics. It must be to create environments—institutions, if you like—in which students are being educated, a different matter entirely.

This last point deserves elaboration, for it contrasts nicely with one of the major premises in the deschooling argument. Many of the more radical critics are fond of reminding their readers that education involves more than schooling—that it can occur in the absence of teachers and courses and classrooms and all of the paraphernalia that we have come to associate with formal schooling. The same argument, incidentally, has recently been adopted as the slogan of several not-so-radical researchers and professors of education who use it to justify turning their attention away from schools and toward other institutions and agencies within our society that perform an educative function.

Now no one can dispute the truism that reminds us of differences between the concepts of education and schooling. Perhaps such a reminder needs to be presented more frequently and more forcefully today than in the past. But there is another truism that needs to be stated with equal force, for it often seems to be overlooked by friend and foe alike. It is that education, in addition to being more than schooling, is also more than learning.

John Dewey, more than any other educator with whom I am familiar, understood supremely both of the cautions to which I have now made reference: that the foundations on which to build a new and constructive view of schooling cannot simply be a reaction to the ailments of our present system and that education involves much more than letting students "do their thing" even when the latter results in significant learning.

Disturbed by the excesses of the reform movement carried out in his name, Dewey pointed out:

"There is always the danger in a new movement that in rejecting the aims and methods of that which it would supplant, it may develop its principles negatively rather than positively and constructively. Then it takes its clew in practice from that which is rejected instead of from the constructive development of its own philosophy."

And, in my judgment, this seems to be precisely what today's would-be reformers are doing. They are saying, in effect, "Here are the features of schooling that are unpleasant. Let us, therefore, make the absence of those features our goal in the design of alternate forms of schooling." The missing element, of course, is a conception of what the process of education leads *toward,* and this can only be supplied by an ethic and a psychology which are conjured in a coherent philosophy or theory of education.

The closest today's critics seem to come to such a conception is their insistence on individual choice and their celebration of man's natural curiosity and his desire to learn. Apparently, if unfettered by institutional constraints, the human spirit will spontaneously seek and achieve those ends that schools are designed to serve. Such is the hope, at any rate. Nor are the critics alone in holding to this belief. Even within our schools themselves a number of persons who call themselves educators seem to be arguing for such a hands-off policy.

Again, it is Dewey who blows the whistle of alarm better than most. Almost 50 years ago he wrote:

There is a present tendency in so-called advanced schools of educational thought . . . to say, in effect, let us surround pupils with certain materials, tools, appliances, etc., and then let pupils respond to these things according to their own desires. Above all, let us not suggest any end or plan to the students; let us not suggest to them what they shall do, for that is an unwarranted trespass upon their sacred intellectual individuality since the essence of such individuality is to set up ends and aims.

Now such a method is really stupid. For it attempts the impossible, which is always stupid; and it misconceives the conditions of independent thinking. There are a multitude of ways of reacting to surrounding conditions and without some guidance from experience these reactions are almost sure to be casual, sporadic, and ultimately fatiguing, accompanied by nervous strain. Since the teacher has presumably a greater background of experience, there is the same presumption of the right of a teacher to make suggestions as to what to do, as there is on the part of a head carpenter to suggest to apprentices something of what they are to do.

Coming from as mild-mannered a man as Dewey, those are strong words indeed. Yet the fact that they are as applicable today as when they first were written suggests that the message they contain remains unheeded by many educational critics both inside and outside the schools. And, I suspect, a major reason why this is so is because to take Dewey's admonition seriously would entail an enormous amount of work and thought on the part of everyone connected with schooling.

It is no easy task to keep our educational purpose in mind while carrying out our day-to-day responsibilities in classrooms and administrative offices; in short, to blend theory and practice. To achieve that end requires nothing less than that each of us, again in Dewey's words, be "possessed by the spirit of an abiding student of education."

Such is the challenge that lies before us if we are to learn from our critics to sidestep some of the pitfalls into which they themselves appear to have fallen. Only then will we truly be able to respond with conviction to those who would claim that schools are passé. Moreover, if we are to avoid a tone of defensiveness and apology, our conviction must be voiced in the language of educational purpose. This means more than empty slogans cloaking an absence of thought, but, rather, a lively and tough-minded discourse that means what it says, that changes as schools change, and that mirrors the reality within them.

Our schools are neither dead nor dying, but neither, unfortunately, are they marked by a degree of vitality and energy that befits the grandeur of their mission. Paradoxically, and even ironically, the writings of those who would bury us may well stimulate such an infusion of new life.

3 The Professional Teacher—A Mischievous Illusion

Harry S. Broudy

The alleged unresponsiveness of the public schools to the wishes of parents, the needs of pupils, and the zeal of reformers has been blamed upon the inertia of bureaucracy, the conservatism of school administrators, and the prejudices of the middle class. However, most editorials, pronouncements of prestigious commissions, and orators at educational conventions sooner or later identify the ultimate, fundamental, basic obstacle to progress as the teacher. Critics who finally locate the sensitive nerve of education in the teacher, of course, are on the right diagnostic route but are led to the further question: why are the teachers of our public schools, both elementary and secondary, so nonadaptive, when it comes to responding to justifiable calls for changes in education?

One way of getting at an answer to this question is to ask another: what sort of competence would teachers have if they were properly responsive to the demands made upon them?

One fairly sure way of getting nowhere with this question is to query teachers, parents, superintendents, supervisors, and pupils about the charac-

From *The Real World of the Public Schools,* copyright © 1972 by Harry S. Broudy. Reprinted by permission of Harcourt Brace Jovanovich, Inc.

teristics of a good teacher. A lot of time and money have been poured down the drain on this kind of research. Instead of providing objective measures of good teaching, the reported traits tell us more about the respondents' psychological history and educational ideology than about the teaching process. One supervisor likes orderly teachers; another is enchanted with enthusiastic ones. Some superintendents find it hard to believe that a pretty young thing can be a poor teacher, but some P-TA mothers find it just as hard to believe she can be a good one. Furthermore, two combinations of the same set of traits may not yield the same judgment.

Even more important than these factors is the psychological bias of the respondent. Invariably the answers indicate what a certain teacher in his own life did to make him feel good or bad about school. And what made him feel good about this teacher? Whatever satisfied some psychological need of the moment, and this satisfier could be anything from a pat on the back to a slap in the face; the "bias" could be anything from a crush on the teacher to hatred of her fiancé. Rarely is the pupil's learning used to measure the goodness of the teaching —even teachers rarely use this as a measure. More often the excitement, eagerness, and interest of the pupils are taken by the teacher as evidence that his teaching is good. This is not a wholly irrelevant way of judging the matter, because given excitement, eagerness, and interest, the chances that learning is going on are better than where there is apathy. But just what is being learned in the excitement, excitement alone does not tell us. Almost any break with school routine—singing popular songs, for example—will generate excitement in a class, but the educational value of rock-and-roll is not thereby established.

A somewhat cynical, but not untypical, way of measuring teaching effectiveness was stated with rare candor by one well-seasoned school superintendent of a small New England city a number of years ago. He put it this way: "Teachers about whom I hear bad things from parents, I rate as poor; they ought not be retained—if they do not already have tenure. Teachers about whom I hear fine things from all quarters, I rate as C. They may be potential troublemakers or bucking for the principal's job. If they get into the newspapers I get really worried." "Who, then," he was asked, "are the teachers you rate A and B, the best teachers?" "Why," he answered, "the teachers about whom I hear nothing."

The single outstanding fact about teachers—especially in American public schools—has been their docility. Until very recently it was tacitly understood that classroom teachers were to carry out policies and programs designed by administrators, principals, and supervisors. A large proportion of the elementary school teachers were female, and unabashed male chauvinism was taken for granted when it came to appointing superintendents and principals, not to speak of membership on school boards.

The superintendent was very much the rooster amid a clucking seraglio of school marms anxious to please him. Together they presented a reassuring example of civic probity and domestic virtue. High school teachers were a different lot. Many of them were male, so that the seraglio metaphor did not apply to them. Instead, they constituted a mildly resentful clutch of mercenaries kept at their posts by financial need, a need exacerbated by the economic law that kept wages down to the amounts that women would work for.

High school teachers of both sexes were somewhat more difficult to manage than their elementary school counterparts, because, as a rule, they held degrees with a major in some discipline. This gave them some sense of intellectual dignity, some of the pride of the specialist, who could look the principal or superintendent in the eye—and tell him that he knew nothing about mathematics or geography or whatever. Furthermore, the subject-matter specialists, for the most part, were preparing their charges for college, and a slight whiff of social superiority swirled around them. Nevertheless, not even these advantages were enough to stiffen their backbones when confronted by the administrative apparatus.

Accordingly, the teacher's role in making decisions was minuscule. Even when the revision of curricula by committees of teachers became customary, only by the greatest courtesy could it be said that *they* made the decisions. This is so because curriculum committees spend most of their time examining what is being done elsewhere and submitting their choices to other committees, which, in turn, consult with review committees, until something called a curriculum guide emerges from the State Department of Instruction or some other equally lofty level in the bureaucracy. This process of constructing curricula by consensus is a bow in the direction of democracy, a bow that becomes a full-fledged genuflection when the total citizenry is invited to participate. Neither the teachers nor the citizens participate because of their special knowledge about what needs to be taught. The citizens give the committee the benefit of their own experience or vent their dissatisfaction with the state of society by demanding that the school teach this or that: the evils of alcohol or the virtues of thrift. The teachers, for their part, bring to curriculum construction their experience and views about the teachability of specific items, and by teachability they do not always mean what can be taught. More often the "teachability" of certain learning tasks depends on whether the pupils, confronted with these tasks will be "turned on" sufficiently to allow the maintenance of some semblance of order in the classroom. The substance or structure of what is to be taught, for most teachers, is either a matter of tradition or something to be determined by the writers of textbooks.

In short, like any other large system, the school lives by rules that are supposed to take care of standard cases. Because the standard school systems are organized by grades, content must be organized into graded sequences. Each grade depends on the one preceding it to "cover" prescribed bits of information or skills. The logistics of instruction require rules about attendance, time periods, and movements through the building. In most schools teachers are required to sign in and out; bulletins flow from the central office; reports are in transit in all directions, at all levels. It is easy to make fun of this routine—the other fellow's logistics are always ludicrously complicated—but obviously no system can do without these rules: a congeries of classrooms having no commerce with one another would not be a school system. I know of no formula by which to balance nicely the logistics and the outcomes to which they are instrumental, but a reliable symptom of imbalance is the preoccupation of administrators with rules and procedures. When their eyes glisten as they describe their command of process, a sound instinct tells the layman to intervene and remind the expert about means and ends.

School operation is so rule-ridden that the teacher's autonomy is restricted to trivialities. About all she can do on her own is make minor adaptations in the curriculum material, in the program of study, and in her own style of teaching. Major changes would almost certainly breed suspicion and brew trouble. Why are rules so important to the system? Because it has no other principle of order.

Lest this be taken as a dark saying or glib cynicism, let us ask what other factors control the activities of the school. For about half of the high school population, acquiring sufficient credits to enter college is a controlling principle—and this, too, is largely governed by rules. But for the other half, this is not an operative principle; even for the college-bound it may not be as definitive as it has been. Systematic study of the intellectual disciplines is under attack. Perhaps it is part of the attack on all existing institutions—social, political, moral. Perhaps it is a phase of the anti-intellectualism that intellectual rebels affect. Whatever the reason, the rational order by which the graded study of subjects articulated the school system is being challenged. Sensitivity to social issues, interdisciplinary approaches, mind blowing, and relevance are not yet adequate substitutes for the order they are challenging.

A science of education and a set of rules derived from it would constitute a rational order of instruction. This kind of intellectual frame maintains order in medicine, engineering, and law. But no such science exists—if by science is meant a set of generally accepted empirical theories. Teaching is not the application of scientifically validated theories. It is more like preparing meals in a restaurant; the menu is prescribed and so are the recipes. Neither the menus nor the recipes are grounded in a coherent theory of nutrition or anything else —except possibly the economics of restaurant keeping or the art of cookery. Accordingly, changes made by management, as well as by employees, can be justified only by success: the general satisfaction of the client. When we say schools have failed, we mean that some adults are unhappy, but their unhappiness may be caused by anything from bussing to achieve integration to a daughter joining a hippie commune.

This somewhat dreary but, I believe, not inaccurate delineation of the teacher's role makes it easy to understand why the pivot of the system is not a pivot at all, but rather a satellite moving in fairly steady and predictable orbits, according to rules determined by almost everyone but the teacher. However, the rhetoric persists. The "good" teacher is supposed to possess arcane knowledge and charisma which overcome all obstacles—economic, social, and psychological—that plague the pupil. The "bad" teacher presumably has neither the knowledge nor the charisma nor the love of children, which makes up for virtually all other lacks.

How far is the rhetoric about teachers from reality? If we take the rhetoric seriously, the teacher is expected to act *in loco parentis, in loco communitatis, in loco humanitatis,* that is, in place of the parent, the community, and the culture—and to do so as an expert in pedagogy.

As representing the parent, the teacher is in the odd position of having to be as concerned about twenty-five or thirty-five children as the natural parent is about one, two, or three children. And, unlike God, who is excused from being concerned about His children as far as their overshoes and temper tantrums go, the schoolteacher is expected to vibrate sympathetically with every child in concrete predicaments of this sort. The blithe idiocy with which we repeat the refrain "Treat every pupil as an individual" is revealed only when we ask how many people does anyone treat as an individual human person. A half dozen is about par for most of us; the modern novel, moreover, often has as its subject our failure to reach even this small number. Indeed, parents are indicted a thousand times a day for not treating their own children as individuals deserving the dignity of persons. Husbands are accused of not treating their wives as persons in their own right. Those who are reluctant to study the evidence of the sociologists and other academicians need only follow the newspaper columns of Dear Abby or Dr. Rose Franzblau for a week or two.

In loco parentis, if it means anything, means playing the role of an ideal parent. As such, the teacher is endowed with an infinite capacity to love all children but freed from the bias that the love of the natural parent is likely to suffer. Good rhetoric, no doubt, but psychologically nonsense. Taken literally, it would make a shambles of teaching, as it would of healing, practicing law, or any other of the humane professions. The mystical glow of the Froebelian kindergarten came from the metaphysical fires of Hegelian idealism; partakers of that mystique and any other have always been few. The image of the teacher as the surrogate of the loving, tender, understanding, wise parent is a tribute to fantasy and, when made a model for public school teaching, breeds a mischievous sentimentalism.

About all that can be said for this notion is that those who dislike young people or who do not want to understand them should not go into teaching. Furthermore, men and women who plan to teach young children over a long period of time had better resign themselves to speaking and perhaps thinking like children for a good part of their waking day. Elementary school teachers often complain that they have been infantilized by their work, an occupational hazard from which clever innovators, who do not work constantly with children, are free.

Perhaps this is why research, theorizing, and large-scale planning in education are not often undertaken by classroom teachers. Teaching may keep one young—if it does not produce premature aging—but it may also preserve immaturity and thereby make more intellectually demanding tasks uncongenial.

So the *in loco parentis* doctrine dribbles down to a legalism that permits teachers to chastise children (under very prescribed circumstances) and to admonish them for their own good without first receiving their consent.

There is, however, another interpretation of *in loco parentis*. Consider Miss F, who is adored by pupil P, because Miss F supplies the affection that his own mother denies him. Miss F might serve as a sister surrogate for some other pupils and for others as a love object. In other words, teachers can serve *in loco parentis* and of other members of the family, actual or potential. Whether or not this surrogation is psychologically healthy either for the teacher or the pupil is debatable.

Certainly teachers should not use pupils to make up for their own psychic deprivations; certainly they should not—like overpossessive mothers—make pupils overly dependent on them. At this stage, I think you will agree, the question "What should be the proper relation between pupil and teacher?" becomes hopelessly vague. When the question is modified so as to read: "What should be the relation between a teacher and each of thirty pupils?" the query becomes absurd. Thus much of the writing on this theme, it goes without saying, is absurd.

The peculiar relation between teacher and pupil is an old mystery. If it is not like that between parent and child, lover and the beloved, master and servant, what is it? The terms "guide" and "midwife" are only two of many suggested to describe the essence of the relationship, and in some situations, such as the Socratic dialogue or the great research man and his graduate students, these metaphors are apt. But young pupils are not on journeys and are not pregnant with the kinds of ideas that require a Socratic midwife—at least it takes quite a stretch of the imagination to think of children's gropings in this way. In our time, perhaps, the professional-to-client relationshi is more suggestie of what many in the educational enterprise seek. Students appreciate a relationship with someone who is concerned about them as individuals, but who does not consider them as psychological burdens or crutches. The occupant of such a role, however, needs not only time to think of pupils as individuals but also a theoretical understanding that does not confuse concern with sentimental identification. If his teaching resembles therapy, it cures through knowledge and insight. But first and last the teacher is responsible for instruction.

Not much less confusing than the *in loco parentis* doctrine is that of *in loco communitatis*. This claims that the teacher represents the community mores and morals, which, presumably, the pupil is to make his own. The teacher is expected to discharge this role by being a model of community-approved behavior and, it is made plain, by inculcating communal expectations. She is somehow to reinforce these standards with appropriate praise and blame.

The first type of enactment is now less enforceable than once was the case. Not more than twenty-five years ago, schoolteachers were expected to stay out of bars, cocktail lounges, gambling halls, and places featuring erotic entertainment. The younger teachers, of course, resented these expectations more than the older ones; the latter more often than not had already absorbed the mores of the community and had no apparent trouble serving as sufficiently luminous exemplars of them. This was all the more understandable because teachers in the public schools were recruited neither from the upper classes nor from skid row—social strata in which the most deviant social behavior was likely to be found.

As to producing middle-class virtue, the public school teacher had neither qualms nor special efficacy. She or he merely reinforced by speech and attitude what the community had already made habitual. The teacher praised honesty, bravery, kindness, loyalty, patriotism, and hard work—as did the textbooks. If I have doubt about the teacher's special efficacy in moral education, it is because in those instances in which pupils had not been habituated by the family and the community, reformation rarely occurred. When in the sixties the younger generation defied its parents and the community elders by flaunting long hair and unconventional dress, the impotence of both the school and the family in enforcing the mores was revealed. In that moment of truth it became clear that *morality* had become identified in the minds of the community with middle-class manners, an identification that neither the young nor the courts would countenance.

If the teacher no longer acts *in loco communitatis* as regards the mores of dress, speech, and social sentiments, does it make any sense to speak of him as representing the community's value system in general? A little, but not much. Which of the numerous value schemata that now divide the community should the teacher represent? That of the WASPs of the upper, the middle, or the working class? The intellectuals of the left, middle, or right? The blacks militant or the blacks integrationist? The Chicanos, Puerto Ricans, Indians? America as a melting pot of cultural differences is no longer a popular notion. Some still hope for a savory stew in which diverse ingredients retain their identity while giving up enough of their essence to produce a pervasive flavor. Many reject even this much unity—so long as the capitalistic economy and its supervening establishments remain intact. Others fear that the unity of a Communist state would be worse than no unity at all.

Of all these doubts and questionings, the crack in the ideal of an American, New-World, democratic culture is the most serious. Cultural pluralism is nothing new in the world; neither is pluralism kept together by a conquering despot. The novelty of the American dream was a cultural unity chosen or accepted freely by people with a variety of ethnic origins—the unity of the American Creed as celebrated and worried over in the late 1940s by Gunnar Myrdal in *An American Dilemma*.

For the teacher to act *in loco communitatis* some such ideal must be accepted by all the divergent groups. Perhaps it is still accepted by a majority of Americans; repeated polls say so. Yet the minorities who reject the ideal are loud and powerful. They make the media, as well as the college campus and the intellectual journals, reverberate with their rejections of any unity. The old-fashioned liberals are not only tired but a little frightened as well. Just as the longer hair style captured even conservative middle-agers, so the liberal thinks a bit longer before risking the scorn of his more radical colleagues. A beard gives him a bit more courage and much more credibility when uttering his verities, but falling out of fashion kills a doctrine more surely than error. That the fashion-makers are not a majority of the people does not diminish the power of the fashions they set. As the decade of the seventies gets underway, there is no question as to what is fashionable: a cultural pluralism; a rejection of structure and of the established order and its norms. In such a climate, to speak of the teacher as representing the norms of the community is meaningless.

The third expectation that teachers are supposed to fulfill is that of serving *in loco humanitatis*. The humanities in their original sense signified the best that man had thought and wrought and said—*humanitas* was the opposite of barbaritas. The Greek and Latin classics were thought to make the difference between truly human beings and barbarians. With the help of Cicero this notion held sway for centuries in the Western world. The idea still whispers in the halls of the academy when the noise of the scientific machinery permits it to be heard; it still persuades people to buy the great books and visit the museums for a look at Greek statuary. The plays of Sophocles and Euripides are staged every so often, but the idea, as Cicero held it, and as it shaped the curriculum of schools up until, say, the beginning of this century, is quite dead; the motions we discern in it are induced by classicists, not by the classics. The teacher as the representative of the classical ideals of Greece and Rome, accordingly, is virtually nonexistent.

The classical ideal of *humanitas* has been displaced by the ideal of knowledge in a broader sense. Rather than regarding education as the absorption of a small set of ancient literary and philosophical masterpieces, standard humanistic education today looks to the mastery of the major intellectual disciplines to fashion the mind of man. To think the way the scientist does, to perceive and imagine as the artist and poet do—these are the contemporary goals of the humanities. The humanities may not stress technology, but they must never be maneuvered into the position of having to say that it is permissible for a humanist to think as witch doctors and astrologers do about physical events.

The authority of the classical writers is now vested in the *cognoscenti* of each of the disciplines and the arts; to be an educated man is to think and perceive and imagine and feel somewhat as they do. Education is the induction of the young into these ways of thinking and feeling. It is this version of the humanities that has guided what is loosely called the liberal arts and science curriculum in the colleges. Is this the *humanitas* that the teacher is supposed to represent?

In a way, yes. This was the point behind the movement to require teachers to have a good general education before undertaking more "professional" studies. The same motive is responsible for the requirement of some professional schools that at least the first two years of college be devoted to finishing up or polishing off general education. Insofar as teachers have increased their exposure to the disciplines, I believe they do begin to qualify as being *in loco humanitatis*. Insofar as this exposure has been narrow, specialized, and professional, they are probably not good examples of the all-round-educated person. If the exposure has not been successful, it is because it is virtually impossible to find on any "good" college campus very much study undertaken for what Aristotle would have called self-cultivation, or, better, the cultivation of one's human potentialities. Most of what is dubbed liberal arts and sciences in college catalogues is a sequence of courses taught by professionals to preprofessionals, or to imaginary preprofessionals called majors.

Nevertheless, until recently it has made sense to say that the teachers in our schools—at all levels—should represent the best that is being thought and said and felt in our culture. It meant approximating the forms of thought and feeling as embodied in the learned and wise of our time. These norms were held to be valid for man as man, not for whites alone or for the rich alone. They did presuppose leisure for self-cultivation but did not presuppose that all but a few would be denied that leisure. With secondary schooling becoming well-nigh universal in this country, and with more than half of the high school graduates giving higher education a try, this ideal, for the first time in history, began to be more than a mere ideal in a democratic society.

Yet, as this is being written in the early seventies, this version of humanism is also being challenged, and, to the degree that its validity is brought into question, the expectation that the teacher will serve *in loco humanitatis* also loses its meaning.

When C. P. Snow reactivated interest in the ancient rift between the scientific and literary cultures, he was talking about scientists versus literary people, philosophers, historians, and artists; between those who delved into the ways of things—and men as things—on the one hand, and those interested in the ways men coped with men—and things—on the other. Snow decided that the future was with the scientists; they could understand what literary men said, but what could literary people do with the language of science? He did not anticipate the dethronement of science in the hearts of the young rebels in the late sixties. They also thought of themselves as humanists and certainly as humanitarians. Yet they resembled the humanists whom Snow had in mind so little that the major cleavage in education today is not between scientific and humanistic studies, but rather between the old-line standard humanists and the new, or existential, humanists.

The infighting between them rages on the college campus and in the political arena, and it has now filtered down into the elementary and secondary schools. I know of no brief way to make the distinction between the standard and the existential humanists that will not oversimplify the issue and that will not draw protests from those who do not find themselves exclusively in one camp or the other. Yet a rough line of demarcation can be drawn on the basis of what each side takes to be the criterion of what is to be called "human."

The classical humanist finds the mark of humanity in man's conquest of the impulsive demands of his physiological drives. The key to the human strategy from Plato on has been self-mastery, the control of commitment and action by reason. Reason to rule the appetites and emotion to reinforce the decrees of reason was and, I believe, still is the formula for liberal humanism—and it was to apply in all departments of life, private and public, individual and social; it acknowledged no cultural exceptions. The cosmos "followed" this law as inexorably as it "followed" the physical laws, even though, and perhaps precisely because, man was free to try to break that law.

Accordingly, the classical humanist looks to the masterworks of literature, philosophy, and art for the formulation of the law and men's experience with it. To induct the new generation into the community of men involves teaching the young to understand and cherish these monuments to the human adventure.

The human adventure is the story of how our biological needs and impulses have been transformed—almost beyond recognition. Take any activity in which we share our animality with other species—feeding, shelter seeking, fighting, reproducing, nurturing the young—and apply human consciousness (reason, memory, and imagination) to it. A peculiar and extraordinary change takes place. Feeding becomes dining, acquiring in the process aesthetic, religious, and social values. The houses we build, we hope, will provide adequate shelter, but how much of the cost of a dwelling is justified by its sheltering properties alone? As soon as they could, the pioneers added the amenities to the essentials of feeding and sheltering. Perhaps the greatest transformation of all has to do with the physiological act of sex. In other animals instinct and physiological mechanisms take care of most of this transaction; in humans surprisingly little sexual activity is explained by either instinct or physiological mechanism. Mostly, psychiatrists tell us, sex is "in the head," where imagination has lodged it. Fighting has been adorned, by imagination, with courage and heroism. It is an instrument of national policy, not merely a means to food and a mate.

These transformations are sublimations of animality, but the very same imagination, reason, and memory can transform biological drives into subanimal behavior. Eating can become gluttony; the *fear of hunger* can become an excuse for aggrandizement and unbridled cruelty. Man can devise forms of combat so frightful that even the thought of annihilation of the entire species does not deter him. Sex can become lust as well as love; it can be driven to the perverse and the bizarre, as imagination invents new forms of stimulation for jaded appetites.

It it this potentiality for the transformation of our nature to the superanimal and subanimal that gives dramatic tension to the human adventure. The direction in which man should go was clear to Plato and Aristotle, Vittorino da Feltre and Montaigne, to Emerson, Ruskin, Matthew Arnold, and the long array of writers who can be thought of as humanists in the classical sense of the word. Do the new humanists reject the classical answer to the human question? It is hard to say. When both sides talk about the kind of individual life and society they would regard as good and admirable, one finds them agreeing. Neither side can abide the injustice, cruelty, bestiality, and folly of men, but it is not easy to assimilate the writers listed above with Nietzsche, Sartre, Genet, Fanon, Marcuse, and their followers on the campus.

The difference is that the existential humanists do not want to wait for the cosmos to carry out its design, or for the second coming, or for the whatever distant millennium. They do not regard the Platonic self-mastery through ordered thought and feeling as the glory of the human species; they prefer freedom from all preconceived restraints. This freedom creates a compelling need to commit oneself to a significant deed—one that will authenticate the self. One must change the evil situation now and not stop with the understanding of it. Too much understanding is a temptation to forgiveness, and to forgive the evil of the world is precisely the temptation to which the new militant humanists believe the classical humanist yields. The scholarly humanist, confronted by evil, goes back to his study to study some more (or he appoints a committee to study) while the poor become more wretched, the environment is ruined, and men wreak violence on each other and ultimately upon themselves. A neohumanist is a classical humanist gone berserk, and, freaked out in this frenzy, he may swing from superanimal to subanimal behavior to make his point. Freedom *from* the order of society and *from* the norms of the culture, and even *from* old ideals provide the sign that one is existing authentically, indeed, that one is existing at all as a human being. The regression from dining to casual feeding; from marital fidelity to uninhibited serial sex; from thinking to touching; from self-mastery to self-expression—these, often allied with drugs to deaden inhibition and deny limits, seem to be the signs of humanity for some of the new militant humanists.

And where in this struggle are the scientists? They, too, would like to be classed with the humanists, but with which kind? Scientists can do one of two things: assert that their knowledge is our most potent tool for humanization and thus ally themselves with the classical humanists; or separate their science from their human "being" and join the neohumanists in action programs, which may or may not be directly related to their roles as scientists.

In academe this struggle has taken the form of an attack on and in defense of structured courses, structured curricula, and the structured private life of students. The neohumanists urge us to make the human problem the curriculum. To the classical humanists, who regard the living tradition of the intellectual and artistic disciplines as the essence of achieved humanity, the rejection of the disciplines is a rejection of all order—of the very norms of humanity and humanism. In politics—on the campus and off—the struggle is between alternative ways of achieving social change. In the elementary and secondary schools, the struggle is between a curriculum based on academic disciplines and a curriculum—if one can call it that—devoted to freeing pupils from the demands of conformity to the establishment—moral, economic, social, and political. Is the goal of schooling to teach and learn biology, chemistry, literature, mathematics, history, and the like, or, in the argot of the moment, is it to become an uninhibited, caring, sensitive person? The Holt-Kozol-Friedenberg-Goodman writings on the schools, it seems to me, leave little doubt as to the nature of the issue—and perhaps of their answers as well.

The split between the old and the new humanism, accordingly, has made it difficult to say in what sense the teacher shall act *in loco humanitatis*, but, as is usual in these matters, the probable answer is that the teacher will be asked to represent both the new and the old humanism and, as is also probable, will succeed in doing neither.

We now have, I hope, a fairly clear summary of what we expect from teachers. First, there is the over-all expectation that the teacher be an expert in teaching; second, that he represent the ideal parent; third, that he represent the community at its ideal best; fourth, that he represent the human being at his best. But it is not at all clear just what these expectations demand in the way of competence and the sort of training that would reasonably insure such competence.

Roughly, the person envisioned by these demands is a good man skilled in teaching, to paraphrase Quintilian's formula for the orator as a "good man skilled in speaking." More concretely, the modern teacher is expected to be a person with a good general education (the old humanistic studies), acting as a professional, that is, applying what educators (or educationists) know to teaching the content of the disciplines he has mastered, and all the while acting as a warm, child-loving father-, mother-, brother-surrogate who "relates" to human beings (the new humanism). These three types of demands make up the bundle we call the ideal, professional teacher who should be in every classroom. . .

4 Characteristics of Good Teachers and Implications for Teacher Education

Don Hamachek

It is, I think, a sad commentary about our educational system that it keeps announcing both publicly and privately that "good" and "poor" teachers cannot be distinguished one from the other. Probably no issue in education has been so voluminously researched as has teacher effectiveness and considerations which enhance or restrict this effectiveness. Nonetheless, we still read that we cannot tell the good guys from the bad guys. For example, Biddle and Ellena[2] in their book, *Contemporary Research on Teacher Effectiveness*, begin by stating that "the problem of teacher effectiveness is so complex that no one today knows what *The Competent Teacher* is." I think we *do* know what the competent—or

Reprinted from *Phi Delta Kappan*, 50 (6): 341–345 (February 1969), by permission of author and publisher.

effective, or good, or whatever you care to call him—teacher is, and in the remainder of this paper I will be as specific as possible in citing *why* I think we know along with implications for our teacher-education programs.

WHAT THE RESEARCH SAYS

By and large, most research efforts aimed at investigating teacher effectiveness have attempted to probe one or more of the following dimensions of teacher personality and behavior: (1) personal characteristics, (2) instructional procedures and interaction styles, (3) perception of self, (4) perceptions of others. Because of space limits this is by no means an exhaustive review of the research related to the problem, but it is, I think, representative of the kind and variety of research findings linked to questions of teacher effectiveness.

Personal Characteristics of Good Versus Poor Teachers

We would probably agree that it is quite possible to have two teachers of equal intelligence, training, and grasp of subject matter who nevertheless differ considerably in the results they achieve with students. Part of the difference can be accounted for by the effect of a teacher's personality on the learners. What kinds of personality do students respond to?

Hart[7] conducted a study based upon the opinions of 3,725 high school seniors concerning best-liked and least-liked teachers and found a total of 43 different reasons for "liking Teacher A best" and 30 different reasons for "liking Teacher Z least." Not surprisingly, over 51 percent of the students said that they liked best those teachers who were "helpful in school work, who explained lessons and assignments clearly, and who used examples in teaching." Also, better than 40 percent responded favorably to teachers with a "sense of humor." Those teachers assessed most negatively were "unable to explain clearly, were partial to brighter students, and had superior, aloof, overbearing attitudes." In addition, over 50 percent of the respondents mentioned behaviors such as "too cross, crabby, grouchy, and sarcastic" as reasons for disliking many teachers. Interestingly enough, mastery of subject matter, which is vital but badly overemphasized by specialists, ranked sixteenth on both lists. Somehow students seem willing to take more or less for granted that a teacher "knows" his material. What seems to make a difference is the teacher's personal style in *communicating* what he knows. Studies by Witty[14] and Bousfield[3] tend to support these conclusions at both the high school *and* college level.

Having desirable personal qualities is one thing, but what are the results of rigorous tests of whether the teacher's having them makes any difference in the performance of students?

Cogan[4] found that warm, considerate teachers got an unusual amount of original poetry and art from their high school students. Reed[10] found that teachers higher in a capacity for warmth favorably affected their pupils' interests in science. Using scores from achievement tests as their criterion measure, Heil, Powell, and Fiefer[8] compared various teacher-pupil personality combinations and found that the well-integrated (healthy, well-rounded, flexible) teachers were most effective with *all* types of students. Spaulding[12] found that the self-concepts of elementary school children were apt to be higher and more positive in classrooms in which the teacher was "socially integrative" and "learner supportive."

In essence, I think the evidence is quite clear when it comes to sorting out good or effective from bad or ineffective teachers on the basis of personal characteristics. Effective teachers appear to be those who are, shall we say, "human" in the fullest sense of the word. They have a sense of humor, are fair, empathetic, more democratic than autocratic, and apparently are more able to relate easily and naturally to students on either a one-to-one or group basis. Their classrooms seem to reflect miniature enterprise operations in the sense that they are more open, spontaneous, and adaptable to change. Ineffective teachers apparently lack a sense of humor, grow impatient easily, use cutting, ego-reducing comments in class, are less well-integrated, are inclined to be somewhat authoritarian, and are generally less sensitive to the needs of their students. Indeed, research related to authoritarianism suggests that the bureaucratic conduct and rigid overtones of the ineffective teacher's classroom are desperate measures to support the weak pillars of his own personality structure.

Instructional Procedures and Interaction Styles of Good Versus Poor Teachers

If there really are polar extremes such as "good" or "poor" teachers, then we can reasonably assume that these teachers differ not only in personal characteristics but in the way they conduct themselves in the classroom.

Flanders[6] found that classrooms in which achievement and attitudes were superior were likely to be conducted by teachers who did not blindly pursue a single behavioral-instructional path to the exclusion of other possibilities. In other words, the more successful teachers were better able to range along a continuum of interaction styles which varied from fairly active, dominative support on the one hand to a more reflective, discriminating support on the other. Interestingly, those teachers who were *not* successful were the very ones who were inclined to use the same interaction styles in a more or less rigid fashion.

Barr[1] discovered that not only did poor teachers make more assignments than good teachers but, almost without exception, they made some sort of textbook assignment as part of their unyielding daily procedure. The majority of good teachers used more outside books and problem-project assignments. When the text was assigned they were more likely to supplement it with topics, questions, or other references.

Research findings related to interaction styles variously called "learner-centered" or "teacher-centered" point to similar conclusions. In general, it appears that the amount of cognitive gain is largely unaffected by the autocratic or democratic tendencies of the instructor. However, when affective gains are considered, the results are somewhat different. For example, Stern[13] reviewed 34 studies comparing nondirective with directive instruction and concluded:

> Regardless of whether the investigator was concerned with attitudes toward the cultural out group, toward other participants in the class, or toward the self, the results generally have indicated that nondirective instruction facilitates a shift in a more favorable, acceptant direction.

When it comes to classroom behavior, interaction patterns, and teaching styles, good or effective teachers seem to reflect more of the following behaviors:

1. Willingness to be flexible, to be direct or indirect as the situation demands
2. Ability to perceive the world from the student's point of view
3. Ability to "personalize" their teaching
4. Willingness to experiment, to try out new things
5. Skill in asking questions (as opposed to seeing self as a kind of answering service)
6. Knowledge of subject matter and related areas
7. Provision of well-established examination procedures
8. Provision of definite study helps
9. Reflection of an appreciative attitude (evidenced by nods, comments, smiles, etc.)
10. Use of conversational manner in teaching—informal, easy style

Self-Perceptions of Good Versus Poor Teachers

We probably do not have to go any further than our own personal life experiences to know that the way we see, regard, and feel about ourselves has an enormous impact on both our private and public lives. How about good and poor teachers? How do they see themselves?

Ryans[11] found that there are, indeed, differences between the self-related reports of teachers with high emotional stability and those with low emotional stability. For example, the more emotionally stable teachers (1) more frequently named self-confidence and cheerfulness as dominant traits in themselves, (2) said they liked active contact with other people, (3) expressed interests in hobbies and handicrafts, (4) reported their childhoods to be happy experiences.

On the other hand, teachers with lower emotional maturity scores (1) had unhappy memories of childhood, (2) seemed *not* to prefer contact with others, (3) were more directive and authoritarian, (4) expressed less self-confidence.

We can be even more specific. Combs,[5] in his book *The Professional Education of Teachers,* cites several studies which reached similar conclusions about the way good teachers typically see themselves, as follows:

1. Good teachers see themselves as identified with people rather than withdrawn, removed, apart from, or alienated from others.
2. Good teachers feel basically adequate rather than inadequate. They do not see themselves as generally unable to cope with problems.
3. Good teachers feel trustworthy rather than untrustworthy. They see themselves as reliable, dependable individuals with the potential for coping with events as they happen.
4. Good teachers see themselves as wanted rather than unwanted. They see themselves as likable and attractive (in a personal, not a physical sense) as opposed to feeling ignored and rejected.
5. Good teachers see themselves as worthy rather than unworthy. They see themselves as people of consequence, dignity, and integrity as opposed to feeling they matter little, can be overlooked and discounted.

In the broadest sense of the word, good teachers are more likely to see themselves as good people. Their self-perceptions are, for the most part, positive, tinged with an air of optimism and colored with tones of healthy self-acceptance. I dare say that self-perceptions of good teachers are not unlike the self-perceptions of any basically healthy person, whether he be a good bricklayer, a good manager, a good doctor, a good lawyer, a good experimental psychologist, or you name it. Clinical evidence has told us time and again that any person is more apt to be happier, more productive, and more effective when he is able to see himself as fundamentally and basically "enough."

Perceptions of Others by Good Versus Poor Teachers

Research is showing us that not only do good and poor teachers view themselves differently, there are also some characteristic differences in the way they perceive others. For example, Ryans[11] reported several studies which have produced findings that are in agreement when it comes to sorting out the differences between how good and poor teachers view others. He found, among other things, that outstandingly "good" teachers rated significantly higher than notably "poor" teachers in at least five different ways with respect to how they viewed others. The good teachers had (1) more favorable opinions of students, (2) more favorable opinions of democratic classroom behavior, (3) more favorable opinions of administrators and colleagues, (4) a greater expressed liking for personal contacts with other people, (5) more favorable estimates of other people generally. That is, they expressed belief that very few students are difficult behavior problems, that very few people are influenced in their opinions and attitudes toward others by feelings of jealousy, and that most teachers are willing to assume their full share of extra duties outside of school.

Interestingly, the characteristics that distinguished the "lowly assessed" teacher group suggested that the relatively "ineffective" teacher is self-centered, anxious, and restricted. One is left with the distinct impression that poor or ineffective teachers have more than the usual number of paranoid defenses.

It comes as no surprise that how we perceive others is highly dependent on how we perceive ourselves. If a potential teacher (or anyone else for that matter) likes himself, trusts himself, and has confidence in himself, he is likely to see others in somewhat this same light. Research is beginning to tell us what common sense has always told us; namely, people grow, flourish, and develop much more easily when in relationship with someone who projects an inherent trust and belief in their capacity to become what they have the potential to become.

It seems to me that we can sketch at least five interrelated generalizations from what research is telling us about how good teachers differ from poor teachers when it comes to how they perceive others.

1. They seem to have generally more positive views of others—students, colleagues, and administrators.
2. They do not seem to be as prone to view others as critical, attacking people with ulterior motives; rather they are seen as potentially friendly and worthy in their own right.
3. They have a more favorable view of democratic classroom procedures.
4. They seem to have the ability and capacity to see things as they seem to others—i.e., the ability to see things from the other person's point of view.
5. They do not seem to see students as persons "you do things to" but rather as individuals capable of doing for themselves once they feel trusted, respected, and valued.

WHO, THEN, IS A GOOD TEACHER?

1. A good teacher is a good person. Simple and true. A good teacher rather likes life, is reasonably at peace with himself, has a sense of humor, and enjoys other people. If I interpret the research correctly, what it says is that there is no one best better-than-all-others type of teacher. Nonetheless there are clearly distinguishable "good" and "poor" teachers. Among other things, a good teacher is good because he does not seem to be dominated by a narcissistic self which demands a spotlight, or a neurotic need for power and authority, or a host of anxieties and tremblings which reduce him from the master of his class to its mechanic.

2. The good teacher is flexible. By far the single most repeated adjective used to describe good teachers is "flexibility." Either implicitly or explicitly (most often the latter), this characteristic emerges time and again over all others when good teaching is discussed in the research. In other words, the good teacher does not seem to be overwhelmed by a single point of view or approach to the point of intellectual myopia. A good teacher knows that he cannot be just one sort of person and use just one kind of approach if he intends to meet the multiple needs of his students. Good teachers are, in a sense, "total" teachers. That is, they seem able to be what they have to be to meet the demands of the moment. They seem able to move with the shifting tides of their own needs, the student's, and do what has to be done to handle the situation. A total teacher can be firm when necessary (say "no" and mean it) or permissive (say "why not try it your way?" and mean that, too) when appropriate. It depends on many things, and good teachers seem to know the difference.

THE NEED FOR "TOTAL" TEACHERS

There probably is not an educational psychology course taught which does not in some way, deal with the highly complex area of individual differences. Even the most unsophisticated undergraduate is aware that people differ in readiness and capacity to handle academic learning. For the most part, our educational technology (audio-visual aids, programmed texts, teaching machines, etc.) is making significant advances designed to assist teachers in coping with intellectual differences among students. We have been making strides in the direction of offering flexible programs and curricula, but we are somewhat remiss when it comes to preparing flexible, "total" teachers. Just as there are intellectual differences among students, there are also personality and self-concept differences which can have just as much impact on achievement. If this is true, then perhaps we need to do more about preparing teachers who are sensitive to the nature of these differences and who are able to take them into account as they plan for their classes.

The point here is that what is important for one student is not important to another. This is one reason why cookbook formulas for good teachers are of so little value and why teaching is inevitably something of an art. The choice of instructional methods makes a big difference for certain kinds of pupils, and a search for the "best" way to teach can succeed only when learners' intellectual and personality differences are taken into account. Available evidence does not support the belief that successful teaching is possible only through the use of some specific methodology. A reasonable inference from existing data is that methods which provide for adaptation to individual differences, encourage student initiative, and stimulate individual and group participation are superior to methods which do not. In order for things of this sort to happen, perhaps what we need first of all are flexible, "total" teachers who are capable of planning around people as they are around ideas.

IMPLICATIONS FOR TEACHER EDUCATION

Research is teaching us many things about the differences between good and poor teachers, and I see at least four related implications for teacher education programs.

1. If it is true that good teachers are good because they view teaching as primarily a human process involving human relationships and human meanings, then this may imply that we should spend at least as much time exposing and sensitizing teacher candidates to the subtle complexities of personality structure as we do to introducing them to the structure of knowledge itself. Does this mean personality development, group dynamics, basic counseling processes, sensitivity training, and techniques such as life-space interviewing and encounter grouping?

2. If it is true that good teachers have a positive view of themselves and others, then this may suggest that we provide more opportunities for teacher candidates to acquire more positive self-other perceptions. Self-concept research tells us that how one feels about himself is learned. If it is learned, it is teachable. Too often, those of us in teacher education are dominated by a concern for long-term goals, while the student is fundamentally motivated by short-term goals. Forecasting what a student will need to know six months or two years from now, we operate on the assumption that he, too, perceives such goals as meaningful. It seems logical enough, but unfortunately it doesn't work out too well in practice. Hence much of what we may do with our teacher candidates is non-self-related—that is, to the student it doesn't seem connected with his own life, time, and needs. Rather than talk about group processes in the abstract, why can't we first assist students to a deeper understanding of their own roles in groups in which they already participate? Rather than simply theorize and cite research evidence related to individual differences, why not also encourage students to analyze the individual differences which exist in this class at this time and then allow them to express and discuss what these differences mean at a more personal level? If one values the self-concept idea at all, then there are literally endless ways to encourage more positive self-other perceptions through teaching strategies aimed at personalizing what goes on in a classroom. Indeed, Jersild[9] has demonstrated that when "teachers face themselves," they feel more adequate as individuals and function more effectively as teachers.

3. If it is true that good teachers are well-informed, then it is clear that we must neither negate nor relax our efforts to provide them with as rich an intellectual background as is possible. Teachers are usually knowledgeable people, and knowledge inculcation is the aspect of preparation with which teacher education has traditionally been most successful. Nonetheless, teachers rarely fail because of lack of knowledge. They fail more often because they are unable to communicate what they know so that it makes a difference to their students. Which brings us to our final implication for teacher-education programs.

4. If it is true that good teachers are able to communicate what they know in a manner that makes sense to their students, then we must assist our teacher candidates both through example and appropriate experiences to the most effective ways of doing this. Communication is not just a process of presenting information. It is also a function of discovery and the development of personal meanings. I wonder what would happen to our expectations of the teacher's role if we viewed him less as dispenser, answerer, coercer, and provoker and more as stimulator, questioner, challenger, and puzzler. With the former, the emphasis is on "giving to," while with the latter the focus is on "guiding to." In developing ability to hold and keep attention, not to mention techniques of encouraging people to adopt the reflective, thoughtful mood, I wonder what the departments of speech, theater, and drama on our college and university campuses could teach us? We expose our students to theories of learning and personality; perhaps what we need to do now is develop some "theories of presentation" with the help of those who know this field best.

This paper has attempted to point out that even though there is no single best or worst kind of teacher, there are clearly distinguishable characteristics associated with "good" and "bad" teachers. There is no one *best* kind of teaching because there is no *one kind* of student. Nonetheless, there seems to be enough evidence to suggest that whether the criteria for good teaching is on the basis of student and/or peer evaluations or in terms of student achievement gains, there are characteristics between both which consistently overlap. That is, the good teacher is able to influence both student feeling and achievement in positive ways.

Research is teaching us many things about the differences between good and bad teachers and there are many ways we can put these research findings into our teacher-education programs.

Good teachers do exist and can be identified. Perhaps the next most fruitful vineyard for research is in the classrooms of good teachers so we can determine, by whatever tools we have, just what makes them good in the first place.

NOTES
1. A. S. Barr, *Characteristic Differences in the Teaching Performance of Good and Poor Teachers of the Social Studies.* Bloomington, Ill.: The Public School Publishing Co., 1929.
2. B. J. Biddle and W. J. Ellena, *Contemporary Research on Teacher Effectiveness.* New York: Holt, Rinehart, and Winston, 1964, p. 2.
3. W. A. Bousfield, "Student's Rating on Qualities Considered Desirable in College Professors," *School and Society,* February 24, 1940, pp. 253–56.
4. M. L. Cogan, "The Behavior of Teachers and the Productive Behavior of Their Pupils," *Journal of Experimental Education,* December, 1958, pp. 89–124.
5. A. W. Combs, *The Professional Education of Teachers.* Boston: Allyn and Bacon, 1965, pp. 70–71.
6. N. A. Flanders, *Teacher Influence, Pupil Attitudes and Achievement:*

Studies in Interaction Analysis. University of Minnesota, U. S. Office of Education Cooperative Research Project No. 397, 1960.

7. W. F. Hart, *Teachers and Teaching,* New York: Macmillan, 1934, pp. 131–32.

8. L. M. Heil, M. Powell, and I. Feifer, *Characteristics of Teacher Behavior Related to the Achievement of Children in Several Elementary Grades.* Washington, D.C.: Office of Education, Cooperative Research Branch, 1960.

9. A. T. Jersild, *When Teachers Face Themselves.* New York: Bureau of Publications, Teachers College, Columbia University, 1955.

10. H. B. Reed, "Implications for Science Education of a Teacher Competence Research," *Science Education,* December, 1962, pp. 473–86.

11. D. G. Ryans, "Prediction of Teacher Effectiveness," *Encyclopedia of Educational Research,* 3rd Edition. New York: Macmillan, 1960, pp. 1, 486–90.

12. R. Spaulding, "Achievement, Creativity, and Self-Concept Correlates of Teacher-Pupil Transactions in Elementary Schools." University of Illinois, U. S. Office of Education Cooperative Research Project No. 1352, 1963.

13. G. C. Stern, "Measuring Non-Cognitive Variables in Research on Teaching," in *Handbook of Research on Teaching,* N. L. Gage (ed.) Chicago: Rand McNally, 1963, p. 427.

14. P. Witty, "An Analysis of the Personality Traits of the Effective Teacher," *Journal of Educational Research,* May, 1947, pp. 662–71.

5 Teacher Surplus and Teacher Shortage

William S. Graybeal

The casual reader of educational literature may be perplexed by the seeming conflict in pronouncements about the current status of supply of and demand for public school teachers. Some observers, including the Research Division of the National Education Association, have reported that there is now a surplus of qualified teachers for most assignments, an adequate supply in several assignment areas, and shortages in a few others. Other observers, again including the NEA Research Division, have reported a continuation of teacher shortages this year; that a large shortage of teachers would exist if the public schools met minimum standards of quality in programs and staffing. The primary difference

Reprinted (with marginal omissions) from *Phi Delta Kappan,* 53 (2): 82–85 (October 1971), by permission of author and publisher.

in these conclusions results from a difference in the assumptions underlying the estimate of the demand for qualified teachers.

The NEA announcement of *surpluses* reflects the comparison of the supply of qualified teachers with the numbers of teachers who *actually will* be employed for a given school year. The difference between the number of applicants and the number of positions being filled gives a picture of actual employment opportunities awaiting new graduates prepared to teach and former teachers desiring to reenter teaching. This estimate of the demand for teachers includes the new teachers needed for positions related to school enrollments and for replacement of teachers leaving active employment.

The announcement of continuing teacher *shortages* is based on the comparison of the supply of qualified teachers with the numbers of teachers who *should be* employed in a given school session to attain a specified standard of educational quality at that time. This is a theoretical estimate—the shortage does not reflect the number of actual positions which will be filled as quickly as qualified applicants are available. It is useful, however, for long-term planning and evaluation. Comparison of the estimated supply with this estimate of the demand provides an indication of the possible impact of current teacher supply upon continued progress in improvement of education.

If the projected standard of quality in education is realistic in likelihood of attainment, continuing growth in the supply of new teachers accompanied by relatively small growth in school enrollments will provide sufficient staff to meet this standard in the foreseeable future.

The existence of a practical limit to the amount of financial support likely to be directed to public education should be recognized. Otherwise the projected standards of minimum quality in education programs and staffing are only speculative, since it is unlikely that they will ever be attained. Long-term planning is not meaningful if it is based on the assumption that there will always be sufficient teaching positions created to provide employment for all interested people who meet minimum qualifications for entering teaching.

The projection of an attainable standard of minimum quality in educational programs and staffing does provide, however, a long-term goal toward which such progress and the adequacy of present and future supply may be evaluated accurately. The results of this evaluation provide information useful to institutions as they plan for future enrollments and programs. It will also be extremely valuable to college freshmen as they attempt to select programs leading to employment after their graduation three or four years from now.

The NEA report of a teacher oversupply two years ago resulted from the observation of (1) an *actual* surplus of qualified applicants for open positions, and (2) the outlook that unless present trends are changed, the supply of qualified applicants will also exceed the quality-based level of demand within the near future. For the first time in recent history the five-year outlook is for *actual* surpluses which, if accumulated, would provide more teachers than needed to attain a standard of minimum quality.

Because this sharp change in the future supply of qualified teachers calls for serious thought and action in adjusting some of the factors influencing teacher supply and demand, the NEA has established a task force which is reviewing the implications of the teacher manpower situation. The task force will provide direction to NEA efforts to accomplish more complete utilization of available teacher manpower, assist unemployed teachers, and guard against possible deleterious outcomes of a teacher surplus.

There is no question that the supply of graduates prepared to teach also is inadequate for the number of teaching-related jobs which *should be* created. Large numbers of additional jobs should be created to assure day-care services for pre-school children, to improve recreational and educational experiences for people in every age group of the population from pre-school to "golden age," and to assist large numbers of people now underparticipating in the benefits of American life (culturally different; physically, mentally, and emotionally disadvantaged; socially maladjusted; etc.). If society were to allocate sufficient resources to create enough of these additional jobs, the personnel requirements would likely exceed the estimated future surpluses of teachers. However, the present-day teacher education programs may not provide the best preparation for these teaching-related occupations. It might be more efficient to create the needed jobs in these areas and then to organize programs to prepare people for each of these areas as a specialty. This would relate their preparation directly to their future assignments and would encourage them to enter these occupations directly rather than to accept such assignments as a second choice because of difficulties in finding a teaching position.

The following paragraphs summarize the considerations underlying the NEA Research Division's estimates of teacher supply and demand. Details about these estimates and the specific figures are given in the annual NEA Research Division report, *Teacher Supply and Demand in Public Schools*. The projections and the considerations underlying them are reported in the October *NEA Research Bulletin*. [*See Figure 1.*]

THE SUPPLY

In addition to currently employed staff, the present supply of teachers comprises former teachers who have interrupted their careers; college graduates completing preparation to enter teaching positions for the first time; graduates who have postponed entry into teaching; former teachers desiring to return to teaching from supervisory, administrative, or supporting positions; and those ready to enter teaching as a second career.

Of the public school teachers employed in 1965–66, 87.4% were employed as teachers the preceding year, 8.5% were attending college or university full time, 1.6% were engaged in homemaking or child-rearing on a full-time basis, 1.1% were working in a nonteaching occupation, and the remainder were in military service, unemployed and seeking work, or in other classifications.

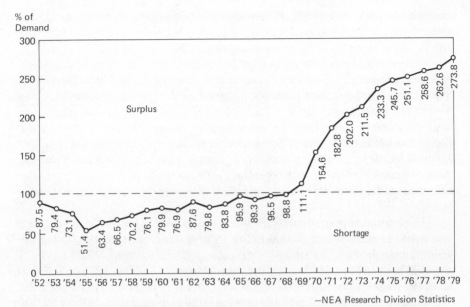

-NEA Research Division Statistics

FIGURE 1.   Supply of Beginning Teachers as Percent Of Normal Demand, 1952 to 1979, According to Present Trends

These estimates were obtained during a period of general teacher shortage and may not be accurate for a period in which the supply is equal to the demand for new teachers. Some of those attending college or university full time the preceding year were experienced teachers who had interrupted their careers to acquire advanced preparation. However, it is clear that the majority of new teachers (persons employed for a given school year who were not employed as teachers anywhere the preceding school year) came from the graduating classes of colleges and universities.

National estimates of the new supply of college and university graduates completing preparation to teach for the first time with minimum certification requirements have been reported annually by the NEA Research Division for 24 years. The numbers of graduates prepared to teach have represented from 26.7% (in 1950) to 36.2% (in 1971) of all graduates receiving the bachelor's and first professional degree.

NEA Research Division projections for the 1970's are for teacher education graduates to be 37% of the projected numbers of graduates receiving the bachelor's and first professional degree. Unless there is a considerable change in the emphasis given to teacher education, it seems likely that future numbers of graduates prepared to teach will continue to grow at about the same rate as the total number of college graduates.

Reflecting the growth in total number of college graduates, the supply of graduates prepared to teach in 1971 (305,711) is more than twice as large as was observed in 1961 (129,188). Projections of college and university graduates show that by 1978 the annual number of graduates prepared to teach (397,000) will be three times as large as the number in 1961.

Not all teacher-education graduates normally enter teaching immediately following graduation. Even in times of critical shortage, more than one-fourth of these prospective teachers postpone entering or decide not to enter teaching during the year following their graduation. Thus we estimate the number of beginning teachers available for entry (supply) in any period in terms of the percent of all teacher education graduates *known* to have entered teaching immediately following their graduation during a period of teacher shortage. Active interest in employment as teachers is projected to be 83.3% of graduates prepared for the elementary level and 69.2% of those prepared for the secondary level.

The annual supply of qualified graduates available for teaching positions was between 65,000 and 90,000 in the 1950's; it increased to 198,000 in the 1960's; it reached 217,750 in 1970; it is projected to grow from 229,053 in 1971 to 266,000 in 1975; it could continue to grow from 277,000 in 1976 to 308,000 in 1979. These projections show the annual supply of beginning teachers in the 1970's to be between two and three times as large as the annual supply of 80,000 to 90,000 observed during the late 1950's.

The supply of qualified persons in the pool of unemployed teachers during a given school session is difficult to estimate accurately. The 1960 U.S. Bureau of the Census reported 304,460 persons as elementary- and secondary-school teachers not gainfully employed at the time of the census. These were people who had completed at least four years of college. An assumption that this group contains the 20-year accumulation of about 1.5% of the teaching staff employed in the public schools provides an estimate that 439,000 persons were in this pool in 1971. This source of supply will continue to grow by at least 2,000 persons each year, reflecting the growth in the total teaching staff during the past 20 years.

The number of reentering teachers employed in 1960 was 18.3% of the persons estimated to be in this pool. Because the year 1960 was in a period of general teacher shortage, this rate of entry may provide an estimate of the supply from this source if attractive positions were available. It would have meant the employment of 80,400 former teachers this fall, about 16,900 more than the number actually employed.

ESTIMATES OF NORMAL DEMAND

The demand for new teachers to replace those leaving through normal turnover is estimated to be about 8% of the total number of teachers each year. This is derived from two studies by the U.S. Office of Education and from a series of sample surveys conducted by the NEA Research Division. Because these estimates were derived during a period of improvements in educational quality, projections using these estimates are likely to reflect a continuation of the rate of these improvements.

The numbers of experienced teachers reentering teaching after at least one year away from it have been about 3% of the total number of teachers employed the preceding year.

Normal demand, therefore, to replace teachers leaving the profession is estimated to be about 8% of the total number of teachers, with reentering teachers filling three-eighths and beginning teachers filling the remaining five-eighths of these positions.

The number of teachers needed to handle enrollment growth was projected on the basis of recent trends of improvement in the pupil-teacher ratio. Because the estimated demand for reentering teachers is based on turnover, the demand for teachers to handle enrollment growth is treated as demand for beginning teachers.

The demand for new (beginning and reentering) teachers for replacement and enrollment change is the *actual* demand for teachers for a given year. The distribution of this actual demand among subject areas and grade levels is estimated by applying the distribution of the numbers of new teachers reported to have been employed the preceding year (23 states are currently able to report this information).

Because the number of births each year began to decline in 1962 and continued to decline each year until 1969, the enrollment potential for the public schools in the 1970's will not increase significantly. The projected growth in the total number of public school teachers between 1971 and 1979 (24,000 positions) will not be as large as the growth in teachers employed in *any one* of the 10 years immediately prior to 1970 (average annual growth of 64,200 positions). As a result, the major source of demand for new teachers during the 1970's will not be increased enrollments but improvements in staffing quality and replacement of teachers in normal turnover. The total annual demand for beginning teachers after 1971 will be between 108,000 and 115,900 through 1979, less than half as large as the projected supply in each of these years (average annual supply of 271,200 between 1972 and 1979).

QUALITY-BASED ESTIMATES

The estimated demand for new teachers to attain minimum quality in educational programs and staffing comprises the normal demand described above plus the new teachers needed to reduce the number of oversize classes, to replace teachers having substandard qualifications, to enlarge school offerings and programs for pupils not now being served (kindergarten, special education, courses not offered because of shortage of qualified teachers), and to replace teachers misassigned for a major portion of their time. Precise standards for these components, however, have not been announced and validated.

During the period of teacher shortage, NEA Research Division estimates were based on the following standards for class size and minimum educational qualifications for teaching: The maximum acceptable teacher load has been 34 pupils per class in elementary grades or a teaching load of 199 pupils per day in secondary grades. The minimum acceptable educational qualification has been the bachelor's degree. An acceptable sign of progress toward providing special education programs has been the number of teachers needed to serve half of the children requiring but not currently having special education services in a single year.

In periods of widespread teacher shortage there was little question that these were standards for rock-bottom *minimum* quality in education programs and staffing. It was accepted that each component of these standards was more than justified and that needs were much greater than the levels projected. However, in these years there were not sufficient numbers of qualified teachers to fill even the normal vacancies. In the current period of teacher surplus, with an adequate supply of qualified teachers available for most assignments, additional research and evaluation should guide decisions about the relative effectiveness of establishing a higher minimum acceptable level of quality in each of these areas. However, it should be remembered that current economic, financial, and employment trends do not suggest attainment of even the former standard for minimum quality in the immediate future, much less an improved standard.

Attainment of these minimum standards in the fall of 1971 would have required 351,200 beginning teachers, 122,100 more than the supply. But the accumulated surpluses of beginning teachers in the fall of 1969 and the fall of 1970 included 96,900 persons. This number is almost equal to the number of beginning teachers needed in 1971 to attain the minimum levels of educational quality. These facts show that unless the annual supply of beginning teachers is reduced for years following 1971, or unless the quality of educational programs and services is improved to levels above these minimum standards, the period of teacher surplus would begin in the fall of 1972 even though these minimum standards of quality are achieved.

The class size component of this minimum standard probably has least professional acceptance. A very desirable revision—maximum class size of 24 in elementary grades and maximum teaching load of 124 in secondary grades—would be a professionally more acceptable *minimum* standard. Further reduction would also be desirable to meet a professionally acceptable standard for most effective instruction.

Achievement of such a revised minimum standard (based on class size maximums listed above) would have required the employment of 729,900 beginning teachers in the fall of 1971, 500,800 more than the number available at that time. This revised standard would have required the addition of 565,800 teaching positions, an increase of 27.7% over the total number of teachers in public schools in 1971.

The number of beginning teachers needed to attain this revised standard of minimum quality is approximately equal to the projected surpluses of beginning teachers between 1970 and 1974 (573,100) persons. Our present course will provide adequate potential staff to attain this revised standard of minimum quality in 1974, at which time the projected continuing growth in teacher supply would create a period of teacher surpluses beginning with that year.

Present trends are for future annual supplies of beginning teachers to be considerably larger than normal demand. The present margin is sufficient for supplying the increased numbers of beginning teachers which will be needed if the rates of school improvements are increased. The likelihood of an increasingly abundant supply of beginning teachers in the future gives reason for the profession to direct attention to two goals: (1) increasing the demand for beginning teachers through rapid improvements in educational quality, and (2) selectively decreasing the future numbers of graduates prepared to teach. In view of the prospect of a surplus, it should be remembered that there will continue to be a need for at least 100,000 beginning teachers annually for the next decade.

6 The Classroom Teacher – 1980
William D. Southworth

Parity with doctors and lawyers, which teachers have longed for since World War II, will be reached by 1980—but not under the conditions that teachers readily foresee, nor conditions which they will necessarily approve. Parity will come about in preparation, compensation, and standards of performance.

Preparation for teaching will be a six-year preparation. The first four years will be a liberal arts program. The fifth year will be confined to education courses, and the sixth will be an internship year.

The extension of the preparation period is almost obvious if one studies current requirements for certification of teachers in the 50 states. All the states, with the exception of four, require a bachelor's degree for certification; and those states not specifically requiring it require specialized training that in many ways is more exacting than the bachelor's degree requirement. Current certification standards must be considered in light of what took place before they were instituted.

It was only fifteen years ago that there was an attempt to reduce the length of preparation for certification for teaching in Wisconsin from two years to one year. The proposed reduction was supposed to develop a greater supply of

Reprinted from *The Clearing House*, 47 (6): 327–331 (February 1973), by permission of author and publisher.

teachers based on the simplistic economic idea that if more teachers became available by setting realistic (lower) standards, teachers would cost less to hire, and school costs would be reduced.

One western state was requiring only some summer training after high school graduation for certification to teach.

The attempt in Wisconsin was defeated; and today Wisconsin requires the bachelor's degree, double the preparation of fifteen years back. The western state learned that not only did reducing standards for certification not make more teachers available, it reduced the number of people willing to enter teaching because serious-minded, capable people did not want to enter a "profession" that required only a summer's preparation.

The trend clearly points toward holding current standards for certification. In fact, it points toward increasing those standards, and for a number of reasons:

1. There is an overage of teachers that will continue through the remainder of the 1970's, and these teachers are four-year graduates. It hardly makes sense to think of lowering standards when there is a surplus of teachers who meet, and in many cases exceed, the four-year requirement.
2. With increased teachers' salaries mandated by current salary schedules, school boards can be more selective and can set up the requirements of satisfactory teaching experience, graduate work, and even an advanced degree for its incoming teachers. There appears to be a simple *quid pro quo* here; teachers will get better salaries, and school boards will get better teaching. And is it necessary to add the corollary that as teachers' salaries increase, the teaching profession becomes attractive to serious-minded, capable people who did not consider entering the profession in the past?

The debate about the content of teacher preparation is an ancient one. On the one side, the academicians maintain that people cannot teach unless they themselves are educated, that the primary need for teachers is to be educated themselves, that the *means and methods* of teaching are not complicated nor complex, and that the means and methods can be learned easily, on the job. On the other side, the professors of the teacher-training institutions hold that prospective teachers must be taught *how* to teach, that it is not fair to children for their teachers to learn on the job what they should have learned in pre-service training. The teacher-preparation plan for 1980 satisfies the arguments of both sides.

By 1980, the usual pattern for teacher preparation will be a liberal arts undergraduate program. The completion of the liberal arts degree will be considered to be just the preliminary to teaching, strictly antecedent to the master's degree with its concomitant of permanent certification.

The fifth year will be confined strictly to professional preparation through education courses. There will be an expansion of preparation in reading for elementary teachers, for example, and the inclusion of many courses long advocated by educational leaders but excluded by the time limitation of the four-year period of preparation. And a 33-hour master's degree will allow the inclusion of broadly expanded professional courses in the teacher preparation program, thus completing the marriage of liberal arts and professional courses.

The argument for the sixth-year internship will be predicated on two bases. First, the comparison with the clerkship in law and the internship in medicine will be made. The common attraction for all three areas—law, medicine, and education—will be remuneration. Since beginning teachers' salaries in 1980 can reasonably be anticipated to be $15,000, there will be strong competition for teaching positions, difficulty in getting into teaching, and greater difficulty in staying in the profession. Since fringe benefits will be added to the beginning teachers' salary of $15,000, and those benefits can be fairly computed as being $4,000, the monetary attraction to teaching will eliminate one barrier of the past that caused many people not to enter teaching.

The internship will be helpful for both the tyro teacher and for the school board for which he works. The tyro will have a small stipend while he is learning, in a broadened student-teacher role, knowing that there are fertile financial fields ahead, and that he must prepare himself well if he is to succeed as a teacher. He will surely recognize what veteran teachers and administrators aver, that student teaching is the most important part of the preparation for teaching. A school board will be willing to pay the small stipend because the tyro will furnish important pedagogical services, from classroom instruction to working in the school office. The capable principal will be able to devise a learning program for the tyro teacher that will have wider bounds than those of the usual student teacher arrangement—to the benefit of all directly concerned with the educational process, teachers, supervisors, administrators, parents, and school boards.

As there are teachers today who favor the increased salaries but not increased standards of personal teaching effectiveness, so there will be teachers of the 1980's who will favor increased salaries but not stricter supervision of their work. While it is still true that inadequate supervision concerns itself about housekeeping and heights of shades, and deserves the contempt that it has so well earned, there are several developments in supervision working now that will become standard supervising practice in the 1980's:

1. Better supervision will be carried on by better prepared and more capable supervisors who will work closely with teachers as colleagues, as *primus inter pares*. The standards for better supervision, and better supervisors, will be even greater than the standards for better teaching because the supervisors will be better paid than the teachers, they will hold greater responsibility for the instructional program than the teachers and will thus be held more strictly accountable th the teachers.
2. Routine supervision and routine supervisors will be as outmoded as routine teaching and routine teachers. In the progress of the 1970's they will have been left behind, and they will learn that what they are doing is

passé. It will be comparable to the feelings of insecurity that the normal school graduates developed as they continued in the profession that required the bachelor's degree for new people entering the profession. However, those truly prepared who practice what they believe wil open wide vistas for remarkable pupil development. And in this new atmosphere for learning, the only ones who need fear are teachers who are: (a) incompetent, (b) lazy, (c) disgruntled, or (d) less than 75 percent effective.

The teachers of 1980 will resist the new pattern of supervision, but will have to accept it, and will become reasonably comfortable with it. They will accept the new pattern because the pattern will be the result of compromise between their teachers' association and the school boards. Also, they will have been trained for standards of excellence upon which the new supervision is based.

The school boards ill argue that increased salaries require increased measurable productivity. The teachers' associations will accept the argument of increased measurable productivity of teachers because they must recognize the inevitability of teacher accountability. The teachers' association will fight against improper and non-measuring measuring instruments, but they will agree that the attractiveness of increased salary and fringe benefits for teachers must be accompanied by a measurable increased effectiveness of the classroom teachers.

The teaching profession will become more closely allied with law and medicine through the increased standards for those who enter the teaching profession. The twins of status and remuneration have allowed law and medicine a critical selectivity of the students entering those two professions. Teaching has not enjoyed comparable selectivity because the external rewards in teaching are not comparable to those in law and medicine; but by 1980, with vastly increased status and remuneration there will be a selectivity for those that enter teaching that will compare favorably.

One other major factor comprising the syndrome of selectivity of students for teaching will be the continuing teacher overage. The easy entree into teaching, as exemplified by the low average standardized test scores of students entering teaching, will have disappeared because the profession will, by 1980, combine increased status and remuneration with critical competition to secure measurably more capable students than those entering the profession today.

The classroom teacher of 1980 will feel even greater self-confidence than his counterpart today because he will enter teaching only after satisfying critical screening procedures by a teacher-training institution, surpassing high cutting scores on standardized tests, and becoming convinced that he is now a member of a profession in the strictest, truest sense of the term. He will never be termed a semi-professional as has his counterpart of today.

There will be greater liaison among the teacher-training institutions and the development of more nearly comparable standards for admission to their teacher-training programs. At the same time, the joint efforts of administrators and teachers in the field, working with the college authorities, will eliminate the callous acceptance of students into such overcrowded fields as social studies. The people working in the field and those in the teacher-training institutions will determine yearly anticipated needs for new teachers, and will advise students of their prospects for employment once they have become qualified to teach. Further, personnel of the teacher-training institutions and the professionals in the field will work jointly in determining the *retention* of students in preparation programs. The current irresponsibility on the part of the professionals to the would-be professionals, as exemplified by indifference to the future employment of the would-be professionals, will be replaced by a more effective evaluation of student progress and concrete actions to secure teaching positions for the newcomers.

There will continue to be a need for tenure, and there will be tenure for the classroom teacher of 1980; but that tenure will be different from the tenure generally known today. The tenure of 1980 will have renewable provisions predicated on proven teaching effectiveness.

What the form that "proven teaching effectiveness" will take is not only moot, it is cloudy—and for several reasons. Those objecting to a renewal of tenure concept will point out that lawyers and physicians do not have to show effectiveness in their professions in order to continue to practice their professions, and that renewable tenure would be discriminatory, illegal, and unfair. The burgeoning teachers' organizations will fight against renewable tenure with the knowledge that some of their people could not meet all the physical, psychical, and pedagogical standards of renewable tenure determinations.

The counter argument, the argument that will be accepted in state law, will be that lawyers and physicians are generally entrepreneurs who prosper only as they are effective, that they do not ordinarily become paid employees of a governmental unit. Even more compelling will be the argument that clients go to the lawyers and the physicians of their own choice, and are not required to accept pre-selected lawyers and physicians as are parents who must accept the choice of teachers for their children by a governmental official, the principal.

The standards for renewable tenure will be set into state law after combined groups of teachers, administrators, college officials, and parents have agreed upon standards for tenure. A regular review arrangement will be made for those seeking renewal of tenure, predicated on written, tri-yearly evaluations of the teacher's effectiveness by a committee of the senior administrator of the school and two of the colleagues of the teacher being evaluated. Though refusal of renewal of tenure will be unusual, the knowledge that an evaluation for renewing of tenure will be made will have a healthy effect on the profession, and will promote greater support among the taxpaying citizenry.

The teacher of 1980 will not retire after 20 years of teaching because he will be enjoying a good salary, good working conditions, and will not want to leave his profession in his forties. Further, though he will be able to take his pension and take another job, he will find that the second job will be an unskilled one, and that the pay from the new job, plus his pension from teaching will not induce him to leave teaching. He will discover that teaching will be more pleasant and remunerative than will the job that a pensioner can secure.

By 1980 the teaching profession will reach the status of law and medicine. Teachers will finally secure the recognition in the public mind that they have sought for so long. Teachers and teaching will not change drastically from what they are today. Improved financial remuneration, and higher standards for admission to, and retention in, the profession will combine to bring teaching into a new light of public acceptance; and this increased public acceptance of teaching will insure teaching's place of continuing major importance in American life by the end of the second century of American independence.

■■ Planning for Teaching

No task of teaching is more important than the one addressed in this part. For, certainly, the kinds of plans made in thousands of classrooms across the country will influence significantly what millions of students learn and become. Yet planning is probably the one task most teachers spend least time on.

Many reasons, of course, account for teachers' spending too little time on planning, and many of these reasons are beyond their control. But one reason common among teachers is their belief that making plans for what is taught is not their responsibility. They believe, in other words, that these kinds of plans are and should be made at the national, state, and local levels, and not at the level of individual classrooms and at the discretion of individual teachers. This belief is the focus of selection 7 by Hough and Duncan. They make the point that individual teachers are in a position to determine what is taught in their classrooms, and that they would be acting irresponsibly if they abandoned this position. But they also emphasize that decisions about what is taught should never be made solely on the basis of teachers' personal preferences. Rather, in determining what is taught, a delicate balance must be forged between what teachers think and what the community at large thinks is most important.

But what is most important? What should be taught? What are schools for? One potential answer to these questions is given by Ebel in article 8. Ebel, it seems, is concerned that schools are trying to do too much for too many. He argues that schools were built and maintained for the primary purpose of helping students learn, and not for the purpose of serving as custodial institutions, adjustment centers, recreational facilities, or social research agencies. He argues further that if schools persist in trying to fill all these roles, they will succeed in none.

Heath is of the opinion that there is danger in perceiving the purposes of schooling too narrowly. In selection 9, he implies that schools should have two major foci: academic and affective. And he maintains that only when these two areas are given equal attention will students be educated in accordance with the principles of human growth and development. One such principle is that a person grows and develops as a total organism; in other words, that each facet of a person's development affects and is affected by every other facet. Consequently, according to Heath, when schools attempt to educate the mind and leave to chance the development of values and feelings, or when schools overemphasize affective education, they contribute, however innocently, to youth's disenchantment on the one hand and anti-intellectualism on the other.

Like Heath, Foshay, in article 10, draws upon the principles of developmental psychology in reflecting upon the question of what it means to be human. In addition, he asks the question of what it means to teach. From analyzing and synthesizing the answers to these questions, Foshay concludes that most schools, through the goals they espouse and the efforts they encourage, have a very simplistic perception of living and learning. In my opinion, Foshay's conclusions are similar though not identical to Heath's, but vastly different from Ebel's. In comparing and contrasting these conclusions, the reader should begin to understand the complexity of that question—What are schools for?

Although educators disagree on many aspects of schooling, they do seem to agree that much of the content taught in schools is irrelevant. Van Til, in article 11, presents two alternatives to teachers who wish to make their instructional content more meaningful. In theory, at least, both alternatives are amazingly simple. The first is to replace irrelevant content, and the second is to adapt it. I note, however, that in actual practice neither alternative is widely used. Perhaps the major reason is that many teachers are either unwilling or unable to find the additional planning time that each approach necessitates. Van Til's statement that there are no easy panaceas is as true for this aspect of education as it is for most others.

One form of education, though, is currently being touted by some as the answer to schools' problems. This particular panacea, open education, has had many predecessors; Barth, in selection 12, mentions several: team teaching, nongrading, differentiated staffing, and performance contracting. To be sure, Barth is a strong advocate of open education. But he is convinced—as I am—that merely adopting new jargon or changing the design of classrooms will not automatically result in openness. What is needed first is a philosophical com-

mitment to the basic assumptions underlying the open education concept. Without such a commitment, no amount of teacher and/or administrative planning will prove very effective; and even with it, there is no guarantee of success.

In articles 13 and 14, the reader's attention is directed to probably the most widely and hotly debated topic in education of the last fifteen or so years. The debate is on the use of behavioral objectives (often called instructional, mastery, measurable, or performance objectives). Popham, in article 13, begins by stating that the only reason teachers exist is to change or modify students' behavior. Consequently, according to Popham, it only makes sense for teachers to identify specifically those behavioral changes they intend to make. Raths, in article 14, takes the opposite position; namely, that it is not the major function of teachers to change students' behavior in specific predetermined ways. Which of the two positions is correct? Or is some kind of compromise possible and desirable? These are not incidental questions. The kinds of plans teachers make will be influenced significantly by the answers.

7 Role of the Teacher in Determining What Is Taught

John B. Hough and James K. Duncan

There are many teachers who . . . believe and behave in ways that would lead others to believe that they cannot and do not make important decisions regarding what is taught in their classrooms. They are so bound to the suggested content and time schedule of their school system's course of study that they do not make the responsible professional decisions that they as teachers should make. For example, such a teacher might say, "I can't spend any more time on the New Deal period; I am given only two weeks to finish it." At the other extreme are those teachers who believe that they are responsible to no one but themselves. They teach what they want and disregard their responsibility to both their students and society.

Yet, when the classroom door is closed, the teacher and his students are able to determine the curriculum. They *can* decide what shall be taught and the emphasis that should be placed upon it. Teachers who believe that they have no latitude with respect to selecting particular content or developing their own instructional objectives operate under perceptions that simply do not coincide with reality. They customarily have wide latitude in these regards.

To summarize: few teachers, except in their private roles as citizens and occasionally as members of national and state commissions, are involved in helping to determine the broad goals of education. Few teachers are directly involved in determining the course objectives of education or the broad selection of the content of instruction. Many teachers are involved, however, in determining the units of study and emphasis that will be placed on content in those units of study. In addition, *all* teachers have a wide latitude to determine what will go on in their classes on a day-to-day basis. Effective teachers take all the latitude they need to help their students meet the objectives of education.

This is a great responsibility. It is not a charge that can be taken lightly. It must be worked out in the best interest of the people whom the teacher serves —his students and the people in the communities at the local, state, and national level. In the process of selecting what should be taught, the teacher must keep his responsibility clearly in mind. He does not have the right to make irresponsible decisions concerning what he will teach. For example, no teacher has the right to teach those things which are of interest to him alone, solely because they are of interest to him. Obviously, no teacher can go on day after day teaching those

From Chapter 2 from *Teaching: Description and Analysis,* by John B. Hough and James K. Duncan. Copyright © 1970 by Addison-Wesley Publishing Company, Inc., Reading, Massachusetts. Reprinted by permission of Addison-Wesley.

things which are not of interest to him, but no teacher has the right to select from his field of study those things which he enjoys teaching without reference to the needs and goals of his students or the communities that he serves. Certainly, however, the most exciting times in teaching are those when the teacher *and* the students are working on things that are of mutual interest to them.

The home-economics teacher in a lower-class urban community who holds objectives that deal with middle-class etiquette must ask herself in whose best interest these objectives are proposed. The mathematics teacher who would make an honor section out of his ninth-grade lower-ability algebra class by introducing profound mathematical concepts and moving the students at a pace far beyond their capacities also must ask himself whose needs he is trying to meet—his or his students. The social-studies teacher in a problems-of-democracy class who turns his lectern into a pulpit for his own political ideology must ask himself the hard questions, "Is this in the best interest of my students? Are my objectives, in fact, congruent with the goals of the people I serve?"

These are indeed difficult questions to answer, for teachers do not serve themselves alone, a single community, or a solitary student. The teacher cannot escape his responsibilities to himself, to all his students, and to all the communities that he serves.

Deciding what should be taught is a basic curriculum decision. What is taught in the public schools should be consistent with the goals of education as expressed by the communities that the teacher serves; and the students are the most important single group among those he serves. The needs and goals of these students and the needs and goals of the other communities he serves must be clarified in the teacher's mind to create the delicate balance from which he makes professional decisions regarding what will be taught on a day-by-day basis. Though he is indeed the master of his classroom, he must not create a classroom world which is anarchistic and unrelated to the outside world. He must respond to the challenge in a responsible way that is congruent with his own values.

8 What Are Schools For?

Robert L. Ebel

When the history of our times is written, it may designate the two decades following World War II as the golden age of American education. Never before was education more highly valued. Never before was so much of it so readily available to so many. Never before had it been supported so generously. Never before was so much expected of it.

But in this eighth decade of the twentieth century public education in this country appears to be in trouble. Taxpayers are revolting against the skyrocketing costs of education. Schools are being denied the funds they say they need for quality education. Teachers are uniting to press demands for higher pay and easier working conditions.

College and high school students have rebelled against what they call "the Establishment," resisting and overturning regulations, demanding pupil-directed rather than teacher-directed education, and turning in some cases to drink, drugs, and delinquency. Minorities are demanding equal treatment, which is surely their right. But when integration makes social differences more visible, and when equality of opportunity is not followed quickly by equality of achievement, frustration turns to anger which sometimes leads to violence.

Surely these problems are serious enough. But I believe there is one yet more serious, because it lies closer to the heart of our whole educational enterprise. We seem to have lost sight of, or become confused about, our main function as educators, our principal goal, our reason for existence. We have no good answer that we are sure of and can agree on to the question, What are schools for?

It may seem presumptuous of me to suggest that I know the answer to this question. Yet the answer I will give is the answer that an overwhelming majority of our fellow citizens would also give. It is the answer that would have been given by most educators of the past who established and operated schools. Indeed, the only reason the question needs to be asked and answered at this time is that some influential educators have been conned into accepting wrong answers to the question. Let me mention a few of these wrong answers:

- Schools are not custodial institutions responsible for coping with emotionally disturbed or incorrigible young people, for keeping nonstudents off the streets or out of the job market.
- Schools are not adjustment centers, responsible for helping young people

Reprinted from *Phi Delta Kappan,* 54 (1): 3-7 (September 1972), by permission of author and publisher.

develop favorable self-concepts, solve personal problems, and come to terms with life.

• Schools are not recreational facilities designed to entertain and amuse, to cultivate the enjoyment of freedom, to help young people find strength through joy.

• Schools are not social research agencies, to which a society can properly delegate responsibility for the discovery of solutions to the problems that are currently troubling the society.

I do not deny that society needs to be concerned about some of the things just mentioned. What I do deny is that schools were built and are maintained primarily to solve such problems. I deny that schools are good places in which to seek solutions, or that they have demonstrated much success in finding them. Schools have a very important special mission. If they accept responsibility for solving many of the other problems that trouble some young people, they are likely to fail in their primary mission, without having much success in solving the rest of our social problems.

Then what is the right answer to the question, What are schools for? I believe it is that schools are for learning, and that what ought to be learned mainly is useful knowledge.

Not all educators agree. Some of them discount the value of knowledge in the modern world. They say we ought to strive for the cultivation of intellectual skills. Others claim that schools have concentrated too much on knowledge, to the neglect of values, attitudes, and such affective dispositions. Still others argue that the purpose of education is to change behavior. They would assess its effectiveness by examining the pupil's behavior or performance. Let us consider these three alternatives in reverse order.

If the schools are to be accountable for the performance of their pupils, the question that immediately arises is, What performance? A direct answer to this question is, The performance you've been trying to teach. But that answer is not as simple or as obviously correct as it seems at first glance. Many schools have not been primarily concerned with teaching pupils to perform. They have been trying to develop their pupil's knowledge, understanding, attitudes, interests, and ideals; their cognitive capabilities and affective dispositions rather than their performances. Those who manage such schools would agree that capabilities and dispositions can only be assessed by observing performances, but they would insist that the performances themselves are not the goals of achievement, only the indicators of it. A teacher who is concerned with the pupil's cognitive capabilities and affective dispositions will teach quite differently, they point out, than one whose attention is focused solely on the pupil's performances. And, if performances are not goals but only indicators, we should choose the ones to use in assessment on the basis of their effectiveness as indicators. Clearly we cannot choose them in terms of the amount of effort we made to develop them.

But, if we reject performance goals, another question arises: What should be the relative emphasis placed on affective dispositions as opposed to cognitive capabilities? Here is another issue that divides professional educators. To some, how the pupil feels—his happiness, his interest, his self-concept, his yearnings—are what should most concern teachers. To others the pupil's cognitive resources and capabilities are the main concern. Both would agree that cognition and affect interact, and that no school ought to concentrate solely on one and ignore the other. But they disagree on which should receive primary emphasis.

In trying to resolve this issue it may be helpful to begin by observing that the instructional programs of almost all schools are aimed directly at the cultivation of cognitive competence. Pupils are taught how to read and to use mathematics, how to write and to express perceptions, feelings, ideas, and desires in writing, to be acquainted with history and to understand science. The pupil's affective dispositions, his feelings, attitudes, interests, etc., constitute conditions that facilitate or inhibit cognitive achievement. They may be enhanced by success or impaired by failure. But they are by-products, not the main products, of the instructional effort. It is almost impossible to find any school that has planned and successfully operated an instructional program aimed primarily at the attainment of affective goals.

That this situation exists does not prove that it ought to exist. But it does suggest that there may be reasons. And we need not look too far to discover what they probably are.

Feelings are essentially unteachable. They can not be passed along from teacher to learner in the way that information is transmitted. Nor can the learner acquire them by pursuing them directly as he might acquire understanding by study. Feelings are almost always the consequence of something—of success or failure, of duty done or duty ignored, of danger encountered or danger escaped. Further, good feelings (and bad feelings also, fortunately) are seldom if ever permanent possessions. They tend to be highly ephemeral. The surest prediction that one can make when he feels particularly good, strong, wise, or happy is that sooner or later he is going to feel bad, weak, foolish, or sad. In these circumstances it is hardly surprising that feelings are difficult to teach.

Nor do they need to be taught. A new-born infant has, or quickly develops, a full complement of them—pain, rage, satiety, drowsiness, vitality, joy, love, and all the rest. Experience may attach these feelings to new objects. It may teach the wisdom of curbing the expression of certain feelings at inappropriate times or in inappropriate ways. And while such attachments and curbings may be desirable, and may be seen as part of the task of the school, they hardly qualify as one of its major missions.

The school has in fact a much more important educational mission than affective education, one which in the current cultural climate and educational fashion is being badly neglected. I refer to moral education—the inculcation in the young of the accumulated moral wisdom of the race. Some of our young people have been allowed to grow up as virtual moral illiterates. And as Joseph Junell points out elsewhere in this *Kappan,* we are paying a heavy price for this neglect as the youth of our society become alienated, turn to revolt, and threaten the destruction of our social fabric.

This change in our perception of the function of the school is reflected in our statements of educational objectives. A century ago Horace Mann, Herbert Spencer, and most others agreed that there were three main aspects of education: intellectual, moral, and physical. Today the main aspects identified by our taxonomies of objectives are cognitive, affective, and psychomotor. The first and third elements in these two triads are essentially identical. The second elements are quite different. The change reflects a shift in emphasis away from the pupil's duties and toward his feelings.

Why has this come about? Perhaps because of the current emphasis in our society on individual liberty rather than on personal responsibility. Perhaps because we have felt it necessary to be more concerned with civil rights than with civic duties. Perhaps because innovation and change look better to us than tradition and stability. Perhaps because we have come to trust and honor the vigor of youth more than the wisdom of age.

In all these things we may have been misled. As we view the contemporary culture in this country it is hard to see how the changes that have taken place in our moral values during the last half century have brought any visible improvement in the quality of our lives. It may be time for the pendulum to start swinging back toward an emphasis on responsibility, on stability, on wisdom. Older people are not always wiser people, but wisdom does grow with experience, and experience does accumulate with age.

Schools have much to contribute to moral education if they choose to do so, and if the courts and the public will let them. The rules of conduct and discipline adopted and enforced in the school, the models of excellence and humanity provided by the teachers, can be powerful influences in moral education. The study of history can teach pupils a decent respect for the lessons in morality that long experience has gradually taught the human race. Schools in the Soviet Union today appear to be doing a much more effective job of moral education than we have done in recent years. This fact alone may be enough to discredit moral education in some eyes. But concern for moral education has also been expressed by educational leaders in the democracies.

Albert North Whitehead[1] put the matter this way at the end of his essay on the aims of education:

> "The essence of education is that it be religious."
> "Pray, what is religious education?"
> "A religious education is an education which inculcates duty and reverence. Duty arises from our potential control over the course of events. Where attainable knowledge could have changed the issue, ignorance has the guilt of vice. And the foundation of reverence is this

---

[1] *The Aims of Education* (New York: The Macmillan Company, 1929).

perception, that the present holds within itself the complete sum of existence, backwards and forwards, that whole amplitude of time which is eternity."

If these views are correct, moral education deserves a much higher priority among the tasks of the school than does affective education. But it does not deserve the highest priority. That spot must be reserved for the cultivation of cognitive competence. Human beings need strong moral foundations, as part of their cultural heritage. They also need a structure of knowledge as part of their intellectual heritage. What schools were primarily built to do, and what they are most capable of doing well, is to help the student develop cognitive competence.

What is cognitive competence? Two distinctly different answers have been given. One is that it requires acquisition of knowledge. The other is that it requires development of intellectual skills. Here is another issue on which educational specialists are divided.

To avoid confusion or superficiality on this issue it is necessary to be quite clear on the meanings attached to the terms *knowledge* and *intellectual skills*. Knowledge, as the term is used here, is not synonymous with information. Knowledge is built out of information by thinking. It is an integrated structure of relationships among concepts and propositions. A teacher can give his students information. He cannot give them knowledge. A student must earn the right to say "I know" by his own thoughtful efforts to understand.

Whatever a person experiences directly in living or vicariously by reading or listening can become part of his knowledge. It will become part of his knowledge if he succeeds in integrating that experience into the structure of his knowledge, so that it makes sense, is likely to be remembered, and will be available for use when needed. Knowledge is essentially a private possession. Information can be made public. Knowledge cannot. Hence it would be more appropriate to speak of a modern-day information explosion than of a knowledge explosion.

The term *intellectual skills* has also been used with a variety of meanings. Further, those who use it often do not say, precisely and clearly, what they mean by it. Most of them seem not to mean skill in specific operations, such as spelling a word, adding two fractions, diagraming a sentence, or balancing a chemical equation. They are likely to conceive of intellectual skills in much broader terms, such as observing, classifying, measuring, communicating, predicting, inferring, experimenting, formulating hypotheses, and interpreting data.

It seems clear that these broader intellectual skills cannot be developed or used very effectively apart from substantial bodies of relevant knowledge. To be skillful in formulating hypotheses about the cause of a patient's persistent headaches, one needs to know a considerable amount of neurology, anatomy, and physiology, as much as possible about the known disorders that cause headaches, and a great deal about the history and habits of the person who is suffering them. That is, to show a particular intellectual skill a person must possess the relevant knowledge. (Note well at this point that a person cannot look up the knowledge he needs, for knowledge, in the sense of the term as we use it, cannot be looked up. Only information can be looked up. Knowledge has to be built by the knower himself.) And, if he does possess the relevant knowledge, what else does he need in order to show the desired skill?

Intellectual skill that goes beyond knowledge can be developed in specific operations like spelling a word or adding fractions. But the more general (and variable from instance to instance) the operation becomes, the less likely it is that a person's intellectual skills will go far beyond his knowledge.

Those who advocate the development of intellectual skills as the principal cognitive aim of education often express the belief (or hope) that these skills will be broadly transferrable from one area of subject matter to another. But if the subjects are quite different, the transfer is likely to be quite limited. Who would hire a man well trained in the measurement of personal characteristics for the job of measuring stellar distances and compositions?

Those who advocate the cultivation of knowledge as the central focus of our educational efforts are sometimes asked, "What about wisdom? Isn't that more important than knowledge?"

To provide a satisfactory answer to this question we need to say clearly what we mean when we speak of wisdom. In some situations wisdom is simply an alias for good fortune. He who calls the plays in a football game, who designs a new automobile, or who plays the stock market is likely to be well acquainted with this kind of wisdom—and with its constant companion, folly. If an action that might turn out badly in fact turns out well, we call it an act of wisdom. If it turns out badly, it was clearly an act of folly.

But there is more than this to the relation of knowledge to wisdom. C. I. Lewis of Harvard has expressed that relation in this way:

> Where ability to make correct judgments of value is concerned, we more typically speak of wisdom, perhaps, than of knowledge. And "wisdom" connotes one character which is not knowledge at all, though it is quality inculcated by experience; the temper, namely, which avoids perversity in intentions, and the insufficiently considered in actions. But for the rest, wisdom and knowledge are distinct merely because there is so much of knowledge which, for any given individual or under the circumstances which obtain, is relatively inessential to judgment of values and to success in action. Thus a man may be pop-eyed with correct information and still lack wisdom, because his information has little bearing on those judgments of relative value which he is called upon to make, or because he lacks capacity to discriminate the practically important from the unimportant, or to apply his information to concrete problems of action. And men of humble attainments so far as breadth of information goes may still be wise by their correct apprehension of such values as lie open to them and of the roads to these. But surely wisdom is a type of knowledge;

that type which is oriented on the important and the valuable. The wise man is he who knows where good lies, and how to act so that it may be attained.[2]

I take Professor Lewis to mean that, apart from the rectitude in purposes and the deliberateness in action that experience must teach, wisdom in action is dependent on relevant knowledge. If that is so, the best the schools can do to foster wisdom is to help students cultivate knowledge.

Our conclusion at this point is that schools should continue to emphasize cognitive achievements as the vast majority of them have been doing. Some of you may not be willing to accept this conclusion. You may believe some other goal deserves higher priority in the work of the school, perhaps something like general ability to think (apart from any particular body of knowledge), or perhaps having the proper affective dispositions, or stable personal adjustment, or simply love of learning.

If you do, you ought to be prepared to explain how different degrees of attainment of the goal you would support can be determined. For if you can not do this, if you claim your favored goal is intangible and hence unmeasurable, there is room for strong suspicion that it may not really be very important (since it has no clearly observable concomitants or consequences to render it tangible and measurable). Or perhaps the problem is that you don't have a very concrete idea of what it is you propose as a goal.

Let us return to the question of what schools are for, and in particular, for what they should be accountable. It follows from what has been said about the purposes of schooling, and about the cooperation required from the student if those purposes are to be achieved, that the school should not accept responsibility for the learning achievement of every individual pupil. The essential condition for learning is the purposeful activity, the willingness to work hard to learn, of the individual learner. Learning is not a gift any school can give. It is a prize the learner himself must pursue. If a pupil is unwilling or unable to make the effort required, he will learn little in even the best school.

Does this mean that a school should give the student maximum freedom to learn, that it should abandon prescribed curricula and course content in favor of independent study on projects selected by the pupils themselves? I do not think so. Surely all learning must be done by the learner himself, but a good teacher can motivate, direct, and assist the learning process to great advantage. For a school to model its instructional program after the kind of free learning pupils do on their own out of school is to abandon most of its special value as a school, most of its very reason for existence.

Harry Broudy and John Palmer, discussing the demise of the kind of progressive education advocated by Dewey's disciple William H. Kilpatrick, had this to say about the predecessors of our contemporary free schools and open classrooms:

[2] C. I. Lewis, *An Analysis of Knowledge and Valuation* (LaSalle, Ill.: Open Court, 1946).

A technically sophisticated society simply does not dare leave the acquisition of systematized knowledge to concomitant learning, the by-products of projects that are themselves wholesome slices of juvenile life. Intelligence without systematized knowledge will do only for the most ordinary, everyday problems. International amity, survival in our atomic age, automation, racial integration, are not common everyday problems to which common-sense knowledge and a sense of decency are adequate.[3]

Like Broudy and Palmer, I believe that command of useful knowledge is likely to be achieved most rapidly and most surely when the individual pupil's effort to learn is motivated, guided, and assisted by expert instruction. Such instruction is most likely to occur, and to be most efficient and effective, when given in classes, not to individuals singly.

If the school is not held to account for the success of each of its pupils in learning, for what should it be accountable? I would say that it should accept responsibility for providing a favorable learning environment. Such an environment, in my view, is one in which the student's efforts to learn are:

1. guided and assisted by a capable, enthusiastic teacher;
2. facilitated by an abundance of books, films, apparatus, equipment, and other instructional materials;
3. stimulated and rewarded by both formal and informal recognition of achievement; and
4. reinforced by the example and the help of other interested, hardworking students.

The first two of these aspects of a favorable learning environment are unlikely to be seriously questioned. But perhaps a word or two needs to be said in defense of the other two. First, what of the need for formal recognition and reward of achievement as a stimulus of efforts to achieve?

In the long run learning may be its own reward. But the experience of generations of good teachers has shown that in the short run learning is greatly facilitated by more immediate recognition and rewards. This means words of praise and of reproof, which good teachers have used from ancient time. It means tests and grades, reports and honors, diplomas and degrees. These formal means and occasions for recognizing and rewarding achievement are built into our system of education. We will do well to retain them, to disregard the perennial advice of educational reformers that such so-called extrinsic incentives to achievement be abandoned—unless, of course, we are also willing to abandon excellence as a goal for our efforts.

Next, what of the influence of classmates in either stimulating, assisting, and

[3] Harry S. Broudy and John R. Palmer, *Exemplars of Teaching Method* (Chicago: Rand McNally, 1965).

rewarding efforts to achieve, or disparaging and ridiculing those efforts? In the experience of many teachers these positive or negative influences can be very strong. Of course a teacher's attitudes and behavior can tend to encourage or discourage learning. But much also depends on the attitudes the students bring with them to the class. If they are interested and prepared to work hard, learning can be productive fun. If not, learning is likely to be listless and unproductive.

There may be some teachers with a magic touch that can convert an uninterested, unwilling class into a group of eager learners. I myself have encountered such teachers only in movies or novels. Surely they are too rare to count on for solving the problems of motivation to learn, especially in some of the more difficult situations. For the most part, motivation to learn is an attitude a student has or lacks well before a particular course of instruction ever begins.

Going to school is an opportunity, and ought to be so regarded by all pupils. The good intentions which led us to enact compulsory schooling laws have trapped us. School attendance can be made compulsory. School learning can not be. So some of our classrooms are loaded with youth who have no wish to be there, whose aim is not to learn but to escape from learning. Such a classroom is not a favorable learning environment.

The remedy is obvious. No upper grade or high school young person ought to be allowed in a class unless he wants to take advantage of the opportunity it offers. Keeping him there under compulsion will do him no good, and will do others in the class harm. Compulsory school attendance laws were never intended to create such a problem for teachers and school officials. Have we the wit to recognize the source of this problem, and the courage to act to correct it?

Let me now recapitulate what I have tried to say about what schools are for.

1. Public education in America today is in trouble.

2. Though many conditions contribute to our present difficulties, the fundamental cause is our own confusions concerning the central purpose of our activities.

3. Schools have been far too willing to accept responsibility for solving all of the problems of young people, for meeting all of their immediate needs. That schools have failed to discharge these obligations successfully is clearly evident.

4. Schools are for learning. They should bend most of their efforts to the facilitation of learning.

5. The kind of learning on which schools should concentrate most of their efforts is cognitive competence, the command of useful knowledge.

6. Knowledge is a structure of relationships among concepts. It must be built by the learner himself as he seeks understanding of the information he has received.

7. Affective dispositions are important by-products of all human experience, but they seldom are or should be the principal targets of our

educational efforts. We should be much more concerned with moral education than with affective education.

8. Intellectual skills are more often praised as educational goals than defined clearly enough to be taught effectively. Broadly general intellectual skills are mainly hypothetical constructs which are hard to demonstrate in real life. Highly specific intellectual skills are simply aspects of knowledge.
9. Wisdom depends primarily on knowledge, secondarily on experience.
10. Schools should not accept responsibility for the success of every pupil in learning, since that success depends so much on the pupil's own efforts.
11. Learning is a personal activity which each student must carry on for himself.
12. Individual learning is greatly facilitated by group instruction.
13. Schools should be held accountable for providing a good learning environment, which consists of a) capable, enthusiastic teachers, b) abundant and appropriate instructional materials, c) formal recognition and reward of achievement, and d) a class of willing learners.
14. Since learning cannot be made compulsory, school attendance ought not to be compulsory either.

Schools ought to be held accountable. One way or another, they surely will be held accountable. If they persist in trying to do too many things, things they were not designed and are not equipped to do well, things that in some cases can not be done at all, they will show up badly when called to account. But there is one very important thing they were designed and are equipped to do well, and that many schools have done very well in the past. That is to cultivate cognitive competence, to foster the learning of useful knowledge. If they keep this as their primary aim, and do not allow unwilling learners to sabotage the learning process, they are likely to give an excellent accounting of their effectiveness and worth.

9 Affective Education: Aesthetics and Discipline

Douglas H. Heath

The affective education movement is a response to deep currents of student dissatisfaction with and alienation from the education they are receiving. As a goal for education the term is inadequate. "Affective education" is more a rallying slogan with several different meanings than a well-defined program for action. It is a diffuse, poorly formulated, gutsy reaction to the excessive and exclusive academicism that has dominated our educational values since Sputnik. Affective education is in danger of becoming an ephemeral fad. As a movement, it risks encouraging the same types of excesses that our faddish enslavement to academic excellence committed. If we do not clearly understand the causes for its dramatic flowering in the past several years, we may snuff out the spirit of affective education through injudicious excess. Finally, affective education is a potentially dangerous innovation that may accentuate unhealthy development.

Despite these strictures and too polemical statements, the affective education movement is today's most needed catalyst for humanizing our schools. Its principal thrust is to enable students to become more whole and so more healthy human beings. It has not been sharply defined. Like its currently popular cognates, "humanistic education," "teaching for personal growth," and "confluent education," affective education seeks to create more powerful ways to nurture and integrate a youth's feelings and values with his intellectual development. I have emphasized the negative aspects of the movement to warn us that it could become but another passing fad unless it is grounded on a reasoned rationale and unless its substantive program is linked to a valid theory of human development.

Four questions must be examined if we are to integrate the affective or humanistic education movement with our academic purposes and methods: What are the societal and psychological forces compelling educators to become concerned with the affective growth of their students? Can the principal meanings of affective education be more sharply delineated? Why is affective education a potentially dangerous movement? And most critically, how can affective education be grounded on a theoretical rationale that integrates it with the academic purposes of schools?

Reprinted from *The School Review*, 80 (3): 353–372 (May 1972), by permission of the author and The University of Chicago Press. Copyright © 1972 by The University of Chicago Press.

Three profound societal changes are fueling the affective education movement. The first is the widening awareness of the psychological discontinuity between the type of emerging society we have been developing and our mode of educating our youth. Educators have not really confronted seriously the implications that an increasingly affluent, leisure-oriented, interdependent, impersonal society have for the way we should educate. Our youth are closer to the psychological effects of such a society than we. They are experiencing the irrelevance of their traditional academic education for living in a society which will demand qualities not being cultivated in our schools. What qualities? They need deeper and more autonomous interests to direct and organize their energies in a society that will not require as many hours of their time to earn money to survive; interpersonal skills for forming intimate relationships more readily in a society that increasingly is converting our relations to "I-It," that is, "I-machine" types of relationships, and guiding values that give a purpose for living in a society whose mythic traditions and institutional forms are losing their authority.

There are other changes occurring in our society which we are ignoring but which make our traditional educational practices increasingly archaic. Take just one profound change: the liberation of both men and women from traditional concepts of masculinity and femininity. The American concept of masculinity has had devastatingly unhealthy psychological effects on many men. Thankfully, it is becoming obsolescent for this younger generation.[1] One of the unintended but powerful effects of the affective education movement will be to accelerate that obsolescence. It will help boys, as well as girls, develop a greater sensitivity to their feelings and a wider range of channels through which to express them than boys, in particular, have now. (Only within the past eight years have colleges provided modern dance classes for males.) What do our schools do to intensify the unhealthy effects of our culture's obsolescent concepts of masculinity and femininity? Do we subtly compel girls to play with dolls and boys with blocks? Do we keep girls from playing football and boys from learning child care and cooking? Do we thereby teach a girl to suppress her aggressive energies and a boy to inhibit his tender nurturant feelings? The affective education movement seeks to release and nurture a youth's emotions, not to block and cripple them to fit a social stereotype or adult hang-up.

The second cause of the affective education movement is in the nature of the deepening estrangements from society contemporary youth are experiencing. Increasingly, our almost exclusive mode of didactic teaching, that is, reliance on verbal abstract symbolic manipulation, is out of phase with the emerging needs of youth. I cite only four profound estrangements occurring that affective education in its different forms seeks to heal. The first is the gulf between vicarious and direct experience that television, especially, has accentuated. The average seventeen-year-old has seen more than 17,000 hours of television. Such viewing teaches passivity in mode of perception as well as in gratification of wishes. Television does not educate for initiative, coping behavior, and action. Adolescents are revolting against traditional forms of teaching, like lecturing. They are satiated with being talked at, with learning *about,* with being manipulated by external forces. They need to experience vividly and immediately, to act, to make their education more than just a verbal game. Affective education emphasizes the importance of experiencing the abstractions of education in the gut and in action.

A second related form of alienation occurring in youth is their growing dependence on increasingly intense stimulation to "turn them on." They are being emptied of their inner resources to deal with their boredom. Many youths are estranged from their passions and so do not feel like alive, vital persons. To feel alive they need the excitement of loud stereos, drugs, vandalism, and violence. Children exhaust novelty more rapidly these days. Nursery school teachers tell me they now bring out new toys sooner in the year than they used to in order to keep their children interested. The danger of providing such rich, colorful, attractive environments for children is that we may satiate them and create *ennui* in the long run. Affective education seeks to help a youth develop stronger emotional resources that will serve as abiding interests in his life so that he will not be so dependent on external incentives and programs.

The third estrangement fueling the demands of students for affective education is a change in their relation to time. Their time perspective is becoming foreshortened as they become alienated from a sense of history as well as of destiny. The past and the future are not as salient directing forces in their lives as they may have been for their parents. The consequence is that youth no longer accept the values of hard work, patience, tolerance of frustration for a future reward, and the mastery of disciplined craftsmanship—qualities necessary to the perfection of skill, but qualities which depend upon a sense of a "reliable future" to sustain one while mastering the tedious discipline involved. Affective education involves experiencing the immediacy of one's body now—not just talking about one's feelings yesterday or about what one might encounter tomorrow.

Finally, their fourth estrangement is from traditional forms of authority. No longer do role, status, age, wealth, and sex convey authority to increasing numbers of youth. Their emerging criterion of authority is, at its root, an aesthetic one. The dynamics of the aesthetic way of life have been described this way: "Each single experience is judged from the standpoint of grace, symmetry, or fitness. He regards life as a procession of events; each single impression is enjoyed for its own sake. He need not be a creative artist nor need he be effete. In social affairs he may be said to be interested in persons but not in the welfare of persons; he tends toward individualism and self-sufficiency. Aesthetic people . . . oppose political activity when it makes for the repression of individuality."[2] What is authoritative to a youth is the beauty, style, and grace with which a person lives his life. If an adventure or a person is "beautiful," though it land a person in jail or he be a bum, that alone is the justification of that adventure or of that person's life. That is the emerging meaning of "authority." Our society is undergoing a profound transition in its values. Rather than valuing what a person does or even becomes, our youth may be increasingly valuing as primary what a person is. Any educational movement, like affective education, that enhances the authority of one's own subjectivity will powerfully confirm to a youth the validity of his own emotional evaluations.

The third and last primary cause of the affective education movement is the violation by educators of a fundamental principle of healthy development. Since Sputnik, we have so pushed verbal, abstract, and symbolic development in our schools that we have distorted the growth of our youth. Such an emphasis is very deep in our schools, even in our elementary ones: accelerated mathematics and reading programs, efforts to introduce reading in some nursery schools, the abandonment or devaluation of play as well as of social group activities, introduction of sociology into third grade, the specialization of elementary school teachers. I recall a sixth grade mathematics teacher who boasted he was able to teach his children the principles he was working out in his master's thesis. Certainly we can teach students to go through our symbolic rituals and games, but frequently such abstract learning is too divorced from experience. My college freshmen have had calculus in high school but do not know how to apply it. It sits like a foreign body in their memories—never assimilated into their bones. The basic principle of growth we have violated is that a person grows as an organism, not just as a head. Too accentuated development in one sector of the personality, as in abstract verbal ability, at the expense of development in other sectors, as in one's feelings and social relationships, begins to induce resistance to further development in that sector until compensatory development has occurred in the neglected areas of the personality. The virulent anti-intellectualism of some of our most intelligent youth, the beginning flood of our best students leaving high school early, the retreat to drugs and sex are, in part, efforts to reclaim a sense of primitive wholeness that the hyperconscious rationality of our educational program has "sicklied over with the pale cast of thought." The affective education movement, by sanctioning the emergence of nonrational, even primitive, childlike emotions is a strong corrective experience for many youth.

What are the consequences of the growing discontinuity between the psychological demands of our emerging society, the growing estrangements of our youth, and the distortion of the growth process? One is the chaotic, sometimes driven, frenetic search for new educational and social forms by which to recover a greater sense of wholeness. Another is the flight of youth from the entreprenurial, the competitive, the aggressive, the coping and mastering, the perfectionistic, and even the rational and the logical. They search the psychedelic, the aesthetic, subjective, expressive world of private feelings and impulse to heal their inner estrangements and create a more integrative way of life for coping with what they consider a dehumanizing society. They are swinging from an Apollonian to a Dionysian mode of life.

Such are some of the dimensions of the ferment out of which the affective education movement has sprung.

But just what do we mean by affective education? The phrase has been applied to a variety of contemporary trends, some of which have their roots deep in the history of American education. Four interrelated educational trends now in process capture its spirit.

First, affective education is the education of affects, or feelings and emotions. Educators have been educating affects since the Athenians first insisted every youth learn to play the lyre. Music teachers have tried to nurture musical sensitivity and appreciative feelings for years. Curricular pilot studies are now underway to sensitize students in more systematic ways to rhythmic, artistic, and dance patterns in order to cultivate artistic judgment. But I have yet to discover an adequate rationale for identifying the specific types of feelings to be nurtured and refined. Psychology is of little help. It has no adequate theory of emotion. Emotion does have many functions. It stirs and incites us. Simulation games are frequently used in the classroom to involve a youth emotionally so he will become interested in more academic topics. Emotion has an expressive function. Its expression reduces tensions. The rigorous athletic programs of some boarding schools are frequently defended because they "drain off" urgent sexual and aggressive impulses. Emotions also direct behavior. Our values and convictions are relatively stable emotionalized preferences and beliefs that guide behavior. Prior to the demise of progressive education and of the influence of church-controlled education, the principal thrust of American education was the development of character and values. Some religious schools still seek to cultivate emotional commitment to certain parochial values. Since Sputnik, in particular, most schools have become defensive about educating for character development and have passively slipped under the shadow of academic excellence, abandoning character development to chance. One focus of affective education is to bring value issues back into the curriculum. Although Glasser and others[3] have proposed some means by which to help children learn how to deal with certain types of value issues, no one of whom I am aware has presented any rationale for the types of values for which we should educate.

A second focus of affective education is to make the learning process less abstract and deductive and more concretely experiential and inductive. Field trips to the zoo, the integrated day- or British infant-school model, or, for adolescents, apprenticeship types of experiences or a semester abroad seek to take advantage of more inductive experiential forms of learning. These approaches are not new. Their renaissance is due to the increasing didactic abstractness of the teacher-dominated classroom and of formalistic teaching methods that accompany a too-verbal curriculum. Such experiential learning takes much more teaching skill than most of us realize. Most trips to the nearby bird sanctuary or Washington, D.C., are passive experiences frequently not adequately reflected upon or integrated into the ongoing curriculum. Many are a waste of time. The National Council of Churches has recently sponsored a project to develop new models of seminary education.[4] Most of the models involve a form of direct action work with real problems. The students claimed they learned more than they ever did in seminary. They certainly became more alive persons. Yet, the participating faculty failed to discover how to reflect theologically about such experiences in order to integrate them with the conceptual content of the curriculum. Raw, unadulterated, experiencing may be entertaining and exciting but it must be reflected upon, ideas and principles abstracted out of it, and feelings symbolized if education is to occur. As much effort should go into reflecting about an experience as into the experiencing itself. Otherwise, affective education risks being only a fun game that leads nowhere.

A third related meaning of affective education is to make learning a more organismic experience rather than only cerebral exercise. Learning does not stick if it is only verbal and not integrated into action. Piaget has been telling us for years that a youth learns best when many sensory modalities, most readily activated in action, are simultaneously involved in learning. Too much academic learning is primarily visual and aural. The progressive loss of enthusiasm and joy in our schools as students move from kindergarten through college is due in part to the enforced constriction of physical movement (students must sit for hours), of vocal activity (students must be quiet), and of other sensory modalities. The integrated day program does have releasing effects, and its principles already are seeping into the secondary school. It recovers what Dewey and Whitehead always insisted upon. We do not know if we have learned something until we act upon what we have learned. And when we act, we act as a thinking, feeling, sensing, deciding organism. Now, I do not mean we should schedule an hour a week for art, another hour for music, several hours for dance, and one for sensitizing experiences. Such specialization only fragments further the principle of integrated or organismic learning. We must find ways to integrate music and art, dance and action, with our geography, English, and mathematics. A Canadian college now has an integrated physical education–mathematics program. Gymnastic exercises have been developed that physically take students through certain abstract mathematical groupings.

The fourth and last meaning of affective education is the belated recognition that man is fundamentally a social being whose humanity needs to be nurtured and educed, and that we do not help him become more human using inhuman or impersonal methods of learning. While TV and computer-assisted instruction have a place, the central arena for growth is the interaction of a student with another human being. It is not just that listening, discussing, arguing, criticizing, and telling some other responding person provide the primary spur to intellectual development—an insight we have been ignoring in our schools; it is that such experiences also humanize a person. Is it more important for a youth to spend 75 percent of his class time being taught more information by television, programmed learning materials, and computer consoles than it is to learn how to listen, really listen, to someone else, to learn how to accept his viewpoint, to understand, to care and cooperate with someone else? Affective education insists we reorder our goals to recognize the centrality of a human and humane learning environment. Affective education also means we teachers learn *how* to help children communicate; *how* to work out personal problems that block their development; *how* to reflect about their relationships with others. Most of us really do not help any of our students learn these skills of being and doing in our classrooms.

Given such reasonable and hopeful shifts in emphases in our schools, why is affective education a potentially dangerous innovation? It is potentially dangerous for several reasons. By releasing and cultivating emotional involvement, confronting values, providing youth with experiences that involve their feelings, many teachers will discover they themselves become more emotionally involved in their teaching. Affective education cannot be effective if a teacher does not allow himself to become vulnerable to his own feelings. And that will require greater maturity of us.

A quote from an instructor of seminary students who initiated an experiential seminar illustrates how much more open we must become to our own feelings if we are to help our students mature:

> I experienced an extraordinary degree of both tension and rapport between myself and the seminar members. Two factors stand out . . . which contributed to more dynamic interaction in this seminar than in my previous teaching experience. One was the intensity of personal investment in the project by the trainees. The other was the degree of transparency in my teaching style. When I was able to be open with seminar members about my own anxieties and frustrations, hopes and mixed motivations, an important learning experience seemed to occur. This experience seems to confirm the wisdom of the advice which a recent graduate gave me; in commenting on improving my teaching, he put it straight, "I hope you'll let it all hang out!" What feels like weakness often turns out to be strength.

Those who work with children may not encounter the intensity and indiscriminate expression of feelings that teachers unexpectedly meet when they initiate more experiential forms of education with older students. Adolescents have been so emotionally suppressed in the classroom for years that some literally just cannot contain their own explosiveness when no longer protected by traditional aseptic classroom rituals. So the first danger is that teachers will find their ability to deal maturely with their own feelings challenged.

A second danger results from the depth of the estrangement of some youth from their own impulses and feelings. When given the opportunity to participate experientially they find the arousal of their own feelings to be so seductively integrating that they resist any effort to take an objective, logical, rational, evaluative attitude toward their experience. Affective education risks intensifying anti-intellectualism—hopefully only temporarily until its cathartic effect has been diminished.

A third danger, particularly for adolescents, though the seeds for it are sown when they are younger, is that affective education may accentuate the potential for narcissism that is already quite strong in today's students. My own studies with American students, confirmed by studies with Italians and Turks, suggest that too developed an aesthetic attitude (as we see in psychedelia) in an adolescent may be symptomatic of an excessive self-centeredness and preoccupation with the subjective at the expense of forming skills and attitudes that tie him to reality or to others. The consequence is that an education that accentuates the immersion of the self in feelings, that justifies beauty as the only criterion of worth, that stimulates self-sufficiency, may have immaturing effects—unless we locate such education within a more powerfully social and caring context.

A fourth related danger is that stimulating aesthetic expression without encouraging the development of skills to transform its subjectivism into some socially communicable form risks intensifying an already strong trend toward dilettantism. Too many of today's youth believe emotional expressiveness is creative. They ignore the fact that creativity involves not only accessibility to aesthetic impulses but also disciplined craftsmanship in communicating such impulses and the insight into some form. Affective education demands much maturity of students, for it requires them to master skills for integrating potentially disturbing feelings and conflicts. This is a much more demanding educational task than to master skills for handling nonpersonal, nondisruptive information. But my evidence, at any rate, is very clear. A characteristic f maturity is the ability to use one's logical, ordered, thought processes to resolve personally disruptive and emotional situations.[5] The ability to master French verbs has no elation to maturity.

Another related danger is that affective education when injudiciously introduced could confirm students' impressions that freedom means the absence of restraint—to be free to be whatever one's emotional impulses dictate —Summerhillian style. I recall visiting a twelfth grade class where the teacher thought complete absence of expectations on his part provided optimal conditions for students to become mature. The reality was that the students were aimless, apathetic, and dispirited. Genuine freedom comes from acquiring the attitudes, motives, and skills that increase one's options for making choices—an insight many youth today reject because to acquire such skills requires the patience, tolerance for frustration, and persistent search for excellence that deny to them the pleasures they associate with freedom from expectations.

The final potential danger is that affective education, however we define it, becomes a substitute for academic excellence as *the* goal of education. Both academic and affective development are partial goals. In reacting against the sterility of academicism, we risk plunging into the fecundity of an undisciplined aestheticism that is nonintegrative of a youth's intellectual talents.

Our goal should be to further the educability of a youth, to help him learn those attitudes, motives, and skills which allow him to be open to continued experiencing and growth. Educability is not equivalent to high academic aptitude, or an A average, nor to a dilettantish abandonment to every impulse that emerges into consciousness. The primary determinants of educability are the qualities that make for emotional maturity.

So the last principal question now becomes, "How does a youth mature?" On what model of healthy development can we ground affective education and so integrate it with academic development? At this point I will describe a complex model of maturing too simply, but it will in broad outline suggest the values for which we should educate if we wish to educate for educability.[6] To illustrate the applicability of the model to affective education, I will describe those qualities central to a disciplined aesthetic attitude.

When are we most educable? When we are children before we have become encrusted with our society's patterned modes of perceiving and thinking, and with personal biases, prejudices, and defenses that serve to close us off from new experiences and new growth. As adolescents and young adults we recover some of our pristine educability when we so open ourselves to the presence of another that we lose ourselves. That is when we are most defenseless. Being in love is one such educable state. All of us know our students are most open to new growth when there is a deeply caring, not sentimental, love between us and them. We are also most open when we are in a meditative prayerful relation with our own inner worlds. My understanding of man tells me the deepest source of the creative-aesthetic impulse is in our less conscious and more primitive inner world, and that we make contact with it through a receptive meditative attitude. Not until we learn how to reach and touch and then channel and witness our inner voices will we be truly educable. If a youth learns how to develop such accessibility to his inner powers and integrates such forces and insights with more social modes of communication, then I have no fear for him. He will have developed a capacity for resiliency and autonomy that will enable him to cure his estrangements and create his own adaptations to his unknown society of the future. He will come into control of his growth.

To educate for educability then means travelling two routes: creating a loving relationship with our students and cultivating a religiously reverent receptivity to the inward presence that is integrated with communicable skills.

So how does a youth mature and how do we help him develop a disciplined aestheticism as exemplified in meditation?

Growth is initiated when we confront a problem, when we are frustrated, bewildered, and unsure about how to proceed. Such frustration spurs us to reflect, to inquire, to think. As a child matures he becomes increasingly able to put into symbolic form—in art, music, words, numbers, gestures, dance—his experience. The evidence is clear: mature persons are more understanding of others, more accurately understand themselves, and are able to reflect more adequately about problems.[7] The first task when educating for educability is to help a youth overcome both the social and personal blocks to symbolizing his own experience. Affective education must not only teach a youth how to derepress or deinhibit his feelings but also how to keep such feelings under his conscious control. When we seal off parts of ourselves we also close ourselves off to other persons and other experiences.

We learn very early what stance to take toward our feelings. Hence, educators must begin to educate affectively with elementary school children. How do we help a first and a second grader to keep open to their own feelings and impulses and learn how to differentiate between and then symbolize the inchoate feelings they have? We begin by teaching them to learn to listen more carefully outwardly and then help them transfer those skills to learning how to listen inwardly. Well, how? Some teachers take their children for silent walks in nearby woods or streets where they sit quietly to listen and remember as many different sounds as they can hear. Of course we stay within the concentration span of small children. If being quiet is too challenging, then begin visually by asking each child to discover on a walk as many different colors as he can, and then describe them. The principle is to sensitize a child in various sensory modalities to his external world. Then some morning begin with a quiet time in the classroom. Darken the room. Have each child put his head in his arms and close his eyes. Then ask him to imagine a TV screen and turn on Channel 5 to see what is going on. Many children will not see anything. We may be surprised how much TV has emptied the imaginative capacity of our youth. So we might make up a vivid four- or five-line story and ask the children to imagine a picture for the story. We might even initiate short guided meditation periods on certain themes or take the children on an imaginal trip inside their bodies, helping them to become aware of what their hungry stomach or cramped tense left ankle is feeling, or we could play music that induces certain moods and have the children try to describe their feelings. We need to help students of all ages learn to differentiate and then label their feelings if they are later to gain intellectual control over them. As a student progresses from elementary to secondary school we could, in our meditative curricular plan, begin to use Zen and Yoga principles to teach him how to shut out distractions, that is, concentrate his consciousness, or how to empty his conscious mind to become more open to the imaginal richness that constantly goes on at the periphery of consciousness. Within a few years, schools and colleges will be offering courses on meditation. Fanciful? Not at all. One of the exciting frontiers of psychological research is the demonstration that man can secure much greater access to and control over his consciousness through meditation than most of us have thought possible.[8]

What are the values we will be teaching? We will be teaching openness and honesty; we will be teaching a youth the skills of being true to his own feeling experience.

The second facet of maturing is developed in the search for ways to solve a problem through reflection as we learn to take symbolically another person's point of view and so to break out of our self-centeredness. We come to understand a problem, another person, even ourselves, from a multiplicity of perspectives. Some philosophers identify this development as at the heart of becoming educated. For its consequence is the transcendence of the self and the development of a sense of shared humanness. In furthering this more allocentric skill, I would help my students learn how to listen to and anticipate another's experiences. Once a class had been together for some time, we could use many games to cultivate this skill. Jimmy could try to act like Jane in certain situations; Susie could try to predict Margie's reaction. We could use role-playing and psychodrama techniques to help students learn how the teacher feels or how students perceive us as teachers; we could take the role of Susie and act out the way we see her acting. Boys could take the role of girls and have the girls decide how accurately the boys experienced being a girl. But we do not really learn how another person feels unless we learn to listen with him. So I would create ways to teach my first graders to listen to other children—a noble and basic educable skill most of us never systematically try to cultivate. In small circles during our meditative time, I would encourage each child to say only· a word or two to describe his image or feeling of the moment. Then we could play a game of recalling exactly what every other child in the circle said. I might repeat one child's words to discover who could identify who said them. Or the children might pair up so that one could share a dream he had the night before and then the other could try to repeat it to him. As the children became more comfortable speaking spontaneously about their images and feelings, I would have longer unprogrammed and undirected meditative periods in which a child or teacher could spontaneously share with the others some thought or feeling. Of course, we would not force a child to participate or punish him if his imaginal life was very barren or if he did not want to share.

The values we would be teaching? Understanding, acceptance, tolerance, respect, and caring—basic allocentric values that are intrinsic to developing an educable attitude.

The third dimension that defines maturing is the combining into a feasible relationship, different possible attributes, perspectives, and alternative solutions of a problem. We begin the process of linking, combining, fitting together, and integrating to find the most economical, simple, harmonious solution. A more mature person thinks relationally, is more consistent, has "himself together," and so can act spontaneously. Much of formal education is devoted to helping a youth create relationships, identify similarities from dissimilarities, become more consistent in what he says and does. The depth of our mutuality, our sense of we-ness, manifests the degree to which we have developed integrative interpersonal skills. In our meditative group, I would encourage, by personal example, students to learn how to combine their feelings and images with other modalities of expression. In English we might begin a period of five minutes of meditation, and when a youth had imaginally created an image he liked he could draw it or describe it verbally. Or n our corporate meditative group, I would encourage the students, by personal example too, to communicate their feelings through music or dance, thus helping them learn how to communicate and integrate thoughts and feelings with some socialized modality. Or if the class had been having a fantasy-sharing time, one youth might try to act out nonverbally the dream of his partner for the others to guess.

The values we would be teaching are harder to define for they involve the wholeness, the harmonizing, the relatedness of living. Consistency, flexibility, integrity, and perhaps even grace and harmony are surely involved.

The last two dimensions that describe how a youth matures healthily are stability and personal autonomy. His reading skill becomes so stabilized that he can now independently use that skill for learning social studies. Or his multiplication tables become so stable, he can without hesitation correctly answer 6×7 and 7×6. He builds up very slowly a more stable concept of himself that gives him a sense of inner centeredness or certainty. His relations with others become less mercurial; he begins to develop more enduring friendships. As a result of these growth experiences he becomes more his own person, more in control of his talents and emotions; he becomes a more self-directed autonomous person, though not a self-centered one, because he has also been developing allocentrically.

How do we create more stable and autonomous meditative skills? When we begin to shift our sensitizing experiences with the external to the internal world we enhance the process of stabilization. That is, we help students become independent of external stimulation for maintaining their ability to concentrate. We might deliberately create distractions during our meditation period to teach the students to ignore them. We might have a gong and sound it very very quietly and then more and more loudly until no youth reported he could hold onto an image he had had in his mind. We might try to meditate close to lunch time, better yet, at the close of the day, to see how long the group could remain quiet and imaginally productive. If a group of starving second graders could have a productive meditative period for five minutes we would really have something. Make that tenth graders!

To encourage autonomy of meditation I would begin at different times of the week, like during regular class time, when tension or an argument was in the making or we were blocked by a problem, to introduce quiet meditative times. I would encourage students to let their inner controls go, let their imaginations run more freely, and spontaneously report any alternative solutions that emerged. I do not know why we do not use meditative periods more frequently in our classrooms. Think what might happen to the quality of our discussions if both we and our students had the opportunity to sit quietly and think before speaking. I would hope such educable skills of inward listening, imaginative sensitization, and receptivity could be transferred to other activities of the class, or better yet, that the students themselves would suggest such transfer. Finally, I would have a quiet corner in the school to which a youth could go at any time he felt like having a meditation period. Then I would really know he had internalized the discipline of opening himself to his own inner world.

And the values we would be teaching? Persistence, steadfastness, independence, and courage.

The values of honesty, understanding, caring, integrity, steadfastness, and courage are intrinsic to developing an educable attitude. If the most brilliant academician is dishonest, or intolerant, or unsympathetic to contradictory viewpoints, or cheats, or is inconsistent, or does not stand up for what he believes, how successful have we, his teachers, been?

If we decide to help a youth learn how to integrate his feelings and values with his intellect, then we will not shy from questions like these:

What is our school doing that inhibits, suppresses, blocks the development of honesty, understanding, caring, integrity, steadfastness, and courage in our students? What are we doing to cultivate such values? A maturing youth has energy free for enthusiasms, curiosity, and joyful commitment. Are our eleventh graders as enthusiastic, curious, and joyful in our classrooms as are the first graders? If not, why not? What have we been doing to make them less mature and so less educable?

What is our school doing to help our students become more accessible to their inner world—to their feelings, impulses, and imaginations—the first stage of nurturing creativity? What systematic curricular plan do we have for helping students escape the narcissism latent in such accessibility to the subjective? How do we help them put their inner worlds into some more social, communicable form—the second stage of becoming creative?

Do we really educate for educability? Or are we blindly following the ritual of a narrow academicism preparing our students only for college and graduate school? Or are we cavalierly playing emotional games with them? We need to educate a youth, not just his head nor just his heart. The promise of affective education is that it will stimulate us to recover the person lost among our abstractions; its danger is that it may devalue man's most promising adaptive and educable skill: a disciplined intellect.

NOTES
1. D. H. Heath, "Is Masculinity Becoming Obsolescent?" *The Journal,* Boys' Clubs (Summer 1970), pp. 4–11.
2. G. W. Allport, P. E. Vernon, and G. Lindzey, *Study of Values* (Manual), 3rd ed. (Boston: Houghton Mifflin Co., 1960), p. 4.
3. W. Glasser, *Schools Without Failure* (New York: Harper & Row, 1969); L. E. Raths, et al., *Values and Teaching* (Columbus, Ohio: Charles E. Merrill Publishing Co., 1966).
4. Conference on Pastoral Ministry of the Church in the 1970's. Sponsored by the National Council of Churches and the W. Clement and Jessie V. Stone Foundation, 1968–71.
5. D. H. Heath, *Explorations of Maturity: Studies of Mature and Immature College Men* (New York: Appleton-Century-Crofts, 1965).
6. D. H. Heath, *Humanizing Schools: New Directions, New Decisions* (New York: Hayden Book Co., 1971). Describes the model of development in more detail and illustrates how it provides a rationale for introducing innovation into the curriculum. *Growing Up in College* (San Francisco: Jossey-Bass, Inc., 1968). Tests the applicability of the model for organizing the growth experience in college as well as describes how the educational determinants of healthy growth can be identified.
7. See nn. 5 and 6 above.
8. B. L. Collier, "Brain Power: The Case for Bio-feedback Training," *Saturday Review,* April 10, 1971.

10 Curriculum Design for the Humane School

Arthur W. Foshay

The eloquent writing of the past few years on the theme of the humane school could result in yet another educational fad, with its accompanying rituals, jargon, and ultimate disillusionment. This theme, especially, invites pompous nonsense, and we have already heard enough.

Let's hope it won't happen. That the schools are in many ways inhumane is easy to demonstrate. The idea that they need not be is one of the most inviting now on our minds. To avoid another disillusioning fad, we need to begin the process of turning our big shambles of an institution into the kind of nurturing social tool we have always intended it to be. And to do this, we need tools.

One such tool is an approach to curriculum design and evaluation that explicitly relates the human condition to the necessary goals of teaching. The purpose of this paper is to offer such an approach for the consideration of the profession.

To begin, we have to cope somehow with the word, "humane." How shall it be understood? Socially? Theologically? Physically? Since the beginning of civilization, the classicists have asked "What is Man?" and their answers are spread before us in the history of ideas, in literature, in the arts. The question is so broad that it seems beyond us educationists; we wait for some agreement among the authorities, but we know it will never come. Under these circumstances, lest we merely wait, we have to nerve ourselves and make an answer of our own—one we can use until a better one appears. One source we have often used has been developmental psychology, which has served us well: it underlies the kindergarten and nursery school curriculum which many of us feel has been our most successful attempt at curriculum design. It has nourished the growth of guidance programs. We turn to it repeatedly as we attempt to design other programs. Where would some of the best current programs be, for example, without Piaget? Let us turn to it again.

Research in developmental psychology falls into recognizable categories. According to such research, man develops intellectually, emotionally, socially, aesthetically, spiritually, and physically. Most of the research we educationists are aware of lies in the first three categories, but there is good and useful work in the second three also. While the psychologists never intended it, they imply that man is an intellectual, emotional, social, aesthetic, spiritual and physical creature.

Reprinted from *Theory into Practice*, 10 (3): 204–207 (June 1971), by permission of author and publisher.

For our purposes, these categories have certain advantages. They do not grow from any particular philosophical or theological system, and need not conform to any particular set of limiting assumptions. They are open-ended and pragmatic. Most important, they define themselves empirically. Since what we try to do in schools is open-ended and pragmatic, and since we try to act according to what appears to happen instead of only in terms of what ought to happen, these categories may well serve to hold the term "humane" still for us long enough to carry on some work. Let's try them out here, at least in principle, and see what they yield. We'll come back to what they mean in a moment.

Before we do so, however, let us consider another set of categories, for in the interaction of the two sets we may find a helpful approach to curriculum design and evaluation.

THE OPERATIONAL GOALS OF TEACHING

This second set of categories deals with the intentions teachers have that are independent of the subject matter they are working with at any given moment. We shall consider four: fluency, manipulation, confidence/value, and persistence.

Fluency

One goal of any teacher is that students become familiar with the symbol system, vocabulary, media, and the typical phenomena associated with the content he seeks to teach. Children have to be fluent with the skills of word recognition, or no reading occurs. They have to be used to the geographer's system of notation, or there will be no thinking about geography. And so on. Fluency does not necessarily precede everything else in teaching—it may grow through time and experience—but it is always a necessary operational teaching goal.

Manipulation

Teachers also seek to lead students to manipulate the data out of which content is made. Word recognition is not reading, even if Rudolf Flesch does not know the difference. To read is to draw understanding from a page—to manipulate the symbol system in such a way as to interpret it. An art experience does not consist of becoming familiar with the various art media and their properties. It consists of manipulating them in such a way as to make an art object. And so on. The ability to manipulate the data, which we often call "understanding," is a universal teaching goal.

Confidence/Value

Teachers also seek to instill confidence in students—confidence that they can manipulate the data on their own. At the same time, teachers hope students will value the ability they acquire. Not only do we want students to "do" math, we want them to be confident that they can do it, and to believe in its value to them. If we fail to produce this condition, students may (as many do) learn to "do" math, and at the same time learn to dislike it. When we are teaching the way we know how to, we build confidence and value by repeatedly putting students on their own in the content, while calling their attention to the satisfactions associated with being on their own. We make the whole affair rewarding.

Persistence

If a student is fluent, has learned to manipulate the content, and has developed confidence and value, then we hope he will persist in "doing" the content after formal instruction has stopped. We hope the student who has learned to think historically will continue to do so, and that the budding pianist will play for pleasure on his own, later. While our failures in this area are grievous, they are not universal. The attrition of budding pianists is shocking; so is the attrition of budding mathematicians. But many children who learn to read go on reading, and there is much evidence that lifelong persistence is kindled in school in science, the arts, athletics and other fields.

THE PSYCHOLOGICAL CATEGORIES

Now let us reconsider the categories of developmental psychology mentioned earlier. Each of them must be understood in some operational manner, if they are to be used operationally—and that is our intent here.

Intellectual

Bloom's *Taxonomy of Educational Objectives: Cognitive Domain* serves as an elaboration of what this category includes. Most of us can claim a considerable acquaintance with it: we recognize the difference between Scheffler's "knowing that" and "knowing how"; we accept Bloom's "higher" and "lower" intellectual activities. For more than fifty years, educational literature and teacher education programs have stressed the importance of problem solving and critical thinking as attributes to be pursued in curriculum development. We need not elaborate on it here.

Emotional

The idea that there is an emotional life that is not merely a pollution of the intellectual life is of our century. Samuel Johnson's *Dictionary* (1755) defines passion merely as a disturbance of the reason; we know better. The emotional development of children and young people has been a major preoccupation of the researchers and observers in developmental psychology for more than two generations. For us educationists, it is a familiar domain, though still in need of extensive exploration.

Social

The social development of children and young people has not been researched as extensively as the intellectual and the emotional, but there is a considerable body of knowledge nevertheless. Social development deals with the social mechanisms children use in their dealings with one another, with their understanding of authority and external social structures, and with their view of the social self.

Aesthetic

The idea that there is such a thing as aesthetic development came to prominence much more recently than did the ideas of intellectual, emotional, and social development. There were pioneering studies of aesthetic development in the twenties and thirties, but the field has never attracted as much attention as the three most popular fields. In general, to borrow from Harry Broudy, aesthetic development consists of increasingly finer discriminations in the sensuous, formal, technical, and expressive meanings of art objects, whether produced by oneself or others, and whether visual, tactile, dramatic, poetic, or kinesthetic. Aesthetic behavior is universal. Even the arrangement of a conventional classroom conforms to an aesthetic judgment of some kind, usually highly conventional and trite. People speak, dress, eat, conduct their love lives, and interact according to aesthetic judgments. Aesthetic development is part of the whole man.

Spiritual

By "spiritual" we refer to what man does about his awe. We are awestruck creatures: we can ask questions that cannot be answered intellectually, emotionally, socially, aesthetically, or physically—questions that require not an answer, but a confrontation and an acknowledgement. The meaning of human existence, the possibility of a conscience, the concept of infinity ("Where is the end of the sky?"), Job's questions, all are examples. Religious practices and forms help us confront and acknowledge such questions. The answers, or the responses to them exist for many of us as spiritual practice. All men are spiritual, even if not religious. One dare not deny this quality of what it is to be human.

Physical

The significance of the fact that we are physical beings has not been examined in nearly the depth the fact demands. Anyone who has worked with children has had to recognize the fact that they need to come to terms with their own bodies. As they mature, their "body image" changes, and with it their view of themselves. Years ago, in a book called *Children's Social Values,* I reported that some children saw themselves as physical creatures, from the neck up. Others have made similar findings. But an adolescent clearly sees himself in a full-length mirror. We offer little or no help to children's sense of themselves as physical beings, except (and for a small minority) in athletic programs. However, for the purposes of our analysis here, we should acknowledge that the physical self is a prominent part of the whole self, and call for more research on its significance as it interacts with the other qualities that enter into the human condition.

A MODEL FOR CURRICULUM DESIGN AND EVALUATION

All this leads us to a design for the construction and evaluation of the curriculum. The six elements of the human condition from developmental psychology and the four elements of the operational goals of teaching may be arranged on a grid [as shown in Figure 1].

	Fluency	Manipulation	Confidence/ Value	Persistence
INTELLECTUAL	1a	2a	3a	4a
EMOTIONAL	1b	2b	3b	4b
SOCIAL	1c	2c	3c	4c
AESTHETIC	1d	2d	3d	4d
SPIRITUAL	1e	2e	3e	4e
PHYSICAL	1f	2f	3f	4f

FIGURE 1. A Grid for Curriculum Design and Evaluation

Where these qualities intersect, curriculum questions are raised. For example, cell 1a raises the question, "How does fluency in a given field contribute to the intellectual growth of a student?" Cell 3c raises the question, "How does confidence and value in a given field contribute to the social growth of a student?" Cell 4f raises the question, "How does persistence in a given field contribute to the sense of physical self of a student?"

All together, there are 24 cells in the grid, hence 24 questions to be confronted by the curriculum planner and the curriculum evaluator. Note that the great preponderance of our current curriculum design and evaluation efforts deal with only two of the cells—1a and 2a. That is, we ask in the main only that our curriculum efforts answer the question, "How do fluency and manipulation in a given subject field contribute to the intellectual growth of the student?" Our failure to deal with the other 22 questions implied by this analysis explains in some degree why students are "turned off" by the curriculum, and why the stereotype of the academic person held by the public is so pejorative.

The whole man is much more than an intellectual creature. If not, we should all be monstrous, for a monster is a creature with some of its attributes exaggerated and others missing. Our peculiar pedagogical monster is what is ordinarily called a pedant—someone who is concerned with purely intellectual matters (often ritualized, as in the case of the grammarian) at the expense of growth in the other five aspects of human existence. He may be a towering intellect, but emotionally and socially, not to mention other qualities, he is an infant. Hence his naiveté and puerility.

So one thing the grid tells us is that we have projected a monstrous version of the human condition by our failure to examine seriously 22 out of the 24 elements that belong in comprehensive curriculum design and evaluation. No wonder we are concerned with making the school humane!

Another observation to be made about the grid is that there are areas of it about which we know very little. We know much less about the aesthetic, spiritual, and physical aspects of growth than we do about the others. Our current evaluation schemes tend to leave out the areas of confidence/value and persistence. That whole quadrant of the grid that includes cells 3d through 3f, and 4d through 4f, is difficult to deal with for this reason. By contrast, the quadrant that includes cells 1a through 1c, and 2a through 2c, is much more familiar to us and correspondingly easier to deal with. The diagonal from 1a to 4f is a line of increasingly sparse knowledge and increasing difficulty. It obviously would repay researchers and curriculum developers to attend to it.

What does it mean to be human? We have answered that question here with the principal dimensions of the research in developmental psychology. What does it mean to teach? We have answered that question here with a four-category analysis. Where the two intersect, we have found questions, some of them perplexing, that offer a kind of map for curriculum development and evaluation for those of us who would develop a curriculum for the humane school we all seek. This is a proposal for analysis, nothing more. It will be interesting to see where it takes us.

11 The Key Word Is Relevance

William Van Til

Let us begin with an admission: Some of the content we teach in American schools is not as relevant as it might be to the lives of the young people we teach, to the society in which they are growing up, or to the clarification of democratic values.

Some illustrations are obvious. For instance, one of the many Puerto Rican schools I visited during a New York University survey of education in Puerto Rico was in a village high in the mountains of the interior. The villagers were very poor and afflicted with the problems that go with poverty—poor nutrition, inefficient agriculture, dilapidated housing, bad health, and the rest.

Only a handful of young people of the village and the surrounding countryside ever enrolled in any kind of educational institution beyond high school. Yet, what were the young people studying in the secondary school in this little mountain village? In a social studies class, they were memorizing lists of products of South American countries. Their mathematics work had no relationship to the problems they might encounter in the school shop or at home or elsewhere. In an English class, students were reading eighteenth and nineteenth century British novels: At the time of my visit one class was dissecting *Ivanhoe*. (This mountain school and community, I hasten to say, was not typical; many other Puerto Rican schools were more relevant to learners, society, and values, and many other communities had higher living standards.)

Recognizing the lack of relevance in education in an exotic, faraway setting is easy. Such was the case when I visited a home economics class in a town of mud hovels in Iran: The girls were making scrapbooks of pictures (clipped from very old magazines) that portrayed the clothes and foods of prosperous Americans and Europeans.

The closer to home we get, however, the harder it becomes for a teacher to recognize irrelevance. Take Doris Smith and Harry Jones, for instance. She teaches in the suburbs in the Midwestern United States; he, in the slums of a West Coast city. Both of them would quickly recognize the lack of meaning in the two faraway examples cited. Yet, both might have difficulty recognizing that they have their own problems in making the content of their classes meaningful to some students.

Doris Smith teaches social studies in an affluent suburb that is among the

Reprinted from *Today's Education: NEA Journal*, 58(1): 14–17 (January 1969), by permission of author and publisher.

first places where new national projects and proposals are tried. A genuine innovator, she uses a variety of methods and materials with versatility. She uses simulation techniques, for example, and has just completed an academic game with her eleventh graders. The game deals with economics; the players adopt roles and the ones who make the most money are the winners.

Margaret, one of Miss Smith's better students, went through the motions of the game but was fundamentally uninvolved. Why? Because, like Benjamin in *The Graduate,* Margaret had painfully learned from the lives of her parents and their friends that affluence did not necessarily result in a good life. Why, wondered Margaret, were teachers blind to what was most relevant to young people? For instance, why didn't the teacher see that the most important thing about this game would be to examine the materialistic goals which were taken for granted as desirable?

During follow-up discussions, Miss Smith raised questions with the class about the strategy of moves made during the game. Margaret's responses were correct but unrelated to her concern for values.

Harry Jones teaches language arts in an intermediate school in a slum neighborhood. Though Mr. Jones is white and most of his students are black, racial differences have not been a barrier to mutual liking and respect. The class is now reading a selection in a new anthology which is quite appropriate to the level of the students' reading abilities. Mr. Jones notices that Jess isn't reading the assigned selection, but instead is simply leafing through the pages. It isn't as though I'd asked the class to read dull, difficult material simply because it's supposed to be an English classic, Harry thinks. I guess Jess just doesn't care.

Jess is thinking: I can't find black men in this book. Where's the brothers? This is Whitey's book. How can a good guy like Mr. Jones be so dumb? Not for me, baby.

"What are you doing, Jess?" asks Harry. "Just lookin'," says Jess.

Good teachers though they are, even Miss Smith and Mr. Jones sometimes attempt to teach content that is unrelated to the lives of learners. Some teachers have even greater difficulty in achieving relevance than do methodologically skilled Doris and well-liked Harry. Classes do exist in your community and mine in which an uninterrupted academic content bores young people. Classes do exist where subject matter is quite unrelated to the dilemmas and struggles and aspirations of many prospective learners.

The teacher who realizes that his content of instruction isn't meaningful has two viable alternatives. He can change his content from the irrelevant to the relevant. Or, if he cannot change the required content, he can teach it in such a way as to give it relevance.

Yes, a third possibility does exist. One can continue with the meaningless content, break his heart trying to teach, and achieve very little.

A teacher does not need extensive instruction in educational psychology to realize that his teaching must be connected with the student's background, drives, and life if any learning is to take place. Experience soon teaches a teacher this axiom.

The obvious and sensible thing to do is to replace the irrelevant with the relevant through changing the content. Remember, for instance, the poverty-stricken Puerto Rican mountain village in which the students were memorizing products, being taught mathematics without application, and reading *Ivanhoe*. Here was a setting characterized by a host of problems in the areas of health, sanitation, housing, nutrition, safety, use of resources, production, and consumption. Here were Puerto Rican youngsters who would face bewildering life problems including those presented by the continuing restless migration from the rural ways of the *barrio* to the urbanized ways of San Juan; from the hospitable island of their birth to the impersonal, tenement-lined canyons of New York City, with its strange folkways and less-than-warm welcome to those regarded as "foreigners."

Reality could be introduced into their education. In social studies, students might well learn of the real problems of the village, the island, the mainland. In mathematics, they might see a relationship between mathematics and the problems they encounter in school shop and in their homes. In English classes, students might well acquire the bilinguality they need by reading English-language newspapers and magazines, as well as books of fiction and nonfiction by Puerto Rican and mainland Americans, plus a sampling of British authors. Fortunately, the better Puerto Rican schools do introduce such realities into their programs.

In mainland America, too, the obvious and sensible approach is to change the content if it is not germane. Most educators will readily grant that a teacher must begin at the actual level of accomplishment of those who are to be educated—not to stay there but begin there. Most will grant that pitching the learning at an unreasonable level is an exercise in futility. But additionally we must recognize the vital importance of selecting suitable content.

The curriculum should be made more relevant to the lives of the children and youth for whom the curriculum exists. Through their reading materials, for example, city children must often meet people like themselves, rather than always encounterthe legendary Dick and Jane and Spot of suburban life. The world of the city must itself become part of the subject matter if young city dwellers are to improve human relations, develop citizenship, widen horizons, and meet the problems of urban living. In Harry Jones's class, and those of his colleagues, surely the contributions of Negro-Americans should be an integral part of the American literature curriculum for both Negroes and whites.

Nor are the suburbs exempt from the blight of irrelevance. Though some suburban young people have an economic head start in life, they, too, are sometimes cheated. When communities are bland and homogenized and indifferent to reality, the young are sometimes cheated of the opportunity to know people of varied races, religions, nationality backgrounds, and social classes.

When high school students are regarded as college fodder, they are sometimes cheated of sufficient experience in home economics, music, fine arts, and industrial arts. When the only god worshipped is academic success in formal learning, students are sometimes cheated of the opportunity to explore seriously their allegiances to values, their relationships to the adult world, their ways of finding satisfaction, and their participation in political action and social change.

"But," a teacher may say, "I cannot change the required content to make it relevant. I am not a board of regents or a local board of education or a curriculum bigwig attached to the central office staff." He may add, "I am just a humble teacher, a prisoner of the syllabus, the required textbook, and the system in which I am caught. Deviation is not permitted. THEY would not allow it."

Maybe so, but I doubt it. Before the teacher resigns himself to a prisoner's life, he might wish to reexamine his chains. Perhaps they are not as strong as he assumes.

In today's world, more and more educators and laymen are realizing that not all of the answers to the problem of curriculum are in. Since the early 1960's, increasing numbers of educators have attempted to develop curriculums that are more important to the culturally disadvantaged or, in a plainer phrase, the poor.

Now recognition is growing that we are far from having achieved the best of all possible worlds with respect to the education of the economically advantaged. In 1969, still more educators will be looking for curriculums appropriate for young people from affluent backgrounds. Paradoxically, today's disenchanted young people, including democratic activists and serious and sensitive students as well as hippies and nihilists and revolutionaries, stem mostly from the middle and upper classes.

. . .

In those cases where, through a variety of circumstances, the chains do prove real and teachers simply must use some prescribed content which is not as relevant as they would wish it to be, how can they make their work more meaningful?

Rather than making fundamental changes in the content, some teachers use the second alternative mentioned and adapt the content to make it more relevant. Illustrations are legion: In literature, teaching *Julius Caesar* in relationship to contemporary dictatorships; in history, preparing and contrasting attitudes toward past American wars with present attitudes on war in Viet Nam; in biology, relating the study of human blood to false claims and misleading mythologies as to blood differences between races; in modern languages, teaching the culture as part of the culture's language; in language arts, stressing those readings in anthologies which have most meaning to the particular learners. Miss Smith, for instance, could have discussed with the class the value assumptions behind the economic game that was the required content.

Some readers may ask for the prescription good teachers use for adaptation of content. There isn't any. Sorry about that. If there were a single sovereign remedy, it would have been discovered long ago. The good teacher uses his intelligence in relating the required content to the world of the learner. Good teachers have been doing so for a long time; adaptation is no revolutionary doctrine.

In making content more relevant, there is no substitute for knowing the social realities which characterize the environment of the student. There is no substitute for knowing the learner as an individual. There is no substitute for having a philosophy which gives direction to the educational enterprise. So armed, one can relate much of the content to the learner, the class, the school, and the community.

12 So You Want to Change to an Open Classroom

Roland S. Barth

Another educational wave is breaking on American shores. Whether termed "integrated day," "Leicestershire Plan," "informal classroom," or "open education," it promises new and radical methods of teaching, learning, and organizing the schools.[1] Many American educators who do not shy from promises of new solutions to old problems are preparing to ride the crest of the wave. In New York State, for instance, the commissioner of education, the chancellor of New York City schools, and the president of the state branch of the American Federation of Teachers have all expressed their intent to make the state's classrooms open classrooms. Schools of education in such varied places as North Dakota, Connecticut, Massachusetts, New York, and Ohio are tooling up to prepare the masses of teachers for these masses of anticipated open classrooms.

Some educators are disposed to search for the new, the different, the flashy, the radical, or the revolutionary. Once an idea or a practice, such as "team teaching," "nongrading," and (more recently) "differentiated staffing" and "performance contracting," has been so labeled by the Establishment, many teachers and administrators are quick to adopt it. More precisely, these educators are quick to assimilate new ideas into their cognitive and operational

For an elaboration of the ideas contained in this article and a discussion of the problems of implementing open classrooms, see Barth, R. S., *Open Education and the American School*, Agathon Press, Inc., 1973.

Reprinted from *Phi Delta Kappan,* 53 (2): 97–99 (October 1971), by permission of author and publisher.

framework. But in so doing they often distort the original conception without recognizing either the distortion or the assumptions violated by the distortion. This seems to happen partly because the educator has taken on the verbal, superficial abstraction of a new idea without going through a concomitant personal reorientation of attitude and behavior. Vocabulary and rhetoric are easily changed; basic beliefs and institutions all too often remain little affected. If open education is to have a fundamental and positive effect on American education, and if changes are to be consciously made, rhetoric and good intentions will not suffice.

There is no doubt that a climate potentially hospitable to fresh alternatives to our floundering educational system exists in this country. It is even possible that, in this brief moment in time, open education may have the opportunity to prove itself. However, a crash program is dangerous. Implementing foreign ideas and practices is a precarious business, and I fear the present opportunity will be abused or misused. Indeed, many attempts to implement open classrooms in America have already been buried with the epitaphs "sloppy permissivism," "neoprogressive," "Communist," "anarchical," or "laissez-faire." An even more discouraging although not surprising consequence has been to push educational practice further away from open education than was the case prior to the attempt at implementation.

Most educators who say they want open education are ready to change *appearances*. They install printing presses, tables in place of desks, classes in corridors, nature study. They adopt the *vocabulary:* "integrated day," "interest areas," "free choice," and "student initiated learning." However, few have understanding of, let alone commitment to, the philosophical, personal, and professional roots from which these practices and phrases have sprung, and upon which they depend so completely for their success. It is my belief that changing appearances to more closely resemble some British classrooms without understanding and accepting the rationale underlying these changes will lead inevitably to failure and conflict among children, teachers, administrators, and parents. American education can withstand no more failure, even in the name of reform or revolution.

I would like to suggest that before you jump on the open classroom surfboard, a precarious vehicle appropriate neither for all people nor for all situations, you pause long enough to consider the following statements and to examine your own reactions to them. Your reactions may reveal salient attitudes about children, learning, and knowledge. I have found that successful open educators in both England and America tend to take similar positions on these statements. Where do you stand?

ASSUMPTIONS ABOUT LEARNING AND KNOWLEDGE[2]

INSTRUCTIONS: Make a mark somewhere along each line which best represents your own feelings about each statement.

Example: School serves the wishes and needs of adults better than it does the wishes and needs of children.

---

strongly agree   agree   no strong feeling   disagree   strongly disagree

I. Assumptions About Children's Learning

MOTIVATION
Assumption 1: Children are innately curious and will explore their environment without adult intervention.

---

strongly agree   agree   no strong feeling   disagree   strongly disagree

Assumption 2: Exploratory behavior is self-perpetuating.

---

strongly agree   agree   no strong feeling   disagree   strongly disagree

CONDITIONS FOR LEARNING
Assumption 3: The child will display natural exploratory behavior if he is not threatened.

---

strongly agree   agree   no strong feeling   disagree   strongly disagree

Assumption 4: Confidence in self is highly related to capacity for learning and for making important choices affecting one's learning.

---

strongly agree   agree   no strong feeling   disagree   strongly disagree

Assumption 5: Active exploration in a rich environment, offering a wide array of manipulative materials, will facilitate children's learning.

---

strongly agree   agree   no strong feeling   disagree   strongly disagree

Assumption 6: Play is not distinguished from work as the predominant mode of learning in early childhood.

---

strongly agree   agree   no strong feeling   disagree   strongly disagree

Assumption 7: Children have both the competence and the right to make significant decisions concerning their own learning.

---

strongly agree   agree   no strong feeling   disagree   strongly disagree

Assumption 8: Children will be likely to learn if they are given considerable choice in the selection of the materials they wish to work with and in the choice of questions they wish to pursue with respect to those materials.

strongly agree   agree   no strong feeling   disagree   strongly disagree

Assumption 9: Given the opportunity, children will choose to engage in activities which will be of high interest to them.

strongly agree   agree   no strong feeling   disagree   strongly disagree

Assumption 10: If a child is fully involved in and is having fun with an activity, learning is taking place.

strongly agree   agree   no strong feeling   disagree   strongly disagree

SOCIAL LEARNING
Assumption 11: When two or more children are interested in exploring the same problem or the same materials, they will often choose to collaborate in some way.

strongly agree   agree   no strong feeling   disagree   strongly disagree

Assumption 12: When a child learns something which is important to him, he will wish to share it with others.

strongly agree   agree   no strong feeling   disagree   strongly disagree

INTELLECTUAL DEVELOPMENT
Assumption 13: Concept formation proceeds very slowly.

strongly agree   agree   no strong feeling   disagree   strongly disagree

Assumption 14: Children learn and develop intellectually not only at their own rate but in their own style.

strongly agree   agree   no strong feeling   disagree   strongly disagree

Assumption 15: Children pass through similar stages of intellectual development, each in his own way and at his own rate and in his own time.

strongly agree   agree   no strong feeling   disagree   strongly disagree

Assumption 16: Intellectual growth and development take place through a sequence of concrete experiences followed by abstractions.

strongly agree   agree   no strong feeling   disagree   strongly disagree

Assumption 17: Verbal abstractions should follow direct experience with objects and ideas, not precede them or substitute for them.

strongly agree   agree   no strong feeling   disagree   strongly disagree

EVALUATION
Assumption 18: The preferred source of verification for a child's solution to a problem comes through the materials he is working with.

strongly agree   agree   no strong feeling   disagree   strongly disagree

Assumption 19: Errors are necessarily a part of the learning process; they are to be expected and even desired, for they contain information essential for further learning.

strongly agree   agree   no strong feeling   disagree   strongly disagree

Assumption 20: Those qualities of a person's learning which can be carefully measured are not necessarily the most important.

strongly agree   agree   no strong feeling   disagree   strongly disagree

Assumption 21: Objective measures of performance may have a negative effect upon learning.

strongly agree   agree   no strong feeling   disagree   strongly disagree

Assumption 22: Learning is best assessed intuitively, by direct observation.

strongly agree   agree   no strong feeling   disagree   strongly disagree

Assumption 23: The best way of evaluating the effect of the school experience on the child is to observe him over a long period of time.

strongly agree   agree   no strong feeling   disagree   strongly disagree

Assumption 24: The best measure of a child's work is his work.

strongly agree   agree   no strong feeling   disagree   strongly disagree

II. ASSUMPTIONS ABOUT KNOWLEDGE

Assumption 25: The quality of being is more important than the quality of knowing; knowledge is a means of education, not its end. The final test of an education is what a man *is,* not what he *knows.*

strongly agree   agree   no strong feeling   disagree   strongly disagree

Assumption 26: Knowledge is a function of one's personal integration of experience and therefore does not fall into neatly separate categories or "disciplines."

strongly agree   agree   no strong feeling   disagree   strongly disagree

Assumption 27: The structure of knowledge is personal and idiosyncratic; it is a function of the synthesis of each individual's experience with the world.

strongly agree   agree   no strong feeling   disagree   strongly disagree

Assumption 28: Little or no knowledge exists which it is essential for everyone to acquire.

strongly agree   agree   no strong feeling   disagree   strongly disagree

Assumption 29: It is possible, even likely, that an individual may learn and possess knowledge of a phenomenon and yet be unable to display it publicly. Knowledge resides with the knower, not in its public expression.

strongly agree   agree   no strong feeling   disagree   strongly disagree

Most open educators, British and American, "strongly agree" with most of these statements.[3] I think it is possible to learn a great deal both about open education and about oneself by taking a position with respect to these different statements. While it would be folly to argue that strong agreement assures success in developing an open classroom, or, on the other hand, that strong disagreement predicts failure, the assumptions are, I believe, closely related to open education practices. Consequently, I feel that for those sympathetic to the assumptions, success at a difficult job will be more likely. For the educator to attempt to adopt practices which depend for their success upon general adherence to these beliefs without actually adhering to them is, at the very least, dangerous.

At the same time, we must be careful not to assume that an "official" British or U.S. government-inspected type of open classroom or set of beliefs exists which is the standard for all others. Indeed, what is exciting about British open classrooms is the *diversity* in thinking and behavior for children and adults —from person to person, class to class, and school to school. The important point here is that the likelihood of successfully developing an open classroom increases as those concerned agree with the basic assumptions underlying open education practices. It is impossible to "role play" such a fundamentally distinct teaching responsibility.

For some people, then, drawing attention to these assumptions may terminate interest in open education. All to the good; a well-organized, consistent, teacher-directed classroom probably has a far less harmful influence upon children than a well-intentioned but sloppy, permissive, and chaotic attempt at an open classroom in which teacher and child must live with contradiction and conflict. For other people, awareness of these assumptions may stimulate confidence and competence in their attempts to change what happens to children in school.

In the final analysis, the success of a widespread movement toward open education in this country rests not upon agreement with any philosophical position but with satisfactory answers to several important questions: For what kinds of people—teachers, administrators, parents, children—is the open classroom appropriate and valuable? What happens to children in open classrooms? Can teachers be *trained* for open classrooms? How can the resistance from children, teachers, administrators, and parents—inevitable among those not committed to open education's assumptions and practices—be surmounted? And finally, should participation in an open classroom be *required* of teachers, children, parents, and administrators?

NOTES
1. For a fuller description of this movement, see Roland S. Barth and Charles H. Rathbone, annotated bibliographies: "The Open School: A Way of Thinking About Children, Learning and Knowledge," *The Center Forum*, Vol. 3, No. 7, July, 1969, a publication of the Center for Urban Education, New York City; and "A Bibliography of Open Education, Early Childhood Education Study," jointly published by the Advisory for Open Education and the Education Development Center, Newton, Mass., 1971.
2. From Roland S. Barth, *"Open Education,"* unpublished doctoral dissertation, Harvard Graduate School of Education, 1970.
3. Since these assumptions were assembled, I have "tested" them with several British primary teachers, headmasters, and inspectors and with an equal number of American proponents of open education. To date, although many qualifications in language have been suggested, there has not been a case where an individual has said of one of the assumptions, "No, that is contrary to what I believe about children, learning, or knowledge."

13 Practical Ways of Improving Curriculum Via Measurable Objectives

W. James Popham

Measurable instructional objectives are designed to counteract what is to me the most serious deficit in American education today, namely, a preoccupation with process without assessment of consequences. Measurable objectives are designed in part to alleviate that particular difficulty. There are at least three realms in which measurable objectives have considerable potential dividends: in curriculum (what goals are selected); in instruction (how to accomplish those goals); and in evaluation (determining whether objectives of the instructional sequence have been realized). I will try to suggest ways in which measurable objectives can be of utility in all three areas.

It is perhaps because I am a convert to this position that I feel viscerally, as well as believe rationally, that measurable objectives have been the most significant instructional advance in the past 10 years.

At UCLA I have invested my energy in giving the prospective teachers with whom I work a simple framework for organizing their thinking about the decisions they have to make in their teaching. This framework, which I call a criterion-referenced instructional model, has four components: (1) specifying objectives, (2) preassessing the learner to see where he is in relation to the objectives, (3) designing some kind of instructional sequence that you think will get him there, and (4) evaluating whether the instructional sequences worked. In this model, the role of the objective is paramount, because objectives have in them the possibility of clarifying instructional intents. Of course, people have admonished for years that we have to have a road map to see where we are going before we can get there. There are other glorious platitudes. But the kind of objective with which I was acquainted when I was learning how to teach was a broad, nebulous goal which may look good on the PTA back-to-school night but will not modify instructional behavior a bit. I remember learning as a prospective high school teacher about the Seven Cardinal Principles of Secondary Education. You remember "command of fundamental processes" (that always sounded evil to me), the "worthy use of leisure time," etc. The time I was first called into a principal's office during my initial high school teaching job, the principal asked, "What are your objectives as a high school teacher?" The only

Reprinted from *The Bulletin of the National Association of Secondary School Principals,* 55 (355): 76–90 (May 1971), by permission of author and publisher.

thing I could think of to say was "command of fundamental processes." In other words, I could quote what I had read and learned but it did not make any difference in my instruction. My instruction was organized around one question and one question only, What will I do today? What will I do in that class? What will I do tomorrow? My preoccupation was with filling time. The thing I feared most was not having enough to do to fill up a period. The question I should have been asking, of course, is, What do I want the learners to become?

WHY THE TEACHER EXISTS

That little four-step model I have identified is predicated on a central assumption that the only reason a teacher exists in a classroom is to modify human beings. If he lectures with the skill of Cicero or leads discussions with the competence of Carl Rogers, and yet the students leave the class unchanged, he is an instructional failure. That assumption, therefore, permits me to say that if changing learners is our task, then it makes sense to articulate the intended changes with a great deal of clarity. Measurable instructional objectives are simply a way of making our instructional intentions more explicit.

There should be no guessing. You should not have a broad goal like, "The student will understand democracy" or "The student will become familiar with American history" or "The student will appreciate music." Why? Because you cannot tell what they mean. You can start with them, but you have to go on to describe in what measurable form you can determine whether the student has achieved the objectives. To me, such precise objectives held much promise. I became very enamored of them. Among memorabilia of my love affair with behavioral objectives are the bumper stickers I had prepared, saying, "HELP STAMP OUT NONBEHAVIORAL OBJECTIVES!" I gave these to my students and they put them on their cars (if they wanted an A). I included, as you can see, an exclamation point at the end of the phrase. Later, I removed the exclamation point, to indicate my increasingly moderate position.

During this time I was pushing behavioral objectives with the zeal of a new convert. People would say to me, "Should all the objectives be stated behaviorally?" I would reply, "Of course. Unless you state all the objectives behaviorally you cannot do anything with them." I was pounding the gospel pretty hard.

WHY BEHAVIORAL OBJECTIVES NOT USED

It was at this time that I was invited by the Peace Corps to go to Ethiopia to see how the four-step instructional model was working. I would pop in on Peace Corps Volunteers we had trained at UCLA and ask, "How is it going? Are you using objectives?" On one occasion we went to a little village south of the capital. I walked down the street and there was a fellow who obviously couldn't remember my name but said, "Hello, Dr . . . . Objectives." When I talked to him at greater length about instructional objectives he said, "Well, I do *not* use them, of course. That's a very good gig you are on back there at UCLA. Keep it up. It's good for the home troops. But I am simply too damn busy to employ them." That phrase, "too damn busy," gnawed at me for a couple of months thereafter. As I talked to my former students, many of whom had left my class knowing very well what a behavioral objective is—some even rather fond of measurable objectives—I found that few of these people employed them. They were all too terribly busy. They were too harassed to take time to generate their own instructional objectives.

The task of producing precise objectives *is* an onerous one. It requires special skill, too. There are many people who can write the simplest, lowest-level measurable objective and think they are good at writing objectives. But they realy are not. It takes some talent and training to be able to write objectives that are both measurable and at the same time worth accomplishing.

One of the dangers with measurable objectives, and particularly among administrators who try to impose them on their staffs, is that they read a little book by Robert Mager and think they know it all. In spite of its overall beneficial impact, the Mager book has far too many low-level objectives in it. The reader is led to believe that if he writes a simple objective such as, "The student will list the names of five Houston houses of ill repute," it is a good objective merely because it is measurable. Obviously, this is a low-level objective. It deals with an inappropriate topic and it ought not to be pursued. The fact that it is measurable does not mean it is good.

THE INSTRUCTIONAL OBJECTIVES EXCHANGE

To have teachers generate their own worthwhile, measurable objectives is simply asking too much; and it is for this reason that we have established, as a nonprofit agency in Los Angeles, the Instructional Objectives Exchange.* It is a beginning, an attempt to gather together, in bank-like fashion, collections of objectives for particular subjects and grade levels. We want to give teachers a collection of objectives and say, "Here, select those which you think appropriate to your situation. If you want to add objectives, that's fine, but at least the collection relieves you of some of the burden of preparing all your own measurable objectives."

I haven't shifted from my former position in thinking that measurable objectives are a fantastic, practical ally of the educator. But I do believe it is unrealistic to ask your teaching staffs to think them up in their spare time. They do not have the time for it.

If you cannot find objectives to suit your fancy in the Instructional Objectives Exchange, stimulate others so that the teachers gathering resources together will generate pools of alternate objectives. Then when you ask teachers to

* Box 24095, Los Angeles, Calif. 90024.

organize their instruction around measurable objectives, they can do so via the selection rather than the instruction route.

In addition to having objectives which are measurable, I strongly urge you to prepare measures for all the objectives so selected. Objectives without measures are somewhat akin to revolvers without bullets. You can scare a few people with them, but when it comes down to the final moment, you cannot really accomplish what you may have to. It seems to me that many people are now enthusiastically supporting measurable objectives, getting lists of them, and then doing nothing with them. If we want teachers to live in a virtuous instructional fashion, we will have to make it easy for them not to sin. I should not dabble with moral theology, but I really believe that one way to get a person to live the good life instructionally is to make it very easy for him. If you give the teachers measurable objectives from which they can select, and accompanying test items, very likely they will use such objectives and test items. If you ask them to generate their own objectives and test items, I do not think they will be used.

HOW TO USE PRECISE OBJECTIVES

Now, how do you use these precise objectives? I suggested earlier that there are three arenas, at least, in which instructional objectives can be employed. The first of these is the curriculum. On common-sense grounds alone it should be apparent that, because there is less ambiguity associated with it, it is easy to determine whether a measurable objective ought to be pursued. Let me illustrate in social science. Let us say that the teacher announces this objective: to make my students better able to function in tomorrow's dynamic democracy. Well, how could you possibly fault that? It sounds so profound. It has all the majesty of years of study associated with it. And yet, if you found out what behavior modifications were actually being made in the kids as a result of a year with that teacher, you might discover that nothing beyond true-false test-taking skills were developed.

In all the curriculum courses I have ever taken, generalities prevailed. I never left such a course knowing specifically how I would go about selecting an objective; but there are now ways available to us as a consequence of developing pools of measurable objectives. In the old days, when you wanted to determine what an objective should be, very frequently you would start with some generalization drawn from the subject matter. You could, if you were insightful, develop an objective from it. We now say to teachers, learners, and others, "Here is a list of measurable objectives. Because they are measurable, you can understand precisely what we have in mind. Take these measurable objectives and simply rate them on a five-point scale." One can thus very economically get estimates of what diferent kinds of clienteles believe are the objectives that ought to be pursued in the school. We have taken arrays of objectives, let us say 100 objectives in mathematics, maybe 50 in social science—whatever the subject is—and have asked different groups (parents, teachers, learners) to rate the importance of them. We then ask futurists to rate the objectives they think would be suitable for the 1980's; that is, we use "councils of the future," as recommended by Alvin Toffler. We then pool and average these different ratings to find out which objectives are preferred by the various groups. Thus if you think student preferences are far more important than parental preferences, you can jack up the weighting of the student ratings. In other words, you can play a technically defensible game.

Let us imagine you have a list of 20 objectives that seem to be strongly preferred by two or three of these groups. You should make these objectives the center, but not the entirety, of your instructional activities. In addition, you will assess the current status of the learners with respect to those objectives. You will find out what the pupils can already do. Having access to that information, plus your knowledge of what various groups think ought to be pursued, gives you a fantastic plus in choosing what objectives should be pursued for your school.

We find that in Los Angeles schools, particularly in inner-city schools, the preferences of parents are far different from what the school administrators think they are. We find that what the kids want is often quite unanticipated by the teachers. That is, the teachers are not very good predictors of what objectives the children think ought to be pursued. But they do not have to be good predictors now, because we can give them the preference information. Then, looking at such a data array, the teacher can make a better choice. Thus we have a valuable curricular use for measurable objectives.

DESIGNING AN INSTRUCTIONAL SEQUENCE

Let us now turn to instruction. In designing an instructional sequence to accomplish one of these objectives, the objectives hopefully selected by a defensible technique, one might proceed almost haphazardly. That is, he can just sit down and say, "I think this will work," and try an instructional sequence. If it does not work, he can try something different next time. But if he has a measurable objective, he is tremendously advantaged in the following ways:

By knowing precisely the kind of learner behavior he wants to have emerge as a consequence of instruction, he can give the learner practice in that behavior during instruction. Psychological studies galore suggest that the best possible way to get a learner to behave in a particular fashion is to give him practice in behaving in that fashion. If the teacher knows what the terminal behavior is, it will be easier to get the learner to practice it. For example, when I formerly taught a statistics course, what I wanted my students to be able to do at the end of the course was to be able, when given hypothetical problems in research, to suggest the correct statistical analysis for the data at hand. In other words, they had to call for a coefficient of correlation, an analysis of variance, a T-test, or whatever it was. When I started teaching, the only time I gave them that particular kind of problem was on the final examination. How absurd! What I should have done, and what I have done recently, is to give them that kind of practice all the way through the course. I know what the desired terminal behavior is, so I give them much practice in doing it. And, quite obviously, they can do it at the end of the course.

Another tremendous advantage is that you can let the learners know what the objectives are. We call this "revelation of objectives," and it sounds almost theological; but all it means is that you tell the students, "Here are the objectives that will be accomplished in the course. If you can behave in these ways after instruction, you will get a fine grade in the course." Now, students are not used to that. As a consequence, they will often ask you, "Where is the *real* exam?" When you give them an exam based on the objectives, they cannot really believe that you are going to play fair. But when you allow them to focus their energy on relevant tasks, you will find that many more students can accomplish the objectives. When you let your teachers know that revealing objectives and providing appropriate practice to students can yield great dividends, you will help them instructionally. Further, it will have a wholesome impact on the teacher himself.

I submit a personal experience from my days on the faculty at San Francisco State College. I was teaching a course there with 18 measurable objectives, which I presented to the students at the start of the course. I said, "We may add objectives, in which case I will tell you. But these are the 18 course goals. If you are able to perform these behaviors at the end of the course, you will get an A. My responsibility will be to get you to achieve these objectives. Let us progress." And we did. Things went pretty well. About half way through the course, however, I was telling a story which, if not raucously funny, was at least mildly levity-laden. The kids were laughing. Then one youngster in the back of the room said, "Dr. Popham, could you please tell us to which of the 18 course objectives your past 10 minutes' worth of remarks were directed?" Well, I should have failed the wise guy, because you cannot have that kind of crud going on in your course. These may have been the first seeds of revolt at San Francisco State College.

What amazed me was the fact that the learners were so highly conscious of the 18 objectives. In my teaching I still try to include an occasional story, but at least I am aware of why I am doing it, e.g., to keep the positive affect going. Concentration on the objectives allows me to cut out much irrelevance in a course. In a sense, the students are also monitoring me to see that I do in fact make the course pertinent to the course goals. They can also question the goals. I have a session at the start of almost all of my classes where I allow students, if they think they have the sophistication, to discuss the kinds of objectives I have announced for them. And we sometimes add objectives as a consequence of this interaction. But when the objectives are clearly explicated, away we roar. Because I provide relevant practice for the students, after letting them know what the objectives are, most of them do very well in my classes.

When I finished graduate school, I was not very fond of the education department. I wear a Mickey Mouse watch now to indicate what my department is. People say to me, "You teach at UCLA?" I say, "Yes." "What department?" I show them the watch and they say, "Oh, education." In one period of my life I tried to have "academic standards." I would give my fair share of D's and F's. I would walk over to the registrar's office and plop down my D's and F's. The registrar's assistant would look up at me and say, "D's and F's—in an education course?" And I would snicker and walk out with my head held high. Well, after what has happened at UCLA, with the focus on relevant practice, providing objectives, and so on, I give an immense number of A's and B's. I gave something like 87 percent A's the last time I taught a course. There were 200 students. Now when I go to the registrar's office to turn in my grades, they giggle and I crawl out. I no longer get the psychic rewards associated with giving F's. But having precise objectives does provide instructional dividends.

EVALUATING THE QUALITY OF INSTRUCTION

Now we turn to evaluation, something which I think should be of particular interest to principals. I don't mean evaluation of learners in the sense that we are going to give them A's or B's. In this instance I mean evaluation of the quality of instruction, that is, evaluation of the instructional plan that the teacher designs and implements. In general, unachieved objectives reflect inadequacies in instruction—deficiencies in the teacher, not deficiencies in the kids. I don't know how many times I have heard my colleagues say to me, "Students did terribly on the final examination." They blame poor performance on almost anything but themselves. They ascribe it to an inattentive group, or poor genes, or anything but their own deficiencies. But in my own classes I try to promote a fairly healthy guilt complex among teachers. When objectives are not achieved, the first person who is deficient is the teacher. Adopting this rationale gives the teacher a basis for judging success. Achieved objectives may suggest augmenting the goals, but unachieved objectives mean something was wrong instructionally. Thus the teacher has a tangible criterion against which to judge the efficacy of his instruction, and that is more than a trivial tool in a teacher's repertoire, because very few of us have the skill to discern when we are teaching effectively.

I used to think that there were certain students in my classes who were in complete tune with me, who knew everything that was going on in my head, because they would nod at just the right time, that is, every time I said something that I thought very insightful. They would murmur and nod at everything I said that I thought worthwhile. But these nodders, I eventually discovered, invariably failed my final examination, suggesting that they had some kind of neck muscle defect. The thing is, I could not tell whether I was teaching very efficiently. But by having a rigorous criterion against which to judge his instruction, that is, whether or not the objective has been achieved, a teacher has a basic requirement for self-improvement.

A CRITERION FOR JUDGING THE TEACHER

Furthermore, the principal has a far better technique for discerning whether the teacher is functioning effectively in the classroom. I submit that the majority of administrator ratings are applied according to this scheme: The principal or supervisor visits the teacher's classroom and discerns what the teacher is doing. If the teacher's procedures parallel those he himself used during his stellar days in the classroom, then that teacher is judged a rousing success. But rating ought not be derived that way. We *do* have better ways now. And these better ways involve determining whether the teacher is bringing about defensible behavior changes in learners.

There is ample evidence to document the fact that there is not a single instructional procedure that works invariably with kids. Teachers are far too heterogeneous. Kids are far too different. Objectives vary. Instructional environments vary. The whole process is too particularized for us to say, "That is a good teaching technique." Rather, what you can say is: "For these learners, for this objective, for that teacher, in this situation, this was the desirable behavior change produced."

I have reached the position where, to accomplish a defensible behavior change in learners, I will accept any instructional means whatever, short of those which are morally reprehensible (and, since I live in Los Angeles, I don't even know what the phrase "morally reprehensible" means). In other words, I guess I would not let teachers beat kids over the heads with a two-by-four or shock them, but if they want to use techniques different from those I would choose, so long as they produce the right kinds of behavior change in kids, I will not fault them. For example, I have a colleague at UCLA who teaches a course in a very nondirective fashion. Students ask questions of her and she will rarely respond. She will say something like, "It is more important what *you* think the answer is"—the whole Rogerian bit. When kids ask me the answer, I usually tell them. Yet, at the end of our different courses, the learners end up being able to do the same thing. Vastly different approaches: the same result.

What I am suggesting is that, with the teacher whom you have to evaluate, you should first agree on worthwhile objectives; then student achievement of those objectives should be the prime, although not the exclusive, determiner of that teacher's success.

THE CONTRACT PLAN

John McNeil of UCLA has developed a scheme that he calls a contract plan of instructional evaluation of student teachers. A student teacher sits down with his supervising teacher and describes essentially what objectives he has and the precise measures that can be used to indicate whether those objectives have been achieved. If the supervising teacher agrees with this particular scheme, both parties sign the contract. If the objectives have been achieved at the end of instruction, irrespective of the instructional techniques employed, the student teacher gets an A. The scheme is working beautifully. Let me explain why. At first I thought the student teachers would be resistant to this approach. After all, it puts their instructional effectiveness on the line. I thought they would not like it. But they do. The reason they prefer this approach is that they know what the criteria are. They do not have to fear capriciously employed criteria when they are being evaluated. The game has established rules, and they respond favorably. Of course there are some who do not respond favorably, some who cannot change kids' behavior although they think they are teaching beautifully. Those people *should* be unhappy. A contract scheme or some variant, where a chief criterion of teacher efficiency is whether that teacher can accomplish objectives is, I submit, a real advance over what school people are doing now.

A DISCONCERTING EXPERIMENT

I have been very dissatisfied with teacher competence measures over the years. This has been my main research interest. In an article in the January, 1971, *American Educational Research Journal* I described what we call performance tests of teaching skills. Because teachers vary in their instructional techniques, we set up a series of very explicit instructional objectives in three different fields: social science, electronics, and automobile mechanics. For these teacher performance tests, we gave the objectives and some resource materials to the teachers. They could use the resource materials or not. The choice was theirs. We said, "Teach to these objectives in a real high school class, accomplishing the objectives any way you like, using any pedagogical techniques you wish, but accomplishing the objectives. Change the kids in these given ways." They undertook this task. Now, my interest was in verifying whether this performance-test approach to assessing teaching skill was worth anything. If it was, it should at least have the power to discriminate between grossly different groups, such as experienced teachers and people off the street. If we put these two groups in a similar situation, have them teach to these performance tests, we could clearly show that the experienced teachers would outperform the people off the street, I theorized.

You have anticipated the results, I am sure. In three separate replications, we have as yet been unable to find a group of people off the street whom the experienced teacher can outperform.

The reason that teachers are no better able to modify learner behavior than are people off the street—housewives, TV repairmen, garage mechanics—is pretty clear. In the first place, I was naive to think there would be a difference. If you think about it, teachers have not been trained in teacher preparatory institutions to be skill behavior modifiers. They are not reinforced for it once they are in the schools. The reward system in the schools does not focus heavily on whether the teacher can modify the behavior of the learner. As a consequence, teachers don't do very well. Assuming that my conclusions will be corroborated, and I really think they will, it becomes clear that teachers are not currently very good at changing kids.

The implications of this statement are, I think, very significant. We cannot let the situation continue. Every reasonably good profession has some unique skill that its members alone can perform. Our unique skill should be to change learners. I submit that we do not have the skill at our disposal. We have to promote it within the teachers with whom we are working. I think measurable objectives can be one way of helping us in the three arenas that I have mentioned thus far.

There are some problems with measurable objectives, however, with which you should be more than slightly conversant. One is this: It is much harder to use measurable objectives in the kind of scheme I have described than to teach the way teachers normally do. To think in precise terms of how you want to change learners, and to devise instructional procedures relevant to those aspirations, and then to find out whether or not it actually has worked—that is difficult.

FILMSTRIP-TAPE PROGRAM ON INSTRUCTIONAL OBJECTIVES

Not long ago I took a filmstrip-tape program on instructional objectives * to the Ford Foundation and proposed that we translate it and several others into Spanish so that they could be used by Latin American educators and others. I was the typical beneficent North American. The Ford Foundation gave me a little money and I did the job. It was not a cavalier translation. I hired very proficient people and they did all the clever little things. They took out the picture of the American flag, they removed all references to the Monroe Doctrine, they changed Yogi Berra to Pele. They inserted all the clever nuances. I was proud of what they were doing.

In this country, pre-test performers hit around 40 percent, post-test around 90 percent. We tried the translated version with Mexican prospective teachers. The results: pre-test 35 percent, post-test 36 percent. The change was in the right direction, but you could hardly call it a quantum leap. That was a devastating experience for me. I was so proud of that program. But I had to confess to myself that I was doing something drastically wrong. Had it not been for the precise objectives and the measures based on those objectives, I would have left that instructional situation trying to sell or give away the program.

What I am suggesting is that using the measurable objective approach often yields rather tragic instances of failure. You have to expect it. I suggest also that it takes a lot of time to use this approach. As long as we are asking high school teachers to teach five periods a day, with heaven knows how many kids, they

---

*Available, along with other filmstrip-tape programs from Vimcet Associates, Box 24714, Los Angeles, Calif. 90024.

will not be able to bring the level of rational planning to the instructional enterprise that it demands. They cannot think rigorously about instruction; they cannot plan it or evaluate it. I submit that right now if we gave them more time, the only thing that would increase is the coffee consumption, because they don't have the competence to use the increased time more efficiently. I suggest that two things have to happen, One, you have to give the teachers more time, but at the same time you have to give them the skills necessary to use that time more efficiently.

Let me suggest some very simple things that one can do. You can set up short-term performance tests, tests that would take no more than a half an hour of instructional time, and have teachers try to accomplish those objectives in front of other teachers. The teacher tries to achieve the objectives, either succeeds or fails, and then the group openly critiques the performance, thereby supplying the teacher with the arsenal of tools necessary for him to accomplish the objectives. This should be a nonevaluative, nonpunitive session. It is open and collegial. I think you have to give the teachers this kind of support.

ARE BEHAVIORAL GOALS DEHUMANIZING?

Further, I submit that additional time is a necessary while not sufficient condition. There are people who object to measurable objectives today because they argue that this is a dehumanizing approach to education. They proclaim humanistic goals to the point that I think is distressing. I think it is distressing because cleavage to precise objectives is essentially a neutral position. All it suggests is that you want to be clear about your instructional intents. If you wish to involve learners in determining what the instructional intent should be, I have already suggested that it can be done. If you want to accomplish some terribly humane goals, I submit to you that you can do it far better with precise, clear goals in mind. There is a certain tyranny in vagueness. If you do not know what is happening, you cannot object to it. But with clear goals, all concerned participants can enter the open arena and debate whether the objectives are sound.

What I have been trying to suggest throughout is that in the areas of curriculum, evaluation, and instruction, there are very practical advantages in the use of precise instructional objectives. As I look back at the 1960's, it seems to me the decade was an era when a tremendous amount of visible support emerged for measurable objectives. There was a coalescing of advocacy for measurable objectives, but without much practical implementation. Then as I look at the 1970's, it seems to me that this could be the decade that yields the dividends. Right now they are within our grasp. But it will take vigorous support from many educational leaders to achieve the real improvements in American education that can be accomplished through the use of measurable objectives.

14 Teaching Without Specific Objectives

James D. Raths

A central issue in the curriculum field is the dilemma, perhaps over-simplified, between *discipline* and *freedom*. Lawrence S. Kubie stated it most clearly:

> To put the question even more specifically, the educator must ask, "How can I equip the child with the facts and the tools which he will need in life, without interfering with the freedom with which he will be able to use them after he has acquired them?" We have learned that both input-overload through the excessive use of grill and drill, and input-underload through excessive permissiveness, may tumble the learner into the same abyss of paralysis and ignorance (1).

The aim of this paper is to argue that by accepting the basic assumption that the *primary* purpose of schooling is to change the behavior of students in specific predetermined ways, schools are only making the problem defined by Kubie more acute. In addition, this paper asserts that activities may be justified for inclusion in the curriculum on grounds other than those based on the efficacy of the activity for specifically changing the behaviors of students. It is also proposed that schools, while accepting a minimum number of training responsibilities, should take as their *major* purpose one of involving students in activities which have no preset objectives, but which meet other specified criteria.

TEACHING FOR BEHAVIORAL OBJECTIVES

Regardless of the underlying bases on which curricula are selected for inclusion in a program, a major problem is that of justifying the activities children are asked to experience. Clearly, the selection process always involves subjective and value-related judgments.

Consider the junior high school teacher of science in his efforts to defend the behavioral objectives of his program. He may argue that a particular objective is justified on the grounds that it is related to student success in senior high school; that the objective has traditionally been taught as a part of the cur-

From *Educational Leadership*, 28 (7): 714–720 (April 1971). Reprinted with permission of the Association for Supervision and Curriculum Development and James D. Raths. Copyright © 1971 by the Association for Supervision and Curriculum Development.

riculum; that it reflects the behavior of scientists and as such is important to his students; or more simply, that the objective is "in the book." None of these justifications, either singly or collectively, seems especially convincing.

The problem is seen most clearly in the affective domain. Lay persons and professionals alike have long asked, "What values should be taught?" Krathwohl, Bloom, and Masia (2) have argued that one reason which partially accounts for the erosion of affective objectives in our schools is that teachers hesitate to impose values on their students through the lever of giving grades. On the other hand, teachers seem to feel that manipulating students in the cognitive domain is ethical. For instance, a science teacher may want his students to acquire behaviors associated with the scientific method. Manifestly, there is no one scientific method, just as there is no one view of justice, yet teachers seem to feel no compunction about "forcing" students to learn the scientific method they have in mind while shying away from teaching one view of justice.

It is important in terms of the central thesis of this paper to consider the long range implications a teacher and his students must accept once it has been decided that all students are to acquire a specific instructional objective. The teacher's task becomes at once difficult and tedious. He must inform his students of the objective to which they are expected to aspire; he must convince them of the relevance of this objective to their lives; he must give students the opportunity to practice the behavior being taught; he must diagnose individual difficulties encountered by members of his group; he must make prescriptions of assignments based on his diagnoses and repeat the cycle again and again. Needless to say, this "method" of instruction has proved itself effective, if not provocative. It is the training paradigm perfected during both World Wars and utilized extensively in the armed forces and in industry to prepare persons for specific responsibilities.

It is the rare teacher who implements this procedure with the precision implied by the foregoing description. Few teachers have the energy, the knowledge important for making diagnoses, the memory needed to recall prescriptions, or the feedback capabilities of a computer. The ultimate training program is the research-based IPI model used experimentally in a few schools throughout the country. This observation is not meant to fault teachers as a group but merely to observe that in terms of the ways schools are organized, for example, teacher-student ratios, availability of special technical assistance, etc., only the most gifted and dedicated teachers can offer an effective training procedure to students. So instead of a rigorous training paradigm, most students are presented with "grill and drill" techniques, as cited by Kubie, repetitious to some and meaningless to others. Yet even if all programs could be set up on the basis of behavioral objectives and even if strict training paradigms could be established to meet the objectives, who could argue that such a program would be other than tedious and ultimately stultifying? This last comment applies both to the students and to the teacher. Usually, teaching for objectives is dull work. Most of the student responses are familiar ones and are anticipated by a teacher who is fully aware of the range of possible problems students might meet in acquiring the behavior. Hopefully, both teachers and students aspire to something other than this.

TEACHING WITHOUT SPECIFIC OBJECTIVES

To suggest that teachers plan programs without specific instructional objectives seems to fly in the face of many sacred beliefs—those dealing with progress, efficiency, success, and even rationality. On the other hand, such a proposal evidently does not fly in the face of current practices. Much to the distress of empiricists (3,4), teachers do from time to time invite children to participate in activities for which specific behavioral objectives are rarely preset. Examples of some of these activities include taking field trips, acting in dramatic presentations, having free periods in school, participating in school governments, putting out a class newspaper, and many others. While teachers evidently hope that students, as individuals, will acquire learnings from these activities, the learnings are generally not preset nor are they imposed on all the children in the class.

Instead, teachers may intend that these activities will provide students with some of the skills they will need in life, either through the direct experience they undergo in the classroom in carrying out the activity or through subsequent follow-up activities. In addition, teachers learn to expect that some children will become bored with any single activity—whatever it is. This response can be found in most classrooms at any one time and teachers simply make plans to involve those students suffering from momentary ennui in other provocative activities later in the day or week.

While carrying out a program composed of such activities, a teacher must perform many important and difficult tasks, but the functions seem less perfunctory and more challenging than those carried out under the training regimen described previously. A teacher must listen to the comments and questions of his students with the intent of clarifying their views and perceptions; he must encourage students to reflect upon their experiences through writings, poetry, drawings, and discussions; he must react to their responses in ways that suggest individual activites students may consider in following up on their experiences. In these ways, teachers provide an environment that is sufficiently evocative to encourage children to become informed and capable, but in individual ways that would be difficult to anticipate either in the central offices of a board of education or in the test construction laboratories located at Palo Alto or Iowa City.

CRITERIA FOR WORTHWHILE ACTIVITIES

If we accept the argument that the major focus of our schools should be away from activities designed to bring about specific behavioral changes in students, then on what basis can activities be justified for inclusion in the curricula of our schools? This section advances some criteria for identifying activities that seem to have some inherent worth. The criteria set down here for identifying worthwhile activities are not advanced to convince anyone of their wisdom as a set or individually, but merely to suggest value statements that might be used to justify the selection of particular activities in a curriculum.

The value statements are couched in terms that can best be used in the following manner. As a teacher contemplates an activity for his classroom, each of the value statements may suggest ways the activity might be altered. For instance, if a teacher were to consider an assignment which requires students to write a report on Brazil, he might revise his assignment to include one or more of the value dimensions suggested by the criteria. With all other things being equal, the revised assignment would be considered, according to these criteria, more worthwhile than the original one.

A relevant question to raise at this point is, "Worthwhile for whom?" The answer necessarily is for the child and for society. While there can be no empirical support for this response, neither can any other activity or behavioral objective be justified through data.

1. *All other things being equal, one activity is more worthwhile than another if it permits children to make informed choices in carrying out the activity and to reflect on the consequences of their choices.*

An activity that requires children to select topics for study, resources for use, or media for the display of ideas, after some exploration of alternatives, is more worthwhile than one that provides children with no opportunities or another that gives choices at rather mundane levels, for example, a choice of now or this afternoon, or using a pen or pencil.

2. *All other things being equal, one activity is more worthwhile than another if it assigns to students active roles in the learning situation rather than passive ones.*

An activity that channels students' energies into such roles as panel members, researchers, orators, observers, reporters, interviewers, actors, surveyors, performers, role players, or participants in simulation exercises such as games is more worthwhile than one which assigns students to tasks such as listening in class to the teacher, filling out a ditto sheet, responding to a drill session, or participating in a routine teacher-led discussion.

3. *All other things being equal, one activity is more worthwhile than another if it asks students to engage in inquiry into ideas, applications of intellectual processes, or current problems, either personal or social.*

An activity that directs children to become acquainted with ideas that transcend traditional curricular areas, ideas such as truth, beauty, worth, justice, or self-worth; one that focuses children on intellectual processes such as testing hypotheses, identifying assumptions, or creating original pieces of work which communicate personal ideas or emotions; or one that raises questions about current social problems such as pollution, war and peace, or of personal human relations is more worthwhile than one that is directed toward places (Mexico or Africa), objects (birds or simple machines), or persons (Columbus or Shakespeare).

4. *All other things being equal, one activity is more worthwhile than another if it involves children with realia.*

An activity that encourages children to touch, handle, apply, manipulate, examine, and collect real objects, materials, and artifacts either in the classroom or on field trips is more worthwhile than one that involves children in the use of pictures, models, or narrative accounts.

5. *All other things being equal, one activity is more worthwhile than another if completion of the activity may be accomplished successfully by children at several different levels of ability.*

An activity that can be completed successfully by children of diverse interests and intellectual backgrounds is more worthwhile than one which specifies in rigid terms only one successful outcome of the activity. Examples of the former are thinking assignments such as imagining, comparing, classifying, or summarizing, all of which allow youngsters to operate on their own levels without imposing a single standard on the outcomes.

6. *All other things being equal, one activity is more worthwhile than another if it asks students to examine in a new setting an idea, an application of an intellectual process, or a current problem which has been previously studied.*

An activity that builds on previous student work by directing a focus into *novel* locations, *new* subject matter areas, or *different* contexts is more worthwhile than one that is completely unrelated to the previous work of the students. (This position is an example of one that is impossible to build into every activity presented to students. Obviously a balance is needed between new areas of study and those which are related to previous work. Value dimension number six asserts the need for some continuity in a program.)

7. *All other things being equal, one activity is more worthwhile than another if it requires students to examine topics or issues that citizens in our society do not normally examine—and that are typically ignored by the major communication media in the nation.*

An activity that deals with matters of sex, religion, war and peace, the profit motive, treatment of minorities, the workings of the courts, the responsiveness of local governments to the needs of the people, the social responsibilities of public corporations, foreign influences in American media, social class, and similar issues is more worthwhile than an activity which deals with mundane "school topics" such as quadratic equations or short stories—topics usually considered safe and traditional.

8. *All other things being equal, one activity is more worthwhile than another if it involves students and faculty members in "risk" taking—not a risk of life or limb, but a risk of success or failure.*

Activities that may receive criticism from supervisors and parents on the basis of "what's usually done," that may fail because of unforeseen events or conditions, are more worthwhile than activities that are relatively risk-free —using approaches which are condoned openly by the community and the school administration and which have served teachers well in the past.

9. *All other things being equal, one activity is more worthwhile than another if it requires students to rewrite, rehearse, and polish their initial efforts.*

Rather than having students perceive assignments as "tasks to complete," activities should provide time and opportunity for students to revise their themes in the light of criticism, rehearse a play in front of an audience, or practice an interviewing technique to be used in a project so that they will begin to see the value of doing a task well. Activities that communicate to students that their efforts are approximations of perfect work—and that efforts can be made to improve their work—are more worthwhile than ones that merely suggest that once an assignment is completed the first time, it is finished.

10. *All other things being equal, one activity is more worthwhile than another if it involves students in the application and mastery of meaningful rules, standards, or disciplines.*

Using standards derived from students as well as authorities, panel discussions can be disciplined by procedures; reporting of data can be disciplined by considerations of control; essays can be regulated by considerations of style and syntax. Activities which foster a sense of meaningful discipline, either imposed or chosen by the children themselves, are more worthwhile than ones that ignore the need for the application of meaningful rules or standards.

11. *All other things being equal, one activity is more worthwhile than another if it gives students a chance to share the planning, the carrying out of a plan, or the results of an activity with others.*

One facet of the current trends in individualizing instruction found in some programs is that of minimizing the chance for children to work in groups and to learn the problems inherent in any situation that calls for individual desires to yield at times to group requirements. An activity that asks children to play a role in sharing responsibilities with others is more worthwhile than one which limits such opportunity.

12. *All other things being equal, one activity is more worthwhile than another if it is relevant to the expressed purposes of the students.*

While a prizing of children's purposes might well be protected by the value dimension previously expressed, of providing choices for children, it is important enough to stress in a value dimension of its own. As students are invited to express their own interests and to define problems in which they feel a personal involvement, and as the activities of the curriculum reflect those interests, the ensuing activity will be more worthwhile than one that is based on attributions of interests and concerns made by teachers.

Obviously, not all of the value components identified in this section can be built into a single activity. Also, not all the values listed deserve the same amount of emphasis in terms of time within a given program. For example, some assignments involving "risk" may be titillating for students and teachers, but a program which has more than a few activities reflecting the "risk" value would probably be out of balance. Finally, the list above is not exhaustive. It is meant to illustrate values that might be used in defining a program of worthwhile activities. The value-criteria are merely working hypotheses at this time, subject to analysis if not empirical testing. Others are encouraged to develop their own set of criteria.

CAVEAT

It must be emphasized that all teachers, whether working at the first grade level or in graduate school, generally need to do some teaching for objectives as well as some teaching without specific objectives. Whitehead has suggested that in terms of the rhythm of education, many more of the tasks assigned to younger children should be justified on non-instrumental values, while those assigned at the upper levels might reasonably contain more performance-related activities (5).

EVALUATION

All of the foregoing is not to suggest that school programs need not be evaluated. As in the past, those activities which are justified in terms of the objectives they are designed to meet can be evaluated through criterion-referenced achievement tests. Other procedures need to be developed to describe school programs in terms of the characteristics of the activities which comprise the programs. The following procedure might serve as a way of communicating information about a given course or program which would be meaningful to administrators and parents.

Assume that a teacher accepted as the major values of his program those previously identified in this paper. (Presumably, this procedure could be used for any set of values.) He could periodically describe his program using a chart similar to the one presented in Table 1. The chart could be completed according to the following ground rules:

> *Column 1:* This column would simply number the activity for purposes of identification.
> *Column 2:* This notation would place the activity in the sequence of activities carried out during the reporting period.
> *Column 3:* This entry would be another way of labeling the topics under study for purposes of identification.
> *Column 4:* The number of students who successfully completed the activity would be entered here to communicate the extent to which all students in the class were involved with the activity.
> *Column 5:* To give emphasis to the centrality of the activity to the

TABLE 1.   Teacher's Log

Subject:........... Teacher's Name:.................... Unit:............ Dates: From ...... To ....

(1)	(2)	(3)	(4) Number of students completing activity	(5) Estimated number of hours of participation per student	(6) Justified by criteria (Check those relevant) 1 2 3 4 5 6 7 8 9 10 11 12
Activity number	Dates	Title of activity			
1	Jan. 8	Experiment with electricity	15	2 hrs.	x x x x x

scope of the course, the estimation of the average number of hours students spent on the activity would be entered in this column.

Column 6: In this column, teachers would check those components of the activity which in their eyes serve to justify it in their program. In the example entered in the table, the teacher has justified an activity, not in terms of what students can do on finishing it that they could not do before, but on the grounds that it gave students a chance to make a choice (#1); involved them in active roles (#2); included experiences with realia (#4); provided various levels of achievement which could be judged as successful (#5); and required students to apply meaningful standards to their work (#10).

If each line of every teacher's log were punched on a computer card, a program could easily be written which would yield output describing the percentage of time spent on each activity, and the number of children who were involved with programs under each value dimension. At present, no generalizations are available which could be used to rate definitively a given course description as adequate or inadequate, based on these data. Nevertheless, if a science program profile indicated that almost no time was spent with students in active roles, if students were almost never involved with realia, and if students had few opportunities to apply meaningful rules or standards to their work, then a person sharing the values espoused in this paper would have serious reservations about the quality of that particular science program.

In summary, the argument has been presented that an activity can be justified in terms other than those associated with its instrumental value for changing the behavior of students. In addition, this paper has presented a set of criteria for identifying worthwhile activities, proposed a modest procedure for describing programs in terms of those criteria, and issued an invitation for others to present alternative criteria. Most of all, it has asked that some concern be directed toward the quality of opportunities for experiences offered through our schools.

REFERENCES
1. Lawrence S. Kubie. "Research on Protecting Preconscious Functions in Education."(n.d.) Mimeo. p. 4. Also see this paper in: A. Harry Passow, editor. *Nurturing Individual Potential.* Washington, D.C.: Association for Supervision and Curriculum Development, 1964. pp. 28–42.
2. D. R. Krathwohl, B. S. Bloom, and B. B. Masia. *Taxonomy of Educational Objectives Handbook II: Affective Domain.* New York: David McKay Company, Inc., 1964. p. 16.
3. W. James Popham. *The Teacher-Empiricist.* Los Angeles: Aegeus Press, 1965.
4. Henry H. Walbesser. *Constructing Behavioral Objectives.* College Park: Bureau of Educational Research and Field Services, University of Maryland, 1970.
5. A. N. Whitehead. *The Aims of Education.* New York: Mentor Books, 1929. pp. 27ff.

III Teaching for Thinking and Feeling

As indicated in Part II of this book, many educators disagree on the relative importance of the schools' major goals. Few educators, though, deny that some combination of cognitive and affective goals is desirable. Even fewer claim that teaching is possible without such a combination. It is essential, then, that the reader be aware that when he does teach, he teaches for both thinking and feeling, and he does so whether by design or by accident.

In article 15, Combs comments on an increasingly documentable fact—that human beings can be and can achieve much more than was ever thought possible. And yet, Combs notes, in today's world there are children who will never have the slightest chance of becoming what they could be. These are children who are limited—limited by their physiology, by their lack of opportunity, by their lack of needs satisfaction, by their damaged self-concepts, and by their lack of suitable challenges. Do the schools share the responsibility for creating and perpetuating these limits? And can the schools realistically be expected to help overcome them? According to Combs, the answer to both questions is yes. In the remainder of this part, and throughout other parts of this

121

book, the reader will become acquainted with instructional ideas and guidelines that can assist him in helping students realize whatever potentialities they have.

If teachers are to help students realize their intellectual potential, they must first have an understanding of what intelligence is and how it develops. In selection 16, Lavatelli and her associates claim that the starting point for such an understanding must be Jean Piaget's developmental theory of intelligence. To be sure, Piaget's theory has had in recent years significant influence on educational thought and practice. And unquestionably teachers do need to understand what a developmental theory of intelligence is and, more important, what its implications are. For this kind of understanding, Lavatelli and her associates are quite right in asserting that teachers need to know Piaget.

Measuring intelligence by means of IQ tests is common educational practice. But is it a legitimate practice? Do IQ tests, in fact, measure intelligence? Are they designed to do so? Are IQ tests culturally biased? Do people who score the same on an IQ test have the same intellectual abilities? What influence does heredity have on intellectual capacity? What influence does the environment have? Are there racial or ethnic differences in intellectual capacity? Are there ways of assessing intelligence other than through the use of IQ tests? In selection 17, Zack addresses these questions. Some are easily answered; others are not; a few, even, may be unanswerable. But if teachers are to use and interpret IQ tests wisely, they need to know what answers there are, and they need to be aware of the areas where answers are yet unknown.

As stated earlier, fostering students' ability to think is a pivotal goal of schools. But what exactly does the term "think" mean? Or does it have different meanings? According to Bayles, article 18, "think" can be used in at least four different ways. From least to most complex, these are (1) to have a passing feeling, (2) to indicate sheer memorization, (3) to signify understanding, and (4) to represent reflective thought. Bayles states that "teaching students how to think" usually means that teachers make assignments and ask questions that call for memorization and understanding. But, he claims, neither of these accomplishes its purpose; namely, teaches students how to think. Rather, memorizing and understanding only help students learn what to think. This distinction, according to Bayles, is far from trivial. I believe that teaching students how to think, teaching them to think reflectively, will require instructional strategies of a considerably different order from the ones most commonly used today.

Helping students learn to think through the use of classroom questioning techniques is the focus of article 19, by Sanders. Using as a basis Bloom's classification scheme for identifying six types of thinking (knowledge, comprehension, application, analysis, synthesis, and evaluation), Sanders asks and answers a series of key questions. These include: Do different types of questions require that students use different types of thinking? Can teachers be trained to ask different types of questions? Can higher level questions be asked at all grade levels and in all subject areas? And does the use of higher level questions always result in higher levels of learning? Of course, the reader should understand that knowing the answers to these questions is only the first step. Developing the *skills and attitudes needed to apply the answers is the next, and by far the more complex, process.*

Many educators have long assumed that a key factor in influencing students' ability to think and learn is the expectations of teachers. Not until recently, however, have studies been conducted to determine the validity of this assumption. In article 20, Brophy and Good summarize the results of some of these investigations. In general, Brophy and Good conclude that there is ample research evidence now available to prove that what teachers believe about their students' capabilities does have a measurable effect on how teachers treat students and on what they actually achieve. They conclude, in other words, that teachers' expectations function as self-fulfilling prophecies. Such a conclusion has implications for teaching that cannot be overstressed.

If one of education's major goals is to help students achieve their full potential as human beings, then education must provide the opportunities, climate, and experiences youngsters need in order to test out who and what they are and who and what they want to become. One potential type of testing-out process is described briefly by Howe, article 21. He states that teachers must provide opportunities for youngsters at all age and grade levels: (1) to fantasize ("If I were . . ."), (2) to game ("Let's pretend . . ."), (3) to encounter (trying it out), and (4) to actualize (playing for keeps). To many readers, these four processes may sound more like what youngsters do on the playground or on the street corner than in the classroom. Perhaps, though, that itself is the major point. For implicit in Howe's article is the conviction that these processes are much too important, that the goal of self-definition is much too critical, to be left to chance.

Certainly, a significant part of teaching for feeling is teaching for valuing. But how do teachers determine which values to teach, and, after that, how do they go about teaching them? These are the two main questions Simon considers in article 22. He is of the opinion, first, that there is no one "right" set of values and, second, that attempts to teach values through indoctrination have simply failed. Simon reasons, therefore, that what teachers should do is help students formulate and clarify their own values, and he proposes five instructional strategies that can be used for this purpose.

One of the most vocal critics of traditional forms of schooling is John Holt. In selection 23, Holt comments on a key educational question. How much freedom should students have in determining what they study? Holt's biases are clearly seen. The reader may not agree with Holt's views, but he would do himself great disservice if, in teaching for thinking and feeling, he failed to give them due consideration.

15 New Concepts of Human Potentials: New Challenge for Teachers

Arthur W. Combs

We are living in a world today with new ideas about the nature of human capacity, about what is possible for human beings. These revolutionary ideas pose vast new challenges to people who work with children.

Each of us behaves in terms of his beliefs about other people. If you believe a man is honest, you will trust him; if you don't believe he is honest, you will not. And any kind of change in our beliefs about what is possible for people must have far-reaching implications for every aspect of life. It makes a lot of difference, for example, whether you believe that children are able or unable. If you believe they are able, you *let* them. But if you don't believe they are able, you don't dare let them.

We now understand that a human organism is like an engineer's bridge. When an engineer constructs a bridge he builds in a safety factor some ten or fifteen times over what the bridge will ever be expected to withstand. He overbuilds it; in the same way the human organism is also overbuilt. Each of us has vastly more capacity than we ever dreamed of. Most of us use only a very small portion of our possibilities.

Today we know that intelligence itself can be created. If you doubt this, let me recommend J. McVicker Hunt's book, *Intelligence and Experience*, which reviews the evidence of why we now understand this is true. We know, for example, that the longer a child has been in an institution, the lower his IQ; when you put him in a rich environment, his IQ rises. We know that when we provide opportunities for people in the ghettos their intelligence levels rise. We know that between World War I and World War II the intelligence levels of men taken into the armed forces rose significantly. How do you suppose that happened? (It certainly *didn't* happen by selective breeding, because we still pick our mates in the same old sloppy way we always did, by falling in love.) This change came about as a consequence of changes in our society and in the way we have learned to deal with human beings.

The idea that intelligence is not fixed and immutable is tremendously exciting for all of us working with young people. It means that you and I are not the victims of the child's intelligence; we are in the business of creating it! It

Reprinted from *Childhood Education*, 47 (7): 349–355 (April 1971), by permission of Arthur W. Combs and the Association for Childhood Education International, 3615 Wisconsin Avenue, N.W., Washington, D.C. Copyright © 1971 by the Association.

means also that the Great Society LBJ talked about, and the rest of us hoped for, is possible. It changes our thinking in many directions. Take our conception of the gifted. If intelligence is something that can be created, the gifted child is our outstanding accomplishment, the child with whom we have been enormously successful. Our job is not to find such children and give them special nourishment, but to find out how we did it and get about the business of producing more of them as quickly as we can.

With all this change in our conception of what is possible, however, we still have children who are deeply limited, who are not achieving, who are not finding the kinds of life we know is possible. We know that a child can live in an expanded world and be unable to profit by it. Limits exist.

PHYSIOLOGICAL LIMITS

Let's take a look at some of those limits. *First,* we know that children are limited by their physiology. In order to be able to use the world, one needs a body in good condition. People in medicine today are talking not just about being sick or being well but about the concept of high-level wellness. We know what could be done for children physically and yet we go on talking about cutting budgets for school lunches. We have starving children in our land; we have children living on Indian reservations without enough to eat. And yet the cost of one single helicopter shot down over Vietnam would feed thousands and thousands of children a free lunch every day for months and months. Not long ago I was at Cape Kennedy and as our beautiful rocket lifted off the pad the man from NASA said, "There goes 329 million dollars!" I thought of what we could do with that kind of money for education.

We have enough know-how and wealth to provide every child in this country with the ultimate in physical health. What kind of world could we produce if we provided for every child adequate care and nutrition? What kind of new generation would we have before us?

OPPORTUNITY

Second, we know that realization of human capacities is limited by lack of opportunity. The child's world is determined by the opportunities he has had and his knowledge acquired as a consequence of experience. But the experience of the child is dependent upon us. Earl Kelley once said, "Whenever we start to worry about the next generation, we need to remind ourselves they were all right when we got them." You and I provide opportunity for children. The information explosion has given us magnificent techniques for providing young people with opportunities; but still some—many—live with no opportunity in the midst of such riches. In the ghettos children are living who do not develop language because nobody is there for them to speak to. Some children are left alone all day every day in a one-room apartment while Mother and Father (if there is one) go to work. Nobody speaks to these children and they grow up without the language development so significant and important for full intellectual growth.

At the University of Florida Ira Gordon is doing some fascinating experiments on early childhood stimulation. Beginning with babies at the age of six weeks, he shows their mothers how to provide them with opportunities for a more stimulating environment, using things found in the home. He is finding that when he provides these children with increased stimulation, even those from the most deprived kinds of home situations show increased intelligence levels.

We now know that human capacities increase with use and atrophy with disuse; that if we do not provide the opportunities for a person to utilize what he has, it dies aborning. Too many of our schools, which are supposed to provide stimulation for children, are deadly dull, monotonous and stupifying. Simply providing schools is no guarantee that children will be able to use them.

Here we are, a nation on wheels, and yet we cannot find ways to expand the world of the ghetto child. Some even fight tooth and nail to prevent the movement of children to enriching experience. The principle is clear—from the psychologist's point of view, human behavior is a function of opportunity. What kind of world could we create if we were really to provide every child with opportunities to experience the kinds of things that would make it possible for him to develop his ultimate capacities?

HUMAN NEEDS

A *third* thing psychologists know about limitations upon human beings has to do with human needs. Each of us is continuously searching for the satisfaction of his needs, which in turn provides us with drive and direction, motivations for obtaining further experience. We know that human needs exist in a hierarchy from those very basic ones like staying alive and getting enough to eat on up to those beautiful ones like love and self-fulfillment. But we also know that you can't do much with higher needs until lower ones are taken care of. You can't think much about nice ideas of democracy on an empty belly. The child who comes to school worried because Mama went to the hospital last night is in no condition to learn the principal exports of Venezuela.

We know today that human failure, maladjustment, stupidity, criminality are often consequences of deprivation. As Abe Maslow once put it, the deviant behavior of the maladjusted represents "the screams of the tortured at the crushing of their psychological bones." What a statement! Illness, physiologically, is a failure of the body to be able to satisfy its need for growth and health. In the same fashion, psychological illness is a failure of the organism to achieve its human needs for self-fulfillment.

Now, we don't say about a child when he is physically ill, "Let's give this child all the diseases we can as early as possible." We say, "Let's keep this child from getting the disease as long as we possibly can." Or, as with a vaccination or an immunization, we give him the disease in such an attentuated form that he will be successful with it and better able to deal with the real thing when it comes along.

But look what we do psychologically. Some children fail every day of their lives—are *forced* to fail, by the conditions they are placed in. We know today that illness is a lack of fulfillment physiologically or psychologically.

We have known for a long time that people behave in terms of their needs and yet we have not really implemented that fact in our dealings with youngsters. We have created schools that are largely irrelevant, out of touch with the needs of the kids. In our schools we have said, "I'm not interested in what you think about that, Jimmy; what does the book say?" Which is a way of saying to him that his needs are unimportant and without value.

Donald Snygg once described the illness of American education in these terms: "We are madly providing children with answers to problems they ain't got yet." We are often unwilling to fulfill people's needs. Instead we insist that they be right *now* what we hope to make them one day. Take for example what we do to the delinquent, who for fifteen years has been learning "Nobody likes me, nobody wants me, nobody cares about me" and who comes to the conclusion, "Well, I don't care about nobody neither!" He comes lunging into the office acting surly and ill mannered. We say to him, "Now, look here, young man, you behave yourself! Sit up there! Be polite!" In his society being polite would ruin him.

We are asking him to be today what the school ought someday to help him become. This is like going to the doctor's and being told, "Go away and get better, and come back and I'll help you!" No wonder we have children who feel their needs are not being satisfied in schools! To drop out is intelligent in that kind of circumstance (it's ridiculous to subject yourself to conditions that have nothing to offer you).

One of the things we have been discovering in our studies of self-actualizing people who are able to be all kinds of things, who are successful and happy and satisfied, effective in the community, is that they are people who grew up with needs fulfilled. As a consequence they are better adjusted, more stable, more successful. We also know that when we help other poeple to fulfill their needs they fulfill ours too. I ask again, what kind of world could we create if we were really to put our minds to the problem of helping every child fulfill his basic needs for love, affection, physiological health, opportunity?

SELF-CONCEPT

The *fourth* limitation that we know hampers people in expanding their world has to do with the self-concept, which we now recognize as perhaps the most important single factor in determining what a person is able to do under any given circumstance. People behave in terms of their self-concept. What a person believes about himself affects everything he does, even what he sees and hears—and, hence, is of tremendous significance in determining how effectively he will be able to deal with the world in which he lives.

Intelligence itself is a function of a person's self-concept. Those who have positive self-concepts because they feel good about themselves are *able* to try, to be creative, to go out into the blue and make use of their world. They have a better approach to life, are more open to their experiences and being more open are more likely to have better answers—which is what we mean by intelligence.

We know also that what a person believes about himself will determine whether he is likely to be well adjusted or badly adjusted. Well-adjusted people see themselves as liked, wanted, acceptable and able, dignified and worthy, whereas the maladjusted are those who see themselves as unwanted, unliked, unacceptable, unable and undignified. A positive view of self provides a tremendous resource for a person to be able to make the fullest possible use of his world.

But, of course, the self is something we learn. You learn who you are, what you are, from the significant others in your life—the ways people have treated you. We can ask, therefore: How can a child feel liked unless someone likes him? How can a child feel wanted unless somebody wants him? How can a child feel acceptable unless someone accepts him? And how can a child feel able unless somewhere he has some success? Thousands of people in our society are trapped, prisoners of their own perception, believing they can only do x-much. Then the rest of us see them only doing x-much, so we say "That is an x-much person"—which only proves what he already thought in the first place! Millions of people in this world are walking around with beliefs about themselves that are self-limiting, self-destructive. It is so also with children in all school subjects.

Let's take reading, for example. Most children who come to the reading clinic do not have anything wrong with their eyes. They are children who *believe* they can't read. Because they believe they can't read, they don't try; because they don't get any practice, they don't do it very well. Then, when the teacher asks them to read, they don't read very well and the teacher says, "My goodness, Jimmy, you don't read very well." And to add to that, we bring the parents in on the act by sending home a failing grade so they can tell him also.

Somehow, we have to find ways of breaking out of this vicious circle in which people are trapped, as James Agee said, "like mirrors locked face to face in an infinite corridor of despair."

A child brings his self-concept with him—he doesn't park it at the door; whatever we do affects his self-concept, even when we are teaching him mathematics, languages, or how to roller skate. If the self-concept is as important as psychologists are telling us today, then you and I must pay attention to it. The laws of learning cannot be suspended because they are inconvenient—they go right on in spite of us. We need to ask ourselves, "What are we teaching?"

Take the child who is reading at the third-grade level in the sixth grade. Day after day, hour after hour, week after week he is condemned to one failure experience after another—because you and I cannot adjust to a third-grade reader who happens to be twelve years old.

If the self-concept is learned, then in order to help children grow effectively we've got to find ways of helping them see themselves in positive fashion. In the answers to the questions I've stated before (how can a child feel liked unless someone likes him and how can he feel successful unless somewhere he has success), we'll discover what we need to do to help the child expand his world.

CHALLENGE AND THREAT

A *fifth* factor that influences how well a person can make use of the world in which he lives has to do with challenge and threat. I remember asking a little girl, "What did you learn today?" "Nothing," she replied, "but was my teacher mad! Wow!" She illustrated a very important psychological point, that a person being threatened can pay attention to nothing but that which threatens him. His capacity to perceive is narrowed down to the object of threat. Obviously, this condition is precisely the opposite of what we seek in expanding a child's world. We don't want him to narrow his perceptions; we want him to open them up.

When people are threatened they are also forced to defend their existing position. The hotter the argument gets, the more a person sticks to the position he had in the first place. Again, this is directly antithetical to everything we are seeking to accomplish in helping a person use his world effectively.

What do we mean by threat? People feel challenged when confronted with a problem that interests them and with which they believe they have a chance to succeed. People feel threatened when confronted with a problem they do not feel able to handle. Whether a child feels challenged or threatened is not a question of how it looks to his teacher—it's a question of how it looks to him.

Whether a person feels challenged or threatened determines how effectively he will be able to make use of the world in which he lives. Our problem then becomes one of finding ways to challenge people without threatening them. Again I ask, what kind of world could we create if we were really to put our minds to the problem of finding ways of challenging children without threatening them?

RECAPITULATION

After all, what children make of the world is dependent on us, on you and me. Science has provided us with answers and directions. These exciting new concepts of what is possible for human beings are world shaking. No human interaction is in vain unless we make it so. Every good experience a person is given is given him forever.

To help a deeply deprived child is like helping a child to fill up a deep pit. It takes a lot of giving and sometimes it is necessary to go on in sheer faith that eventually it will make a difference. So it is with deeply deprived people. A single thing you do on a nice Tuesday afternoon may not be enough; but neither is that good thing ever in vain, unless you make it so. Unfortunately we sometimes get into too much of a hurry.

For instance, take the "delinquent" I was talking about earlier who feels, "Nobody likes me, nobody wants me, nobody cares about me; well, I don't care about nobody neither." A well-meaning teacher comes along and says, "Eddie, I like you," and Eddie swears at her. Why? Because all his life all his experiences have taught him that he can't trust people who talk like that. He thinks, "Either she's lying and in that case she deserves to get punished, or she is making fun of me and in that case she deserves it all the more." So he swears at the teacher and she clouts him across the mouth—which, of course, just proves what he thought in the first place: she didn't mean it either!

Somehow we have to recognize that every good experience is given forever—but somebody has to start. We talk much about rejected children at school. And teachers who say, "What can I do with a child from a home like that?"

In my own clinical experience I have seen children change their homes because of their experience in school. Let me give you an illustration. Eddie Smith is unhappy, bugging his mother, driving her nuts. He comes to school, where he has a teacher who makes him feel just a little bit better. As a result, when Eddie goes home he doesn't bug Mama quite so much. In turn Mama, because she finds Eddie is a little bit better that day, doesn't take it out on Papa when he comes home. Papa finds that Mama is a little bit nicer tonight than she has been lately, so when he sits down to read the paper and his daughter wants to climb onto his lap, instead of pushing her away he says, "OK, honey, come on." She climbs up in his lap and has a good experience too. Because she feels better about her daddy, she doesn't tease Eddie so much (he was our problem in the first place!). I have seen it happen.

Many teachers believe that what they do is unimportant. This is never so! It is never unimportant because you cannot "unexperience" a good experience. Even a holding operation can be a positive thing. When everything in a child's life is pushing him downhill and all you do is keep him as bad as he is, that's progress. Fritz Redl, talking about juvenile delinquents, once put it very nicely when he said, "There's not much difference between a good child and a naughty child, but there is a world of difference between a naughty child and a real tough delinquent." And then he said, "Gee, if we could just keep them naughty!" I find that very reassuring.

With our new understanding of human potential, we now understand that stupidity and maladjustment are not "the will of God" but the *lack* of will of man. A theological concept holds that a man has not sinned if he doesn't know any better. In previous times our production of stupid and depraved people was excusable because we didn't know. That excuse no longer exists! We now know that constant deprivation leads to depravity, while *being given* leads to growth. In the light of that knowledge, we live in grievous sin if we do not act upon it. If we do not help the next generation to expand its world, we have failed everyone—the child, the parents, our institutions, the nation itself. It is in our own best interest to help expand the world of children. But, even if we do not act upon our new understandings for such selfish reasons, we ought to do it anyhow—just because we love them.

16 The Developmental Theory of Piaget

Celia Stendler Lavatelli, Walter J. Moore, and Theodore Kaltsounis

THE DEVELOPMENTAL THEORY OF PIAGET

Jean Piaget is a Swiss psychologist who, with his colleagues, has been studying the development of intelligence for over forty years. He has formulated a theory that has done for mental development what Freud did for the field of personality development. The starting point today for the serious student of the development of intelligence is the theory of Piaget, and his descriptions of stages in that development.

The Sensorimotor Stage

In contrast to the now discarded belief that intelligence is fixed at birth, Piaget, like most modern psychologists, believes that intelligence develops as the human organism carries on transactions upon objects or events in the environment. The human infant is born with a very large cortical area (the so-called gray matter of the brain where intelligent processes go on), but with few inborn responses. The infant comes into the world capable of reflex activity. Some of the reflexes, like that of the knee jerk, are not altered by experience. Others, however, like grasping, sucking, and reflexes involved in vision, are modified as the infant exercises them in response to stimulation. With the exercise, the infant assimilates information about objects and accommodates developing mental structures accordingly. That is, contact with an object modifies the activity of the reflex. The infant, for example, accommodates the

From *Elementary School Curriculum* by Celia Stendler Lavatelli, Walter J. Moore, and Theodore Kaltsounis. Copyright © 1972 by Holt, Rinehart and Winston, Inc. Reprinted by permission of Holt, Rinehart and Winston, Inc.

grasping reflex to the shape of the object to be grasped, curving the fingers in one way for a long narrow object and differently to grasp a ring. The exercise of the reflexes serves as needed aliment for the reflex; as Piaget (1963) points out with respect to the eye, "Light is nourishment for the eye . . . the eye needs light images just as the whole body needs chemical nourishment" (pp.42–43). And, as the reflexes are nourished by exercise, there is a tendency toward spontaneous repetition. Grasping leads to more grasping and looking to more looking. "The more a child has seen and heard, the more he wants to see and hear," is Piaget's way of summarizing the circular reaction of the first acquired adaptations. Through sensorimotor channels the infant is taking in information about the world, and the more he takes in, the more he wants.

The exercise of acquired adaptations leads to fresh discoveries, "every discovery historically entails a series of others." As the infant carries on activities with his environment, new behavior patterns are formed by differentiation and adaptation of preceding ones. Put an obstacle in the way of what a young infant is trying to grasp and he will abandon his attempt to find the object; out-of-sight is out-of-mind, for he lacks the concept of permanence of object. With experience, however, he comes to realize that objects *do* have permanence, and he will search for an object that an adult has shown him and then removed. Later, he may put to work here a response previously acquired in some other situation —that of pushing away or striking at the barrier in order to reach his goal. Parents and baby-sitters may recall the first time the baby discovered that striking at or pushing away an adult hand made it possible for him to reach the object which he now knows continues to exist.

During the first eighteen months, the infant carries on countless transactions involving space, time, matter, and causality. He assimilates information from these transactions, and because there are regularities and order in the physical world, mental structures become transformed as they accommodate themselves to new information. A baby tries to pull a ruler through the bars of the playpen. He discovers that held horizontally the ruler will not go through, but turned vertically it will. The discovery stimulates practice, and the infant may carry on a directed apprenticeship with variously shaped objects, and by twisting and turning them, assimilate information about how an object relates to space.

Piaget labels this early stage of intelligence, "sensorimotor intelligence." Sensorimotor intelligence is the intelligence of action; the infant "thinks" with action. If one moves a teddy bear from a chair to a bed while the infant looks on, and then says, "Where's teddy?", the baby will look first in the direction of the chair and then the bed. He does not have the capability for representational thought, for representing in his mind the displacement just carried out. He can carry on a series of displacements, of shifting data about, *but only in his actions* and not in his mind. He can move a toy physically, but he cannot visualize the move.

But according to the way in which Piaget traces the development of intelligent behavior in infancy, gradually the child comes to think about an action as he carries it out. Give an eighteen-month-old baby a closed box that he has never opened before and he does not grope for a solution. Rather, he puts to use the various schemata he has acquired for opening things, until he finds the correct one. This capacity to think out an action before representing it Piaget calls "mental invention." At this same stage the infant is capable of "representation"—that is, he has the capacity for imagining the environment other than as he directly perceives it. If the baby is asked, "Where's mommy?", after mommy has just left the room, he will point to the door she has passed through and say, "Dere mommy." He can conserve a part of the external world as a mental image, at least for a short time. And with the advent of language, events are increasingly represented linguistically, so that actions that previously had to be carried out in the sensorimotor system can now be carried out in thought.

The reader may wonder why we are concerned with the infancy period in a chapter on thinking processes of school-age children. The five-to-twelve-year-old is, after all, well beyond the stage of sensorimotor intelligence. For teachers, however, development in this first stage raises the interesting question of whether complex operations must first be enacted physically before they can be internalized. Bruner has written persuasively of such an enactive process in learning. He discusses the question of representation, or how a child gets to conserve past experience, in a model: "What is meant by representation? What does it mean to translate experience into a model of the world? Let me suggest that there are probably three ways in which human beings accomplish this feat: The first is through action. We know many things for which we have no imagery and no words, and they are very hard to teach to anybody by the use of either words or diagrams and pictures. If you have tried to coach somebody at tennis or skiing or to teach a child to ride a bike, you will have been struck by the wordlessness and the diagrammatic impotence of the teaching process. . . . There is a second system of representation that depends upon visual or other sensory organization and upon the use of summarizing images. We may . . . grope our way through a maze of toggle switches and then at a certain point in overlearning come to recognize a visualizable path or pattern. We have come to talk about the first form of representation as *enactive,* the second as *iconic*. . . . Finally, there is representation in words or language. Its hallmark is that it is symbolic in nature, with certain features of symbolic systems that are only now coming to be understood" (Bruner, 1966, pp. 10–11).

There is the question of whether only motor skills, like playing tennis or swimming, depend upon sensorimotor action, or whether certain cognitive skills do also. This is a question that must eventually be answered by research. However, teachers would do well to keep the question in mind and to experiment themselves to find which kinds of learnings demand a sensorimotor underpinning. Learnings having to do with space almost certainly do. The large floor maps that first-grade children draw, and then walk their way from place to place on, very probably help them to become oriented in space. Kindergarten children who set the table, and in doing so must transform a place-setting 180°, keeping spoon, napkin, and cup in the same position relative to the diner, are building into their motor systems a concept of relativity. Perhaps the reason it is difficult for adults to make certain transformations in thought is because a sensorimotor underpinning for the operation is missing.

The Preoperational Stage

Piaget finds thinking processes changing with environmental transactions. The preoperational stage extends roughly from four to seven years of age. (There are, of course, individual differences in the ages of children at a particular stage.) At this stage the child does not perform operations of thought upon data when confronted with a problem. If three dolls of various sizes were placed before the child, he could immediately pick out the largest. But if we say, "Amy is larger than Susie and Susie is smaller than Mary; which one is largest?" he cannot compare the three because he cannot "serialize" (that is, he cannot place the three dolls in his mind in order of size). If we show him a box of wooden beads, eighteen of which are red and two of which are yellow, and ask him if there are more wooden beads or more red ones, he will say, "More red ones, because there are only two yellow ones." He cannot keep the whole in mind when one of the parts is so obviously larger than the other. If presented with a matrix puzzle where he must consider several properties of a figure (perhaps size and color), he will choose on the basis of one property alone, the one that stands out visually. Serializing, classifying by more than one attribute, dealing with whole-part relations, are logical operations the young child is not yet capable of mastering.

From research in Geneva and elsewhere, certain characteristics of mental processes at the preoperational stage have been identified (Stendler, 1966, pp. 8–11):

"1. *The child is perceptually oriented;* he makes judgments in terms of how things *look* to him. He may, for example, be confused in thinking about space by the objects placed in that space. When given a problem where two lines of ten sequential sticks are laid out in parallel rows, he will see that both are equal in length; that two dolls, walking along each path, would walk the same distance. But if one of the rows is rearranged in this fashion:

and the child is again asked if each doll takes as long a walk as the other, the child says, "No." Even when he counts the segments, he denies equality; the child does not see that there is a logical necessity by which ten must equal ten. Piaget has shown that this same type of perceptual judgment enters into the preoperational child's thinking about space, time, number, and causality. It is only as the child goes beyond his perceptions to perform displacements upon the data in his mind (for example, visualizing the second row of sticks straightened out again) that ability to conserve length even with a change in appearance appears.

"2. *The child centers on one variable only, usually the variable that stands out visually; he lacks the ability to coordinate variables.* For example, a kindergarten child is pouring juice into paper cups. The standard-size cups run out, and the teacher substitutes some that are much higher but are also smaller in diameter. As the children drink their juice, several comment on the fact that Jimmy, Eddie, and Danny have more juice. Why? Because those children have cups that are taller. The dimension of height, not width, stands out. The child's thinking is rigid; he does not perform operations on what he sees. Later he will reason that "higher than" is compensated for by "skinnier than," and that both kinds of cups may hold the same amount of juice. This ability to see reciprocal changes in two sets of data is an important logical tool available to older children but not to the preoperational child.

"3. *The child has difficulty in realizing that an object can possess more than one property, and that multiple classifications are possible.* It is hard for the child to see that one can live in Los Angeles and in California at the same time, that a bird is also an animal, and that, since there are animals other than birds, there are logically *more* animals in the world than there are birds. The operation of combining elements to form a whole and then seeing a part in relation to the whole has not as yet developed, and so hierarchical relationships cannot be mastered.

"So far, this consideration of preoperational thinking has been largely negative. We have seen that the child lacks the ability to combine parts into a whole, to put parts together in different ways, and to reverse processes. What, then, can the child do? The development of logical processes is not at a standstill during this period; there are some positive accomplishments. We see, for example, the rudiments of classification: the child can make collections of things on the basis of some criterion; he can also shift that criterion. Thus, if we present a kindergarten child with a collection of pink and blue squares and circles, some large and some small, and ask him to sort them into two piles with those in each pile being alike in some way, he can usually make two different collections on the bases of color and shape (a few children discover the third criterion of size). Such an ability, of course, is essential to the formulation of classes and eventually of a hierarchy of classes.

"The child is also beginning to arrange things in a series. He can compare two members of a set when they are in a consecutive order; he knows that Tuesday comes after Monday. But since Friday comes after Tuesday, which is after Monday, does Friday also come after Monday? This operation, involving seeing logical relations between things or events that are arranged in a series, is not yet possible to the preoperational child, but experiences with seriation are preparatory to the development of such operations. The "inching up" that an older pupil does in trying to establish equilibrium between two parts of a physical system (add a little to one side; then add a little to the other) is an example of a more sophisticated use of seriation.

The Concrete-Operational Stage

"Between seven and eleven years of age on the average, as the child assimilates information from his actions and accommodates mental structures to the new information, thinking processes change. The child abandons his perceptual judgments, and thought takes on certain logical properties. Piaget calls this stage the stage of *concrete operations,* because, while the child uses logical operations, the content of his thinking is concrete rather than abstract. One of the mental operations that develops is that of combining elements; the child begins to put two and two together figuratively as well as literally. He uses this combining operation to discover (though not until toward the end of this stage) that a substance like sugar added to water will make the water level rise, and that the water level will stay up even after the sugar dissolves. It dawns on the pupil that matter combined with matter produces more matter, that matter doesn't disappear into nothingness.

"Another property of logical thought is that elements of a whole can be associated in various ways without changing the total. Thus, in the problem of the ten sticks, the segments can be "associated" in a straight line or a zigzag line, but the total distance of the path to be covered remains the same, or is conserved. And in studying science, the pupil can use the associative operation to discover how to keep a system in equilibrium—how, for example, when a muscle is flexed, it becomes shorter but thicker; when relaxed, it is longer but thinner. In each case, the total amount of muscle remains the same; the amount of matter is conserved, though its shape is changed.

"A third property of logical thought is that of identity. The identity operation is basically a null operation; the child can mentally cancel out the effects of any operation by combining it with its opposite. He uses such an identity operation to reason that the effects of adding a force to one side of a balanced tug-of-war can be canceled out by adding a force to the other side (at the preoperational stage, he could solve the problem only by taking away the extra force that had been added). The pupil can also reason, as he thinks about a flexed muscle, that, since nothing has been added to the muscle and nothing has been taken away, then quantity of matter is identical before and after the flexing. An extension of the identity operation is the one-to-one correspondence a pupil carries on to establish identity between two sets. Is the spider an insect? The pupil must compare each characteristic in the set of insect characteristics with each in the spider set, on a one-to-one basis, to answer the question.

"Of all the properties of logical thinking, one of the most critical to develop is that of reversibility. Often when we are engaged in a discussion, it is necessary to go back in thought to the starting point and to compare what was said in the beginning with what is being said now. Children must be able to go back in thought, for example, when they are reading to find the answer to a question, so that they can compare what they are reading with what they started out to find."

The Stage of Formal Operations

Thinking processes change again at around eleven or twelve years of age, with the biggest change being the manner of attack on problems. Given a particular problem, a child at the level of concrete operations is likely to test out a possible solution, reject it if it does not fit, try another, and so forth. A student at the level of formal operations, however, "begins his consideration of the problem at hand by trying to envisage all the possible relations which could hold true in the data and then attempts, through a combination of experimentation and logical analysis, to find out which of these possible relations in fact do hold true. Reality is thus conceived of as a special subset within the totality of things which the data would admit as hypotheses" (Flavell, 1963, p. 204). He is capable of propositional thinking, of identifying the variables needed for testing, and putting them in a form for testing. This may be by *implication:* "If I try two mixtures in the hummingbird feeder, both of which are sweet and one of which is red while the other is colorless, and if the hummingbirds are attracted to the red, perhaps it is redness to which they respond." Or, it may be by *identity:* "I can test for redness by hanging up various red objects some of which are not food to see to which ones the hummingbirds will be attracted." Or the adolescent may use in his thinking processes *conjunction* (it's *either* this *or* that) or *disjunction* (it's this but *not* that) as he tests reality.

Piaget also points out that at the stage of formal operations the student can use a *combinatorial analysis* to make sure that all possible variables and combinations of variables have been tested. The student is not content with testing variable *A, B,* and *C;* he knows that he must also test for *A* and *B* together, or *A* and *C,* or any of the other combinations. We come back to specific examples of both combinatorial analysis and propositional thinking later in this chapter.

IMPLICATIONS OF PIAGET'S DEVELOPMENTAL THEORY FOR INSTRUCTION

Disequilibrium as a Condition for Learning

It is clear from research findings that there are individual differences in children's ability to think logically, with some children being severely retarded in logical development. Can the schools intervene to foster maximum development? And, if so, what can teachers do?

Piaget makes it quite clear that maturation alone is not a guarantee of development; we cannot anticipate that children by virtue of having reached a certain age will have reached a certain state in logical development. Studies done in Martinique of culturally disadvantaged children showed a four-year delay in development over the Geneva norms. Nor is exposure to a particular experience enough. Deutsch found children of migratory workers, who had crossed the country many times as their parents followed the crops, whose knowledge of the geography of the region was minimal. Nor does instruction that depends upon verbal transmission apparently guarantee emergence of logical structures; readers of this text have probably had the experience themselves of listening to or reading about a clear account of the scientific discovery of a Nobel prize winner and feeling that they were understanding the explanation, only to find it totally impossible to explain the phenomenon to others.

How, then, *is* knowledge acquired and intellective development facilitated? For Piaget, twin processes of assimilation and accommodation are involved. As he acts upon his environment, the child assimilates certain elements into already existing mental structures. Equilibrium in mental organization is upset, the mental structures change to accommodate the new data, and equilibrium is restored. An analogy to homeostatic processes involved in temperature control may be helpful. As the body cools, temperature equilibrium is upset. Information on changes in the state of the system is assimilated in the hypothalamus, and the autonomic nervous system accommodates by setting in motion certain changes that enable the body to take care of the cooling. Blood vessels close to the skin contract so that less surface area is exposed to the cold; shivering increases production of heat in the body. In a somewhat comparable manner, one can postulate homeostasis in mental structures involving a sequence of assimilation — disequilibrium — accommodation — equilibrium. The obvious difference is that, whereas temperature adjustments are automatic and structures in the autonomic nervous system are not permanently altered as a result of the cycle, in the case of intelligence, there are changes in existing mental structures, and even new structures emerge at certain transition points in development.

Self-activity is crucial in the equilibration model described above. If equilibrium is to be achieved at a higher level, then the child must be mentally active; *he* must transform the data. The elements to be incorporated may be present in an experience, or the child may be told of the error in his thinking, but unless the mind is actively engaged in wrestling with data, no accommodation, or *false* accommodation, occurs. Children, like adults, are not convinced by being told they are wrong, nor by merely seeking evidence that contradicts their thinking. They have to act upon the data and transform them, and in so doing, make their own discoveries. As Piaget puts it, knowledge is not a copy of reality; to know something one must modify reality.

Does the foregoing presentation with its emphasis upon self-activity imply that such activity must be physical? Can the child carry on transactions in his mind, or must they always be upon actual objects? This question has already been raised in connection with sensorimotor intelligence, and again a reminder for the reader may be in order. Activity for Piaget is the activity of the mind.

Physical activity may support, but mere physical involvement with material objects does not guarantee, mental activity any more than does verbal transmission. Mental activity is ensured when there is disequilibrium. When the learner is confronted with data that are fresh and challenging, or that contradict what he has always believed, he is more likely to carry on mental operations to resolve the dissonance and restore equilibrium. The data may be derived from experimenting with real objects, or they may come from other sources (books, maps, graphs, people), but disequilibrium is the necessary condition for acquisition of knowledge.

How, then, does the teacher create disequilibrium? How does he become a problem maker? He does so by changing the emphasis in his teaching from fact gathering to problem making. Bruner discusses a teaching technique used in the social studies that offers some clues. The topic was the geography of the North Central states and the children involved were fifth graders. Using a conventional approach a teacher might have listed such questions as

> What are the cities with a population over 250,000 in the North Central states and where are they located?
> What are the principal products of these states?
> What are the physical features?

Instead, the teacher in this instance did the following:

> We hit upon the happy idea of presenting this chunk of geography not as a set of knowns, but as a set of unknowns. One class was presented blank maps, containing only tracings of the rivers and lakes of the area as well as the natural resources. They were asked as a first exercise to indicate where the principal cities would be located, where the railroads, and where the main highways. Books and maps were not permitted and "looking up the facts" was cast in a sinful light. Upon completing this exercise, a class discussion was begun in which the children attempted to justify why the major city would be here, a large city there, a railroad on this line, and so on.
>
> The discussion was a hot one. After an hour, and much pleading, permission was given to consult the rolled-up wall map. I will never forget one young student, as he pointed his finger at the foot of Lake Michigan, shouting, "Yippee, *Chicago* is at the end of the pointing-down lake." And another replying, "Well, OK: but Chicago's no good for the rivers and it should be here where there is a big city (St. Louis)." These children were thinking, and learning was an instrument for checking and improving the process. (Bruner, 1966, pp. 80–81)

When children are set to work to answer a question of fact, they must keep the question in mind and look for clues in the text to find the answer. Such mental operations are at a fairly low level. In contrast, in the example that Bruner cites, the mind must perform more complex operations, putting together, comparing and contrasting bits and pieces of information to form a hypothesis that might read, "Maybe cities get built up where two rivers come together." Does this hypothesis check with the facts? Perhaps not. The student may have chosen rivers that are not navigable or that do not lead to raw materials, and he may have to discard his hypothesis. Eventually, however, there *will* be learning, and he *will* acquire new knowledge. Disequilibrium of this kind begins with a problem that cannot be solved by recall of previously learned information.

A state of disequilibrium is motivating. The motivation may stem from what one psychologist calls competence motivation. White (1959) proposes the existence of an intrinsic need to deal competently with the unknown, a need that drives men to climb Mount Everest, monkeys to undo hasps that are fastened to a wooden slab and that open nothing, and children to solve problems and in so doing to acquire knowledge.

Implications of Theory for Planning Curriculum Sequence

Implicit in Piagetian theory is the notion of readiness. Intelligence consists of logical structures that permit the child to solve increasingly complex problems. The learner can have difficulty in mastering subject matter because he does not have ways of using the mind that certain concepts require for mastery. The boy or girl who cannot hold certain variables constant in his mind while another variable is experimentally manipulated is going to have difficulty in following a written description of the procedures of Pasteur. He will have even more difficulty in trying to set up an experiment where he must plan which variables will be held constant and which one will be manipulated. Similarly the child who is not nimble enough in combining classes and reversing an operation will find so-called two-step problems in arithmetic impossible to solve. We used to think that such pupils were stupid or stubborn, or both, or were poorly motivated, or had what we called, for lack of a better name, an "emotional block." One or more of these conditions may indeed be true, but there is gathering evidence that a cognitive deficit, an inability to manipulate data in particular ways, may be the basis of the learning problem.

REFERENCES

Bruner, J. S. *Toward a Theory of Instruction*. Cambridge, Mass.: Harvard University Press, 1966.

Flavell, J. *The Developmental Psychology of Jean Piaget*. Princeton: Van Nostrand, 1963.

Piaget, J. *The Origins of Intelligence in Children*. New York: Norton, 1963.

Stendler, C. B. *The Developmental Approach of Piaget and Its Implications for Science in the Elementary Schools*. The Macmillan Science Series. New York: Macmillan, 1966.

While, R. W. "Motivation Reconsidered: The Concept of Competence." *Psychological Review*, 1959, 66, 297–333.

17 The IQ Debate

Lillian Zach

Intelligence testing, from basis to implications, continues to be the center of heated debate. Despite a history which is almost three quarters of a century long and despite the fact that the IQ is by now a housshold term in America, mental tests are still reeling under the impact of criticisms which term them, among other things, invalid, misleading, and based upon false assumptions of human development.

In a highly controversial article published in December 1969, Arthur Jensen, a professor at the University of California at Berkeley, proposed that compensatory education failed to raise the IQ of black children because of a biological difference in the way these children learn. The topic became incendiary; psychological, edcational, political, and racist groups began interpreting the data to suit their views. Arguments and criticisms continue. Yet, unquestionably, the Stanford-Binet, the Wechsler Scales, and certain group tests do provide useful information, and the tests remain the most relied-on source for sorting children according to their presumed learning ability. Is it any wonder that teachers are uncertain what to believe about intelligence testing?

Binet's original intent was to develop an instrument to determine which children in Paris were retarded and in need of special education. In 1905, he produced the first Binet scale, designed to measure a retarded child's intelligence and compare it to the intelligence of normal children the same age. There was no attempt to determine whether the child's retarded learning was genetic or curable.

In 1912, German psychologist Wilhelm Stern suggested that one could express the developmental level, or mental age, of a given child as the age at which the average child achieved equivalent ability. If mental age (MA) were used as a ratio to the child's chronological age (CA), one could arrive at a brightness index, now called the Intelligence Quotient (IQ).

Like Binet, Stern did not claim that the test measured inborn capacity. In 1914, he wrote, "No series of tests, however skillfully selected it may be, does reach the innate intellectual endowment, stripped of all complications, but rather this endowment, in conjunction with all influences to which the examinee has been subjected up to the moment of testing. And it is just these external influences that are different in the lower social classes. Children of higher social status are much more often in the company of adults, are stimulated in manifold ways, are busy in play and amusement with things that require thinking, acquire a totally different vocabulary, and receive better school instruction. All this must

Reprinted from *Today's Education: NEA Journal,* 61 (6): 40–43 + (September 1972), by permission of author and publisher.

bring it about that they meet the demands of the test better than children of the uncultured classes."

But H. H. Goddard, who brought the test to America in 1910, had a very different viewpoint. Dr. Goddard translated the test into English for use at the Vineland Training School for the mentally defective. Perhaps it was an act of fate that the man who brought mental testing to this country was someone who emphasized the importance of heredity on human behavior.

Goddard was working with grossly defective children, and one can speculate that he was probably not convinced they could be educated. (Further, the chances are they were biologically defective as well as mentally retarded.) Goddard became intrigued with the notion that, being able to measure innate intelligence, we had the means for a sweeping program of social reform, with every man working on his own mental level. Soon, mental testing was adopted in every training school and teachers college in the country. Few stopped to consider that perhaps the innate intelligence which Goddard postulated and the intelligence measured by the test were not the same. Shortly thereafter, in 1916, L. M. Terman revised the Binet Scale at Stanford University to give birth to the Stanford-Binet, the standard of today's intelligence test. The test was revised and updated in 1937 and 1960. The rapid growth of compulsory education in the United States required some means to identify the intellectual capacities of pupils in the schools, and the Stanford-Binet seemed to fill the bill.

When the intelligence test is evaluated solely in terms of its value to meet specifically defined, immediate situations, its usefulness has proven itself. A good case in point can be seen in its use since the start of World War I to screen men for the armed forces. In these instances, the mental test has provided the means for appraising what an individual could do, here and now, as the product of his biological inheritance and his training and background.

But as testing proliferated, some problems became apparent. Testing in America was growing along two separate paths. One was in the real world of the school, the armed forces, and the industrial plant. The other was in the halls of academe, where the basic theoretical issues of intelligence were not yet settled. This lack of a universally accepted theoretical framework led to the anomolous situation in which intelligence is defined as that which intelligence tests test.

Herein lies a dilemma: Intelligence was only vaguely defined by the test maker, but the tests were used to define intelligence. This is perhaps the greatest failure of the testing movement in the United States. The pragmatic value of the mental test is undiminished. Test scores are good indicators of functioning abilities as long as their limitations are clearly understood, but these scores should not be used outside of their immediate significance. The failure lies not in the mental tests themselves, but in the perversion of the test results by investigators and social philosophers who use numbers in support of particular far-reaching positions. It is unfair both to the person tested and to the test itself to say that the scores of any one individual represent support for broad statements concerning human development.

There is nothing inherently wrong with practical definitions as long as they are clearly understood. The tests, after all, were developed to measure those aspects of human behavior which correlate well with scholastic achievement. In order to succeed in school, an individual must demonstrate certain types of abilities. If we develop tests to measure these abilities and if they prove to be valid and reliable instruments, we are measuring some form of intellectual ability. But if we lose sight of what we are measuring and if we claim for the test qualities for which it was never intended, we can be led into invalid implications.

The IQ, like the MA, is nothing but a score. The IQ indicates a child's performance on a test in the same way that a score of 80 on an arithmetic test does, except that intelligence tests purport to measure more general learning skills. Further, the scores merely reflect the child's performance on a specific test at a given time. The difference between the IQ and other test scores is that intelligence tests are standardized. Standardization means that the same test items are developed and revised on a large group, representative of the population for whom the test is designed—U.S. elementary school students, for example. Standardization also requires that the same test be administered under the same carefully controlled conditions to all who take the test. This means that a given child's score can be compared with scores obtained by other children of the same age on whom the test was originally standardized. It also permits prediction of the chances that in later testing a given child will obtain a score which is close to the original score, and further, to what extent a given child's performance is the result of the construction of the test rather than his own ability.

In order to interpret the results of standardized tests, certain fundamental assumptions are implicit. It is assumed, for example, that test norms are fair, since they are based on a representative national sampling of children. But this does not take into consideration the fact that the national sample is weighted heavily by average white children.

Since the mental test purports to measure basic learning capacities, it is also assumed that the items which make up the test are of two types—information which for the most part all children have been exposed to or situations to which no one has been exposed.

For items based upon supposedly equal opportunities of exposure, it is possible to reason that a child who has learned what he has been exposed to is bright; one who has not done so is not bright. Observation tells us that this does not have to be true.

In my own testing experiences, I found that many black children who had just come North gave as response to the question, "Who discovered America?" the answer, "Abraham Lincoln." The response is obviously wrong and adds no points to the IQ score. But does this response mean that this child has no ability to learn or does it merely reflect the child's background? In certain ways, the answer could be considered a meaningful and pertinent response.

For items to which no one has been exposed and which therefore demand "on the spot" learning, similar problems arise. Usually, tests try to utilize nonverbal materials like blocks and puzzles as a way of minimizing factors like education and experience. But these are not equally novel experiences for all children. Many youngsters are familiar with educational toys long before they enter school. (Even more important, and less easy to identify, are factors related to "learning to learn" and test-taking abilities.)

Another assumption is that the mental test is a sampling of behaviors which directly reflect the general capacity for learning. Actually, all available intelligence tests are direct measures only of achievement in learning. We wrongly equate the inferences from scores on IQ tests to some native inherent trait. Many persons think of intelligence as a discrete dimension existing within the individual and believe that different people have different amounts of it. In a certain sense this is true, but one's intelligence is not a characteristic of a person so much as it is a characteristic of the person's behavior. We can only hope to measure or observe manifestations of it.

It is also not possible to add up the elements of someone's intelligence in the same way that you can count the number of fingers on his hand. Although two people can have the same IQ score, they may demonstrate quite different abilities by virtue of the fact that they succeeded on different parts of the test. All too often, undue weight is given to an IQ score, although numerical assignment of a child to a man-made concept, untied to real characteristics of the child, tells us very little. Even more unfortunate, parents and some teachers are led to believe that the IQ concept has deeper significance than its meaning as a score.

Unquestioning faith in descriptive concepts reaches the height of absurdity in the notion of overachievers—a word used to describe children whose classroom performance is higher than their IQ scores would predict. The concept makes no sense at all because it says, in effect, that although these children are achieving, they do not have the ability to do so. Their success is laid to other factors, such as motivation. It's like telling the child who had the highest batting average in the Little League that, on the basis of batting practice, he's really a very poor hitter. He only did it because he wanted to.

The danger in a meaningless concept like overachieving is that children so designated may not receive as positive a recommendation for college as other children with the same grades but higher IQ scores. Few stop to consider that the mehods used to judge ability must have been inadequate and that terms like IQ, MA, and overachievement are man-made.

In view of all the drawbacks, one might reasonably ask, then, why do we continue using mental tests? Even though many have argued for abandoning them, most psychologists still feel that they have value. In most cases, we can describe, evaluate, and even predict certain kinds of behavior much better with tests than without them. The paradox exists that most psychologists, who were responsible for the tests, have never given them as much weight as those in schools and industries who use and misuse them.

While various practical problems were being confronted, the academic world of psychology was still trying to resolve many basic issues about intelligence testing. One of these, the focus of several decades of research, concerned the whole heredity-environment controversy—the battle over nature versus nurture.

Not all psychologists in America were convinced that the IQ was the highly predictive, hereditarily determined measure it was held to be by Goddard and his followers. It wasn't long before studies were reported which demonstrated that not only was the IQ not fixed but that it could be altered with training, experience, and changes in adjustment patterns.

Although research was reported from all over the nation to support one or the other position, two distinct battle camps could be located. One group, at the University of Iowa, came to be known as the environmentalists. The other, at Stanford University, supported the significance of heredity. After a while, it seemed as if the heredity-environment controversy had settled down into a comfortable compromise: Most people were content to accept the notion that the IQ is the result of the interaction between the gene structure and the environment.

Everyone knew that the argument was not settled, however, probably because people were asking the wrong kinds of questions. Instead of asking how *much* is contributed by heredity and environment respectively, they should have been asking *how* each makes its particular contributions.

For example, in our present state of knowledge, nothing will enable a child who is born deaf to hear. How differences in environment can affect his future development, however, is a terribly significant factor: With appropriate educational procedures he can develop into a literate, communicating adult; without them, he can remain illiterate and uncommunicative. Concentrating on heredity versus environment obscures the more important problem of determining how education can help each child best use what he has at his disposal.

In recent years, the black community has become more and more vociferous in its objections to the mental test as being biased against them. The outcry has been especially strong against group testing because these tests depend almost entirely on the child's ability to read. Since the child has to read the questions in order to answer them, blacks question whether the test measures capacity to learn or ability to read. They also argue that IQ tests are self-fulfilling predictions. A child with a low IQ score is placed in slow learning classes, where he learns less, thereby supporting the original score. Prompted by such arguments, many major school systems abandoned group intelligence testing. Individual tests like the Stanford-Binet and the WechslerScales are less subject to criticism, since, hopefully, the trained psychologist ensures that the test is administered properly under an optimum testing climate, and is able to evaluate better to what extent a given child's performance is influenced by emotional, motivational, educational, and socioeconomic factors.

Some people have suggested that we discard the IQ test entirely and substitute for it a battery of achievements tests. The problem is that since the achievement test is a sampling of what a child has learned, usually in specific academic subjects, the achievement battery does not provide much information about general learning skills. Others have looked to new methods of measurement which could meet the limitations and criticisms posed by our current models.

One such method has been developed by John Ertl at the University of Ottawa. Dr. Ertl records the brain response to a flashing light by placing electrodes on the motor cortex. By averaging the responses, which are recorded on a computer so as to eliminate noise, he arrives at a score, known as the *evoked potential*, which he claims is a culture-free index of intellectual functioning.

Several drawbacks can be cited to Ertl's approach. For one thing, he has no strong theoretical rationale to support his hypothesis that more intelligent people respond faster to stimulation than do less intelligent ones. The results he reports may be explained, not by the greater (or lesser) strength of the brain, but by the fact that some people are better able to pay attention and to fixate on the light source. In addition, correlations with IQ, although significant, are low—as are correlations on retesting with the same subject. In view of all this, in my opinion, it is doubtful that Ertl's method can be of real use to the teacher, at least at this time.

Previous attempts had been made at developing culture-free scales. For example, an effort was made to remove the middle-class bias of IQ tests by changing the wording of questions and by introducing content more relevant to the lower-class child's background and life experiences.

The results were unsuccessful, and since the task of developing culture-free tests poses difficult problems, it seemed to make better sense to concentrate on improving the environment of the culturally deprived rather than on changing our tests.

As a result, many special programs were started that were designed to educate children from the lower socioeconomic strata. In too many cases, these programs were established in an atmosphere of emergency, with little planning and with limited knowledge of what should constitute suitable curriculums for such classes. Professional educators were not too surprised, therefore, when these programs failed to raise the IQ of black children.

Using the failure of these programs and an impressive array of statistical data, Dr. Jensen shocked many educators when he proposed that the reason these programs failed can be traced to an hereditary inferiority in black children. The great fear this aroused in the minds of socially oriented psychologists and educators is that it might be possible, by misinterpretation, to obtain "proof" that no matter what compensatory education the black child receives, he remains inferior in intellect. Another possible interpretation is that the schools are not to blame if black children fail to achieve academically.

The IQ Argument: Race, Intelligence, and Education (Library Press, 1971), a recent publication by Hans J. Eysenck, a British psychologist, lends support to Jensen's position. Actually, there was nothing so new about Dr. Jensen's position; it's the old nature-nurture controversy in new clothes. It is a fact that blacks as a group score lower than whites as a group on intelligence tests. It is also a fact, however, as Jensen notes, that many blacks score higher than a very large number of whites. People concentrating on the main conclusions in the article tend to forget this.

I recently received a rather touching letter from a young black boy attending an Ivy League college. He wrote: "I was interested that the specific areas in which Jensen indicated blacks were inherently inferior are precisely those areas in which I scored highest in my class. Maybe it was luck." Even he had lost sight of the fact that the Jensen data refer to averages and not to individuals.

It is unfortunate that.Jensen presented his material within the context of a racial issue, since the emotional impact of this tends to negate all of what he has to say. Despite its incendiary qualities, the Jensen paper has the major merit of reminding us that we are dealing with a biological organism and that the educational environment is only one of the many influences affecting the growth and development of a given individual.

Black people as a group in America are poor, and poor people are subject to all kinds of health risks deriving from prenatal conditions and malnutrition. The relationship between poverty, health, and learning failure is now receiving the attention it deserves. It is becoming clear that not only does malnutrition play a role in retarded intellectual development but that more than one generation may have to be well-fed before all the effects of dietary deficiency are overcome.

Jensen was premature in evaluating just what portion of the black child's biological structure actually resides in the genes. It is difficult to evaluate the amount of damage caused by health hazards resulting from poverty, or to say how even slight changes in environment can produce large changes in behaviors, even where those behaviors are linked to genetics and biology.

Another criticism of the Jensen material is that the public does not have a clear appreciation of just what kinds of information can be validly drawn from hereditability data. The method used by Jensen and Eysenck can only tell what proportion heredity contributes to the variance of a specified trait in a given population under existing conditions. The data cannot tell us the reason for a given child's low intelligence, the origin of ethnic differences in test performance, or what educational intervention programs can accomplish.

Jensen's article should be credited with helping us recognize that compensatory programs of education in their beginning phases were inadequately structured. That he used these poorly planned programs as a basis for postulating hereditary inferiority in blacks is a major weakness. His reasoning could have proceeded the other way. If the programs failed to raise IQ scores, why place the onus on the black child's shoulders? Why not look at what's wrong with the programs?

A peculiar characteristic of American education is that, although we give lip service to meeting the needs of individual children, we seldom follow through with concrete actions. We meet the needs of individual children as long as they respond to the existing curriculum, but when a child fails to learn under the existing structure, we assume there is something wrong with him. If "meeting the needs of individual children" is to become meaningful, we should consider the possibility that perhaps a particular teaching method is all wrong for a particular child.

Certainly, we can't make wholesale prescriptions for black children as if they were all alike. A black child who is not doing well in school may be more like a white child who is similarly unsuccessful than he is like an achieving black child. The problem of understanding learning deficiencies and of locating appropriate pedagogy for overcoming them is not something we know too much about. The storm over the Jensen article may provide the impetus toward working for a true understanding of education and individual differences.

A first step might well be to define our aims and come to grips with why we test. Are we concerned with measuring the amount of cognitive ability an individual is born with, or do we wish to appraise, by sampling performance, the level of adaptive capacities at his disposal?

Do we seek to predict, by way of one or several tests, what an individual will do 20 years from now? Or do we seek to know how and at what stage educational circumstances might be arranged for the individual to achieve his highest level of intellectual functioning ability? Piaget, among others, has never been impressed with standard IQ tests because they do not lead to an understanding of how intelligence functions. His work is not based on predictions, but rather on assessments of the presence or absence of the essential abilities related to intellectual functioning.

Schools must decide what is the purpose of testing. If all we wish is to separate the bright child from the dull child, the brain-damaged from the neurologically intact, the retarded learner from the gifted, and to attach labels to the children in our schools, we can go on using tests the way we always have, and the argument over genes will continue. But if we mean what we say about meeting individual needs, we can put tests to better use.

The intelligence test, not the IQ score, can tell us the level of the child's functioning in a variety of tasks which measure general intelligence and which are intimately correlated with classroom learning. The goal of testing then becomes to describe the developmental level the child has attained. The next step requires that educators and psychologists together formulate the educational environment necessary to raise the child to the next developmental level.

18 Thinking : A Pivotal Goal of Secondary Schools

Ernest E. Bayles

Two or three years ago at a seminar of members of an Education faculty, I was asked what I thought would be the next big development in educational practice. My off-the-cuff answer was, "Reflective Teaching." Some think this answer pretty nostalgic, harking back (?) to Dewey. But what is "Education as Inquiry" anyway? And what do Bruner, Piaget, Schwab, Holt, Kohl, Leonard, Silberman, the National Science Foundation scientists ho are belatedly taking a look at secondary and even elementary education, Fischer, and others, have in mind if not to promote reflective thinking in the schools? Seemingly, we are not "going beyond Dewey," we are merely catching up with him.

But merely to say that we are wanting to "teach people *how* to think rather than *what* to think" is hardly enough, for the word "think" is commonly used in at least four different ways, which we can differentiate with subscripts 1, 2, 3, and 4.

We shall take "think$_1$" to signify what is meant when we say, "I think . . . . ," such as that the weather is uncomfortable or that the world isn't going quite the way I'd like it. Should we not call this usage illegitimate, eve though so common that to avoid it tends to make our speech sound somewhat stilted? We do not in any way infer that we have necessarily thought the matter over; we are merely saying that that is our passing feeling or conviction, what we *believe* at the time of expression. However, I think (?) that we need not proscribe it, because the context in which it occurs is ordinarily so clear that no one is likely to mistake what we man; i.e., I believe.

We shall take "think$_2$" to signify sheer memory, unmodified recall, rote. It indeed represents the cognitive, in that brain activity is presumably at work in effecting it. It is employed when, for example, meeting a former acquaintance and not remembering his name, I say to myself, "Think hard!" But I do not at all mean it in the next two senses.

We shall take "think$_3$" to signify the putting to work of an insight or idea in a way more or less different from previous experience with it. It is not a repeat. It is employment in what we may call a *novel situation*, one never met in exactly that form before. Of course, since very close observation shows all present situations to be more or less different from all past ones, in actuality we never act on the think$_2$ level, though we often closely approach it. This is what we think of as

Reprinted from *The High School Journal*, 55 (6): 243–255 (March 1972), by permission of author and publisher.

transfer; we define it as thinking on the *understanding level,* to be contrasted with think₂ as on the *memory level.*

However, we can perform on the think₃ level without "mulling things over"; without reflecting upon them; with the mere exercise of snap judgment. When a situation and a true signification or meaning (true in the sense of being accurately predictive) occur simultaneously in experience, we behave correctly, non-hesitantly, insightfully, hence on habit level, though never having behaved exactly that way before. This represents the *using* of an insight, not the obtainment of one. This very well represents "straight thinking," but not reflective thinking.

It is at this point that much of educational thought goes awry; failure to differentiate between think₃ and think₄, between understanding-level and reflection-level thinking. The way is fully open for it to happen when the term "critical thinking" is used, and more often than not it does happen. It took me several years, back in the late twenties, to realize the difference, so after forty years of recognition of it I think I can truthfully say I *appreciate* the difference. And I do indeed insist that there is one.

We take "think₄" to signify what has long been called "reflective thinking," Dewey's "complete act of thought." This is not a case of using an insight, but of finding one; not a case of transfer, but of learning. However, not all cases of learning represent reflection, except in the most minimal sense. Learning to think reflectively means *learning to learn by one's self.* The bulk of one's conscious existence is comprised of learning non-reflectively, for since, in living, there is no such phenomenon as exact repetition of what has gone before, every successive instant of existence requires a new insight. And mostly we behave on habit level, hence on the basis of insights that arise as each successive confronting-situation arrives, with no need for "mulling over." Then, too, there are the myriad instances wherein someone instructs us ahead of time regarding what we may need to know later, thereby relieving us of the necessity of figuring them out for ourselves. This we see as the major disadvantage of non-rflective, *understanding-level teaching,* which schools us in *what* to think but not in how to think—it provides the basis for think₃ but not for think₄. Recognition of this distinction enables us when teaching to avoid the anomaly of claiming to teach students how to think when in actuality proceeding in such a way as only to teach them what to think. We can then proceed with assurance of when we are doing which, and thereby do precisely what any given situation requires.

Reflection-level, or reflective, thinking (if and when it comes) takes its rise in a situation wherein a realization of what to do about it fails to arrive *with* the situation. It is like coming to a block in a road with no visible instructions as to how to get around it, or to a fork in a road without knowledge of which one to take. Such a no-road or forked-road situation we call a *problem*—provided we and desirous of finding a way out and proceeding on our journey. An I-don't-know situation is no problem unless we are seriously wanting to know. Most of the puzzles that continually appear in my daily newspaper are no problems for me because I blithely and blissfully pass them by without letting myself get hooked. But, once the hook sinks in, then I have a problem. Mathematics teachers and textbook writers are incessantly talking about problems—i.e., using the word—when indeed what they have in mind is not problems at all; they are merely practice exercises, designed to furnish students a sufficient number of opportunities to "repeat" a process so as to make it sink in. The solving of genuine problems, hence problem solving, is what is meant by reflective thinking. But remember! It must be a problem *for the student;* as long as it is that, it matters not for how many others it is no problem at all.

Thus, the first step in problem-solving or reflection-level teaching is *problem raising.* Then what comes? *Not* what so many are prone to claim—the gathering of data! Oh, of course, since data-gathering comes any and everywhere along the line, some data-gathering is likely to come immediately after problem-raising. However, without data there will be no problem at all; it is that somehow the data just don't "add up" that gives rise to a problem. Systematically, after problem-raising comes problem-solving, and the first step in the latter is to look about for *possible* solutions, schematically called hypotheses.

After the formulation of hypotheses comes the testing, which is much more than a mere matter of gathering raw data and patiently watching until they congeal into an answer. Human mental activity of the most stringent kind is now employed, by which the logical consequences of each hypothesis are worked out in careful detail. *If* such-and-such be true, what must we necessarily expect under given conditions? This is a step mentalistic in nature, akin to the rationalism of pre-Baconian idealistic philosophy and, because of its dependence on human minds actively at work and of its consequent subjectivity, it was rejected by Baconian realists who were insistent on being completely objective, on letting facts speak for themselves. It differs, however, from pre-Baconian rationalism because of the "if"; the rationalists began with a "since," basing their deductions on a proposition already accepted as true rather than on a proposition undergoing test to determine *whether* it be true.

Next comes implementation—setting up whatever conditions the hypotheses call for, critical or crucial conditions such as will differentiate among the various hypotheses, one calling for one set of results and another another. In scientific investigation, this is the step of building whatever machines or other devices are necessary to run an experiment, such as the atomic pile for the original testing of whether man-engineered atomic fission were possible.

Then the wheels are set in motion and the experiment is run. But is it not evident that a great deal of card-stacking has preceded? The difficulty has been pinned down (i.e., the right questions have been asked), hypotheses have been formulated, logical deductions have been drawn, and implementation has been effected. The human element—subjectivity—has played a large and vital role all along the line.

After all this preparation, the passive, unbiased, honest, (shall we call him objective?) observer comes to the fore. But he is asked only the simplest of questions: What did the voltmeter register? What color did the solution become or what kind of precipitate, if any, was thrown down? Did a particular bright spot appear on the photographic film? What did the Geiger counter do when brought near the blast area? No observer need have any idea of what is involved in his observations; of what they may prove or disprove. All he needs is the capacity to make the observation and the honesty to report it as he sees it. The scientific team has done and will do the rest. It makes and announces the conclusions; it judges what has been proven and what disproven. The facts—in this case, the events- —have not spoken; that has been the role of the human beings responsible for conducting the whole enterprise.

This is the problem-raising, problem-solving method of reflective or reflection-level thinking—think₄. And reflective teaching refers to handling classes in such ways as to promote reflective thinking on the part of students. This involves (1) enabling them to get first-hand experience with the process; (2) learning what is involved and how it is done; (3) finding that they themselves are in varying degrees capable of doing it; (4) discovering the advantages to be gained by being reflective as well as when to be so and when not; (5) in the process becoming acquainted with much more educational content than other-wise as well as developing a firmer, more useable understanding of the various principles or generalizations that become the topics of study; and (6) come to realize that such principles or generalizations—the truths of the world—are not authoritarian handouts but are human formulations that achieve credence by the showings they make when put to the test of experience and experiment.

There are several observations that I think should be made at this point. First, what I have been describing is largely the reflective-*scientific* process. But re-flective thinking can be pursued on matters or in fields other than the scientific. Whether a reflective study is scientific or not depends on the criteria employed in judging the validity of the various hypotheses under study or the soundness of the conclusion that is reached. When scientific criteria are employed, then scientific conclusions are reached (of course, if the procedure is sond throughout. When other criteria are employed, reflective conclusions may be reached but they are not necessarily and not likely to be scientific. For example, geometrical theorems based on Euclidian postulates and axioms are quite different from those based on Lobatschewskian or Riemannian, yet all can be reflectively studied and formulated. And none is *necessarily* scientific. In fact, when Einstein cast about for a geometry that would enable him to deal with the vastnesses of interstellar space, he had to reject the Euclidian and employ the Riemannian. Thoroughly valid or truthful Euclidian theorems were simply invalid or false —they are not accurately predictive—when vast stretches of the universe are involved. Similarly, theorems valid for plane geometry are invalid for solid geometry, such as that the sum of the interior angles of a triangle is equal to two right angles. Again, judged on realistic standards, a painting that does not look like the object depicted is a poor one, whereas judged on impressionist stand-ards it may be first quality. Beautiful pentatonic musical harmony ordinarily sounds horrid when judged on the octatonic basis. There are many, many cri-terial bases for reflective study other than the scientific.

Second, abduction: reflective thinking or study is not an inductive procedure. Technically speaking, induction is a straight-line progression from particular to general. It is rather like taking a photograph at night by using time-exposure: by emitting a steady stream of non-varying impressions, stationary objects (the universals) show up with relative clarity, whereas moving or intermittent objects either give blurs or show only faintly. It is a passive recording of events, a survey, that is obtained; a cumulation of impressions, not an experiment. The hypothetico-deductive, experimental procedure, which has been called *abduction* so as to differentiate it from either induction or deduction, posits the receiver of impressions as a selective *taker* rather than a passive recipient.

Abduction moves in a generally inductive direction, starting with a congeries of particulars and moving toward a generalization that systematizes, unifies, or integrates them. It also embodies the objectivism of Baconian realism, taking advantage of all the observational information that can be gathered. On the other hand, it also embodies the mentalism of pre-Baconian idealism, taking advantage of the imaginative, hypothesis-forming, creativity of human minds as well as the process of logical deduction from first premises. But it takes mentalistic proposals as hypothetical, as matters requiring testing; not as cosmic deliverances, which it is blasphemy to question. However, by subjecting both observational and mental contributions to the requirement of standing test, on the basis of whatever criteria are on given occasions taken to be germane, it goes beyond either realism or idealism. Scientific experimentation, for example, places a stringent test on both observation and imagination, hopefully letting neither get away with anything.

Third, inquiry: please let me stress that reflection-level thinking and teaching *primarily* depend on an overall *atmosphere of inquiry* and only secondarily on particular devices that may be used. For example, the mere occurrence of a teacher-lecture does not mean that a class is not being conducted reflectively. On the other hand, student questioning of statements made by teacher or textbook may be in the spirit of revolt rather than of inquiry. As with all devices, a given device may promote one end or objective in one context or configuration, and quite a different one in another. Much of the laboratory work in natural-science classes does not promote the spirit of inquiry at all. If not mere busy work, it may be solely for the purpose of fixating a previously asserted proposition; to *demonstrate that* the teacher is right rather than to *question whether*. A teacher who cannot stand to be challenged or questioned is a teacher who cannot encourage and promote reflective study. And please let me insert there this personal note that, if I do not evoke that kind of response in my classes, I feel that somehow I have failed even to get ideas across.

Returning now to the various meanings of the word think, think₁ (having a belief) is the outcome of either think₃ or think₄, hence teaching on either level is conducive to development of personal beliefs or convictions. But teaching on the think₂ or memory level stays aloof for the most part from developing personal convictions of any kind. It is the haven of refuge for the ivory-tower teacher who chooses to take a stand on nothing. A student may on his own use the information (provided it is such) for the purpose of establishing beliefs of his own, but the teacher is not to be praised or blamed for that. This is a device often employed by teachers who intend thereby to avoid indoctrination, but in that regard it is a false one. Those who employ it are very likely to be guilty of indoctrination by omission rather than by commission; of staying out of the fray and letting those already in take over. This is merely giving way to the strongest indoctrinator; leaving him a free field for peddling his wares, be they good, bad, or indifferent.

Think₂ (or memory-level) teaching is the easy way for teachers. It requires neither knowledge nor much of any other mental capacity on a teacher's part, for he can keep the book before him while the poor student has to sweat it out. This is recitation–re-citation—undefiled; merely repeating a past experience as it *was*, without alteration. Would that we could pass it by as not meriting our attention, but even today it is probably the most used way of teaching. The oft-repeated humbug that one has to have facts before he can think does not hold water, because part of thinking is determining what facts are pertinent and getting those that are required. Moreover, facts gathered at the time they are sensed as necessary, hence appearing in a logical context, are much easier memorized and much longer retained than those obtained by rote. Facts are grist for the thought-mill, and when obtained and employed in context such as that they take on meaning, hence interest, and are not readily forgotten. That logical learning comes easier and stays longer than learning by rote has long been averred by psychologists, as well as by anyone else who has paid the matter some mind.

Think₃ (understanding level) represents the logicalizing or rationalizing of mental content; establishing a logic or a rationale; relating. When a person understands something, he can handle a wide range of situations related thereto but never met before—novel situations. He can think on the if-then or since-then level; deductively. He comprehends a generalization or generality, from which he can deduce implied particulars. Generalized insights, such as these, possess transfer value which makes them widely useful both in reconstructing old experiences and in handling new situations. Moreover, a generality is not a vagueness or vagary at all; a generality can be exactly particularized, a vagueness or vagary cannot.

Teaching on the think₃ or understanding level means handling learners in such ways as to attain the capacity to use generalizations, and the test for such capacity is a learner's capacity to handle novel situations accurately and dependably. But it does not encompass the development of independent learning capacity. Teaching strictly on the think₃ level means starting with a question, but immediately giving the answer. Subsequent study is follow-up; keeping a learner at it until he gives satisfactory evidence of having achieved the understanding.

During the mid-twenties, the Morrison plan was introduced and, for the next ten years or so, was very much in vogue. Presented in 1926 by Morrison's *The Practice of Teaching in the Secondary School,* it popularized "the personality adaptation," units and unit-teaching, "the mastery formula," previews or overviews, workbooks and worksheets, and mastery testing. In its "science-type" units, the personality adaptations to be achieved were the understandings, of which we have just been speaking. Units were areas of subject matter whose learning resulted in a personality adaptation—in science, an understanding. The preview or overview was an introductory lecture, giving the "story of the unit," and the mastery formula was, "teach, test, diagnose difficulties, adjust procedure, teach and test again, until mastery." Morrison was explicit and emphatic that his plan did not countenance memory-level learning and teaching, which he characterized as a "learning perversion." But he was also explicit and emphatic that it did not countenance reflective teaching; though, strangely enough, his measure of completion of secondary education was not the number of adaptations mastered but was the attainment of independent learning ability, the ability to proceed on one's own and to use a teacher in the same way one would use a textbook. Except for this latter unexplained reversal, Morrison's was a plan *par excellence* for teaching on the understanding level.

It seems to be a dictum, accepted by the teaching profession as a whole, that teaching ought to achieve the understanding level, even though so very much of it is still conducted on the memory level. But this seems to be about all that is envisioned, even by those who insist that we should "teach students how to think." And this means teaching only in terms of established ways; not for creation, innovation. Morrison was emphatic on this score. This, however, is the very point at issue in much of the student revolt of today. For them, the "establishment" has not done well by them (or us); let's inaugurate some radical reform. I submit that, if we had really been teaching reflectively during the past years, there would have been no teeth in this argument and it would have gotten nowhere, perhaps not even arisen.

Think₄ (reflective level) represents innovation, the drive toward "progressive reconstruction," the blazing of new paths. Heresy is enthroned not anathematized. The old—the orthodox—is not repudiated out of hand, but is continually brought before the bar of justice and required to put its claims for justification to the test. History is in no way disparaged; what has been done is reviewed for the light it can shed on both the successes and the errors of the past, so that the shortcomings of the past may be avoided for and in the future.

Teaching on the think₄ level means *starting* with a question but not ending when the answer has been obtained. The studying that is done by *both students and teacher* is for the purpose of finding *whether* the teacher's answer is good enough to adopt, not to make sure that it is the one adopted. Reflective teaching means that an investigation is being conducted, not that a demonstration is being staged. It means teaching as inquiry. Instead of serving as the fountainhead of knowledge, the teacher becomes the chairman or director of an investigational body; the beliefs or proposals with which the teacher begins the study to be placed alongside of all others and, if there is any difference, to be subjected to more stringent examination than the others in order to counteract the possible and likely advantage of the teacher's being present and able to protect his own. This, of course, means that, as far as questions under study are concerned, the teacher's convictions (or biases?) must be known by the students so they will know what especially to guard against. Reflective study means arrival at conclusions and convictions, not merely becoming acquainted with all sides of a given matter and letting it terminate there. But it also means that the *study* must be the determinant; not the convictions held by *any*one beforehand. If a teacher *has no* convictions beforehand, how can he be justified in asking students to reach them, even at the end of study? If he has them and doesn't make them known as such, he is in more danger of being indoctrinative than otherwise.

So far, I have been only skirting the question of indoctrination, but in the context of our present discussion it is a question that must not be skirted. By indoctrination, I mean an attempt or a tendency to establish a given doctrine to the exclusion of others; and it makes no difference whether the favored doctrine be good, bad, or indifferent. But reflective study must be such as to determine *what* is right, rather than to demonstrate *who* is right. Therefore, reflective study, be it scientific or some other kind, must be such as to avoid any attempt or tendency to indoctrinate.

There are many who say we should not make a bogy out of indoctrination; they deem it unavoidable, so ask that we indoctrinate in favor of the good and against the bad. However, indoctrination is not only opposed to the very spirit of science; it is opposed also to the spirit of democracy. If the democratic ideal is to mean equality of opportunity on the part of all members of a sovereign group to participate in establishing and reestablishing whatever rules or regulations they deem to be desirable, together with equality of obligation to abide by such rules or regulations until they are revised or revoked, is indoctrination not inherently proscribed? Indoctrination bestows privileged status on the favored doctrine; the antithesis of democracy.

Yet, how can it possibly be avoided? How can human beings resist the very human tendency to view their pet theories—as well as other pets—through rose-colored glasses? We grant that it is not easy, but not that it is impossible. The method is really quite simple. First, of course, there must be the disposition to seek its avoidance; without that, all is lost. Then there must be a recognized and understood method of avoidance, and that is explicit adoption of *criteria*.

A criterion is a standard of judgment or criticism. Whenever we pass a judgment, we have a criterion (or criteria) on which the judgment is based. The trouble, however, is that often (maybe usually?) we are not aware of just what it or they may be; hence, in the interest of understanding what we are doing, it behooves us to bring into focal consciousness just what criteria we are employing. Moreover, our criteria vary from time to time—all the more reason for knowing at any given time just what they are. As teachers, therefore, let us sensitize our students to the fact that human judgments always have critical bases and help them to become able to determine what, from time to time, those criteria are; for certain criteria logically entail certain judgments and others entail others.

Another point: if we wish to test any criterion, we need to apply or employ it in particular cases and ascertain just what judgments it logically requires us to reach. Good judgments grow out of good criteria; bad out of bad. It is a case of "the proof of the pudding." So let us constantly seek to be aware of just what criteria we are using in the various judgments we are continually making, and constantly on the alert to find what criteria we consider good and what not good.

Now we come to the matter of avoidance of indoctrination in classrooms. At one stage or another in the process of testing hypotheses, not necessarily at the beginning, the teacher (as chairman or director of the investigation) needs to raise the question of what criteia are o be used in making the test. In science classes, of course, the scientific truth-criterion will ordinarily be the one that pertains; though I might merely mention in passing that it may not always be.

When a given criterion is consciously adopted for a given judgmental situation, then it is possible to subject all proposals to the same judgmental basis. Special treatment or status is alloted to none. Teacher's ideas, any textbook writer's ideas, the ideas of the various class members or those that any of them have heard bandied about; *all* are to be given equal opportunity to be heard and *all* are required to stand and answer equally before the bar of justice, the criteria in force at the time. It is comparable to a footrace, wherein the course and other conditions are made equal for all and the declared winner is the one that reaches the finish line first. This is democratic, since it satisfies the definition we have given; and, when scientific criteria are in force, it satisfies the requrements for being a scientific investigatin. Conclusions are reached, but conclusions that are justified only in light of the circumstances of the investigation. And, since the showing that a given proposition or proposal makes is what determines its acceptance or rejection—*not* the status of the one responsible for making it—, indoctrination is avoided. This does not make a teacher neutral, unconcerned with what conclusion is reached. He is vitally concerned with maintenance of a fair field, with avoidance of forensic or any other kind of trickery or chicanery, and with carrying the investigation through to the conclusion required by the criteria and announced as, "In light of our investigation, the conclusion appears to be thus and so."

And such procedure not only enables classes to reach particular conclusions non-indoctrinatively, it also enables them to make value-judgments among the various criteria that are or may be so used. And it gives them fair warning of the necessity for knowing, on any given occasion, what criteria are in force; for the fixation of criteria fixates conclusions and woe to him who is unaware of this.

Before leaving the matter of criteria and democratic teaching, let me issue one admonition. In order to maintain democracy in a classroom, the students do not have to vote on what the criteria shall be at any given time. In a democracy, decisions are to be made by the group that has jurisdiction or authority over the matter in question, not by any sub-group having variant ideas of its own. A single classroom is by no means the sole and only group having concern with what goes on within it. This is a point hard for many to understand, and we cannot canvass it fully at this moment. It is anarchy, not democracy, to let each individual classroom go entirely on its own; the same as it would be to permit each and every automobile driver to disregard stoplights if and when he chose.

Science classrooms, for example, are not free to disregard scientific criteria if and when they wish, and it is the business of teachers to see that they do not.

The choosing of criteria is, for a given class, as much of a curriculum matter as is the choosing of topics to be studied, for it is in fact an aspect of the choice of study topics. The "new math" is belated recognition of this; previously, three plus four must be declared as equalling seven, but now youngsters are being led to realize that it may also equal twelve, depending on whether a decimal or a pentimal system or "set" is being used. And the amusing thing is that youngsters often catch the point more quickly than oldsters, including many teachers. But in a given class no child is to be permitted to give any answer between seven and twelve that may serve his fancy and go scot-free with it, for that would vitiate the very purposes of mathematics instruction. As with other aspects of curriculum, student wants, wishes, and desires are not to go unheeded—we are learning that the hard way today—, but choice of criteria for employment at a given time and place is pretty much a matter of professional judgment, and is not to be left to student vote or whim. Perhaps very few missed the jocular nature of one of the Ryatt youngster's suggestions regarding how to determine the sex of the newly acquired cat, "Let's vote on it"; one of the more amusing episodes in the popular comic strip.

This article has already overrun the originally allotted space limitation, so without further ado we rest our case.

19 A Second Look at Classroom Questions

Norris M. Sanders

A modest-looking book edited by B. S. Bloom and published in 1956 suggests a way by which teachers can systematically improve classroom questioning skills. To date, about 250,000 copies of this book have been purchased by educators. A sizeable proportion of candidates for teacher certificates continue to be assigned to read the *Taxonomy of Educational Objectives: Cognitive Domain*.[1] The book has also been a favorite for use in both national and local curriculum development projects.

The heart of Bloom's book is the definition of six kinds of thinking named

Reprinted from *The High School Journal*, 55 (6): 265–277 (March 1972), by permission of author and publisher.

knowledge, comprehension, application, analysis, synthesis, and evaluation. Specified patterns of questions lead to each kind of thinking, so a teacher who masters the six categories can classify the questions he asks in recitation, homework, and evaluation to determine whether students are receiving an adequate variety in thinking experience. A few teachers find that they are intuitively good questioners, but a multitude of research studies shows that the majority of teachers offers a relatively narrow range of questions. The beauty of the taxonomy is that it not only provides a framework with which to measure the variety of questions but it also suggests what should be done to broaden the intellectual offerings. A science teacher, for example, who discovers that he offers few or no questions calling for creative thinking (synthesis) or evaluative thinking can study the nature of questions in these categories and build them into his lessons.

Since the publication of Bloom's book, a number of other plans for classifying classroom thinking and questions have appeared. Some were a modification or redefinition of Bloom's ideas.[2] Others, such as the description of five kinds of questions in Maurice J. Eash's book *Reading and Thinking,* were designed for special teaching areas.[3] Several efforts have been made to simplify Bloom's system by defining fewer categories, such as "remembering," "understanding," and "reasoning." Meredith Gall lists eleven systems for classifying classroom questions and undoubtedly many more have been developed during the last fifteen years.[4] Gall notes that Bloom's Taxonomy best represents the commonalities among the systems.

This article is an effort to review experiences and problems of educators who have been working with patterns of questions in an effort to improve the curriculum.

Have Bloom's categories of questions proven to be applicable to all grade levels, all scholastic aptitude levels, and all subject fields?

The answer is "yes." Both college professors and kindergarten teachers find it possible to lead students to all levels of thinking defined in the taxonomy. Within each category, there are questions appropriate for slow learners and for the scholastically gifted. The same wide range of application has proven true for the various subject fields.

A good indication of the range of areas to which the taxonomy has been applied is found in an annotated bibliography of studies using Bloom's Taxonomy by Richard C. Cox and Carol E. Wildeman.[5] The most recent version includes studies in reading, elementary science, health, biology, chemistry, physics, English, literature, elementary social studies, geography, history, elementary mathematics, industrial arts, home economics, special education, teacher education, medical education, and religious education.

How can the taxonomy of questions be used by a teacher to measure the variety of thinking his questions lead to in recitation, homework, and evaluation?

Educators have found it revealing to classify questions used in instruction as a means of measuring the variety of thinking built into a course. For example, the chapter-end questions in a textbook can be studied in this manner; there are often considerable differences from book to book. Comparing the questions in the daily teaching suggestions with those offered for the end of unit examinations is often revealing. Occasionally a peculiar situation is uncovered where teaching questions are varied, but the examination questions go entirely to memory.

Classroom observation systems, such as Flanders' Interaction Analysis, have been used widely to study oral interactions of students and teacher. The procedure gathers a variety of useful data, but the category under "Indirect Influence" entitled "Asks Questions" does not give sufficient information concerning the levels of thinking. In studying a dozen five-minute segments from tapes of classroom discourse, Laurel Anne Picket found a small negative correlation between the "indirectness" of teachers and the higher cognitive level of questions asked.[6]

Several systems have been devised for measuring the cognitive levels of questions asked in recitation. Bob Burton Brown of Florida State University devised a check-off system entitled the "Florida Taxonomy of Cognitive Behavior" which can be used to record the levels of questions asked by a teacher. Another program combining analysis of questions with other elements of classroom climate is

THE QUESTIONING STRATEGIES OBSERVATION SYSTEM.[7]

For a teacher who wishes to improve his questioning skills or for a supervisor who wants to reveal to teachers a significant element of instruction, a good procedure is simply to record the questions asked in recitation (A teacher can ask a student to write down the daily questions asked in recitation.) One supervisor recorded these questions during a brief segment of a general science class:

Which way does earth spin on axis? (Memory)
What season for U.S. when earth and sun are in this position? (Interpretation) (Demonstrates)
Come up and show how earth and sun are positioned for winter in Argentina. (Translation) (The students are unable to do this so teacher demonstrates.)
What is vernal equinox? (Memory)
Where is Tropic of Cancer? (Memory)
Where is equator? (Memory)

In many class periods, two or three pages of questions are recorded. They retrieve most of the data necessary for meaningful analysis of the cognitive strategy of the teacher.

What variety of thinking was achieved?
What opportunities for good questions were missed?
Were the questions appropriate for the class in terms of difficulty and
interest?
What improvements could be made in wording questions?

Do teachers ask a greater variety of questions after they study one of the classification schemes?

The answer appears to be affirmative—at least within the experimental situation. Burton Grover studied questions asked on tests from elementary and secondary schools in ten school districts in Wisconsin. Eight of the districts had inservice study on questioning techniques. Teachers in the other two districts were not given any special training. The variety of questions asked and the significance of the subject matter on tests were considerably better in social studies, science, and language arts in those districts in which improved questioning techniques were studied by teachers.[8] Ambrose Clegg found that six student teachers who had instruction in questioning skills asked a greater proportion of higher level questions in the classroom than members of a control group who lacked the treatment.[9] The Far Western Laboratory for Educational Research and Development has a mini-course involving micro-teaching on classroom questioning that improves the cognitive level of questioning.[10] A game named *Questioneze* based on Bloom's Taxonomy was found to improve the variety of questions asked by student teachers. The improvement was measured by comparing questions they wrote on a one-page essay before playing the game with those written on another essay after playing the game for three hours.[11]

At least one study suggests that a teacher's knowledge of the structure of questions may not be as important as his enforced attention on the thinking called for by his questions. McCartin and Mees used an electronic device in the ear of a teacher as a means of communicating to him during the process of instruction.[12] Two fourth-grade teachers were told only that the study concerned the way children think. They were given no instruction in levels of questions. The researchers monitored the classes and "beeped" the teachers each time a higher level question was asked. Over a ten-week period, the results showed a "marked change in the desired direction."

Are teachers who study questioning willing and able to implement their skills in the classroom?

Research cited in the previous section establishes that teachers who study the taxonomy can demonstrate their abilities to ask a wider range of questions within the operation of the experiment. However, my experience is that teachers trained in the taxonomy of questions often fail to implement the questioning skills in their classrooms in a pervasive and continuous way. The problem is not that they reject the merit of asking a variety of questions; rather, they find it difficult to put into practice.

The next several sections of the article deal with the following difficulties encountered in attempting to implement questioning skills:

1. The subject content in some courses is not amenable to using a variety of interpretation and application questions without making substantial adjustments.
2. Certain classroom procedures are necessary for success with application, synthesis, and evaluation questions.
3. Using a variety of questions does not solve problems in interpersonal relations nor in motivation. Classes in which students do not want to cooperate with one another or with the teacher are not likely to be improved by the use of a variety of questions.
4. While it is true that there are easy and difficult questions possible in every category of thinking, in practice it frequently turns out that when teachers start asking more higher level questions, they receive more incorrect answers. It is harder to compose questions in higher categories for average and slow students than for bright students.

What kinds of subject matter are needed in a course to facilitate success with interpretation and application questions?

Success with questioning demands the availability of certain kinds of subject matter. Above memory, the crucial category in virtually every subject field is interpretation. Up to fifty to seventy-five per cent of the possibilities for questions above memory fall in this category. The interpretation question asks students to draw inferences, to make comparisons, to take an inductive leap from a sampling of data to a generalization, or, most common of all, to use a *functional idea* in a *new situation*. A "functional idea" is one that can be used to solve, classify, or explain. It is commonly called a rule, law, principle, class, skill, method, process, theory, theorem, or formula. A "new situation" refers to uninterpreted raw data relating to a functional idea. Every subject has raw data. In science it often takes the form of data gathered from observation or experimentation. In social studies there are voting records, daily temperatures at specific geographic locations, prices of food, wages of workers, historical documents, and election campaign advertisements. In foreign languages there are letters, periodicals, and radio broadcasts from abroad. Language arts offers endless sources of oral and written information encountered in everyday experiences.

After a functional idea is introduced, students can practice using it by relating it to raw information. The description of the process by which a student carries out an experiment is excellent raw data to test understanding of the scientific method. The teacher can ask interpretation questions such as these: Does the experimenter use proper sampling techniques? Does the experimenter use appropriate measuring procedures? Does the experimenter use proper controls? Are the conclusions adequately supported by the data? Are there additional conclusions that might have been made? To practice recognizing the principles of free enterprise, the teacher may ask students to find examples of the operation or violation of the principles in the newspaper. To practice recognition of the rules of grammar, the students can evaluate themes written by classmates.

The use of raw information in testing follows the same general procedures as in the practice of instruction. However, in testing, fresh information must be used. For example, if in instruction a teacher has the students practice finding examples of logical fallacies in tape recordings from the "Voice of the People," then in evaluation he could have them perform the same operation but with different recordings. Most tests should include questions based on raw information that students have not seen before. Too often teachers ask students to interpret raw information in instruction but revert to memory questions on the test. Sometimes the reverse mistake is made by requiring students to demonstrate on tests the use of functional ideas that have been explained but never used in instruction.

Textbooks often present little raw data; the responsibility then falls mainly on the teacher. A good approach is for the teacher to identify the main functional ideas and skills taught in his course. Next, he decides the kind of raw data that would illustrate the operation of one or more concepts, or provide practice in a skill. The data is then located either by the teacher or by students as part of an assignment. Sometimes it is possible to make up data. A home economics teacher can compose a fictional menu of a family for one week and ask questions requiring application of principles of nutrition. To test for the use of definitions of social class, a teacher can compose descriptions of individuals or families. Writing fictional data has both advantages and disadvantages. It is often easier to invent data than to find it. When a teacher writes his own raw information, he can tailor it to fit exact needs. On the other hand, fabricated data may be unauthentic.

The problems in finding the proper forms of subject matter vary from course to course. History is difficult to raise to an interpretive level because the emphasis on the chronological narrative by many historians limits the availability of functional ideas. the other social studies have functional ideas that are available to historians, but many feel that putting much emphasis on them dilutes the integrity of history. Geography, political science, sociology, anthropology, and psychology contain functional ideas, but raw data isn't always easily accessible. Of all the social studies, economics offers the easiest opportunities for a variety of thinking. It is full of functional ideas, and raw data is available on most topics.

In the sciences, biology appears most vulnerable to an overemphasis on memory of detail. The stress on nomenclature in the subject means that outside of a few functional topics, such as heredity, classroom questions will probably continue to be more memory oriented than will be true in either chemistry or physics.

In language arts, the study of grammar and usage lends itself to interpretation thinking, but English teachers currently are not enthusiastic about a great emphasis on these topics. Principles of rhetoric and semantics are functional and susceptible to interpretation and application questions. Raw data related to these topics is easily available too. In literature units, there is a temptation to ask too large a proportion of memory and translation questions. There is ample raw data, but the functional concepts are not obvious.

Mathematics teachers have different subject matter problems in seeking justifiable proportions of questions. Through junior high school—or at least up to algebra—the questions asked in the best mathematics programs appear quite varied. Starting with algebra, there is a small proportion of questions applying mathematics to life. The more advanced the program, the more serious the lack of lifelike applications. One group of secondary school math teachers with whom I worked indicated that the mathematics in high school does not relate to life but does prepare students for college mathematics. If this is true, it makes me feel uneasy about the program.

Home economics and industrial arts contain much functional content and offer beautiful opportunities for a variety of thinking. However, the questions in the performance part of the classes often look much better than the parts of the courses calling for written or oral answers. Many physical education teachers have built written tests into their programs, but the emphasis is more on remembering descriptive information than on using concepts.

Getting subject matter organized for questioning is usually a bigger undertaking for teachers than learning the six kinds of questions.

What classroom practices promote successful use of application, synthesis, and evaluation questions?

Application questions are similar to interpretation questions but with one major difference. Both call upon the student to use a functional idea in a new situation. The crucial difference is that an interpretation question stipulates the idea the student is to use, while in an application question, part of the student's problem is to figure out which functional idea to use. Application questions are important, because in life outside of school the teacher isn't present to coach the pupil on which principle to use in a new problem. I observed a beautiful example of how teachers wish students would carry school learning into life. At a high school baccalaureate address, two boys were whispering and jotting down notes. My curiosity was aroused because high school boys don't ordinarily take notes on a graduation speech. Afterward I asked them what they had been doing. They said they had learned a series of logical fallacies in their language arts class and were keeping track of how many were used by the speaker. How pleased their language arts teacher was when I told him.

The best way to promote this kind of transfer of training is to ask application questions in class; but there are some special problems in making them work out. The first is that if students do not understand the purpose of the teacher in asking this kind of question, it seems unfair. The students complain: "Why didn't you tell us we were supposed to use Archimedes principle?" "Why didn't you tell us you were going to count off on our grade for cooking the casserole if we didn't set the table properly?"

Another problem is that it is unreasonable for teachers to expect that students will remember all functional ideas in a course. Application questions should be reserved for the most important ideas. A teacher might think of the problem this way: "If I put the functional ideas in this course in order from the most important to the least important, what would be the ten to twenty at the top of the list that I would most like my students to be using five years from now?" Once these ideas are identified, the teacher should inform the students as to the specific functional ideas that he plans to test on the application level. With a little explanation, students easily see the importance of application questions. One civics teacher explained the nature and importance of application questions to students and then periodically handed out a sheet headed "Fair Warning" with this opening sentence: "For the remainder of this court, be ready at all times to answer application questions on the six principles of United States government and the definitions of liberalism and conservatism." The number of these sets of functional ideas was kept at about a dozen for the entire school year. Students were called upon to use the ideas many times in new situations but without having the teacher remind them to use the idea each time.

The main challenge in synthesis and evaluation questions is not in composing good questions as much as in getting good answers. So often students' responses are superficial. The questioning situation must be nurtured in the classroom to stimulate better thinking. A substantial literature has grown up around both creative thinking and value education. Digging into these sources is more helpful than studying the nature of synthesis and evaluation questions in Bloom.

Do students like a course that provides a variety of thinking?

Constructive interpersonal relationships among students and the teacher is necessary before the variety of questions will contribute to improved learning. Students are more likely to want to learn if at the outset they see where they are going. It isn't enough for teachers to accept the objectives. Students must understand and accept them too. Pupil-teacher planning isn't in vogue but can contribute toward goal clarification. Behaviorally stated goals have the advantage of being more understandable. A common error of teachers is to set goals and procedures appropriate for the middle class but not for the lower class. A study of the attitudes of lower classes toward school, property, ambition, authority, violence, and ethics would help many teachers understand students and thereby improve learning climate.

A curriculum development program that promotes a variety of questions without parallel attention to the feelings and attitudes of students is likely to be of only marginal success.

Will more concentration on higher levels of thinking cause students to get more wrong answers?

Answering a question correctly and then having the answer confirmed as being correct by the teacher is a pleasant experience that happens frequently in classrooms emphasizing memory of facts. When a teacher places more emphasis on interpretation, application, synthesis, and evaluation, great care must be taken to maintain reasonable levels of student success and to create new kinds of feelings of success.

Interpretation and application questions place emphasis on more abstract and complex forms of functional knowledge. In the 1960's, virtually every subject discipline identified its most important functional knowledge—usually under the rubric of "concepts." This was a great contribution in showing teachers what academicians thought the most important ideas were in each discipline. The problem was that seldom were the ideas stated within the language and experience of average and below-average students. The questions for homework, recitation, and tests in national curriculum projects in social studies, science, mathematics, and language arts were frequently varied by standards of the taxonomy, but teachers often found they had to grade on a curve in order to save a majority in their classes from failing. A controversy developed as to whether it was undesirable to have students missing so many questions. Some argued that from the standpoint of grading, the test was no less fair and no less accurate in measuring progress just because a raw score of sixty was worth an "A" on a test with 100 questions. On such a test, it was common for scores of thirty to fifty per cent correct to be passing. This low level of understanding of daily classwork must be frustrating to students even if a passing grade is attained.

When student success levels on questions in higher categories go down, it does not mean that students aren't capable of higher levels of thinking. The problem is more likely associated with the functional ideas. Improving the success level does not require going to lower categories; it means selecting functional ideas with greater care, communicating them within the experience of students, and then having students use the concepts in new situations that they comprehend. The most skillful teachers and the best curriculum programs have proven this can be done.

Do students who are instructed on a higher cognitive level learn more or something of greater value than students taught on a lower cognitive level?

Most educators experimenting with the taxonomy of questions seem willing to accept as self-evident the conclusion that higher level thinking leads to higher level learning. Two recent research studies support this contention.

George T. Ladd and Hans Q. Anderson used a modification of a question classification scheme devised by Smith and Meux to identify twenty "low inquiry" teachers and twenty "high inquiry" teachers of a ninth-grade earth science course.[13] The definitions of low and high inquiry corresponded only roughly to lower and higher level questions in Bloom's Taxonomy. A test made up of both high and low inquiry questions and given to students of the forty teachers showed markedly better scores by students of high inquiry teachers.

In another study, two groups of sixth-graders learned social studies, but, in the course of instruction, one group answered knowledge questions while the other group worked with analysis and evaluation questions.[14] A post test keyed to Bloom's levels of thinking showed better scores on application and evaluation questions by the class that had emphasized higher categories in practice. The two classes did not differ in other categories.

In spite of the positive results of these two experiments, it would be surprising to me if higher level questions were consistently found to lead to higher levels of learning. The known potency of individual differences among students, of varying affective climates in classrooms, of differences in teaching styles and differences in functional knowledge in various subject fields makes it unlikely that higher level questioning will prove advantageous in any kind of global way. The kind of research needed would determine the kinds of students, teachers, and classroom conditions that foster success with higher level questions.

Is a taxonomy of classroom questions just another curriculum fad that will soon fade from the scene?

One of the discouraging aspects of curriculum development in any field is the transitory character of innovations. In the case of the taxonomy of questions, this seems unlikely to occur. The major curriculum innovations of the 1960's did not replace the taxonomy but rather underscored its importance. Experiments in team teaching, for example, showed that teachers who were unskillful at questioning in a self-contained classroom were also unskillful at questioning in an instructional team. Questioning skills must be attacked directly; they are not automatically solved by administrative, technological, and architectural changes.

Other curriculum developments that cannot be successful without systematic concern for classroom questioning are these: educational TV, programmed learning and teaching machines; single concept films, modular scheduling, independent study, individualized instruction, large and small group instruction, pass-fail courses, interaction analysis, change-agent teams, inquiry, simulation, and national assessment. In each of these examples, skillful questioning is a necessary condition (not, however, a sufficient condition) for success.

NOTES
1. Bloom, B. S. (ed.), *Taxonomy of Educational Objectives: Cognitive Domain*, New York: Longmans, Green and Co., 1956.
2. Sanders, Norris M., *Classroom Questions: What Kinds?* New York: Harper and Row, 1966.
3. Eash, Maurice J., *Reading and Thinking*, Garden City, New York: Doubleday and Co., 1967.
4. Gall, Meredith D., "The Use of Questions in Teaching," *Review of Educational Research*, Vol. 40, No. 5, pp. 707–721.
5. Cox, Richard C., and Wildeman, Carol E., *Taxonomy of Educational Objectives: Cognitive Domain: An Annotated Bibliography*, Pittsburgh: Learning Research and Development Center, University of Pittsburgh, 1970.

6. Picket, Laurel Anne, "Can the Level of Cognitive Instruction Be Raised Through Use of Interactive Analysis," *Educational Leadership,* March 1970, pp. 597–600.
7. Morse, Kevin, and Davis, O. L., *The Questioning Strategies Observation System,* Austin, Texas: The Research and Development Center for Teacher Education, University of Texas, May 1970.
8. Grover, Burton, "A Study of Classroom Tests," Cooperative Curriculum Development Center, Manitowoc, Wisconsin, 1969. Mimeographed paper.
9. Clegg, Ambrose A., Jr., "Increasing the Cognitive Level of Classroom Questions in Social Studies: An Application of Bloom's Taxonomy," Paper presented at the annual meeting of the American Educational Research Association, Los Angeles, February 8, 1969.
10. "Overview of Teacher Education Program," Far West Laboratory of Educational Research and Development, Berkeley, California, Mimeographed paper.
11. Rogers, Virginia, "Varying the Cognitive Level of Teachers' Classroom Questions in Social Studies," Paper presented at the annual meeting of the National Council for the Social Studies, Houston, Texas, November, 1969.
12. McCartin, Rosemarie E., and Mees, Hayden, "Raising the Level of Teachers' Questions by Immediate Systematic Feedback," Applied Behavior Change Project, Seattle University, Seattle, Washington, June 1969, Mimeographed paper.
13. Ladd, George T., and Anderson, Hans Q., "Determining the Level of Inquiry of Teachers' Questions," *Journal of Research in Science Teaching,* Vol. 7, No. 4, pp. 395–400.
14. Hunkins, Frances, "The Effects of Analysis and Evaluation Questions on Various Levels of Achievement," Paper presented at the annual meeting of the American Education Research Association, Chicago, 1968.

20 Teacher Expectations: Beyond the Pygmalion Controversy

Jere E. Brophy and Thomas L. Good

Rosenthal and Jacobson's 1968 book, *Pygmalion in the Classroom,* has been hotly debated since its publication. This paper attempts to place the debate in the larger context of research on teacher expectation effects. We believe that further debate on the original study is now academic, because much evidence has accumulated to document the reality of teacher expectation effects and identify some of the mechanisms which explain them.

When *Pygmalion* first appeared, it was uncritically accepted by many educators. However, following several critical reviews and replication failures, this initial overly positive reaction was soon replaced by what we consider to be an overly negative reaction. Subsequent research by many investigators using several different approaches has shown that teachers' expectations sometimes do function as self-fulfilling prophecies.

STUDIES ON INDUCED EXPECTATIONS

Several studies using the Rosenthal and Jacobson method of *inducing* expectations in teachers have shown mixed, mostly negative results as noted by Elashoff and Snow.[1] However, Meichenbaum, Bowers, and Ross found that teachers gave more positive and less negative attention to students identified as "late bloomers" than to matched controls, and that the "late bloomers" out-performed controls on later tests.[2] Beez found that tutors working with Head Start children they thought to be of high ability taught more than tutors working with children they thought to be of low ability, so that the "high ability" students learned more.[3]

Rothbart, Dalfen, and Barrett studied student teachers working with students described either as "lacking in intellectual potential" or as having "considerably greater academic ability."[4] Teachers were more attentive toward the "brighter" students and rated them as having higher intelligence and potential for future success and less need for approval. Rubovits and Maehr, studying undergraduate volunteer teachers working with students labeled as either gifted or nongifted, found that teachers requested more statements, initiated more

Reprinted from *Phi Delta Kappan,* 54(4): 276–278 (December 1972), by permission of authors and publisher.

interactions, and directed more praise toward the "gifted" students.[5] Medinnus and Unruh observed Head Start teachers working with two of their students, one labeled as "high ability" and one as "low ability." The teachers directed more praise and less criticism to the "high ability" students.[6]

Why are expectancy effects obtained in some studies and not in others when certain expectations are induced in teachers? One possibility, of course, is controlled and unknown teacher differences. Another is the scope of the study. Replication failures have occurred mostly in studies which spanned the entire school year and used general achievement tests; the studies showing positive results usually involved only brief contacts between teachers and students and used specific, criterion-referenced tests.

An especially crucial factor is the success of the experimental manipulations. Follow-up interviews by Rosenthal and Jacobson showed that some of the teachers in their study did not remember which students had been designated as "bloomers."[7] Fleming and Anttonen tried to raise teacher expectations by inflating certain student s' IQs by 16 points. However, students with inflated IQs did not outgain their classmates. Follow-up interviews showed that most teachers rejected the inflated IQs as erroneous and thus did not raise their expectations for these students.[8]

The importance of teachers' acceptance of individual expectations was shown even more clearly in two studies by Schrank.[9] He assigned students to five ability groups randomly instead of by measured ability. The "high" group achieved significantly more than the "low" group, and group achievement means fell into position in the same order as the five "ability" labels. The labels had clearly affected the amount that each group learned. Schrank repeated his study two years later (in 1970), but this time teachers were *told* that students were being assigned randomly rather than by ability. However, they were asked to teach the classes as if they had been ability grouped. Despite this attempt to get teachers to simulate ability group teaching, no expectation effects appeared. The implications here seem clear: Information presented to teachers will not affect their expectations unless it is believed to be accurate. If information given by an experimenter is too discrepant from what teachers see in their everyday interactions with students, it will be rejected.

This was one reason for the negative results in the Fleming and Anttonen study, and it may also have been a factor in the many failures to replicate Rosenthal and Jacobson's findings. This points up a serious disadvantage in studies using inducement of teacher expectations: When negative results are obtained, we don't know whether the teachers' expectations did not influence their teaching, or, instead, the treatment failed to induce the desired teacher expectations. The success of experiments involving manipulation of teachers' expectations will vary with the type of information presented, the status and credibility of the presenter, and the personality and ability of the teacher, among other factors. Studies of this type should routinely include follow-ups to assess whether the desired teacher expectations were actually induced by the treatment.

NATURALISTICALLY FORMED EXPECTATIONS

Rather than attempt to induce expectations, several investigators have questioned teachers to discover their naturalistically formed expectations, then related these to teacher-student interaction or to student achievement.

Brophy and Good[10] had first-grade teachers rank their students according to expected achievement. Three high and three low boys, and three high and three low girls were then observed in each class. Clear teacher expectation effects were found. The teachers were more likely to stay with highs after they failed to answer an initial question (by repeating the question, giving a clue, or asking another question). In contrast, they tended to end the interaction by giving the answer or calling on someone else in parallel situations with lows. Differences in teacher feedback reactions were also noted. Teachers failed to give feedback to highs in only 3% of their response opportunities, while the figure for lows was 15%. In addition, highs were more likely to be praised when they answered correctly and less likely to be criticized when they answered incorrectly or failed to respond. These differences were observed even though highs made more correct responses and had fewer failures than lows.

A related set of finds was obtained by Rowe.[11] She asked teachers to name the top five and the bottom five students in their classes, then timed the teachers to see how long they waited for a response after questioning a student. Teachers waited significantly longer for a response from the top group. Thus the students least able to respond had to answer more quickly or lose their chance. When Rowe trained teachers to increase their time-wait, students in the bottom groups began to speak up more often, sometimes enough to change the teachers' expectations.

These studies illustrate how differential expectations are communicated through differential treatment of students. Along with some of the results reviewed earlier, they show a tendency for teachers to be rewarding and encouraging toward high-expectation students and to work for good responses from them. In contrast, they tend to be critical toward low-expectation students and to give up on them too easily when they don't respond quickly.

There are also two studies showing how teachers' naturalistically formed expectations influence student achievement. Palardy asked teachers to indicate whether or not they thought boys could learn to read as well as girls in the first grade. From their responses he identified five teachers who did not believe that boys could do as well as girls and paired these teachers with five others who expected no sex difference. Teachers were paired according to sex, race, experience, type of school, and textbook used for teaching reading. The boys and girls in classrooms of teachers who expected no sex difference achieved equally, but in classrooms of teachers who did not expect boys to do as well as girls, the girls outperformed the boys.[12]

Doyle, Hancock, and Kifer asked first-grade teachers to estimate student IQs shortly before an IQ test was administered. The teachers systematically overestimated girls' IQs and underestimated boys'. Also, reading achievement scores taken at the end of the year showed that students who had been overestimated achieved more than their IQs would predict, while students who had been underestimated achieved less. Thus the teachers produced higher achievement in students for whom they had higher expectations. Furthermore, teachers who generally overestimated their students' IQs produced higher achievement than teachers who generally underestimated them. Thus this study showed both a selective expectation effect operating within each classroom and a more general effect separating high expectation teachers from low expectation teachers.[13]

CONCLUSIONS

In our view the research reviewed leaves little doubt as to the reality of teacher expectation effects. Since *Pygmalion,* much evidence has accumulated to show that teachers' expectations can become self-fulfilling by causing teachers to treat highs appropriately while treating lows in ways that will minimize their learning interests and opportunities. Further proof of the *existence* of teacher expectation effects is not needed; instead, attention should now turn to discovering the causal mechanisms involved and to developing teacher training and intervention strategies that will minimize undesirable expectation effects.[14]

The available data suggest that although expectation effects are quite real, they are neither ubiquitous nor particularly strong in the usual situation. They are not always found, even when the teacher's naturalistically formed expectations are used.[15] Factors causing a teacher to be influenced either more or less by his expectations have not yet been identified, although we suspect that both cognitive and personality factors are involved. Both teacher training and teacher ability seem important. A master teacher with a rich repertoire of skills for diagnosing and remediating learning problems should achieve greater success and be less prone to rationalizing failures than a teacher who is confused and frustrated in the face of difficulty.

Student differences are also involved. Relaxed and active students who frequently initiate contact with teachers will get more attention and are more likely to correct any misconceptions that teachers may have about them. In contrast, quiet, withdrawn students who avoid teachers and do not say much when questioned leave the teachers much more room for error in judging them.

This review has been selective due to space limitations, but we believe that it is representative of the available literature, published and unpublished. (A more extensive review is presented in our forthcoming book.)[16] We conclude from this literature that self-fulfilling prophecy effects of teachers' naturalistically formed expectations are quite real but not universal across teachers or students. They are probably not as strong or important as some enthusiasts would suggest, but they are observable and measurable. They are probably strongest early in the year, before teachers have had much time to observe students. Even across the whole school year, however, teachers' expectations and students' reactions to them are likely to be quite crucial in individual cases, affecting the students' attitudes, self-concepts, and achievement. Thus, we believe this area is well worth further study. In particular, we need data to show *when* and *how* teacher expectations become self-fulfilling. Studies involving naturalistic observation followed by intervention, in which the investigation *helps* rather than simply *manipulates* the teacher, are especially needed.

NOTES

1. Janet Elashoff and Richard Snow, *Pygmalion Reconsidered* (Belmont, Calif.: Charles A. Jones, 1971).

2. Donald Meichenbaum, Kenneth Bowers, and Robert Ross, "A Behavioral Analysis of Teacher Expectancy Effect," *Journal of Personality and Social Psychology,* May, 1969, pp. 306–16.

3. W. Victor Beez, "Influence of Biased Psychological Reports on Teacher Behavior and Pupil Performance," *Proceedings of the Annual Convention of the American Psychological Association,* 1968, pp. 605-606.

4. Myron Rothbart, Susan Dalfen, and Robert Barrett, "Effects of Teacher Expectancy on Student-Teacher Interaction," *Journal of Educational Psychology,* January–February, 1971, pp. 49–54.

5. Pamela Rubovits and Martin Maehr, "Pygmalion Analyzed: Toward an Explanation of the Rosenthal-Jacobson Findings," *Journal of Personality and Social Psychology,* August, 1971, pp. 197–203.

6. Gene Medinnus and Ronald Unruh, "Teacher Expectations and Verbal Communication," paper presented at the annual meeting of the Western Psychological Association, 1970.

7. Robert Rosenthal and Lenore Jacobson, *Pygmalion in the Classroom: Teacher Expectation and Pupils' Intellectual Development* (New York: Holt, Rinehart & Winston, 1968).

8. Elyse Fleming and Ralph Anttonen, "Teacher Expectancy or My Fair Lady," *American Educational Research Journal,* March, 1971, pp. 241–52.

9. Wilburn Schrank, "The Labeling Effect of Ability Grouping," *Journal of Educational Research,* October, 1968, pp. 51, 52: and "A Further Study of the Labeling Effect of Ability Grouping," *Journal of Educational Research,* April, 1970, pp. 358–60.

10. Jere Brophy and Thomas Good, "Teachers' Communication of Differential Expectations for Children's Classroom Performance: Some Behavioral Data," *Journal of Educational Psychology,* September-October, 1970, pp. 365–74.

11. Mary Budd Rowe, "Science, Silence, and Sanctions," *Science and Children,* September, 1969, pp. 11–13.

12. J. Michael Palardy, "What Teachers Believe, What Children Achieve," *Elementary School Journal,* April, 1969, pp. 370–74.

13. Wayne Doyle, Greg Hancock, and Edward Kifer, "Teachers' Perceptions:

Do They Make a Difference?" (paper presented at the annual meeting of the American Educational Research Association, 1971).

14. Thomas Good and Jere Brophy, *Looking in Classrooms* (New York: Harper and Row, in press).

15. Jere Brophy and Thomas Good, *Individual Differences: Toward an Understanding of Classroom Life* (New York: Holt, Rinehart & Winston, in press).

16. Ibid.

21 Educating to Make a Difference

Leland W. Howe

If a person is going to be productive and contribute to our society, he must develop a healthy self-concept, for—so the theory goes—people who believe in themselves and their ability to influence society develop a stake in things. They care; they become committed; they play for keeps; they attempt *to make a difference.*

The literature is full of research studies which support this position. Numerous books and articles have been written exhorting the teacher to pay attention to the self-concept, to help children improve their self-image and become independent thinkers and self-directed persons. Yet it remains for the classroom teacher to do the job, most of the time with few guidelines. Only recently have educators turned their full attention to the problem of "how" in such projects as the Harvard Achievement Motivation Development Project, the Center for Humanistic Education at the University of Massachusetts, and the new experimental teacher education program at Southern Illinois University, to name a few.

Some promising work has been done in the program at SIU. One objective of the program is to develop a meaningful theory as well as a set of procedures (teaching practices) which the classroom teacher at any level can use to help adolescents clarify their goals, values, and beliefs and develop positive self-concepts which result in positive self-directed action.

Reprinted from *Phi Delta Kappan,* 52 (9): 547–549 (May 1971), by permission of author and publisher.

THE THEORY

There are four natural growth stages in the process of self-definition: fantasizing, gaming, encountering, and actualizing.

The first stage, *fantasizing,* begins when children define themselves—who they are, who they want to become, what they want to do— through fantasy. They hear stories about firemen, policemen, scientists, and legendary heroes; they read about older children who go camping and help others in time of need; and they see older brothers, sisters, playmates, and neighbors do important things, and they begin to dream about how they might do likewise. "If I were 16, I would ride my bike to the park and see what I could see"; "If I could be as tall as a tree I would see the little robins in the tree"; "If I had but one wish, I wish I could be . . ."

As children enter adolescence, they begin to formulate their ideal man or woman. "She must be beautiful, courageous, intelligent, and a cheerleader." Fantasy about this girlfriend or that boyfriend often dominates the time spent in and out of school. Adolescents hunt for models of what and who they want to be in novels, history books, world events, and among those around them. They "fall in love" with and idealize their teachers, the president, Abe Lincoln, Nancy Drew, the Beatles, and the best hitter in the class.

Fantasy provides a safe way of telling themselves who they are, what they would like to become, what they value, and what they believe. It is safe because there is little investment in overt behavior. No one but they need know their inner thoughts, so if they change their minds and want to become Billy the Kid instead of Marshal Dillon, they do not have to explain the change to anyone. Nor must they accept the consequences of being a real outlaw. It allows them to go steady with the best-looking boy in the class without getting turned down or dropped if he is really not interested. Fantasy allows the adolescent to try on a new personality in complete privacy. If the fit begins to get too tight, it can be discarded immediately with no one the wiser. In fact, fantasy allows one to be two persons at the same time, one which others know and one which only the mind's eye knows. It allows one to keep respect, get even, and do a dirty deed or a noble one without having to face any of the results of the actual act.

Fantasy allows the adult to build a company, start a school, manage a law firm, and buy stock in IBM without the risk of actually doing so. Fantasy is an exploratory adventure which lets the inner self explore new areas, new vistas, and new ideas in the protective safety of the mind's walls. It is often the beginning of growth in self; it may be the first halting step toward further self-definition. It is the preparation for changes in status, personality, and belief; it is, perhaps, the only fun part of being human which has almost no risks.

However, if healthy self-growth is to continue, the individual must begin the second step—*gaming.* This means testing the fantasy to see if it is realistic. Children and adolescents test the potential consequences of fantasies through a low-risk technique. "Let's pretend," children say. "Let's pretend we're hunting for gold in the Yukon!" "Let's pretend we're married—you be the father and I'll be the mother." Or, on an adult level, "Let's pretend we are in the middle of a race riot. Now as a policeman, what is your duty when . . ."

"Let's pretend" requires the individual to act, but within a situation which is make-believe. It is fantasy acted out where others can see it. Thus it is not as safe as fantasy because others can see what the individual chooses to say or do, and actions are always open to criticism; it can bring scorn, laughter, and ridicule. Yet games are relatively safe, since one can always stop the action. Getting shot and playing dead is no fun in a game of "cops and robbers," so one can always suggest that the game be stopped or the rules changed: "Everybody has to shoot only to wound, not to kill."

The consequences of taking certain actions come alive through the make-believe of games. The player—child, adolescent, or adult—can test new and different ways of behaving. He can behave more aggressively and see how others react. He can be sneaky and sly and see how others like it; he can work harder to get ahead in the game and see if the results are worth the extra effort. Best of all, he can stop the action if the going gets too rough: "I quit!" The option is always open to change the game to another which will produce more desirable outcomes.

"Let's pretend," whether expressed in games like "Monopoly" or "cowboys and Indians" or in role-play on the company's time, allows the player to try on new behavior without the obligation to buy. He can just look, and if he doesn't like what he sees he can turn it in, no questions asked. Though more risky than fantasy, it has the advantage of producing more personal satisfaction; the closer one gets to the self one wants to be, the more meaningful and rich life becomes.

To go all the way toward becoming the desired self—that is the goal. This means graduating from the world of make-believe to the real world of increased risks and benefits. As anyone who has recently done it can testify, the development of new skills, the creation of a new life-style, the formulation of new values, the redoing of one's personality, or the changing of certain behaviors so that one can be successful in a new undertaking can be very frustrating and traumatic. If one has not prepared in advance, it can be overwhelming and sometimes defeating.

One of the most important and effective ways of preparing and testing oneself to see if the goal is worth it, or if one's mettle is strong enough to stand it, is to *encounter,* the third stage. This means trying out certain behavior in the real world of "for keeps," but in such a limited and controlled way that the negative consequences are diminished and the chance to back out is not denied.

Encountering is doing it for real, but only temporarily. It is the testing stage as engagement is a testing stage for marriage. It is here that the self is tried out under actual battle conditions, but without declaring war. This means that the consequences are of a serious nature. One has a stake in the encounter because it is for real. "She might not like the way I kiss her"; "If I take the summer job in the law firm and find out I don't like law, what will I do with my law degree?'' Yet it is not as serious as playing for keeps because one has only made a temporary commitment. "If she doesn't like the way I kiss her, there are plenty of fish in the sea"; or, "Maybe I'll like insurance; anyway, the law degree can't hurt anything."

Adolescents go through a visible stage of encountering when they begin to reject ingrained family values in favor of trying out new ones in an attempt to develop their own value systems. This "natural" stage of rebellion might be brought on by reading *Gone with the Wind* and deciding to make one's life, at least temporarily, more like Scarlett O'Hara's; it might be caused by a confrontation with a teacher who "makes one stop and think," or by admiring a friend from a wealthy family. It might be questioning whether making money is the end all and be all, or whether virginity is worth the wait, or, indeed, worth anything. Encountering might be a vacation with an uncle who offers employment in plastics after graduation; it might be a debate contest in which one tries to assert oneself more aggressively; it might be petting to see if sex is really as dirty as Mom says; it might be a T-group which meets temporarily to help its members study their behavior and become more effective in relating to one another; it might be the first year of teaching without tenure.

At the end of all this is the fourth stage, *actualizing*. This means playing for keeps, going all the way. It is marriage, 10 years of medical practice, investment of one's life savings in the stock market, publication of one's writing, pregnancy, and plastic surgery. Once the action is taken, turning back may be difficult if not impossible. Divorce may be too costly, new employment difficult to find, money hard to recover in a bear market, distribution of one's writing impossible to stop, abortion against the law, and the shock of more surgery too great. Even if one could turn back, the cost of doing so may be excessive.

Of course, playing for keeps is where satisfaction is. It can result in happiness and self-fulfillment. On the other hand, it has the greatest risks—high blood pressure, an ulcer, or accidental death, to say nothing of financial failure and loss of prestige. Yet it is where we all yearn to be. To make a difference—that's where the action is.

These four stages are natural growth stages for self-definition. In defining one's self through goal setting and goal achievement, children, adolescents, and adults go through these stages in an attempt to plan, organize, direct, and evaluate growth of self. The stages tend to be cyclical but nonsequential in occurrence. That is, people tend to go through these stages again and again from early childhood until death, but not in any given order. Fantasy about who one wants to be may follow a meaningful experience with one's grandfather and result in actualization some 10 years later; on the other hand, the experience might generate such a powerful force for change that the testing stage is omitted and actualization is immediate.

As we can all testify, the process of self-definition is extremely complex and perhaps impossible to describe accurately; however, it seems useful to conceive of it as unfolding in the four stages that have been described. These can be arranged along a continuum from low risk and low satisfaction at one end to high risk and high satisfaction at the other, as follows:

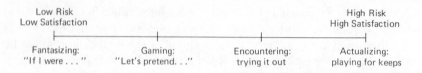

Low Risk
Low Satisfaction

High Risk
High Satisfaction

Fantasizing:
"If I were . . ."

Gaming:
"Let's pretend. . ."

Encountering:
trying it out

Actualizing:
playing for keeps

Risk represents possible negative consequences or setbacks in growth of self; satisfaction represents the possible pleasure to be derived from goal achievement. The relationship between risk and satisfaction tends to be directly proportionate—the higher the degree of possible risk, the higher the degree of possible satisfaction.

MEANING FOR THE TEACHER

Do we as educators want to help children and young people achieve actualization of their full potential as human beings? If the answer is yes, and I think it has to be, then we must provide the opportunities, climate, and encouragement which children and adolescents need in order to safely explore who they are, who they want to be, and what relation to the rest of us and the world of things they want to have. We must help them see beyond their personal blinders— to see and explore new alternatives for behaving, new ways of relating and finding meaning, and new modes of being and becoming. We must provide them with opportunities and encouragement to fantasize, to verbalize their fantasies, to write and talk about them, and to explore them in depth. We must provide opportunities and encouragement to go beyond fantasy; to risk and actualize in games, through encounters, and for keeps—behavior which will make them stronger, more determined, and more zestful human beings. We must help them collect and evaluate information about their effectiveness, and we must help them know their weaknesses as challenges to be taken up with self-confidence.

This means providing children and adolescents with opportunities to "pretend," to game, to role play, to play at being different, to play at being more than what they are, and to extend themselves into new ways of doing, seeing, being, behaving, and becoming. It means creating and building games which are fun and non-threatening but which challenge and give meaning to behavior, and which allow for alternative modes of expression and self-definition. It means following up these kinds of activities with a chance for players to see how they did by evaluating the consequences of their behavior.

It means going beyond fantasy and games to the real thing; we must provide children and adolescents at all levels of schooling with real and meaningful opportunities to "try it out"—to dig in old Indian campsites, to tag along with a policeman for a week, to program a computer, to watch a brain surgeon perform an operation, to manage a gas station for six weeks, to raise food in a garden, to design their own schooling for 10 weeks. In short, we must make the experimental schools without walls a reality for all children and adolescents by constructing controlled situations and experiences in which they can realistically assess their degree of aptitude, interest, and skill for carrying through and playing for keeps.

When we have done this, and done it skillfully, then and only then can we say that we are truly educating to make a difference.

22 Values-Clarification vs. Indoctrination

Sidney B. Simon

Whatever happened to those good old words we once used when we talked of values? Remember how comfortable it was to say *inculcate?* It was a nice, clean, dignified, closely shaved word if there ever was one. Then there was the old standby, *to instill*—usually followed by "the democratic values of our society." Doesn't anyone instill anymore? And what about the word *foster?* In schools, not so very long ago, we used to "foster" all over the place. But nobody does that much anymore. What has happened to the old familiar jargon of value teaching?

What happened was the realization that all the inculcating, instilling, and fostering added up to indoctrination; and despite our best efforts at doing the indoctrinating, we've come to see that it just didn't take. Most of the people who experienced the inculcation, instillation, and fostering seem not the much better for it. They appear to play just as much hanky-panky with income taxes as anyone else, and concerned letters-to-the-editor are not written by them in any greater profusion. They pollute and defoliate; move to the suburbs to escape integration; buy convertibles with vinyl tops that collapse in roll-over accidents;

Reprinted from SOCIAL EDUCATION, 35 (8): 902–905 + (December 1971), by permission of the National Council for the Social Studies and Sidney B. Simon.

For information about current Values Clarification materials or nation-wide training workshops, contact Values Associates, Box 43, Amherst, Massachusetts 01002.

fail to wear seat belts; and commit all kinds of sins even while they are saying the very words that have been dutifully inculcated, instilled, and fostered in them. It *is* discouraging.

At this point, one might ask: "Is it all that bad?" "Aren't they also among the good people who go to the polls in November, read the current events weeklies, and pay their Bankamericard charges on time?" Yes, of course. But in these troubled, confused, and conflicted times, we need people who can do much more than that. We desperately need men and women who know who they are, who know what they want out of life, and who can name their names when controversy rages. We need people who know what is significant and what is trash, and who are not so vulnerable to demagoguery, blandness, or safety.

The indoctrination procedures of the past fail to help people grapple with all the confusion and conflict which abound in these baffling days. For example, in values-clarification, we apply a strategy which is deceptively simple. We ask students to spend some time listing the brand names in their home medicine cabinets. Just think of your own medicine cabinet as you are sitting reading this. What's in it? How many creams, ointments, and salves have you been sold? Do you use a brand-name, buffered product instead of plain old aspirin? How did you get started on that? What about the spray cans? How many are in your aerosol arsenal? What did you use before the product you now spray? How did all those brand names get there? Who bought them? What was the motivating force? How did you learn what to value as seen in your medicine cabinet? As long as you have the door to your cabinet open, why don't you pull out the cosmetic tray? How vulnerable are you to avoiding the hysteria surrounding all of us about getting a wrinkle? Getting old has become such a negative value. Who are the people who fear it?

In place of indoctrination, my associates and I are substituting a *process* approach to the entire area of dealing with values in the schools, which focuses on the process of valuing, not on the transmission of the "right" set of values. We call this approach *values-clarification,* and it is based on the premise that none of us has the "right" set of values to pass on to other people's children. Yes, there may be some things we can all agree upon, and I will grant you some absolutes, but when we begin to operationalize our values, make them show up in how we live our days and spend our nights, then we begin to see the enormous smugness of those people who profess they have the right values for others' children. The issues and hostility generated around hair length and dress and armbands are just the surface absurdity.

More dangerous is the incredible hypocrisy we generate when we live two-faced values and hustle the one right value to children. Think about the hundreds of elementary school teachers who daily stop children from running down the halls. I close my eyes and I see them with their arms outstretched, hands pressing against the chest of kids who put on their "brakes" in order to make the token slowdown until the teacher ducks into the teacher's room for a fast cigarette before all the kids get back to hear the cancer lecture. Think of those teachers preaching to children about the need to take turns and share. "We wait in lines, boys and girls, and we learn to share our crayons and paints in here. And, I don't want to see anybody in my class being a tattletale—except in cases of serious emergency, naturally." The words are all too familiar. I have used them in the old days. I have also seen myself cut into the cafeteria lunch line ahead of third graders. (Take turns? Well, not when we have so few minutes for lunch and always so much to do to get ready for afternoon classes.)

The alternative to indoctrination of values is *not* to do nothing. In this time of the anti-hero, our students need all the help we can give them if they are to make sense of the confusion and conflict inherited from the indoctrinated types. Moreover, we all need help in grappling with the chaos of the international scene, with the polarization of national life—not to mention the right-outside-the-door string of purely local dilemmas.

An approach to this problem is to help students learn a process for the clarification of their values, which is a far cry from indoctrination. The theory behind it can be found in *Values and Teaching* (Louis E. Raths, Merrill Harmin, and Sidney B. Simon, Columbus: Charles E. Merrill, 1966). In the remainder of this article, I will describe some of the strategies we are presently using to help students learn the process of values-clarification and begin lifelong searches for the sets of personal values by which to steer their lives.[1]

FIVE VALUE-CLARIFYING STRATEGIES AND THEIR USE

Strategy #1—Things I Love to Do

Ask students (teacher does it with them) to number from 1–20 on a paper. Then suggest they list, as rapidly as they can, 20 things in life which they really, *really* love to do. Stress that the papers will not be collected and "corrected," and that there is no right answer about what people *should* like. It should be emphasized that in none of values strategies should students be forced to participate. Each has the right to pass. Students may get strangely quiet; and, at first, they may even be baffled by such an unschoollike task as this. Flow with it, and be certain to allow enough time to list what they really love to do. Remember, at no time must the individual's privacy be invaded, and that the right of an individual to pass is sacrosanct.

When everyone has listed his 20 items, the process of coding responses can be started. Here are some suggested codes which you might ask the students to use:

1. Place the $ sign by any item which costs more than $3, each time you do it.

---

[1] Most of these strategies are from a soon-to-be published book, *New Strategies for Clarifying Values* by Sidney B. Simon, Howard Kirschenbaum, and Leland Howe.

2. Put an *R* in front of any item which involves some RISK. The risk might be physical, intellectual, or emotional. (Which things in your own life that are things you love to do require some risk?)

3. Using the code letters *F* and *M*, record which of the items on your list you think your father and mother might have had on their lists if they had been asked to make them at YOUR age.

4. Place either the letter *P* or the letter *A* before each item. The "P" to be used for items which you prefer doing with PEOPLE, the "A" for items which you prefer doing ALONE. (Stress again that there is no right answer. It is important to just become aware of which are your preferences.)

5. Place a number *5* in front of any item which you think would not be on your list 5 years from now.

6. Finally go down through your list and place near each item the date when you did it last.

The discussion which follows this exercise argues more eloquently than almost anything else we can say for values-clarification.

Strategy #2—I Learned That I . . . .

This strategy fits in with the one above. After students have listed and coded their 20 items, the teacher might say, "Look at your list as something which tells a lot about you at this time in your life. What did you learn about yourself as you were going through the strategy? Will you please complete one of these sentences and share with us some of the learning you did?"

I learned that I . . . .
I relearned that I . . . .
I noticed that I . . . .
I was surprised to see that I . . . .
I was disappointed that I . . . .
I was pleased that I . . . .
I realized that I . . . .

The teacher must be willing to make some "I learned that I . . . . " statements, too. And they must not be platitudinous, either. Every effort is made for the values-clarifying teacher to be as honest and as authentic as possible.

"I learned that I . . . ." statements can be used after almost any important value-clarifying strategy. It is a way of getting the student to own the process of the search for values. It should be clear how diametrically opposed "I learned that I . . . ." statements are from indoctrination, although it is possible to misuse this or any clarification strategy to get kids to give back the party line. On the other hand, using this strategy can begin to build that lifetime search for personal meaning into all of our experiences.

Strategy #3—Baker's Dozen

This is a very simple strategy which teaches us something about our personal priorities. The teacher asks each student to list 13, a baker's dozen, of his favorite items around the house which use PLUGS, that is, which require electricity.

When the students have made their lists, the teacher says, "Now, please draw a line through the three which you really could do without if there were suddenly to be a serious power shortage. It's not that you don't like them, but that you could, if you had to, live without them. O.K., now circle the three which really mean the most to you and which you would hold onto until the very end."

It should be clear that again there is no right answer as to what "good" people *should* draw lines through and circle. The main thing is for each of us to know what we want and to see it in the perspective of what we like less.

Strategy #4—"I Urge" Telegrams

The teacher obtains blank Western Union telegram blanks. Or simply has students head a piece of paper with the word *Telegram*. He then says, "Each of you should think of someone in your real life to whom you would send a telegram which begins with these words: I URGE YOU TO . . . . Then finish the telegram and we'll hear some of them."

A great many values issues come out of this simple strategy. Consider some of these telegrams:

> *To my sister:* "I urge you to get your head together and quit using drugs." Nancy. (All telegrams must be signed. It is our affirmation of the need to name your name and to stand up for what you believe in.)
> *To my Sunday School teacher:* "I urge you to quit thinking that you are the only person to know what God wants." Signed, your student Rodney Phillips.
> *To my neighbor on the North Side:* "I urge you to see that we have no other place to play ball and that you not call the cops so often." Signed, Billy Clark.

One of the things that students working with values-clarification learn to do is to find out what they really want. "I urge telegrams" help do that. Just think of the people in your own lives to whom an "I urge telegram" needs to be sent. The second thing students working with values-clarification learn to do is to find *alternative* ways of getting what they need and want. Take the case of Billy Clark's neighbor. The class spent some time brainstorming ways of approaching that neighbor. They talked about how to negotiate with a grouch, and how to try to offer alternatives in your drive to get what you want.

"I urge telegrams" are used several times during the semester. The students keep them on file and after they have done five or six, they are spread out on the desk and "I learned statements" made from the pattern of the messages carried by the telegrams.

Students also learn to use the "I urge you to . . . ." model to get messages across between student and student and between student and teacher.

An assignment I like to use, related to the "I urge telegram," is to have each student get a letter-to-the-editor published in a magazine or newspaper.

Strategy #5—Personal Coat of Arms

Each student is asked to draw a shield shape in preparation for making a personal coat of arms. The teacher could go into the historical significance of shields and coats of arms, but the exercise is designed to help us learn more about some of our most strongly held values and to learn the importance of publicly affirming what we believe, that is, literally wearing our values out front on our shields.

The coat of arms shield is divided into six sections (see figure). The teacher makes it clear that words are to be used only in the sixth block. All the others are to contain pictures. He stresses that it is not an art lesson. Only crude stick figures, etc., need be used. Then he tells what is to go in each of the six sections:

1. Draw two pictures. One to represent something you are very good at and one to show something you *want* to become good at.
2. Make a picture to show one of your values from which you would never budge. This is one about which you feel extremely strong, and which you might never give up.
3. Draw a picture to show a value by which your family lives. Make it one that everyone in your family would probably agree is one of their most important.
4. In this block, imagine that you could achieve anything you wanted, and that whatever you tried to do would be a success. What would you strive to do?
5. Use this block to show one of the values you wished all men would believe, and certainly one in which you believe very deeply.
6. In the last block, you can use words. Use four words which you would like people to say about you behind your back.

The teacher can do several different things at this point. He can have the students share among themselves in little trios or quartets. He can also get the pictures hung up on the walls and get people to take each other on gallery tours to share the coats of arms. A game could be played which would involve trying to guess what the pictures represented. The class might try to make a group coat of arms to represent their living together in that classroom. In any case, the value expressions elicited in this nonverbal way are very exciting and lead to discussions which range far and wide. Incidentally, this strategy is a good one to use with parents to illustrate to them the power of the values-clarification methodology. It makes a meaningful exercise for an evening PTA meeting.

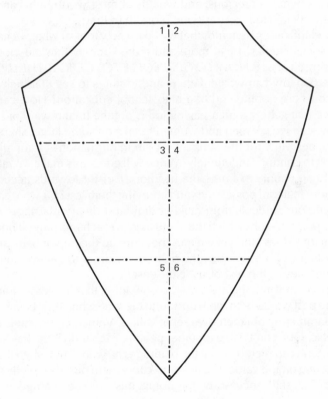

The Coat of Arms strategy illustrates quite well some things common to all of the values-clarification strategies. The teacher sets up an interesting way of eliciting some value responses. He establishes that there is no right answer. The strategy is open-ended and allows students to take the exploration to whatever level they want to take it. Finally, there is a chance to share with each other some of the alternatives that emerge from our searching. This whole process allows each student to focus on areas were he has some work yet to do in order to keep growing. The Coat of Arms can be done several times during the school year and the various shields compared and seen as measures of a student's search.

CONCLUSIONS

The five strategies used as illustrations of what values-clarification is must raise some serious questions in the minds of readers who have more conventional views of what the social studies should be. For one thing, I have used no standard subject-matter content: there is no history, no geography, etc. Yet, if one thinks through what the outcomes of a course will be making use of the five strategies, he will see the student emerging with a deeper sense of who he is, what he wants, what is precious, and what is of most worth in his and others' lives. Has the social studies ever done more than that?

Values-clarification demands that we take a new look at what we have been calling the social studies. I feel more and more strongly that the most severe problem facing all of us is *HOW TO GET PEOPLE TO LOOK AT THE LIVES THEY ARE LEADING.* How can we get fathers and mothers to see that high college-entrance scores are not the end of a high school education? How can we get people to see that getting a high-paying job is not the final reward of a college degree? How can we get men and women to take on some larger share of their personal responsibility for the rampant racism in our nation? Or for allowing a senseless war to continue indefinitely? When will educators make a contribution towards helping people examine the headlong pursuit towards accumulating more and more material possessions and enjoying them less? Or what can we do about keeping our students from making drab and dreary marriages or being trapped into pointless jobs which they hate to go to each morning? It boils down to a concern for values, and yet we must not fall into the trap of believing that if only we could give boys and girls the right set of values to believe, they would avoid the mistakes of the rest of us. Nonsense!

Indoctrination is not the answer. The only thing that indoctrination did for people in the past was to help them postpone the time when they began the hard process of hammering out their own set of values. Values simply can't be given to anyone else. One can't value for other people. Each individual has to find his own values. One can memorize all the platitudes he wants, but when it comes to living and acting on the values, he needs to carve them out of carefully reflected experience. The skills necessary for doing this can be learned in values-clarification.

Perhaps when the reader and author acknowledge how little help they received from their own education about making sense out of life, maybe then they will be willing to help other people's children learn the *process,* a lifetime process, of searching for a viable set of values to live by and perhaps even to die for.

The author is convinced that he can leave his own children no greater inheritance than the gift of knowing how to negotiate the lovely banquet of life ahead of them. That is indeed something of value.

23 The Problem of Choice

John Holt

Teachers very often say to me, "Suppose we tell kids that they now have the freedom to choose what they are going to study, and how and when they are going to study it, and they don't choose anything, don't do anything? Then what do we do?" A good many teachers who have tried to open up their classrooms, usually in a junior high school or high school, have said that this has in fact happened.

First, we should try to see this situation through the eyes of the student. For years he has been playing a school game which looks to him about like this. The teacher holds up a hoop and says "Jump!" He jumps, and if he makes it, he gets a doggy biscuit. Then the teacher raised the hoop a little higher and again says "Jump!" Another jump, another biscuit. Or, perhaps the student makes a feeble pretense of jumping, saying, "I'm jumping as high as I can, this is the best I can do." Or, he may lie on the floor and refuse to jump. But in any case the rules of the game are simple and clear—hoop, jump, biscuit. Now along comes a teacher who says, "We aren't going to play that game anymore, you're going to decide for yourselves what you're going to do." What is the student going to think about this? Almost certainly, he is going to think, "They're hiding the hoop! It was bad enough having to jump through it before, but now I have to find it." Then after a while he is likely to think, "On second thought, maybe I don't have to find it. If I just wait long enough, pretty soon that hoop is going to slip out of its hiding place, and then we'll be back to the old game where at least I know the rules and am comfortable."

In short, if we make this offer of freedom, choice, self-direction to students who have spent much time in traditional schools, most of them will not trust us or believe us. Given their experience, they are quite right not to. A student in a traditional school learns before long in a hundred different ways that the school is not on his side; that it is working, not for him, but for the community and the state; that it is not interested in him except as he serves its purposes; and that among all the reasons for which the adults in the school do things, his happiness, health, and growth are by far the least important. He has probably also learned that most of the adults in the school do not tell him the truth and indeed are not allowed to—unless they are willing to run the risk of being fired, which most of them are not. They are not independent and responsible persons, free to say what they think, feel, believe, or to do what seems reasonable and right. They are employees and spokesmen, telling the children whatever the school administration, the school board, the community, or the legislature want the children to be told. Their job is by whatever means they can to "motivate" the students to do whatever the school wants. So, when a school or teacher says that the students don't have to play the old school game anymore, most of them, certainly those who have not been "good students," will not believe it. They would be very foolish if they did.

We must try to understand and accept this, without getting hurt feelings, or taking it as some very personal kind of rejection. This may be far from easy. A school, or teachers, or teacher, that offers students very much choice has probably gone to some trouble to be able to do so, and even risk—risk of misunderstanding or hostility from parents or community or fellow-teachers. If after we have run this risk to give students some freedom, choice, and control in their learning, they show us that they do not believe or trust us, we may be tempted to think "Well, you weren't worth going to this trouble for in the first place, the hell with you, we'll go on doing things in here the old way if that is what you want." But we must resist this temptation, and keep our offer of freedom and choice out on the table even though at first it is not believed or trusted. It might be helpful, if we feel comfortable doing it, to say to the students that we understand their skepticism and suspicion, and the reasons for it, and are sympathetic rather than hurt or angry. We might even invite them to talk about their reactions to our offer. On the other hand, if students do not believe our offer they may not trust us enough to talk candidly about their reasons for not believing it. Also, they may not really know, well enough to put it into words, why they don't believe it or are afraid to make use of it.

Some may think that in all this talk of trusting and not trusting I am too cynical, making complications where none exist. In some cases, they may be right. There are many schools and classes in which the students, given this chance to plan and direct their own learning and growth, have seen it right away for a good thing and have wasted no time in making good use of it. If only it could be this way everywhere. But from experience we know that it often has not been and is often not going to be. For one thing, in offering freedom and choice to students, we may be trusting them less than we think. Many parents, and more than a few educators, have seized on the idea of the open classroom, freedom, and choice, not as a way of having students direct their own learning, explore the world in the way that seems best to them, but only as a way of getting them to do conventional schoolwork more willingly and hence more rapidly than before. In short, they believe in freedom only as a "motivating" device. This is a cruel deception, bound to lead us to disappointment. If we have such an idea anywhere in our minds, students will be aware of it, even if we are not. They will see the offer as not being real. They will know that the old hoop is still there, but hidden.

Not long ago I saw a vivid example of this. I was invited to a conference, held in a new high school, built only a few years before at a great expense, and already quite famous. The school, like most, was too big, too elaborate, too inflexible, and too ponderous. Handsome enough in its way, but without color, humor, warmth, or grace. Why do we think that humane learning can go on in buildings that look as if they were designed to hold atomic secrets? Inside, the usual bare walls, unrelieved by any decoration or human touch. The big talking point of the school was that it had been designed for a program in which the students would do a great deal of independent learning. Instead of the usual classrooms, there were a number of resource areas and centers—in Mathematics, Physical Sciences, History, and so forth. The idea was that students would have a great deal of unscheduled time that they would be free to use as they wished, going to this or that center. Though the program was only in its second year, we were told it was "not working." The students were not making good use of their time, it was said, just loafing around talking to each other. The school had to cut back on the unscheduled time and schedule more regular classes—for which the building was not well designed.

One student spoke mournfully to me about this. He had two or three very strong interests—photography, writing, and something else. He said, "Last year I had a lot of time, I could really get into these things. This year they have taken more than half of it away, and they'll probably take more away next year. But already my day is so chopped up with classes that I can't really do any serious projects in the darkroom. I might as well forget it." I asked him why the school had changed. He said, "Of course, a lot of the kids weren't doing much of anything. But they didn't give us time to find out what we might want to do. I already knew what I wanted. Most of them didn't. But at least you'd think that they'd let the students who were making good use of the program go on doing what they were interested in. But I can't get out of classes even to do projects. I have to go like everyone else. In another year or two this will just be like any other school."

If the school was sincere in its offer to the students, it was unwise to have lost heart so quickly. What would probably have happened, if they had let it, if they had had the patience to wait for it, is that more and more students, like the one I talked to, would have found things to do that they could put their whole energy into, and that gradually more and more students would have learned about this, followed their example, or been drawn into their activities. Young people naturally like to share what gives them real pleasure and satisfaction. My student friend's interest in photography would certainly in time have touched and enriched the lives of other students. But the school did not allow this to happen.

At another time during the day I was being shown around the school by someone who knew it. We went by one of the biology resources centers. It was lavishly equipped, but with few of the signs—human junk, stuff brought in, bones, skulls, skins, nests, shells—of a place where people really care about what they are doing. Five or six boys and girls were sitting in a group in the middle of the room, talking. My guide looked at them for a while through the door. Then, as we moved away, he said to me sourly, "Doesn't look to me as if they're doing much biology." In his voice there was a world of suspicion and contempt. Worse yet, satisfaction—I knew those kids were no good, and they're proving I'm right. I said mildly that for all we knew they might be talking about biology. He made no comment. I let the matter drop. What seems clear to me even now is that students must from the very first have read and understood the secret feelings of this man and perhaps many others like him. Perhaps they knew that in this school, resource centers or no, they were never really going to be allowed to learn and talk about what really mattered to them. Small wonder most of them decided to escape from the usual grind for whatever time they could.

But lack of trust in us is not the only reason why students may be slow to use the freedom and choice we offer them. Suppose we get over this first hump, and the students believe our offer is genuine. The next problem is that they may not trust themselves enough to be willing to choose. We must not be surprised at this either. They have been taught in school to distrust themselves, and they have learned. It is one of the few things that schools teach well. Everything the traditional school does says clearly to the student that he cannot be trusted to do anything, not even to make the simplest choices about what he will learn or do next or how he will do it. Nothing is left to chance or the student's own design.

To choose is to risk. Faced with a choice, the student may well think, if I have to decide what I'm going to do, how do I know that I will like it or get anything out of it. The choice may be no good. But then I'll have no one else to blame. I can't say, as at least I can if I mess up regular schoolwork, that it was the teacher's fault for asking an unfair question, or not telling me what she really wanted, or not teaching me what I was supposed to know. There is nobody to blame but me. If I fail, it will be my fault. This is too much for most children. They learn in school—another one of the few things they really do learn—that since to fail is the worst thing of all, it is best to take no chances. We must realize that when we ask or invite them to make choices we are asking them to take a risk much larger than the risks we have spent years teaching them never to take. No wonder many of them hang back. This too may be something it would be helpful to talk about.

It is not just the people we call children who find choosing difficult. A few years ago I taught at the Harvard Graduate School of Education a one-semester course called Student-Directed Learning—which came to be called T-52, its number in the catalog. Many of the students were in their early twenties, still on the schooling ladder, but many others were experienced teachers and school administrators, some as old as I was or older. At our first meeting I talked a while about how I saw the course, what I planned to do in it. I had a certain amount of resources and experiences, all having to do with student-directed or open learning, that I was going to put before them. I would talk and lead some class discussions; I had some other people coming in; the class was welcome to find and bring in people of their own. I had some films to show them of alternative schools already at work. I had a list of books and articles about open learning that had seemed to me useful, that I liked, and that I strongly recommended. If they were interested in and wanted to find out more about anything on the list, I would be glad to tell them. I also had a list of places in the area where, in different ways, student-directed learning was going on, and I encouraged them to visit such places, spend as much time there as they wanted and could arrange, and get involved in any way that might seem useful. I also said that the course was

Pass-Fail, that everyone enrolled would get a Pass, that there would be no exams or compulsory written work, that attendance at class sessions was optional.

I urged them to keep a private journal or notes, in whatever form they liked, of thoughts or reactions or observations that came up in the course of their work, inside class or out. I said that I would be very glad to read any such writing that they wanted to share with me. I said that if anyone has some ideas that he wanted to give to everyone, I would give him a ditto stencil, he could write his piece on this, and I would make copies for the whole class. I suggested that we might make up a kind of open journal, rather like the correspondence columns of some British newspapers, and magazines, in which they could write whatever thoughts they wanted others to hear, or respond in various ways to what other people had written. I said that as I found new articles, newspaper stories, or interesting material, I would post them on the walls of the classroom, and invited others to do the same—to use the walls as a kind of open bulletin board. I was full of bright ideas and suggestions.

But having proposed all this, I said that none of this was required. Here were these resources on Student-Directed Learning. They could use all of it, or any parts of it they wished, or substitute something else of their own choosing, or do nothing whatever. The class seemed satisfied with this; indeed, they shouted down one young angry who said that I was dominating the class, and why did they have to sit around and listen to what this guy Holt said, why couldn't they just get themselves together? Why did they have to sit in the chairs in this lecture hall? I said they didn't; sit on the floor or the lecturer's platform, if you like. They all came and sat on the platform. Next class they were back in the chairs—and why not, they were more comfortable.

Anyway, the class seemed to think my offer and plan were reasonable. We went along smoothly enough for six weeks or so. Nobody did any writing, nobody put anything in the journal, nobody took up most of those bright ideas. But the class sessions seemed interesting, and I knew some things were happening outside. Then at one class meeting there was an explosion. Many people in the class began to attack me about the course. They were very angry. You don't care what we think! You never tell us to write anything! You're not interested in our ideas! I repeated the suggestions and offers I had made at the beginning of the course. They said, You don't care about us, *otherwise you'd tell us what to do.* I said I did care about them, that was why I didn't want to tell them what to do. If it was true, and it seemed to be, that many of them had never had the chance to decide for themselves whether to read a book or not, write a paper or not, go to a meeting or not, then I thought it was time they decided.

Later, one of the students sympathetic to me told me about the book problem. He said, "You've no idea what a bind you put us in. Here are all these books on your list. You say they are good, and on the whole we believe you. We'd like to read them. But they are not required, we're not going to be tested on them, and meanwhile here is all this other stuff we have to do at the Ed School, more reading than we can ever get finished, a lot of it probably not as good as the stuff on your list. But those other courses are graded, and we need those grades.

So we'd better read those required books and let these books go. Then we think, 'But Holt says they are good books, and I'll bet they are. I'd like to read them.' 'But I haven't got the time!' 'But it's not fair to Holt not to read any of his reading stuff just because he said we didn't have to!' 'Not fair, hell! He *said* we didn't have to.' 'Yes, but . . . but . . .' The more we think about it, the more guilty we feel for not reading those books, and the madder we get at you for making us feel so guilty." He said all this in a good-natured way, and I laughed, and said I was sorry to make life so difficult, and I hoped someday he might read some of those books.

Part of the point here may be that it doesn't take much sense to talk of "giving freedom" to people. The most we can do is put within reach certain choices, and remove certain coercions and constraints. Whether doing this creates for other people something they sense as release, liberation, opportunity, freedom, or whether it just puts them in a more painful spot than ever, is very much up to them and how they see things. There isn't much we can do to control it. We have to assume, or at least I choose to, that in the long run more choices and fewer constraints, less coercion, less fear, is good for most people—if only because it gives them a chance to look for and maybe find something that they really want.

IV Some Strategies of Teaching

For two reasons, the reader should take careful note of the title of Part IV–"Some Strategies of Teaching." First, teaching strategies in the truest sense constitute all that teachers do in planning, implementing, and evaluating instruction. Teaching strategies, then, are what most of this book is about–not merely Part IV. Second, because of the personalized nature of teaching, there undoubtedly are as many specific strategies as there are teachers. Obviously, all such strategies could never be identified. There are, though, some basic approaches to teaching, some general strategies, that can be identified and that every prospective and practicing teacher should know. Several are considered in Part IV.

If asked, most teachers would acknowledge that their major instructional goal is to individualize instruction. Without waiting to be asked, most would hasten to add that "it's a lot easier said than done." Implied in this statement is that teachers know what individualized instruction is. But do they? According to Mitzel, in article 24, individualized instruction is defined and carried out in different ways by different people. Furthermore, in his view, none of the five most common of these ways is very satisfactory. And yet, the definition and *description of individualized instruction that Mitzel gives would be considered unsatisfactory by others. Indeed, individualized instruction is "a lot easier said than done." Perhaps one reason is that there is so much confusion about what it really is.*

Keuscher, in article 25, believes that the key ingredient in individualized instruction is involving students in all phases of instructional decision making. He believes, in other words, that students need to play a significant role not only in determining how they study (at what speed, for example), but also in selecting what they study. In Keuscher's opinion, most current attempts to individualize instruction pay most attention to the former and little, if any, to the latter.

In article 26, Burns makes two important observations. The first is that many teachers mistakenly think individualized instruction is an all-or-nothing process. Burns claims that there are degrees of individualized instruction, and that teachers need not, and probably should not, try to do everything at once. His second observation centers around a teaching strategy called performance-based instruction. According to Burns, performance-based instruction is a systematic process that has the potential of providing a tailor-made education for all learners. It is the model, he claims, of individualization.

Palardy and Eisele, in article 27, present and examine briefly several assumptions underlying competency- or performance-based programs. They claim that the key to competency-based instruction is specifying in advance terminal learning outcomes. Without this specification, competency-based instruction—as it is now known—is impossible. And yet, the authors note, it is on this very item that most educators disagree. Their debate centers not on whether learning outcomes can be specified in advance, but on whether they should be. Without question, how the debate is resolved will play a major role, not only in determining the future of competency-based education, but also, and more important, in helping clarify the meaning of individualization.

In searching for ways to individualize instruction, many teachers have tried using programmed learning materials. Very probably, some have done so without clearly understanding the rationale underlying the materials or their potential advantages and disadvantages. In article 28, Post takes the position that, conceptually, programmed instruction could have much to offer, but that, in actual practice, it offers little. Post does not blame teachers for this; rather, he blames the programmers. He reasons, first, that programmers take a too narrow view of the learning process and, second, that they write their materials in a totally uninteresting way. Post seems to think that both limitations can be overcome, but it must be added that others do not think so.

Lecture and recitation are not only two of the oldest strategies used by teachers in working with groups of students, but also two of the most criticized. Are all of the criticisms directed at lecture and recitation valid? Are there justifications for teachers' using these techniques and, if so, what are they? These are questions Hyman addresses in selection 29. It is hoped that Hyman's brief analysis of lecture and recitation will serve more as a point of departure for further analysis than as a definitive guide. For these two instructional strategies will unquestionably remain widely used. The question that does remain is to what extent they will be used wisely.

Michels and Hatcher, in article 30, advocate the use of sociodrama as a different approach to teaching and learning. Such an approach is needed, they claim, because many youth are rejecting traditional approaches that they view as outdated and irrelevant. In the article, Michels and Hatcher give several examples of the types of situations that can be presented and analyzed through sociodrama and outline the steps teachers should take in conducting it. It is my belief that perhaps the first of these steps, selecting the situation, is the most crucial. Sociodrama can deal with personal situations of an immediate and sensitive nature, or it can deal with historical and vicarious situations of less controversy. To teachers who are contemplating using sociodrama for the first time, I would strongly recommend the latter type.

In selection 31, Thelen describes a variety of tutoring activities that are currently being conducted in school systems across the nation. He reports that these activities, though taking many different forms, are consistently judged successful. Thelen admits that the basic reason for tutoring's success is unclear, but does suggest that its use in schools is partly a reaction to various forms of discrimination and competition. Thelen concludes by suggesting some potential advantages of tutoring. These include enhancing the self-esteem of tutors, increasing the chances for individualized instruction, and reducing the communication barriers between and among students, teachers, and parents.

In article 32, Dulin describes three methods that can be used to measure the difficulty of reading materials. The Fog Index is used to approximate the difficulty of materials written at or above the seventh grade level. The cloze technique is used to estimate how well students can comprehend material written at any level. And Betts' criteria are used to identify students' independent, instruction, and frustration reading levels. Utilizing some combination of these or similar techniques would seem to be an essential part of teaching today.

24 The IMPENDING Instruction Revolution

Harold E. Mitzel

First, let me explain my choice of the above title. It is fashionable in these days of rhetorical excess to describe change as revolutionary in scope. The mass media remind us daily that revolutions are occurring right under our noses. We hear of (and see) the Social Revolution, the Sexual Revolution, the Technology Revolution, the Student Revolt, the Faculty Revolt, and so on. Apparently any complete or sudden change in the conduct of human affairs, with or without a violent confrontation or an exchange of power, may properly be called a revolution.

It is my thesis that the last three decades of the twentieth century will witness a drastic change in the business of providing instruction in schools and colleges. Change by the year 2000 will be so thoroughgoing that historians will have no difficulty in agreeing that it was a revolution. You will note the omission of words like "teaching" and "learning" in describing the coming revolution. Teaching connotes for most of us an inherently person-mediated activity and the vision of the "stand-up" lecturer comes most immediately to mind. One of the concomitants of the impending change is a major modification of the role of teacher. It is likely that future terms for teacher may be "instructional agent" or "lesson designer" or "instructional programmer." As for learning, we take the position that the word is not a way of describing an *activity* of the student, but rather a way of characterizing change in the student's behavior in some desired direction between two definite time markers. Pask[1] has pointed out that teaching is "exercising control of the instructional environment by arranging scope, sequence, materials, evaluation, and content for students." In other words, instruction is the general term for the process and learning is the product.

My objective is to challenge you with the shape of the instruction revolution, to point out how you as a teacher or administrator can cooperate and cope with it, and to suggest some of the social changes which are currently fueling this revolution.

Reprinted from *Engineering Education*, 60 (7): 749–752 (March 1970), by permission of author and publisher.

[1] G. Pask, "Computer-Assisted Learning and Teaching," paper presented at Seminar on Computer-Based Learning, Leeds University, September 9–12, 1969.

INDIVIDUALIZED INSTRUCTION

At the secondary school level, American educators, beginning with Preston W. Search[2] in the late nineteenth century, have been interested in the goal of individualization. Between 1900 and 1930, disciples of Frederick Burk (see Brubacher[3] and Parkhurst[4]) devised and implemented several laboratory-type plans for self-instruction in the lower schools. These were self-pacing plans for the learner and demanded a great deal of versatility on the part of the teacher. Additional impetus for the theoretical interest of educators in individualization stemmed from the mental testing movement, beginning with the seminal work of Binet[5] about 60 years ago. Early intelligence tests clearly showed differences in speed of task completion among pupils, and these differences were easily confirmed by a teacher's own observations of mental agility. At the practical level, a great deal of individualization took place in rural America's one-room schools. Fifteen to 25 children spread unevenly through ages 6 to 14 necessarily committed the teacher to large doses of individual pupil direction, recitation, and evaluation. With population increases and school consolidations, most village and rural schools began to look like rigidly graded city schools. Teachers found themselves responsible for larger and larger groups of children of approximately the same age and about the same physical size. It is little wonder that some of the zest, enthusiasm, and obviousness of need for individualized teaching was lost. When teachers complained about too-large classes, the lack of time to spend with individual pupils, the wide diversity in pupil ability levels, many not-so-smart administrators introduced "tracking" or "streaming" strategies. Separating children into homogeneous classes according to measured mental ability within age groups has been shown conclusively to fail to increase the achievement level of groups as a whole.[6] Homogeneous ability grouping has, on the other hand, seriously exacerbated social problems connected with race and economic levels by "ghettoizing" classrooms within the schools, even though the schools served racially and economically mixed neighborhoods.

Whereas the common schools have *some* history of experimentation with individualized instruction methods, higher education, led by the large state universities, has pushed the development of mass communication methods in instruction. The large-group lecture and the adaptation of closed-circuit televi-

[2] P. W. Search, "Individual Teaching: The Pueblo Plan," *Education Review*, February, 1894, pp. 154–70.

[3] J. S. Brubacher, *A History of the Problems of Education,* 2nd ed. New York: McGraw-Hill, 1966.

[4] H. H. Parkhurst, *Education on the Dalton Plan.* New York: E. P. Dutton & Co., 1922.

[5] A. Binet and T. Simon, *The Development of Intelligence in Children,* trans. Elizabeth S. Kite. Vineland, N.J.: The Training School, 1916.

[6] J. I. Goodlad in *Encyclopedia of Educational Research,* 3rd ed., ed. C. Harris. New York: Macmillan, 1960.

sion are examples of higher education's trend away from individualized instruction. Of course, the outstanding accomplishments of American university graduate schools could never have been achieved without the cost-savings introduced by mass communications techniques in their undergraduate colleges.

Interest in individualized instruction had a surge about 15 years ago when Harvard's B. F. Skinner[7],[8] advocated an education technology built around the use of rather crude teaching machines. It soon became apparent that there was no particular magic in the machines themselves, since they contained only short linear series of questions and answers to word problems called "frames." These programs were quickly put into book form and the programmed text was born. Although it enjoyed initial success with some highly motivated learners, the programmed text has not caught on in either the lower schools or in higher education as a major instructional device. Industry and the military forces seem to have made the best use of programmed texts, perhaps because of a high degree of motivation on the part of many learners in those situations.

Most recently, an educational technique for the lower schools has been developed out of the work of the Learning Research and Development Center at the University of Pittsburgh. The method, called "individually prescribed instruction" or IPI, is described by Lindvall and Bolvin,[9] by Glaser,[10] and by Cooley and Glaser.[11] Behind the method lies the careful development of a technology based on precise specification and delineation of educational objectives in behavioral terms. Pupils work individually on a precisely scaled set of materials with frequent interspersed diagnostic quizzes.

It must be clear, even after this sketchy review of the history of individualized instruction, that the concept has been pursued in a desultory fashion. I have heard hour-long conversations on individualization by educators who have only the vaguest notion of what is encompassed by the concept. Let me review five *different* concepts of individualization and acknowledge that I am indebted to Tyler[12] for some of these distinctions.

[7] B. F. Skinner, "The Science of Learning and the Art of Teaching," *Harvard Educational Review,* Spring, 1954, pp. 86–97.

[8] B. F. Skinner, "Teaching Machines," *Science,* 128, 1958, pp. 969–77.

[9] C. M. Lindvall and J. O. Bolvin, "Programed Instruction in the Schools: An Application of Programing Principles in Individually Prescribed Instruction," in *Programed Instruction,* ed. P. C. Lange. The Sixty-Sixth Yearbook of the National Society for the Study of Education, Part II. Chicago: The University of Chicago Press, 1967, pp. 217–54.

[10] R. Glaser, *The Education of Individuals.* Pittsburgh, Pa.: Learning Research and Development Center, University of Pittsburgh, 1966.

[11] W. W. Cooley and R. Glaser, "An Information Management System for Individually Prescribed Instruction," Working Paper No. 44, Learning Research and Development Center, University of Pittsburgh, mimeographed, 1968.

[12] R. W. Tyler, "New Directions in Individualizing Instruction," in *The Abington Conference '67 on New Directions in Individualizing Instruction.* Abington, Pa.: The Conference, 1967.

First, most educators agree that instruction is "individual" when the learner is allowed to proceed through content materials at a *self-determined pace that is comfortable for him.* This concept of self-paced instruction is incorporated into all programmed texts and is perhaps easiest to achieve with reading material and hardest to achieve in a setting that presents content by means of lectures, films, and television. Oettinger,[13] in his witty but infuriating little book, *Run, Computer, Run,* refers to this self-pacing concept of individualization as "rate tailoring."

A second concept of individualized instruction is that the learner should be able *to work at times convenient to him.* The hard realities of academic book-keeping with the associated paraphernalia of credits, marks, and time-serving schedules make this concept difficult to implement in colleges or in the common schools.

That a learner should *begin instruction in a given subject at a point appropriate to his past achievement* is a third way of looking at individualization. This concept makes the assumption that progress in learning is linear and that the main task is to locate the learner's present position on a universal continuum. Once properly located, he can then continue to the goal. These notions seem to have their optimum validity for well-ordered content like mathematics or foreign languages. In fact, the advanced placement program, which provides college credit for tested subject matter achievement during secondary school, is a gross attempt to get at this kind of individualization.

A fourth concept of individualization is the idea that *learners are inhibited by a small number of easily identifiable skills or knowledges.* The assumption is that the absence of these skills is diagnosable and that remedial efforts through special instructional units can eliminate the difficulty. Colleges and universities seeking to enroll a higher proportion of their students from among the culturally disadvantaged and the economically deprived will be forced to bring this concept to bear if they wish to maintain current academic standards.

A fifth concept is that individualization can be achieved by *furnishing the learner with a wealth of instructional media from which to choose.* Lectures, audio tapes, films, books, etc., all with the same intellectual content, could theoretically be made available to the learner. The underlying notion is that the learner will instinctively choose the communication medium or combination of media that enable him to do his best work. The research evidence to support this viewpoint and practice is not at all strong.[14] Perhaps even more persuasive than the lack of evidence is the vanity of instructors who cannot understand why a student would choose a film or an audio tape in preference to the instructor's own lively, stimulating, and informative lectures.[15]

[13] A. G. Oettinger and S. Marks, *Run, Computer, Run.* Cambridge, Mass.: Harvard University Press, 1969.

[14] S. N. Postlethwait, "Planning for Better Learning," in *In Search of Leaders,* ed. G. K. Smith, Washington, D.C.: American Association for Higher Education, NEA, 1967, pp. 110–13.

[15] D. T. Tosti and J. T. Ball, *A Behavioral Approach to Instructional Design and Media Selection,* BSD Paper Number 1, Observations in Behavioral Technology, Albuquerque, N.M.: The Behavior Systems Division, Westinghouse Learning Corporation, 1969.

I have reviewed five concepts of individualization which have some credence in education, but by far the most prevalent interpretation is the one of self-pacing, or rate tailoring. These notions lead us directly to the idea of adaptive education in responsive environments, which I want to discuss shortly. But first, one more distinction. "Individual instruction," where one studies in isolation from other learners, should probably be distinguished from "individualized instruction," where the scope, sequence, and time of instruction are tailored in one or more of the five ways I have just described. "Individualized instruction" can still be in a group setting and, in fact, was commonly practiced in rural one-room schools, as mentioned earlier. On the other hand, "individual instruction" can be singularly rigid, monotonous, and unresponsive to the needs of the learner. You could, for instance, take programmed text material which is designed for individualized instruction and put it into an educational television format. Each frame could be shown to a large group of students for a short time, allowing the students to pick a correct option and then going on to another frame. This procedure would be individual instruction with a vengeance. But it forces a kind of lockstep on students of varying abilities and interests that is the antithesis of "individualized instruction."

ADAPTIVE EDUCATION

I predict that the impending instruction revolution will shortly bypass the simple idea of individualizing instruction and move ahead to the more sophisticated notion of providing *adaptive education* for school and college learners. By adaptive education we mean the tailoring of subject matter presentations to fit the special requirements and capabilities of each learner. The ideal is that no learner should stop short of his ultimate achievement in an area of content because of idiosyncratic hang-ups in his particular study strategies.

We have seen how the concept of individualized instruction has been pretty well arrested at the level of encouraging the learner to vary and control his task completion time. Many additional, more psychologically oriented variables will have to be brought into play to achieve the goals of adaptive education, as well as the adoption of individualizing techniques. We know a great deal about individual differences among people in regard to their sensory inputs, their reaction times, their interests, their values and preferences, and their organizational strategies in "mapping" the cognitive world. What we do not know very much about is the extent to which, or how, these easily tested, individual difference variables affect the acquisition and retention of new knowledge. Psychological learning theory has been preoccupied with the study of variables in extremely simple stimulus-response situations, and investigations of meaningful learning phenomena have clearly dealt with human subjects as if they were all cut from the same bolt. The exception to this observation is, of course, the variable of measured mental ability, which has been shown to be related to achievement in conventionally presented instruction and has been carefully controlled in many learning experiments involving human subjects.

Essential to the idea of adaptive education is the means of utilizing new knowledge about individual differences among learners to bring a highly tailored instructional product to the student. As long as we are dealing with static or canned linear presentations such as those contained in books, films, video tapes, and some lectures, there seems to be little incentive to try to discover what modifications in instructional materials would optimize learning for each student. To plug this important gap in the drive toward vastly improved learning, the modern digital computer seems to have great promise. About a decade ago, Rath, Anderson, and Brainerd[16] suggested the application of the computer to teaching tasks and actually programmed some associative learning material. In the intervening decade, a number of major universities, medical schools, industries, and military establishments have been exploring the use of the computer in instruction. Five years ago we instituted a computer-assisted instruction laboratory at Penn State and have been trying to perfect new instructional techniques within the constraints of available hardware and computer operating systems.[17,18,19,20] There are, according to my estimate, some 35 to 40 active computer-assisted instruction (CAI) installations operating in the world today, and fewer than 100 completed, semester-length courses or their equivalent. Almost none of these courses have been constructed according to the ideals I mentioned for adaptive education. Indeed, many of them look like crude, made-over versions of programmed textbooks, but this does not disturb me when I recall that the earliest automobiles were designed to look like carriages without the horses. The fact is that the modern computer's information storage capacity and decision logic have given us a glimpse of what a dynamic, individualized instruction procedure could be, and some insight into how this tool might be brought to bear to achieve an adaptive quality education for every student. We do not claim that the achievement of this goal is just around the corner or that every school and college can implement it by the turn of the

[16] G. J. Rath, N. S. Anderson, and R. C. Brainerd, "The IBM Research Center Teaching Machine Project," in *Automatic Teaching: The State of the Art,* ed. E. H. Galanter, New York: Wiley, 1959, pp. 117–30.

[17] H. E. Mitzel, *The Development and Presentation of Four College Courses by Computer Teleprocessing.* Final Report, Computer-Assisted Instruction Laboratory, The Pennsylvania State University, June 30, 1967. Contract No. OE-4-16-010, New Project No. 5-1194, U.S. Office of Education.

[18] H. E. Mitzel, B. R. Brown, and R. Igo, *The Development and Evaluation of a Teleprocessed Computer-Assisted Instruction Course in the Recognition of Malarial Parasites.* Final Report No. R-I7, Computer-Assisted Instruction Laboratory, The Pennsylvania State University, June 30, 1968. Contract No. N00014-67-A-0385-0003, Office of Naval Research.

[19] H. E. Mitzel, *Experimentation with Computer-Assisted Instruction in Technical Education.* Semi-annual progress report, R-18, Computer-Assisted Instruction Laboratory, The Pennsylvania State University, December 31, 1968.

[20] "Inquiry," Research Report published by Office of the Vice President for Research, Penn State.

century. We do believe that progress toward a program of adaptive education will be the big difference between our best schools and our mediocre ones at the end of the next three decades.

What individual difference variables look most promising for adapting instruction to the individual student via CAI? At Penn State we are testing the idea that a person learns best if he is rewarded for correctness with his most preferred type of reinforcement.[21] Thus some students will, we believe, learn more rapidly if they receive encouragement in the form of adult approval. Others will perform better if they receive actual tokens for excellence at significant places in the program, the tokens being exchangeable for candy, cokes, or other wanted objects. Still others respond to competitive situations in which they are given evidence of the superiority or inferiority of their performance compared to that of their peers. It is a fairly simple matter to determine a learner's reward preference in advance of instruction and to provide him with a computer-based program in which the information feedback is tailored to his psychological preference.

Perhaps the most dynamic and relevant variable on which to base an adaptive program of instruction is the learner's immediate past history of responses. By programming the computer to count and evaluate the correctness of the 10 most recent responses, it is possible to determine what comes next for each learner according to a prearranged schedule. For example, four or fewer correct out of the most recent 10 might dictate branching into shorter teaching steps with heavy prompting and large amounts of practice material. A score of five to seven might indicate the need for just a little more practice material, and eight or more correct out of the 10 most recent problems would suggest movement onto a fast "track" with long strides through the computer-presented content. The dynamic part of this adaptive mechanism is that the computer constantly updates its performance information about each learner by dropping off the learner's response to the tenth problem back as it adds on new performance information from a just-completed problem.

There are two rather distinct strategies for presenting subject matter to learners. One is *deductive,* in which a rule, principle, or generalization is presented, followed by examples. The other strategy is *inductive* and seeks, by means of a careful choice of illustrative examples, to lead the learner into formulating principles and generalizations on his own initiative. In the lower schools, inductive method is called "guided discovery" and has been found useful by many teachers. Our belief at the Penn State CAI Laboratory is that these two presentation strategies have their corollaries in an individual differences variable and that, for some students, learning will be facilitated by the deductive approach; others will learn more rapidly and with better retention if an inductive mode is adopted. A strong program of adaptive education would take these and other identifiable learner variables into account in the instructional process.

[21] C. A. Cartwright and G. P. Cartwright, *Reward Preference Profiles of Elementary School Children,* mimeographed, Computer- Assisted Instruction Laboratory, The Pennsylvania State University, 1969. Paper presented at the meeting of the American Educational Research Association, Los Angeles, February, 1969.

25 Individualization of Instruction: What It Is and What It Isn't

Robert E. Keuscher

There are several generalizations one can make about individualization of instruction today. First, it's "in." Everyone is in favor of individualizing. Second, most teachers will look you squarely in the eye and tell you they are individualizing instruction to some extent in their classrooms. Which leads naturally to the third generalization, that there are easily as many definitions of what individualization is as there are people attempting to do it. Fourth, every major producer of instructional materials and equipment in this country is peddling one or more sure-fire gimmicks to enable teachers to individualize. And last, but surely the most disconcerting, is that very few, if any, of the different modes of individualization or the kits, packages, and programs purported to help teachers individualize, do much of anything for the individual; in fact, they may do much to stifle the learner's initiative, his creativity, and his independence.

INDIVIDUALIZATION IS "IN"

It is easy to account for enthusiasm for individualization of instruction. Primarily, it is a natural reaction against the impersonal, mass-production methods we have been using in education. The idea of a teacher standing before a class of 30 or more youngsters attempting to teach the same lesson to all of them at the same time is preposterous. It defies all we know about the wide range of differences that exist within the group. It negates what we know about motivation, about children's needs, their interests, their creative capabilities. Nor does dividing 30 kids into 3 groups do anything to make instruction more effective. The teacher must get closer to the individual pupil than that—at least ten times closer!

If learning is to be meaningful to children they need a voice in deciding what they study and when and how they study it. Children must see the utility of what they are learning. We're a long way down the road from the time when adults (curriculum committees, textbook writers, teachers) can play God, hand-

Reprinted from *The California Journal for Instructional Improvement*, 14 (2): 53–59 (May 1971), by permission of author.

ing down the decisions as to what students must study "from on high." All we've done with that kind of behavior—and educators are beginning to realize it *finally*—is turn kids off, make exhortation the number one task of teachers, and increase classroom discipline problems. Older students are complaining about "relevancy." The younger children would, too, if they knew the word. Far too much of what we have been handing out as required curriculum is not relevant to children at the time we confront them with it. The term "individualize instruction" to me means bringing the decision-making about curriculum closer to the individual learner. Unless he participates in the decisions, the planning, the goal-setting, let's not pretend we are "individualizing" anything. The term just doesn't apply.

TEACHERS DELUDE THEMSELVES

Most teachers recognize the myriad of differences that exist among children, but they have never really faced the possibility of adequately meeting such a great range of diversity. Rather, they tinker with the organizational structure or the assignment requirements and honestly believe they are individualizing.

It is very difficult for most teachers to visualize a classroom where everyone is busy working alone, in pairs, or in groups of three to eight on a variety of projects spanning several subject areas at one time, while the teacher moves freely about the classroom lending a hand here, making a suggestion there, asking an appropriate question or two here, receiving a progress report there. Teachers who work in this manner tell me they have never known their students so well and have never seen boys and girls so excited about schooling.

Teachers have to quit kidding themselves about how individualization takes place. To really do it, they must know their children like they've never known them before. This means listening to students much more than they have previously, observing students more than they have in the past, and permitting students to incorporate their own needs and interests into the instructional program. The teacher will do far less "teaching" in such a program and much more facilitating, or helping learning take place.

MOST PROGRAMS MISS THEIR MARK

With so many different versions of what constitutes individualized instruction, it is inevitable that most individualized programs fall far short of their mark. One thing is increasingly clear to me as I visit so-called individualized classrooms. There is no possibility of attending to the diversity we find there without increasing many times over the number of options available to students. Children must have choices as to what to study and how to study it.

Providing alternatives for students dictates a different kind of classroom environment than the desk and textbook-dominated rooms we now have, most of them so tidy and formal that they bore the teacher as well as the pupils. "Chalk and talk classrooms," one visiting British educator dubbed these unexciting boxes we cage our children in while we talk and they sit passively and listen. And then we wonder why they begin to turn off as early as second or third grade and learn to dislike school!

Learning should be an exciting activity and to make it so, schools have to be exciting places. There have to be projects for children to do, problems for them to investigate, ideas for them to read and write and calculate about, activities that are fun as well as educational, and experiences to whet the interest of pupils of different levels of maturity, of different backgrounds and cultures. There should be books and books and books—not textbooks, but library books—books so plentiful, so colorful, and so broad in their interest appeal that one would almost defy a child not to find several that turn him on. There should be interest areas for science including experiments with plants and animals, a microscope, a dry cell battery or two, mealworms, tropical fish, perhaps a salt-water aquarium, small animals, rocks, shells, insect collection boxes, and a lot of common, inexpensive science supplies.

There should be a mathematics center. Here is a place where students can weigh, measure, time, and graph their data. It contains yardsticks, tape measures, rulers, a click wheel, balances, two or three different kinds of scales, a stop watch or two, and of course things to weigh and balance—beans, pebbles, nuts, blocks. Also found in such a center are paper, yarn, and other materials necessary for pictorial representation of findings.

There should be a language arts center with all kinds of suggestions and incentives to help motivate children to write. An old typewriter or two is a must for this center as well as the materials needed to make hard back covers for the "books" children will write.

There should be a quiet corner for research or just plain reading. A piece of used carpet, an old sofa or rocking chair, and several large pillows can make this area the most popular in the room.

Other attractions might include a junk art area, the "tinker table" where children dismantle old clocks, radios, and electrical appliances that the teacher has picked up at the repair shop where they were about to be discarded. Also one might find a puppet theater or drama corner, a sewing or knitting center, an educational game area.

Where does one find room for all of this? In the regular classroom! But most or all of the students' desks are removed. Bookcases and tables properly placed divide the room into the various areas and students keep their belongings in tote trays or individual cubby holes in a cabinet along one wall.

Students are encouraged to bring materials for the room. Parents get in on the act. It's surprising what an exciting environment can be built in a short time when everyone pitches in. Surprising, too, will be the different attitude students have about the room when they feel it is "their" room.

It won't take a lot of money to set up a room along the lines suggested. In fact, you will find it much less expensive. The classrooms I visited in Great

Britain were simply "rich" with materials for children to work with despite the fact that the expenditure per pupil is only a small fraction of what we spend in this country.

One thing is certain. You will not need to purchase many of the products currently appearing on the market and advertised as facilitating individualization.

GIMMICKS AND PACKAGES AREN'T THE ANSWER

Most materials and programs marketed in the name of individualization do very little over and beyond adjusting the pace with which the student wades through the prescribed assignments. Everyone covers the same material (what allowances for differences exist here?)—some just go through faster than others.

Another indictment of most programmed or computer-assisted materials is that they teach only those facts and understandings that are going to show up on the tests. Both information and answers are decided beforehand by some "all-knowing" person or group of people who, although they do not know, have never seen, nor ever will see the pupil, has decided what he should learn and the manner in which he should learn it.

Let's face it! What programmed materials do is indoctrinate, with no concern whatsoever for the individual's rights in the matter. And they can indoctrinate for any purpose desired. I'm sure that Adolph Hitler, if he were alive and training German youth today, would be using many of the same kinds of materials and methods that are being urged upon teachers in this country as aids to individualization. Proponents claim their programmed materials and methods to be a more efficient way of educating. They may be right, if we are willing to accept the premise that what we are trying to do is get our students to learn a specified, fixed block of knowledge. But is there such a block of knowledge that everyone must have? If so, who determines what that knowledge is? And is our methodology in exposing the child to that knowledge going to accomplish what is intended? I'm fully convinced that in our zeal to teach some children to read through the high pressure tactics of computer assistance, systems approaches, and programming, we may be raising reading scores but turning children so against reading that they will never enjoy it again as long as they live!

Individualizing instruction along the lines of diagnosis and prescription, pre-testing, and post-testing, through behavioral objectives, is a manipulative method of teaching. It stresses what is to be taught and how it is to be taught with little or no regard for the feelings of the individual. He becomes a pawn in the process. There is NO way we can develop a zest for learning, self-confidence, rational thinking, independence, and responsibility through the programmed approach to learning.

Educators who grasp such methods hoping they'll solve all problems ought to be smarter than that. They should realize that all they are going to reap is more disinterest and alienation. If there is anything children DO NOT NEED at this time, it is more manipulation, more distance between pupil and teacher. Schooling is far too impersonal now. What we need desperately to do today is to PERSONALIZE our teaching.

IT'S WHAT HAPPENS TO THE PERSON THAT MATTERS

Most attempts at individualization fail to do much, if anything, for the individual, his self-concept, his feeling about school. I'm convinced we must start with the learner before we worry about reading or mathematics. If a child doesn't feel pretty good about himself, have some confidence in his ability to succeed, and if he doesn't feel good about school, enjoy being there, look forward to returning each day, find it an exciting, fun place to be, we aren't going to accomplish much with reading or any other content we try to teach. *We must work on first things first.* The child's feelings about himself and about school precede all other concerns.

This cannot be accomplished with a machine, nor can it be programmed . It takes a teacher who gives primacy to the feelings of his children and to the personal development of each member of his class to turn students on to learning. Place that teacher who is personalizing his instruction in the rich environment that every teacher owes his pupils, and learning is going to take place. There is no way to prevent it! Furthermore, creativity will flourish, relationships between students (a great concern to many of the teachers I know today) will become less aggressive and more warmly cooperative, and boys and girls will not only learn to read but learn to love reading!

Personalized teaching (I prefer that term over individualized) is not a program; it's a way of performing in the classroom, based on a set of values about children and schooling. It's not a method; it's an attitude.

Most British schools have moved dramatically in this direction, and I have never seen more turned-on, happy, productive students than those I saw there on a recent visit. Over there, they call it Open Education and I recall one primary school Head who told me, "It's not a program we have, it's a way of living!"

I think it is a way of life based on a genuine concern for our most precious resource, our children. Whether we call it Personalized Instruction or Open Education or stick by the oft-misused term Individualized Instruction, it is urgent that we educators re-examine our programs with special concern for one question regarding what we are now doing—"What is happening to the person in the process?"

READINGS
1. Association for Supervision and Curriculum Development. *To Nurture Humanness.* ASCD Yearbook, 1970.
2. Holt, John. *What Do I Do Monday?* New York: E. P. Dutton & Co., Inc., 1970.
3. Howes, Virgil M., Helen F. Darrow, Robert E. Keuscher, and Louise L. Tyler. *Individualization of Instruction: Exploring Open-Structure.* Los Angeles:

ASUCLA Students' Store, 308 Westwood Plaza, Los Angeles, CA 90024, 1968.
4. Howes, Virgil M., ed. *Individualization of Instruction, A Teaching Strategy.* New York: 1970.
5. Kohl, Herbert R. *The Open Classroom.* New York: The New York Review, 1969.
6. Rogers, Vincent R. *Teaching in the British Primary School.* New York: Macmillan Publishing Co., Inc., 1970.
7. Silberman, Charles. *Crisis in the Classroom,* New York: Random House, 1970.

26 Methods for Individualizing Instruction

Richard Burns

Teachers frequently inquire about individualized instruction—they intuitively feel (and rightly so) that as a method it has a lot to offer in improving classroom learning. However, with present facilities, materials, curricular organization and administrative constrictions, it is difficult to achieve little other than token individualization of learning. In practice, there are degrees of individualized instruction (hereafter designated as I-I) ranging from idealized methods to the use of single operating features which are a start in the right direction.

The basis for believing that I-I is educationally desirable resides in the nature of man. *No two living organisms are alike.* If this statement is true, and all evidence appears to support it, then basically we are lead to the assumptions that:

1. No two learners achieve at the same rate.
2. No two learners achieve using the same study techniques.
3. No two learners solve problems in exactly the same way.
4. No two learners possess the same repertoire of behaviors.
5. No two learners possess the same pattern of interests.
6. No two learners are motivated to achieve to the same degree.
7. No two learners are motivated to achieve the same goals.

Reprinted from *Educational Technology,* 11 (6): 55–56 (June 1971), by permission of publisher.

8. No two learners are ready to learn at the same time.
9. No two learners have exactly the same capacity to learn.

Coupling these nine assumptions with variations in city, home and school environments, it is easy to see how learning for the individual must be, to some degree, unique. Perhaps in reality, small differences between individuals may not demand I-I; however, in many cases the differences are not small, and hundreds of years of educational experience have repeatedly confirmed the futility of looking for the *one* method which, if used by teachers, will reach each learner. No one textbook has been found which will adequately serve a given classroom, no one explanation of a concept reaches each learner, and so on, to each classroom feature or practice. All evidence seems to support the idea that learning is a unique process.

What then is I-I? Earlier it was indicated that there is an ideal concept and, in practice, there are degrees of individualization which do not take into account all the features of the ideal. *Ideally, individualized instruction is a system which tailor-makes learning in terms of learner needs and characteristics*. This is to say, I-I concerns itself mainly with the three variables:

a. objectives;
b. study habits;
c. time.

In relation to the first variable, objectives, I-I is based on the learner: his needs, desires, wishes, skills and motives. Learners need to achieve different goals or objectives in the various areas of their learning. Ideally, I-I attempts to give the learner the opportunity to achieve uniquely in relation to what he already knows and what he is attempting to learn. To provide this type of "tailor-made" instruction for the learners, there must be a minimum of two instructional features present:

a. learner diagnosis;
b. a variety of curricular units (modules, lessons, etc.).

If the learner is to profit (achieve faster, achieve more or remember longer) from I-I, then whatever instruction he receives *must take into account present behaviors and some idea of his objectives*. The student must be given some latitude in selection of his learning objectives. A diagnostic analysis is necessary to establish the subject matter proficiency or subject readiness of the learner. Has he achieved (acquired the proper behaviors) to some minimum level which will permit him to profit from the coming instruction? Also, is the ensuing instruction related or necessary for his (the learner's) education? This implies that what he is to learn is known to be necessary by adults, experts in the field, or is desired by the learner. Some objectives may be attained solely because the learner "wants" to attain them for his personal reasons. Since each learner will *need* and/or *want* different things, a variety of things to be learned must be available. First, there must be rich curricular offerings by way of different subject matter to learn; and second, each learner should be permitted to achieve as far (or deeply) into a subject as his talents permit.

The second variable, study habits, also demands two instructional features, namely:

a. learner diagnosis;
b. a variety of teaching materials and aids.

If the learner is to profit from I-I, then the instruction he receives must take into account his strengths and weaknesses as far as study habits and ability to learn are concerned. His reading level; reading rate; preference for visual, auditory or tactile learning; ability to conclude; ability to summarize; ability to compare; ability to translate; ability to abstract; ability to infer; ability to express himself orally; ability to express himself in writing; and possibly other skills, or lack of them, must be taken into account. In order to effectively implement the results of such a diagnostic analysis of the learner, a variety of teaching materials and aids must be available. Tapes and recorders, filmstrips, film loops, reading materials designed for a variety of levels, maps, charts, drills and dozens of other types of aids need to be readily accessible for learner use. In addition, many teaching strategies should be employed.

Time, the third variable, must be flexible for I-I. Some learners proceed slowly and others rapidly because of a variety of reasons, such as: (1) intelligence, (2) study habits, (3) prior learning, (4) motivation, (5) competitive pressures, (6) social/family pressure, (7) physical/physiological status and (8) additional causes. Synthesizing these three variables into an effective I-I program takes considerable instructional insight, effort and cooperation. The learner must cooperate with the instructor (guider of the learning process), and the instructor must receive administrative support. I-I implies more guidance of learners as they learn and less emphasis on the traditional role of teaching, the imparting of knowledge.

Implementation of this idealized concept of I-I in the classroom is enhanced if the program is subdivided into small, manageable parts and a systematic method for dealing with the parts is established. One common method is to provide the learning sequences in the form of *modules*. Modules are difficult to define, as they vary greatly in their length, composition and degree of organization. Generally, however, and as the term is used here, modules are short (1-3 hours) organized, learning sequences. Each module develops one, or at most a very few, terminal behaviors.

A flow chart of one unit in a modular system is depicted in Figure 1. The learner (L) enters the system and is given a diagnostic test (DE) to determine if he has the necessary behaviors required to profit from the planned instruction. If he does not have the prerequisite behaviors, he is sent for remedial instruction so that he can acquire the entering behaviors. If he has the prerequisites, he then is

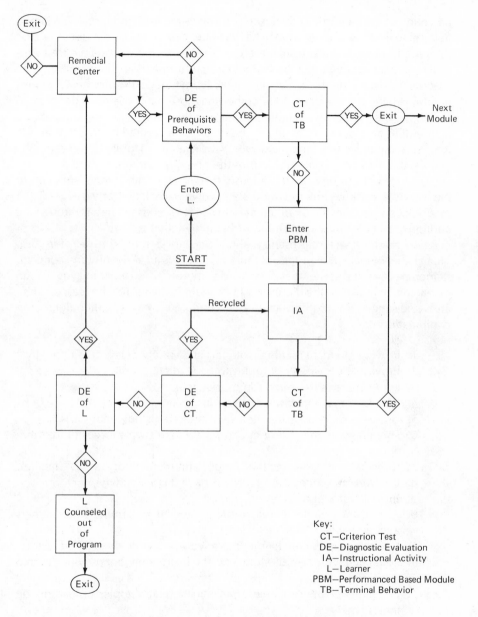

FIGURE 1. Flow Chart—Performance Based Module System

given the criterion test (CT) for the module to determine if he already has the terminal behaviors (TB) the module is intended to develop. If the learner already has the behaviors, he goes to the next module; but if he does not, he enters the performance based modules (PBM) for instruction. After the learner has participated in the instructional activities (IA), he takes the criterion test (CT) again to determine if he has acquired the behaviors intended. If the learner does not pass the criterion test, the test results are examined to see if there is a clue to his problem. If it is thought that the learner can profit from going back through the module (or parts of it), he is recycled. However, if the analysis of his CT shows that he is having great difficulty, another diagnostic analysis is made to try to determine the reason for his failure to learn. If the diagnostic evaluation of the learner (DE of L) points to a cause which can be remedied by instruction, the learner is referred to the remedial center. If the evaluation turns up non-remedial causes, the learner is counseled out of the program (the set of modules) .

The system just described obviously tries to tailor-make the instruction to the learner and allows him to progress at his own pace. If properly designed, the modules can also provide for differences in learning modes or habits through the appropriate choice and application of learning activities.

The modular system presented above was not described to *sell* it *in toto*. That is, do not make the mistake of thinking that I-I is an all-or-nothing concept. Remember, we said earlier that there are degrees of I-I, and anything you can do in teaching which is in the direction of I-I should be helpful to the learner. Here are some suggestions of things that can be done quite easily, either alone or in combination.

1. Provide alternate reading materials at a variety of levels of difficulty.
2. Provide for a variety of topics to be studied.
3. Let learners select some topics they want to study.
4. Let learners help set the goals of instruction.
5. Let learners study using their own preferred study habits.
6. Encourage learners to hunt and locate their own sources of information.
7. Provide for a variety of modes for learning (auditory, visual, tactile).
8. Let learners proceed at their own pace (fast or slowly).
9. Provide tutorial help.
10. Devise and administer diagnostic pre-tests to determine what learners already know.
11. If it is known that the learner has already acquired the desired instructional behaviors, excuse him from the instruction, but provide alternative things to learn.
12. Encourage learners to select and pursue related topics of learning on their own.
13. Provide for supplementary and concurrent projects for students to pursue.
14. Encourage students who are having difficulty in learning to try new, alternative methods of study, until they find study techniques which work for them.
15. Devise and administer diagnostic pretests to ensure that learners pos-

sess the prerequisite knowledges, understandings and skills needed to achieve the next set of things to be learned.

16. Provide a variety of visual, auditory and tactile materials to aid learners.
17. Provide remedial instruction for learners who need it before they attempt to learn new sets of materials.
18. Provide remedial instruction during the learning of the new set of materials.

Individualizing instruction really is nothing more than applying logic to the learning act, and then, by careful planning and organization, providing an efficient method whereby learners have the opportunity to acquire behaviors in their own way at their own rate.

In addition to individualizing the instruction in terms of the three main variables—objectives, study habits and time—it is helpful to consider other factors which will enhance learning. One such factor is response confirmation—feedback and reinforcement; another is application or practice (preferably distributed); a third is readiness.

Methods and teaching strategies also are closely related to I-I. The utilization of team teaching, non-graded instruction, discussion seminars and small group techniques can enhance and contribute to an I-I system. More closely related are micro techniques, flexible scheduling, continuous progress systems, contract methods and independent study. Each of these methods and strategies can contribute in some way to implementing the 18 suggestions for I-I, as listed previously.

In summary, I-I appears to be a natural way of learning, and in the long run it may be the answer to part of the problems currently facing school systems. I-I is not a single thing in practice, which is done or not done, but a concept of instruction which takes into account learners' needs, habits of study and time. With a little effort, each teacher can find some way and time to provide one or more methods, strategies or applications of opportunity pointing in the direction of I-I.

27 Competency Based Education

J. Michael Palardy and James E. Eisele

The dialogue revolving around competency based education (CBE) is having a predictable impact on the educational community. Proponents see in CBE the best chance for needed reform. Critics posit that CBE is mechanistic; that it is based upon an engineering model and, consequently, inappropriate for an area whose goal is to mold better human beings, not to build better submarines, aircraft, or bridges. And others in the educational community, still the majority we suspect, simply do not know enough about CBE to take a definitive, or even tentative, stand.

CBE is defined in various ways. In its simplest form, however, it means that the recipient (the prospective learner) must be able to demonstrate mastery or attainment of specified criteria. These criteria can be stated so that they include areas in the cognitive, affective, and psychomotor domains and encompass all phases of education—from the preprimary to the graduate.

Competency, of course, is the important concept, the *sine qua non* of CBE. The learner will have X number of reading skills, he will differentiate among geometric forms with Y per cent accuracy, he will know Z number of economic concepts, and so on. This is different from the usual approach of saying: Given X amount of time, we will teach the learner to the best of his and our ability. In this latter approach, time is the major limiting factor; in CBE, time is said to be basically inconsequential.

Given this emphasis on competency, CBE may sound anachronistic—a page out of education's past, not a blueprint for its future. But, as conceptualized, CBE is not a return to the days when all learners, regardless of cognitive, social, or emotional differences, were expected to master the same sterile subject matter, in the same rote way, in the same allotment of time. An examination of three of the major assumptions underlying CBE should help clarify this point (1).

ASSUMPTIONS

(1) *CBE should have at its base detailed descriptions of the behavioral outcomes expected of the learner.* Although already alluded to, this assumption

Reprinted from *The Clearing House*, 46 (9): 545–548 (May 1972), by permission of authors and publisher.

deserves additional comment because, of all the assumptions underlying CBE, the emphasis on behavioral outcomes is probably the most controversial.

Behavioral outcomes are variously referred to as behavioral objectives, performance goals, operational objectives, and instructional objectives. But regardless of the nomenclature employed, most would agree that statements of behavioral outcomes should meet three criteria: (a) the behavior itself must be identified, (b) the important conditions under which the behavior is to occur must be defined, and (c) the criterion of acceptable performance must be specified (2).

When these criteria are met, the result looks something like the following:

The student must be able to reply in grammatically correct French to 95% of the French questions that are put to him during an examination (2:50).

Or:

The student must be able to spell correctly at least 80% of the words called out to him during an examination (2:50).

The advantages of stating educational outcomes in behavioral terms are increasingly becoming recognized. Advantages include: giving meaning to broad statements of educational goals, giving direction to the design of instructional strategies, and making obvious the methods used in evaluation. These, proponents argue, are critical elements in the search for a more effective and efficient system of public education.

But critics of behavioral objectives point out several potential dangers. One danger revolves around the issue of responsibility. Does the teacher write his own objectives? Or does he use objectives which have been preestablished by experts? The critics argue that the teacher seldom has time to do the former, and that he jeopardizes the unique aspirations of his class by opting for the latter.

Another potential danger is well stated by Atkin:

If identification of all worthwhile outcomes in behavioral terms comes to be commonly accepted and expected, then it is inevitable that, over time, the curriculum will tend to emphasize those elements which have been thus identified. Important outcomes which are detected only with great difficulty and which are translated only rarely into behavioral terms tend to atrophy. They disappear from the curriculum because we spend all the time allotted to us in teaching explicitly for the more readily specifiable learnings to which we have been directed (3:28).

Because even proponents admit that behavioral outcomes are specified more readily in some areas than in others, for example in the cognitive domain than in the affective, Atkin's concern cannot easily be dismissed.

Other potential dangers, as well as advantages, could be listed. That, however, is not the intent. The intent is only to illustrate that the first, and presumably the most critical, assumption underlying CBE is currently being debated. How that debate is resolved will in large measure determine CBE's future.

(2) *CBE should provide for differences among learners in terms of their accumulated experience, extent of achievement, and rate and style of learning.* In other words, CBE is based on the principle of individualized instruction and learning. Individualization is effected in most such programs within the five-stage framework presented below.

The first stage is establishing for any given school activity, such as a course or a unit of work, a listing of behavioral outcomes. These outcomes are then grouped together and sequenced in some kind of logical order. On the basis of this grouping, a certain number of sets or categories of behavioral outcomes emerges. The sets are often referred to as learning modules. To repeat, each learning module begins with a sequence of behaviorally stated outcomes.

The second stage is diagnosis. Here it is determined whether the prospective learner has the prerequisite competencies to engage in the work set forth in a particular learning module. If the focus of the learning module is long division, for example, the learner must demonstrate that he can add, subtract, and multiply. If the learner lacks one of these skills, he is recycled into other learning modules which have that particular skill as their major focus.

The third stage in the process is pretesting. Assuming that the learner has the prerequisite competencies, he is pretested. The pretests are designed to assess which of the behaviors spelled out in the learning module the learner possesses. If the learner has none of the behaviors, he enters the learning module at its beginning point. If he has some of the behaviors, he enters the module at that point which is commensurate with his level of competence. If the learner has all the behaviors which are spelled out in a particular module, he exits the module and begins work on another.

The fourth stage is a series of alternate learning activities. Obviously, all activities are designed to help lead the learner toward mastery of the module's objectives. Each activity, however, is structured differently in an attempt to accommodate a particular style of learning. Based on how he learns best, then, the learner makes his choice(s) of activities and proceeds.

After the learner has progressed at his own rate through enough activities to give him (and/or his teacher) confidence that he can meet the module's objectives, he asks to be given (or is requested by his teacher to take) a post-test. This is the fifth and final stage in the process. If the results of the post-test are satisfactory, the learner begins work on another module. If the results are unsatisfactory, the learner selects (or is helped to select) learning activities designed to remedy his deficiencies.

(3) *CBE should provide opportunities for the learner to pursue his personal goals.* The intent of this assumption goes beyond the elements of individualiza-

tion described above. That is, it means more than providing the learner with opportunities to make choices among alternate learning activities. In essence, the assumption means that the learner is also given opportunities to make choices among various objectives and, in some instances, to develop his own.

In a competency based program, there are certain objectives or sets of objectives which are required for everyone. For example, each learner must be able to do X, Y, and Z. But there are other objectives, all of which are considered important, but none of which is considered to be as vital as X, Y, or Z, or more valuable to all learners than another. From this latter group of objectives, then, each learner has the freedom and the responsibility to negotiate a program of studies.

Or, suppose that the learner is interested in a particular area of study for which the school has no objectives. In such a case, the learner is encouraged to become involved, along with the professional staff, in designing learning modules in that area. Certainly, the extent of the learner's involvement will be determined by his age and talents.

In addition to the assumptions cited above, two others need to be mentioned, if only in passing. One is that *CBE should be so organized and managed that all persons concerned with or affected by the education of learners share the responsibility for it.* A key concept in CBE, then, is involvement: the involvement of parents, of community groups and institutions, and, of course, of teachers and learners in the design and implementation of programs. Another key concept is accountability. For when one is responsible for the design and implementation of instructional programs, to some extent one must also be accountable for their consequences.

The other assumption is that *CBE should be so organized and managed that it provides for its own continuous evaluation and revision.* This is a critical area. For there is always danger that the efficiency of any instructional program will become equated with its effectiveness and relevance. In other words, an instructional program may appear to be functioning with no apparent flaws, to be maintaining itself with little difficulty, but upon closer examination, the program may not be achieving its stated objectives, or the objectives themselves may be irrelevant. In CBE, then, questions of efficiency, of effectiveness, and of relevance are separate questions, and careful attention is given to asking and answering them as such.

CONCLUSION

Three questions and little space remain. Can CBE be done? Is it being done? Should it be done? In our opinion, the answer to the first question is yes. CBE can be done, and eventually more efficiently than and as economically as most education programs in existence today.

To our best knowledge, the answer to the second question is both yes and no. Yes, CBE is being field tested on a small scale in several educational settings. No, CBE does not constitute the total program of any school we know.

Our answer to the question of whether CBE should be done is, again, both yes and no. On the one hand, we believe that CBE holds great promise as a systematic framework for teaching and learning certain items, such as multiplication tables, word attack skills, social studies facts, principles of letter writing, and so on. Most certainly, we believe that CBE should continue to be field tested.

On the other hand, we have reservations about the ability of CBE programs to come to grips adequately with many aspects of the social, emotional, and high-order cognitive lives of learners. In this respect, we share Macdonald's concern:

> To direct a class to the activity of reading *For Whom the Bell Tolls* by Hemingway makes great sense as a statement of direction. Any number of behavioral objectives could be defined from this activity. However, to direct the study of the novel by determining objectives ahead of time would be to lose the point. The "objectives" are inherent in the material. They involve the meaningful relationships of individual pupils to the whole work or to parts of the work. In other words, this work as an art form transcends the bits and pieces of it. The meaning of this work can be known only as individuals interact with it (4:123).

· · ·

REFERENCES
1. Charles E. Johnson and Gilbert F. Shearron, Directors of the Georgia Educational Models, are responsible for drawing together the assumptions discussed here.
2. Robert F. Mager. *Preparing Instructional Objectives*. San Francisco, California: Fearon Publishers, 1962.
3. J. Myron Atkin. "Behavioral Objectives in Curriculum Design: A Cautionary Note," *The Science Teacher*, May 1968, p. 28.
4. James B. Macdonald and Bernice J. Wolfson. "A Case Against Behavioral Objectives," *The Elementary School Journal*, December 1970, p. 123.

28 How to Stop Programmed Instruction from Boring Learners and Strangling Results

Dudley Post

Everywhere new technology falls short of its promise, short of having the major economic impact predicted. Sometimes—as with computer assisted instruction—the cost of delivery is just too high. Sometimes all the pieces have not been invented, e.g., the electric car. Or, perhaps, the social mechanism/innovations are missing, as with planned communities and metropolitan government.

Programmed instruction is another in the list, for while the concept of programmed writing may be the soundest innovation ever in the educational materials field, its product—programmed instruction (PI)—is being held back by a needlessly narrow theory. Every person who still believes in the undeviating application of prescribed rules of programmed instruction, who believes in strict logic, consistent small frame size, metered response frequency, the 90/90 criterion and other dogma, and who considers these rules/principles the guts of the method, should count himself guilty for the meager acceptance of "pure" PI in the public schools and the aversion of so many learners who have tried it.

The most important long-run contribution of PI (and of performance contracting as well) will probably turn out to be *the assumption that learning is the responsibility of materials, that the author can, to a great extent, control and engineer quality and quantity of learning and is, by extension, accountable for the results,* which is a complete reversal of the teacher-student, author-learner rules. Other lasting contributions of PI are the importance of success and reinforcement, behavioral objectives as a starting and ending point, and building in learner involvement. But such principles have been lost in the scramble to evolve a technology based on the programming technique, when in fact the technique should be subordinate to the underlying principles. This is why arguments over the relative merit of linear vs. branched vs. Crowder PI are misleading and pointless, the real issue being "Is the technique used an effective embodiment (implementation) of learning principles?" The separate schools of PI are legitimately different from one another, as each has different priorities. Branched PI believes errors are instructive; linear, that success and reinforce-

Reprinted from *Educational Technology,* 12 (8): 14–17 (August 1972), by permission of publisher.

ment are more important. Branched likes to save time by skipping at the learner's discretion, while linear believes there cannot be too many sequencing decisions. In practice, of course, these views need not be incompatible, but legitimately different applications of sound learning principles. It is inevitable, of course, that all successful rules and principles will become part of every programmer's tool kit.

Programmed instruction has enjoyed nominal growth since its initial spurt in the early sixties. But its limited acceptance is not all due to those traditional apologists, the difficulty of client education, the high cost per learner hour, or the shortage of trained programmers, the slumping economy. The computer industry has overcome these same obstacles in much more severe form. No, the limitations of PI are more inherent in the technique than they are in administration, yet the limitations show little sign of being admitted, much less corrected. The fact is that programmed instruction is hampered by a narrow theory of learning which, in turn, leads to narrow results.

The PI ballgame is dominated by the linear and the branching players—with adjunct advocates on the sidelines dashing in for an occasional play. Each faction defends its theory as both the correct and the sole bearer of truth. Yet, it is not unreasonable that twenty more factions of PI could appear, and all major ways people learn would still be far from represented.

I apprenticed under two programmers: one, who was used to writing programs for newly literate Spanish-speaking hospital workers, believed in short frames, one-word responses, in simple programs with lots of feedback and *never* too much information. The greatest crime was a program that was too difficult. My other mentor had learned his trade writing bank management programs, and he believed in large frames with multiple responses and frequent blank line, open-ended responses. The greatest crime to him was a boring program. Yet, both felt his was *the* way to write PI, because each had experienced success with his way. Both my mentors were right, but they were only right for their respective learner populations, which were quite different. Variety and interest were rightfully central to bright bankers, while success through repetition was the proper concern of the hospital workers. This shows both the great strength of PI and a reason for its weakness as a technique. Its strength is the principle of adapting materials to the learner population and taking responsibility for their success. Its weakness has constantly been premature overgeneralization; because repetitive reinforcement and constant success and tiny frame size worked with animals, it was expanded to people and indeed basically worked with slow learners. But to assert this as *the* technique for all learners is both unsound and at times absurd.

The worst offender has been Skinner himself, or whatever yo-yo first claimed that conditioned response (CR) explained all learning, an absurd notion for anyone who has learned a sport or to write an original paragraph. CR has led to a rigid overemphasis on frame construction and metronomic responses of consistent size and format, which PI has prided itself on, but is increasingly confined by. The other mainstream of theory—the intrinsic/Crowder/scrambled/branched PI—is based also on sound but incomplete principles.

Learners, this theory asserts, can learn from mistakes and at different rates; some learners even need exposure to different amounts of the same topic. This is a major amendment to the CR litany, yet it too is overasserted as *the* way to program instruction. Given the range of learners and subjects, not to mention the crude state of the art, no major technique should be looked at as either all-inclusive or irrelevant.

The best specific example of a naive, premature, constricting application based on incomplete theory is the 90/90 criterion, which says that 90 percent of all learners must answer 90 percent of the responses correctly for a program to be acceptable. This standard was almost arbitrarily established by the Air Force on the perfectly sound notion that success is a better motivator than failure. But, like so many good ideas, when pushed too far it becomes useless and even destructive. For while people need success, they also need challenge, and the two are a direct trade-off. Studies have repeatedly found that people set themselves an average 60 to 70 percent chance of success in game situations. The range may be higher for learning situations, especially if job-related; but certainly for all but the most insecure or slowest learner, being repeatedly 90 percent correct is not success but boredom.

One of the problems programmed instruction set out to overcome was the failure and discouragement of so many learners, particularly poor ones, with new subject matter. This led to the maxim that success (defined as a correct response) was a good thing and, therefore, the more success the better. But this is a limited view of success. If I asked someone to name the current U.S. President, he would take no pride in saying Richard Nixon; but if I asked him to name all U.S. Presidents, he would be rightly self-congratulatory if he could. Similarly, a learner is not satisfied by being right if it's no challenge, regardless of the newness of the subject matter. And a 90/90 program rolls on like the New Jersey Turnpike, with errors as frequent as stoplights on the same road. It becomes soon apparent to the most dense learner that this thing is rigged, it's made so *anyone* gets the right answer. There can be scant satisfaction after that, save for the deluded author who thinks he has *programmed in* a feeling of success. Again, because success worked with slow learners, it was inappropriately expanded to all learners, whereas in truth challenge is most people's kick, not facile, contrived, effortless success.

This can be said another way by looking at the complement of success —mistakes. There are only five kinds of mistakes in PI, those due to:

1. Carelessness
2. Under-cuing
3. Misleading, poorly written frames (unintentionally difficult)
4. Assuming knowledge the learner lacks
5. Too difficult (intentionally).

Carelessness cannot be eliminated and can only be partially controlled by the programmer; 2 and 4 are poor programming and are the only valid reasons for the 90/90 criterion. These three kinds of mistakes should rightfully be excised from PI land. But programmers also try to eliminate number 5-type mistakes, and this is wrong. Intentionally difficult frames represent challenge and, therefore, the possibility of meaningful success, and should be consciously written *into* programs, not written out. Perhaps in the final stage of revision, after 90/90 has been reached, frames should be removed or deliberately made more difficult, to bring the rate down to 70/90 or 80/90—depending on learner population.

Better than one restrictive standard appropriate to failures and slow learners would be some *set* of several standards, such as 100/60, 80/70, and 80/80, which could serve any target population *as called for*. And if 100/60 proved too easy, say, for a program to train door-to-door salesmen accustomed to one-in-ten odds, a 100/10 standard should be unflinchingly applied. It is subjective learner success the programmer should seek, not compliance with a superannuated rule. The key is motivation, and this is created by challenge, by stimulation, as well as by success. To put the burden all on success is naive and limiting.

A just slightly less important example of over-applying a narrow rule rather than the principle behind it is the ruthless efficiency of PI writing. The strict format, intentional repetition, objectivity and scant imagination of programming's tundra is lengendary (but not unique, as textbook users know). What PI writer has not heard someone say, "I learned a lot from that program, but I'll never take another one."

Mass writing in any field inevitably yields some mediocre products, but contrasted with the average newspaper column, PI is as much fun as the Dewey Decimal User's Guide. Programmers assume that the learning principles alone are powerful and complete enough to do the job and, therefore, the writer should purge any personal style. But this policy leads to suboptimization of the most blatant kind. The writer should be dedicated to holding the learner's attention for the length of the program, and only secondarily working to keep the number of words (and hence learning time) to a minimum—because without the learner's concentration either learning time or the error rate will wander up. Excessive efficiency does not pay off, in terms of learner attitude or even objective measures, when it sacrifices appealing diversions, "irrelevant" ideas, "excessive" examples, anecdotes, historical detail or humor. Whatever makes the material livelier, more appealing, more self-motivating, better written is justified up to some limit, say 30 percent of total frames. PI, after all, grew out of a partial answer to the question "By what principles do people learn?" Yet, given that the principles of PI are not a complete learning theory, it makes just as much sense to approach the matter from the other end and ask: "What do people choose to learn from? What do they enjoy learning from successfully?" Imitate *that* form and its principles, be it good journalism or *Laugh-In*. *Sesame Street* is quite right in modeling its style after what the kids prefer to watch, enjoy and learn from—TV commercials. Commercials are expensively produced and condition the pace and expectations of children, so that any educational medium must compete with these trained expectations. The same is true but less obvious in print. Programmed instruction is competing with everything else the learner has read, and if its interest, pace and style fail to match his conditioned expectations, motivation is lost. No learner gives a handicap to a program because it is educational and, therefore, "good" for him.

There is nothing new about this point. Scientific innovations involving people often maximize a single objective measure of performance at the expense of people's needs, which are harder to measure. Scientific management multiplied worker productivity by helping men to work more intelligently, but went too far in streamlining motions and job organization, and as a result trampled all over the need for variety and challenge, for self-control, each worker's unique pace and style, his unique way of doing the job. It is often said of industrial engineers that they can design a job for maximum efficiency over one hour, but not over 500 hours, because they ignore this human factor. Highway designers straightened out roads to improve safety, but got carried away—and soon drivers were going to sleep on interminable stretches. So now designers *build in curves and variety;* driving time may be slightly longer, but more people want to use the road, and accidents are down. Speed, then, should not be the sole criterion for a highway or a program. For an hour, or maybe four or five hours with highly motivated learners, one can get by with a boring program. But after that the risk of "accidents" goes up, and the learner is likely never to return to such a road.

Perhaps the only solution is to measure subjective reaction and thereby make it a part of objective performance. Perhaps the weight given the subjective side should even increase with longer programs, where motivation becomes more important. Subjective performance has been ignored partly for that catch-all excuse—it is hard to measure. Yet it is a mistake to think learner acceptance is not crucial to PI, just because it is not the learner who makes the purchase decision. As the high schools and universities are being loudly told by their students, without relevant (motivating) subjects, they tune out. John Holt long ago told us his third graders learned nothing unless they were interested in the topic at hand. The same is partially true at the smaller level of PI—putting an obligation on the writer to at least be concerned with minimizing tune-out. If one takes seriously the principle that failure to learn is the material's fault, then failure to be motivated is the material's fault as well.

While it may appear I am condemning programmed instruction, that is not my intent. The point is that credit should go where credit is due. The *concepts* behind PI are far more innovative and powerful than current *practice.* Like performance contracting, the real innovation is probably *accountability*—the idea that the materials rather than the learner are responsible for success. Yet it is the *form* which has been oversold as the real innovation. Setting behavioral objectives and analyzing subject matter rigorously accounts for a majority of the learner time saved by PI, and this is not a new concept or technique but merely a standard of quality and writing procedure. *Revision cylces* and *validation* with learners account for its effectiveness, more than the responses and sequencing.

Someday, after the last conceivable .002 percent of marginal efficiency has been squeezed from programming, some mischievous non-educator will discover that the most effective program is one the learner prefers, just as the best program writers are people who enjoy writing programs. Someday the subjective element will be rediscovered—that creative people with adequate resources make more effective teaching materials than uncreative PI companies, that *Sesame Street's* success is due to mixing entertainment and learning, and that perhaps efforts are best put into making arresting, high-impact, attention-grabbing products and working backwards from that objective rather than forwards from dozens of out-of-date micro-measures of what has worked and assembling them into a scientific and logical, but unpalatable, program.

CONCLUSION

Programmed instruction sells more to industry and military than to schools, not just because the former are more cost conscious and the latter group-paced, but because increasingly students have a choice over how they learn, if not over what they learn also. Business and military still rely on authority—but this is passing, just as it has already passed in the schools: employees will not always learn their job from an unmotivating or boring medium. Programming must keep up with its customers' expectations, not just by becoming "appealing," but by re-examining the limited theory which may guarantee its rejection by a generation bred on the non-linear, involving electronic media. It is all too easy to put off such a re-examination because the paying customer is so rarely the end user of PI. However, the learner's needs cannot be ignored indefinitely. Ask any college president.

29 Recitation and Lecture
Ronald T. Hyman

Lecture and recitation are perhaps the two oldest methods employed by teachers working with groups of students. They are traditional methods and, in addition, stem from a similar view of teaching. In any era of reform and reconsideration of teaching, traditional methods bear the brunt of sharp negative criticism. However, it is precisely in an era of reform that what is valuable in traditional items should be preserved and given careful reexamination and

Reprinted from *Ways of Teaching* by Ronald T. Hyman. Reprinted by permission of the publisher, J. B. Lippincott Company. Copyright 1970.

reformulation. These two methods require respecification of rationale and a new consideration. In this way it is possible to build upon tradition. . . .

It is essential for the teacher who uses the lecture and recitation methods to keep in mind that, though these methods are in common use, their negative image is of long standing. Samuel Johnson, the famous writer and lexicographer, is quoted by his biographer, James Boswell, as saying in 1766,

> *"People have now-a-days got a strange opinion that everything should be taught by lectures. Now, I cannot see that lectures can do so much good as reading the books from which the lectures are taken. I know nothing that can be best taught by lectures, except where experiments are to be shewn. You may teach chymistry by lectures.—You might teach making of shoes by lectures!" (5:337).*

The teacher, in coping with this image, must explore and keep in mind the underlying justifications of these methods. This will aid him in recognizing the nature of the activity he is performing. Hopefully he will then be able to cope with the limitations of the methods, and will be able to utilize their strengths to his best advantage.

UNDERLYING JUSTIFICATIONS

Those who support the lecture and recitation methods of conducting a class are guided by a view of teaching that has several special features. The *first* of these features involves the concept that what the student needs to know (and/or do and/or believe) and can know (and/or do and/or believe) is external to him. The knowledge, for example, that a student needs to possess and can come to possess is actually held by someone else (the teacher) who can transmit it to the student. Knowledge lies outside of the student, not within him. When someone communicates knowledge to the student, the student's mind receives it, assimilates it, and stores it along with other knowledge previously gained. The mind is seen as a never-full receptacle that continually receives, sorts, and interrelates externally-generated stimuli. This view of teaching depicts the mind, according to Scheffler, "essentially as sifting and sorting the external impressions to which it is receptive" (8:132).

Second, teaching is viewed as the activity that brings about the accumulation of the knowledge that is to be utilized by the student as he performs his life's activities. Man is born without knowledge and begins to accumulate it immediately upon birth. Teaching fosters that accumulation of knowledge by giving the student direction and seeing to it that he receives and stores the appropriate knowledge. "The desired end result of teaching is an accumulation in the learner of the basic elements fed in from without, organized and processed in standard ways, but, in any event, not generated by the learner himself" (8:132).

The *third* important feature is the idea the *teacher* has the knowledge to give the student or can easily acquire it when necessary or can readily guide the student to some book or film or the like that contains it. This gives the teacher status with the students for he has what they do not have but need to have. Thus, the teacher serves as the external source of stimuli for the student. The teacher can, furthermore, direct the process of accumulation through considered, deliberate selection and timing of inputs. This earns the teacher further status. It is evident that prestige in this area is related to the social prestige the teacher has by virtue of his very position.

Moreover, and critical to the entire process of teaching, there is the *fourth* idea—that the teacher can transmit his knowledge to the student. The teacher tells what he knows, and the student receives and learns. Teaching is essentially the dispensing of knowledge and thus ideally leads to the eventual elimination of the mystery surrounding the knowledge the teacher has amassed. This concept of teaching and the teacher is illustrated in the diagram below:

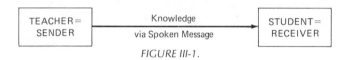

FIGURE III-1.

The skill of the teacher thus amounts to being able to transmit knowledge—usually by means of verbal communication—so that the student not only receives it but accumulates it. The diagram is amplified to become:

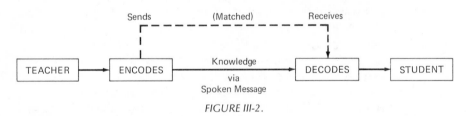

FIGURE III-2.

Of course the teacher assumes, or takes steps to assure: that what he sends is received and decoded by the student; that what he sends, not less, reaches the student; that what he sends arrives with no changes that would confuse or distort; that he can encode, or translate, his knowledge into language that is meaningful to the student; that the student can and does decode the message in such a way as to learn it.

This feeding in of external stimuli further involves the idea that there is congruence and validity in what the student decodes. It must be assumed, for example, that the impressions of an event that the student receives from the teacher are valid and correspond to the event itself; that the student can learn about the event from the stimuli he receives. This is illustrated in Figure III-3. . . .

Note that in Figure III-3 the teacher tells the statements about the event in

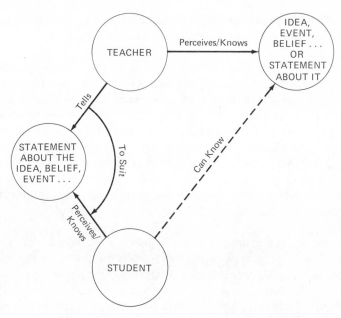

FIGURE III-3.

such a way as to suit the student's ability to perceive. The teacher selects the appropriate level of words, speed, and other controls (6) in order to assure that the student will be able to comprehend the statement about the event.

Fifth, this view of teaching acknowledges that the reception by the student may be either rote reception or meaningful reception (1). The failure to make the distinction between rote reception and meaningful reception is one factor that has led to misunderstanding and the subsequent repudiation of the lecture and recitation methods. "Few pedagogic devices in our time have been repudiated more unequivocally by educational theorists than the method of verbal instruction. It is fashionable in many quarters to characterize verbal learning as parrot-like recitation and rote memorization of isolated facts, and dismiss it disdainfully as an archaic remnant of discredited educational tradition" (1:15).

The distinction between rote reception and meaningful reception leads to the recognition that disapproval of the recitation and lecture methods usually arises from abuses of these methods rather than from the nature of these methods. Ausubel claims that "the weaknesses attributed to the method of verbal instruction do not inhere in the method itself" (1:16). . . . The point here is simply that communication of knowledge via verbal exposition can be meaningful to the student. This is in direct opposition to the view of many of those who discredit the recitation and lecture methods.

Sixth—and this is a very significant feature of the recitation and lecture methods—this view of teaching is entirely consistent with and supportive of the anthropological concept of culture. That is to say, man can communicate the knowledge he has acquired to his offspring. A man's children can benefit from their father's learning provided he can relate it to them. This ability to transmit knowledge is one essential characteristic that sets man off from the lower animals.

"... perhaps the most unique attribute of human culture, which distinguishes it from every other kind of social organization in the animal kingdom, is precisely the fact that the accumulated discoveries of millennia can be transmitted to each succeeding generation in the course of childhood and youth, and need not be discovered anew by each generation. This miracle of culture is made possible only because it is so much less time-consuming to communicate and explain an idea meaningfully to others than to require them to re-discover it by themselves" (4:91).

Seventh, the lecture and recitation methods of teaching are consistent with the concept of the school as agent for transmission of knowledge to students. According to this view, teaching in school should concern itself with communicating to the student the skills, knowledge, and values of his culture, so that he can employ these in his life. The student "is primarily engaged in an effort to learn the same basic subject matter . . . which the scientist had learned in his days. . . . Most of [the student's] time should be taken up with appropriate expository learning" (3:38–39).

Eighth, this view of teaching, moreover, accommodates and encourages efficiency in gaining knowledge. This notion is closely related to the concept of culture mentioned earlier. Teaching by means of lectures is simply an efficient way of teaching a large number of students. This indeed has always been a matter of consideration for teachers, especially teachers in schools. But today, when school enrollment is growing yearly, due to a combination of factors —including increased population—the issue of efficiency is important. Efficiency must be considered in terms of time and cost (2:117). It costs less to teach, via a lecture, a group of 100 students in a single room than it does to teach via some other method that involves small groups in many sessions in many rooms. There are certain experiences "that are too expensive to repeat for subgroups of the course" (7:31). Time and cost efficiency is also gained in the recitation method. The teacher utilizes a common textbook for communicating the desired knowledge, and the students study their textbooks at home or in their free time. This decreases the time required by the teacher for transmitting the desired knowledge.

Ninth, students often are happy when they are considered part of a large group made up of their friends and acquaintances. They want to have the same experiences as their classmates, and they want to share those experiences. They want to experience just what their fellows experience and they want to know just what their fellows know. They feel secure sitting with a large group, and this sense of security and satisfaction promotes learning. Thus, the lecture and recitation methods can be, and often are, justified in terms of satisfying social needs of the student.

Furthermore, during the question-and-answer interplay which may be a part of a lecture but is especially important during the recitation session, the student learns from his classmates. This is not to be denigrated or minimized, for there are many students who benefit greatly from this aspect of the lecture and recitation methods.

REFERENCES
1. Ausubel, David P. "In Defense of Verbal Learning." *Educational Theory* 11:15–25, January 1961.
2. ———. "Learning by Discovery." *Educational Leadership* 20:113–117, November 1962.
3. ———. "Learning by Discovery: Rationale and Mystique." *Bulletin of the National Association of Secondary School Principals* 45:18–58, December 1961.
4. ———. "Some Psychological and Educational Limitations of Learning by Discovery." *New York State Mathematics Teachers Journal* 13:90–108, June 1963.
5. Boswell, James. *The Life of Samuel Johnson, L.L.D.* Oxford ed., vol. 1. London: Henry Frowde, 1904.
6. Gerbner, George. "A Theory of Communication and Its Implications for Teaching." *The Nature of Teaching,* ed. by Louise M. Berman. Milwaukee: University of Wisconsin-Milwaukee, 1963. Pp. 33–47. Reprinted in *Teaching: Vantage Points for Study,* ed. by Ronald T. Hyman. Philadelphia: J. B. Lippincott, 1968. Pp. 18–31.
7. Loud, Oliver S. "Lecture and Discussion in General Education." *Journal of General Education* 8:30–33, October 1954.
8. Scheffler, Israel. "Philosophical Models of Teaching." *Harvard Educational Review* 35:131–143, Spring 1965.

30 Sociodrama in the Classroom—A Different Approach to Learning

T. J. Michels and Nolan C. Hatcher

Imagine that you are a visitor in a classroom where pupils are discussing the problems of cheating in schools. The instructor stops the discussion and initiates a unique classroom drama with the students playing the following roles: the teacher, the student caught cheating, the accessory student, the "tattle-tale" student, the principal, and the mother of the cheating student. After about three minutes of dramatic action, the students are asked to swap roles with one another and other students in the class are inserted into the spontaneously improvised playlet. There are no scripts and no rehearsals. Before a logical conclusion is reached, the instructor rings down the imaginary curtain and asks the class for its reaction to the emotional involvement that has just been experienced. This is sociodrama.

Sociodrama is becoming more appropriate in our schools today, because recently there appears to be a significant movement of youth who are posing basic challenges to existing values and traditional approaches to learning. These young people appear to be attempting to create new life styles in order to preserve their individual identities. In addition, there are increasing demands for all persons to participate more actively in social, cultural, and political programs designed to improve the quality of American life.

Traditional methods of classroom learning are felt by today's youth to be out of step with their real world. The present-day student does not accept many of the past routine learning methods. Social scientists have been telling us for years that this is the case; and yet, until recently, educators have persisted in ignoring the changes in youth and have held to the lock-step, rote learning approach by which they were taught. We are addressing this paper to those educators who are willing to try new and different methods to replace the time-worn teaching methods being rejected by youth. It is the thesis of this paper that sociodrama can fill an important role and serve the useful purpose of helping to solve current educational problems and promote educational objectives.

Sociodrama, the teaching method we are espousing, is a technique whereby situations are acted out by a group. Its purpose is to give a clearer picture of a problem by living the situation. The situation can then be analyzed on the basis of a common experience. Thus, in a sociodrama, the students act the

Reprinted from *The High School Journal*, 55 (4): 151–156 (January 1972), by permission of authors and publisher.

parts of the characters in the problem situation. J. L. Moreno, in his book, *International Handbook of Group Psychotherapy*, states that the exploratory value of sociodrama is only half of its contribution. The second, and even more important part is that a sociodrama can change attitudes as well as provide the vehicle for studying them.

Sociodrama permits the presentation and analysis of situations outside their natural settings and allows the creative meaning of the situations to be investigated. In doing so, it is action oriented instead of being purely verbal or cognitive. Further, it encourages the spontaneous learning process to occur in the here-and-now of the life context of the classroom.

Both sociodrama and psychodrama were developed by J. L. Moreno in the 1930's, but until very recently were applied as techniques in psychotherapy only. Both have been tried recently by far-sighted educators; however, the sociodrama appears to be less threatening to teachers and appears to be more flexible and adaptable to the classroom situation. (Students, on the other hand, have warmly accepted both innovations.) Inasmuch as sociodrama appears to have the greater appeal and broader application to educators, our focus will be on this mode of facilitating learning.

At the outset, we stress the point that no great amount of training or special skills are required of teachers to incorporate sociodrama as a learning method. As a case in point, these writers have learned this approach and incorporated it in their work solely from their own inservice, trial-and-error efforts. Of course, the theoretical concepts were learned in the context of psychotherapy. In the process of learning to use sociodrama in classroom teaching, we have concluded that the theoretical rationale is not a prerequisite for successful adaptation of sociodrama to teaching, and that any teacher who will invest a brief period of time and has the courage to give it a try will find his class taking on a new aura of excitement. For the teacher, the experience will be most rewarding.

TECHNIQUE AND APPLICATION

There appear to be three basic prerequisites to the successful use of sociodrama in the classroom: (1) the class should have a cooperative group feeling, being concerned about the accurate portrayal and understanding of the issue at hand; (2) the students who participate should have some knowledge of the situation and the person they are to represent (knowledge and feel); and (3) the sociodrama should be used as a supplementary technique rather than as an end in itself.

Basically, a sociodrama is an interpersonal situation coupled with role playing. From the role-playing context, sociodrama depends for its success on spontaneity, with no rehearsals, no scripts, and no props. This application of role playing is one in which an individual assumes an identity in a specific moment when he reacts to a specific situation involving other people and their interaction. An example for a class that is studying a unit on the coming of the atomic age might be: The class is given the instructions, "Suppose you are Dr. Robert Oppenheimer, working in a laboratory beneath a football stadium in Chicago, and you are nearing a scientific break-through. You know that you are about to deliver to the world some awesome power never before known to man. What are the thoughts in the minds of yourself and your colleagues?"

Having presented the situation and locale to the class, and with no further instructions, a student is designated to be Dr. Oppenheimer and others his colleagues. They are brought to the front of the class and told to interject their own reactions and values as they assume their designated roles. The teacher's role here would be, perhaps, to inject controversial ideas or issues that may have been actual in the past or have some current application.

An alternative example for a class studying a unit on race relations would be as follows: The students will have previously been assigned specific readings on the subject, and the teacher introduces the sociodrama by illustrating a situation with the following words: "You are a white homeowner in a middle-class suburban community composed of whites only. Your neighbor on the west side is ultra-conservative and outspoken in his beliefs and value judgments (most of his conversation is about conserving racial segregation). The house just to the east of yours has recently been purchased by a middle-class Negro family with whom you have become quite friendly. You are also a friend of your conservative neighbor on the west. The locale for the sociodrama could be your backyard, where you and your white neighbor are having a friendly chat. Your Negro neighbor strolls up and joins the conversation." The teacher of the class, having set the stage, designates the characters and has them carry on with the spontaneous enactment. This example of sociodrama gives the teacher an excellent opportunity to try role reversals and, also to involve a great many students taking the three basic roles involved.

Role reversal, in this case, is done in the following manner: The student in the Negro role is asked to assume that of the white segregationist and vice versa. Students are then asked to continue the discussion as if there had been no interruption and to inject their own, newly reversed feelings.

As the sociodrama continues, other members of the class may be encouraged to go up and stand behind the key characters and whisper their own thoughts and ideas for incorporation into the dialogue.

A key value of the sociodrama is the follow-up or ensuing discussion at its conclusion. The teacher may introduce the discussion period with such open-ended questions as, "What were your feelings or reactions to this situation and to the characters as the drama developed?" or "What key points have you thought of that were apparently overlooked in this drama?"

As may be seen from the above examples, the topics for use in sociodrama are limitless, and may be on the subject of an aspect of social, vocational, and educational problems. Some additional suggestions would be: (1) social skills (rehearsal for a first date, sexual expectations, or boy-girl etiquette); (2) applying for a job; (3) parent-student argument; (4) student-teacher situations; (5) intercultural situations; and (6) actual classroom lessons.

CONDUCTING A SOCIODRAMA

1. *Selection of the Situation.* The situation should be as simple as possible and should involve personalities. The issues should be those that arise from human desires, beliefs, hopes, anxieties and aspirations or problems that occur because people do not understand each other's points of view. These writers have discovered that the sociodrama works best when there are between four and eight persons taking part. The teacher, in planning the sociodrama, should identify approximately three basic roles to be taken. At the same time, he should remain open to the emergence of other roles which may enter the situation as it moves through the drama. Some of the most interesting, thought-provoking outcomes arise from the emergence of spontaneous roles initiated by the students themselves.

2. *Choosing Participants.* When first trying out sociodrama, the teacher should select students who are fairly well informed on the issue to be presented and who are imaginative and articulate. In the early sociodramas, let the shy and retiring persons take minor roles. As the teacher and the class become more proficient and accepting of the technique, effort should be made to bring out the shy types by letting them play the major roles. It is often surprising to note the depth of feeling and ability of such students when they are placed in the more aggressive, assertive roles. Dramatics training is not necessary and may even be found to be detrimental because sociodrama draws upon the individual's own resources. It is helpful to know the background of students so that they can be placed in situations that will most benefit them. For instance, if the problem is one of prejudice, those with marked prejudice could unobtrusively be cast in roles to demonstrate the issues. Inasmuch as the sociodrama is an excellent vehicle for revealing personalities, this technique may have an additional bonus effect for the teacher in that it will help him to know his students better.

3. *Setting the Stage.* There are a variety of approaches to this component of sociodrama. We have found that breaking the class into small groups (four or five in each) and allowing each group to plan the scene serves to involve more individual participation. Having allowed the groups five to ten minutes for private discussions, the teacher calls on one of the groups to perform its sociodrama. An alternative approach is to select the roles and allow these students to leave the room and briefly talk through their method of presentation.

4. *Preparing the Audience.* Each class member should observe the sociodrama as if each one were an active participant. Each member of the audience should be encouraged to ask himself, "Is this the way one would feel in real life?" The teacher should emphasize that in sociodrama no finished product is to be expected.

5. *Acting Out the Situation*. The teacher's role is a blend between being the director and a member of the audience. He should remind students of their roles, if they slip out, and, if the sociodrama appears at a stand-still or impasse, he can either add to or cut short the situation. He should keep emphasizing the students' freedom of expression and allow for an appropriate mixture of reality and creativity. After the drama has developed for about five minutes, the teacher could do a role reversal or substitute new roles or place different students in current roles. These writers have found that their most insightful sociodramas last from five to twenty minutes. When a sociodrama appears to drag, an interesting technique is for the teacher to ask the cast to reenact the scenes as if they occurred at a different place or point in time. For example, the teacher could shift time backward and have a current sociopolitical sociodrama enacted as if Hitler were just ascending to power.

6. *Follow-up*. The sociodrama should be interrupted or stopped prior to a logical conclusion. The teacher thus should find that the class is quite eager for comment. The focus should be on how the class members felt toward the situation and the roles being depicted, why they acted as they did, and what new ideas could have been incorporated with different actors. Many times the teacher and students will feel new knowledge is needed; this tends to stimulate further research before reenactment of the situation. Finally, the participants should be requested to report on how they felt in their respective roles.

The teacher should assure the class that no one is expected to do a perfect job of acting. He should express pleasant surprise at how well the students succeeded in the task. Sociodrama can, in this manner, be a very effective learning device providing both the teacher and the students with an exciting opportunity for joint creative learning experiences.

REFERENCE
1. Moreno, J. L. (Ed.) The International Handbook of Group Psychotherapy. New York: Philosophical Library Inc., 1966.

31 Tutoring by Students[1]

Herbert A. Thelen

During the last several years, a few dozen schools in the United States have experimented with students teaching each other. The purpose seems to be to help the tutor, the tutee, or both. Compared to the tutee, the tutor may or may not be older, brighter, or more maladjusted; of a different socioeconomic class; or attend the same school. The tutor may drag the tutee over teacher-prescribed remedial materials or he may teach a lesson he himself has planned for his pupil; he may serve as drillmaster, friend, consultant, guide, big brother, or teacher. Participants in tutoring programs may be volunteers or they may be selected by authorities; individual classes, or special clubs set up for the purpose may be involved. Tutoring programs have so far been conceived, planned, and supervised by teachers, but there is no reason why students could not shoulder much of this responsibility.

The practice of students helping each other is not new. Friends have always done some homework together—on their own time, outside of school. The "little red school house," in which six to twenty students of all ages studied in one room presided over by a single teacher, relied heavily on students learning from each other—if only by eavesdropping on each other's recitations. Under the Lancastrian Monitorial System of the 1820s, the teacher instructed a group of older students who would in turn drill younger ones on the lesson. Under the project method, teachers may assign tasks to small groups of children partly in the expectation that they will learn from each other.

These practices were developed to instruct the learners. Today's new element is the anticipation of benefits to the tutor. It is hoped that he will develop his own academic skills or understanding further, as he employs them to teach another; that he will form a better character (e.g., attitudes), become better adjusted or more adequate as a person, discover new interests or commitments for his life. At the University of Chicago we became interested in tutoring first graders (six-year olds) as a way to help fifth grade problem pupils in slum schools. We felt that discussion among the tutors about their own teaching experiences would be as valuable as the experience of tutoring.

Three facts prompted this paper: first, that the various tutorial schemes have arisen independently of each other in all parts of a large country; second, that the arrangements for tutoring take a great number of different forms; and third, that the educators (almost to a man) feel that tutoring works. (I can think of no other innovation which has been so consistently perceived as successful.) These three

Reprinted from *The School Review,* 77 (3–4): 229–244 (September-December 1969), by permission of the author and The University of Chicago Press. Copyright © 1969 by the University of Chicago Press.

conditions, taken together, are intriguing. They seem to suggest that there is some widespread societal need, goal, or attitude which may be attained or realized through almost any arrangement of students helping each other. The benefits do not seem to depend on such particulars as subject matter, academic status or competence, or the nature of the lesson plan; what does seem salient is the helping relationship between students which is newly created and formally legitimized by the school authorities.

In the remainder of this paper I shall describe briefly some tutoring activities in different school systems across the nation; speculate on these school activities as responses to certain conditions in modern society; and finally project some further ideas about how the helping relationship might revitalize our schools and invite the reader to both visualize the various phenomena of "tutoring" and appreciate their germinal value for school reform.

THE VARIETIES OF STUDENT TUTORING

In New York City, each of thirty students enrolled in the teacher preparation program at Hunter College tutors one fifth or sixth grader in Public School 158. Each of these children then tutors a third grader on the lesson just taught by the college students. The college students spend six hours a week during one semester in the project: They hold their own seminar for four hours and they tutor and supervise tutors for two hours. The fifth-grade tutor and the third-grade tutee may be selected as having similar learning problems, and the college tutor plans a lesson that will benefit both children. Many benefits are claimed: the regular classroom teacher has assistance in dealing with learning problems of individual pupils; the older pupil gains new respect for himself and the teacher; the college students, invited to experiment with a microcosmic learning situation, are challenged to create learning activities and pedagogical principles.[2]

Also in New York City, Dr. Albert Deering reports that a program called Homework Helper was developed five years ago by Mobilization for Youth, the Lower East Side antipoverty agency, and has been operating in two school districts. It is now being expanded and offered to twenty-nine school districts and within six months it is hoped that 5,000 elementary school tutees and 2,000 high school tutors will be busily at work within about 100 centers set up in neighborhood schools. The cost of the program will be about $1.2 million. According to the *New York Times,*

> The tutors work with the pupils on a one-to-one basis two days each week. They help them with their homework and then give them instruction in reading. High school and elementary teachers are assigned to the centers to supervise the tutors. The tutors are paid up to $2 an hour for their work. . . . A study of the program released last year by Columbia University School of Social Work found that the tutors from slum areas not only helped their pupils but also made great improve-

ments in reading themselves . . . [thus the tutees in the program] showed a 6.2 month gain in their reading levels after 5 months. A control group that had had no tutoring showed the usual slum school rate, a 3.5 month gain in the same period. The tutors improved even more than their pupils. In a seven month period their mean gain in reading level over their control group was a year and seven months.[3]

One of the antipoverty organizations, the National Commission of Resources for Youth, is currently developing plans to pay poor boys to tutor youngsters. This organization sees tutoring as a new kind of job that can be created for fourteen- and fifteen-year-old boys as a way to induct them into the world of work and also to get some money into their pockets.

In University City, Missouri, students of Brittany Junior High School spent five hours a week tutoring youngsters at Blackberry Land and Delmar-Harvard elementary schools. The tutors

began by sitting in small groups and discussing what it means to learn, how they are most comfortable when they learn, what difficulties they had and might expect primary one pupils to have. Then individually and in groups, they set to work at tables and desks to prepare lessons and materials. Two boys cut paper and print flashcards, carefully lettering first year vocabulary. A girl looks at filmstrips through a viewer to decide which she could use and what kind of lesson she might build around it. Three girls sit at a tape recorder and read a young child's story aloud; then listen to and evaluate the playback. Later they will make worksheets for the stories. A boy works with a pegboard, planning a lesson around patterns and colors and numbers. . . . Each child is building an abacus; he will design it and select his own materials and perhaps later create a mathematical teaching lesson around it.[4]

From the typewritten reports of the teachers, we find that:

The tutoring program served definite functions within the general program. Primarily, the tutoring program was a motivational device used to encourage students to learn basic skills. Students thought that they "knew" how to do most of the skills taught in the primary and middle grades. They hesitated about learning primary-level reading and math skills for their own benefit, but they were willing to "relearn" such skills so that they might become tutors. In addition, the tutoring program provided a means for building the self-images of these disabled [underachieving] learners. The students were very enthusiastic about obtaining the status of teacher. This prestige was accentuated by the freedom required for the tutoring schedule; students left the building daily either by bus or by walking across the street to the elementary school. In the eyes of their non-project peers, these activities were highly privileged. Furthermore, the attitudes of the elementary students increased the self-images of the tutors. For the elementary pupils, the tutors were very special. The young children appreciated the academic help, but they also valued the personal attention lavished on them by their tutors. . . . Many of these elementary students did not receive the necessary positive attention of parents or peers, and the junior high students were able to provide this much needed social developmental influence. Moreover, the project students gained social skills as they developed positive relationships with the younger children. . . . Finally, the feeling of being needed further developed a positive self-image for the tutors.[5]

The activities among the tutors are probably as important as the tutoring experience itself. The teachers report that

prior to the tutoring assignment tutors observed elementary classrooms and made reports of their observations. An observation sheet helped the students look at the classroom objectively, and served as the basis for oral reports to the group [of tutors]. . . . Students also practiced being tutors by role playing and critiquing one another's teaching techniques. Students wrote "lesson plans" and presented their lessons for peer criticism. They also learned to listen and sometimes to accept peer criticism. . . . They discussed teaching techniques and considered how they learned specific tasks.[6]

An interesting but unforeseen development was that of dependence of the primary grade child on the junior high school tutor; it is reported that certain of the youngsters refused to work except when their tutor was with them. Weaning procedures are to be devised!

The public schools of Salem, Oregon, report the use of high school and junior high school students to help elementary students. The high school students are recruited from the disadvantaged and sent to help other disadvantaged children for $1.25 per hour. . . . At the other end of the spectrum, Salem has a program, now in its fifteenth year, of selecting certain high school students who are interested in becoming teachers; these students serve as cadet teachers, helping the regular teacher in elementary school classrooms. The program is elaborate and has many features of college-level teacher preparation programs.

In Portland, Oregon, there is an elementary school program called Student Team Action and a program for using student assistants of high school age in high school classrooms. The Student Team Action program follows the now familiar pattern. The local newspaper reports as follows:

Mr. Carl Fleming's sixth grade class at Fernwood School taught a lesson on simple machines to Miss Blanche Green's second grade in a demonstration of Student Team Action. Student Team Action is a one-to-one correspondence between upper and primary students. Students become involved in "doing" rather than "memorizing" and plan their own presentation, method, and materials. Special ability is not a pre-requisite to teaching, as one entire class teaches individual students in another. The role of teacher is changed from transmitting knowledge to the role of the helper who facilitates learning. All subjects are adaptable to this teaching method—science, math, creative writing, and even physical education. . . . Interested parents and educators will have a chance to see this program, instigated by Mr. J. Carl Fleming of Fernwood School, put into action when 140 students will take part in a demonstration, Thursday, January 18, in the school cafeteria at 7:30 PM.[7]

"The Wilson Student Assistant Program" at Woodrow Wilson High School is a very large operation. William D. Proppe, principal, has this to say:

There are so many innovations in education that one is hard pressed to discern those which are only novelty from those which are viable and will have a pervasive effect. Our program developed out of a series of nagging concerns that young people of today were growing increasingly self-centered and materialistic, that the trend seemed to be for young people to become spectators rather than participants in the education process, that faculties and students needed to work closer together in a common goal of education, and that students seldom have the opportunity to be of service to someone else.

A study of the conventional high school reveals a seven-period day. It is usual for most college bound students to take six subjects and, with a lunch period, their day is complete. The students taking five subjects had a study hall, and it was from this reservoir that the traditional student help was recruited to do the menial tasks around the school. Inadvertently schools throughout the nation established a stigma on being of help at school for it was only the noncollege bound who were recruited to work in the bookroom, work in the office, and act as Audio-visual projectionists. At Wilson, we simply added a period to the day so that the college bound students could take their six subjects, have their lunch period, and still have a period in which they could be of assistance to the teachers, tutor students, and participate directly in the instructional process. Last year, in our student body of 2,000, one student in four was working as a student assistant, and the kinds of activities in which they were involved included large group presentations, small group presentations, individual tutoring, correction of homework, secretarial help in the office, operation of the Closed Circuit Television equipment, etc. . . . If the interest of the several hundred school administrators who have visited our school to see our program in operation may be used as a criterion, I believe that a workshop on the use of students in the teaching process would capture the fancy of many educators, and might prove to be the most significant new emphasis in education of this decade.[8]

An extensive questionnaire was used to evaluate the program. The results were generally very positive. The tabulations show that only two first-year high school students participated as against 106 fourth-year or senior students. Of the total involved in the program, three-fifths (ninety-six) were girls; four-fifths (134) said they would like to participate another year. Of the thirty-six who would not care to participate again, only eleven gave dissatisfaction with the project among their reasons. The overwhelming majority of the students reported that they had been helpful to the supervising teacher, that they had worked fairly hard, that they had really prepared the lessons they would teach, that they helped at least one other student make progress during the year, that the majority of the class they had taught viewed them with respect. The most common criticism, mentioned by slightly less than half the group, was that they had "too few duties and had to spend time sitting around, waiting." It is interesting that these students clearly were aware of other students who resisted help, whose "personality" was difficult to deal with, and whose "background" made them hard to understand or teach.

At the Bellevue School in Santa Rosa, California, Mrs. Irma Nyby, a remedial reading teacher, has solicited the help of fifth and sixth graders for her first graders. Five tutors come in during each of three periods of the day; they have a tutoring corner, separated from the rest of the classroom. Initially, the tutors were girl members of a service club, and they helped recruit additional students who had behavior or academic problems. It was not hard to get these students to help "as the prospect of leaving class made volunteers of most of them." The upper-grade teachers were also glad to have their problem children volunteer.

The tutoring activities were varied. In addition to some of those already mentioned, Mrs. Nyby found that filmstrips which projected stories with sentence-length captions on each frame were especially useful for reading practice. Occasionally tutors would work with a small group of first graders, as in producing a dramatic show using puppets as actors. Among the noteworthy effects of the tutoring, the teacher writes of one child who overcame her inability to talk in a group; one who overcame her indifference to school; one of Mexican-American background who needed help to understand our language; one outgoing behavior problem who was assigned a tutor with similar problems which they outgrew together; one "frightened and immature baby" who was taken on by a girl and emerged as a "happy delightful little fellow, participating with much satisfaction."[9]

The program had won a place in the school. The major problem it has yet to solve is that of finding enough time for the tutors to compare notes with each other and form insights based on their experiences with the younger children.

In Overland Park, Kansas, fourth to sixth graders are used to teach arithmetic to first to third graders who are falling behind. According to Adelyn C. Muller, "creator and director of the three-year-old program, 'Obviously some of these kids are good teachers. We've cut the category of those who need improvement by 75 per cent.'" The report goes on:

> Given the responsibility of teaching, a child changes quite a bit—he matures overnight, dresses better, is more considerate, becomes a better young citizen. And, somehow, the exercise of teaching seems to make him a sharper learner of his own school work. He's awarded an official "Cadet Teacher Certificate," and he wants to make certain he deserves it.[10]

Volunteers in South High School, Downers Grove, Illinois agreed to be "friends" with volunteers in Kingsley Elementary School.

> The high school students would not be tutors or teachers, or even "big brothers and sisters," but friends—people with whom the children could talk, play games, read, and, as time went on, perhaps get some academic help. The high school students would come during elementary school hours twice a week, during free periods or at the end of a class day. . . . While all the friends do not meet at the same time, we do have to set up "stations" for thirteen sets of friends on Tuesdays and Thursdays at 3:00 PM, the time that has proved most convenient for many high school students. Desks and chairs are placed in corners, in low-traffic parts of corridors, and in any unused special purpose rooms. A walk through the school at these times presents a most unusual and altogether delightful picture: clusters of children here and there, each little group enveloped in the privacy of its own concerns and activities, with an animation and an absorption in one another that testify to the meaningfulness of the relationship. . . . On any one afternoon the following might be observed: a young child reading to his friend, discussing his story, or the older one reading to the younger; two friends working together with water colors or tempera, or some other art medium; several little girls being taught cake decorating by a high school girl; a pair working with arithmetic flash cards (in a couple of instances the younger child "drilled" the older until he [the younger] felt secure enough himself in the relationship to try answering them himself); groups playing games; a high school student singing with some little ones; a science experiment in process in the school kitchen; two little girls busy at portable sewing machines while two others cut out simple patterns, all supervised by a high school girl; a dramatization being worked out; a youngster dictating an original story to his friend who takes it down on a typewriter; a pair proofreading the younger child's report.[11]

In Baltimore, Maryland, ten senior high school students, members of Future Teachers of America, "practice taught" in two elementary schools, eventually reaching 350 elementary school children. All ten cadet teachers are now en-rolled in regular college programs, preparing to be teachers.[12]

Finally, to complete our sample of student-helping activities, in Bethpage, Long Island, is a different pattern of students helping each other within interage classes. All the students in the John H. West Elementary School are in classes which have "a two- or three-year-age spread. For example, one class might have 6- 7- 8-year-olds, 7- 8- 9-year-olds, or 9- 10- 11-year-olds, etc." Thus a child might be put into a class in which he is among the youngest or the oldest students, depending on his needs, or a brother and sister might be in the same class. Moreover, subgrouping within the class is extremely flexible. Grade levels are constantly disregarded. A child who needs to review some basic skills moves to the group that is learning the skill he needs, whether it be phonics, spelling, punctuation, number work, or something else. The interage class is intended to capitalize on maximum *heterogeneity,* in sharp contrast to the increasing ten-dency to group students *homogeneously* (by I.Q. or achievement). Because of this heterogeneity, there are always some students who know enough more than others to be helpful to them. There is also considerable "osmosis" as in the little old red school house, where children overheard each other's lessons. Both fast and slow learners form part of the classroom society; each has a place, and the fast one is not exploited nor the slow one stigmatized. Clearly the interage class is an imaginative application of recent knowledge of the operation of small groups. Also arrangements such as this expand the "helping relationship" into the en-tire school day, rather than into just a few hours of specially arranged tutor-ing.[13]

The innovations I have described arose spontaneously and simultaneously in many parts of the country. They were not stimulated by a central directive from Washington, a dramatic book, or an authoritative bit of research. What accounts for this emergence? Did the innovators sense some new promise, some spirit of the age waiting to be born? Are these practices in some sense prophetic, the harbingers of a new understanding, condition, or period in education? These questions are practical, not poetical; if we can identify whatever it is that makes these practices so exciting and somehow appropriate to our times, then we can build on that knowledge to bring about much more effectively the reconstruction needed in education. Let us then identify some of the novel elements which seem most significant and inquire into their meanings in and for the larger society.

Meeting Individual Needs. In the United States there is a growing realiza-tion that our nation is divided into two societies: the productive and the non-productive (or the affluent and the poor). The technological system of business, industry, knowledge, and bureaucratic rationality has developed its own set of demands which a person must meet if he is to be part of the productive society. If he fails to meet these demands, he is doomed to public welfare, to a life of alienation from the societal mainstream. The passport from nonproductive to productive societies is the diploma of graduation from high school. This is the single most important document in the life of a child from a poor family, and the obstacles to his achieving it are hard for a middle-class person—who can get that credential almost automatically—to believe. Of the barriers, the most important are anachronistic school curricula and methods of teaching. Such curricula and teaching methods make demands for middle-class manners; impulse control; speech fluency, vocabulary, and syntax; planning; parental help with homework, etc.—and the performances that will meet these demands are not automatically within the repertoire of the poor.

The highest priority of the schools is to get each student to stay in school, to learn to read, and to earn a high school diploma. This will call for a great amount of attention to individuals; for a great deal more teaching than now exists. Yet there is no insurmountable problem of means: there are suitable reading materials, teaching programs, and audiovisual aids in unprecedented variety and quality. The shortage is of teachers, not materials or know-how. Student tutoring seems to be a promising answer, especially if it were built into the school day on a regularly scheduled basis.

Combating Prejudice. All children have to contend with the requirement of a high school diploma; in addition, many children have to contend with prejudice and discrimination. These children tend to be poor and of these, the most victimized are also Negroes. Discrimination in school takes several forms: first, the methods of teaching were designed for middle-class children and are simply unsuitable for children of poverty; second, schools which are attended by Negroes tend to be poorer in resources and teaching skills than those attended by whites; third, when both races attend the same schools they tend to be divided into "homogeneous ability groups" which quite effectively segregate the races. Whatever the apparent educational reasons for homogeneous ability grouping, the fact is that research fails to show that children achieve more when thus segregated, and observation shows that children in the upper groups are socialized into the productive society, while those in the lower tracks are inducted into the welfare or nonproductive society.

Against this background, student tutoring looks promising as a way to eliminate two of the three forms of discrimination. With respect to suitable methods of teaching, the tutor can be an older child from the same socioeconomic background or culture as the tutee, thus eliminating the culture barrier. With respect to the lower-level teaching skill in predominantly Negro schools, student tutors could help beef up the teaching, but the only real cure for bad teaching is good teaching. With regard to the lower economic support of Negro schools, no method of instruction would directly ameliorate the situation, but the values and attitudes behind tutoring could, over time, develop strong school-community relationships and through this, more community support. Third, as the report on interage grouping shows, student tutoring built into the regular classroom learning process actually capitalizes on heterogeneity and therefore is a method through which racial and class integration can be achieved. It is especially intriguing to think of the possibilities of Negroes helping whites, of younger children helping older ones, and of ethnic minority members helping the majority.

Cooperation versus Competition. Our country was built on the notion that individuals compete, on the basis of merit or ability, for power, money, and other goods, and, conversely, that family position, titles, precedence, etc., are irrelevant to the rights and privileges one may enjoy. This meritocratic system served two functions: It laid down the rules by which the best man would win—to the advantage of himself and his community; it solved the problem of how to distribute such rewards as social position, money, and amenities of living. The experience of school is one continuous unremitting competition for "achievement," by which we mean grades and entry into further schools. With the population explosion, the affluence of the productive segment, and the increasing skill demands of industrial society, the competition for places in the better colleges and university graduate schools has become painful and crippling; the aim of education has become the passing of tests rather than the development of individual creative potentials that are vital to our country's survival.

Now this entire system is breaking down. It is breaking down because one of the major assumptions on which the meritocratic system is based is no longer tenable: the assumption that goods and services are "scarce"; that there is not enough to go around. The fact is that after eight years of continuous relentless prosperity, we *do* have enough to go around; enough food, television sets, cars, books—everything. Competition is no longer required as the basis for distributing goods.

To return to tutoring, students learning through *helping* each other is a very promising alternative to learning through *competing with* each other. And it also makes the acquisition of knowledge and skills valuable, not in the service of competition for grades but as the means for personally significant interaction with others.

Creative Adaptation. The survival of any institution, whether it be a club, factory, or nation, depends on its responsiveness to changing conditions in itself and its environment. Our society has become stalemated, and there is a sense of drift and despair. The reasons are not hard to find. First, there has been a great increase in size and complexity of all operations, whether they be educational, religious, industrial, military, etc. The complexity reflects a fantastically expanded range of publicly recognized goals and concerns. Every decision has vast and unknowable consequences. To cite one, in the most oversimplified terms possible: Shall we spend a billion dollars in Vietnam or in thirty large cities at home? At the local level, shall we bring ten Negro students by bus to attend an all white school? For each person or goal favored by a decision, several other persons or goals are bound to be disfavored. For every goal there are interested parties or "vested interests," and the trick is to satisfy each sufficiently to keep its support—but not to the extent of antagonizing others. And when a decision *is* made, it has to be implemented by very large cumbersome machinery in which many parts must act semi-independently and yet in concert. It is no wonder that the problem of getting action and change is formidable.

The matter is further aggravated by institutionalization of attitudes and prejudices. There has been very little real dialogue between institutions for many years. There is a lot more variation *within* our major political parties than there is *between* them; in fact, as someone pointed out, the only real difference is that one is "in" and the other "out." Each institution of society goes its own way, following its own logic, insight, and traditions; its major responsibility is to be self-perpetuating, as, for example, the army, the schools, and the Education associations. By now every institution from the teacher in your local school to the military general staff responds as if by habit to everything that happens. In avoiding any effective *revolution* we have also become refugees from *evolution*.

The reaction to this sense of societal stalemate, with its accompanying sense of lack of individual autonomy, has followed predictable lines. The predictive principle is that when the formal organization of a school, factory, government, or nation becomes nonfunctional, informal organizations begin to form and take over. People turn to each other, to their friends; they share feelings and concerns; they gradually define their targets for change; they involve more people—thus runs the natural history of social movements. And it is thus, through voluntary "psychic" or interpersonal interaction, that new ideas are born and gradually turn into genuine alternative policies for action.

The description of stalemate and institutional unresponsiveness that I have just given fits the school very well. It is true that many changes are made in procedures and techniques—including the introduction of student tutoring—but it is very rarely the case that anything of the innovation remains after the innovator leaves. But student tutoring seems to me to be especially promising as a focal point for change, for new ideas and inspiration within the school. It depends on an entirely new kind of interaction among students under conditions such that revealing feedback can be obtained by the teacher. It calls for teachers to cooperate across grade lines in an enterprise that is to the advantage of both. It invites recognition of all sorts of individual characteristics of pupils that are usually ignored; and it makes creative thinking about lesson plans and activities the norm rather than the exception. It is also likely to interest and involve the parent group, thus creating a reference group or "imaginal audience" whose expectations will help maintain action.

There are many more connections that could be suggested between events emerging in the large society and the helping arrangements emerging in schools. Interesting as it would be to develop the analogy or identity further, our real point is rather different: to develop some basis for forecasting the educative possibilities of the helping experiences. To the extent that these experiences in school are archetypal representations of significant encounters the student will have in the larger society their educational potential is worth trying to realize. Our little analysis convinces us that participation and understanding of oneself in the school helping situations may be helpful, if not actually required, for one to become educated for the modern world; that it will be worthwhile, as we experiment with the helping relationships among students, to recognize and demand that the student recognize those qualities and principles which are also viable in the larger society and which may be its best hope.

FURTHER POSSIBILITIES AND POTENTIALS

We have been considering the possibility that the emergence of the helping relationships in schools is partly a response to the state of affairs in the larger society. I have implied that since the school is a microcosm of the total system the things wrong with the larger society are also wrong with the schools. And that the actions taken to solve school problems—such as coping with prejudice, preventing dropouts, and getting cooperation—may be exactly the sort of actions needed in the broader community.

I should like now to suggest a variety of aspects of the helping relationship that seem to me to suggest some of the richness and flexibility of its utilization in schools.

1. *The establishment of teaching and learning as a common goal, shared by parents, teachers, and pupils.*(While any common goal to which everyone is committed would revitalize schools, teaching and learning seems especially appropriate as the highest priority goal for schools.) As more and more pupils, parents, and teachers participate together in innumerable helping processes, they will begin to make common cause, to have more concerns in common, to develop a common realm of discourse. They will also begin putting themselves in the place of the other, thus making possible a higher degree of sympathy and trust; and this in turn would reinforce the sense of common purpose.

2. *Reduction of cross-cultural, cross-generational, and authority barriers to communication.* As common purpose develops, tolerable heterogeneity increases. A common purpose acts like a super authority to adjudicate arguments and differences. To the extent, for example, that the tutor and tutee are committed to the same goal, any conflict between them can be resolved by seeing which of the contesting positions will facilitate best the goal they both want. But without such a goal, differences can be resolved only through power; through domination by one party and submission by the other. The other way in which the barriers can be reduced is by lessening the friction-generating differences between parties. Thus having the tutor and tutee both students, both from the same socioeconomic class, and both free to make suggestions and plan together, would go a long way toward reducing many of the barriers that usually separate teacher and class.

3. *Changing the social-psychological "climate" of the school from competitiveness to concern for each other; reduction of anxiety which distorts children's views of each other and themselves.* This would begin to come about with the development of processes of cooperative inquiry. The basis of concern would be the recognition that each person has a "place," that his views are needed, his feelings relevant, his suggestions worth poring over. Persons are needed to the extent that they are in fact interdependent with others and are aware of it. The tutoring process seems to me to be one in which a high degree of awareness of the other in relation to the self can be easily fostered.

4. *Enhancing the ego strength and self-esteem of the tutors.* To the comfort

of feeling supported, we now add the development of one's own sense of adequacy, of strength within himself. Most of the adults who have watched tutoring are impressed with the serious behavior of even generally irrepressible tutors and with the extent of their gratification when their tutoring is successful. It seems clear that in some way tutoring builds on strengths children have rather than continually exacerbating their weaknesses. In the case of poor Negro children, whose school experience has been largely one failure after another, the success of tutoring suggests some kind of strength not tapped in other activities. We believe it is related to the sense of family and the obligations siblings feel for each other. In a sense the tutoring experience is not only successful in its own limited terms, it is also a validation of the child as a member of a family—and this is a very deep and fundamental belongingness.

5. *Helping the students find a meaningful use of subject matter, thus assimilating it better and even coming to want more of it.* In the helping relationship, knowledge is the currency of interaction. It is not just to store away in memory and then disgorge on an examination. Nor is it merely to make deductions about remote things like chemical reactions. Knowledge has its humane uses: for having interactive stimulation, being able to dominate, being able to reach out and make contact with others through talking about something interesting to both.

6. *Giving children an opportunity to take an adult role, and to imagine what it would be like to be part of the productive society.* Our experience with slum children is that their discovery that there might be a place for them in the world of work is tremendously rewarding. Any observation or technique that builds up their experience as "adult" is rewarding; and, given half a chance, the students will elaborate their performance with adult fantasies. Supervision offered from one adult to another is likely to be received much more graciously than the same criticism from adult to child. "Teaching certificates" handed out after so many hours of "practice teaching" would seem to be demanded by the logic of the situation; certainly they are well received by both children and parents.

7. *Training indigenous potential leaders for their community.* "Leadership training" used to be listed as an educational objective for schools, but that was a long time ago. Yet the ability to lead and the ability to follow are both aspects of interdependence, and there is much to be said for tutoring as a way to make both visible. These understandings would be proper topics to discuss in a seminar of tutors who meet to talk over their experiences, get "hold" of them, and compare notes on techniques. There are communities such as inner-city slums, whose citizens are virtually without leadership of any kind, and for these communities it is extremely important that indigenous leadership be encouraged to develop. Tutoring, as a kind of thought-about experience of caring about and guiding less able persons, would seem to be an obvious candidate for the training program.

8. *Increasing by a very large factor the amount of teaching going on in the school.* The amount of teaching theoretically possible in a school is limited by the number of pupils and by the teacher's ingenuity in getting manageable

"lessons" planned. Teaching is easy when the learner is dealing directly with materials or events, in which case the teacher is on the sidelines illuminating the child's experience with such comments as seem necessary. On the other hand, teaching is very difficult when the learner must deal mostly with the teacher and only through him with the real world. Thus the amount of teaching that children can do would be greatly increased by making all courses "laboratory" courses, making use of role playing, projective techniques, pupil observations of the world, etc.

9. *Individualizing instruction.* When the tutor and tutee sit eyeball-to-eyeball, the tutor can give his full attention to the tutee and can respond to him without worrying about what is being communicated to other children. This greater and more unalloyed responsiveness is one way of increasing the individualization of instruction. Another way is to allow the tutee choice among activities, materials, etc.; decisions are easy to reach when only one person's wishes have to be consulted. If the tutor has somewhat more skill, he may attempt diagnosis of "where the tutee went wrong," and then plan a lesson pinpointed to the deficiency. But mostly I am impressed by the humane responsiveness of the tutors; it is through this that the tutee can learn to become human.

10. *Giving the younger child a big brother or sister who can guide him during the year, as if he were an adopted sibling.* I am eager to find out under what circumstances the tutoring relationship may turn into a semipermanent voluntary pact, and what activities have to be undertaken in order to maintain the pact. Lying between the big brother and the tutor is some sort of counselor role, and this can vary between the image of the therapist and that of the social worker. Assuming that the relationship develops beyond tutoring, it will also be interesting to see how large a social unit the big brother becomes involved with. Will he become part of the tutee's family? or will he be involved only with this one child?

11. *Tutoring-advising on a standby basis.* It is one thing to schedule helping hours, but what about making tutors available for unexpected crises? These might be academic, as when a student suddenly needs to be able to spell; or the crisis could be emotional, a time when a fellow really needs a friend. The standby tutor might take over with the upset child, leaving the teacher free to cope with the class; or the tutor might take the class and allow the teacher to devote full attention to the upset child. Classes that are known to have serious problem children might be assigned one or more tutors so that crises could be unobtrusively headed off before reaching hurricane proportions.

12. *Picking up cues for teaching of tutees.* I am thinking here of poor children that teachers do not know how to "reach." It might turn out that other children can reach them far more readily than the teacher can, and it would be useful to know why. With a large number of "teachers" available, with them attempting to describe their experiences, and with the teacher leading them in a seminar on their own teaching and also supervising their teaching, it seems inevitable that useful hints can be picked up.

13. *Expanding the tutoring system to include parents, college students, etc.*

The point is that once the tutoring system has been set up, it will be relatively easy to make room in it for selected parents, college students, etc. One might hope also that artists, small business men, and others might be tempted to work up a few lessons of their own to administer to small groups of students who would come to see them in their natural habitats. The Hunter College plan, described in the first section, seems especially sensible, with a variety of persons being allowed for one reason or another to take the role currently occupied by college girls.

14. *Learning how to learn.* Here tutorial activity would be used as a way to get the child to develop his own insights into the teaching-learning process so that he can cooperate more effectively with his own teachers. In this view, the tutor might be viewed by the tutee simply as a teacher or even drillmaster, but the tutee would see himself as conducting an investigation into the teaching-learning process. This investigation would be of the type known as action research, in which one sizes up the situation, decides what to do, does it, observes the response, and then corrects his strategy. The experience of teaching as action research may remain in the child's psychic archives as a model for him in dealing with many other social problems he will encounter.

NOTES

1. The investigation reported here was partially supported by a grant from the National Institute of Mental Health for a study of "Small Group Methods to Adapt Problem Students."
2. "10-Year-Olds Are Tutoring 7-Year-Olds," *Education News,* January 22, 1968, p. 8.
3. *New York Times,* October 29, 1967.
4. "Underachievers in the Junior High," *Impact* (published by the School District of University City, Missouri) 4, no. 2 (1967): 12–13.
5. "Evaluation Report: The Tutoring Program. A Comprehensive Remedial and Developmental Program for Disabled Learners at the Junior High School Level. July 5, 1967." University City, Mo.: Brittany Junior High School. (Provided by William R. Page.)
6. Ibid.
7. Clipping (entire) from local Portland newspaper (date cut off).
8. Personal letter from Principal William D. Proppe, December 27, 1967.
9. Letter, dated January 30, 1968, and thermofaxed report "Student-Tutor Program for First Graders" (n.d.)—both from Mrs. Irma Nyby.
10. John G. Rogers, "A School Where Kids Are Teachers," *Parade,* July 2, 1967, pp. 8–9.
11. Mrs. Ella Konikow, "High School Friend Program," mimeographed (Downers Grove, Ill. n.d.).
12. Personal letter from Assistant Superintendent Sidney Chernak, enclosing mimeographed report from Mrs. Worden, January 18, 1968.
13. Marie J. Yerry, "Interage Classes in the Plainedge School District," planographed, illustrated (Bethpage, N.Y.).

32 Measuring the Difficulty of Reading Materials

Kenneth L. Dulin

A continuing problem for every . . . teacher is the matching of reading materials to the reading abilities of particular individuals and groups. Daily decisions must be made as to which selections should be read by all the students, which would be particularly valuable to slow students, and which would be challenging and enriching for the more able within the group. Faced with a range of at least four or five grade levels of reading ability among their students, many teachers find this problem almost as crucial as the selection of course content *per se.*

Sometimes what the teacher wants is a *grade-level* estimate of the difficulty of a piece of material—8.0, 9.5, 10.4, or perhaps "college-level or above." For this purpose, readability formulas are quite effective. A representative sample can be taken from a textbook or article, a syntactical and lexical analysis made, and a "grade-level" of difficulty designated for the material. A departmental curriculum committee, for example, when examining new textbooks for possible adoption, can make good use of this approach.

At other times, a judgment needs to be made in terms of a *particular group of readers.* Here, the theoretical grade-level of the material is relatively unimportant. The decision to be made is simply a pragmatic one: Can my class handle this material, or *not*? For this problem, the "cloze" technique works well.

Finally, a *completely individual decision* must sometimes be made: Can one individual reader read a particular piece of material comfortably and effectively? For this problem, too, an easy method is available.

THE FOG INDEX

To determine the approximate grade-level of difficulty for any piece of writing, the Fog Index formula is easy to use and quite reliable. Its usefulness, however, is limited to secondary-level materials; to measure materials written at or below the sixth-grade level, formulas like the Dale-Chall or the Flesch Reading Ease should be consulted.

The steps to be followed in computing a Fog Index are as follows:

1. Take several samples of approximately 100 words each, spaced about evenly throughout the article or book. It is best to follow some sort of

Reprinted from *Reading Improvement,* 8 (1): 3–6 (Spring 1971), by permission of author and publisher.

randomization procedure, beginning at the 100th page, the 200th page, and so on.

2. Divide the number of words in the total sample by the number of complete-thought sentences. This gives you your first input factor: *average sentence length*. Note, however, that complete thoughts are often linked together by a comma, a semicolon, or a colon; as such, they should be counted as separate sentences: this sentence you are reading is an example of this, and should therefore be considered as three sentences instead of as one.

3. Next, count the number of words that have three or more syllables. Do not, however, count (a) proper nouns, (b) compound words that are combinations of short, easy words like "basketball" or "butterfly" (unless, of course, one of the words that makes up the compound word has three or more syllables in itself like "readability"), or (c) verb forms that have been made into three syllables by adding -ed, or -es, such as *decided* or *refuses*. Also, in determining how many syllables a word contains, count them as most people would pronounce the word. Few readers, for example, will pronounce "evening," "every," "interest," or "general" as three-syllable words, even though many dictionaries would consider them so. If a word is repeated, count it each time it occurs.

4. Next, divide this number of "hard words" by the number of words in the total sample. This gives you your second input factor: *percentage of hard words*. This figure should be computed to four decimal places, so that it will still be to two places after you have moved the decimal place two places to the right to convert the decimal fraction to a percentage.

5. Now, add together these two factors, and multiply the sum by .4 (four-tenths). This gives you the grade placement score for the total sample. Any final score above 17.0 should be considered simply as 17th grade.

The following example would, of course, be too brief to be very reliable, but it does illustrate the process:

The growth of **political** parties in America was a **natural concomitant** to the **coalescence** of special interest groups. // **Citizens** who shared common **economic** or **philosophical ideologies** tended quite **naturally** to wish to **perpetuate** them through law. // Thus, Jefferson's Democratic-Republican party came to **represent** the rural areas, // and Hamilton's Federalists came to **represent** the **affluent, metropolitan communities.** // Though Washington never **offically** joined either group, he supported the Federalists more often than not (71 words)

71 words ÷ 5 sentences = 14.20 average sentence length
16 hard words ÷ 71 words total = 22.54% hard words

Sum of these two factors = 36.74
36.74 × .4 = 14.696 = 14.7 grade level

THE CLOZE TECHNIQUE

This system gives a good estimate of how well a particular group can handle a piece of material. Rather than predicting a certain grade level of difficulty, it indicates about how well the group would score on a well-constructed multiple-choice test covering the same material. The steps to be followed are these:

1. Take a set of samples from throughout the selection to be tested. If you plan on checking the material with one class (30 *n. so readers),the total sample must be at least 625 words in length. For several classes, 500 words is probably a large enough sample.*
2. Type out the total sample, substituting for each fifth word (words 5, 10, 15, 20, and so on) a 15-space blank. Your final product will look something like this: "As a teaching area, _____ Arts draws upon all _____ ways human communicate with _____ other: speaking, listening, reading _____ writing. The effective teacher _____ Language Arts, then, is _____ who's able to bring _____ all these separate activities _____ such a way as _____ focus upon their one _____ factor: thinking."
   To do a really good job, you could make five forms of this exercise, omitting words 2, 6, 11, etc., on Form Two, words 3, 7, 12, etc., on Form Three, and so on, and then averaging the results of al five. For classroom purposes, however, one form will generally do a good job.
3. Now distribute the exercise(s) to the class, and give them all the time they need to replace the omitted words as best they can. After they are through, average the number of words *exactly replaced* (no synonyms allowed) by the group. Divide this average by the total number of blanks to get *average percentage of words replaced.*
4. Multiply this figure by 1.67, and you will have a good estimate of the *average comprehension* you can expect from the group. Anything below 80–85 percent potential comprehension (approximately 50 percent exact replacement) indicates that the material is probably too difficult for this particular group.

BETTS' READING LEVELS

For an individual measure for a particular student, Emmett Betts' criteria for Independent, Instructional and Frustrational Reading Levels can be used:

1. From the material in question (a text, an article, a library book) select a representative sample of about 100 words in length. If possible, avoid the very beginning of a selection, since this is often not representative.
2. Have the student read this sample orally to you at sight (no previous-silent reading). Note how many words per 100 give him trouble, and then ask him five general comprehension questions on the ideas or narrative presented.
3. If the reader can attack and pronounce easily at least 99 percent of the words and answer at least four of your five questions, the material is written at his *Independent* Reading Level. This means that he can probably read the selection on his own with relatively little help from you.
4. If he has trouble with more than one word per hundred but less than five (99 percent to 95 percent) and can answer three or four of your five questions, the material is written at his *Instructional* Reading Level. This means that with teacher help (introduction of the tough words, guiding questions provided, etc.) he can probably handle the material adequately.
5. If his performance falls short of this measure (less than 95 percent word-attack proficiency and/or less than 50 percent comprehension) the material is written at his *Frustrational* Reading Level and should not be used even with teacher help.

For those who might wish to investigate more fully these three systems, the following sources would be good beginning points:

READABILITY FORMULAS
1. Flesch, Rudolph. *How To Test Readability.* New York: Harper and Brothers, 1951.
2. Fry, Edward. "A Readability Formula That Saves Time," *Journal of Reading,* 11:513–16, April 1968.
3. Gunning, Robert. *The Technique of Clear Writing.* New York: McGraw-Hill, 1968.
4. Klare, George R. *The Measurement of Readability.* Ames: The Iowa State University Press, 1963.
5. McLaughlin, Harry G. "SMOG Grading—A New Readability Formula," *Journal of Reading,* 12:639–646, May 1969.

CLOZE TECHNIQUE
1. Bormuth, John R. "The Cloze Readability Procedure," *Elementary English,* 45:429–36, April 1968.
2. Bormuth, John R. "Comparable Cloze and Multiple Choice Comprehension Test Scores," *Journal of Reading,* 10:291–99, February 1967.
3. Bormuth, John R. "Optimum Sample Size and Cloze Test Length in Readabil-

ity Measurement," *Journal of Educational Measurement,* 2:111–116, June 1965.
4. Rankin, Earl F., Jr. "The Cloze Procedure—A Survey of the Research," in E. L. Thurston and L. E. Hafner (Eds.) *The Philosophical and Sociological Bases of Reading,* National Reading Conference Proceedings, 8:131–144 1959.
5. Taylor, Wilson L. "'Cloze Procedure': A New Tool for Measuring Readability," *Journalism Quarterly,* 30:415–433, Fall 1953.

BETTS' READING LEVELS
1. Betts, Emmett A. *Foundations of Reading Instruction* New York: American Book Company, 1957.
2. Johnson, Marjorie S., and Kress, Roy A. *Informal Reading Inventories.* Newark, Delaware: International Reading Association, 1965.

V Motivating and Managing in Teaching

In Part V, an attempt is made to focus specifically on two topics: motivating students and managing their behavior. In some other books on teaching, these two topics seem to be dealt with superficially–almost as though they were not thought to be important enough for serious study. But obviously I think they are and, more important, I think most teachers would agree.

To begin to appreciate the complexity of motivation, you will need to study article 33, by Frymier, carefully. In it he presents and analyzes a theoretical model of academic motivation, a concept he defines as that which gives direction and intensity to human behavior in an educational context. The model itself consists of three dimensions: approach-avoidance, internal-external, and intake-output. These three dimensions constitute, respectively, the source, the form, and the direction of motivation. The key point, according to Frymier, is that it is the pattern of relationships among these dimensions, and not any single dimension, that yields a valid picture of students' motivation.

One of the obvious effects of inadequate academic motivation is the failure of some students to achieve up to capacity. Yet it is fallacious to assume that all underachievement is caused by insufficient motivation. In article 34, Allen points out that some students underachieve because of too intense motivation, others because of emotional insecurity, and still others because of their distaste for academic competition. Allen's thesis–that underachievement is many-sided–needs to be understood by all teachers, but particularly by those inclined to believe that all that the underachiever need do is "to try a little harder."

In article 35, Frieder reviews some key teaching tasks. These include formulating objectives, diagnosing needs, prescribing activities, instructing, motivating, and evaluating. Frieder maintains that the one task carried out least well is motivating. In order to do it better, he urges that teachers learn and apply the basic rules of contingency contracting. Contingency contracts are arrangements between teachers and students where students know in advance that "if they do X, they will be rewarded with Y." Based on Frieder's remarks, you might assume, first, that it is relatively easy to design and use contingency contracts and, second, that the theory underlying their use is widely accepted. Either assumption would be erroneous.

Glasser, in article 36, maintains that those techniques which motivated students in the past will simply not work with today's youth. These youth, Glasser claims, are primarily searching for a role (not, as in the past, for a goal), for a sense of identity (not for security), and for recognition as human beings (not for status). Because of these factors, Glasser argues, to attempt to motivate students in traditional ways—particularly through fear or threats of failure–is and will continue to be ineffective. What Glasser advocates is a general educational/motivational approach he calls "schools without failure." In both theory and practice, the key element in such an approach is total commitment to the idea that no student should or ever will fail. Admittedly, for many teachers this is not an easy approach either to understand or to implement. And like contingency contracting in Frieder's article, there are some who reject it totally.

Hundreds of times hourly teachers communicate with students in both verbal and nonverbal ways. Communicating verbally, of course, has long been recognized as important and has consequently been the subject of careful esearch; but communicating nonverbally, at least until recently it seems, has not been. Koch, in article 37, makes several observations about nonverbal communication in the classroom. He notes, for example, that what teachers say (verbally) and how they say it (nonverbally) often disagree. In most cases where there is disagreement, Koch says, the nonverbal message is more powerful. The nonverbal message, in other words, is actually the one intended and the one received. Koch notes too that most teachers seem to be better nonverbal decoders than encoders; that is, they seem to be more adept at receiving messages than at sending them. Koch's major thesis is that teachers' nonverbal communication can serve as a powerful motivational and managerial tool. It is my belief that an awareness of his thesis is prerequisite to effective teaching.

Selections 38 and 39 deal with the managerial task most teachers call discipline. In selection 38, Palardy and Mudrey define discipline as what teachers do in response to three questions: (1) What do teachers do to prevent behavior problems? (2) What do they do when behavior problems occur? and (3)

What do they do to prevent behavior problems from recurring? Palardy and Mudrey state there are four basic approaches teachers can use in answering these questions: the permissive, the authoritarian, the behavioristic, and the diagnostic. It is the last of these approaches, the diagnostic, that the writers most strongly endorse.

From having studied the article by Palardy and Mudrey, you will be acquainted with the management process known as behavior modification. In behavior modification, two principal techniques are used: rewards and extinction procedures. Clarizio, in selection 39, observes how each of these techniques is often misused by teachers and offers a series of guidelines regarding how each should be used. You should take careful note of the different points of view expressed in selections 38 and 39, with the former emphasizing a diagnostic approach to discipline and the latter a behavioristic approach. You should note too how contingency contracts, which were mentioned earlier as a motivational tool, can also be used as a management technique.

33 Motivation: The Mainspring and Gyroscope of Learning

Jack R. Frymier

A CONCEPT OF MOTIVATION

Motivation gives both direction and intensity to behavior. Motivation to learn gives direction and intensity to human behavior in an educational context. Motivation to learn in school gives direction and intensity to students' behavior in a school situation. The purpose of this paper will be to explore these ideas in such a way that people interested in and concerned about education and schooling may find them useful.

Motives relate to the "why" of human behavior. What people do, how they do it, when or where it is done are all important, but *why* people do what they do is the motivational question.

Why do people pollute the rivers and air?
Why do nations go to war?
Why does one man murder another?
Why do workers go on strike?
Why do some students try to learn in school?
Why do some students not try to learn in school?
Why do teachers teach?

These are all motivational questions. But to say that "motivation gives both direction and intensity to behavior" is to beg the question: "What is motivation?" To be more precise we have to say that motivation is *that which* gives direction and intensity to behavior. And motivation to learn is *that which* gives direction and intensity to human behavior in an educational context. And motivation to learn in school is *that which* gives direction and intensity to students' behavior in a school situation.

Three things are important in this discussion thus far. Motivation is an *inferred* construct (i.e., that which). *Direction* implies selection from possible variations in purposes or goals. *Intensity* implies possible variation in terms of degree of effort or energy put forth to attain the goal. Each of these three factors is discussed below.

Reprinted from *Theory into Practice,* 9 (1): 23–32 (February 1970), by permission of author and publisher.

Motivation Is Inferred

To say that motivation is *that which* gives direction and intensity to behavior is not very helpful, but describing and understanding "motivation" or "motivation to learn" or "motivation to learn in school" must begin at that point.

In many ways, the problem is similar to the one we face in dealing with intelligence in an educational setting. We always *infer* the nature and degree of intelligence from observations of a student's behavior. No one really knows what intelligence is, so we simply watch what a student does (or study his performance on standardized tests) and then make inferences about his intellectual ability. We never actually measure his intelligence, but only how he uses *that which* he has. We have to use the same process to understand that which gives direction and intensity to what young people do in school.

However, over the years the power of the concept of intelligence has become so great that few persons have ever attempted research studies without starting from the assumption that measured ability (i.e., IQ) is the most influential variable involved.

This is unfortunate. The great strides in understanding of human intelligence have contributed immeasurably to our knowledge of what man is and how he learns. But an educational blind spot seems to have developed along with these advances in research on intellectual abilities. IQ scores appear to be exact, while other variables such as motivation or personality or cognitive style seem slippery and difficult to pin down with precision. The correlations between IQ and achievement, however, always leave much to be desired. Students who score high on measures of IQ *tend* to do better in school than students whose measured IQ is low (the fact that the original criterion measure for measured intelligence was teacher judgment of achievement in school would account for some if not most of that notion), but discrepancies persistently occur. All of the research in the area of underachievement, for example, reflects both an awareness of and a probing interest in the fact that some students do *not* do as well as they *ought to,* when the "ought to" is defined in terms of measured aptitude or IQ. Something else must be involved.

Most educators account for the difference between *predicted* achievement and *actual* achievement by postulating the concept of motivation. In other words, motivation is invariably inferred from observations of behavior, usually in conjunction with a consideration of ability or IQ.

In the conventional wisdom of education, "motivation" and "ability" are recognized as relatively discrete phenomena. Because research and instrument development have proceeded unevenly and much more rapidly in the area of intelligence than in the area of motivation, however, our understanding of learning ability is much greater than our understanding of motivation to learn. Both are inferred constructs, however, but while "ability" summarizes observations about what an organism *can do,* "motivation" summarizes observations about what an organism *will do* or *wants to do*. This brings us to a consideration of the "direction" and "intensity" factors described above.

Motivation Gives Direction to Behavior

Behavior is purposive. Life is not without direction, and motives flow from the wellspring of life itself. They are energy in action; philosophy and physiology fused. Motivation gives direction to behavior.

Our concern here, however, is with "motivation" in an educational sense, such as "motivation to learn" or "motivation to learn in school." These differentiations, although apparently simple, are actually quite complex. "Education" is not "schooling," and though educators are concerned with learning, "schooling" does not necessarily result in "education." The point is made because children who are "motivated to learn in school" may actually be motivated to "get good marks," "do as they are told," "obey the rules," "write neatly," "be punctual," or any one of a hundred things which may or may not be related to "education," but which they have "learned in school." For the purpose of this paper, "motivation to learn" rather than "motivation" or "motivation to learn in school" will be explored. There are obvious relationships between these concepts, and every effort will be made to relate "learning" to "learning in school" in such a way that the concepts have both clarity and utility.

This writer views educational purposes as hierarchically related, with the most general statement being: The basic *purpose of schools is to help children learn*. But *helping children learn means helping children learn:*

1. To value learning.
2. To want to learn.
3. How to learn.
4. To value knowledge.
5. To acquire knowledge.
6. To understand knowledge.
7. To behave according to knowledge.

The ultimate objective of the educational effort is to help youngsters learn to *behave* according to the best knowledge that is available at any given point in time. And "motivation to learn" ought to aim people in that direction.

But helping people behave according to factual knowledge is not possible unless people *understand* that knowledge, unless they give meaning to that knowledge based upon their own past experience. Meaning always comes from the individual and what he has already learned. Understanding represents the union of past experience and new stimuli in the learner's mind.

Because acquisition of knowledge precedes understanding, schools must help youngsters *acquire knowledge*. Helping children acquire information and knowledge is an educational objective that must be realized before those students can proceed to objectives such as understanding and behaving.

In the same way, helping children acquire knowledge is hardly meaningful unless those children, *value knowledge first.* Unless they believe in the importance and value of information and facts and knowledge, mere acquisition is pointless.

This logic goes even further. Valuing knowledge is not possible unless youngsters have *learned how to learn.* That is, the skills of learning are not only means to more noble ends but purposes in their own right.

Learning how to learn, however, is meaningless if students have not *learned to want to learn.* In other words, learning to want to learn is an educational objective.

Helping children learn to want to learn, though, presumes that the children *value learning,* which is the most basic educational objective of all. Unless children have learned to believe in the value of learning as a human activity, nothing else will count much anyway.

To begin with the idea that motivation is that which gives direction and intensity to behavior is not to suggest, therefore, that the direction is aimless or unknown. Quite the contrary. "Motivation to learn" means many things, and the general direction in which such learning should lead, according to the values and understandings of this writer, has been sketched in above.

Because these purposes are functionally related to one another, however, there is an inexorable logic to the direction which has been defined. This logic leads toward the idea of "rational man" (i.e., man who uses the power of intelligence in such a way that his actions and thought are consistent with factual knowledge), and then, presumably, to "the good life." Thus it is consistent with the heritage of Western man struggling to realize that which is both "good" and "true."

Motivation presumes valuing, and values are learned behaviors; thus motivation, at least in part, is learned and it can be taught. Motivation gives direction to behavior.

Motivation Gives Intensity to Behavior

In the human organism, intensity implies effort, activity, energy output. If values are the part of motivation which gives direction to human behavior, what causes the organism to strive? To initiate? To carry through? Five factors seem especially important:

1. Availability and quality of stimuli.
2. Perceptual openness.
3. Handling of dissonance.
4. Physiological functioning.
5. Anxiety.

Research studies have repeatedly shown that motivation is either affected by or a function of the number, quality, richness, intricacy, uniqueness, and complexity of *stimulus material*. The organism needs stimulation. When it is deprived of stimuli, the organism seeks stimuli or even makes its own. Over extended periods of time, those organisms which exist in stimulus-deprived environments develop lower mental abilities (i.e., their intelligence deteriorates) or in extreme cases they die. On the other hand, those which exist and function in stimulus environments which are rich and varied develop higher mental abilities (i.e., their intelligence increases). Organisms of all levels and kinds are attracted to rich stimulus sources, especially sources which are extensive, varied, and novel.

A second factor which affects the intensity of motivation is the personality structure of the learner, and especially his *openness* to experience. Those persons who are maximally perceptive, adequate, and relatively unthreatened are drawn to the new and the novel and the unknown. Those who are psychologically "closed," who have extensive defense mechanisms and perceptual barriers, tend to repel new stimuli. Openness is a function of self-concept and manifests itself especially in the response of the organism to stress or threat, but the open individual is more curious, more inquiring, more excited, more "motivated," if you please.

If openness might be considered the extent to which the organism is perceptually capable of receiving and processing stimuli, the style or manner in which he *handles dissonance* or ambiguous stimuli is another factor which affects the intensity of motivation. Dissonance may appear in either one or both of two forms, and the way in which the individual copes with either affects his motivation. On the one hand, there may be a discrepancy between where the individual is (or what he has or what he knows or what he can do) and what he wants in the valuing sense. Inconsistencies, anomalies, and ambiguities appeal to those persons who are psychologically open, and they work to resolve the dissonance. Likewise, when the individual senses that where he is and where he wants to go are not the same in terms of his value framework, he acts to resolve those kinds of inconsistencies, too. In other words, both cognitive dissonance and affective dissonance contribute to motivation.

The *physiological functioning* of the individual is another factor which affects the intensity of his motivation to learn. Basal metabolic rate, endurance, cardiovascular functioning, strength, and the like all play a part in affecting motivation.

Anxiety is another factor which affects the intensity of behavior. Anxiety is apprehensiveness in any given situation, and results from the interaction of the individual's concept of self, the number and quality of stimuli, and the dissonance which is perceived. A certain degree of anxiety seems to lure the learner forward into the learning task. Too much anxiety unquestionably drives him away. When the individual finds himself confronted with an ambiguous or value conflict situation, he becomes uncomfortable and apprehensive. Whether the anxiety induced attracts him forward or drives him back is partially a function of the type and extent of the dissonance involved, partially a function of the adequacy and security of the self, and partially a function of the number and type of stimuli present. Those persons who have clear, strong, positive concepts of self are capable of perceiving and coping with greater dissonance and with more stimuli than those with less clear, weaker, more negative views of self. As related to motivation, the important point is that there is a curvilinear relationship between anxiety and achievement behavior. This means that motivation can be too "high." Too much motivation, in other words, gets in the way of a student's learning. Stated more precisely, the relationship between achievement and motivation is curvilinear rather than linear; thus, there is a point beyond which motivation is debilitating rather than facilitating of learning. For this reason motivation should probably be thought of in optimal rather than maximal terms.

Too many stimuli, too much dissonance, too much uniqueness and novelty and ambiguity overwhelm the learner and he withdraws from rather than pro-ceeds toward the learning task. For example, an individual may respond to cognitive overload (i.e., too many stimuli) in many ways. He may queue the stimuli and deal with them one at a time. He may respond randomly to whatever stimulus presents itself into his perceptual field. He may group stimuli into broad categories and respond to the categorizations rather than to the stimuli them-selves. He may cease activity and wait for the overload to dissipate. Or he may withdraw. Cognitive "stuffing" or extreme dissonance do not affect motivation in positive ways, in other words. They impede learning. But no stimuli or too few stimuli or no dissonance at all result in inappropriate behaviors, too.

Students who are too highly motivated may focus on a very narrow segment of their educational world and miss the relationships in learning which are so important. They are less able to see the patterns and make meaningful interpreta-tions of the complexities of the learning stimuli. Students whose motivation to learn is too low are unable to focus their perceptual energies long enough or clearly enough to engage in the kinds of experiences which are conducive to learning.

Many of the things discussed thus far suggest that motivation is a relatively constant phenomenon: it does not change much, except over extended periods of time. Values, cognitive style, perceptual defenses, and self-concept, for example, are all relatively durable. They will change, but generally only slowly. Interest and perseverance are related to but different from motivation. Interest is basically short-term commitment. Perseverance is basically working style. The optimally motivated youngster may have difficulty persisting and may even lack interest in the immediate task at hand, but still be motivated to learn. And the opposite might also be true.

In summary, motivation to learn is that which gives both direction and intensity to human behavior in an educational context. As such, motivation can only be inferred; it is a function of values and educational purposes; and it is affected by the kind and quality of stimuli available, openness to experience and perceptual style, dissonance, anxiety, and the physiological functioning of the individual learner involved. Furthermore, it is probably durable rather than fragile, and because of a variety of factors, motivation needs to be thought of in optimal rather than maximal terms, since too much motivation evidently "gets in the way" of positive learning. The point is, motivation to learn is complex and elusive.

In this section there has been an attempt to delineate the complexities and to "nail down" some of the elusive factors. In the following section a theoretical model of motivation is described.

A THEORETICAL MODEL OF ACADEMIC MOTIVATION

Although it has been implied, it has not been stated explicitly that motivation to learn is only one of many types of human motivation. That point must be made now. Research in the area of motivation has identified many kinds of human motives: affiliative, achievement, sex, hunger, power, economic, aesthetic, and the like. The purpose of this section is to outline a theory of motivation which relates to learning in an academic setting. This might be described as academic motivation.

The term "academic motivation," however, may be too narrow. In the conventional academic setting, students are motivated in many different ways, not all of which are positive. For example, some students are obsessed with a desire to "get good grades," but to presume that "grades" relate directly to "learning" as it was outlined above is certainly questionable in some cases, at least. It is true that students whose motivations to learn are positive will tend, on the average, to learn more, and thus, they will generally receive higher marks from their teachers than students whose motivations to learn are otherwise. But it is also true that some youngsters become puppetlike and parrotlike in the educational context, simply in order to "get good grades," and one is forced to conclude that their conformity behaviors are basically unhealthy and undesirable. However, the fact that some students "do as they are told" in order to benefit positively from the experience and learn, thus conforming in the best rather than the worst sense of that term, complicates the matter still further.

The point of this discussion is that what causes students to strive in school and what factors are considered when teachers "grade" their achievement are complex and interrelated, and must be dealt with in terms of the complexities and interrelationships which are involved. For instance, the fact that research studies have repeatedly demonstrated that students' grades are a function of achievement, congruence with teachers' values, socioeconomic background, intelligence, social acceptance, and motivation, among other things, tends to negate the usefulness of many existing measures of academic motivation which have been validated almost exclusively against grade point average as a criterion. Such instruments may very well measure the "motivation to get good grades," but to equate the factor with "motivation to learn" would be a mistake of the most serious order, in the opinion of this writer. That such instruments often correlate positively with conformity and negatively with creativity simply underscores the point in another way.

The discussion which follows, therefore, attempts to delineate some of the nuances of "academic motivation" in the best sense of that term. Those who equate "striving for good grades" or "following instructions" with "academic motivation" will find the theoretical model outlined below broader and more comprehensive than their view. On the other hand, those who equate "motivation" in general with "academic motivation" in particular will find the model much narrower and more restrictive than their global view. The attempt here is to deal with motivation in the academic realm in such a way that it is differentiated from motivation in general and from such specifics as the desire to get good grades.

Overview of the Theoretical Model

Academic motivation has several dimensions. Three are described below. These "dimensions" might ultimately prove to be "factors" in the statistical sense of that term, and there may very well be more than three. At the present time, however, the three basic dimensions of academic motivation seem to be *internal-external, intake-output,* and *approach-avoidance.* The labels are arbitrary. The dimensions appear to be real. A graphic portrayal of the model is the traditional three-dimensional cube, as shown in Figure 1.

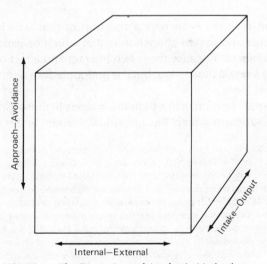

FIGURE 1. The Dimensions of Academic Motivation

Dichotomizing each dimension into its polarized categories,[1] we get a two-by-two-by-two graphic model, as outlined in Figure 2.

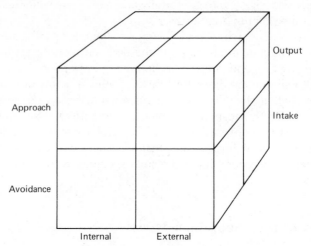

FIGURE 2. A Theoretical Model of Academic Motivation

Described this way, the model seems to have eight "cells" or "categories." Before these categories are described, however, each dimension will be set forth in more detail.

Internal-External Dimension

Motivation to learn is in part a function of that which lies within the individual learner and in part a function of that which he experiences from his learning environment. Because these two interact and affect one another, they are considered a single dimension, but it is undoubtedly a dimension with many aspects or many parts.

The "internal" portion of this dimension refers to those aspects of personality and value structure which the individual learner brings with him to the

---

[1] This logical breaking of each dimension into dichotomous "categories" tends to negate the concept of "dimension," which implies points along a continuum rather than dichotomized extremes. It is assumed that the "dimension" concept is consistent with the reality, and this notion must be maintained. For purposes of discussion, however, the dichotomized categories approach lends itself more readily to verbal description, conceptual manipulation, and analysis. Such an approach does a severe disservice to the complex realities of each dimension, but it is hoped that such intellectual gymnastics will enable us to be more insightful regarding the reality over time. The approach should be viewed strictly as a research and conceptual tool, therefore, rather than "the way things really are," and as we come to know more about the reality through further research and theorizing, then we will be in a position to modify the scheme and be both more precise and more sophisticated on the basis of empirical data.

learning situation. Self-concept, perceptual style, belief-system, and the like make up the internal part of academic motivation.

The "external" portion of this dimension refers to the environment as a stimulus source, and only those stimuli which are available within the immediate external environment are considered relevant: textbooks, parental approval, facial expressions of the teacher, filmstrips, blackboard diagrams, teacher talk, reference materials in the school or home library, peer reactions, quality of language spoken in the home, number of new ideas encountered during the day, and the like.

The internal-external dimension appears to reflect the *source* of academic motivation. That is, motivation to learn is in part a function of what resides within the individual and in part a function of the external world he encounters. Some positively motivated youngsters seem to draw most heavily upon forces located within themselves to enhance their learning. They believe in learning and knowledge, for example. They are intrigued by the new and novel; ambiguity and uncertainty excite them. They feel adequate, unthreatened, and secure.

Other students, equally well motivated, seem to be positively affected by the quality and quantity of stimuli which they experience in school. Exciting lectures, fascinating movies, vivid illustrations, and intense discussions are likely to spark these students' efforts.

To say it in still another way, some students apparently draw primarily upon external factors. Still others draw heavily upon both. In other words, as far as the internal-external dimension is concerned, there does not seem to be one "right" balance or ratio of internal and external factors, but there undoubtedly is a "right" direction to both of these factors. That is, a student whose motivation to learn is positive almost inevitably evidences "good mental health" and functions most productively in a rich and varied stimulus environment. Youngsters who hold negative feelings about themselves, who are insecure, frightened, inadequate people or who repeatedly encounter a barren stimulus situation —limited number or poor quality of ideas, books, discussions, pictures—are much less apt to be positively motivated to learn. However it is described, the internal-external dimension seems to be the *source* of academic motivation.

Intake-Output Dimension

Motivation to learn manifests itself in many ways, and these manifestations are encompassed here by what is called the intake-output dimension or what might be called the consumption-production aspect of academic motivation. Some students seem moved to consume the learning world around them, while others are producers, in the main.

Students who are avid readers and thoughtful listeners—who seek information and new experience in every way—are "intake" types. Other students are "output" people. They write. They talk a lot. They generate ideas and concepts. Their motivations propel them to active rather than passive roles.

The intake-output dimension, then, seems to reflect the *form* or *style* of academic motivation; the actual substance of motivated behavior when it appears. Again, there is probably no "right" form of academic motivation, although there are undoubtedly various types of persons. That is, some positively motivated students are intake persons, in the main, whereas other students are output people, primarily. Still others reflect a balance between these two styles. Negative academic motivations would probably reflect themselves in very different behaviors.

Approach-Avoidance Dimension

Any careful study of learning in an academic setting suggests clearly that some students move toward teacher approval, stimulus ambiguity, novelty, social acceptance, and the like, while other students move away from such things. The approach-avoidance dimension, therefore, seems to be the *directional* dimension of academic motivation. However, once again the positive and negative aspects of the directional dimension are complex and not easily ascertained or understood. Though some students move toward "good grades" and teacher approval, for instance, other students move away from such phenomena, but either group of students might be identified as "positively motivated" or "negatively motivated," depending upon the other factors which are involved. Even though the approach-avoidance dimension suggests directionality, therefore, that concept applies to the behavior of the learners in relation to the attainment or rejection of certain objectives or goals, irrespective of whether an outside observer would categorize those goals as related to positive or negative motivation.

The point is, some students who are positively motivated move toward good grades and teacher approval whereas other students who are positively motivated move away from such factors or do not move at all, and the differences probably reside in whether the *source* of motivation for the individual is primarily internal or external or whether the motivation is mainly intake or output in form. In other words, the *directional* dimension (i.e., approach-avoidance) is only meaningful when understood in relationship to the other dimensions: it is the interaction of this dimension with the other dimensions which reveals whether a student's motivation is positive or negative. To say it still another way, it is the *pattern* of relationships among dimensions which is crucial.

Relationships Among Dimensions

Any observer of the educational scene knows that some students whose motivation to learn is positive may move toward (approach) reading (intake) an exciting novel (external stimulus) whereas other youngsters who are also positively motivated might move away from (avoidance) teacher approval (external stimulus) in order to generate (output) a graphic description of social equality for a history course, for example.

The concepts of "positive" and "negative" motivation, therefore, are only meaningful if the pattern of relationships among dimensions is considered. Some internal factors are positive, some internal factors are negative. Some external factors are positive, some external factors are negative. The same thing is true for approach, avoidance, intake, and output aspects of the other dimensions. Some positive forms of academic motivation express themselves in certain types of intake or output or approach or avoidance behaviors in response to various internal and external sources. But negative motivation is expressed through such behaviors also, so it is only through a consideration of the precise pattern of relationships among dimensions which brings meaning and utility to the concept of academic motivation.

If we go back to our schematic diagram in Figure 2, the two-by-two-by-two outline describes eight specific cells. [See Figure 2a]

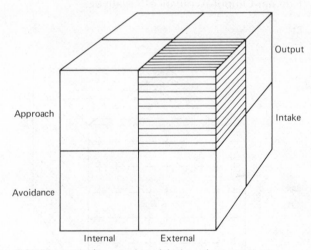

FIGURE 2a. A Theoretical Model of Academic Motivation

This time, however, one of the cells has been singled out and identified by special markings. This is the external-intake-approach cell. Suppose we take a special view of just that one cell and try to conceptualize it in both positive and negative ways. Figure 3 outlines how such an approach might be graphically portrayed.

This diagram suggests pictorially that it is possible to think about the various dimensions of academic motivation both in relationship to one another and in positive and negative terms. Employing such a logical approach, it is immediately evident that there are 16 different facets to academic motivation according to the theory we have described:

1. Internal-Intake-Approach-Positive
2. Internal-Intake-Avoidance-Positive
3. Internal-Output-Approach-Positive
4. Internal-Output-Avoidance-Positive
5. External-Intake-Approach-Positive
6. External-Intake-Avoidance-Positive
7. External-Output-Approach-Positive
8. External-Output-Avoidance-Positive
9. Internal-Intake-Approach-Negative
10. Internal-Intake-Avoidance-Negative
11. Internal-Output-Approach-Negative
12. Internal-Output-Avoidance-Negative
13. External-Intake-Approach-Negative
14. External-Intake-Avoidance-Negative
15. External-Output-Approach-Negative
16. External-Output-Avoidance-Negative

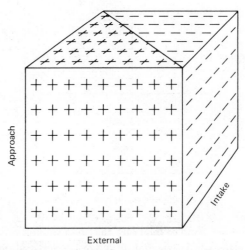

FIGURE 3.   Positive and Negative Aspects of a Motivational Cell

The best that can be done at the present time is to hypothesize along lines such as these and to develop instruments and procedures to test these hypotheses carefully. With the development of new and different instruments, the dimensions themselves will become more obvious or modified as empirical data are fed back to test the theoretical model which has been described.

The following are illustrations of behaviors within the framework of the individual dimensions set forth. An elaboration of such listings might be an appropriate point at which to begin. The primary thesis described above, though, dare not be forgotten: It is the *pattern of relationships* among the dimensions *which is foremost rather than the specific incidents or specific behaviors themselves.* Even so, a consideration of such specific behaviors may be one place to start.

Positive Examples of the Internal-External Dimension

(I) Sense of worth
(I) Feeling of acceptance
(I) Ability to tolerate ambiguity
(I) Positive concept of other persons
(I) Lack of prejudice
(I) Belief in the importance of information
(I) Minimum of defense mechanisms
(E) Variety of points of view
(E) Validity of information
(E) Variation in sequence of stimuli
(E) Multi-sensory stimuli
(E) Accessibility of stimuli

Negative Examples of Internal-External Dimension

(I) Excessive anxiety or fear
(I) Jumping to conclusions
(I) Fear or dislike of authority per se
(E) Limited sources of information
(E) Information embedded in other stimuli (hard to get at)
(E) Sequencing of stimuli unduly repetitive
(E) Validity postulated with few or no external referents

Positive Examples of Intake-Output Dimension

(I) Voracious reading
(I) Sensitive, attentive listening
(I) Surprise when confronted with novelty
(I) Question-asking for information
(I) Browsing in the library
(O) Writing extensively
(O) Practicing skills

(O) "Arguing" fine points in a discussion

(I-O) "Insisting" that contrary views be presented

Negative Examples of Intake-Output Dimension

(I) "Being quiet" but not "hearing"

(I) "Reading the assignment" without comprehension

(I) Inattentiveness

(O) Disruptive talk during discussion

(O) "Talking about boys" all the time (for girls)

(O) Throwing spitballs

(O) "Telling teacher off"

Positive Examples of Approach-Avoidance Dimension

(Ap) Attending at non-required lectures, museums, etc.

(Ap) Ordering information source by mail

(Ap) Seeking out persons with opposing points of view

(Ap) Establishing and following definite study routines

(Av) Dropping a course which is "poorly taught"

(Av) Turning off radio during study hours

(Av) Staying away from "the gang" some of the time

Negative Examples of Approach-Avoidance Dimension

(Ap) Going to movies instead of doing homework

(Ap) Doing homework just to get teacher's approval

(Ap) Copying from seatmate during examination

(Ap) Excessive talking with friends on the telephone

(Av) Dropping out of school

(Av) Daydreaming

(Av) "Giving up" during test

(Av) Reluctance to ask questions when in doubt

Three things, at least, are important about these listings. First, they are neither complete nor discrete nor adequately described in the limited space here. Second, only the interactions among the dimensions are ultimately of assistance to the person who wants a valid conceptualization of academic motivation. Third, all ignore what must be a very important, mediating-type behavior (e.g., what happens in the mind of the student between intake and output activities, for example, or how the internal personality characteristics affect the processing of external stimuli). The first point can be clarified only through further discussion and extensive research, the second point has been emphasized before, and the third point illustrates the relationship between learning theory and motivation theory.

IMPLICATIONS FOR TEACHING AND RESEARCH

What motivates students to learn? What can teachers do to affect students' motivation? What can teachers do to match their instructional efforts with the motivations their students bring to school? These questions are pertinent and real. The discussion which follows explores some of the implications of the concept of motivation that has been described for teaching and research.

Motivation to learn is a function of values, stimulation, personality structure, dissonance, and anxiety, among other things. Because these factors can be affected or controlled, at least in part, by the teacher, implications for teaching become obvious. What teachers say, how they say it, and the values which they reflect in their daily teaching all become perceivable substances from the learner's point of view. They are the feedback which students use to build their own conceptions of self.

Recent studies in the area of teacher behavior, for example, indicate that every teacher interacts with his class hundreds of times each day. Most of these interactions are so rapid that they are not deliberate or planned. The teacher is a very deliberate person before school starts in the morning, when he is conceptualizing and planning his efforts for the day. Furthermore, the teacher is a very rational, thoughtful person after school is over in the afternoon, as he reflects on how his plans went, what events, occurred, and the like. But all day long the teacher is literally "bouncing" off the class: "Johnny, go to the board." "Betty, open your book." "Yes, Mary, what do you want?" "Say that again so everybody can hear you." "Tom, stop whispering, please." Hour after hour, day after day, the teacher "bounces" off his class hundreds and hundreds of times. And every "bounce" is feedback to the students in his group.

Some teachers have a basic "bouncing style" which is positive, while others are more negative, in the main. That is, some teachers' style of interacting is such that they feed a steady stream of positive feedback to the group: "Good work." "Keep it up." "That's fine, now do it once more so everyone else can see exactly how to solve that kind of problem." Other teachers have a response mode which is essentially negative: "What is the matter with you, John?" "Why don't you keep quiet back there?" "Shut up." "Billy, for heaven's sake, everybody else has finished. Why haven't you?"

Feedback is the "stuff" out of which self-concept and values are built. Teachers must be aware of the kinds of feedback they provide for their students to perceive. The formal types (e.g., grades received in courses taken, written notices to parents) are important, but equally important are the thousands and thousands of specific instructions, demands, responses, and reactions which teachers make regularly and generally without careful thought.

If motivation presumes values, and if values give direction toward particular objectives or learning goals, then educators' conceptions of objectives and purposes become central to any consideration of what will help students learn to want to learn in school. Goals have at least two qualities—clarity and acceptability—and teachers probably have considerable control over the former but little if any control over the latter; thus the motivational problems in school emerge.

Working to "clarify goals" and "state objectives precisely in behavioral terms" will help students learn to want to learn *if* the goals are acceptable to them. But confronting students with clearly stated objectives will only increase their discomfort and resistance toward the school if the goals are inappropriate or unacceptable from their point of view. Meaningful involvement and relevant curricula are probably more directly related to acceptability of goals than clarity of goals. Teachers should generate objectives out of student concerns rather than subject matter concerns, it would seem. The relationship of motivation and teaching and goals must be sorted out more carefully than we have done heretofore. Thinking along this line, therefore, questions which need to be explored through careful research can be identified:

What curricular experiences, what organizational strategies, what evaluative procedures will be most likely to affect the development of motivational factors over extended periods of time? Does the "right answer philosophy," which seems to characterize so many classroom teachers' examinations and so many schools' operating policies, teach youngsters to be intolerant of ambiguity, and thus develop more negative motivations to learn in school? Does the increasing obviousness of the vocational aspects of curriculum, from the students' point of view, cause students' motivations to change over time? (For example, even advanced mathematics or foreign languages tend to be seen by high school students as courses which are essential for them to go to college and get a degree in order to make more money.) Is it possible for young people to value the abstract or the aesthetic or the general if their parents or teachers do not reflect these values in the structure of the building or in the attitudes and actions of those "significant others" who are involved?

Will cognitive growth and mastery learning affect a youngster's concept of self in positive ways? Can students learn to be more "open" and less defensive as they encounter the novel and the unknown? What sequencing and pacing of information will be most conducive to the development in a learner of the desire to learn?

Theory development, test development, curriculum development, and student development must go hand in hand. This paper has set forth some theoretical conceptualizations about academic motivation. The implications for teaching and educational practice have been sketched in outline form. Researchers, test constructors, and educational developers must generate hypotheses to test in the laboratory and in the classroom from this point on. Motivation to learn gives direction and intensity to human behavior in an educational context. We need to know more and more about why people do what they do when they learn or teach or administer or supervise in a school. Can we strive for a "breakthrough" in our understanding of motivation? We must.

34 Underachievement Is Many-Sided

Dean A. Allen

While counselors in high schools and colleges have doubtless found some practical utility in the concept of *underachievement* (particularly as a goad to promising but turned-off students), and while researchers in educational psychology have produced literally hundreds of studies dealing with it, the concept remains ill-defined and flimsy. It is obvious, of course, that academic performance depends in large part on such nonintellectual factors as attitudes, motivation, emotional states, and the like, yet our efforts to determine more precisely the personality correlates of academic underachievement have yielded disappointingly meager results. Why is this?

We have been wedded to a conceptual basis for classifying students as achievers and underachievers which is much too simple—essentially, some comparison of expected grades and actual grades—and have left unexamined the underlying psychologically meaningful bases for this categorization. The standard research approach has been to lump together all those students who do not earn grades up to the level expected of them and then to contrast their scores on personality inventories, surveys of family background, or other social-psychological measures with the scores of students whose grades are up to predicted level. But this ignores most of what we know about both student psychology and the social climate in today's schools. Until an attempt is made to discriminate among subtypes of underachievers and achievers, or, better yet, we discard these terms entirely in favor of more sophisticated concepts, research results based simply on the statistical discrepancy between predicted grades and earned grades are quite likely to remain theoretically trivial and practically useless for counselors. As a first approximation, some of the subtypes which might be taken into account are suggested below.

SOME UNDERACHIEVERS

1. *The student with new directions.* For some students, grades are not even fallible measures of achievement; they are no measures at all. These students aren't trying for high grades. One often finds in talking with students, even those with high aptitude and high achievement, no more than a grudging acceptance of grades as criteria of achievement or of learning. Grades represent to them only

Reprinted from *The Personnel and Guidance Journal,* 49 (7): 529–532 (March 1971), by permission of author and publisher. Copyright (©) 1971 by the American Personnel and Guidance Association.

another part of the burdensome official school machinery. They feel—and in all likelihood correctly—that grades are at best crudely related to "real learning" and that there is much more to be done, learned, and experienced in college or high school than is reflected in course grades.

Although we can write off this sentiment in some cases as rationalization for inadequate achievement, or as too precious idealism (unwillingness to accept the practicalities of our competitive educational system), or as misguided and self-defeating rebellion against parent-surrogate authorities, it is not entirely wrong-headed. There are plenty of faculty members who admit to the same sort of distaste for and mistrust of school-room grades as the sole measure of academic (much less, human) excellence. And in their public utterances teachers and counselors often admonish students to concern themselves with something more worthy than mere grades. Before we assign the pejorative, slightly despairing label "underachiever" to a student, we ought to know what it is he aims to achieve. He may, in fact, be achieving exactly what he wants, even if it is not what we want.

Students may have as major achievement motives, instead of or in addition to earning high grades, any of dozens of goals, activities, or states of being. To attain status in athletics, campus politics, dramatics, or fraternity social life is a recognizable alternative to grade-slaving but is somehow lost in studies of underachievement. To gain self-understanding, moral excellence, popularity, sexual experience, vocational skills, artistic competence, or a marriage partner—these may be compelling motives, and their accomplishment, or indeed their wholehearted pursuit even without final accomplishment, may be fully as rewarding as striving for top grades in courses. This is not to say that these alternative goals are equally meritorious; usually they are not from the point of view of the classroom instructor. But for many students these goals have at least phenomenological reality and value—probably have even more than that when seen in the context of lifetime importance.

There are plenty of students whose direction in high school or college is not what it was in the earlier grades. Their legitimate aims are now wider, or deeper, than the achievement of high marks. With a sigh of relief, perhaps, and with a welcome expansion of horizons, they strive now to be something different from what they were, not just more of what they already were. And the striving behavior in itself can be rewarding. From this point of view, indeed, studying and learning yield their own gratifications for some students while the grades received are felt to be anticlimactic, irrelevant, even destructive. Current efforts by students to change grading systems by such devices as pass/fail options reflect this concern for self-propelled learning in place of grade-grubbing.

To describe these goal-directed, productive, and personally satisfied students as underachievers is to miss the point as well as to betray our own pedantic orthodoxy. These "new directions" students are quite unlike the two subgroups described below, but standard research procedures and the campus Establishment catch them all in the same statistical net.

2. *The anxious underachiever.* Any number of papers on the psychodynamics of underachievement have demonstrated the academically destructive effects of underlying—often unconscious—self-disparagement, anxiety, and displaced hostility. The authors' interpretations are derived from contacts with students who have sought counseling and would doubtless apply to many others with the same problems who do not reach counselors. But this is a special group who sense some conflict within themselves. These are the self-identified underachievers, the sufferers from some form of anxiety and personal dissatisfaction related to schoolwork.

The point here is that these driven grade-conscious young people are a subtype among the statistically identified underachievers, individuals who work hard at their studies but, for psychological reasons, fail to achieve success. They are worried about their relatively poor performance in distinct contrast to the "new directions" students, who are not worried. The psychology of underachievement is not clarified by research which merges the two groups.

3. *The all-round ineffective student.* Although the focus of thinking in this field has been primarily academic, it is probably the case that many underachieving students are generally unproductive, that is, fail to make use of any of their talents, are unable to fulfill their needs for self-development and self-expression, and may be unengaged, alienated, and frustrated in many areas of living beyond the classroom. These students feel that they are doing nothing well or with defensive cynicism may declare that there is nothing worth doing well. Underachievement as narrowly conceived is only one aspect, and by no means the most significant, of these more pervasive difficulties.

Here the underachievement researchers have identified some of the right people but for the wrong reasons and with the wrong intent; the condition is misinterpreted if thought of as simple "failure to live up to predicted grade level." The problem may not be basically academic at all but a massive retreat from any involvement, from competition, from deep friendships, from enthusiastic engagement in living. While much of value has been written in other contexts about student apathy, identity-diffusion, noncommitment, absurdity, loss of purpose, and the like, almost nothing of any sophistication has found its way into the years of routine investigations of underachievement.

4. *Other underachievers.* Further subgroups of ineffective students, familiar enough to working counselors, could be briefly described: the immature, indolent college freshmen who found high school undemanding and good grades easy to come by, who knocked off the College Boards without effort, but who lack the persistent staying-power and self-discipline required for college courses; the rebels whose provocative contempt for the System leads to academic failure and disciplinary retribution; and the severely disturbed neurotic and psychotic students whose heads are somewhere else. The variations are not merely stylistic nor are the individuals merely interchangeable components to be arbitrarily indexed together as "underachievers;" these are essentially different psychological phenomena.

SOME ACHIEVERS

5. *The anxious achiever.* On the other side of the arbitrary achiever–underachiever division are the students made miserably unhappy by grades which are in fact quite up to predicted level. These are the psychological, but not statistical, underachievers. They are more like the "anxious under-achievers" of Group 2 than are the latter like the statistically underachieving but personally satisfied "new directions" students in Group 1. Yet typical under-achievement research sorts out the groups in the wrong way by failing to draw the lines along psychologically valid dimensions.

6. *The apathetic achiever.* At the risk of appearing to elaborate categories for the sake of argument, we may call attention to the group of students whose grades are adequate but whose involvement in the life of the mind is minimal. They dutifully earn the grade point averages forecast for them and so meet our criterion of *achievement,* but they are quite as uninvolved in the educational enterprise as are some groups of underachievers. These apathetic, perhaps disillusioned drones (and the academic environments which seem to produce them in large numbers) are much in need of study, yet here again underachieve-ment thinking with its single-minded allegiance to the criteria of test scores and grade point averages has shuffled students into meaningless congeries. Groups 5 and 6 are thrown together (along with a hypothetical Group 7—the normal, contented, suitably ambitious achievers whose school and college grades are neatly in line) as if their earning of statistically predicted grade point averages assured their psychological similarity.

THE REAL PROBLEM

The main trouble with research on underachievement is not that our statisti-cal techniques need refinement. Here, as in much of present-day psychology, we are glutted with method and starved for ideas. Our understanding and definition of achievement have too closely reflected our ingroup biases: on the one hand toward easy quantifiability, and on the other hand toward the assump-tion that grades are the *desiderata* of education. The very term *underachiever* carries implications of personal failure, defiance, emotional disorder, or irre-sponsibility, as if our statistically derived forecasts of school and college grades were prescriptive and potentially valid save for some quirk of personality. The net results of dozens of research reports have been the designation of groups of students who have little in common beyond their predicted-grade/earned-grade discrepancy and the confounding of personality characteristics which stem from this misclassification.

One further aspect of underachievement, especially research in the field, deserves comment. The effort to find personality measures which identify stu-dents whose goals are strictly classroom achievement and whose narrow range of growth potential can be encompassed within earned grades and test scores seems something like the search for an efficient loyalty oath, a device to purify the academic atmosphere by screening out the unpredictables. If the effort were successful and if the results were taken literally and applied widely, under-achievement research might have dangerously self-fulfilling consequences. We might come to believe our own unacknowledged assumptions about the "right way" for students to achieve. And worse, we might then use our measuring rods to induct selectively into our schools and colleges only those students who could be counted on to conform to these narrow assumptions. So perhaps it is just as well that this field of applied educational–psychological research remains so sterile.

35 Motivator: Least Developed of Teacher Roles

Brian Frieder

The students of Socrates learned by listening to Socrates, listening to their peers, and by looking at various scrolls. Students today learn by listening to their Socrates (but usually sans the Socratic method), listening to their peers, and looking at various scrolls. There is really only one difference: Socrates was asked to do too much for too few, while today's teacher is asked to do too much for too many. And though hemlock is no longer considered a feasible solution to the problem, society is nearly as displeased with the results of education today as it was then (although the reasons are perhaps different).

The issue is not that we cannot teach some children nor that some children cannot learn. Students do learn, even in traditional, musty old classrooms. In an absolute sense, there is probably as much student learning going on in a slum school as in the most highly innovative classroom: some children learn to read while others learn to avoid reading training; some learn mathematics while others learn that mathematics is irrelevant to their lives; some learn American history while others learn to pass American history tests; and some strengthen their egos, while others have their egos deflated.

All children learn; the issue is whether or not we can teach children what we want them to know. There are a number of prerequisites to solving this

Reprinted from *Educational Technology*, 10(2): 28–36 (February 1970), by permission of publisher.

problem: we must, for example, decide what it is, exactly, that we want children to learn; which children already know it; how we can teach it to the rest; and how we will know when they have learned it. In fact, there are so many areas of concern in the field of education, and they overlap so widely, that one of the first necessities in attempting to solve the problem of teaching children what we want them to know is developing an organized approach to the problem.

Extensive work has been done with one such approach—a classification model of the activities that are both necessary and sufficient to a formal learning environment. Its components have been drawn together over the years by Drs. Lloyd Homme and Donald Tosti, colleagues at the Behavior Systems Division of the Westinghouse Learning Corporation. They call their model PRIME: **PR**escription, **I**nstruction, **M**otivation and **E**valuation.[1] I prefer to further break down their prescriptive function into objectives formulation, diagnosis and prescription. Thus restated, the acronym reads O D PRIME.

O D PRIME is a simple but complete classification of the events that must and do occur in any formal learning situation.

O = formulation of objectives of learning activities
D = diagnosis of learner's instructional needs
PR = prescription of instructional activities for the learner
 I = instruction of the learner
M = motivation of the learner
E = evaluation of learner's degree of achievement of objectives.

O D PRIME is a total system; each of the six components it contains works in conjunction with and is dependent on all of the others. But many advances in educational technology have been made through isolating one of the components for intensive research and development and then reintegrating it into the total system. With each such integration has generally come a new or restructured teacher role. Learning theorists have made great strides in analyzing motivation as an isolated learning variable, but little has been done by educators to integrate such findings into the educational system as a specific component. While many educators often refer to the motivating potential of a particular instructional medium or strategy, the teacher's role as a motivator has not been any more specifically defined than it was in Socrates' day.

This article will concentrate on the teacher's separate role in motivating children to learn. Because this role is so intimately connected with the other components of a learning system, it is necessary to first briefly review each component.

OBJECTIVES FORMULATION

In any formal learning environment, someone or some group determines the objectives of learning; it is the existence of objectives that sets a formal learning environment apart from a random learning environment. Even in free schools, objectives exist, though they may be as simple as the creation of students who do their things or who dig the life-style of those who run the school; without objectives there is no reason to establish the school.

Teachers are usually expected to work from a list of generalized objectives: teach reading, teach writing, evoke appreciation for good literature; teach grammar and other language skills; review American literature; promote sharing and the American way; awaken creativity; teach the student to become a logical, critical thinker and an independent learner; help him to respect himself and his fellow human beings. Translating these into everyday learning experience is generally left to the individual teacher's intuition and judgment. Promoting the American way may be served by one teacher through daily display of the flag and by another teacher through a six-week anti-Communism unit.

The problem is not that there are no objectives; the problem is that objectives are rarely stated in a **meaningful way**.[2] The teacher's role as a motivator would be greatly enhanced if she knew precisely what it was she was motivating children to learn. She often finds she has motivated them to learn things she did not intend them to learn.

DIAGNOSIS

The second component of a formal learning system is diagnosis: someone or some group diagnoses the learner's current characteristics—i.e., assesses his performance levels, learning styles and rates, self-image, attention span, physical health, or any other variable that might conceivably affect his learning. Diagnosis is closely related to objectives: first, the student is diagnosed in terms of objectives that already exist—for example, if reading is a system objective, then the incoming student's reading level will be diagnosed; and second, new objectives may arise from factors diagnosed randomly—for example, creating a positive self-image was probably not an objective of education until some diagnostician demonstrated that Johnny's reading problem might, in reality, be a self-image problem.

Several groups of persons, both inside and outside the formal learning system, are involved in diagnosis; and each of these persons or groups usually has its own set of objectives for the learner. Sometimes formal analysis of data is employed; more often diagnosis is an informal, intuitive teacher process. In either case, problems exist. Carl B. Smith recently wrote, "In diagnosing . . ., educational research falls far short of the sophistication found in medical diagnosis and treatment."[3] Smith implies that this is due to the relatively lower research expenditure for educational diagnosis.[4]

Despite advances made in the standardization of diagnostic instruments, a teacher's daily application of motivational devices—whether praise or punishment—will continue to be misapplied in many instances, until she knows more about where her students are in relation to where she wants them to go.

PRESCRIPTION

The third factor in any formal learning environment is prescription. Some-one or some group prescribes learning activities: read this book, take that field trip, listen to this lecture. Once again, a number of prescribers exist—from teachers to state textbook-selection committees to computer programs.

Prescription, of course, depends on objectives and on diagnosis: the pre-scriber must know what constitutes good educational health for the learner—for example, what level of reading ability is desirable for him; and he must perceive the current state of the learner's educational health—for example, what level of reading ability he has already attained. He must then select the instructional unit that will take the learner from the diagnosed level to the desired level.[5] Many alternatives are currently available to the prescriber in the areas of instructional media and strategies; but despite the advances in diagnosis and instruction, research has provided little concrete information about the prescriber's task —putting diagnosis and instruction together to reach objectives.

Training institutions make teachers aware of a multitude of problem diag-noses (including the extremes of dyslexia, malnutrition, bilingualism) and of a multitude of instructional media; but there are almost no guidelines for deciding which medium is most suitable for delivering what content to which student. Thus, audio-visual instruction at typical teacher colleges consists largely of procedures for finding and ordering materials and equipment and directions for operating machines.

If there is any single component of the O D PRIME system that has been as neglected as motivation in terms of sound componential development and integration, it is the area of prescription. As with motivation, prescriptive deci-sions on a day-to-day basis are left to the teacher's intuition, with little prepara-tion or concrete advice from educational technologists and researchers.

INSTRUCTION

The fourth classification of learning factors is instruction. Instruction occurs in every classroom. It may be direct, as when instruction in addition takes the form of a set of addition problems to be worked by the students; or it may be indirect, as when instruction in honesty takes the form of a daily display of honesty by the teacher. Instruction is, of course, related to all of the previous components. Objectives, diagnosis and prescription determine, in theory, what form instruction will take. Once again, a variety of persons contribute to instruc-tion, including film makers, teachers, students, computer programmers and novelists.

The phrase "educational technology" connotes, for most laymen, dazzling new instructional hardware. Educational technology also includes, of course, subtleties of instructional strategy, content and curriculum objectives' sequence, diagnostic and evaluative techniques, and prescriptive decision-making. But the most visible innovations in education have occurred in the area of instructional media. The development of instructional media has undergone two distinct stages, but as yet has not been able to struggle through a needed third stage. Much initial effort concentrated on the display properties of the media—that is, attempts were made to make it pretty. Books were printed with more pictures and color or made into movies; movies were made in Kodachrome with full orchestration. This stage continues today. The second stage, developed in the 1950's, focused more on reliability of the instructional media to produce results. This effort concentrated on the student response to the media, and the most notable movement in this stage was the development of programmed instruction.

The third stage, not yet reached, consists of discrimination between reliable instructional technologies. The systems concept of equifinality holds that there are usually several ways in which a single objective can be reached—and some must be better than others. This seems to be the case in education; if a student cannot read his way to an objective from a book, it can be told to him in a lecture or on a film, or read to him by a peer-tutor. Thus, any one of these alternatives may be better than reading, unless, of course, we can teach the student to read. The trade-offs between teaching a student to read and then having him read, or lecturing the content to him, are not made very clear in the milieu that surrounds instructional innovation. As Tosti and Ball have pointed out, a great deal of mythology must be dispelled from instructional media before this third and vital stage will be reached.[6]

Despite the new media, instruction in the typical classroom is still primarily Socrates-to-student. The teacher is the most overworked instructional medium, yet is seldom viewed as such. She initially came under attack as the new media were developed to replace or help her, and she now comes under attack on the grounds that she does not properly use the media available to her; yet little has been told to her about which is better and which is best. These discriminations will depend upon the particular type of learner in question, the time and money available for the learning, and a host of other generally unspecified factors. This data is badly needed by prescribers—data without which our advances in implementing instructional technology are, at best, half useful.

Earlier it was stated that motivation has usually been subsumed under the other components in a formal learning system, and little advance has been made in terms of developing a specific teacher role as a motivator. This fact is best seen in the two stages of instructional media development. The primary reason cited for making the display properties of an instructional medium more attractive was to enhance motivation. While this may have succeeded in motivating some students, there are still students, much to the English teacher's chagrin, who are not turned on to Hamlet, even Burton's. The developers of programmed instruction, concentrating on student response, depended heavily upon the student's constant perception of his success as a motivating force. Yet, some students find working through programmed instruction rather tedious, and the rates at which they progress through the material often drop off; after initial showcase displays of speed, they soon lose concentration and make more errors, requiring more time in remedial tracks. The Hawthorne effect noted with many mechanical display devices has not yet been bottled and maintained.

EVALUATION

Evaluation of learning, the final category save motivation, must exist in a formal learning environment; it is the system's check on all of the other factors. Evaluation reveals whether or not diagnosis, prescription and instruction are, in fact, resulting in student achievement of objectives.

Evaluation, like diagnosis, can be objective and controlled—the S.A.T., the G.R.E. and other standardized, nationally normed measures are examples. But most daily, ongoing evaluative procedures are frankly unreliable: loosely constructed pop quizzes, a teacher's casual observation of laboratory sessions, a counselor's notes jotted down hurriedly after an interview, the comment of a parent disappointed in his child's progress, the B given to Joe because he tried so hard, the C given to Jim because he's lazy.

In a very real sense, there is currently no reason for evaluation to be precise, objective and controlled. As long as objectives continue to be stated in vague, general terms, no one really knows what is to be evaluated anyway; little is gained by striving for more precise evaluation of nothing. But, by the same token, there is little reason to improve diagnosis, prescription, objectives formulation and instruction without concurrent improvement of evaluation, since evaluation is the only way to be sure that efforts in the first four fields are paying off.

In the absence of knowledge of a student's success, praise and/or punishment become meaningless motivational devices. Unfortunately, they are applied meaninglessly, but for the recipient are very meaningful—and tend to cause him to act in specific ways, many of which were not desired nor intended by the instructor.

A TOTAL SYSTEM

The five components treated above, plus motivation, simply apply common sense labels to events that must and do occur in any formal learning environment. Each activity may be done poorly or well; events may occur in an order different from the one set out here; there may be one student or 1,000 students involved in the learning environment; the learners may be homogeneously or heterogeneously grouped; the events may be initiated by teachers, machines, or learners themselves. But all learning activities, whether in Socrates' day or in a modern classroom, can be classified into these six categories.[7]

It is worth reiterating that O D PRIME is a total system. The quality of the learning output of the system depends not only on the quality but also on the compatibility of all the parts, just as the quality of stereo reproduction depends on the quality and compatibility of all the components of the stereo system. Improvement in any one of the O D PRIME components will produce higher-fidelity learning, but only within the constraints of compatibility; overloading one component can produce diminishing returns. For example, constant improvement in instructional strategies without also improving instructional materials gives the same effect as a new stereo set with a 20-year old record: one hears scratches better. The usefulness of a background model can be seen in this analogy; often a new set picks up scratches that went unnoticed with the old one. A new approach to analyzing instructional systems can turn up hidden problems in the old approaches.

I have singled out motivation as the uniquely neglected component of the O D PRIME system. Research, I have stated, has certainly been done, but attempts to implement that research have always linked motivation to a particular component, rather than allowing it to function as a full sub-system, in full articulation with all of the other components of the total system.

The following will describe a significant part of the research into motivation, while treating motivation as a full-fledged sub-system, and describing its interaction with the other five components of the total O D PRIME system.

Behavior theory assumes that all behaviors are learned responses. The environment in which a child is raised develops his behavioral repertoire by giving him "payoffs" or rewards for certain behaviors. Peers, for example, pay off an individual by giving him status; peer-status may reinforce getting good grades, or it may reinforce school avoidance. Generally peers reinforce what has been promoted as appropriate behavior by adults. Parents may orally reinforce consistent job-attendance behaviors at the same time that their actions reinforce get-by-on-the-job behaviors. Other adults may condemn a child's escapism in glue-sniffing, while they engage in escapism themselves on a daily basis in front of the television set. Oral reinforcement quickly wears thin in the face of contrary adult behavior.

Since both desirable and undesirable behaviors are learned, both can be modified by the application of learning principles. Persistent undesirable behavior, it is argued, has three causes: (1) positive reinforcement of such behavior; (2) failure to reinforce desired behavior; and (3) inappropriate or excessive use of aversive stimulation and punishment.

Certainly, in our society, desired behaviors, or social "shalls," are usually not reinforced. "Shalls" are generally stated in very hazy terms, if at all, and promised payoffs for "shall" behaviors are vague. But undesirable social behaviors, or "shall-nots," are stated very precisely, and the punishments for shall-not behaviors are made abundantly clear.

In actual practice, however, the promised punishment for an undesirable act is seldom as swift and consistent as the positive payoff for the same act. Stealing liquor, for example, may go unpunished by parents forever if the culprit is never identified or if the theft is unsuspected, but peer recognition (in certain peer groups) for stealing liquor is immediate and consistent.

Attempts to correct undesirable behavior usually stress punishment, but experimentation with punishment as a conditioner of learning indicates that it is difficult to use and is often transitory in effect. Learned behavior disappears shortly after the punishment is withdrawn; but other, often bizarre, side behaviors are produced when punishment is the motivator applied.

It is assumed in the behavioral model that undesirable behavior can best be modified by consistent application of the same principles of positive reinforcement that produce behaviors—both desirable and undesirable—in the environment-at-large. While generalizations are not sufficiently advanced to account for all behaviors and intrapsychic events, it is argued that one need not concern himself with these phenomena to apply the principles effectively.

CONTINGENCY MANAGEMENT

Many educators associate the behavioral label with early behavioral research into rats, pellets and shock, and fail to recognize developing sophistication and advances that have been made. One very fruitful advance with direct classroom application is an instructional system known as Contingency Management.[8]

By the 1960's, Contingency Management was well-defined and operational. The system has its roots in reinforcement learning theory and the Premack[9] principle, which says that "for any pair of responses, the more probable one will reinforce the less probable one." The technology of Contingency Management applied in a classroom is simply the management of the learning environment so that rewards (reinforcements) are contingent upon (dependent upon) the execution of certain behaviors (such as the completion of a learning task or unit).

An explicit system of contracting between the student and teacher for curriculum and available time has been developed. Given a prepared range of tasks for one day, the student determines the order in which he will do the tasks and the reinforcements he will experience upon completion of a prespecified degree of proficiency in each task.

In the Contingency Management framework, such terms as wish, complex, self-concept, unconscious needs, etc., are viewed as inferences about the inner-mental apparatus that often confuse rather than clarify. Thus, no underlying psychodynamic explanations or mediating constructs are involved in the behavioral model. Intervention is directed at the subject's observable behaviors and behavior rates. As B. F. Skinner has stated, "self-knowledge is at best a by-product of contingencies; it is not a cause of behavior generated by them."[10] For example, the youngster with a positive outlook on his future, who is confident of his ability to succeed, might be diagnosed psycho-dynamically as having a strong self-concept or ego strength. The modern behaviorist would contend that the youngster exhibits self-confidence because of a history of reinforced behaviors. That he has positive feelings about himself is a product of these contingencies and his subsequent behavior, not a mystically created or inherited factor, and therefore he engaged in these behaviors in a compatible way.

In essence, the behavioral model contends that if the subject's "self-image" is weak, pointing this fact out to him and discussing its causation with him has less effect than going directly to the weakening behaviors and assisting him to replace them with others that produce results both he and society can live with. Since self-awareness is regarded as a by-product of behavior with influence on the course of events, the behavioral model attends primarily to the observable stimuli and the observable responses. To change behavior, the behaviorist tries to determine what behavior he wants to occur, what stimuli are to control it, and what reinforcers are to be made contingent upon the response. Traditionally, negative contingencies have been favored to achieve the goal of motivating children to perform tasks whose desirability is determined by adults. The contract in such cases is, "To avoid punishment, you must perform such and such a task." Homme advocates positive contingencies only. The contract in this case is, "As soon as you demonstrate that you have learned a little more, you may do something which is even more desirable."[11]

Positive contingency contracts are used every day. When one goes shopping, takes a job, or hires an employee, positive contingency contracts are involved. Our everyday life is largely run by positive contracts. Wherever such contracts meet the criteria of fairness and honesty, they will serve important needs for interpersonal relations.

The ultimate objective of behavior motivation technology is the shifting of motivation management techniques to self-management techniques. The reason for bringing up the ultimate objective at this time is to reassure the readers who may be dubious about the whole area of motivation management. They may be saying to themselves, "Students should be motivated by a desire to succeed, not by the promise of a reward," or "This sounds like bribery to me," or "If I apply contingency contracting systematically now, won't the child grow up expecting rewards for every little thing he does?" But experience has proved otherwise; in fact, with a wide variety of reinforcing behaviors available, students concentrate more on the learning objectives than on the reinforcers which are always present. This is certainly far removed from the tendency to pursue grades (often the only tangible reinforcer in schools) in lieu of objective achievement.

Generally, children in a contingency managed environment do not display the timid or aggressive behaviors of children performing under duress and coercion, nor do they exhibit the demanding and spoiled characteristics of those who are used to receiving unearned benefits. There is a delight and joy in the activities of children who have a feeling of willing and conscious accomplishment and well-deserved rewards.

The terms of a contingency contract must offer as a reward an experience which is highly desirable and not obtainable outside the conditions of the contract. If the terms on the student's side of the contract lead to such experiences, the probability that the student will perform the same activity in the future will increase (and this is very important when the tasks are aversive to the student), and a behavior which is already strong will be maintained (and this is important when the student already has some motivation to do the tasks the system requires, so that he does not lose his motivation).

These rules will be true as long as the terms of the contract hold and as long as the characteristics of desirability and attainability of the experience do not change. If the experience offered becomes less desirable, or if the same experience becomes attainable in other ways, the experience will lose its potential as a reinforcer.

There are many kinds of reinforcers. Some reinforcers make it possible for an individual to engage in a desired activity. A person is likely to perform a relatively boring and uninteresting task if the payoff is the opportunity to do something more interesting and entertaining. For example, driving for miles through holiday traffic is not a rewarding task, but thousands do this to get to a place to perform enjoyable activities which otherwise would not be available to them. Generally, reinforcers are things the individual does or likes to do. Other reinforcers involve things that happen to the individual. The phrase, reinforcing event, is broad enough to include all possibilities. It must be clearly understood, however, that only the student can say what event is reinforcing to him at a given time; and his choice tomorrow may not be the same as today's. Thus, for a class of 30 students a wide variety of reinforcers must be available.

Rules of contracting are not entirely unknown to the average teacher or parent. In fact, much of the system of contingency contracting is summed up in "Grandma's Law," which states: "First clean up your plate, and then you may have your dessert."

Although the majority of parents and educators have always used these rules in the management of relationships between adults and children, they have not been explicitly stated nor have they been used consistently or systematically.

RULES OF CONTINGENCY CONTRACTING

The role of the teacher as a motivation manager can be summarized in Homme's ten basic rules of contingency contracting. The first five refer to use of the reward in contracting, while the last five describe characteristics of proper contracting that the teacher should employ.

Rule 1: Reward Immediately

This applies particularly early in the game, when the child is just learning about contracting. Initial contracts should demand a small bit of behavior followed by a progress check to see whether the behavior has been performed to the contractor's specifications. If so, the reward should be offered immediately. It is important that the presentation of the reinforcer be contingent only on the adequate performance of the behavior and not on the passage of time.

Rule 2: Reward Small Approximations

Again, this is especially important early in the contracting. If the initial performance requested from the student is a small part or a simple-to-perform approximation of the ultimate performance objective, no difficulties will be encountered. But if the performance requested is too difficult for the student to perform, no amount of reward will help. In fact, the major difficulty with contingency contracting in every-day situations is that the contract manager does not settle for approximation at the outset. Such a contract says, "Do all the arithmetic problems at the end of the chapter correctly, and then you may read the novel." The systematic motivation manager is more apt to say, "Do the first two problems correctly, and then you may read for five minutes." When he is training a new employee, the employer always has to reward approximations. If the new employee were to be rewarded only for expert performance at the start, he would never be paid and would probably void the contract by leaving the job.

Rule 3: Reward Frequently with Small Reinforcers

This is an especially important consideration for the classroom teacher with a number of students to deal with simultaneously. Attention spans vary with each student and each task; each day or each hour, any one student's attention span varies. The teacher should recognize this in her own repertoire.

Strategically, tasks must be structured around the shortest common denominator of attention. The teacher will find that students who are capable of longer consecutive task efforts will soon approach her and contract to do several small tasks in a row for a longer (or combined-value) reinforcer. Students will operate at their own level, if allowed to do so, because the attention span will vary for each student each day. The wise motivation manager will have tasks and contingencies small enough to always be able to meet this low denomination.

Where the teacher desires to specifically increase the number of consecutive tasks a student can attend to, contingencies can be arranged accordingly. The teacher must be very clear in her mind that this is her objective, however. Further, she should carefully observe and note the average task span that each of her students arrives at in a free situation before she begins; only in this way can she be sure she even wants to increase it, and measures her success if she decides it is a worthwhile objective.

Rule 4: Reward Accomplishment Rather than Obedience

A contract should say, "If you accomplish X, you will be rewarded with Y," not, "If you do what I tell you to do, I will reward you with X." Reward for accomplishments leads to independence. Reward for obedience leads to continued dependence on the person from whom the child takes orders. Of course, this latter type of obedience can be an objective desired by educational systems; and, in fact, it too frequently becomes one of the few objectives actually achieved by students. This is due to grade-gifts, praise and bestowal of other privileges on students who attend conscientiously to pleasing the teachers rather than to learning.

Rule 5: Reward the Performance After It Occurs, Not Before

In contingency management, the first-work-then-play sequence occurs not once, twice, or three times a day, but a dozen times a day. But in less carefully controlled situations, the order of events is often reversed, leading to bad contracts—for example, "Just one more game of cards (a reinforcing activity), and then you must do your homework (a task event);" or "Stop watching television (a reinforcing event), and carry out this trash (a task event)." The examples illustrate that events do not automatically break down into small units and arrange themselves in the correct order. The teacher must exercise planning and agility to maintain the proper order.

Rule 6: Be Fair

The terms of the contract must be fair. Both sides of the agreement ("If you will do X, I will do Y") must be of equal weight. "If you get all A's throughout the school year, I will take you to the movies," is an unfair contract. On the other hand, "If you sit quietly for two minutes, I will take you to the movies," is also unbalanced and unfair. In general, the amount of reward must be equal to the amount of performance. What terms constitute equality will be determined by negotiation between the parties, as in many other areas of life.

Rule 7: Be Clear

The terms on both sides of the agreement must be explicitly stated. An example of an unclear contract is, "Do a few arithmetic problems, and then we will do something more interesting." Clearly-stated this contract says, "Do ten arithmetic problems correctly, and then we will watch the Popeye Cartoon." The child must always know how much performance is expected of him and what he, in turn, can expect as a payoff.

Rule 8: Be Honest

An honest contract is one which is carried out immediately and according to the terms specified in the contract. The teacher often finds it difficult to maintain her efforts as a motivation manager over a long period of time—it takes constant alertness to observe the rules. This is especially true once the students have begun to respond favorably; the teacher tends to let down. She must not contract for what she cannot deliver.

Rule 9: Be Positive

Contracts should not resemble "I will not do X, if you will do Y." The terms of the contract should contribute something to the child's experience rather than take something away from him, Habits of years make it very easy for the teacher to fall into negative contracting, especially as the teacher becomes tired or the contract is made to rectify a negative student behavior. "Pay attention or I will keep you after school," is a negative contract (as well as a vague one—for how long must the students pay attention, and for how long will they stay after school?).

Rule 10: Use Contracting Systematically

The laws of contingency management work whether one applies them systematically or is essentially ignorant of their existence. And they work at all times, not just during arithmetic period, the reading lesson, or school hours in general. A reinforcement following a bit of behavior will strengthen that behavior, whether it occurs at home or at school and whether a teacher or parent desires such behavior to be strengthened or not. Behavior occurs; it is reinforced, ignored, or punished, and thereby strengthened or weakened accordingly. The teacher cannot avoid this occurrence; she should become cognizant of the rules so as to minimize damage to students as well as enhance their learning. If one is to utilize contingency management, systematization is necessary; the manager must ask himself for almost every behavior he requests, "What is the payoff for this child?"

CONCLUSION

Once contracting has been established as a motivation-management procedure, it should be maintained, and care should be taken not to reward undesirable acts. Unwanted behavior can be eliminated by never reinforcing it or by reinforcing behavior which is incompatible with the undesirable behavior (e.g., a student who constantly leaves his seat to sharpen pencils can be highly reinforced for using ball-point pens). Again, punishment can and does work, but it frequently causes bizarre and unwanted side effects; undesirable traits often reappear soon after punishment is removed. When punishment operates as a successful motivator, it operates by the same rules as positive rewards, consistently applied. Since each is difficult to use well, and reinforcement has other socially-desirable consequences, reinforcement is highly preferable to punishment.

Contingency management has been successful with head starters, retarded children, adult vocational students and advanced college students; only the list of potential reinforcers varies. The rules of contingency contracting have the fortunate property of ignoring race, creed, income, age, condition of home life, nutrition and similar variables. Contingency management has been successfully employed in all of the following tasks:

Teaching composition to college students;
Teaching basic math to middle-class children;
Teaching English reading to Spanish-speaking poverty children;
Teaching welding to ghetto-level, unemployed adults;
Teaching verbalization to retarded children;
Creating positive self-images in reform school inmates;
Teaching live and sharing behaviors to aggressive, tantrum-prone children; and
Teaching self-supportive and cooperative behaviors to catatonic schizophrenics who had demonstrated no response whatsoever to many years of traditional psychotherapy.

The number and kind of reinforcers available to the teacher as a motivation manager are limited only by student and teacher imagination (and the social value system). In addition to reinforcers currently used by teachers (grades, praise, privileges and honors), they can include playing with games and toys, leaving school, looking out the window, talking with a friend, sleeping, listening to records, watching movies and making money, to name a few. Reading novels can be used to reinforce doing math, if novel reading is liked by the student and math is disliked; for another student, doing math can be a reinforcer for reading novels. Shop work or lab work, if liked by the student, can be made contingent upon successful completion of short (not year-long) amounts of text work.

The motivation manager role of the teacher can be employed in a new, specially-designed classroom with sliding partitions, or in a basement store-front school with leaking pipes. Some successful programs have employed a fully-equipped recreation room manned by para-professionsla or monitored by closed-circuit TV adjacent to the classroom. Students engaged in learning tasks in the classroom and, upon evaluation of their success, took a break in the recreation room. They went back and forth many times a day, spending half of their time in the recreation room; their concentration in the classroom was such that they nevertheless gained several years in academic progress in five weeks.[12] Others have operated in a traditional class setting, where reinforcements were confined to quiet, at-the-desk activities of the student's choosing.[13]

The functions of a teacher as a motivational manager can operate in conjunction with a wide variety of teacher roles from the other five categories.

Instruction and evaluation can be accomplished entirely by a computer display and program, for example. Because most computer managed instruction consists of small learning units leading toward small clusters of objectives which are tested regularly, this particular mix is highly compatible; the motivation manager already has small break points around which to contract with the student for reinforcing activities. Such a contract might read, "Do unit X, pass the progress test at 90 percent, and then you may do Y (student's preferred activity) for N minutes." Such a mixture could add a great deal of power to sound computer managed programs that now must depend only on clear learning objectives and tasks and on the Hawthorne effect for motivational impact. A computer can even evaluate student progress and tell the successful student to take a break (reinforcer) or offer him a list of appealing activities from which to choose his next occupation. A computer might have difficulty getting the student back to the console for his next learning task without human aid, however.

The teacher can also use a traditional text or lecture for instructional purposes. In this situation, the contract might read, "Listen to the lecture for N minutes and pass a short quiz at 90 percent and then you may relax, look out the window, or talk with a friend for N minutes." Or the contract might state, "Read these N pages of your text, come to my desk, and answer N questions correctly, and then you may . . . ," and so on.

In either example, when the student fails to meet the stated performance criterion (e.g., 90 percent), the teacher (or a computer program) schedules remediation before the reinforcer is delivered. Remediation can be as informal as an oral review of the quiz or as formal as a branch-programming assignment to an item-analyzed remedial unit. Failure to pass, however, should immediately cause the teacher to question the student's placement (is it too advanced?); the material (can he learn from this type of format?, does it teach what is tested?); and the test item (does it test what's taught or desired?). If the problem is none of the above, a conscientious motivation manager must ask whether the payoff makes it worth attending to the task. The burden is always on the system to prove that it is smart before it judges the student as dumb; obviously, a remedial track that contains the same shortcoming as the lesson the student failed will probably fail as well.

The motivation manager role of a teacher seems most powerful and reliable when combined with behavioral objectives, multi-level and multi-instrument diagnosis and evaluation, and single or multi-media instructional materials that contain the properties of sophisticated programmed materials. (Remember, the teacher herself has a role as an instructional medium and can structure such a role with the properties of good programming). This is not surprising since these seem to be the most powerful and reliable developments to come from advances in educational technology. But, just as the single addition of specifying behavioral objectives or the single addition of programmed materials to the traditional learning environment can provide a significant increase in student learning, so too can the mere addition to the environment of a teacher trained in her role as a motivation manager.

REFERENCES

1. Tosti, Donald T. "*PRIME—A General Model for Instructional Systems,*" *NSPI Journal,* Vol. VII, No. 2, February, 1968.

2. At one time I thought that educators are resistant to specifying objectives in terms of desired student behaviors because teaching in this context seems too limiting and unexciting. I tend now, however, to believe that much of the resistance has another cause: educators are afraid of specific objectives because they provide a real measure of teaching ability. It is interesting, too, to speculate that the recent thrusts of education into the affective domain, where many educators believe that behavioral specification of objectives is impossible, may be a reaction to increasing demands for such specification of objectives in the cognitive domain.

3. "Let's Be Practical About Reading," *American Education,* US HEW-OE, August/September, 1969, p. 28.

4. But educators do not seem to perceive the extent to which the medical profession uses treatment, rather than consideration of causes, in the diagnostic process. That is, instead of knowing that X symptoms equal Y disease, many successful medical diagnosticians rely on the knowledge that X symptoms usually respond to A, B, or C treatment. A is tried, and if the patient fails to respond, B is tried and then C. When positive response is noted, the problem is thus diagnosed not as Y disease, but as one of N factors that responds to treatment A. Perhaps this technique could aid educators in generating more treatment successes for the same diagnostic dollars.

5. Prescriptions made from vague or inaccurate diagnoses obviously can lead to the application of inappropriate treatments; but the potentially disastrous results of taking the wrong medicine can be mitigated if the diagnosis-by-treatment approach noted above is employed. What is required is frequent rechecking of the patient for positive response; if response is negative, the old treatment must be discontinued and new prescriptions tried. But, in education, evaluation is usually postponed for weeks, semesters, or even years, and many patients die.

6. Tosti, D. & Ball, J. *A Behavioral Approach to Instructional Design and Media Selection,* Albuquerque, New Mexico: Westinghouse Learning Corporation, 1969.

7. The reader will be hard-pressed to find any activity of a classroom teacher that does not fit somewhere in these simple categories. Housekeeping chores, for example, are motivational (pretty atmosphere), and roll-taking is diagnostic (is student present for learning activity?). The degree of stretching necessary to fit an observed activity into this model may be a reasonable measure of the relevancy of that activity.

8. Homme, L. *What Behavioral Engineering Is.* Albuquerque, New Mexico: Westinghouse Learning Corporation, 1969.

9. Premack, D. Toward Empirical Behavior Laws: I. Positive Reinforcement. *Psychological Review,* 1959, 66, 219–233.

10. Holland, J. G. & Skinner, B. F. *The Analysis of Behavior,* New York: McGraw-Hill Book Co., 1961.
11. The basis of the remaining segment of this paper draws heavily on many of Lloyd Homme's works, especially his ten rules of contingency contracting. See, *How to Use Contingency Contracting in the Classroom,* Research Press, USA, 1969.
12. *A Report to the Project Director of Upward Bound, University of Albuquerque.* Westinghouse Learning Corporation, 1968; and same report to *Florida A & M University,* Tallahassee, Florida, Westinghouse Learning Corporation, 1969.
13. *Teaching Contingency Management to Teachers of Underachieving Adolescents–Final Report.* Office of Education, Contract No. OE 1-6-061530-1934, Westinghouse Learning Corporation, 1968.

36 The Role of the Teacher in Society

William Glasser

What I would like to speak about tonight are some things I have done in education and how they might apply to people in business education. I have worked in education for about seven years myself, and during that time I have espoused a certain philosophy which is probably broadly covered under the catch phrase, "schools without failure." These kinds of schools are becoming more common around the country now as we work mostly with elementary schools to help young children develop the idea that they can succeed in school and move ahead with this success and with confidence to do better things. If a child gets off to a bad start, it is obvious that it is going to be hard to work with him. You in business education quite often get people that have been shunted into your department—especially in high schools—because someone says they are not going to do well in academics and should go into business. I suppose business classes and shops catch a certain number of students who themselves are more or less committed to failure in school. And so they fail again in your place—and give you a very difficult time in trying to work with them.

Reprinted from *Business Education Forum,* 26 (7):37–42 (April 1972), by permission of author and publisher.

What I am trying to do is prevent this from happening. But so long as it continues to happen, you have to learn, I suppose, how to handle people who come to your departments without too much motivation. The whole concept of schools without failure is a motivation concept. The idea is to motivate people to want to learn.

My own work was mostly in elementary schools. I had developed a reputation while working in corrections and dealing with kids who were in trouble. Eventually, I was asked to come into a school system. This was back in 1965. I went into the first school system as a consulting psychiatrist, a kind of "babe in the woods" in the education thing. I had come from the reform school, and I didn't know much about what I was going to run into in public schools.

The first thing they did is they put me in a room with a nasty little kid. I remember that this kid and I were sitting in a room. He was looking at me and I was looking at him. Evidently this kid was out of adjustment; and they hoped I would adjust him. Well, I didn't even want to sit in the same room with him, so I said, "Take this kid away." I asked if they had many more kids like this one, and they said they had a lot just like him. I wanted to quit right then and there, and if they had let me quit, I wouldn't be here talking now. I would have left the schools.

But they didn't let me quit. They were kind of desperate, and they said, "You don't have to sit in the room with the kid, but can you offer us anything?" I came up with some statements like, "Yes, I think I can give you some advice." That is always easy, and it is the safe thing to do—I didn't want to do any more than that to start with. But they asked what advice I had. I said, "I think you ought to stop irritating the kids." I don't think that is the advice that they wanted to hear, but that was what I was offering, And they said, "What do you mean, irritating them?" I said, "Well, you have a lot of kids around here who are irritated." Yes, they agreed with that. And I said, "I think you are irritating them." "What are we doing?" they asked. I said, "I think you are failing them, and I think that is irritating them." And so we argued this back and forth for quite a while. I held to my guns, and we got into this long hassle. "How can you stop failing them, if they are failing?" they wanted to know. And I said, "Is it doing any good?" And they said, "No." So I said, "Then, just stop it." And then they said, "How?" And I said, "I don't know. I never figured out how to start it. I never failed anybody. I come from a reform school—nobody failed in reform school. You flunked into that place, not out of it. There was no way you could fail out of it." They were willing to pass the nasty kids who knew something, and even pass the nice kids who knew nothing, but the nasty kids who knew nothing—they are the ones that really failed. And I suggested that even those kids don't fail. So they said, "What shall we do?"

This gets on to some of the things that I suggested. "Make friends with them." (Now this was a long time ago—maybe schools are more friendly today, but then, this came as quite a little shock.) "Make friends with the kids? What do you mean?" "I don't think I mean anything special," I said. "Just make friends." I don't know whether there is any difference between making friends with kids and making friends with anybody else, and I have held to that pretty much: that if we want to motivate children to work in today's schools, we have to make friends with them. And people asked, "Well, how do you do that?"

So I analyzed friendship. There are three things that you ordinarily do to make friends with people. One is to treat them kindly and with courtesy and consideration. I said, "Do this at all times and under all circumstances, regardless of how the child treats you." We say we are the professional people, so we have to take this responsibility. It will give you a certain power that you have never had before. It is very difficult for a child to continue to act up or misbehave or give you a hard time if you always treat him with kindness and consideration.

"The second part," I said, "is that friends ordinarily have a few laughs when they are together. I think we ought to have a few laughs in the classroom—maybe not make it a laugh-in, but once or twice a week to have a laugh won't hurt anything." I had been going in and out of some fairly grim classrooms and I told them that kids want to laugh, whether in elementary school or in business classes. You don't have to do much to get them to laugh. It doesn't take any great comedian—just a few very poor jokes will get them laughing. So they said, "All right, we will do that. What is the third thing?"

The third thing is the hardest, and I am not sure how it applies to business education, yet I feel it does apply. I think it applies because again it has to do with motivating the children and young people to learn. I don't think you can always assume that everyone that comes into your classroom is going to be highly motivated or that you can teach as if they are. I think we have an obligation not only to teach but also to motivate. And this is a point where there are areas of disagreement. Many teachers are from the old school and believe that the student is either motivated and learns or else fails. That's it! And there is nothing basically wrong with that idea providing there are reasonable places for the failures to go.

But more and more in our society there are fewer places for children and young people who fail to go. So when you fail someone in your class in business, whatever particular phase of this course you teach, where can that student go? Now you may say, that is not my problem, that is his. He failed. And of course he did. But the point is that our job is not so much to concern ourselves with failing or not failing him, but to motivate him so that he will do the work. I think that teachers in all courses, all disciplines, have this obligation.

So we got into this motivation bit, and the motivation, of course, will come partly from being kind and courteous and having a few laughs. But the hardest thing to do in motivating young people is to talk with them: to set-up a time when you talk. I suggest to elementary schools that this happen every day. The class gets into a circle and they talk. In secondary schools and colleges, however, the students resent it if you try to talk too much with them. But they also resent it, I believe—although they don't know how to voice their resentment—when you don't talk with them very much. They want to have some conversation with you as a teacher and with each other about anything that is of some interest and has some reasonable connection with business or something relevant to their lives. If you will have these kinds of conversations periodically, maybe even on a basis of once a week, you will motivate many more people to work hard in your class.

And as I started saying this, people said: "When I was going to school no one had to motivate me. I was motivated." You know, the old story which we all tell. And maybe we were motivated when we were going to school, and for that I would say great! But we can't assume that because we and the people that went to school with us were motivated, today's students are the same way. What I am suggesting is something that will motivate students who tend to be less motivated than we were.

WHY WE WERE MOTIVATED

People ask why we were motivated. I think the answer is pretty clear. If you are about my age, in the mid forties or even a little younger or older, we were motivated because we were scared. It is a good reason, and it is an ancient and traditional motivater, and it works as long as people are scared. But if people aren't scared, it doesn't work.

The teachers said to me that the ancient and traditional motivaters of fear and threats that had always been used in education quite effectively didn't seem to be working anymore. Principals came to me and asked what I learned working in prisons that they might use in schools to scare kids—they asked this in all sincerity. And I said that in prisons we were scared of them. We tried to treat them nice. We thought that would be best for everybody.

Well, if the fear is gone, then the question immediately asked is, Where is the fear? What happened to it? Where did it go? I think we have to begin to examine the society in which we live, and I think that if we understand the society, we have a much better chance to work more effectively with our students and to understand some reasons why they are the way they are and why they aren't scared.

The students you are teaching for the most part are not too frightened. They may be motivated or not motivated, but if you attempt to motivate them through fear or threats or failure or some methods that used to work, you will find that this is no longer as effective. That's because the students themselves have changed—there really has been a change. And I would like to tell you a little bit about this change because it is going to affect your personal life and the lives of your students dramatically in the next few years.

The historical basis for the change is really too long to go into at the present time. But sometime after World War II, about 1950, give or take a few years, the major motivation of almost all the young people suddenly shifted, and a new motivation began to spring up. The old motivation—the one we were used to, the one that most schools and teachers depended upon—began to become secondary to the new motivation. When teachers first said to me that kids have changed, I kind of pooh-poohed this idea. Then I began to listen, I began to look, and I began to think that maybe they had changed. Maybe my kids are really a lot different than I was, and maybe your children are much different from the way you were. The difference was something I couldn't pinpoint.

By this time I had written the book, *Schools Without Failure,* that told teachers to get involved with kids, to stop failing them, to make education relevant and thoughtful. And teachers asked me why. "Nobody got involved with me," they said. "My education wasn't particularly relevant and certainly no one broke his back to make it thoughtful. Why do we have to do this particular thing now?" And I told them, "I don't know, but I think it will work."

In the schools I was working in, mostly elementary schools, I promised them if they would do these things the discipline problems in the school would drop to almost nothing and the children would be motivated to learn. And the teachers decided to give it a try. I didn't know whether it would work or not, but I had to say something or I wouldn't have gotten anywhere. In schools where they took me really to heart, it did work. Children who were previously very unmotivated began to want to learn and the discipline problems dropped off.

When people saw this, they began to believe that I was right, that some change had taken place, and they kept asking me why these things tork and what change has taken place and other questions that I couldn't answer because I did not know. I had written a book, but I didn't know the answers, and it was bothering me. Bothering me because I should have known why my ideas worked, what the difference was—and I was worried someone else would find out before I did. And it seemed that would be kind of embarrassing.

ROLE NOT GOAL

So I started to do some extensive reading and finally found the answer in a statement by Marshall McLuhan: the students are searching for a role, not a goal. To me, that simple explanation was profound! This was what I had been looking for. This was why the things I was advocating—simple things like making friends with the students and making the education sensible—were necessary now even though they weren't necessary when I went to school. I learned—whether the teacher was friendly or not. I learned the most nonsensical things in school, and I was happy to learn them. I was goal oriented, and I wanted to get that diploma! I was frightened of not getting it. I was not searching for a role, for verification of me as a person. I was searching for a specific goal which I felt would lead to security and success, and then perhaps later in life I would be able to find a role for myself.

My major motivation was the major motivation of the people who have lived in the world for the past 10,000 years. Almost everyone, except the very rich, the very powerful, or the very intellectual people, was as I was: goal oriented. Get the job done, gain the security from getting the job done, and then afterwards, worry about who you are as an individual or how to lead a fuller, richer, more enjoyable, more satisfying, human kind of a life. That came second. In other words, the natural sequence of things for 10,000 years had been goal before role, and McLuhan was saying the students are in turmoil because they want to change this natural order of things and have role precede goal. By that he meant that they want to be recognized as individuals, as human beings, as people who stand for something even before they start doing the job.

The traditional sequence had been to do the job and then get the pat on the head. Now I am sure that every single person who teaches, if he has a good goal-oriented student working away and doing the job, is more than happy to give him a pat on the head when he does a good job. That is natural; that is the way our whole system was set up, and all our institutions are based upon that ancient and traditional order of things. The only problem is that those people who presently inhabit our institutions, those people for whom our institutions are created—the students—have changed that order. They now say: Pay some attention to me, verify me, accept me as a human being, and then I will work at the task that you lay out for me. What they are really saying in rather simple terms is pat me on the head first and then I will do the job. And that is contrary to what most of us have believed most of our lives. We say, "Never. You do the job first." And they say, "Unless you give me some recognition that I count for something and you accept me as a person, I am not going to do the job."

If we examine the institutions of our society, and school of course is probably the major institution in terms of involving people and investments of money, we find that they always reflect that society, and they tend to reflect it even after things have changed. And we have suddenly moved into a new society with almost no preparation—a society where, as McLuhan says, role probably now precedes goal. And our institutions have nowhere begun to accept, or even to become aware of, this change. I go into school after school and point this out, and I find a few people agreeing. "Maybe that is why I succeeded working with that one kid," they say. "Remember that kid! Gee, that kid I couldn't really get to. Suddenly I said the heck with pushing and pushing and pushing him to do the work and I spent a few minutes each day just making friends with him, and all of a sudden he started doing the work. He began to move in a way that all the threats and the various sanctions and everything else I did could not accomplish. I spent a few minutes making friends with him —simply saying okay, kid, I will give you some recognition as a human being and I accept you. He then became motivated to do the work because he related to me and believed the work made some sense."

BUSINESS EDUCATION MAKES SENSE

In your particular field, what you ordinarily teach makes a great deal of sense. It is quite easily applicable to the world as people see it around them. The whole concept of business in a society like ours is a very relevant and valid one. The only thing you have to make sure of is that your students will learn the concept, and so again, I am getting back to motivation. And I claim that each year, as you struggle with your new classes in typing or shorthand or bookkeeping or accounting or business and management practices, you will see more and more students say: "I really have no interest in this work unless I gain some recognition here that I am a human being"—and this is true whether you are at a higher level in a university or just at the beginning level in a junior or senior high school. They won't say this to you directly, I suppose, but they will behave as if that's the case. You will come home at the end of the day after hammering away at this class, and your head will hurt, and you will wonder why it is so hard. You are doing the same things you always did, and it is so much harder. The mistake is in assuming that the students' motivation is the same as it always was. The only students very much like that anymore are getting their recognition someplace else. There are a few goal-oriented students in your classes; but I don't believe there is any place in the system, even in the professional schools, where teachers can count on that old motivation being valid for many, and it will be less each year. And you are going to have to do something whether you teach business, typing, shorthand. biology, mathematics, law, medicine, whatever. I don't think it makes a particle of difference. Even if the shop courses, something is going to have to be done. Even football and basketball coaches are going to have to let these students know not only that they care but also that they are going to spend a certain amount of time getting to know them and helping them get to know each other.

For 10,000 years of what we call civilization, people really were struggling for security and were terribly frightened of insecurity. After World War II and the prosperity that followed, there was an increased concern for the rights of people as people—concern by our law, by our courts, and by society as a whole. We began practicing more democracy than we had ever really practiced before. So what we are seeing now is more freedom, more respect for people, and yet more griping and complaining about there not being enough. Because a little nourishes a little more. So with more security and enough money so that people don't have to worry about food in their bellies and a roof over their heads, with more concern for the rights of people as people, and with the increasing and tremendous influence of television upon this whole culture, I think we have seen 500 million people who comprise what we loosely call the Western World very quickly move into a society where almost everybody is now role oriented. You are and I am.

But there is a big difference between us and our students. We became role oriented through increasing security. We became secure enough so we could move into concerning ourselves with our humanity, with our identity, with who we are. But as the older people of the society, we went through the traditional sequence—for us goal preceded role.

MESSAGE OF TELEVISION

All your students, whether you teach college or high school, in almost all cases had security as they grew. They have lived in a time when there has been an obvious concern about human rights. And they have been born and raised with television, with lots of time to watch it. And the message of television is very strong. The message is: Everything is all right. There are a few little places where it doesn't say this, but mostly that is what TV says, and people listen to it. TV says you are important, you ought to enjoy yourself! It says use our product, and it will make a better human being out of you, a more acceptable person, a sexier, better smelling, more sociable individual.

If you remember the old TV ads, you can see how the tradition changed in television. Television changed from goal to role in about 1951. (Schools haven't changed yet, and I found out about the change in 1969, which goes to show you how quickly people who are not at the forefront of things find out.) The old ads, if you remember, used to say that the products would give you more for your money. They didn't say what was better or worse, but they said you got more. That was the goal-oriented advertisement. (Comparable advertisements in today's paper are classified ads or ads for certain types of clothing and food.) Then TV advertisers began to feel that people weren't that interested in saving a dime. Everybody had a dime. Who cared? And it didn't seem important anymore whether they offered much or little. What they had to do was satisfy people's needs. They had a serious problem trying to do that with some products. And so they said, "This we may never do, but maybe we can make them think we are doing it. And that will be good enough because reality is what we think it is, and as long as we hammer the message home enough and as long as they need certain roles defined, they will buy anything that might give them that feeling." So they designed new ads that showed people using the products and always enjoying themselves—always being fulfilled in some way. And the point is that it worked dramatically well.

This is the change in the society mirrored by TV advertisements, all of which prove that if you want to sell a product that has no utility value, you have got to tie it to "role." There is absolutely no other way to sell it. And products of low utility have high profit. It is almost directly proportional—as utility goes down, profit goes up, and if you tie a product's use to a human need, like popularity, you can sell tremendous quantities of the product.

But that is all history now. The important part is that advertisements will mirror and reflect the basic wants and needs of the people. If they don't do this, the companies will go broke.

So with this change in society and because of television, the increased concern for human rights, and the fact that people are secure, the old fear left, and young people are no longer scared. When the fear left, another innate motivation that had been kept in check for 10,000 years came forth. This was the intrinsic motivation: I want to be involved with my fellowman, I want to be respected for the person I am, and I can take a chance and make that my main motivation because I am secure now. And what we are seeing in our schools, reflected in your classes and all classes, is increasingly this kind of student—the student for whom the old motivaters don't work, the student for whom you have to develop new motivaters. A student who will ask questions and say, "Where does this affect me? Does this make sense? Is this going to be meaningful in my life?" As well as the student who says, "I want you to have some concern and care for me as a human being within this class."

I see this in all schools; therefore, I am willing to make this suggestion: that the schools change to adapt to the motivation of these students. Institutions don't like to change, because they have tradition on their side. But I think that what you are seeing is the need for this change. I am not reflecting something that I predict will happen; I am reflecting something that has happened and is continuing to happen. And if you go into a teacher's room—whether it is a class in business English or typing or shorthand or bookkeeping or accounting or management principles or whatever—and you see a class working very hard and dedicated to the job, check the teacher out carefully and see if this teacher isn't making some provision in his teaching day or teaching week to recognize these students as human beings. Also see if this teacher isn't teaching essentially without failure. Because the whole concept of failure is vital to this concept of role.

SECURITY OR INSECURITY

There are in society two kinds of things that you can have, security or insecurity. If you have insecurity you are just grubbing for survival and terrified, and the fear of this will motivate people to grub for security. But that is a very tangible thing. Security is much more tangible than what's happened now. Now we have people attempting to gain a successful identity for themselves—a feeling that "I am a successful, worthwhile human being . . . I have security." And they can gain a successful identity providing they get feedback from the people around them that success is possible for them. But if they get feedback from the people around them that they are failures or they are not doing the job or they are not really performing as they should, they don't take this in the old sense. The old sense was, Okay, I am doing badly on the job, so I had better improve. Now they say, I must be a failure as a person. And I talk to children over and over again who got low grades in school, and I ask them what low grades mean, and they say it means that I am no good—and I am a failure.

And I think increasingly you will see as you perhaps teach in the traditional way (although in business education the traditional way is easily, easily changed) that giving students very low grades instead of motivating them is taken as a personal thing. Students are looking for a role, and if they can't find a role as a success, they will take on the role as a failure and say, See you verified me as a failure. What do failures do? Well, failures don't work very hard. They don't really buckle down and do the job that has to be done. They work at failing. They live with failure, and they reinforce themselves as failures. And then they can say in a certain perverse sense, well at least I succeeded at failing. And you are struggling in many cases with students who are tremendously successful at failing. When you continue failing them, you give them the ultimate reinforcement.

And so what I suggested years ago when I went into public schools, I suggest now in your schools just as much: Don't give them a chance to get this label. Say, "There are no failures in my class. You cannot fail here." That will shake them up to start with a little bit, I'll tell you that! That goes against the way almost all of you have been taught yourselves, and really what many of you believe. You say if he does a bum job, he ought to be failed. I have no right to send him out into the world unless he knows his stuff. Well, that is true. But you also have to understand that if you fail him, he will still not learn his stuff in most cases.

SCHOOL WITHOUT FAILURE

A school without failure is not at all a school with all success or guarantee of success. You don't give a person a good grade or a good report for doing bad work. But you don't fail him either. And this is a difficult concept for many people to understand. The old concept that just because you don't succeed you necessarily have to fail has to be gotten rid of. What you have to do is make this concept clear to your class: that you haven't succeeded, but in this class nobody fails. That is motivating. Then you are not labeling the person a failure. You are putting the tag where it should be—on his work, not on him, and saying, "You haven't succeeded yet." Use this idea of time. "Yet" is a word which connotes time. And when you do that, the person has no choice but to continue moving ahead.

It is a very motivating kind of situation. Because you say to him, "I care for you, I want to talk with you, I want to get to know you, and I am not going to fail you. But I won't give you credit for this course until you do the job." People understand that; it is realistic, it is sensible, and it is motivating. And they say, "Well, what if I never do the job?"

Then you will say, "You will never get credit for the course. That is obvious. But I am not going to fail you. I see no sense in failing you. You are not a failure at typing, you just haven't yet learned to typing. It has nothing to do with failure. I don't know anything about failure. If you set out to drive from Chicago to Toledo, you don't fail Toledo if you don't get there. You just haven't gotten there yet, that's all. If you want to get there, then get going and get there. We don't care how long it takes, that is your decision. We will do everything possible to expedite the course."

People tell me that everybody will stop working and just clog up the class and do nothing. Well, they won't. They won't. They will continue to work and work harder perhaps than they have ever worked before. You have to have faith that people really want to succeed, that success is highly motivating. But we have to take away the concept of failure and get across to the class only this concept—I can make it; I can succeed here; this teacher is here to teach me; this teacher is here to get to know me, to explain what I am doing, and talk with me about what I am doing, how it relates to the world, and how it might make sense. But there is no failure here at all. And if I take a little longer, I will take a little longer. Who is the one that suffers if I take longer? Well, if it is hard work, I will have to suffer a little longer until I learn it.

It is a highly motivating way to operate, but as I say, it goes against the ethics and principles of traditional schooling, which is if the kid is supposed to type a certain number of words by a certain day and he doesn't do it, we give him a low or failing grade. In the past when he was frightened, this might have motivated him, but right now it tends to reinforce the concept: I am not doing very well and that is it; I may as well stop. And I think you find yourself in that situation with an increasing number of students.

With this in mind, I began to be able to tell people that the reason you don't fail people is you don't wnat them to identify as failures. The reason you make friends with them is that getting involved and treating them with kindness and courtesy and having a few laughs are the things that reinforce this thing which I call identity or role. These are the basic reinforcing things. You can only gain a feeling of verification through another human being whom you respect verifying you. That is absolutely the only way it can happen.

If we do that, we motivate the person to say: I am a success, I am a person. Now, as a person who is moderately successful, what should I do? Well, I had better do the things that will give me further success. This teacher says that his course is definitely a good course and I elected to take it anyway, so I will work for these goals because I am a competent person. I won't be failed here. I will be respected and treated well here, and these goals make good sense. And if I reach these goals it will make me a better person.

And I think that is absolutely true and you have every reason to reinforce that, of course. The teacher says, "I will respect you further as you work further and do the job. But I respect you in the beginning and I won't threaten you with failure."

There are the basic concepts of the school without failure. They are concepts which are strongly related to the new world in which we live. Some people say that this world isn't going to last very long. Maybe we will have a long depression and go back to the old fear of insecurity. Maybe we will. I can't say that we won't But the point is that most of the young people you are dealing with now are being raised in homes where their mothers and fathers have concerned themselves very seriously with making sure they get the best possible life, whether they are in the poorest homes or the wealthiest homes. They have reinforced them as people who are important, and they expect to get the same reinforcement when they come to school.

You don't have to do that much. Spend a few moments at the beginning of the class just to let the kid know: I do care about you as a person, you won't fail, the work here is fair, it is honestly laid out, work at your own speed, and I will help you as much as possible. And I will talk to you and make friends with you and respect you along the way.

A SIMPLE MESSAGE

Well this is a terribly simple message for the most part. What I am trying to do is to explain why this simple message is necessary. It is necessary because we have moved into a world where we have more security and where there is going to be even more concern for security. And as security goes up, then we can move into this next major concern: How can we establish ourselves as human beings? And if we can establish ourselves as successful human beings, as people who really stand for something and mean something, and then do something not only for ourselves but for others, then we can have a good world in this new world. If we establish ourselves as failing human beings, as people who gain our recognition only because we fail or because of the things we do which are harmful to ourselves and destructive to others—if too many people gain recognition and gain an identity that way, then we will have a world which is really not very worthwhile living in.

Unfortunately, at the present time our schools generally are the largest manufacturers of young-people failures—although business courses are probably the least offenders here. Our traditional schools do a good job of teaching kids they are failures. And if they continue to do that, then our schools will be the principal impediment to this new society we are trying to create. I think our schools can change. It doesn't cost any more. It will probably cost less. It just means our recognition that the student is now a human being when he come to school and can be motivated most by reinforcing that concept and then explaining to him reasonably and sensibly what he has to do further to reinforce himself and to get a job done.

37 The Teacher and Nonverbal Communication

Robert Koch

I'm going to talk about nonverbal communication. Sometimes it is called "body-language," but that is not entirely accurate—there is more than the body involved, as you shall see.

Anthropologists term it *kinesics*.[1] They have been working in this area for a long time. Then it spread to counselors and psychologists and now it is beginning to filter through to teachers. Strangely, such breakthroughs often come from other disciplines. It is said that the computer scientists told the neurologists how the brain circuits had to function.

What is nonverbal language? It is any message we send or receive outside of words. It may be an "agreed-upon-before" signal such as the umpire's "You're out," or something so common to our culture that everyone understands it, like the teacher's "Shh," her finger to her lips. The hippy's hair, a teen-ager screeching his tires rounding a turn, a large number of cookbooks in a home, and being first to pick up the restaurant check are all nonverbal signs. It would take a large book to contain them.

Is a single nonverbal signal always valid? No; nonverbal observers prefer to judge it in context, just as they would a word. A frown, for instance, might mean concentration or it might denote annoyance. A white face could have several causes.

Don't sell nonverbal decoding short; it gets at the real truth as you shall soon see. It would not take us long to determine whether the white face came from cold, fear, sickness, or a long lack of sun, and when we know nonverbally, we know for sure.

I first got interested in nonverbal communication from a statement of Freud.[2] He said that a patient might lie with words, but the therapist would know the truth from the nonverbal signals. I thought about it a minute and decided, "Well, I wouldn't," and began reading in the area.

Most nonverbal encoding and decoding is largely unconscious with a sprinkling of conscious decoding. An example: You grip the arms of the dentist's chair, unaware of the act. He sees and knows you are nervous, aware of what he saw. You might deny being nervous (verbally) either because you are not aware

[1] Birdwhistell, R. *Kinesics and Context.* University of Pennsylvania Press, September, 1970.

[2] Freud, S. *Psychopathology of Everyday Life.* New York: Macmillan, 1914.

Reprinted from *Theory into Practice*, 10(4):231–236 (October 1971,) by permission of author and publisher.

that you are, or because our culture frowns upon being a sissy. But your gripping hands spoke the truth and the dentist ignores your verbal denial.

I could say that nonverbal communication is brand new. No university offers a course. But a very few groups are aware. Sensitivity group leaders know of its powers. Better-trained police use it. Actors certainly do. Conmen and other brainy-type criminals are adept. But in the schools, if anyone knows about the use of nonverbal, it is the counselor. However, most teachers never heard of nonverbal other than their "reading" a few student-sent cues.

Of those above, mentioned as consciously using nonverbal cues, it seems they largely decode. The policeman watches for guilt signs, but does not consider what nonverbal cues he is sending to the suspect. The teacher and the counselor perform in like manner. In fact, that is about as extensively as most of us ever use nonverbal. Only the actor and the criminal, of the groups mentioned, are concerned with sending.

Strangely, these two groups want to fool us—to make us believe things that are not really so. Is it bad, then, to send nonverbal messages knowingly? As with words, nonverbal can be good or bad.

So the study of nonverbal is new, yet it is as old as the hills. It was the first language, even before grunts came into vogue. It really is not new to teachers. They use it all the time, but they need to refine their decoding and to encode consciously.

They know it is good to smile at a student, so they do. After a while it becomes a habit. There is nothing necessarily "fakey" or wrong about one's deliberately smiling at a student. We should, then, see the deliberate use of other nonverbal signals in the same light.

We asked one teacher to deliberately try moving closer to students when they were working in small groups at tables. She reported that it was very hard to do. She felt conspicuous and ill at ease, and so uncomfortable that she would have given up on further attempts had not she gotten immediate, positive feedback from her students. They sent her messages that they liked the warmth and interest that her closer proximity engendered. In a short time, drawing near to students became a natural act for her.

A second teacher, however, tried too much too soon. She determined to touch students to unleash the tremendous power of tactility. Two obstacles stood in the way of success: First of all she had great inhibitions against becoming that intimate, having been raised in a nonexhibitionistic, reserved home. No doubt she sent out conflicting nonverbal statements when she attempted to touch. To the student receiving the positive nonverbal touch, it would seem almost as if she had patted him with one hand and pinched with the other! Secondly, such a teacher, unused to touching, would probably not be able to sense need for touch in a student or the opposite, a horror of being touched.

The last is exactly what happened at this brave teacher's first attempt. She touched a student who did not welcome it and he told her so! She was dismayed and crushed. The student who did not wish to be touched was sending out nonverbal signals, had she been able to read them. One signal of such people is that they will retreat if another draws too close. It is as though we each have an invisible bubble about us. Edward Hall calls this our "personal space."[3] It is of a different size for each person; we grow uneasy if another steps into our bubble.

Teachers do unconsciously read a lot of their students' nonverbal messages, and consciously read some,[4] but their use of conscious sending is practically nil.

What they are not aware of, is the fact that they are unconsciously sending messages to their students in a constant chatter. One can "shut-up" verbally, but not nonverbally. Even a silence speaks.[5]

Teachers probably use nonverbal mostly to verify verbal statements and to detect sincerity and emotion. For instance, a fellow teacher says, "I *really* worry about my failing students," and we believe her, or we don't. We turn to nonverbal, whether we realize it or not, for verification.

A student tells the counselor that he hates his father. The counselor believes him. . . . or he does not. If he does not believe him, perhaps the counselor cannot tell us why—he may call it a "hunch." A counselor who was sophisticated in the use of nonverbal decoding might have explained, "The student's posture wasn't quite like a hating person's, and the gestures were too expansive and violent. These denote anger, yes, but not real hate."

We use nonverbal to "read" actions too far away to hear the words or when there are no words. The other day while testing seventh graders I observed certain nonverbal signals. When some students wanted to copy an answer from another, they would casually glance at the wall clock, innocently enough, but before lowering their gazes, their eyes would dart about, locating the proctors. The change-of-pace of the eye movements exposed them. Students who merely wished to know the time did not change their rhythm.

Others would hold their heads too stationary as they peered out of the tops of their eyes at a paper across the table. It is quite a difficult task to copy in such a manner.

First of all, peering out of the tops of the eyes is not natural. Also when copying from across the table everything is reversed or inverted; and lastly, we prefer to be about fourteen inches away for clear vision of small objects.

These last gave themselves away by having to hold their heads too stationary while they spotted the answer they sought under unnatural conditions.

All of us make tiny head movements continuously. We can detect when such movements stop in another. There seems to be an instinct to "freeze" if we sense danger or if we are about to attack. We have apparently inherited the instinct to note stoppage of all motion in our companions.

Other students in the above situation would look at another's test, but somehow the nonverbal told me that all was well. Checking, I would find that these pupils were through with the test or were on a different part.

If possible, I check out the validity of my decoding of nonverbal signals. For

---

[3] Hall, E. T. *The Silent Language.* Garden City: Doubleday, 1959.

[4] Galloway, C. College of Education, Ohio State University, (in correspondence).

[5] Ibid.

example, the other day I made a statement about promotion of failing students to the next grade. I was speaking to Mrs. Van Etten, a media and materials expert at George Peabody College in Nashville. Her shoulders gave a litle twisting movement and there was a minute eye-flicker.

I read this as saying she didn't agree with my statement, and I turned to Mr. Donald Petrie, a student of nonverbal, and asked him to decode the nonverbal we had seen. He agreed with my interpretation. Then we asked Mrs. Van Etten, and she laughingly admitted that we had read her nonverbal correctly.

This raises the question, can you be conned? Are there people who can lie verbally and convince you by making their nonverbal congruent? Yes, there are. Bette Davis does it all the time. She says, "I love you—I hate you—I'm tired," and the audience believes her.

Certain criminals, successful salesmen, good poker players, and actors can fool us if they choose to. Some students certainly lie to teachers, and many go undetected because teachers are not nonverbal experts. Sometimes people think they are "putting one over," but an expert in nonverbal usually knows.

I read of a certain Chinese jade dealer who watched the nonverbal of customers, especially the eye-pupil size. Customers would enter the shop and examine several pieces (indifferently, they thought), but the dealer knew which piece they *really* wanted and jacked the price up.

Why should teachers be interested in nonverbal communication? Besides adding depth to interactions with adults, there are two reasons of special note to teachers.

First, if we merely listen to the words of children, we are only partly understanding. Children are not so verbal as adults and often do a poor job of expressing themselves. A child begins life a totally nonverbal person and gradually grows to use verbal expression. The younger he is, or the less intelligent, the less he will be adept at expressing himself verbally.

An analogy: If the speaker's mike kept cutting on and off at a lecture so we only heard parts, we should come away only partially informed. A lot of what a child tells us has the mike shut off if we are inept at decoding nonverbal signals.

Ernest Siegel claims that most special-education children are even less adept at verbal than normals, but are quite alert and keen in the use of nonverbal. He adds, however, that there is an occasional special-education child who has no concept that movements, facial expressions, etc., are sending messages.[6]

Siegel gives as an example an unsavory child, nose running, face dirty, hungry for love, who rubbed up against a shrinking, white-faced teacher, never dreaming that he repelled her. He says such children have to be taught what their actions and those of others mean.

To complicate the fact that children do not send messages completely via the verbal medium, teachers are adept in using the verbal and rather inept in nonverbal.

[6] Siegel, E. New York City, Homebound Teachers, (in correspondence).

Teachers are a very, very verbal group of people. They, in large part, are the ones who took to reading "like a duck to water." Perhaps, for this reason—they sense the great power of words—they thus depend on words to the degree that they seem to be weaker in the use of nonverbal.

In an unpublished study, laborers knew more about a person being observed during an interview than teachers did. Convicts know more about hired personnel than the prison psychiatrist does.[7] In fact, one warden near Denver has convicts interview prospective employees, and follows their advice, to the chagrin of the personnel office.

Before hiring, the personnel office has tests and interviews, letters of application and letters of recommendation—all verbal. The convicts, perhaps forced to learn nonverbal in the ghetto to survive, bypass the verbal (which can be all lies) and get at the truth.

I have said one reason for you to be aware of nonverbal is so that you can understand better what children say.

The second reason to understand nonverbal is that teachers would like to know that they send positive signals that "turn the kids on," and avoid sending negative, "turn-them-off signals."

None reading this will deny that children have two talents: They can predict coming bad weather and they are past-masters at "psyching us out." Ask any fifth grader which subject his teacher likes to teach and which she does not, and who the teacher's pets are, and whom she does not like, and the student will tell you! Now we know the teacher did not say (verbally) these things, so they had to be nonverbally stated and read by the child.

These answers may come as a surprise to the teacher. She may not have been aware that she did not like to teach arithmetic, but upon pondering, agreed.

Even worse, a teacher can so devalue a subject that a negative imprinting carries on into other school years. Parents can devalue the whole idea of school—turn the child off—and do it all nonverbally.

Such parents protest, "We tell him to study so he can get ahead." But nonverbally they may be saying otherwise.

I observed one parent approach his boy who was oiling a baseball mitt. He stood beside the boy, a hand on his shoulder, and talked about the merits of neatsfoot oil on leather.

When the lad switched to home-work, the father excused himself and went outside to prune the shrubbery. School work was devaluated.

It was mentioned earlier that the fifth grade student would be able to name his classmates who were "teacher's pets" and those who were not favored. The teacher's training and her middle-class morality dictate to her conscious mind. A dirty child, a dull one, a dark-skinned one, even disturbed or a disturbing one is entitled to acceptance and dignity. So she *says* the *right words*. But her unconscious mind knows differently and directs the nonverbal actions that tell the students "the real score."

[7] Christensen, J. President emeritus, Community College, Wyoming, (in conference).

Dr. Palomares tells of an experiment he conducted.[8] First he culled out teachers who were frank about their certain dislikes. He chose only those who claimed fair treatment and admitted no prejudice of any kind.

Then he video-taped them while teaching. When they saw and heard themselves, nearly all were amazed—they had broken nonverbal rules and belied their previous claims.

To partially explain the above, if teachers know a rule, their conscious minds and their sense of fairness refuse to let them break the rule. Example: They would not call a child, "Stupid." They know that rule. But perhaps they do not know that. . . . spending just a mite more time criticizing his blackboard example than is done for others speaks volumes.

The teacher may protest (in the last example), "But I *told* the student that he had pleased me!" We must remember that the nonverbal message is so much stronger than the verbal that if there is an incongruity, the *nonverbal is believed!*[9]

I am reminded of Owen Wister's Virginian when he told the other cowboy to smile when calling him a dirty name. Here we have an example of the more powerful nonverbal wiping-out the defined meaning of the words.

When the verbal and nonverbal do not agree, it is called the "double-bind." If a mother says, "I love you," but nonverbally says it is not so, the child believes the nonverbal. Dr. Ray Birdwhistell reports filming a mother pinning a diaper on her baby.[10] It had been determined earlier that the mother rejected her child on an unconscious level. Slowing down the film showed a "double-bind" in action, but with all components being nonverbal.

If a teacher says, "I like you and I know you can do this work," but her nonverbal says, "But you and I both know I don't and you can't," the latter is believed by the child.

The "double-bind" theme cannot be developed further here due to space, but it is so important in mental health that some claim it is one cause of childhood schizophrenia.

I find teachers are divided in their opinions as to whether a teacher should know things about incoming students at the beginning of the year. Some are afraid that if they know I.Q.'s and behavior and so on, their expectancy will be actualized.

They are right! A mysterious phenomenon seems to exist in teaching. It seems teachers can "will" a child to learn, or they can squelch his progress (though trying hard to teach in either case), and what the child accomplishes correlates with teachers' expectancies. The pupils' meeting teachers' expectancies has been shown with mice and with rats and later with children.[11]

---

[8] Palomares, U. Human Development Laboratories, San Diego, (in lecture).

[9] Galloway, C. College of Education, Ohio State University, (in correspondence).

[10] Birdwhistell, R. *Kinesics and Context.* University of Pennsylvania Press, September, 1970.

[11] Christensen, J. President emeritus, Community College, Wyoming, (in conference).

Rist, R. Student Social Class and Teacher Expectations: Self-fulfilling Prophesy in Ghetto Education. *Harvard Review,* August, 1970, 40, 411–451.

I propose that short of the occult, the "willing a child to learn," and the fact that a child will meet a teacher's expectancy can only be explained by bringing in nonverbal. Teachers *must* be, in such cases, telling the child with nonverbal signals, that they expect him to achieve, or to fail, etc. Dr. Charles Galloway at Ohio State University supports my theory.[12]

Dr. Nicholas Long, speaking at the University of New Mexico in the *Guidance Greats Program*, claimed that students' good or bad behavior often can be attributed to the same thing—teachers' expectancies passed on to the students via nonverbal cues.

Since this article is of a survey nature, intended to whet teachers' curiosity and make them aware of nonverbal—that is the first step, become aware[13]—subtleties and refinements will not be dealt with.

For instance, it can be told of two persons, who is of the superior rank and who is subservient by noticing the changes in the length of the sentences used, or how one enters a room when the other is already inside.

Perhaps the reader already uses subtle nonverbal cues without being aware. In an interesting experiment at an army base they mixed unknown sergeants, wearing privates' uniforms, in with groups of new soldiers. Each sergeant was only told to take a shower with his group. Observers watched the naked men. The privates acted subservient to the sergeants. They made way, stood aside, and clearly showed that they saw them as "somebodies."[14]

Some basics in nonverbal communication:

Gestures: Most people think of hand gestures when gestures are mentioned, but there are foot, body, head, and facial gestures. Some gestures stand alone as in pointing, and others back-up verbal expressions as in saying, "It's over there," and pointing simultaneously. The verbal lags just behind the gesture in these cases. In spoofing an 1890 melodrama, for comic effect, the director has the actors reverse the sequence. The audience does not know why it is funny, but it is.

Posture: Standing or sitting, posture denotes inner feelings such as weariness, alertness, and relaxation. There are refinements such as, should a person suddenly shift positions on a chair and sit up straighter, he may have disagreed with the speaker or he may have switched sides in the argument.

Eyes: It is claimed that the eyes are the best nonverbal cue of all.[15] When one's pupil enlarges, one likes what he is looking at, or a student has the answer of the question asked. Anthropologists claim an attacker can be spotted and separated from a bluffer by the gaze combined with facial color, and that sexual invitation is reflected in the eyes.[16] People who claimed to like wild "mod"

[12] Galloway, C. College of Education, Ohio State University, (in correspondence).

[13] Galloway, C. *The Instructor,* 77, No. 8, April, 1968, 37–42.

[14] Christensen, J. President emeritus, Community College, Wyoming, (in conference).

[15] Hess, E. Pupil Size as Related to Interest Value of Visual Stimuli. *Science,* 1960, 132, No. 3423, 349–350.

[16] Morris, D. *The Naked Ape.* New York: Delta Press, 1969.

paintings, but really did not, have been exposed by eye-pupil photography.

Skin: Many signals are sent with skin changes such as pallor, perspiration, redness, and blushing.

Proximity: In general, we stay away from those we dislike or fear. It can also be related to one's poor self-image. Thus, the closer a teacher gets to a student, the better, keeping in mind the student's "personal space-bubble" mentioned earlier.

Tactility: Touching, when it is desired by the student, and when it is a natural act with the teacher, is a most powerful nonverbal act. At times it is the only way to reach a child.[17] Special-education children often need much touching, even hugging. Since, in our society, touching in certain combinations of sexes and ages might be misconstrued as sexual (by adults, not children), a teacher can achieve positive results with smiles, proximity, warm voice, and eye use.

Voice: At first glance, voice seems to be verbal, but interwoven around and among the words are tone, intonation, volume, pitch, hesitations, quivering, silence, etc. Emotions come through such as anger, fear, or enthusiasm. Many silent-picture stars became unemployed at the advent of "talking pictures," some because their voices did not sound well, but some because they could not match their voices to the emotion wanted by the director. The public would reject these actors.

Dress: Clothes and jewelry speak volumes about how the wearer sees himself or how he wants the observers to see him. Whole books have been written about the impact of dress.[18]

Breathing: Breathing reflects inner feelings such as excitement. When you think the nurse is uncommonly long in counting your pulse rate, she is spending half of the time counting and observing your breathing.

Time: The use of time tells us things. It was mentioned earlier in the case of the teacher who criticized a student for a longer time than he did others. Being early or late or *exactly* on time tells the psychologist (or the principal) things about a teacher. There are many other examples, and no doubt many that I have not observed.

Materials: If a teacher uses work-books as "busy work," individualizes reading instead of depending upon a basal reader, wants all themes typed, has a number line taped to each child's desk—each of these and hundreds more, tells something about the teacher. I do not pretend to be able to decipher each, but teachers could ask themselves, "What am I saying nonverbally to students, parents, and other staff when I give thirty-two identical science books to the thirty-two students in my room?" Such questions will give insight.

Methods: The same thinking as was applied to materials will be profitable about methods.

---

[17] *Good Housekeeping,* August, 1971, 14–24.

[18] Flugel, J. *The Psychology of Clothes.* London: Hogarth. 1930.

Actions: The coach who runs the score up to 40 to 0 is telling us things about his security; the librarian who won't let books be taken home because they get dirty is also telling us of her values. The reader, upon reflection, can supply dozens more.

How can your school begin to apply the principles of positive nonverbal communication? It has been mentioned that the first step is awareness of the existence of nonverbal language. After reading this tonight, you'll begin to notice nonverbal signals tomorrow. As with any skill, you will improve rapidly with basics; refinement will take more time. It is a fascinating study bringing satisfactions.

38 Discipline: Four Approaches

J. Michael Palardy and James E. Mudrey

What approaches can teachers use in dealing with discipline—one of their most demanding and most complex responsibilities? We begin with the knowledge that there are no easy answers to discipline problems. But we also begin convinced that, generally, there are right and wrong approaches to finding answers.

Discipline is defined in various ways. Our definition can best be given by asking three questions: What can teachers do to prevent behavior problems? What can teachers do when behavior problems occur? What can teachers do to prevent behavior problems from recurring? Discipline is what teachers do in response to these three questions.

Ours is not one of the more encompassing definitions. In fact, some object strenuously to the idea that discipline, as in our definition, deals only with behavior problems. We are aware of this objection and of the limitation of our definition, but we make no apologies. Teachers are asking these three questions. We think that they deserve a response.

There are four basic approaches to discipline: the permissive, the authoritarian, the behavioristic, and the diagnostic.

Reprinted from *The Elementary School Journal,* 73 (6): 297–305 (March 1973), by permission of the authors and The University of Chicago Press. Copyright © 1973 by the University of Chicago Press.

THE PERMISSIVE APPROACH

One school of thought has a simple answer to the discipline questions. The answer is, "Do nothing." What can teachers do to prevent behavior problems? Nothing. What can teachers do when behavior probl ems occur? Nothing. What can teachers do to prevent behavior problems from recurring? Nothing.

Why do nothing? Some advocates of the permissive approach believe that if pupils are meaningfully involved in a relevant curriculum they will not misbehave. This is to say that, given the right conditions, all children will always behave. This is not so. Others believe that pupils must feel free to do what they want whenever they want. For pupils to feel otherwise, they say, inhibits their natural, God-given pattern of development. This, too, is not so. Psychologists are convinced that all pupils, for the sake of their mental health, need set limits for behavior.

Consequently, although permissiveness is one approach to discipline, it is not, in our opinion, a realistic, or an educational, or a responsible approach. Pupils cannot do what they want whenever they want.

THE AUTHORITARIAN APPROACH

If permissiveness is at one end of the discipline continuum, authoritarianism is at the other. The authoritarian approach assumes that most pupils are going to misbehave as often as they can. Given this assumption, what can teachers do to prevent behavior problems. The answer given here is not all inclusive, but it is representative enough to give the general idea.

Since pupils are going to misbehave as often as they can, teachers have to prepare for the worst. One way of preparing is to have a multitude of classroom rules, designed and communicated in such a way that pupils know immediately that they have an inferior status. The more rules, the better. Teachers must let pupils know that deviations from rules will not be tolerated. Teachers must be tough, they must act tough. They must demand respect and should not worry about earning it. They must keep their distance from pupils because friendliness, warmth, understanding, and interest breed problems. Teachers must let each pupil know that they carry a big stick and will use it at the slightest provocation.

Ridiculing pupils, embarrassing them, questioning their integrity are other good authoritarian techniques. These, too, are going to help prevent behavior problems. So the advocates of authoritarianism would have teachers believe!

But what can teachers do when misbehavior does occur? And what can teachers do to prevent it from recurring? The answer is obvious. Teachers must get tougher. They must become more rigid, more abrasive. They must impose more rules.

Effective teachers know that this approach does not work. Why should it?

Human beings learn to act in the manner in which they are treated. If they are treated like criminals, they act like criminals.

But even if the authoritarian approach did work, should teachers use it? Our answer is no. Because the approach is inhumane. If schools can function only by being inhumane to pupils, we have to wonder about the legitimacy of having schools at all.

We have stated that permissiveness and authoritarianism are two approaches to discipline. We have also stated that in our opinion neither approach is legitimate. Since the score now reads two approaches down and two to go, we think it might be reassuring at this point to state that the remaining approaches, behavioristic and diagnostic, are legitimate—not equally legitimate, in our estimation, but legitimate nonetheless.

THE BEHAVIORISTIC APPROACH

The psychology of behaviorism has been a key force in American education for at least fifty years. But as it relates to discipline, behaviorism has only recently captured widespread attention. As is often true, attention has grown because of a new name. In this case, the new name is *behavior modification*.

The purpose of behavior modification is to reshape behavior—for example, to change pupils' behavior patterns from undesirable to desirable. Supposedly, this change or reshaping is effected through four basic steps.

Before describing these four steps, we need to point out that the purpose and the techniques of behavior modification deal only with the last two questions on discipline. Behavior modification gives teachers no guidelines for preventing behavior problems. Behavior modification gives teachers guidelines only for dealing with behavior problems when they occur and for preventing their recurrence.

The first of the four steps in reshaping behavior is identification of the behavior problem. Teachers must identify the specific behavior they find undesirable. The key is to be specific. It is not sufficient for teachers to say that Johnny misbehaves. Rather, they must pinpoint the specific way he misbehaves. For example, he keeps getting out of his seat during reading class; he throws spitwads at Harry; he bullies Joe on the playground; he comes to class late three days a week. The more specifically the behavior is identified, the better.

The second step is identification of the appropriate behavior. Teachers must identify the specific way they want the pupil to act. In almost every case, such identification is the reverse of the undesired behavior. For example, Johnny remains seated during reading class; he refrains from throwing spitwads; he comes to class on time. This step may seem to be a duplication of effort, but for behavior modification the step is critically important.

The third step is the use of reward. When the pupil behaves in the way that was spelled out in the second step, teachers must reward him, they must pay him off. To return to our example, not even Johnny is out of his seat every minute of every reading class. When Johnny is seated, it is important for teachers to reward him.

The point is simple, but often missed. Good behavior is not necessarily its own reward. When teachers object to a pupil's behavior, they typically tell him "not to do it again." Then, when the pupil does what he has been told not to do teachers usually react, often by punishing. But when the pupil does what he is supposed to do, teachers tend to do nothing. Thinking that good behavior is its own reward, teachers fail to commend the pupil for his good conduct. According to the behavioristic approach, the omission is deadly. For only when teachers actively and consistently reward appropriate behavior will they succeed in eliminating misbehavior.

The fourth and final step is the use of extinction procedures to help eliminate the inappropriate behavior identified in the first step. The key words are *to help eliminate.* Let's return to Johnny. He has two choices in reading class: to sit or not to sit. Even if teachers consistently reward Johnny when he chooses to sit, there will be occasions, particularly at first, when he will choose not to. When Johnny opts to leave his seat, teachers can do one of two things. They can either ignore his behavior or react to it. Each of these responses is what behaviorists refer to as an extinction procedure.

Critics often ask why teachers should ever ignore inappropriate behavior. As one example, suppose that Johnny gets out of his seat during reading class to attract attention. When teachers react to his behavior by saying, "Johnny, please sit down!" what have they done? They have given him exactly what he wants —attention. In essence, they have rewarded Johnny for behaving inappropriately. Even worse, they have reinforced his knowledge that, whenever he wants attention, all he has to do to get it is to misbehave. There are times, then, when reacting to misbehavior has an effect entirely different from the one intended.

Other types of misbehavior, of course, demand that teachers react. They cannot simply stand by and watch a pupil destroy or deface school property. They have to stop him. Subsequently, they may even think it necessary to punish him. But it is important to note that reacting is not synonymous with punishing. Reminding Johnny that he is supposed to be seated during reading class is reacting. Keeping him in at recess because he needed reminding is punishing. To repeat, teachers can react to misbehavior without punishing.

The key to behavior modification is not the use of punishment, but the use of reward. Pupils can be conditioned to act in desirable ways if teachers will reward them for acting in these ways. Then, as pupils begin to be conditioned, their need for reward lessens. At first, Johnny needs immediate and frequent payoffs for staying in his seat. Later, as he becomes conditioned to remaining seated, the payoffs can and should become less frequent. Finally, it is hoped, the conditioning process will work so well that payoffs will no longer be necessary.

Is this a legitimate hope? Does behavior modification work? We think it does, but not to the degree or with the frequency behaviorists predict. For the approach, in our opinion, has several serious flaws. The most significant is that only the symptoms of behavior problems are dealt with, not their causes.

Stated bluntly, but not unjustly, proponents of behavior modification argue that teachers are wasting time in trying to discover and treat the underlying causes of behavior. From the point of view of advocates of behavior modification, teachers can be effective if they deal only with the behavior itself. What does this mean when teachers observe Johnny sleeping in math class every other day? Primarily, it means that they should begin rewarding him for staying awake. It does not mean that they should try to find out why he sleeps. Whether he is bored, or malnourished, or fatigued, or on dope, or rebellious, or just plain lazy—each a possible cause of his sleepiness—is irrelevant for behaviorists. But for us, and for the pupil, the cause seems critically important. As long as the cause of the child's problem is undiagnosed and untreated, he is hurting and sooner or later symptoms of that hurt will emerge.

THE DIAGNOSTIC APPROACH

To us, the most comprehensive and legitimate approach to discipline is what we call *the diagnostic approach.* Contrary to behavior modification, this approach assumes that there can be lasting effects on certain behavior problems only after their causes are ferreted out and treated. Unlike behavior modification, the diagnostic approach responds to the first question on discipline.

According to the diagnostic approach, what can teachers do to prevent behavior problems? What are some strategies of prevention? We have listed nine strategies which, in our opinion, are essential. But we need to emphasize that others are possible. We also must emphasize that preventive strategies are not failure free. Even if all the preventive strategies described here are used, behavior problems may still emerge. But from the diagnostic point of view and our own, if the strategies described here are used, the number of these problems will be significantly reduced.

Prevention

Here are nine strategies to prevent discipline problems:

1. Teachers must feel comfortable with themselves, their pupils, and their subject matter. The major reason, we think, that student teachers and first-year teachers often have difficulties with discipline is their uneasiness—uneasiness with themselves because being on the other side of that desk, particularly at first, is no easy task; uneasiness with their pupils because they may be "so different" or "so little;" uneasiness with their subject matter because, in terms of the real world, college methods courses often leave much to be desired. But regardless of

the cause, and regardless of the teachers' years of experience, teachers who are uneasy are going to communicate that uneasiness to their pupils. When this happens, the door to restlessness among pupils is wide open.

2. Teachers must believe in their pupils' capacity and propensity for appropriate classroom conduct. For according to sociologists, teachers' beliefs serve as "self-fulfilling prophecies." If teachers believe that pupils can and will act in socially acceptable ways, pupils will do so. But if teachers believe, for any number of reasons, that pupils neither can nor will behave appropriately, they will in fact misbehave. The principle of the self-fulfilling prophecy is profoundly, and often painfully, clear: the tendency of pupils, as of every social group, is to live and act as others expect them to live and act.

3. Teachers must insure that their instructional activities are interesting and relevant. The words *interesting* and *relevant* may be overworked in educational literature, but there can be no mistaking their importance. Nor can there be any mistaking the fact that dreary classrooms, monotonous routines, irrelevant, antiquated content, and boring methods of presentation are more characteristic of more educational settings than most care to admit. There is little doubt that these characteristics are major causes of misbehavior. Some pupils, to be sure, become acculturated to drabness in school life, learn to play the game, and become model citizens in school. But just as certainly, and possibly even more expectedly, other pupils become indifferent, rebel, and become troublemakers.

4. Teachers must match their instructional activities with their pupils' capabilities. Behavior problems are often the result of the teachers' failure to adapt their instruction to their pupils' capabilities. When pupils are handed materials that are too difficult, when pupils are required to complete assignments for which they lack readiness, when pupils are given directions they cannot possibly understand, is it any wonder that some become frustrated and cause problems? We think not. When other pupils are assigned tasks that insult their intelligence, is it any wonder that they lose interest and cause trouble? Again, we think not. Teachers must see to it that all pupils are challenged. Failing this, teachers should at least lay the blame for misbehavior where the blame belongs.

5. Teachers must involve their pupils in setting up "the rules." There are two major reasons for following this practice, one long range and one short term. From the long-range perspective, a democracy requires that citizens have the skills to participate actively and intelligently in group decision-making. Schools, in our opinion, are potentially the single best medium through which children can practice and master these skills in a gradual, nonthreatening way. From the short-term perspective, when groups of individuals help make the decisions that affect their lives, they are more likely to live within the framework of these decisions. Groups of pupils are no exception. Pupils who help set up the rules and regulations of the classroom better understand the necessity of having the rules and are more committed to following them than pupils who have no voice in classroom rules.

6. Teachers must make certain that their pupils know and understand "the routine." No two teachers hold the same set of expectations for pupils. No two

teachers have the same classroom routine. Given differing expectations and differing routines, the problem confronting pupils is real. In this day of team teaching, departmentalization, open space, and hosts of grouping patterns, even the youngest pupils daily come into contact with two or more teachers. Pupils must remember not only what routine to follow, but also whose routine. This is no easy task, but one that teachers often take for granted. Too frequently, teachers make the mistake of assuming that their standards for proper behavior are the only standards for proper behavior. In fact, though, behavior is relative, and its appropriateness can be determined only in context. Given differing routines or contexts, what one teacher perceives as proper behavior another teacher may perceive as misbehavior. And pupils are caught in the middle.

7. Teachers must identify their problem times. When do pupils tend to act up? When they first get to class? Or toward the end of the period? On the playground? In the lunchroom? In the halls? With the music teacher? In mathematics, or reading, or science? On Monday, or Wednesday, or Friday? The day before or after a big test? Knowing when the problem times are is an important first step in planning to prevent them.

8. Teachers must remember that pupils are not "little adults." Rather, in the elementary school, they are children ranging in age from five or six to twelve or thirteen. These children cannot be expected to display the same control over their behavior as adults. Yet, in too many instances, they are expected to display more. There is no doubt that teachers would save their pupils much frustration, and themselves many headaches, if they refrained from insisting on proper adult conduct from nonadults.

9. Teachers must give evidence that they genuinely respect their pupils. Teachers do not give such evidence when they complain about pupils in the halls and lounges; when they laugh at pupils behind their backs; when they tell pupils in hundreds of ways that their culture is deficient, that their homes are inadequate; when they do not take time to make a home visit or prepare an extra lesson that Johnny and Mary need. The list could go on, but the point is unmistakable. Teachers do not give evidence that they respect pupils by voicing platitudes. Teachers give evidence only through their actions, and only through these actions will they succeed in earning pupils' respect. To earn it is probably the most important preventive strategy of all.

These nine strategies are measures teachers can and must take to prevent behavior problems. But even with these measures, behavior problems will still emerge. When they do, what guidelines does the diagnostic approach give teachers? What can teachers do when behavior problems occur?

Intervention

According to the diagnostic approach, there is no one method of dealing with behavior problems, just as there is no one method of preventing them. There is no single strategy of intervention that works every time. Rather, there are many intervention strategies, and only teachers themselves can assess which ones work best in various situations. There are, however, seven strategies that we believe should be in every teacher's repertory. Again, these seven strategies in no way constitute a comprehensive list, but they do provide teachers with as sound a point of departure as we think there is.

1. The use of nonverbal techniques, particularly at the beginning stages of misbehavior, can be an effective way of letting pupils know that one or all of them had better settle down. Eye contact, body posture, facial expression, and silence are probably the most noteworthy of these techniques. Verbal techniques can also be effective. But they are so overused that their impact is questionable. Witness the number of teachers who intersperse every other sentence with "sh."

2. When a pupil is misbehaving, merely walking up to him and standing beside him for five or ten seconds can frequently bring about the desired result. When this technique is used, few pupils fail to get the message, and even fewer are brazen enough to disregard it.

3. Removing the source of a disturbance can bring about the desired result. One form of removal is the "take-it-away type." The teacher may take away rubber bands, water pistols, food, and contraband reading materials. Most teachers are familiar with this form of removal. Another form of removal is the "let-it-run-its-course type." Teachers may be less familiar with this type. Almost daily, in the classroom and outside, there are phenomena that pupils are naturally interested in, that they naturally give their attention to. Hailstorms, ambulance sirens, Johnny's new shoes, Mary's coiffure, Mrs. Smith's student teacher are a few examples. When such attractions capture pupils' attention, the surest way of recapturing it is simply to let pupils have a few minutes of exploration.

4. Pointing out to pupils the consequence of their misbehavior can be an effective method of intervention. The key is to find the right consequence. To tell Johnny that he will have a terrible time with long division if he does not stop horsing around in second-grade addition is probably not a very meaningful consequence to him. But to tell him that he will not be able to sit next to Billy might be. Matching the pupil with the right consequence is no easy task. But making false matches yields no benefits whatsoever.

5. The use of behavior-modification techniques can be an effective method of intervention. These techniques, as well as some of their limitations, were described earlier.

6. Asking a pupil to leave the room can be an important intervention strategy. This technique has a single purpose: to give the pupil a chance to cool off. Asking him to run an errand, sending him to get a drink, telling him to walk around the playground are all legitimate tactics. Trying to deal with a pupil who is on the verge of losing self-control is almost inevitably a lost cause. In such situations teachers often become angry and lose their own self-control.

7. Punishing pupils can be a necessary and an effective strategy. But when punishment is being considered, five principles should be kept in mind:

First, punishment should be used sparingly. The more often punishment is used, the less effective it becomes. Teachers who frequently resort to punishment find that they have to punish more often and more severely just to maintain the status quo.

Second, punishment should never constitute retaliation. It is beneath the dignity of professionals to punish pupils to get back at them. Teachers who do so do not belong in education.

Third, subject matter should not be used as punishment. In most cases, requiring pupils to do another page of mathematics or to write an extra book report reduces the chance that they will develop favorable attitudes in these areas. In the long run, much more is lost than gained.

Fourth, mass punishment should not be used. Teachers should never punish the entire class for the transgressions of a few members. Many teachers fall into this trap; few escape without some loss of respect.

Fifth, corporal punishment should not be used. We know that there are strong differences of opinion about whether corporal punishment is effective. We happen to believe that it is generally ineffective. But this is not the key point. The key is that corporal punishment, by those who support its use, is intended to be a last-ditch effort to change behavior. The implication is that if corporal punishment fails, nothing else can be done. This implication, from the diagnostic point of view and our own, is anathema.

According to the diagnostic approach, then, if the strategies of prevention and intervention are used, most common forms of misbehavior can either be eliminated or be dealt with effectively. But some behavior problems cannot be. These are the problems that are symptoms of underlying causes and, consequently, continue to recur until the causes are diagnosed and treated.

Diagnosis

There is no quick, easy, or fail-proof formula for diagnosing the causes of pupils' behavior problems. But there is one absolutely essential step: to learn as much as possible about the pupils. To do so, teachers must draw on all possible sources of information. These include achievement and intelligence tests, social and psychological inventories, attendance records, cumulative folders, previous teachers, clergymen, parents, relatives, siblings, peers, social workers, visiting teachers, medical personnel, employers, coaches, and, most important of all, the pupils themselves.

After the information from these sources has been gathered and analyzed, it is our contention that teachers can make a reasonably reliable determination of the causes of most behavior problems. It is also our contention that teachers can then take steps to help eliminate these causes and the resulting behavioral symptoms. But, as we said earlier, neither of these contentions is universally supported.

Most critics of this approach argue that the whole effort of diagnosis is a waste of time and energy because nothing can be done anyway. These critics are quick to assert that teachers cannot force parents to love their children or to feed them adequately, that teachers cannot mend broken homes, that teachers cannot keep Joe's father off the bottle or Mary's mother off the streets.

But we disagree with this argument. First, because it assumes that the causes of behavior problems are never school related or school induced. Like it or not, many are.

Second, even if the diagnosis shows that the causes are not school related or school induced, much can still be done. Pupils' ego needs can be met in school, their self-respect enhanced, their enjoyment of life increased. In school, pupils can be given love and can learn to give it in return. Schools can provide food and clothing. They can make medical, dental, and psychological referrals. They can contact community action programs, welfare departments, civic organizations, churches, and even law-enforcement agencies. Schools can provide for adult education, sex education, and early education. We disagree that diagnosis is a waste of time because nothing can be done! This logic has long been refuted by schools and teachers who have done all these things and more.

We said that there are no easy answers to discipline problems. We know that we have proven ourselves right, but hope that in the process we have helped.

39 The Use of Reward and Extinction Procedures

Harvey F. Clarizio

THE USE OF REWARD

If a behavior results in what we want, we are inclined to repeat it. Behavior, n other words, is in large measure determined by its consequences. For example, if an acting-out student can attract the attention of others by blurting out answers in class, he will probably not raise his hand and wait his turn. Likewise, if he raises his hand and the teacher does not call on him because he has already taken other students' turns, the acting-out child is not likely to follow the "raise your hand" rule. All behaviors must have a payoff of some kind—the attracting of attention, the gaining of power, the expression of hostility toward those we do not like, being left alone (Dreikurs, 1969)—or we discontinue them. If a trouble-some behavior, for example, whining, occurs frequently, one can be certain that it has worked, that it has been positively reinforced, or else the misbehavior would not be worth our time and energy.

The giving of rewards constitutes one of the most valuable tools teachers have at their disposal. Teachers have long recognized the importance of rewards and often use them to change behavior. Thus the teacher who says, "I see that Johnny is ready to begin his math now that recess is over" is rewarding Johnny for his attentiveness and studiousness.

One of the merits of this approach stems from its applicability to all students. It is not just for the antisocial student, the culturally disadvantaged, the brain-injured, the emotionally disturbed, or for the normal child. For every student, regardless of the label we attach to him, needs ample rewards if he is to behave and to achieve in school.

Despite the efficacy and apparent simplicity of this technique, we oftne misuse it. Basically, there are two ways in which we violate this principle——through sins of commission and through sins of omission. The former refers to the rewarding of unwanted behavior, whereas the latter refers to the failure to reward desired behavior. Their consequences are nicely illustrated by the study of Madsen and his associates (1968) on sit-down commands. These investigators dealt with a student behavior that has plagued teachers for years, namely, the students' standing up when they are supposed to be working. First, the investigators observed how frequently the target behavior—standing up inappropriately—occurred during a given time interval so as to have a base line for later comparisons. Two types of teacher behavior were also recorded: (a) the number of times that teachers told students to sit down or that they gave reprimands for stand up behaviors, and (b) the number of times a teacher praised students for sitting down. The teachers then were instructed to give "sit down" commands whenever the child was inappropriately out of his seat. During this phase of the experiment, "sit down" commands tripled. What happened? Did the incidence of standing behavior decrease? No, instead it rose dramatically, presumably, because the "sit down" commands served as a reinforcer for the behavior that the demands were to eliminate. The teachers were then instructed to return to their earlier ways of coping with this type of disruptive behavior. The rate of standing behavior fell to its original level. Another "sit down" phase was instituted, and standing behaviors again increased. In the final phase of the program, teachers were given the following rule:

"Give *praise* and *attention* to behaviors which facilitate learning. Tell the child what he is being praised for. Try to reinforce behaviors incompatible with those you wish to decrease (praise: sitting in seat and working properly, sitting with feet on floor and facing front, etc.)."

Under this regimen wherein desired behavior is strengthened and undesirable behavior is weakened, stand-up behaviors decreased to the point that there were approximately 100 less instances of it per 20-minute period! In addition to pointing out the misuse and proper use of reward, this study highlights the importance of dealing with *specific* behaviors, the potency of catching children at being good, and the technique of strengthening appropriate behaviors that compete with inappropriate behaviors.

Classroom observations reveal that even experienced teachers "sin" by commission and omission. Reflect for a moment on the following "sins of commission." How many times do you in a typical day reinforce:

the negativistic student by "arguing" with him, the aggressive student by paying attention to him, the dependent student by doing things for him, or the whiny student by eventually giving in to him?

Consider the following "sins of omission." How often do you pay attenion to:

the talkative child when he is quiet, the hyperactive child when he is in his seat, or the irresponsible student when he turns in an assignment?

How often do you phone or jot the parent a note when the disorderly child had a good day?

Do you ever send the problem child to the office so that the principal can reinforce the student's acceptable behavior?

How often do you put the child's name on the board when he is good?

It is easy to understand how teachers inadvertently reward undesirable behavior. As many of us know too well, it is natural to pay attention to the problem behavior regardless of how busy we may be. Generally, the teacher gets reinforced for yelling or threatening the acting-out student in that these tactics on the teacher's part lead to short-term changes in the student's behavior. Unfortunately, however, even though the student may desist momentarily, the troublesome behavior may actually accidentally be strengthened in that it effectively elicits teacher attention. Just as teachers train students, students also train teachers. In this case, they train us to shout and to become upset over them. Such attention, although unpleasant, is nonetheless better than none. Since both the teacher and the student are reinforced for their behaviors, they continue using them. Ideally, or ultimately, teachers should pay attention to disorderly students only when they do what teachers want them to do.

We all realize that we should reward desirable behavior, but there are discrepancies between what we know and what we do. The question arises as to why we miss so many opportunities to strengthen the very kind of behaviors that we want to develop in our students. Four explanations come to mind.

One reason is that we develop such negative perceptions of the misbehaving pupil that we do not see what he does right. It is his misbehavior that catches our eye. We do not expect this kind of child to behave and thus we do not see his proper conduct. Perception is a very selective process. On many occasions I have asked teachers what a disorderly student does right. The standard reply is nothing or not much. Yet, when given a description of an average day's events, it is apparent that the student engages in many behaviors that the teacher could commend. But we simply fail to notice him when he quiets down or slows down.

Second, even when we do see him behave, it is very difficult to reward someone who gives us a bad time. We are simply not inclined to do so. It is hard to be nice to people who are not nice to us. This reaction on our part makes it difficult for us to reward such a child. How many times have we, on seeing a disorderly child behaving, said to ourselves something to the effect that, "This won't last long. He'll be back to his old tricks before long." Let's face it—the disorderly pupil makes our job doubly difficult. Our days go well when he is absent, and we give a sigh of relief when he does not put in an appearance in the morning. Third, the teacher has a natural tendency to "let-down," and catch her breath once the problem child does quiet down. We are quite content to leave him alone once he settles down. Or else we feel, justifiably so, that we must start paying attention to the other 30 students in the class. After all, we are group workers.

Finally, we simply expect all students to behave. After all, we reason, is it not the student's role to meet our expectations? Why should we give the disorderly student extra payoffs when he is only doing what everyone else in the class does without apparent reward. Giving extra privileges, we reason, is unfair to the other students.[1] This type of cultural value relating to a middle class sense of duty and fairness interferes with our becoming effective sources of reward ftr students. While teachers feel that it is fair to individualize classroom instruction in reading, or math, they feel that it is unjust to individualize their policies regarding classroom discipline. We often are quite willing to gear academic kinds of instruction to the student's intellectual readiness but frequently we are unwilling to adjust discipline practices to the child's level of social and emotional readiness.

· · · · ·

EXTINCTION PROCEDURES

Just as a substantial body of research shows that the presentation of rewards can facilitate the acquisition and maintenance of given behaviors, a growing body of literature is demonstrating that extinction—simply removing the reward that usually accompanies the misbehavior—can reduce or eliminate troublesome behaviors. If behavior is learned through the giving of rewards, then it can be unlearned by taking the rewards away. If a given behavior no longer has its intended effect, its frequency tends to diminish.

[1] Many teachers view rewards as "bribes." The equating of these two terms overlooks an important distinction between them. Bribes are designed to produce morally corrupt behaviors whereas rewards, as referred to here, are used to develop and to strengthen socially appropriate behaviors.

As Hunter (1967), points out, "We don't keep on doing something that doesn't work." If the troublesome student acts out and nothing happens, he soon gets the message and abandons the particular maladaptive way. In short, simply removing the rewarding consequences of an act constitutes an effective way of weakening it. As we shall learn, this technique has been found effective with a wide variety of behavior.

Despite the simplicity and potency of this principle, teachers often fail to use it to its best advantage. Hopefully, a fuller understanding of the cautions and guidelines regarding the use of this technique will enable teachers to apply it to better advantage.

Caution and Guidelines

EFFICIENCY AND EFFECTIVENESS

Although unacceptable behavior can be weakened by the nonrewarded repetition of a response, extinction if used as the sole method is not always the most economical and effective means to produce behavioral change, as we indicate in our discussion below.

Therefore, it is often wise to use extinction in conjunction with other techniques. One especially effective combination involves the simultaneous use of extinction and reward. The teacher might, for instance, ignore the child when he talks out of turn in class but might make a favorable comment about his answers when he speaks out in ways that are consistent with classroom ground rules. For example, "That's a good point, Jim" or "Jim, thank you for waiting your turn," whenever he raises his hand to answer or otherwise waits his turn. If the youngster has not yet learned to raise his hand, the teacher might assist him. For instance, whenever she notices him about to blurt something, she might say in a friendly voice something like, "Jim, did you want to raise your hand to say something?" Or the teacher might say, "Jim, I know you have something you want to say. We'll get to you in just a bit." Then the teacher might call on him in 20 to 30 seconds (gradually this interval could be increased) and say, "Thank you for waiting, Jim. Now, let's hear what you have to say."

A good rule of thumb is to reinforce desirable behaviors, for example, cooperativeness, which are incompatible with and compete with undesirable behaviors, for example, negativistic behavior. A student cannot be both cooperative and negativistic simultaneously. One junior high school teacher after years of yelling, pleading, and belittling, decided to say nothing to the students who forgot to bring the necessary supplies to class (not even a sign of reproach) and to give a daily "A" to book bringers. Within a five-day period, this teacher solved a problem that had annoyed her throughout five years of teaching by positively rewarding a desirable behavior (bringing supplies) which competed with unwanted behavior (forgetting supplies).

THE OLD MISBEHAVIOR CAN RETURN

We should point out that the term extinction is probably a misnomer, since extinguished behavior is displaced rather than permanently lost. Moreover, if the original undesirable misbehavior is again reinforced, it is often easily reinstated. This difficulty can be overcome through the use of additional extinction trials, however. For example, one teacher had, for all practical purposes, eliminated tantrum behavior in Jane, a third grade student, by ignoring her temper outbursts. The teacher was ill for a week. On her return she found that Jane was up to her old tricks again. The teacher later confirmed her suspicions, namely, that the substitute teacher had inadvertently strengthened tantrum behavior by attending to it. Nevertheless, the regular teacher again was able to reduce these episodes to a minimal frequency through the reinstatement of her ignoring policy.

What should the teacher do when old habits reoccur after they have been supposedly eliminated? Although you may be inclined to blow your top and thereby to reinforce the misbehavior, you should simply lay the unwanted behavior to rest once again by withholding reinforcement, that is, you should undertake another series of extinction trials. Fortunately, the unwanted behavior can usually be more readily extinguished on the second series of extinction trials.

OCCASIONAL REWARD

One of the primary factors in the reappearance of undesirable behavior is occasional or intermittent reward. As noted earlier in our discussion of intermittent reinforcement behaviors, troublesome or otherwise, once these behaviors have been established, they can be maintained or even strengthened even though they are only occasionally reinforced. What sometimes happens is that many deviant behaviors, for example, talking out loud in class, are occasionally reinforced either directly or vicariously and are thereby set up on an intermittent reinforcement schedule. Thus, instead of abolishing the behavior via extinction as intended, there is a rise in the frequency and intensity of deviant responses via intermittent reinforcement. On some occasions, a given teacher may be inconsistent in his ignoring of a certain behavior. For instance, he may become angry when the disorderly student talks out loud in class and, consequently, may pay attention to the behavior by scolding. On other occasions, there may be inconsistency between teachers. This type of inconsistency is most likely to occur in elementary schools in conjunction with team-taught courses and in junior and senior high school where students typically have several teachers. Remember that any rewards given during the extinction process will reinstate the misbehavior and, frequently, at a higher level than if extinction had not been attempted (Bandura, 1969).

INABILITY TO IGNORE MISBEHAVIOR

This brings us to a related point, namely, that it is especially difficult for teachers to ignore behavior deviations. We are good detectives and we quickly spot (and attend to) rule violations. It is as though we are compelled to respond to misbehavior. "George, get back to your seat." "Mary, you've been at the pencil sharpener long enough." "Bob, stop pestering your neighbors and get back to work." "Tom, do you always have to be moving around in your desk?" "Barry, how long are you going to keep tapping that pencil?" "Carol, sit up straight." "Bill, watch your feet." "Steve, scoot your chair over." As you know now, teacher attention can often strengthen the undesirable behavior. Although teachers have little difficulty in grasping the value of ignoring (and thereby of removing the reward for the deviant behavior), they have considerable difficulty in implementing this idea. As one teacher related, "As a practice teacher, I vowed that I would not hen like my supervising teacher but found myself doing it too once I got on the job." Being aware of the value of ignoring is one matter, and practicing to ignore is quite another. Ignoring requires rigorous self-control.

If teachers are to derive the maximum benefit from extinction procedures, they must learn not to respond to all undesirable behavior.[2] In all likelihood, many classroom transgressions could be safely ignored. Motor behaviors such as getting out of the seat, standing up, wandering around the room, and moving chairs could probably be ignored. Irrelevant verbalizations or noises such as conversations with others, answering without raising one's hand, crying, whistling, and coughing also can fall into the category of behaviors to which the teacher should not respond. Oppositional tactics, for example, negativism, represent another major class of behaviors to which no heed should be paid (Madsen et. al., 1968). The teacher, even though he might initially feel uncomfortable, will do a more adequate job of managing classroom behavior if he can learn to avoid responding to certain misbehaviors. Remember that teacher disapproval can strengthen deviant behavior, whereas ignoring it can weaken such behavior by removing the pay off. The student has to learn that unacceptable behavior is worth nothing.

Should a teacher ignore all undesirable behavior? If not, how will he know what behaviors to ignore? The general guidelines that follow should prove of value in helping teachers answer these questions. There are certain types of behavior that the teacher cannot ignore. Included among them are behaviors that are injurious to self or others and inappropriate behaviors for which the teacher cannot for various reasons remove the reward, that is, self-rewarding behaviors and behaviors rewarded by the peer group. Hunter (1967) suggests that if a given misbehavior is relatively new, one can probably ignore it. On the other hand, if the misbehavior occurs with a high degree of consistency and is of long standing, extinction procedures may prove inadequate. If the misbehavior happens frequently and is of long standing, one can be reasonably sure that it is being reinforced. Either other social agents such as the peer group are making these deviances worth the student's while or his behavior is rewarding in and of itself, for example, sleeping in class, laughing, and hitting. As we indicate later, it

---

[2] Because it is unlikely that a teacher will ignore all instances of a given misbehavior, extinction procedures should be combined with the positive reinforcement of acceptable behaviors.

might well be necessary to use some form of punishment to deal effectively with behavior that is intense and/or frequent. For now, remember that ignoring works only when the reward is attention. When systematic teacher ignoring fails, it is likely that the misbehavior is being maintained by something other than teacher attention, and that some other change in the classroom environment will be needed to discourage the behavior.

PEER REWARDED BEHAVIOR

Some comments relative to peer group extinction deserve mention at this point. Conversations with and observations of teachers indicate that they frequently do not come to grips with the problem of the peer group. More often than not, teachers allow the peer group to reinforce undesirable behavior. For instance, if a boy clowns in class and three to four other students generally respond with laughter, teachers rarely enlist the assistance of these students in extinguishing the undesired behavior. Just as peer group rewards can serve as powerful strengtheners of behavior, group extinction procedures also can serve as powerful weakeners of behavior, as is illustrated in the case of George, a first grader who was described as immature, disruptive, and poorly motivated by his teacher. The following announcement was made to George's class.

George does not learn as much as he can because he has really not learned how to sit still and work. This is a "how-to-work-box" that will help him to practice working. When he sits still and works, the light flashes up here like this (demonstrates) and the counter clicks. When that happens it means that George has earned one M&M candy. When he is all done working today, we will take all of the candy he earns and divide it up among all of you. If you want George to earn a lot of candy, then don't pay any attention to him if he acts silly, talks to you, or gets up out of his seat. O.K.? Now, let's see how much candy George can earn. (Patterson, 1969).

Although every teacher might not have a "how to work box" nor wish to pass out M&M candy, he could still make use of group extinction procedures by finding incentives more natural to the classroom setting which could be used for the peer group's ignoring of inappropriate behavior. Again, notice the simultaneous use of positive reinforcement and extinction procedures.

SELF-REINFORCING BEHAVIOR

Occasionally the reward for misbehavior comes from the act itself. Consequently, it is sometimes extremely difficult to keep maladaptive behaviors from being reinforced. For instance, the aggressive pupil who kicks the teacher or a classmate cannot help but be reinforced by the look of pain on the victim's face. Furthermore, even if the victim somehow manages to keep a straight face, the kicker knows that he has inflicted pain, and this knowledge in itself can be reinforcing. Looking out the window, having a good belly laugh, or having a conquering hero daydream are all intrinsically rewarding. When dealing with behavior that contains its own satisfactions, it is necessary to punish the undesirable behavior to suppress it temporarily and to reward incompatible positive behaviors. For example, the aggressive student may have to relinquish certain classroom privileges, such as playing with his peers, when he acts out. Yet, every effort should be made to reward his cooperative or friendly interactions.

INTENSE MISBEHAVIOR

There are also situations in which we cannot wait for a behavior to fizzle out through repeated nonreward. This limitation is particularly characteristic of situations wherein the dangers of emotional contagion and severe injury to self or others are distinct possibilities. In these cases, immediate action is called for, and some form of punishment (for example, isolation or physical restraint) is probably the method of choice.

ORIGINAL MISBEHAVIOR INCREASES

The teacher should fully expect that misbehavior, if it does not increase in frequency or in intensity, will remain at a high level during the initial stages of the extinction process. The old adage that things will get worse before they get better certainly pertains here. Temper tantrums may well soar to frightening intensities, initially mild dependency demands may culminate in a sharp kick in the shins, and negative attention-getting behavior may assume increasingly ludicrous forms (Bandura, 1969). This state of affairs should not discourage the teacher, since the initial rise in undesired behavior is a sign that the extinction process is working. As the vigorous misbehavior proves unsuccessful, it will gradually taper off and alternative ways of behavior will emerge.

The systematic application of extinction procedures is essential. The teacher must be consistent and must stick to his guns, since the troublesome child believes on the basis of his past experience that he will get his way if he persists. He has hope of attaining the customary reward for his misbehavior. Eventually, he figures, the teacher will give in, accidently or intentionally. Since the student has had luck with his tactics before, he is going to try them again and again. The message to teachers is clear—stick to your guns.

NEW MISBEHAVIORS SOMETIMES EMERGE

The extinction of a given maladaptive behavior constitutes no guarantee in and of itself that desirable behavior will automatically appear. As dominant modes of behavior are extinguished, the student will use alternative courses of action that have proved successful on previous occasions in similar circumstances. The use of extinction alone poses no special problems provided that the alternative responses in the student's repertoire are acceptable to the teacher. A problem does arise, however, when the new responses are also maladaptive. If this situation arises, the teacher may be faced with the laborious task of extinguishing a long succession of unacceptable behavior patterns. For example, one student turned to verbal impersonations of the teacher after his pantomiming had

TABLE 4.1.   A Summary of Cautions and Guidelines Regarding Extinction Procedures

Caution	Guideline
Not always economical or effective if used alone	Combine extinction with other methods, especially the rewarding of incompatible behaviors.
Old habits can reoccur	Lay problem to rest again through an additional extinction series.
Occasional reward	Be consistent. Make sure you are not the reinforcing agent.
Inability to ignore unwanted behavior	Practice not responding to all misbehavior.
Peer rewarded behavior	Enlist support of peer group.
Self-reinforcing behavior	Combine extinction with other methods such as reward of competing responses and punishment.
Intense misbehavior	Some form of punishment may be the method of choice.
Original misbehavior increases	Expect this initial rise. Continue to apply extinction procedures systematically.
New misbehaviors sometimes emerge	Combine extinction procedures with other methods that foster desired behavior (social modeling, reward).

gone unrewarded. It was necessary, therefore, for the teacher to extinguish the verbal impersonations too. The teacher can avoid the problems associated with extinguishing a long succession of inappropriate behaviors by combining extinction procedures with other methods that foster more effective modes of adjustment (Bandura, 1969).

Because teachers have not always taken into account the above-mentioned cautions and guidelines, they have sometimes become discouraged in their use of this technique. We have seen many teachers become disheartened in trying to implement the school counselor's advice not to reward maladaptive behaviors. What usually happens, unless the above precautions are taken, is that the teachers' efforts to extinguish unacceptable student behaviors themselves undergo extinction. A summary of cautions and guidelines is presented in Table 4.1.

In conclusion, the rate and effectiveness of extinction as an intervention technique are dictated by several factors. Among them are (1) the irregularity with which the maladaptive behavior has been rewarded in the past (recall that the occasional reward of an established behavior makes extinction a more arduous process); (2) the ease with which the teacher can identify and remove the rewards that are maintaining the maladaptive behavior; (3) the availability of alternative modes of behaving in the student's repertoire or in those opened up to him by the teacher; (4) the amount of effort needed to misbehave (theoretically, one might expect violent, extended tantrum behavior to extinguish more readily than whining behavior, since the former requires more energy and effort on the student's part); (5) the student's level of deprivation during the extinction process (the class clown, for example, after a short illness that kept him out of school might well relinquish his need for peer approval—social deprivation level—is higher now that he missed his buddies); (6) the extent to which extinction procedures are combined with other behavior modification methods such as positive reinforcement, social modeling, punishment, and desensitization; (7) the teacher's ability ignore certain kinds of misbehavior, and (8) the teacher's ability to apply extinction techniques in a consistent and systematic way.

REFERENCES

Bandura, A. *Principles of Behavior Modification.* New York: Holt, Rinehart and Winston, Inc., 1969.

Hunter, M. *Reinforcement.* El Segundo, Calif.: TIP Publications, 1967.

Madsen, C. H., W. C. Becker, and D. R. Thomas, "Rules, Praise, and Ignoring: Elements of Elementary Classroom Control," *Journal of Applied Behavior Analysis,* 1968, 1, 139–150.

Patterson, G. "Teaching Parents to Be Behavior Modifiers in the Classroom," in J. Krumboltz and C. Thoresen (eds.), *Behavioral Counseling.* New York: Holt, Rinehart and Winston, Inc., 1969, pp. 155–161.

VI Understanding and Teaching the "Different" Student

Perhaps the greatest single challenge today's educator faces is understanding and teaching "different" students. Among others, these are students who are economically disadvantaged, who are emotionally disturbed, and who have exceptionally high or low academic potential. These are students who in the past benefited least from education. These are students in whose present education lies an important key to a better future.

Articles 40, 41, and 42 focus on the economically disadvantaged. In article 40, Ornstein states that in the United States there are approximately 28 million school-age children living in poverty. These children, according to Ornstein, suffer from poor self-esteem, from social and environmental deprivation, from inadequate medical attention and parental supervision, from prejudicial and discriminatory treatment, and from experiential and educational deficiencies. I believe that although Ornstein is generally correct in his portrayal of disadvantaged youth, he does on occasions overgeneralize. You must identify these overgeneralizations if you are to acquire a valid understanding of poverty and its causes and effects.

In article 41, Hesburgh claims that there are serious inequities in the educational opportunities afforded advantaged and disadvantaged students, and that these inequities are as much the fault of schools as they are of society. Educators are at fault, Hesburgh reasons, first, because the majority of experimental and innovative programs have been conducted in schools that serve advantaged students; second, because the majority of "better educated" teachers have been assigned to work in these schools; and third–and by far the most important–because school officials have attempted to maintain zoning patterns that separate differing racial and economic groups. Hesburgh's challenge to educators is to take the initiative in rectifying these conditions and, in the process, to help mold a better society.

In article 42, Erickson, Bryan, and Walker make several observations. They note, for example, that economically disadvantaged students are not culturally deprived or culturally disadvantaged, and that they are not so much educationally disadvantaged as they are educationally excluded. The authors also note that desegregating schools by mixing school populations on the basis of race has not resulted in the academic and social benefits some educators had predicted. If such benefits are to be derived, the authors imply, schools must be integrated not only on the basis of race, but also on the basis of socioeconomic class.

So long as schools remain segregated, however, many teachers may never have occasion to work with the economically disadvantaged. But at one time or another all teachers will work with youngsters who are emotionally disturbed and who have very high or low academic potential. In articles 43 through 47, attention is given to the unique learning needs these youngsters have and to the special instructional problems they pose.

In article 43, Morse distinguishes between different types of disturbed students, examines some of the more usual causes underlying their behavior, and identifies several techniques that have proved relatively effective in teaching and counseling them. Morse is convinced that regular classroom teachers cannot and should not be expected to function as psychotherapists. But he seems equally convinced that teachers can and must learn to form with disturbed students the types of relationships that are themselves therapeutic.

In article 44, Kline structures his remarks on two major premises. The first is that there are great numbers of students who have severe learning disabilities. In reading alone, Kline claims, there are 8 million such students. The second is that educators have failed miserably in diagnosing the causes of learning problems and in prescribing appropriate remedial treatment. Kline suggests, for example, that 90 per cent of all reading disabilities can be attributed to ineffective teaching. In my opinion, although Kline's remarks are at times unduly harsh and occasionally inconsistent, his two major premises are sound.

Karnes, in article 45, identifies some of the characteristics of slow-learning students. Compared to average students, according to Karnes, slow learners tend to have more physical defects, poorer reasoning abilities, shorter attention spans, poorer work habits and motivation, less social and emotional maturity, less proficiency in the communication skills, and more and greater feelings of insecurity and inadequacy. In other words, Karnes is saying that slow learners generally tend to be behind average students in most, if not all, areas that affect their ability to function in the classroom.

But just as slow learners may be too far behind their age-mates, gifted and creative students may be too far ahead! Lyon, in article 46, and Torrance, in article 47, illustrate this latter point. In most regular classrooms, these authors claim, the special talents of gifted students are unrecognized, their preferred methods of learning frowned upon, their high energy levels squelched, their ideas and ideals criticized, and their emotional security threatened. Despite these conditions, the authors claim, some talented students manage to realize their potential. Most, however, fall far short. In this era of great national concern for the wise and efficient use of natural resources, both Lyon and Torrance seem bewildered by the fact that the greatest resource of all–human resources–is in the main being mishandled.

40 Who Are the Disadvantaged?

Allan C. Ornstein

In a vicious, stubborn cycle, the fact that [certain groups]⸌are financially disadvantaged causes other disadvantages, and the fact that they have so many other disadvantages gives rise to and increases their financial deprivation.⸍

The majority are white, although non-white minorities suffer the most intense and concentrated number of disadvantages. In a spectrum of grim blight, they stretch across the country, from North to South, from coast to coast, hidden in rural waste lands and submerged in urban squalor. Although the magnitude and the number of their disadvantages vary with the level of their income, many live on the fringe, in a bleak no-man's land, human exiles from the rest of America.

Now the disadvantaged youth, and by this I mean about 40 per cent of the 70 million Americans, (16) seem doomed to become the next generation of disadvantaged Americans. Although their only real chance of changing their fortune is by taking advantage of educational opportunities available to them, most of them drop out of school or graduate as functional illiterates. (40)

The problem is the same everywhere. The schools have been unable to educate or equip these children for today's world. (40) Their access to occupational opportunity and a better life is impossible, because they do not have "the vocational training and background of skills and knowledge to get and keep a job." (38) Since these youngsters cannot obtain a job except of the most inferior quality, they never get a chance to break away from their misfortune. It is foolish, therefore, to hope for a brighter future where every indication leads us to expect a worsening trend. Midway through the sixties, then, the nation is confronted with a most dangerous problem: As Harrington puts it, "An enormous concentration of young people who, if they do not receive immediate help, may well be the source of a kind of heredity (deprivation) new to American society." (25, p. 183)

It is now appropriate to consider more specific aspects of this deprivation; perhaps, then, we will be able to surmise a solution to this foreboding crisis.

SELF DEPRIVATION

Disadvantaged children often have injured personalities. Many lack a sense of self-esteem, self-praise, and self-importance. Many have low and unrealistic

Reprinted from *Journal of Secondary Education*, 41 (4): 154–163 (April 1966), by permission of author and publisher.

aspiration levels. "They feel," according to Kvaraceus, "like nothing and nobody, unwanted and unnecessary." (32) They have feelings of guilt and shame, and have limited trust in adults. (31)

Disadvantaged children are usually too demoralized and frustrated, and too powerless to combat the forces that confuse and ensnare their lives. (22) They "know" they are failures, and they are convinced they always will be. They live in defeat and despair, and feel inferior and exiled from the prevailing society. The majority are too disillusioned and dispirited to care. They have been rejected and discouraged too many times to have any ideas of hope or ambition. (39) They will not even try to do what is necessary to escape their deprivation—stay in school, for instance.

Also, the disadvantaged cannot cope with humiliation, nor can they assimilate an attack on their dignity or values. Resentment, intense anxiety, and often direct hostility are manifested among these adolescents. (21) Any aspect of authority: their parents, their teachers, the law, the school, is a direct target for their anger. Similarly, emotional disorders requiring specialized treatment are common among many of these children. (31, 39)

One of my colleagues described these children: "They know they are being left out of the mainstream. They're sophisticated and naive at the same time. They know they have little opportunity and yet they want the American dream—a job, a car, a T.V., a little recognition." Another colleague added, "'The Star-Spangled Banner' doesn't mean a thing for these children, and when they say 'liberty and justice for all' they know damn well they're not getting their full share."

SOCIAL DEPRIVATION

Disadvantaged youth are often uncommitted to the larger society and uncontrolled by its values. Unable to participate successfully in the life of the larger society, they feel unwanted and rejected, and often turn to delinquent sub-cultures. "In these sub-cultures," writes Olsen, "the youngster's need for status and acceptance is satisfied." (38) Here he is respected, and his lack of a sense of identification with the general American culture is reinforced to the point that he is all but lost to his society. (38, 44)

In this connection, Richard Cloward and Lloyd Ohlin have set forth a theory that explains juvenile delinquency essentially as a response to deprivation. Given a society with a certain core of values shared by all which emphasizes achievement and status, and given certain classes of youth that are deprived of the means to participate or obtain success, there is a high manifestation of antisocial behavior. (7)

The negative values evidenced by these children begin to develop at an early age. Tenenbaum (49) and Cavan (4) maintain that it is not surprising to find disadvantaged children of six or seven smoking and sniffing airplane glue, and young teenage boys and girls openly engaging in sex play, drinking, gambling, and stealing. By the same token, Salisbury is of the opinion that many by their early teens make excellent prospects for dope and vice; in fact, both go hand in hand. "First the girl is 'hooked' to drugs," he writes. "Then, she is put into prostitution to earn money for her drugs." (45, p. 79)

What makes matters worse is that the parents are often tolerant and uncritical of such behavior. Some are too busy working or caring for a host of other sons and daughters, but others are engaged in the same activities as their children. For example, Cavan asserts that "the free sexual activities of the adolescent girl may simply repeat the activities of her mother; the girl herself may be illegitimate." (4)

The outcome is that disadvantaged youth accept and often boast of their deviant behavior. Many are proud of, rather than disturbed by, their actions. In reacting as they do, then, these children are merely expressing contempt and striking out against those who reject them. For this reason, it is not uncommon to find depressed areas saturated with gangs. Writes Salisbury, "There is only one place where the youngsters can star. It's not at home, not in school. It's in the street." (45, p. 52)

To be sure, these are the same boys who turn schools into blackboard jungles, who extort protection money from younger children, who rape a thirteen-year-old girl in the bathroom, who make zip guns in shop, who knife the monitor in the hallway, and who attack the teacher who tries to bring them order. (39, 45)

ENVIRONMENTAL DEPRIVATION

The disadvantaged are hidden along the rural countryside in wooden shanties over the hills and out of sight from major turnpikes. They are also submerged in the garbage-strewn ghettos of our large cities. Indeed, the physical conditions are depressing in both areas.

In rural and urban slums, whole families are boxed into one or two rooms, paying high rentals to a landlord they never see. There is no running water, no bath or inside toilet, no heat in winter, except what the kitchen stove delivers, no refrigerator, no icebox. (33, 45) Two or three children may sleep on the same bed. Living space is cramped and overcrowded, denying any form of privacy and sensitizing children to adult sexual behavior. Maintains Crosby, "Often young girls are victims of adults. They become mothers when they are children. Illegitimacy is accepted." (9)

Not rarely, children three or four years old sit out on their front stoops late at night. In the backwoods of Georgia or on the streets in Harlem, the reason is the same. They cannot go to bed. Someone is sitting on it. Until the adults are ready for bed, there is no place for them to sleep. Consequently, many school children will fall asleep in class because they have not fully slept at night.

Here it is important to add that many city slums have been ripped down and replaced by low-cost housing projects. In many cases, however, this practice has made the environment worse, concentrating it almost exclusively with the most crippled and deviant segment of our population.

By screening the applicants to eliminate those with even modest wages, the community becomes a receptacle for the poorest and most deprived elements in our society. (45, 52) Fort Greene, for instance, the largest low-income (Negro and Puerto Rican) housing project in the United States, has almost 50 per cent of its families on welfare. (24) As soon as a family income rises above a minimum figure, it is forced to leave, replaced by a needy family, more than likely on relief and incapable of helping itself, with probably one or more of its members engaged in some type of antisocial behavior. The whole community is a reservoir for what Conant characterizes as "social dynamite," and there are hundreds of urban communities like this across the country.

Thus it is that the home and street of the ghetto are despairing complements. Few successful adult models are available for the children to emulate. Deviant behavior and social problems also are frequent, and are worsening at a frightening pace. This is reflected in statistics on delinquency and crime, unemployment, welfare, alcoholism, prostitution, drug addiction, illegitimacy, illiteracy, disease, and broken homes.

PARENTAL DEPRIVATION

Most disadvantaged children are members of families with many problems: divorce, desertion, unemployment, chronic sickness, mental illness, delinquency, and alcoholism. Their parents or the adults they live with regard as normal and natural such things as poverty, dependence on relief agencies, free sex relations, illegitimate children, and physical combat. (4, 26, 34) Not surprisingly, the children reared in these homes also accept these conditions, all of which are marginal to delinquent behavior.

Most damaging to the child is family instability. "Children in the same family group," declares Crosby, "sometimes have a number of different fathers. These youngsters are accustomed to seeing a succession of men in the home whose relations with the mother are transitory." (3) In the same vein, Cavan writes, "Many children live within several families during their lives. Many have never lived with both parents." (4)

Frequently, the mother assumes the male role, as breadwinner and as the one who metes out harsh and suppressive forms of punishment. (15) She usually works even when the family is not split. The children are denied the benefits of her affection and love. (17, 23) The atmosphere at home is indifferent and hostile. There is little kindness or supervision. The children, therefore, are free to roam the streets. The images of their parents are images of despair, frustration, and enforced idleness. They detach themselves from their parents, and they acquire independence outside the home. They rebel against teachers and the rest of the adult world, and they adopt interests in conflict with those of the school.

HYGIENIC DEPRIVATION

There is a high rate of illness and malnutrition among disadvantaged groups. Many are ignorant of good health practices and are unable to pay for any type of medical care. (15) Their standards of sanitation and cleanliness are atypical with respect to the dominant society. (14) Medical and dental checks will show hundreds of children who have never brushed their teeth or bathed regularly. (20)

A large number of these children are also improperly and irregularly fed. They go to bed hungry, they get up hungry, and they go to school hungry. They do not know what it means to go for one day with a full stomach. Their only complete meal is obtained in school; in fact, the school serves as a broadway for free lunch.

One study of low-class children indicated that 30 per cent of the group under 13 years of age had no milk. In another study, one-quarter of the children had no vegetables or fruits in the vitamin C category. More than half were suffering from vitamin A deficiencies. Similarly, a large number of the children were suffering from one form of malnutrition or another; gum and tongue conditions, rickets, and acne, for a few examples. (50)

It is depressing. The majority of the children who enter my classroom come with shabby and spoiled clothing. Their shirts and blouses are torn; buttons are missing; zippers do not work. When it rains some of them do not come to school, because they have holes in their shoes. On Fridays there are some who do not come to school, because they have no white shirt or blouse, and cannot be admitted to the assembly.

Thus there is a common denominator among these children; not enough proper medical care, not enough proper food, and not enough clothing.

RACIAL DEPRIVATION

Besides being faced with an intricate number of disadvantages, non-white minorities suffer from discrimination and prejudices. This, in turn, intensifies their other disadvantages and institutionalizes their financial deprivation. In most instances, minority groups must accept a lower or inferior position because of norms and vertically imposed definitions the larger society sets up. Furthermore, they conform to expectations of the society although conformity is directly opposed to their own self-interest. Asserts Hines, "An acquiescence in degradation takes place which becomes internalized and accepted wholly or in part by the discriminated group as part of its own way of life." (27)

With regard to Negro children, numerous tests indicate negative consciousness and unmistakable rejection of their skin color in preschool years. (6, 13, 28) Other tests also show that preschool white children ascribe inferior roles and low status to Negroes. (1, 2) At a very young age, then, Negro children learn that they belong to the wrong group and are worth very little according to the standards of the larger society.

Negro children have some contact with the world outside their ghetto, through mass-media communication: movies, radio, television, newspapers, magazines, and comic books. From these and other sources, they learn that they are considered by the prevailing society to have a second-class status. (38) In this connection Jefferson says, "They would like to think well of themselves but often tend to evaluate themselves according to standards used by other groups. These mixed feelings lead to self-hatred and rejection of their group, hostility toward other groups, and a generalized pattern of personality difficulties." (29)

Their attendance at a segregated school also adds to their "inferiority." (5) It should be noted, however, that many large cities spend extra money on these schools. New York City, for example, spends an extra $65 million yearly on "special services" for its 400 thousand disadvantaged children. (51) Nevertheless, segregated schools are generally inferior; more important, the children realize that they are being rejected and prevented from associating with children in the larger part of the community.

Corresponding problems exist among other minority groups. Spanish-speaking children, for example, are subjected to perhaps more discrimination. In addition, first-generation Mexican and Puerto Rican children have linguistic problems. Many are torn between two opposing cultures; therefore, they suffer from "anomie." (3, 43, 52) Their whole life situation, too, encourages the conviction that they cannot improve their condition very much by school or hard work.

EXPERIENCE DEPRIVATION

For the greater part, the disadvantaged are handicapped by a lack of information and awareness about any part of the world except their own limited one. From his study, Deutsch found that 65 per cent of the slum children have never been more than twenty-five blocks away from home, that half reported their homes were not supplied with writing pens, and the majority had no books, except for some comic books and magazines. (18) Similarly, many of these children have never been to the movies, eaten in a restaurant, or ridden in a bus except to school. Some have never had a birthday party, some do not even know their own birthdays; likewise some begin school without knowing their own names. (15, 20, 31)

It should be noted that the youngsters' physical surroundings are also impoverished, thus retarding all types of cultural stimulus and background. As Deutsch points out, most disadvantaged children have limited experiences, a scarcity of objects to manipulate, and a limited number of colors and forms to discriminate. (19)

This stimulus and background deficiency is a primary cause for the child's learning and school retardation. Writes Deutsch, "A child . . . who has been deprived of a substantial portion of the variety which he is maturationally capable of responding to is likely to be deficient in the equipment required for learning." (19) In the same vein, Piaget's developmental theory makes clear that the more limited a youngster's experiences are, the less he is likely to be interested in learning. (30, 41, 42)

EDUCATION DEPRIVATION

Besides lacking the requisite experience for learning basic skills, most disadvantaged youth are handicapped by numerous other factors which foster their school failure. Their depressed conditions have a deleterious effect upon their mental health. (19, 39) The fact that many come from crowded and noisy homes inhibits the development of their auditory and visual discrimination, and causes inattentiveness in school. (19, 42) Also, the combination of their impoverished environment and limited experiences hinders the development of their memory and language skills. (10, 35, 36, 41)

In many instances the assumption is made that when these children begin school they have developed skills necessary for learning. The truth is, however, many are unable to speak in whole sentences and are unable to find sense in their teacher's statements or in the stories in their primer. (36) Many cannot perceive the difference between letters and numbers. Ordinary concepts, such as near and far, or even the difference between red and blue, are meaningless. To attempt to teach these children how to read before they can visualize different letters is absurd. The assumption, then, that they are ready for learning, is the cause for more frustration, and when continued and compounded year after year, it is the cause of school failure.

True, the parents of most disadvantaged youth have been unable to provide the background and initial experience for formal learning; nonetheless, the parents are not against education. At worst, they see no need for it and are indifferent. Writes Mitchell, "Many have hope for their children but have little formal education themselves and know very little about studies or how to help their children. Most parents care a great deal; but care without knowledge. . . . (34)

Thus the experience deprivation of these children is compounded by the inadequacies of their parents. By the third grade, a large number are retarded one or more years in the basic skills. Their failure manifests a change in behavior. When they enter junior high school, they are openly defiant and their minds are closed. Passed from one grade to another, without any basis in knowledge or achievement, many lose interest in school; moreover, the longer they stay in school the more discouraged they become.

The outcome is that the majority of disadvantaged youth leave school or are suspended at an early age. In the poorest areas of the large cities about 60 to 70 per cent of the pupils drop out from school before graduation. (8) In discussing this point, Sexton found in her study that the dropout rate for low-income urban children is six times higher than that of middle-class children. (47) Rural areas have even higher dropout figures. (12, 37) Among Texas Mexicans, for example, the average education limit is six years of schooling, and the chances are that it is constantly interrupted, and inferior. (3, 25)

SUMMARY

Although no one program can itself lead to a solution to deprivation on a mass scale, education is most important, because without it there is no hope that the disadvantaged will ever acquire skills to hold a decent job so that they can break from their complex web of impoverishment. Unquestionably, more money is needed to be spent, more on elementary schools than in college, and more money in slum and rural schools than in suburban schools. Right now the situation is reversed. (46) Nevertheless, the political and economic power structure on all governmental levels is at present willing to spend large sums of money on the experimentation and research for the education of the disadvantaged. They are willing not because they have suddenly become humanitarian, but because they are afraid of the consequences if they do not. (40) For this reason, almost any school system or college can obtain today a federal grant which is focused on the educational needs of disadvantaged children.

But money is not enough, unless it is channeled wisely. The fact that the disadvantaged have an integral chain of handicaps means that the whole child must be considered. Higher Horizons' type of programs, prekindergarten education, after-school-study centers, and the like, have very rarely, if ever, been fully effective. In the next few years, we will spend billions of dollars on similar educational programs. Unless all the integral number of disadvantages of these children are taken into account our new efforts will also fail.

Indeed, time is running out. "This is our last chance," writes one educator. "We cannot afford another generation as ignorant as we are." The demands of our society necessitate that we educate our disadvantaged youth. As Shaw put it, "The preservation of our democratic way of life, the demands of our economy, and the mental health of our people all require that we learn how to educate these children effectively." (48)

REFERENCES

1. Ammons, R. B., "Reactions in a Projective Doll Play Interview of White Males Two to Six Years of Age to Differences in Skin Color and Facial Factors," *Journal of Genetic Psychology*. Vol. LXXVI (1950), pp. 323–341.
2. Blake, Robert; Dennis, Wayne, "The Development of Stereotypes Concerning the Negro," *Journal of Abnormal and Social Psychology*, Vol. XXXVIII (1943), pp. 525–531.

3. Burma, John H., "Spanish-Speaking Children," in Eli Ginsberg, *The Nation's Children*, Vol. III (New York: Columbia University Press, 1960), pp. 78–102.

4. Cavan, Ruth S., "Negro Family Disorganization and Juvenile Delinquency," *Journal of Negro Education*, Summer 1959, pp. 230–239.

5. Clark, Kenneth B., *Prejudice and Your Child* (Boston: Beacon Press, 1936).

6. Clark, Kenneth B.; Clark, Mamie J., "The Development of Consciousness in Negro Pre-School Children," *Journal of Social Psychology*, Vol. X (1939), pp. 591–599.

7. Cloward, Richard A.; Ohlin, Lloyd E., *Delinquency and Opportunity* (Glencoe, Illinois: Free Press, 1960).

8. Conant, James B., *Slums & Suburbs* (New York: McGraw-Hill, 1961).

9. Crosby, Muriel, "A Portrait of Blight," *Educational Leadership*, February 1963, pp. 300–304.

10. Cutts, Warren G., "Special Language Problems of the Culturally Disadvantaged," *Clearing House*, October 1962, pp. 80–83.

11. Dai, Bingham, "Some Problems of Personality Development Among Negro Children," in C. Klucholn and H. A. Murray, *Personality in Nature, Society and Culture* (New York: Knopf, 1956), pp. 545–566.

12. Daniel, Walter G., "Problems of Disadvantaged Youth, Urban and Rural," *Journal of Negro Education*, Summer 1964, pp. 218–224.

13. Davis, Allison, "The Socialization of the American Negro Child and Adolescent," *Journal of Negro Education*, July 1939, pp. 264–275.

14. Davis, Michael M.; Smythe, Hugh H., "Providing Adequate Health Services to Negroes," *Journal of Negro Education*, Summer 1949, pp. 283–290.

15. Della-Dora, Delmo, "The Culturally Disadvantaged: Educational Implications of Certain Social Cultural Phenomena," *Exceptional Children*, May 1962, pp. 467–472.

16. Department of Commerce, Bureau of the Census, *Current Population Report*, Series 1–227, No. 96; Series 1–601, No. 225; Series 1–604, No. 226.

17. Deutsch, Martin, "Some Considerations as to the Contributions of Social Personality and Racial Factors to School Retardation in Minority Group Children," paper read at the American Psychology Association, Chicago, September 1956.

18. Deutsch, Martin, "Minority Group and Class Structure as Related to Social and Personality Factors in Scholastic Achievement," Mimeographed, No. 2, Ithaca, New York: Society for Applied Anthropology, 1960.

19. Deutsch, Martin, "The Disadvantaged Child and the Learning Process," in A. Harry Passow, *Education in Depressed Areas* (New York: Columbia University Press, 1964), pp. 163–179.

20. Ford Foundation Reprint, "Stirrings in the Big Cities: The Great Cities Project," Mimeographed, New York: Ford Foundation, 1962.

21. Friedenberg, Edgar Z., *The Vanishing Adolescent* (New York: Dell Publishing Co., 1962).

22. Galbraith, John K., *The Affluent Society* (Boston: Houghton Mifflin, 1958).
23. Goff, Regina M., "The Curriculum as a Source of Psychological Strength for the Negro Child," *Education Administration and Supervision*, May 1952, pp. 299–301.
24. Guidance Department, Sands Junior High School, Fort Greene, Brooklyn, New York.
25. Harrington, Michael, *The Other America* (Baltimore: Penguin Books, 1964).
26. Health and Welfare Council of the Baltimore Area, Inc., A Letter to Ourselves; A Master Plan for Human Redevelopment, Mimeographed. Baltimore: The Council, January 18, 1962, p. 3.
27. Hines, Ralph, "Social Expectations and Cultural Deprivation," *Journal of Negro Education*, Spring 1964, pp. 136–142.
28. Horowitz, Ruth E., "Racial Aspects of Self-Identification in Nursery School Children," *Journal of Psychology*, Vol. VIII (1940), pp. 91–99.
29. Jefferson, Ruth, "Some Obstacles to Racial Integration," *Journal of Negro Education*, Summer 1957, pp. 145–154.
30. Hunt, J. McV., *Intelligence and Experience* (New York: Ronald Press, 1961).
31. Krugman, Judith I., "Cultural Deprivation and Child Development," *High Points*, November 1956, pp. 5–20.
32. Kvaraceus, William C., "Alienated Youth Here and Abroad," *Phi Delta Kappan*, November 1963, pp. 87–90.
33. Masse, Benjamin L., "Poverty, U.S.A.," *America*, July 20, 1963, pp. 73–75.
34. Mitchell, Charles, "The Culturally Deprived Child—A Matter of Concern," *Childhood Education*, May 1962, pp. 412–420.
35. Newton, Eunice, "The Culturally Deprived Child in our Verbal Schools," *Journal of Negro Education*, Fall 1962, pp. 184–187.
36. Newton, Eunice, "Verbal Destitution: The Pivotal Barrier to Learning," *Journal of Negro Education*, Fall 1960, pp. 497–499.
37. O'Hara, James M., "Disadvantaged Newcomers to the City," *NEA Journal*, April 1963, pp. 25–27.
38. Olsen, James, "Children of the Ghetto," *High Points*, March 1964, pp. 25–33.
39. Ornstein, Allan C., "Effective Schools for Disadvantaged Children," *Journal of Secondary Education*, March 1965, pp. 105–109.
40. Ornstein, Allan C., "Program Revision for Culturally Disadvantaged Children," *Journal of Negro Education*, Spring 1966.
41. Piaget, J., *The Language and Thought of the Child* (New York: Humanities Press, 1926).
42. Piaget, J., *The Origins of Intelligence in Children* (New York: International Universities Press, 1952).
43. *Puerto Rican Profiles* (New York: Board of Education of the City of New York, July 7, 1964).
44. Redl, Fritz, *Children Who Hate* (Glencoe, Illinois: Free Press, 1951).

45. Salisbury, Harrison E., *The Shook-Up Generation* (Greenwich, Connecticut: Fawcett Publications, 1959).
46. Sexton, Patricia, "Comments on Three Cities," *Integrated Education*, August 1963, pp. 27–32.
47. Sexton, Patricia, *Education and Income* (New York: Viking Press, 1961).
48. Shaw, Frederick, "Educating Culturally Deprived Youth in Urban Centers," *Phi Delta Kappan*, November 1963, pp. 91–97.
49. Tenenbaum, Samuel, "The Teacher, the Middle-Class, the Lower- Class," *Phi Delta Kappan*, November 1963, pp. 82–86.
50. "The Nutritional Status of Negroes," Study by Nutrition Branch and Program Analysis Branch, Division of Chronic Disease, Public Health, F. S. A., *Journal of Negro Education*, Summer 1949, pp. 291–304.
51. *The Public Schools of New York City Staff Bulletin*, Vol. III, January 11, 1965.
52. Wakefield, Dan, *Island in the City* (New York: Corinth Books, 1965).

41 The Challenge to Education

Theodore M. Hesburgh

We Americans place enormous faith in education and we make many demands upon our educators. We ask them to accomplish almost super-human feats—not only to teach our children the basic skills necessary to earn a livelihood in modern-day society but also to be a moving force in the process of healing the social divisions that exist. This is nothing new. These are the tasks which Americans traditionally have asked educators to perform, not just to teach the "3 R's", but to serve also, in Horace Mann's words, as "the great equalizer of the conditions of men—the balance wheel of the social machinery."[1]

There is a substantial question whether schools are capable of carrying out these responsibilities—indeed whether they ever did carry them out in the past. There are many who claim that our schools were primarily responsible for molding the diverse groups of immigrants who flocked to this country during the

[1] 12th Annual Report of Horace Mann as Secretary of the Massachusetts State Board of Education (1848), in *Discussions in American History*, 318 (Commager ed. 1958).

Reprinted from *The Journal of Negro Education*, 40 (3): 290–296 (Summer 1971), by permission of author and publisher.

late 19th and early 20th centuries into full and productive participants in American society. As one group of educators put it: "When the need arose to make one nation out of many communities of foreign origin, the people turned to the public schools, and their faith was justified."[2] Other commentators take a less glowing view of the role that education played. Some go so far as to contend that the millions of immigrants and their descendants succeeded in spite of the schools rather than because of their efforts. In their view the schools failed to adapt to the immigrants' basic needs, disdaining the rich variety of language and culture they brought, seeking instead to force them into a mold of antiseptic sameness.

Whatever the merits of this argument over the past, there is little question that today, by whatever standard their performance is measured, our schools are failing. Just in terms of teaching children basic verbal and technical skills—by far the easiest part of the task society has entrusted to them—the schools are not succeeding. To be sure, privileged suburban children are acquiring these skills, but the schools deserve little credit for this. For these children, academic achievement usually is an integral part of the affluent environment in which they have been nurtured. Teaching them is no great challenge. Indeed, there are some who are convinced that these children would learn as much without benefit of attending class at all.

What of the children brought up in environments in which affluence is unknown and academic achievement is rare—Appalachian white children newly arrived in the cities, black children brought up in the ghettos of our giant urban centers, and brown children living in the barrios of the Southwest? This is the main challenge to education today and our educators are not meeting it. Many of these children, even at the early age at which they enter school, already have grown accustomed to failure and hopelessness. This is what they see about them, and it is what they already have come to expect for themselves. The schools, instead of altering this cycle of defeat, are tending to perpetuate it. As Dr. Kenneth B. Clark has put it: "The total pattern of failure, inefficiency, academic and vocational retardation is a part of the cycle of rejection, despair, and hopelessness in which low-status children are perceived as uneducable, while they, in turn, perceive school personnel and officials as adversaries."[3]

Education also must serve a broader function than providing children with the technical tools necessary to compete in the technological society of modern-day America. It is a function which one commentator recently described as to "Prepare people not just to earn a living but also to live a life—a creative, humane, and sensitive life."[4] Here the failure of schools is even greater.

[2] Educational Policies Division of the National Education Association and the American Association of School Educators, *Education and the Search for Equal Opportunity* 4 (1965).

[3] Alex C. Sherriffs and Kenneth B. Clark, *How Relevant Is Education in America Today* (Washington: American Institute for Public Policy Research, 1970), p. 42.

[4] Charles E. Silberman, *Crisis in the Classroom: The Remaking of American Education* (New York: Random House, 1970), p. 114.

Thus the privileged child, while he may acquire the skills necessary to pass ever more difficult technical examinations, learns little that will equip him to become a responsible citizen capable of making judgments on the basis of factors other than narrow self-interest. The less privileged child—black, brown, and white —all too often is neither equipped to pass tests nor to develop his own inner resources to the fullest. In short, all of our children are being shortchanged and are being ill-equipped to make the society they will inherit a better one than we, their parents, will have left.

Having made this harsh indictment of our system of public education, let me concede that the problems with education can by no means be laid entirely at the doorstep of the schools. Many factors bear on a child's education and the values he develops as he grows into adulthood. Only a part of them is acquired in school. Most of his educational experience is gained from the environment in which he lives, and the values he adopts are more strongly influenced by the society that surrounds him than by the school, in which he spends only a part of his time.

Thus children who come from well-educated, highly motivated families begin school with a distinct advantage over fellow students from less advantaged homes. As the monumental report of the U.S. Office of Education, *Equality of Educational Opportunity*,[5] demonstrated, a child's own family background is a far stronger influence on his academic achievement and aspirations than any factor within the control of the schools.

By the same token, there are severe limits to the capacity of schools to instill moral and humane values in children when these children see gross injustices and inhumanity in the larger society which claims most of his time. For many minority children, the reality of racial injustice breeds a sense of hopelessness and frustration that can thwart the efforts of even the most creative teachers and principals. For affluent children of majority families, the great disparities between the principles of freedom and equality they are taught in school and society's failure to live up to those principles foster cynicism and the conviction that the values taught in school are irrelevant to those necessary for success in the real world.

Schools necessarily exist in the larger society of which they are a part and the injustices of society are mirrored in the schools themselves. Just as housing in our metropolitan areas is racially and economically segregated, so are the schools which exist in these metropolitan areas. Just as the various institutions of our society are geared to serve the needs and ambitions of the white middle-class child of conventional upbringing, so are the schools. In short, the failure of the schools reflects the failure of the larger society. In a true sense we are getting what we deserve.

I have heard some people complain that to demand that the schools overcome the realities of society is to expect them to accomplish miracles. Before we can reasonably expect the schools to carry out their critical role as

---

⁵ U.S. Office of Education, *Equality of Educational Opportunity* (1966).

"the balance wheel of the social machinery," they add, society, itself, must be drastically altered. Through my own experience as an educator, I recognize the enormous burden that we are asking the schools to shoulder—that we are, indeed, asking them to perform miracles. Through my experience as an active participant in the cause of civil rights and an observer of the social and economic injustices that exist in our society, I also recognize the need for drastic changes and a reordering of the priorities which govern the Nation and the lives of the people who live in it.

But having conceded that the failure of our system of education must be attributed in large part to the conditions that exist in society—conditions totally outside the control of the schools—the fact remains that the schools are far from blameless. Educators have been much too eager to shift the blame elsewhere, seeking to absolve themselves entirely of responsibility for the inadequate education the children entrusted to their care receive. This simply will not wash. For educators, in effect, to wring their hands in despair and assert that society has created conditions which make it impossible for them to carry out their assigned task represents an unacceptable abdication of responsibility. The schools, for better or for worse, play a unique and pivotal role in shaping a child's future. As the President pointed out last year: "It is a place not only of learning but also of living—where a child's friendships center, where he learns to measure himself against others, to share, to compete, to cooperate—and it is the one institution above all others with which the parent shares his child."[6]

The school is the most important public institution bearing on a child's development as an informed, educated person and as a human being. Through the school, the opportunity is presented to intervene at an early stage in a child's development for purposes of breaking the cycle of poverty and hopelessness which is the preordained fate of so many children, and to instill dedication to the principles of morality and humanity in all children so that they will seek to change, rather than accept, the hypocrisy they see about them.

The obstacles that impede the educational process are real enough. I do not accept the proposition, however, that they are insurmountable or that the schools are helpless in the face of them. For example, while the finding of the Office of Education report that the most important factor bearing on a child's performance and aspirations is his individual family background—a factor totally outside control of the school—means that there are limits to what the schools reasonably can be expected to accomplish, this finding hardly negates the role that schools can play, nor does it justify counsels of despair on the part of educators. For that report also found that there are other factors, within the control of schools, that also bear significantly on the child's performance.

The kind of curriculum and the quality of facilities available in the school contribute substantially to the learning process, for they shape the basic tools of education and the environment in which it takes place.

[6] Statement by the President on Elementary and Secondary School Desegregation, March 24, 1970.

The ability of teachers is an even stronger factor, again within the control of the schools. Each of us undoubtedly remembers at least one or two teachers in the course of our progress through the schools who, through their dedication and enthusiasm, caught our imagination and made education an adventure rather than an endless exercise in drudgery.

By far the most important school factor that bears on the learning process is the nature of a child's fellow students. As the Office of Education report demonstrated, and as the Commission on Civil Rights report on "Racial Isolation in the Public Schools" confirmed, there is a significant difference in the performance and aspirations of school children, depending upon the social and economic background of their classmates. This is particularly true for disadvantaged children. That is, a disadvantaged child attending school with children, a majority of whom are from advantaged backgrounds, is likely to do substantially better both in school and in later life than a similarly situated child attending school with other disadvantaged children. What this key finding bears out is the almost self-evident fact that school children learn as much from each other as they do from teachers and textbooks.

Given these key findings, none of which should be a revelation, it is apparent that the schools are not helpless in the face of the inequities that exist in the larger society. Decisions by school officials and others involved in the educational process can make a difference, despite the ills of society, in contributing to the healthy development of all children in their charge. Yet in so many cases the decisions that have been made have tended to perpetuate the very inequities of which educators complain.

Let us take the matter of curriculum and other educational techniques to encourage the child and to inspire in him a love of learning. By and large, innovations and experimental approaches in education have been conducted in schools that serve children of white affluent families—those who typically need them the least. In schools in which minority children are concentrated, innovations are rare and the learning process is conducted in an atmosphere of dullness and hostility. One reason offered for this lack of innovation in schools that serve children of the ghettos and barrios has been inadequate financial resources to undertake them. In 1965 Congress enacted the landmark Elementary and Secondary Act, earmarking substantial amounts of money specifically for the purpose of improving the quality of education afforded to disadvantaged children. To be sure, the amount of money provided has not been as much as we would like or need—it rarely is—but it should have afforded educators an opportunity to make significant changes and to implement many of the innovative ideas that have been circulating in the educational community.

The experience under this legislation, however, has been disappointing. Some school officials have squandered the money on purposes totally unrelated to educational improvements. (In one case, the funds were deposited in a bank and left there to draw interest.) Others have restricted the use of funds to the purchase of new school hardware which, while satisfying the appetite for gadgetry that many of us have, has only limited value in improving the quality of education.

These inequities also are perpetuated in the assignment of teachers. Teachers who are young, better educated, and more inclined to attempt innovative approaches to education tend to teach in schools that serve children of the affluent, while children of the ghettos and barrios tend to be served by less able teachers, many of whom view education solely in terms of the need for order and discipline. For these teachers, the school too often is seen more as a house of correction than an institution of learning, and the children too often are treated more as a faceless mass of bodies than as individuals each with unique hopes and ambitions that must be carefully nurtured and cultivated. Here again, a key element in the educational process has been carried out in a way that, at best, acquiesces in the perpetuation of inequity.

Perhaps the most distressing failure of the schools has been in their willing acceptance of racial and economic segregation as the inevitable pattern of school attendance. Although segregation represents the typical residential pattern in metropolitan areas, it need not be so for school attendance. It is only when school officials impose geographic zoning as the sole criterion that determines which school a child shall attend that segregated patterns of residence are inevitably reflected in the schools. It is as though school officials operate on the principle that schools, which, in fact, belong to the entire community, are somehow the exclusive property of those who happen to live in the immediate neighborhood. This, of course, is a principle which has no basis in law. It also makes no sense in terms of educational policy. By thus educating children of different racial and economic backgrounds separately, the schools are failing to take advantage of their greatest asset—the children themselves. This acceptance of educational duality has tragic implications for the country's future.

Several years ago, Mrs. Frankie M. Freeman, a member of the U.S. Commission on Civil Rights, stated what those implications were. She said: "We are now on a collision course which may produce within our borders two alienated and unequal nations confronting each other across a widening gulf created by a dual educational system based upon income and race."[7]

In the years since Commissioner Freeman stated that warning, we have remained on a collision course and educators have done little on their own to help the country veer from it.

The picture that I have described is far from an encouraging one. It is as though we in the profession of education have somehow lost our way and are merely going through the motions, rather than undertaking our tasks with enthusiasm and creativity. Timidity and defeatism have become all too often the hallmark of educators and the noble purposes of the profession we have entered are being distorted. If education is to assume again the role that was once claimed for it—"healer of great social divisions"—it will have to be mainly

---

[7] U.S. Commission on Civil Rights, *Racial Isolation in the Public Schools* 215 (1967).

through the efforts of educators themselves, and these efforts must be undertaken on several levels.

We must be prepared to try experimental approaches to education in an effort to fire the imagination of children whose experience in school has left them apathetic and uninterested. We must do this even though it can be anticipated that some of these new approaches will fail.

We must train those who enter the profession of teaching to regard assignment to ghetto and barrio schools as the great challenge and adventure that it can be, rather than an onerous chore to be avoided.

We must initiate school attendance techniques that seek to overcome the segregated residential patterns that exist and assure that children of all races and economic backgrounds learn together and know each other as equals.

Above all, we must develop the strength and will to assume leadership roles in our communities and no longer act on the assumption that the expressions of prejudice and narrow self-interest voiced by some reflect the will of the community at large.

I recognize that all this is easy to say. Some may think it represents hopeless idealism. I would agree, at least in part. It does represent the ideal. I cannot concede, however, that it is hopeless. For if education is not to serve as the catalyst for salutary change in our society, then the chances for such change are slim. There simply is no other institution in society capable of serving this function.

I recognize also that what I have suggested amounts to an enormous burden for educators and that for them to accept it requires considerable backbone and courage. It is much easier to go along with the status quo. But the plain fact is that the status quo is leading to disaster and can no longer be tolerated. Backbone and courage are essential ingredients for any educator worth his salt. The rewards and satisfactions experienced by those who possess these ingredients are enormous. There also are risks for those who dare to use them. The stakes, however, are such that the risks must be taken. Those of us who have followed the calling of education must dare, for, in large part, the future well-being of the country depends upon how well we perform.

42 The Educability of Dominant Groups

Edsel L. Erickson, Clifford E. Bryan,
and Lewis Walker

One of the greatest single issues in our tradition concerns the notion that all persons and subcultures should have an equal opportunity to share in the societal distribution of rewards. Along with increased recognition that the nation's educational system represents one of the few remaining avenues of vertical mobility, more and more attention has been focused on the fact that minority-group children from the lower social classes often receive considerably less benefit from their school experiences than do more privileged children. The issue is why. (Of course, a great deal has been written explaining why some subcultures are "more equal than others.")

For generations our society has been plagued with false biological explanations for subcultural differences. Education and social science, reflecting the parochialism of the dominant Euro-American culture, have explained the unfortunate condition of Afro-American, Mexican-American, Puerto Rican-American, Indian-American, and other minority-American children on the basis of genetic inferiority. Gradually, however, with an occasional throwback or backlash, educators and scientists by the 1960's began seriously to challenge the absurdity of biological explanations and to shift to other equally absurd social-class explanations.

One approach particularly in vogue in the early sixties, when the war on poverty began, was the theme that many children are "culturally deprived" when they enter school. From the "culturally deprived" view, white middle-class children are assumed to have the benefit of exposure to a more enriched culture than are lower-class (especially nonwhite) children. From this perspective, it is said that young black pupils may not know what a "square meal" is, or an egg, or an orange, or the proper definition of a "muffler," etc. The implications for educators who took the culturally deprived perspective were that these "deprived" children should somehow have their lives "enriched," that they should be exposed to and thereby internalize middle-class cultural values; such exposure would compensate for their "cultural deprivation." To the proponents of this perspective came the sharp reply that minority children come from a culture just as everyone else does—a full, rich, multifaceted culture—and they are *not* deprived. The argument is that minority group subcultures are merely

Reprinted from *Phi Delta Kappan*, 53 (5): 319–321 (January 1972), by permission of authors and publisher.

different from those subcultures in which they are expected to compete. It is just as necessary, according to this point of view, for educators to learn and understand the lower-class culture as it is for lower-class children to learn to compete in terms of the middle-class culture.

Thereby it was concluded that if lower-class children were not " culturally deprived," they were at least "culturally disadvantaged." Hence it was acknowledged for a time by many educators and social scientists that lower-class children do, in fact, come from a full, rich culture: Children from the inner-city areas, it was observed, even spoke their own unique style of language ("ghettoese") . Since their culture is assumed to be *different* from that on which our educational assumptions and processes are based, however, the students in question were placed at a disadvantage. The implications for education, then, were that such children should learn to participate in *two* cultures; they should become *bilingual,* i.e., be able to speak ghettoese as well as the dominant vernacular. Other critics raised the objection, however, that this was *not* the case; lower-class children learned certain coping mechanisms necessary for their survival in the lower-class setting—in their own social milieu, then, they were advantaged indeed. To insist, they contended, that an ethnic or lower-class cultural background placed them at a disadvantage was to imply a rejection of their cultural heritage that would lead to self-hatred.

A new argument was then advanced: Perhaps such children were not "deprived" and perhaps they were not even "disadvantaged" by their culture. But they were at least "educationally disadvantaged. " In other words, when such children were expected to perform in the academic arena, their prior preparation was such that other children had an advantage over them. One of the more recent rejoinders to this idea is that the blame lies in the *other* direction— such children have been *excluded.* Their parental families have been excluded from conditions conducive to stability (jobs, educational qualifications, adequate housing, suitable incomes, health care), and the children themselves have been excluded from quality education at every level of the formal education system (shortage of supplies, inadequate facilities, inexperienced teachers, lack of funds, overcrowded classrooms, etc.). Therefore, lower-class and black children have problems, not because their heritage has placed them at a disadvantage, but because the larger society has both unintentionally and willfully excluded them from the societal distribution of rewards. The implications of this approach for education, then, are that the larger society must *include* the children and their families; accountability and responsibility are placed on the larger society and school rather than on the children alone. Illustrative of the increased attention being placed on society and the educational system in particular as a culprit is the recent work of Ray Rist.[1] In a three-year longitudinal observational study, he provided an examination of the

---

[1] Ray C. Rist, "Student Social Class and Teacher Expectations: The Self-Fulfilling Prophecy in Ghetto Education," *Harvard Educational Review,* August, 1970, pp. 411–49.

caste system of the classroom and the class system of the larger society. Although many studies have demonstrated that academic achievement is associated with social class, Rist's project is one of the few that have attempted to ascertain just how the school helps to reinforce the class structure of the larger society.

Rist began his study at the kindergarten level. The setting was an inner-city school in which all of the teachers as well as the students were black. He sought to determine which kinds of expectations and social interactions gave rise to the social organization of class. He assumed that, even at the kindergarten level, there would emerge certain patterns of behavior, expectations of performance, and a mutually accepted stratification system which would differentiate between those doing well and those doing poorly. Of particular importance would be the relation of the teacher's expectations of potential academic performance to the social status of the student.

It was found that the black kindergarten teacher assigned her new students to three different tables; the first table was close to the teacher and to the instructional materials, while the others were progressively farther away. There were some common characteristics associated with the students seated at each table. Those at the first table were clean and well-groomed while those at the second and third tables were considerably less so. Those at the last table smelled of urine, had darker skins, and had either matted or unprocessed hair.

Several other important characteristics were associated with the assigned seating positions. The children who began to develop as classroom leaders were placed at the first table. They were at greater ease in speaking to the teacher. They were not only much more verbal but displayed a greater command of standard American English. The less verbal children at the other two tables, in the few responses they did give to the teacher, used ghettoese rather than "school language." Finally, there were a number of social status differences. The children at the first table came from families with higher incomes and higher levels of education. They had considerably fewer siblings. The teacher informed the observer that children at the first table were the "fast learners" while those at the two tables farthest from her "had no idea of what was going on in the classroom."

What is of even greater importance, however, is the fact that this particular seating arrangement was also the basic pattern in the first and second grades. As the pupils progressed through school, those who were seated at the second and third tables were joined by students who had "failed" and were retained at their respective grade level. The seating arrangements and the physical setting of the classroom virtually ensured that the "poor" students received less communication from the teachers (the teachers directed their conversation toward those nearest them), were not involved in class activities (the pupils at the first table often denounced the others for their inappropriate responses, hence discouraging further attempts), and received less frequent instruction (those at the last table often were seated in such a position that they could not even see the materials presented in class or instructions written on the chalkboard).

Rist found that the students largely internalized definitions of themselves provided by the teachers. At the beginning of the kindergarten year, for example, the students related to each other on a fairly egalitarian basis. After being assigned seating positions, and after the teacher's definitions of "high" and "low" learning potential had been communicated to the students, there was a distinct qualitative difference in the patterns of interaction between the students. Those at the first table began to call the others "dumb" and "stupid." Furthermore, those at the remaining two tables used such terms in referring to each other. The "good" pupils began to direct a great deal of hostility towards the "poor" students; and the "poor" students developed a considerable amount of overt and covert conflict among themselves.

Rist concluded that what develops as a "caste" within the classrooms appears to emerge in the larger society as "class." The low-income children segregated as a caste of "unclean and intellectually inferior" persons may very well be those who become the car washers, dishwashers, welfare recipients, and unemployed and underemployed in the larger society. Hence the public school system (even in an all-black setting) not only mirrors the configurations of the larger society but also significantly contributes to maintaining them. Rist's study is unique in that it documents the operations of this particular phenomenon on a microcosmic level within a minority group subsystem. Black students who bore physical evidence of lower socioeconomic backgrounds were exposed to socialization processes in the school which gave certainty to the fact that they would occupy lower social status positions as adults; similarly, students from "better" families are selectively educated for "better" future positions.

Rist's study is of great importance, for it provides a great deal of insight and holds a number of implications for the current concerns over school desegregation. A major philosophical consideration underlying this particular intervention attempt is that of providing minority-group children the opportunity to become exposed to middle-class norms and values by placing them in middle-class schools (which are generally white).

While it is apparent that racial or economic segregation is often imposed by providing separate schools for children, it is not so well recognized that the practice of simply placing students of differing races or classes together does not mean that desegregation has taken place in any meaningful way. In the U.S. federal intervention programs have sought to desegregate simply by placing students of different races in the same school.

For the most part, the aims of such federal programs, i.e., racial desegregation of the schools, have been justified by the conclusion that dominant-group norms influence the behavior of the individual. The primary idea has been that minority-group children shall acquire middle-class academic values when placed in a middle-class normative milieu. Many studies have come to the conclusion that schools which serve an exclusively all-black lower-class student clientele are currently characterized in predominantly white Western societies by a social climate which militates against high levels of academic achievement.[2] Some studies[3] indicate that when lower-class black students are in a primarily middle-class school their academic achievement approaches that of the middle-class norms. Very often, then, efforts to provide a more equal opportunity in education for lower-class children have resulted in proposals for mixing school populations on the basis of race. Very often, heightened racial conflict has accompanied this mixing. Why? According to many authorities, the mixing should provide better education for the minority-group children. But often it does not. Why?

These negative results may be partially attributable to erroneous assumptions. Perhaps by making these assumptions explicit we can come to a greater understanding of what is happening.

It is frequently assumed, for example, that since most black people are lower class, most whites are middle class.

This is a very wrong assumption. Although it has been estimated that nearly 75% of all black people would fall into the lower socioeconomic stratum, there is a much greater absolute number of whites who are lower class.

Although the *proportion* of blacks who are lower class is greater than the *proportion* of whites in that social category, the sheer number of lower-class whites far exceeds that of the number of black people. Very often, then, when students are mixed merely on the basis of color composition, lower-class black children are merely mixed in with lower-class white children. One large city in Michigan undertook a very conscientious attempt to desegregate its public schools. One after another, each school exploded. It was only *after* such futile attempts that some researchers surveyed the entire student population in that city. It was found that nearly 40% of all school-aged children attended either private or parochial schools; the wealthier children—those who are generally the more socially liberal—had been removed from the public schools. In effect, this meant that those who were left in the public schools, those who were to be "desegregated" and who, it was hoped, would be able to modify the academic behavior of the black children, were likely to have the same kinds of problems as those who were introduced into their schools, even though they were white.

We have learned a great deal from the birth and death of various terms which have been used to describe poor youths and from studies such as those by Rist and research that documents the relationship between race, social class, and integration. However, we are still left with the task of reorganizing the educational Establishment so that it will facilitate the achievement of students who belong to America's ethnic minority groups. This is the major challenge for the seventies.

---

[2] Wilbur B. Brookover and Edsel L. Erickson, *Society, Schools, and Learning*. Boston: Allyn and Bacon, 1969, pp. 80–96.

[3] James Coleman et al., *Equality of Educational Opportunity*. Washington, D.C.: U.S. Office of Education, National Center for Educational Statistics, Government Printing Office.

43　Disturbed Youngsters in the Classroom

William C. Morse

"John can make a shambles of my classroom. The only way I can get anyplace talking with him is away from the group. Then he explains very clearly why he does various things. He usually admits that they were dumb things to do, but there is no carryover. He already has a court record.

"And then there are Beth and George. Beth is so quiet and dreamy that she seems here only when I press her with questions and then she drifts away. George is another story. His conversations are non sequiturs. He asks the strangest questions—and always with a worried look. The psychologist has referred him for intensive treatment, but there is a long waiting list. Most of the time I can almost keep on top of the situation, but there are days when I don't seem to be getting anywhere."

An experienced teacher was describing her classroom. Almost any teacher in almost any school could paint a similar picture, and although the percentage of Johns, Beths, and Georges in the typical classroom is small, it does not take huge numbers of disturbed youngsters to create a critical mass that can confound a teacher and convert a classroom to chaos.

What can a teacher do that will be helpful to the disturbed children in the classroom and at the same time will keep them from disrupting the rest of the class? Source books are not available for teaching attitudes, values, identification, or empathic behavior. Advice ranges from the assured behavior modifiers who direct the teacher to "train" the pupils to the proponents of a leave-them-alone-and-they'll-all-come-home-to-Summerhill philosophy.

These answers are too simple. If the schools are to meet their responsibility toward all children, teachers and schools must change. Teachers need to understand what causes the disturbed children in their classes to be that way. They need to develop new teaching skills and to find new ways of using resources. School systems need to look for new ways to use the resources—the time, space, techniques, and personnel—now available and to add new resources.

UNDERSTANDING DISTURBED PUPILS

Some children are disturbed both in their home-community life and in school. Their difficulties are pervasive—with them wherever they go. For exam-

Reprinted from *Today's Education: NEA Journal*, 58 (4): 30–37 (April 1969), by permission of author and publisher.

ple, many a youngster who is rejected and unwanted in his family feels the same way in school.

In other children, disturbance shows up at home or at school but not in both situations. Ralph, for instance, is a skilled leader on the playground and in his neighborhood and gets along reasonably well in his fatherless home. He chafes under the pressure of school routines, however. He is in constant contest with conformity demands and has no interest in school learning. Generally speaking, he is happy-go-lucky and forgets a school disciplinary episode almost before it is over.

Other children who feel supported and do very well in school have difficulties elsewhere. The school is sometimes central in problem behavior and sometimes peripheral, but the aim is to make the school compensatory whenever possible.

The behavior symptoms a child displays are not an automatic revelation of the causes of that behavior. To plan effectively for a disturbed child, the teacher needs not only to see accurately what the youngster does but to understand why he does it. This requires the teacher to do some diagnostic thinking and to gain the ability to see life through the eyes of the pupil.

Let us apply diagnostic thinking first to pupils who are aggressive toward peers, perhaps toward the teacher, and even toward school requirements —pupils who display what is called "acting-out behavior." Children with this broad range of symptoms are the most frequent referrals to special services and special classes. They may provoke fights, break rules, and generally defy the teacher. Older youngsters often turn sullen and hostile. Acting-out children prevent others from working, may react with an outburst if required to conform, and are ready to rebel at a moment's notice.

Since this type of behavior can make conducting classes impossible, no one should be surprised that teachers find it the most vexing difficulty.

When teachers explore beyond the generalized acting-out symptoms, they find some common patterns.

Sometimes aggressiveness results from a lack of adequate socialization. Our culture is producing increasing numbers of children who have never developed social concerns for others, who still function on an impulse basis, doing what they want to do when they feel like it. For one reason or another they lack a suitable prototype for basic identification. Sometimes they take on an omnipotent character—"No one can make me." At best they are narcissistic, bent on following their own desires; at worst they are without the capacity to feel for others. They practice a primitive hedonism.

Sometimes, these children come from indulgent, protective families and become embittered when crossed. When one is asked why he did something, he is likely to say, "I felt like it," until he learns it goes over better to say that he doesn't know why.

Because his delinquent and destructive behavior may stem from a lack of incorporated norms and values, the child with a defect in socialization needs a benign but strong surveillance, so that he is held accountable for misbehavior.

He requires clear and specific limits, enforced without anger or harshness. At the same time, he needs models, such as a "big brother," teachers, and older youths, to set an example of proper behavior.

The process of rehabilitation of the unsocialized child is slow and rough, with many periods of regression, because the school is asking the child to give up immediate gratification for long-term goals and to replace self-seeking with consideration for the rights of others. Frequently these youngsters make their first attachment to a single strong teacher and will comply only with his demands. Generalized trust builds slowly. Substantial correction, especially at adolescence, is most difficult. Since the school is the major conformity agent of society, it becomes the natural battleground.

A subgroup among the aggressive children is composed of youngsters who lack social skills but have the capacity to learn them because they have been cared about and loved at home, even though their families have been too disorganized to teach adequate behavior. They are not so much anticonforming as they are untutored in social skills. Role playing and demonstrations by models are useful to show such children the behavior expected of them.

While the reduction of acting-out behavior through teaching basic socialization is difficult, teachers still must try. Learning to value the rights of others is essential for members of a democratic society and recent follow-up studies indicate that neither individual treatment nor institutional custody is a satisfactory approach for such youth.

Another common cause of acting-out behavior is alienation. Estrangement from the educational establishment is occurring more and more frequently. Sometimes, from their very first day, these students find no gratification in the school experience, and their disinterest turns to hostility. The teacher sees these youngsters as problems in motivation. "They just don't seem to care about anything they should be doing."

For the most part, these are not weak children, and they are often well-accepted by peers outside of school. Having found life engaging elsewhere, they can't wait to get at it. One sixth grader had already figured out the number of days until he could quit school. Cars, money, the opposite sex, jobs—these are high demands of the alienated adolescent.

Youngsters like this are usually first admonished, then suspended to "shape them up." Suspension actually works in reverse, since they want out in the first place. If the youngsters are not suspended, too many teachers handle the problem by demanding nothing and letting them do just about as they please.

The better way of resolving the difficulty would be to undertake a thorough examination of the curriculum to see what could be altered. A junior high school pupil, already conducting a profitable business of his own, found nothing in classes with any meaning to him. With visions of establishing himself as an adult, he finally ran away with his girl friend.

Education is turning off an increasing number of able and intellectual youths. Such disenchantment was evidenced first at the college level, but it has already seeped down to the junior high. Many young people feel that school is a meaningless scramble for grades and graduation instead of the authentic education experience they seek. What often needs to be done is to make over the school rather than the pupil, but some teachers still rigidly follow the current curriculum as though it were sacred.

In some children, acting-out behavior in school is reaction to failure. No one wants to fail or even be in a marginal position, and yet thousands get failure messages every school day. The child comes to hate the establishment that makes him a failure, so he strikes back. Some failed first at home, where nothing they did was as good as what a sibling did—where no matter how hard they tried, they failed. The hatred such children feel for adults at home may transfer to their teachers, who may never have been in the least unfair.

The amount of defiling and belittling, to say nothing of direct abuse, that children suffer in our supposedly child-favoring culture comes as a shock to many a protected teacher. If the cause of acting-out behavior is in the home, then acting out in school is merely a displacement, but the acting-out child gets a reputation that is passed along ahead of him and he lives up to it.

School can be too taxing for certain children, grading too severe, and teacher's help too scarce. Although they get along well at home, children with mild learning disabilities or limited academic ability frequently drift into frustration at school. Some of the slow-developing early primary pupils or late-blooming adolescents in junior high are too immature to meet expectations. The solution is for the school to adjust to the pupil by proper pacing. Many of these pupils change surprisingly when a perceptive teacher builds in success.

Still other children who act out are anxious about their lives in general. Often they are hyperactive, driven to release tension through physical activity. They are oversensitive, easily distracted, and given to disruptive behavior. After misbehaving, they feel guilty and promise never to repeat the offense, but in a subsequent period of anxiety they do repeat it, acting out in order to dissipate tension.

Some of this group actually seek punishment because they feel they are bad and should pay the penalty. This feeling of guilt may stem from wrong things they have done or merely thought of doing. For instance, one boy, who was being stimulated by a seductive mother, used to blow up in math class, where concentration was required. He could do the math, but not when he was upset. It took the social worker a long time to help him work this out.

A special category of anxiousness, found with increasing frequency in suburbia, is achievement neurosis. In order to meet overt or covert expectations, pupils who have this affliction feel compelled to be on top. They have lost the satisfaction of learning as its own reward; grades are to prove they are as good as their parents want them to be. These youngsters are frequently tense and driven and overvalue the academic. Their parents are forever inquiring, "How well is John doing?"

Children who are driven in this way need to be made to feel better about themselves. Some of them demand much attention, always seeking resubstantiation by adult approval. If the source of the damaged self-picture is an over-demanding home or neighborhood, it is often difficult to provide enough compensatory success in school to allay it. This is where counselors, psychiatrists, psychologists, school social workers, or referral agencies play their part.

By now it is easy to see why any two acting-out children may not need the same type of help from the teacher. But teachers' concerns are not limited to those who directly disrupt the educational process, for the profession is equally attuned to pupils who have given up. While withdrawn children may not cause the teacher managerial difficulty, they, too, are in need of special assistance.

Many unhappy, depressed youngsters are in school today. Basically, these youngsters have very low self-esteem; they have somehow been taught by life that they are good-for-nothing and important to nobody. Often, internal preoccupation takes over, and they drift into a world of fantasy. They absorb the support sensitive teachers give, but often this is not sufficient to strengthen them to a point where they can sustain themselves.

Sometimes students are confirmed losers. They just know they will fail and usually contrive to make their anticipations come true. Others come to rely on fate rather than on their own efforts. As one youngster put it: "Fifty-fifty, I pass or I flunk. It depends on the breaks." So why put forth any effort?

Another group of the withdrawn children are the lonely ones. The loner drifts by himself at recess or eats alone in the junior high cafeteria or has no one to talk to about his high school lessons. Because he feels that nobody would care, he sees no point in trying to make friends. Many youngsters who are scapegoats in their peer group come from among the lonely ones, especially if they have some physical problem such as overweight, a tic, or odd looks. In these cases, the way the teacher manages the group life in the classroom is just as important as individual attention and counseling.

DEALING WITH DISTURBED PUPILS

No magic, no single cure, no shortcut will solve the problems of disturbed children in the schools. The job demands an extension of the individualization that is the essence of good school practice. This calls for teacher time and specially planned curricular experiences. To provide these, many school systems will add a new resource—the psychological, social-work, or psychiatric consultant. Conflict between specialists and regular classroom teachers used to be commonplace, but teachers have now discovered a new way to use the specialists' help, replacing long discourses on "how Johnny got that way" with discussions of what can be done now, in the classroom.

Frequently, a curriculum expert and the principal should join the teacher and the special consultant in discussions about a disturbed child. Remedial action should be based on study of the deviant youngster's classroom behavior and of his basic personality. Clinical insights provide the backdrop for practical planning.

When the problem is caused not by the school but by the child's home situation, the remedial goal is to have the school provide a supportive environment that will compensate, in part, for what is lacking or negative. Referral services to agencies that can offer individual therapy are vital also. They are not enough, however. Group work agencies, boys' clubs, and big brothers can help the unsocialized child who does not have serious internal conflicts. Such a child is in dire need of basic identification building.

Many disturbed children who can function within normal bounds and utilize the regular classroom much of the time lapse occasionally into disruptive behavior that throws the classroom into chaos. Some schools—secondary as well as elementary—deal with this problem by having a special teacher, trained to work with the disturbed in both academic and behavioral spheres, to whom such a child goes during a crisis. This teacher works with him in a special classroom where he can receive assistance on both individual and small group bases.

While the issue is still current, the crisis teacher and the child discuss the matter, much after the fashion of crisis intervention in community mental health. Close liaison with the regular teacher is, of course, mandatory. Referrals to a school or community service for intensive individual work may be needed, but the crisis teacher is the key person to support the regular classroom teacher and the pupil and to coordinate the entire effort in time of stress. When the pupil has gained control and/or is able to do the task in question, he returns to the regular classroom.

NEEDED CHANGES

The task is to examine the classroom environment and the teacher's role. What changes will improve the helping index?

No one has any idea of making the teacher into a psychotherapist, although many disturbed students form a profound relationship with their teachers. The function of the teacher is to provide pupils with a reasonable human relationship (in itself therapeutic) and the opportunity to grow through academic accomplishment and social learning.

Achievement is therapeutic for a child, especially when he has achieved little or nothing in the past. Having an adult who cares about him and who helps him when he falters instead of getting angry and rejecting him is certainly helpful. Peer acceptance in the classroom has lasting significance for the lonely child.

In this sense, therapeutic intervention has always been a part of school, but some children need much more. Providing that more will require three things:

1. The schools will have to reexamine how the curriculum, methodology, and experiences can be bent to enhance growth and minimize failure.
2. Teachers will have to learn new skills.

3. Teachers will have to become more open about their feelings toward disturbed children, because externalizing attitudes is a necessary step in changing negative feelings.

Since the school operation itself provokes a considerable amount of school difficulty, what is taught and how it is taught will require adjustment. Pupils need short assignments that interest them and that they are capable of doing. Not only the level of difficulty but the rate of learning should be attuned to the child, with provision for remedial teaching of what he has missed.

Individualization for the alienated youngster requires new subject matter that is relevant rather than merely different. Some children with learning disabilities require the use of self-tutoring devices. Iconoclastic curriculums, such as cooperative work programs for older youths, are needed.

Although most behaviorists avoid considering disturbed children in any but symptomatic terms, they offer the teacher two most useful guidelines.

First, they tell teachers to study what the child actually does. Observation of how and to what the pupil responds often shows that much of what the teacher is doing is quite beside his intent. Many disturbed children are adept at controlling teachers by getting them to make inappropriate responses, thus reinforcing just what the teacher wishes to eliminate. If the pupil cares more about having *some* kind of relationship with the teacher than he does about *what* kind of relationship he has, he can get teacher attention by misbehavior. Thus, a teacher encourages repeat performances of an undesirable behavior even as he tells a pupil not to behave that way.

Second, behaviorists emphasize that many pupils do not operate on the basis of high-level gratifications, such as love of learning. Teachers must deal with them on their own motivational level. For example, the attention span and motivation of some who need concrete rewards suddenly improves when the teacher recognizes this need. Free time earned for work done or proper behavior may help get children started who have never had any real success before. They forget their "can't do" to earn free time. Behavior that approximates being acceptable is worth rewarding at first.

Punishment, the major reward many disturbed children receive, is a poor teaching device. Low grades seldom work as a challenge. Emphasis needs to be on accomplishments rather than on failures. Many teachers, wedded to the illusion of homogeneity, have a hard job learning to help these children achieve by accommodating to the special range they present in ability, rate, motivation, and interests. Sometimes the range can be narrowed. In junior and senior high, for example, a student can be assigned in every course to the teacher and the content best suited to him.

When nothing else works, something may be gained by asking a child to do only what interests him. One pupil studied nothing but the Civil War. Another drew pictures. This was no real solution, but the teacher survived and the other students could do their work. Desperate conditions require desperate measures, and it is better to have a student reading about the Civil War than conducting a war with the teacher.

Teachers of classes that include disturbed children need to be particularly skilled in group management. The capacity to establish a work orientation for the class as a whole that will provide psychological insulation is one of the most critical skills in a class that includes disturbed children. Jacob Kounin and his associates have found out that the same teachers are successful in managing both disturbed and normal students.

These teachers focus on the group and its learning activities, actively solicit feedback, concentrate on more than one thing at a time, and select the proper targets for their interventions. The high degree of involvement reduces negative contagion from the disturbed pupils and provides the needed reserve for the teacher to work out the marginal situations that develop.

The first questions a teacher needs to ask are, "How meaningful is the work to these pupils? Can they do it? Do I understand the various roles and relationships in the class well enough to be able to emphasize the things that will maintain stability instead of reacting in a haphazard way to everything that happens?"

The successful teacher knows how to use grouping itself as a tool.

1. Some classroom groups are particularly stable and constitute a reservoir of peer help for the distraught pupil; other groups have such a thin shell of control that one acting-out pupil means a breakdown. If most members of a class offer support, they can calm down a lot of misbehavior as well as serve as models of proper action.

2. Pupils whose behavior frightens their own age peers and makes them anxious may not bother slightly older children, so upgrouping a disturbed child may reduce negative group effects.

3. Sometimes the size of the group is important. Classes with several disturbed pupils should be smaller than others. In fairly large schools, three or four teachers of the same grade or course can arrange to have one small class for those who need it by making the other classes somewhat larger.

4. When a class needs relief from a pupil's disturbing antics, sending the offender to another class for a visit may be helpful. The teacher needs to make advance provisions for doing this. He also needs to know when to intervene in this way and to find out what the child does that makes his classmates anxious and angry.

Of course, any kind of exclusion must be used with extreme care. It would be ill-advised for a youngster who wanted out in the first place, or one who was so fearful as to be traumatized. Sometimes, however, planned exclusion can produce controls in a youngster.

Teachers need to develop skill in talking productively with children. They spend a great deal of time in verbal interaction with their students and, unfortunately, the typical verbal interplay is largely a waste. Fritz Redl has pioneered with what he calls "life-space interviewing," a technique that is particularly well suited to helping the teacher of disturbed children put an end to the undesirable behavior or at least to take steps in that direction.

The content of life-space interviewing focuses on the ego level and the behavior experience in the "life-space" shared by teacher and student. The technique provides an opportunity for diagnostic exploration, mild probing, and planning for the future on the basis of realistic appraisal. First the teacher asks the pupil for his perception of what happened, and then, step by step, examines what can be done to clarify reality. This leads to specific strategies which can serve to reduce recurrences. Of course, not all students will respond, but this style prevents moralizing on the one hand and passive acceptance on the other. The same principles can be used with groups for classroom problem solving.

Classroom problem solving brings up the concept of crisis intervention. Youngsters are most teachable at a time of conflict, when they are searching for a resolution. Being able to use the crisis at hand and knowing how to talk effectively to children are two skills basic to any classroom management of disturbed pupils. Behind this rests a new concept of acceptance. Psychological acceptance means responding to the student in order to facilitate his adopting more acceptable patterns of behavior. This may mean more strict enforcement of regulations, more listening to his concerns, or doing whatever is relevant to his self-concept and nature.

Three qualities seem to be critical in order for a teacher to develop the right interpersonal relationship with disturbed students: strength to stand testing without giving in or becoming hostile, a belief that the youngster can change (this eliminates the self-fulfilling prophesy of failure that many teachers imply, if only on the unconscious level), and a recognition that the classroom is a good place for helping youngsters. Of course, certain teachers seem to have natural talent with particular types of disturbed children. Definitive teachers, for example, are most successful with insurgent pupils, while a quiet teacher may get closer to frightened youngsters.

Disturbed children require an inordinate amount of teacher time, so there is never enough to go around. Several plans have been used to add teacher power. Frequently, children low in confidence and self-esteem benefit from one-to-one sessions, cause no disruptions during them, and focus on the task. Sometimes, with a mature class, a teacher can borrow a little special time for such students, but in most cases this is just not possible. Often the only feasible learning condition for them is a tutorial, manned by a community volunteer, a teacher aide, or an older student, with the teacher supervising and designing the lesson material.

Other means of stretching the busy teacher's time include the use of a self-tutoring device, task cards setting up individual projects, and prerecorded tapes with lessons and answers. A peer may serve as tutor-listener if proper pairing can be arranged.

Parents are a teacher's resource more often than we have believed. Programs for disturbed students, particularly the alienated ones, are reaching out to include the home. Rather than letting behavior difficulties continue to a point where a student must be excluded, the schools now, at an early stage of a difficulty, schedule conferences in which parents, student, teacher, and a mental health specialist participate. The assumption is that all parties really want to solve the difficulty, and the support of the home may be critical. When parents are hostile to the pupil, the hostility is less likely to provoke unfortunate behavior if the matter can be talked out and plans drawn up to meet the difficulties. While no punches are pulled, the issue is to teach the child what he *must* learn rather than revert to punitive handling.

Help may be needed outside the classroom. Here a "big brother" or "big sister" may be most important in providing not only reasonable recreation but identification as well. Assistance with homework, especially at the junior and senior high levels, may be the only road to survival.

A wise teacher keeps time flexible in planning for the disturbed youngster. Some children may be able to benefit from one hour of school but no longer. Some can make it through the morning but fall apart before the afternoon is under way.

Wise use of space is important. For example, some disturbed students benefit from having offices or study cubicles to reduce distraction. On the other hand, some need to see others and observe what is going on in order to feel less anxious.

The more flexible the concept of space in the teacher's mind, the more he can use this resource to serve the disturbed student. Dividing the room into work centers for various subgroups is one technique. Using the hall not as a punitive place but as a stimulus control may be appropriate. Some older youngsters can do their work better in the library, while others would roam the halls if not under surveillance.

Above all, the teacher and the school need to bear in mind that, for a disturbed child, being able to escape temporarily from group pressures is often the key to survival. Each school should have a place and, if possible, a person for a disturbed child to go to at a time of crisis.

Even with the most able consultation and highly skilled teaching it may not be possible to help a child in the regular school setting, and unless he can be helped—not merely contained—in the classroom, he should not be there. The teacher's survival and the other children's welfare, as well as his own, are at stake.

For children who still fail to respond in the regular classroom after everything feasible has been done, the next step is the special class. Such classes provide relief for the whole school system and, generally speaking, they offer the disturbed pupils more individualized planning, with the result that pupil behavior and achievement improve. Some recent research, however, suggests that the improvement tends to disappear when the pupil returns to the mainstream. Indeed, the special class is far from being a panacea. It often helps least the unsocialized youngster, who needs so much, and sometimes it includes very disturbed children, even though the general consensus is that psychotic children need more help than a special class can give.

The special class falls short of the mark for other reasons. Frequently, special class curriculums do not include individual work and family contacts, although classroom work alone is usually not enough. Further, many public school teachers do not have the assistants they need to conduct a special class successfully.

And the special class bears a stigma. Students seldom see the value of being "special" and attitude is a critical part of the impact. Particularly at the secondary level, they resist being set apart. To adolescents, the stigma is so oppressive to their whole quest for a self (and a normal self) that it generates a great deal of friction. The stigma is strengthened because teachers and school administrations are seldom eager to welcome back a "cured" student. Nevertheless, special class provisions, if properly handled and staffed, are part of the sequence of support needed in every school program.

When all is said and done, most disturbed children are, and will continue to be, in the regular classroom, and, like it or not, classrooms and teaching will have to change if the schools are to fulfill their ever-increasing responsibility for the social and emotional development of children.

44 The Adolescents with Learning Problems: How Long Must They Wait?

Carl L. Kline

A significant number of our youth are being ravaged by learning disabilities, a disaster of great proportion and with major societal implications. In general, our collective efforts to deal with various "people problems" have failed dismally. For decades our determined efforts to discover the incidence of various human problems have mostly resulted in our discovering the extent of our failures. Perhaps what has been accomplished is nothing more than a pseudosophisticated body count. Labeling people and placing them in stereotyped groups has created the illusion that we understand their problems. Having invented this artificial system, we have come to believe in it. Entrapped

Reprinted from *Journal of Learning Disabilities*, 5 (5): 262–271 (May 1972), by permission of author and publisher.

in our own fantasies, we are now part of the problem instead of part of the solution.

Even though this characterizes what has been happening in the field of learning disabilities, few among us choose to see what is going on. By resorting to such labels as "generation gap" and "alienated youth," we avoid facing the problems of young people, and we evade our responsibility to young people with learning disabilities calling them "slow learners," "neurotic," or "poorly motivated." Fortunately, extensive studies, such as those recently reported by the Joint Commission on Mental Health of Children, are placing these problems in better perspective. In a sense the same basic factors are operating to create and to perpetuate most of our major "people problems." The Joint Commission named racism as the number one mental health problem in the United States. This report, along with the work of Silberman, Coles, and others, spells out the fact that racism, poverty, violence, and war cannot be separated from other major problems, including educational problems. A generation having 15 percent of its population made up of angry, functional illiterates is going to be part of all of these problems, and will not contribute to their solution. Yet upon the solution of these problems rests the future of mankind.

Unfortunately, adult society resembles the three monkeys who see no evil, hear no evil, speak no evil. Bob Dylan's message doesn't get through, and inadequate recognition is given to the fact that "the times they are a changin'." Actually the same repressive measures are used against children with learning disabilities as are used against black people and against the poor: the problem is ignored, it is met with inappropriate or inadequate measures, and the children are blamed for having the problem. Further, these children are segregated into classroom ghettos.

Experts continue to argue over whether a given "case" of reading disability should be called primary or secondary. And we omnipotently decide whether the cause is "minimal cerebral dysfunction" or "developmental neurological dysfunction." But the truth is that, in the deepest sense, the existence of 8,000,000 children and young people with reading disabilities in the United States is a societal problem of the first order, requiring a global approach if real progress is ever to occur. Perhaps it is time to be less concerned about the labels and more about solving the problem.

For several decades we have known that the incidence of severe reading disability is upwards of 15 percent of our children and youth. We have known that it is a major cause of emotional problems in children. Dr. Leon Eisenberg, Chairman of the Department of Psychiatry at Harvard, and others have been telling us this. Silberman (1964) has told us that reading disability is the major factor in juvenile delinquency. In fact, 75 percent of the youngsters in juvenile court have severe reading problems. Yet, in the face of all of this, how much headway has been made in resolving the problem? If anything, the problem is growing. If we know so much about the problem, why hasn't it been solved? If we don't know enough to solve it, why don't we find out?

These same questions can be asked about the other major problems identified by our society: racism, pollution, poverty, and war. I suggest that the same human dilemmas underlie all of these by-products of our uncivilized state. Do we somehow *need* these problems? If not, why do we allow them to exist?

The findings and recommendations of the Dept. of HEW National Advisory Committee on Dyslexia and Related Reading Disorders were published in a booklet entitled *Reading Disorders in the United States*. This study brings the subject into focus in terms of the realities of its existence and the problems it reflects. The report also makes some constructive recommendations for change.

The report concluded that the nation's effort to teach reading is mostly an ill-defined, directionless, uncoordinated "patchwork affair," lacking urgency. Some of the findings relevant to this paper include the following: (1) Fifteen percent of the children in our schools have severe reading disabilities. (2) The enrollment in the primary and secondary grades of our public schools is 51,500,000. The average annual cost per child is $696.00. If one child in 20 (5 percent) is not promoted, the national loss expressed in economic terms alone is $1.7 billion. (3) Children of adequate intelligence but retarded in reading often perform adequately in nonreading school work during the early grades. However, as the years of reading failure build up feelings of inadequacy and dissatisfaction with school, their overall academic work is severely affected. (4) A follow-up study shows that sixth-grade underachievers continue to be underachievers in the ninth grade, with a resulting tendency to drop out. (5) The American Association of Junior Colleges has estimated that from one third to one half of their new students have significant reading problems and that 20 percent of their new students in the most disadvantaged areas are unable to profit from their present remedial programs, so severe is their handicap. (6) Every year some 700,000 children drop out of public school. (7) Sixty percent of the enrollees in the Job Corps Urban Centers have less than a sixth grade reading ability, and about 20 percent of them read below the third grade level. (8) Seventy-five percent of juvenile delinquents are significantly retarded in reading. The 1968 cost for detention of a juvenile delinquent in a Federal institution was $6,935 per man year. (9) The retention of reading underachievers costs the nation's public education system in excess of one billion dollars every year. (10) Unless the causes of failure are determined and specific remedial instruction is provided, a child profits little from repeating the same grade. (Recently, I saw a little boy who had repeated grade one and was now repeating grade two for the third time. Despite an IQ of 118 he still was unable to read from a preprimer and he knew nothing about phonics.) (11) The present state of affairs is such that there can be no assurance that a diagnostic study will be accurate nor that related remedial instruction will be sufficient to meet a child's needs. Unfortunately today's situation opens the way to exploitation and to well-meaning but ineffective effort.

Based upon the estimated incidence of 8 million children in the United States having severe reading disability (Botel estimated 15 million), I have calculated what it would cost to provide effective remediation for these children. At an average of 90 hours per student and at a minimum cost of $5.00 per hour, the cost would be 4 billion dollars. This is only five percent of the cost of the Vietnam war for one year. . . .

All of these comments, facts, and figures lead us to the realization that we are discussing a complex societal problem with enormous implications socially, economically, and psychiatrically. It is evident that reading disability must be viewed on a developmental continuum. The world doesn't stop so that children can get off. Nor does the process of education stop; it may get distorted, it may change scenes, but it goes on. One illusion that disturbs our ability to meet the problem is that education only goes on in the schools. Actually we are all educators and therefore responsible for all facets of the education of children. If our schools are inadequate, it is our failure. It is every person's responsibility to do something about learning disabilities. Leaving it up to the education system is like leaving it up to an elephant to rid itself of its own fleas.

Realizing then that the adolescent with a learning problem is on the move—that he or she is moving along the developmental road—we are in a better position to understand. Immediately we have the advantage of seeing the problem in broad perspective instead of narrowly viewing one dimension. This means that not only can we view the problem as it exists now, but also we enable ourselves to see the relationship of the problem to past experience and to the struggle to develop on into the future.

Are there any unique features to be singled out as characteristic of learning disabilities in adolescents? This question can best be answered by a consideration of the varieties of learning problems seen in this age group. The following grouping is adapted from Rhoda Lorand's chapter on "Therapy of Learning Problems" in the book *Adolescents* by Lorand and Schneer.

1. *Chronic Dyslexics.* Most adolescent learning problems are the result of long-standing reading difficulties which have always slowed the child's progress to varying degrees. In milder cases the problem may first become apparent in the upper grades where so much of the work depends on good reading ability, and where the pressure of time is added. The youth who requires triple the amount of time to complete a reading assignment obviously is greatly handicapped.

2. *The Mini-Effort Group.* There are many bright children who have managed quite well in the primary grades where minimal effort produced adequate or even above-average grades, but who find in junior high or high school that they are unable to produce the sustained effort necessary to succeed. Some are rather narcissistic youngsters who have gotten what they want with little or no effort and now feel put upon because they are required to produce.

3. *The Over-Indulged.* Another group of bright children have been brought up in an overpermissive environment where they never had to work for or postpone gratification. When confronted with the necessity to endure the tension of working toward mastering knowledge, they become impatient, discouraged, or anxious. Not infrequently these children give up and turn their attention to activities in which they can secure immediate gratification. They may feign contempt for their fellow students who are achieving well. Often they turn to such providers of quick gratification as drugs, sex, and delinquency.

4. *The Can't Lose Group.* Another group of rather immature children withdraw from scholastic endeavor because they can't bear to have their performance compared unfavorably with someone else's. By not doing the work, they can tell themselves and others, "If I bothered to study I would do well." These children often learn without difficulty when tutored privately.

5. *The Smart Big Brother Group.* It is not uncommon to find a younger sibling of a successful older student feeling unable to live up to the record of his brother or sister. When the older child graduates, the younger one may show a sudden upward spurt in achievement level.

6. *The Afraid-to-be-Curious.* Adolescents whose childhood curiosity was mishandled are prone to develop learning difficulties in certain subjects. Subjects such as biology and science can be very threatening to the youngster who is struggling against allowing the emergence of repressed childhood curiosity about sex.

7. *The Emotionally-Traumatized.* The fact that a youth can be so disturbed by traumatic occurrences at home that he is unable to concentrate seems almost too obvious to mention. The student who has been doing well in school and whose performance suddenly drops is usually caught up in an acute emotional crisis, often home-centered. Young people caught up in teen-age romances and the associated crisis can suffer temporary disturbance in academic performance. Sometimes the young person comes to the doctor because of his loss of ability to achieve in school, not recognizing the source of the problem.

8. *The Afraid-to-Know.* The need *not* to know is a primary difficulty in some children with learning disabilities. The child attempts to avoid unbearable pain by trying not to know what is going on. To learn means to learn painful facts; therefore all learning is feared and avoided. Adult models often unwittingly teach children this avoidance technique. Many adults are experts at pretending that problems don't exist, scrupulously avoiding reading or talking about them. Teachers often are guilty of this maneuver, helping the parents and child to avoid facing the problem of a reading disability by denying that it exists. I see many angry parents of teen-age boys and girls who want to know why the school personnel didn't identify the problem sooner. Often parents will state that they have consistently raised the question of reading disability with the child's teachers, only to be told that the child will outgrow it or that they, the parents, are overanxious or overambitious for their child.

9. *The Love-to-be-Loved Group.* Some emotionally deprived children who suddenly find themselves attractive in adolescence derive so much gratification from dates, admiration, and physical contact—from feeling attractive and lovable for the first time in their lives—that they cannot combine these experiences with less gratifying academic experiences, so that their scholastic achievement is poor.

10. *The Psychiatrically-Ill.* Children with severe, specific emotional illness or personality disturbance may suffer reading disabilities and other learning disabilities as a direct result of these disturbances. Difficulty in handling aggres-

sion with excessive guilt and anxiety over hostile, destructive, or sadistic impulses and fantasies is a common finding. These children probably comprise only about two percent of cases, but it is important to identify them when this exists.

A common prototype of reading disabilities seen in adolescents is the bright high school student who reads at or near grade level, but who has a spelling disability, is a slow reader, who misreads some words, omits words, substitutes words, and occasionally reverses. Often these youngsters are unidentified dyslexics. Despite their borderline performance in school, their minimal interest in school, and their lack of interest in outside reading, they are dismissed as "underachievers." These youngsters are apt to be placed in "X" classes, which are made up of a heterogeneous mixture of undiagnosed youngsters who are underachieving, misbehaving, or both. These classes are often dubbed the "dum dum" classes and shunned by the teachers whenever possible. The teachers who lack the seniority to avoid these classes tolerate being assigned to them. Assuming that these children can't learn and don't want to learn, the teacher concentrates on maintaining discipline, and the negative reinforcement process continues.

Adolescents with learning disabilities are grossly misunderstood and even more grossly neglected. The rather feeble diagnostic and remedial therapy programs which exist in most school systems usually have to concentrate on a small segment of the school population. Quite properly they concentrate their efforts on younger children, usually in the first three or four grades. By the time the developmental process brings the child into his teens he either becomes a dropout, gets sick, or suffers the humiliation of being one of the "dum dums."

Parents who have struggled to find help for these youngsters often have given up by this time. Sometimes they assume that the child just doesn't have it. At this point many bright children with considerable potential get channeled into nonacademic programs. The more intelligent and sensitive the youngster, the more easily he is hurt and the more likely that he will seek socially unacceptable alternatives.

As is known, learning disabilities of all kinds appear to affect more boys than girls in a ratio of about 4:1. In my experience, in the teen-age population the ratio narrows. Because of the greater variety of problems which cause academic difficulties in this age group, proportionately more girls are affected. This does not mean that the sex distribution changes for dyslexia.

One more adolescent group needs to be paid attention to, a group not accounted for in any of the categories just described. Many intelligent youngsters who are emotionally mature, come from stable family backgrounds, and who do not suffer with a specific reading disability are rebelling against the school system and dropping out, some as early as age 14, others in grades 11 or 12 or on up at the university level. I see many distressed parents of such youngsters, desperately seeking help to find ways to get their son or daughter back into the mainstream. Many of these young people become temporary transients or join "hippie" groups or communes. Some turn to drugs as a means of attempting to find something, usually themselves. I focus for a few moments on this group because I feel that they are the vanguard of the real problem we are faced with. They may help us to see that the system, not the children, is the problem. And we are the system. If there is still a world twenty years from now, will we still be nit-picking about such concepts as minimal cerebral dysfunction while thousands of desperate youngsters are doomed by a society which demands literacy, but makes it impossible to achieve?

These so-called alienated young people are spelling it out for us, but we are so dyslexic we can't read the message. It is the system. Dr. Conant of Harvard has told us this, and a rash of recent books have been spelling it out quite dramatically: Silberman in *Crisis in the Classroom;* Bronfenbrenner in *Two Worlds of Childhood;* Richette in *The Throwaway Children;* Kozol in *Death at an Early Age;* Postman and Weingartner in *Teaching As a Subversive Activity,* and many others. Is anyone getting the message?

In my opinion, the truth—the message—is that the existing school system is irrational, ineffectual, authoritarian, inept, smug, defensive, and undereducated. I suspect that ineffective teaching and poor methodology cause about 90 percent of the reading disabilities in our schools. Rigid, unimaginative, often boorish and irrelevant educational programs in primary and secondary classrooms slash down many not already demolished by failing to learn to read. If we are ever going to meet this enormous overall problem, we are going to have to get busy with preventive measures where it's at: in the system. Remember, the school system is what the society wants it to be; it is an extension of the ego of the society.

Before closing this presentation, it seems important to make some additional comments about the epidemic of reading disabilities in our society. Illich has stated that "as you spend more than a certain amount of money people cease to be capable of reading. And there seems to be—for all subject matters—a certain point at which you create, with further investment, more learning difficulties." In effect he was saying that the more money spent, the higher the incidence of reading disability. There are some impressive examples around to substantiate his idea. Many expensive programs involving large capital expenditures have been sold to school boards under the guise of being cure-alls for learning problems. For example, the open classroom, which has proved enriching for some children, is actually destructive to dyslexics who need structured programs and classrooms. The open classroom concept was not properly researched before being put into action. And, many schools have bought expensive equipment such as tachistoscopes, trampolines, balance boards, and a variety of so-called perceptual-motor training gimmicks in the hope of remediating reading problems. Current research is discrediting much of the theory and practice upon which the use of many of these materials is based.

With the best of motivation, many school boards have provided funds to establish large special education departments. The contribution of these people has in some instances been limited and even destructive. Frankly, some schools of education admit not knowing how to train special educators, or what to train them for.

In the Report of the Joint Commission on Mental Health of Children, a good deal was said about problems in the education system. Some very thoughtful, carefully considered recommendations were made. Here are a few which I desire to give special emphasis to here:

1. The goals for education should be focused on developmental processes in childhood: sensitivity to the world around; cognitive power and intellectual mastering of the symbolic systems; synthesis of cognitive and affective experiences; differentiated reaction to people; adaptation to requirements of social situations, self-understanding, and moral judgment. *Achievement criteria are partial, inadequate measures of development.*

2. Instructional methods and technology should be evaluated before adoption by two criteria: (a) productivity in advancing intellectual power and (b) positive value for associated emotional factors related to personality. (These criteria would eliminate the use of operant conditioning as a method for treatment of reading disability.)

3. Learning activities should be designed for independent pursuit by an actively involved child; should afford varied possibilities to observe, discover, invent, and choose; should avoid complete dependence on verbal, vicarious transmission of information.

4. Learning activities should encompass and integrate thinking and feeling experiences; children should have opportunity to express feeling directly in relation to people in school and for indirect re-expression in symbolic form, through creative activities.

5. The organization of learning tasks should make maximal use of the peer group process: for evolving codes of special interaction, for working through interpersonal reactions, for experience in being part of a forum for the discussion of ideas.

6. The authority structure should be flexible and rational, not arbitrary, not invested in status and position; it should exclude threat, humiliation or retaliatory punishment; children should participate in formulating regulations; methods of control should be corrective, relevant, and nonpunitive.

7. Genuine work experiences serving the school and the community should be included as an integral part of the curriculum; the work should be perceived by the children as realistically essential and as a sign of their acceptance into the world of adult concerns. Projects of cross-age teaching are an example of intraschool work activities that have had positive results.

8. The moral climate of the school should be built around attitudes of mutual trust, respect, and "fair-play" as the basis for judgment and behavior; children should be exposed to diversity of points of view and helped to build up moral principles for judging and guiding behavior; values openly advocated by schools must not be violated covertly.

Bronfenbrenner has emphasized some of the same ideas. He feels that the teacher should serve as a model and that it also is her responsibility to seek out, organize, develop, and coordinate the activities of other appropriate models and reinforcing agents both within the classroom and outside. Teachers who are poorly paid, treated as subordinates, and given little freedom and autonomy by the school administration cannot help but reflect their true position and their influence on their pupils is reduced.

Bronfenbrenner makes this very strong statement, with which I totally agree: "It is not primarily the needs of problem children or the disadvantaged that call for change in American schools. If the radical innovations that are required are not introduced, it will be all children who will be culturally deprived—not of cognitive stimulation, but of their humanity" (p. 158).

Finally, as pointed out in the Report of the Joint Commission on Mental Health, we need to open up the adult world to children and youth. "For too long now we have clung to history and tradition and considered school as a separate society responsible for all aspects of child care. This view of the school has been reinforced by our tendency to seal off children, adolescents, and youth into worlds separate from those of adults. We frequently have taken the irrational and overly protective attitude that children and adolescents are radically different from adults, that they should be shielded from the dangers and pleasures of the adult world, that their (falsely presumed) childish innocence should be preserved. It is obvious, too, that many adults do not want to be bothered with the strains of closely relating to children and dealing with their strong emotions, their high energy levels, and their drive for exploration, mastery and self-determination. Many adults would rather provide *for* children, as for example, through the schools, than interact closely *with them*. However, this sealing of children into separate societies leads to a discontinuity in the growth experience, a lack of integration of the many parts of the world with which the child comes in contact, twisted perceptions of reality and a learned incapacity to relate to adults. The only effective way to prepare children and youth for adult society is to give them increasing opportunities to have contact with it, to share in many aspects of community life, and to have a more open, realistic learning experience in school."

In 1846 Horace Mann made a very prophetic statement: "They, then, who knowingly withhold sustenance from a new born child, and he dies, are guilty of infanticide. And, by the same reasoning, they who refuse to enlighten the intellect of a rising generation, are guilty of degrading the human race! They who refuse to train up children in the way they should go, are training up incendiaries and madmen to destroy property and life, and to invade and pollute the sanctuaries of society."

Eight million children are waiting. How long will we keep them waiting? How long will they be content to wait?

REFERENCES

1. Botel, M.: Paper read at Syracusan University Meeting, Frontiers of Education, 1957.
2. Bronfenbrenner, Urie: *Two Worlds of Childhood, U.S. and U.S.S.R.* New York: Russell Sage Foundation, 1970.
3. Bywaters, Dorothy M.: *Language Training for Adolescents.* Cambridge: Educators Publ. Co., 1967.
4. Coles, Robert: *Children of Crisis.* Atlantic-Little Brown, 1967.
5. Conant, James: *Slums and Suburbs.* New York: McGraw Hill, 1961.
6. Department of Health, Education & Welfare National Advisory Committee on Dyslexia and Related Reading Disorders: *Reading Disorders in the United States.* Washington, D.C.: Gov't Printing Office, 1969.
7. Eisenberg, Leon: In: John Money (Ed.), *The Disabled Reader.* Baltimore: Johns Hopkins Press, 1966.
8. Gillingham, Anna, and Stillman, Bessie: *Remedial Training for Children with Specified Disability in Reading, Spelling and Penmanship.* Cambridge: Educators Publ. Co., 1967.
9. Illich, Ivan: *Toward a Society Without Schools. A Center Occasional Paper.* Palo Alto, Calif.: Center for Study of Democratic Institutions, 1971.
10. Joint Commission on Mental Health of Children in U.S.: *Crisis in Child Mental Health: Challenge for the 1970's.* New York: Harper and Row, 1970.
11. Kozol, J.: *Death at an Early Age. The Destruction of Hearts and Minds of Negro Children in the Boston Public Schools.* Boston: Houghton Mifflin, 1969.
12. Lorand, Rhoda: *Therapy of Learning Problems.* In: Sandor Lorand and Henry Schneer (eds.), *Adolescents.* New York: Harper-Hoeber, 1961.
13. Mann, Horace: In: C. Silberman, *Crisis in the Classroom.* New York: Random House, 1970.
14. Meerlo, J. A.: *Reading Block and Television Apathy; An Alarm for Parent.* Mental Hygiene, Oct., 1962.
15. Postman, N., and Weingartner, C.: *Teaching as a Subversive Activity.* New York: Delacorte Press, 1969.
16. Richette, Lisa A.: *The Throwaway Children.* Philadelphia: Lippincott, 1969.
17. Schmideberg, Melitta: *Searchlights on Delinquency.* New York: International Univ. Press, 1949, 174–189.
18. Silberman, Charles: *Crisis·in Black and White.* New York: Random House, 1964.
19. Silberman, Charles: *Crisis in the Classroom.* New York: Random House, 1970.

45 The Slow Learner...
What Are His Characteristics
and Needs?

Merle B. Karnes

Slow learners are children who learn at a less rapid rate than the normal but not as slowly as the educable mentally retarded. They are sometimes referred to as dull-normal or intellectually backward children. One criterion in determining whether or not a child is a slow learner is his intelligence quotient, which may range anywhere from 75 to 90.

In addition to a slow rate of learning, the following characteristics are attributed to slow learners as a group. (Not all slow learners, of course, possess all these characteristics, but it is important to consider them in planning an instructional program for these children.)

• The slow learner tends to have more physical defects than the average child. Defects of hearing and speech may interfere with a child's learning. One possible reason for more physical defects among slow learners is that a large percentage come from low-income families where prenatal and postnatal care is inadequate. In addition, when there is a weakness or defect in one area, it is common to find defects in other areas of development. In contrast, an intellectually gifted child is likely to be superior in all aspects of development. Referral to agencies and community resources available to assist the family in correcting physical defects of the child is important.

• The slow learner is consistently below grade level in academic progress. Even when the slow learner is working at a level commensurate with his mental age, he can be expected to achieve only about the seventh or eighth grade level when he is 16. He can learn more, but the material to be learned cannot be more difficult. Also, the range of individual differences among slow learners increases with age. Usually, the slow learner lags further and further behind his more able peers, making it more and more difficult for the school to differentiate instruction to meet his specific needs. The higher up the educational ladder this child goes, the more difficulty the school has in changing the regular curriculum to accommodate his slow rate of learning.

• The slow learner's reasoning ability is poorer than that of the normal child. He is slow to see cause and effect relationships, to make inferences, to draw logical and valid conclusions, to transfer learning, and to generalize.

Reprinted from *Today's Education: NEA Journal*, 59 (3): 42–44 (March 1970), by permission of author and publisher.

Slow learners need meaningful educational experiences geared to their stage of development and ample opportunity to develop reasoning skills. They also need much teacher guidance in order to see meaningful associations. A multisensory approach seems to be particularly appropriate in making learning experiences more concrete. The quality of learning experiences is far more important to the slow learner than the quantity of experiences.

• Short attention span seems to typify this group of children. However, the short attention span is often due to poor instruction rather than to a defect in the slow learner. When materials are interesting and when success is possible, the attention span of the slow learner tends to be adequate.

• Poor retention is still another weakness of slow learners. Slow learners are noticeably below par in both immediate and delayed memory. They need more repetition to reinforce learning. With slow learners, overlearning is especially important. It is crucial that these children have opportunities to practice skills and to use knowledge in various meaningful contexts to ensure permanency of learning.

• Unlike brighter children, slow learners do not learn incidentally as a rule. If they are not specifically taught, they are unlikely to learn by themselves. Those learnings felt to be important to current and future academic success and adjustment must never be left to chance but must be taught systematically and sequentially. Careful planning by the teacher is a must to facilitate learning among slow learners.

• Poor work habits and poor motivation to learn characterize slow learners, who find it difficult to persist independently until a task is completed. Activities should be carefully chosen so that success is possible and so that a minimum amount of time is required for the completion of a task. Recognition for completion of tasks is important to encourage future efforts. The complexities of the task and the amount of time necessary for completion can be increased as the slow learner matures and progresses.

• Slow learners respond to immediate goals rather than to delayed ones. These children must see a reason here and now for engaging in a task. A reward or gratification that is postponed for a week or a month is meaningless. For example, learning arithmetic makes sense to slow learners who need to know arithmetic facts to hold their jobs in certain work-study programs. When they see no immediate, tangible need for learning the facts, they are not likely to apply themselves.

• The slow learner has poorly developed language and communication skills. He needs many opportunities to practice language. He learns by talking about meaningful, firsthand experiences involving what he has seen, what he has heard, what he has done, and what he plans to do.

He needs a stimulating school environment where he has many things to talk about. In this way, he increases his vocabulary and improves in his ability to communicate ideas to others. The greater his facility in the use of words, the more effective his thinking will become.

• Socially and emotionally, slow learners tend to be less mature than their brighter peers. Approximately 50 percent have poor personal adjustment. Many are discipline problems. They have considerable difficulty controlling their emotions and perceiving how their actions affect others. Acquiring social competence is an important goal for these children throughout their school attendance. They need more counseling services to help them to understand themselves as well as to set realistic goals for themselves. Especially, they need more vocational guidance. The slow learners need teachers who accept them and who provide a warm, friendly atmosphere where they can feel secure and have a sense of belonging.

• Slow learners feel less confident and less adequate than average children. To build up feelings of adequacy and personal worth, it is essential to give them immediate feedback as to the correctness of their responses. They need more praise and encouragement than their brighter peers. Tangible evidence of progress should be made available in such forms as graphs, positive notes to pupil and parents, positive verbal evaluations by teachers and other pupils, positive comparisons of present work with previous.

• They have a hard time following directions. This problem presents considerable difficulty in school. Since their memory spans are comparatively short, the teacher should make sure that the directions he gives are specific and definite. He should consider carefully how many directions to give at any one time and keep them within each child's ability to follow them successfully.

• Slow learners are not as curious and creative as their more able peers. Since achievement and creative thinking have a high correlation, slow learners should be encouraged to develop their creative abilities, especially in language and thinking. They should be encouraged to ask questions and to think through various ways of solving problems. In addition, self-expression through art and music activities can provide outlets that are satisfying and rewarding to them.

• A large percentage of slow learners come from disadvantaged homes. These homes often have a multiplicity of problems that affect the child's adjustment. Referral to social agencies can often improve home conditions and thereby help provide the slow learner with an improved atmosphere for learning.

A poor environment can depress a child's intellectual functioning. Teaching parents how to assist their slow learner in developing his potential to the fullest should be a goal of any educational program for slow learners.

• Slow learners are capable of being followers but have limited leadership potentials. Schools must aim to help slow learners make valid decisions as to whom they wish to follow. Learning to be good followers is important to them, especially in achieving personal objectives and democratic goals.

Identification of the slow learner should begin early. As a general rule, slow learners are slow in beginning to sit, walk, and talk. While the IQ derived from an individual intelligence test administered by a qualified person is possibly the best single index of a slow rate of learning, it by no means should be considered infallible. Furthermore, in many instances, a psychologist will not be available to administer an individual intelligence test to slow learners. Group intelligence tests, supplemented by cumulative records, information from parents, and objective teacher observations based on a checklist of characteristics of slow learners, can identify almost every slow learner.

Despite their lowered intellectual potential, slow learners are not a homogeneous group. Each has his desires, goals, skills, and differences that make him a unique individual. Planning, programing for, and educating slow learners requires an individualized approach. With such an approach, slow learners can learn academic skills essential for effective daily living. It is up to the schools to respond to the challenge.

46 Talent Down the Drain
Harold C. Lyon, Jr.

Every community has its share of youngsters who are so bright and sparkling that they stand out as individuals apart. Educators categorize them as "gifted and talented," and estimates are that more than two million such boys and girls are to be found among the nation's elementary and secondary schools.

They are usually regarded with a mixture of awe and envy, and the assumption is that they will breeze through high school and college and inevitably achieve distinguished careers. Given their exceptional head start, the odds are that many of these youngsters will indeed be more successful than most. But the process will not be inevitable or automatic, and the record suggests that thousands upon thousands of them will be lost in the shuffle unless teachers and school administrators can find ways to help them realize their potential.

The fact is that the gifted and talented youngster tends to see himself as standing out not as a beacon but as a sore thumb. Being "different" is a heavy burden, and many of these young people find themselves unable to deal with it alone. Contrary to the general impression, they need help.

Bob Evans is a reasonably representative example. Bob has an IQ of 145, putting him in the intellectual stratosphere at the midwestern high school he attends, but it's nip and tuck whether he will graduate with his class next spring. In the classroom his behavior has been sometimes comic, more often eccentric, and almost always disruptive. Written off by his teachers as hopelessly uncooperative, he busied himself learning to write and read Russian on his own, although he cannot speak that language because he has never heard it spoken. Subsequently he buried himself in physics—so deeply, in fact, that he failed

Reprinted from *American Education*, 8 (8): 13–16 (October 1972), by permission of author and publisher.

courses in algebra and simple geometry because he was unable to summon up the discipline of doing his assignments along with the other students.

Within the last year or so, however, Bob seems to have started settling down, thanks chiefly to a counselor named James Blair. Patiently and with a careful blend of praise and urging, Blair has been trying to get Bob to understand that certain kinds of behavior are unacceptable, inappropriate, and—a telling point with Bob—immature. Last summer with Blair's help Bob got a job testing experimental equipment in an electronics laboratory. The experience clearly did much to demonstrate to him the practical necessity of completing an assigned piece of work without bothering others, and with Blair's continuing counsel and friendship Bob will probably meet all the requirements for a diploma.

But Bob is one of a fortunate few. At present only four percent of the two million gifted and talented youth receive planned, expert guidance and encouragement—either through special education classes they attend several times a week or through the interest of an adult who is willing to spend a good deal of time helping them resolve the tensions that being "different" consistently generate. The remainder, particularly those who are under constant pressure to conform, are as likely as not to lead lives of bored, frustrated mediocrity, or worse, brilliant criminality.

It is paradoxical that in a time of widespread concern for the waste and destruction of water, air, and land, we are wasting through neglect the very natural resources that might do most to help improve the quality of our culture and assure strong leadership for the future. The extent of this neglect is suggested by a recent Office of Education report to Congress which reveals among other things that the departments of education in only ten states have anyone engaged full time in identifying and helping the gifted.

The low priority given to these students at the state level is symptomatic of what goes on in the local community, and to a large degree it seems to be based on the old saw—stemming from a day when it was evidently assumed that human beings were no more complex than a bottle of milk—which holds that "cream always rises to the top." As is demonstrated in the recent OE study and in others that preceded it, the cream represented by the gifted and talented may indeed rise if there are human beings who create a warm, supportive atmosphere, who show the way to emotional balance and constructive spontaneity, and who help the brilliant learn to be at ease with their brilliance—in short, if there is guidance and support and understanding from a teacher or a counselor or parent or other respected adult. Otherwise, the chances are unfortunately high that the "cream" will become homogenized with the average, and that the special talents and gifts will get lost, or even curdled.

In addition to the "rising cream" notion there is another major reason why youngsters with outsize abilities are often neglected and submerged. It arises from a somewhat astonishing apprehension on the part of many parents and teachers and other school people that these young people will form an elite and come to dominate their classmates and make them feel inferior. The fact is, however, that feelings of inferiority are much more commonly found among the bright and talented than among the average, perhaps because the latter are not as keenly aware of how much there is to know. As the Office of Education report points out, special programs for the gifted "have not produced arrogant, selfish snobs" but have instead "extended a sense of reality, wholesome humility, self-respect and respect for others." And the report further notes that "contrary to widespread belief, these students cannot ordinarily excel without assistance."

Another erroneous assumption holds that such youngsters uniformly come from privileged backgrounds. Not so. Unusual intellectual and creative capacities are to be found in every strata of society and at every economic level, though of course the potential of boys and girls from the inner-city or from poverty-stricken rural areas is more likely to go unnoticed. No matter what the background, however, this potential has a delicate quality about it. It cannot survive educational neglect. Moreover, the withering that results from such neglect is likely to carry with it severe psychological damage. The challenge lies first in identifying the gifted youngster and then in helping him understand, accept and ultimately capitalize on the circumstance of being "different."

Meeting this challenge is no easy proposition, since the gifted and talented come in a bewildering variety of shapes and sizes and inclinations. It can be said in general, however, that they display exceptional interest in exploring fundamental suppositions and issues, in creating new uses for both familiar and unusual materials, and in developing new and original interpretations of standard ideas and sounds. They develop intellectual independence and integrity early in their lives and are more concerned than others of their age with abstract concepts and ethical problems. Making a contribution is often more important to them than special recognition.

An outstanding characteristic of many of the gifted is versatility. If their energies have not been exhausted by trying to resist the pressure to conform, they stand out as people capable of doing many things superbly well. Often, in fact, their versatility creates problems in choosing a career.

The other side of the coin is that these young people seem to be exceptionally susceptible to the deadening effect of an atmosphere barren of stimulation. While their intellectual and emotional development can be rapid, someone or something needs to provide continual opportunity for discovery. Thus while the OE report notes that about half of the gifted have taught themselves to read before entering school—some of them as early as two years and many by the age of four—it must be understood that this accomplishment can take place only if someone has cared enough to read to the child and get him started.

An equally important and more complex matter is that of nurturing the gifted youngster's psyche. Just as we all tend to see ourselves in terms of how others react to us, the gifted and talented often acquire a low opinion of themselves because their difference typically produces a mixture of awe, fear, teasing, and ridicule among their classmates. The resulting loss of self-esteem can become a lifelong companion of the gifted, a deterrent that holds their best and most daring ideas firmly in check.

One attempt to deal with this problem has consisted of establishing separate schools for these young people. Critics complain, however, that not only are such schools expensive but also they simply postpone the problem and, by doing so, may in fact intensify it. Where everyone is unusual, no one is unusual—the argument goes—and a person emerging from such a cocoon is likely to find himself completely incapable of dealing with the realities of the everyday world of work. Additionally, the gifted have something to contribute to, and gain from, their average classmates.

Clearly, we have much to learn about helping the gifted and talented, and a long way to go before we can halt the waste of their potential contributions. Such a move is now under way, and the Office of Education stands ready to lend a hand in this effort to the states and to local communities.

U.S. Commissioner of Education, Sidney P. Marland, Jr., has focused national attention on the importance of recognizing the special needs of the gifted and talented. One basic goal, to be accomplished within the next five years, is to double the number of such youngsters receiving direct and sustained help.

As part of this effort, OE's Office for the Gifted and Talented—in the Bureau of Education for the Handicapped—is seeking to encourage the strengthening of State Departments of Education in this field, so that every state—and not just the present ten—have at least one full-time staff member assigned to dealing with programs for the gifted and talented. Such programs are eligible for support through Titles I, III, and V of the Elementary and Secondary Education Act, as provided through Public Law 91-230.

Similarly, OE is moving toward the establishment of a network of prominent citizens who understand the problems confronting gifted or talented but under-educated persons and are ready to lend leadership in halting the waste of their talent. The plan calls for the formation of regional "action teams" composed of representatives of the ten OE regional offices and of state consultants. Joining them will be professionals associated with a recently established National Leadership Training Institute for the Gifted and Talented—distinguished people from many fields whose participation can do much to give visibility to the problem and generate local action—plus volunteers, interested parent groups, and others.

Meanwhile plans are going forward for the Office of the Gifted and Talented together with OE's Bureau of Adult, Vocational, and Technical Education to fund an Institute of Career Education for the Gifted, with the goal of developing relevant career models. Vocational and technical training traditionally have been thought of in terms of those who presumably lack the mental muscle for admission to college. Today such training is recognized as a step into the world of work as valuable to the gifted as to other students.

Another activity calls for underwriting, to the extent that money ceilings permit, applied research that builds on a range of exploratory research that has been carried out in the past few years. One such investigation is now under way through a contract awarded to the Southwest Educational Development Laboratory in Austin, Texas, to develop effective methods of identifying gifted minority group members whose capacities are obscured by the disadvantaged circumstances of their lives. Recognizing that standard testing instruments may fail to indicate the potential of black or chicano children burdened with a language problem, the plan calls for developing and packaging prototype materials for use by state education departments.

Working with the private sector, apprenticeships are being developed for disadvantaged gifted and talented students so that they can be freed to tackle university training at however accelerated a pace they choose. As an example of this apprenticeship, an Exploration Scholarship program for gifted students oriented toward science was jointly established by Office of Education and the private, nonprofit Explorers Club. Last summer the 44 final scholarship winners, young people between the ages of 14 and 21, accompanied well-known scientists on expeditions ranging from archeological digs in Israel to a scrutiny of volcanoes in the Congo and a study of the Aleut Indians in Alaska. In addition to OE and the Explorers Club, support for the scholarships came from Educational Expeditions International and the Department of the Interior's Bureau of Indian Affairs. (Eleven of the 44 scholarships, incidentally, were reserved for American Indians.) The plan calls for conducting these competitions for a period of five years, to reach a total of 350 scholarships.

Attention is also being given to the crucial matter of teacher training. Indications are that the gifted fare best if they have teachers who are themselves gifted and whose egos are strong and sure. The need is for teachers with "natural authority" as contrasted with "status authority"—humanistic teachers whose influence stems not from a title or an academic degree but from a capacity to share their feelings and even their imperfections as well as their knowledge and experience. Too often the tendency is to push the gifted child down the cognitive track and to neglect those affective aspects of learning that help make the individual a truly human being.

In these specific activities and in the general movement to be more responsive to the needs of the gifted and talented, the objective is to develop citizens who are whole. As we have seen, a common dilemma among these young people is how to achieve an effective balance between their intellects and their emotions. By being "different" they are especially subject to a sense of rejection by others and in turn rejection of themselves. Somehow we must learn to help them get their hearts and heads in tandem, and by doing so contribute toward strengthening our society and serving mankind.

The words of Senator Jacob Javits of New York before a recent meeting of the Council for Exceptional Children are worth remembering:

"I hope that all of us will work, not just to develop intellectual eggheads among our gifted children, but to provide opportunities for them to develop their capacities for love, empathy, and communication with their fellow men. Without the development of these neglected traits, the brightest individual is greatly handicapped and much of his potential lost."

47 Creative Kids

E. Paul Torrance

In most classrooms, highly creative children are handicapped by their creativeness and are regarded as behavior problems. Frequently, such children are diagnosed as having learning disabilities. For these reasons, I have suggested that highly creative children be designated as a new category of handicapped children in the field of special education.

Many of the behavior problems of highly creative children stem from differences between them and other children and between them and their teachers. Their learning difficulties arise from incompatibility between their abilities and learning preferences and the system of school rewards and methods of teaching.

If brought together with other creatively gifted youngsters, the chances are that they would no longer be misfits. If taught in ways compatible with their abilities and interests, their achievement might soar and their problems fade out. These things have happened in enough cases to give encouragement.

A variety of studies document the fact that creatively gifted children are handicapped in most schools as they now operate. One study showed that fourth grade pupils who were on the honor roll achieved lower scores on tests of creative thinking than did their peers who were not on the honor roll.

A similar investigation in higher education showed that college freshmen in honors programs scored lower on tests of creative thinking than their peers who were not in honors programs.

In another study, creatively gifted fourth and fifth grade children were shown to be handicapped in learning a commonly used type of programmed material in language arts. Still another study demonstrated, however, that certain kinds of curriculum tasks—open-ended and difficult ones—facilitate the learning of creatively gifted youngsters more than that of their less creative classmates.

In conducting research in elementary schools, I have frequently found creatively gifted children relegated to a circle of "hopeless" children in the rear of the room to keep them out of the way, seated right next to the teacher's desk so that their every behavior can be observed and controlled, and standing in the corner or in the principal's office because of deviant behavior.

In some instances, identification of such children as creatively gifted has changed the teacher's perception of them and consequently his relationship with them. This has been a turning point in the educational careers of such children.

Reprinted from *Today's Education: NEA Journal*, 61 (1): 25–28 (January 1972), by permission of author and publisher.

Tests of creative thinking ability can be useful in helping teachers and other educational workers become aware of creative potentialities that might otherwise be overlooked, but teachers need not be dependent upon tests for this purpose. At all educational levels, observable behaviors mark certain children as being highly creative.

At the preprimary and primary level, the creative child is full of the spirit of wonder and magic and is willing to attempt difficult tasks. He is testing his limits, however, and does not obsessively attempt the difficult. He is neither compulsively conforming nor nonconforming but is free to make choices in terms of what is true, right, or beautiful. Rather than learning solely by authority, he prefers to learn in creative ways by questioning, inquiring, searching, manipulating, and experimenting. He is always trying to find out how things really work.

When he learns in creative ways, he becomes completely absorbed and has a long attention span. Serious problems are likely to arise when anyone tries to drag him away from some of these absorbing activities. He has an amazing capacity to organize and reorganize things. He can tolerate disorder for a time but, if given a chance, he will soon establish his own organization. He will return to familiar things and see them in different ways and in greater depth.

The creative preprimary or primary child may insist on learning in creative ways rather than by authority and may fail to learn altogether if teachers insist that he learn only by authority in predetermined ways. Such children may hesitate to respond in class and remain silent, but nonetheless they may be making excellent use of these uncommunicative periods. The teacher who begins to take a new look at such students is always amazed at how much information they possess and how deeply they think about things.

Although many creative preprimary and primary children appear to be overactive, on occasion they can also sit still for longer periods of time than their less creative peers. At first they may be content to look at something from a distance, but quite soon they have to have a closer look, even at the risk of severe punishment. Creative children use fantasy to solve many of their developmental problems. They are terrific story tellers and can compose songs, poems, and stories charmingly and excitingly.

It is illuminating to consider the common characteristics of creative children in intermediate and junior high school grades. During this period, the creative child's independent thinking gets him into difficulty in the average classroom.

Most creative children who hold onto their creativity and do not surrender to conformity pressures have a strong self-image. They know what their capabilities and limitations are much better than do their less creative peers. Such children may appear haughty just because they are confident of their ability to perceive reality—to see that the emperor wears no clothes—and to do things that others regard as too difficult for them. Other creative children have feelings of inadequacy and unworthiness—especially those who are high in creativity but average or low in intelligence.

Creative children in the intermediate grades and junior high years may at times appear very grown-up and at other times very childlike. This seems to be almost necessary for their creativity.

They are likely to express unconventional ideas and engage in fanciful and imaginative activities. They respond emotionally and spontaneously to their environment and become absorbed and involved in it. They are at the same time more sensitive and more independent, as well as more masculine and more feminine than other children. They also show high levels of attention span, concentration, and interest.

The high energy level of most creative children in the intermediate grades and junior high school years is most noticeable. Their energy seems almost limitless. Their high curiosity and exploratory behavior continue, but by this time most of them have learned restraint, for otherwise they are in trouble. During this period, creative children tend to go all out with activities they consider worthwhile.

What appears to be a strong tendency toward disruptive and attention-seeking behavior usually stems from outright boredom or a strong desire to propose novel, divergent possibilities.

It is not difficult to see why the creative child, endowed with the characteristics discussed thus far, is severely handicapped in the average classroom. This statement is not a criticism of teachers in these average classrooms nor an attempt to arouse feelings of guilt. I sympathize with teachers regarding the problems generated by creative children. However, such problems have many satisfactory solutions, a number of which my associates and I have actually tested.

The following suggestions offer some interventions teachers may use to assist creative children at all levels of education. A teacher may—

• Help the creative child find a refuge somewhere in the system. Because of his social role, a teacher may not be able to provide this himself. To survive, however, the child must have one.

Society is very harsh in its treatment of the creative child or young person, who almost inescapably will come into conflict with authorities in the system or establishment. He will experience frustration and must therefore have some source of encouragement and support. He must have the right to fail without being ostracized or ruined. The teacher may be unable to serve as this refuge, but he can listen and he can help the creative child find such a refuge.

• Assist the creative child in finding a sponsor or patron, especially if his family fails to understand and encourage him. It has been said frequently that wherever creativity occurs and persists, there is always some sponsor or patron who saw to it that the creative young person got a chance.

Providing such sponsors or patrons seems to be especially crucial in working with creatively gifted children from disadvantaged families. Frequently, creative individuals or families in a community are happy to become patrons or sponsors for such children.

• Make sure that the creative child's potentialities are recognized and acknowledged. Evidence strongly suggests that this is something teachers can do which makes a real difference.

Teachers can recognize and acknowledge creative potentialities in many ways. Testing programs may help, and a child's creative excellence can also be recognized in writing, art, music, science, and the like.

• Guide the creative child in understanding and accepting his divergence—his sensitivity, his capacity to be disturbed, his tendency to become involved and committed and to seek new and original solutions. Perhaps this is one of the most important ways a teacher can help such a child.

All of us suffer from infringements upon our personal freedom. No one has complete freedom, but restrictions irk us. The creative child experiences more than his share of these restrictions, and he is also likely to feel irked more frequently and intensely than most children. Since engaging in energetic behavior to change a situation helps the creative child to feel less helpless, he is likely to engage in such behavior more frequently than other children. He needs help in recognizing that his actions aggravate rather than relieve his actual state of helplessness.

Teachers must also recognize that creative children find certain kinds of misbehavior exciting. Under restrictive and dull teaching, misbehavior offers possibilities for excitement in an otherwise monotonous, despairing existence. The dangers involved in such misbehavior call for use of skills and talents that might otherwise go unused. One way to keep creative children from misbehaving is to engage them in difficult, exciting, and worthwhile activities.

• Encourage the creative child to find legitimate ways of expressing himself and communicating his ideas. If teachers at all levels of education were more accustomed to and skilled in listening to students and had more respect for their ideas, most young people probably would not find it necessary to riot, destroy, or otherwise alienate themselves from society.

Some experts on delinquency believe that the future criminal is frequently a child who has little chance to use his creative abilities in socially acceptable ways and who therefore uses his potentialities to plan and carry out an illegal act. In my opinion, the curriculum at any educational level or in any subject has possibilities for providing equally exciting and certainly more rewarding outlets for these potentialities.

Teachers cannot meet all of the special needs of creative children. This is too much to expect, and, indeed, many teachers feel that their influence makes little difference because family, community, and other agencies have such a powerful impact.

It seems to me that the kinds of interventions I have just described will make a difference in the lives of creative children, if applied, but there is much that the teacher cannot do. It may be necessary, therefore, for the teacher to help creative students gain access to resources outside the classroom.

It is important for creative children to develop motivations and skills for continued learning. Librarians in the school and at the public library can be helpful in developing skills for finding out things and in sustaining motivation.

The motivations of creative children are such that they easily acquire many of the concepts and skills for doing research in the areas where their talents lie. Teachers who are not familiar with these areas will need to help children find someone who can teach them. (Most business, educational, and community leaders are generous in teaching creative children.)

Sponsoring creative writing clubs, dramatic groups, science clubs, Junior Great Books Clubs, and other special interest groups that children initiate is one way of meeting some of their needs in regular school programs. Such activities can be nonevaluative, with emphasis placed on the positive, constructive, growth aspects of the experience.

If there is a school psychologist, counselor, or someone else in the school system or in the community who can work with groups of parents, family resources for working with creative children may also be tapped. A PTA, a church group, a mental health organization, or the like may sponsor such activities. The role of the teacher may be to interest a sponsor in taking on an activity or service of this kind. Development of creative family relationships and teaching the skills of creative problem solving might be a new focus for all work with parents.

A teacher can help creative children establish working relationships with people in the community. Volunteer groups in the community, including senior citizen groups, professional associations, and business and industrial organizations, are a rich resource for working with creative children. Such groups rarely refuse reasonable requests and frequently accept unreasonable ones. Community groups are especially effective in providing creative writing, dramatics, and dance, as well as musical and art experiences. Usually, however, it is a teacher's initiative that makes such resources available to a particular creative child.

VII Evaluating in Teaching

Although it is common practice in books dealing with teaching to reserve a discussion of evaluation for the last chapter or section, it may be just as common a mistake—or, at least, it may be misleading. For evaluation constitutes a necessary part of everything teachers do. Teachers evaluate (make judgments about) the plans they make, the strategies they use, the students they instruct, the motivation and management processes they employ, and the techniques they use to assess performance and to assign grades. You need to understand, in other words, that evaluation in teaching is a continuous and interrelated process. The articles included in this part should help lead you toward such an understanding.

In article 48, Dyer illustrates how the use of tests can assist teachers in improving instruction. Dyer points out that the teaching-learning process is a continuous experiment whose success depends on feedback. Feedback enables teachers to keep readings on their students in much the same way as a thermostat keeps readings on a room's temperature. The quality of the feedback that teachers obtain determines their ability to plan and implement instructional strategies consistent with students' capabilities and needs. Tests, obviously, provide teachers with one means of obtaining such feedback. Testing, Dyer emphasizes, should not be considered peripheral to the instructional process—something to be done after the fact; rather, it must be seen as central to the process—something to be done before additional steps can be taken.

Travers, in selection 49, begins by stating "that any program should have means built into it for determination of the extent to which the goals of the program are being achieved."[1] He then identifies five general approaches that are used to judge the effectiveness of programs in education: (1) assessing what students do after they graduate, (2) appraising what they do in simulated settings, (3) observing their behavior in school-related situations, (4) evaluating their performance on teacher-made tests, and (5) judging their performance on standardized tests. Travers' analysis of these approaches should help the reader see that evaluating the effectiveness of schools' programs is and must be a multifaceted process.

In selection 50, Airasian and Madaus identify and define four different forms of student evaluation: (1) placement, (2) formative, (3) diagnostic, and (4) summative. Perhaps the differences between them can be presented most clearly by examining their respective purposes. The purpose of (1) placement evaluation is to assign students to the most appropriate point in an instructional sequence by determining the degree to which they possess or lack needed behaviors or skills. The purpose of (2) formative evaluation is to provide teachers with feedback concerning students' progress. The purpose of (3) diagnostic evaluation is to identify students whose progress is being adversely affected by physical, social, or emotional problems unrelated to classroom instruction. The purpose of (4) summative evaluation is to certify or grade students at the conclusion of instruction. The authors note that it is the last of these forms which is most commonly used. And yet it is probably the least important in terms of enhancing students' learning!

In article 51, Millman distinguishes between two types of measurement techniques, norm-referenced and criterion-referenced. Norm-referenced techniques are used to assess students' performance in relationship to the performance of other students; criterion-referenced techniques are used to assess students' performance in relationship to specified standards. Millman's opinion, as well as mine, is that norm-referenced evaluation is proving to be a major stumbling block to individualized instruction. Making comparisons among students— which by design or accident is the end product of normative evaluation—is the antithesis of individualized instruction; providing opportunities for and making judgments about individual students' progress toward reasonable goals is its ideal. Without some form of criterion assessment, the latter is impossible.

[1] Robert M. W. Travers, *Educational Psychology: A Scientific Foundation for Educational Practice* (New York: Macmillan Publishing Co., Inc., 1973), p. 209.

The use of norm-referenced marking systems, along with the graded pattern of school organization, has been a chief contributor to a perennial educational problem. The problem is whether teachers should promote or retain students who are achieving below grade-level expectations. Mouly, in selection 52, points out that three reasons are generally given as justification for failing students. The first is that failure, or the threat of it, will motivate students; the second is that by failing them classroom standards will be maintained; and the third is that nonpromoted students will do better academically in succeeding years. None of these reasons, according to Mouly, is tenable.

In article 53, Nash focuses on a concept that has recently received the widespread attention of educators and lay personnel alike. This concept, accountability, means that institutions generally should be held responsible for what they purport to do. As it applies specifically to education, accountability means that if schools claim to teach certain skills, educators must be held responsible when and if these skills are not learned. In other words, if students fail, it is the fault of their schools and teachers. But can the general concept of accountability be applied to education? Is educational accountability possible? Is it desirable? Nash addresses these questions by posing four others: in an educational setting, who is accountable, for what are they accountable, to whom are they accountable, and when are they accountable? Nash's answers to these questions should provide you with the needed framework for analyzing further one of today's most central and controversial issues.

Amidon, in article 54, describes and illustrates the use of a process known as interaction analysis. Basically, interaction analysis is a categorization system for quantifying and analyzing teacher-student verbal interaction in the classroom. Many claim the major advantage of this system is that it provides teachers amount of classroom time—talking. Other categorization systems are also available. Each focuses on particular aspects of the teaching-learning process, each has the potential of providing feedback to teachers, and each—like interaction analysis—has advantages and disadvantages. Regardless of the system, though, the point is that some form of feedback would seem to be prerequisite to improving instruction.

48 Needed Changes to Sweeten the Impact of Testing

Henry S. Dyer

There are no doubt a good many things that can and should be done to promote right thinking and proper conduct among the users of tests. This paper considers two approaches that might be helpful. The first has to do with getting people to look behind the numbers commonly associated with tests, and the second with getting them to see tests as an integral part of the educational process.

To suggest that it is important to get behind the numbers is to suggest that the kind of pupil performance a test score stands for runs the risk of being lost from sight under the statistical superstructure of scales and norms and other interpretive data that get erected upon it. This is not to say that the superstructure is unnecessary or that a firm grip on the meaning of the numbers can be dispensed with in trying to understand students or in trying to get them to understand themselves. On the contrary, the art of statistical thinking and careful inference is absolutely fundamental to the proper use of test results, and the neglect of this art or the failure to exercise it constitutes a serious failure of professional responsibility.

But a thoroughgoing awareness of the probabilistic nature of the numbers that go with tests is not in itself sufficient for obtaining a full sense of what they mean. A test score, however expressed, points in two directions at once. Through norms, scales, contingency tables, and the like, it points *outward* to populations with which the student may be compared and to situations in which the level of his performance may be predicted or estimated. But a score also points *inward* to the processes that lie behind it, that is, to the specific mental operations that have generated the score. In the practical application of tests, the pragmatic tradition, which has had such a strong effect on educational developments of all kinds in this country, has led to a neglect of the meaning to be derived from that aspect of a test score that points inward. We have been so concerned with using test scores to classify students in one way or another or to predict how they will make out, academically or otherwise, that we have, I think, paid far too little attention to the details of behavior that a test score presumably summarizes.

This is particularly true in the case of tests of general intelligence. Piaget (1963, pp. 153–154), referring to Binet's work, has called attention to the problem in these words:

Reprinted from *The Personnel and Guidance Journal,* 45 (8): 776–780 (April 1967), by permission of author and publisher. Copyright © 1967 by the American Personnel and Guidance Association.

It is indisputable that these tests of mental age have on the whole lived up to what was expected of them: a rapid and convenient estimation of an individual's general level. But it is no less obvious that they simply measure a "yield" without reaching constructive operations themselves. . . . Intelligence conceived in these terms [i.e., in mental age terms] is essentially a value-judgment applied to complex behavior.

To put it another way, the normative score—that is, the single number that we call a mental age—may be a quick and easy way of seeing how a child's test performance compares with that of other children, but, in itself, it tells nothing at all about the nature of the performance on which the children are being compared.

This kind of blind comparison, with its implication of a value judgment, has had much to do with making test scores unpleasant to many recipients. It slaps a label on a child and leaves him and his parents with the impression that there is nothing that he or his teachers can do about it. It regards mental age—or worse still, the IQ—as an unmodifiable *condition* of achievement rather than as a "yield" of the educational process that can itself be affected, in part at least, by what happens in the classroom. It overlooks the fact that, if the school is to be something more than a device for sorting pupils into convenient categories, it must take some part of the responsibility for developing pupils' intelligence, instead of relying on the genes and the accidents of the environment to do the whole job. If it is to assume this responsibility, it will have to go behind the numbers on tests to try to understand in detail *how* pupils are thinking and *what* in detail might be done to help them think better.

We speak glibly of "abstract thinking," but we too rarely look at how children handle the specific tasks on tests so as to get a feeling for the actual mental operations that are involved in their thinking. A small study by Connolly and Wantman (1964) has demonstrated not only how one can get behind the numbers, but also what a wealth of information can be found there. They simply asked students to talk their thoughts into a tape recorder while reasoning their way through items on an aptitude test. They show that playbacks of the material can be assigned with reasonably good reliability to descriptive categories of mental behavior that can do much to give a student's score substantive meaning.

THE PERCEPTION OF TESTING AS PART OF THE EDUCATIONAL PROCESS

If a school is to perceive itself as engaged in educating pupils, and not just housing them while they grow up, it needs to acquire the view that testing, taken in the broadest sense, is indispensable to teaching. For years we have been giving lip service to the notion that testing is an "integral part of the educational process," but in fact a considerable part of the testing that goes on in schools is divorced from teaching. It has become a part of the mystique of the school psychologist and the guidance counselor, and usually yields only incidental information for use in the actual management of instruction. This may explain why many teachers perceive standardized tests as either threatening or irrelevant.

What is needed is some sort of conceptual model of the teaching-learning process that puts testing right in the middle of that process. The model proposed is based on a conception of education as a comprehensive system of control and communication in which those responsible for instructing and guiding the pupil—teachers, counselors, administrators—are provided with a continuous flow of information about the needs of students, the relevant factors in their life situations that affect their development, and the day-to-day effects of the educational program on their growth as persons and as citizens. The kind of control system implied is an extension to education of the system of control and communication in animals and machines that Norbert Wiener (1948) described 19 years ago in *Cybernetics*. In that revolutionary book, Wiener brought into general usage the notion of *feedback*. Testing can be usefully thought of as the means for providing feedback in the process of instruction.

Wiener cites the ordinary thermostat as a simple example of a control device that supplies self-correcting feedback. When the temperature of a room drops, the thermostat flashes a signal to the heater to get going; when the temperature rises to a certain level, the thermostat tells the heater to cease firing. Education does not have communication and control devices as efficient and as dependable as a thermostat. And the reason is obvious: educational systems are a billion times more complicated than heating systems. In a heating system the controls can be automatic and mechanical; in an educational system the controls must be largely voluntary and must depend upon frequent and intelligent human intervention. The feedback required to keep a heater responsive to the needs of a household is of one kind only—temperature readings. The kinds of feedback needed to keep an educational system responsive to the needs of the learner are practically infinite: they include readings on the hopes, aspirations, frustrations, fears, physical condition, attitudes, values, interests, skills, abilities, past accomplishments, and current levels of achievement of every student a teacher faces in his classes. They should provide usable information on how all of these qualities, traits, characteristics, and behavior tendencies are changing from moment to moment, from hour to hour, from week to week, and from year to year. They should tell how students are interacting with each other, with their teachers, and with the materials of instruction, so as to make possible reasonably dependable inferences about what procedures and what materials are producing what kinds of effects on what kinds of youngsters. They should tell what is happening in the home and elsewhere that may be facilitating or impeding the student's development as a person and as a functioning member of society.

Of course, such complex varieties of feedback are not now available and are unlikely to be available for a long time to come, if ever. Testing (and its first cousin, programmed instruction) is still a couple of light years away from the instrumentation necessary to furnish the kinds of feedback required to keep the educational process fully effective at all times for all pupils. As a systems analyst would say, it is scarcely sufficiently refined to "close the feedback loop" in all particulars. But the inadequacy of tests is hardly an argument for their abandonment as tools of teaching, as some of the critics of testing seem to imply. It is an argument, rather, for extracting all the information there is in the instruments available and supplementing as best one can by looking and listening for any clues to be had about what is going on "out there" in the minds of students.

This conception of testing as part of a communication and control system is shown schematically in the chart labeled "Testing in the Educational Process" (Figure 1). The chart attempts to show how tests can or should function in any kind of instructional system, whether one conceives of such a "system" as the total collection of activities that constitute the school system of an entire state, or as the collection of activities that go on in a single classroom, or as something between the two.

The model has five elements: I for the instructor, S for the student, E for the student's environment, F for the feedback, and t for points in time. The student environment (E) is between the horizontal lines. It is not to be thought of as static, but as a continuous stream of events impinging on the life and growth of the student, changing as he changes during the course of time. The four boxes labeled S stand for a single student at successive points in time. The four boxes labeled I may represent a single instructor or a succession of different instructors,

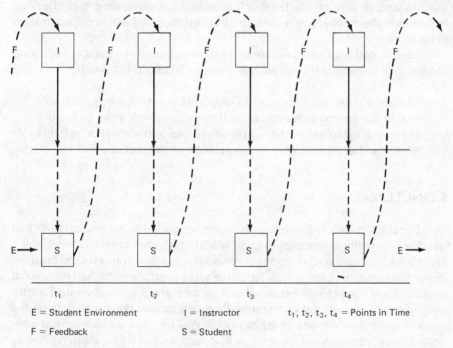

E = Student Environment	I = Instructor	t_1, t_2, t_3, t_4 = Points in Time
F = Feedback	S = Student	

FIGURE 1. Testing in the Educational Process

depending on how long the time intervals happen to be and on how the educational program may be organized. If the interval between t_1 and t_2 is 10 minutes, say, then presumably the instructor at both points is one and the same person who is getting the feedback *(F)* from his own efforts with the student. If the interval between t_3 and t_4 is two years, then the instructor in the first instance may be a high school teacher and the instructor in the second instance a college teacher, in which case the feedback is the possible information link that, it is hoped, will prevent the student from becoming a lost soul as he crosses the Great Divide between high school and college.

The arrows pointing from the instructor to the student are meant to suggest that the essence of instruction consists in manipulating the environment so as to provide the student with maturing experiences. This is to say that the most any instructor can do is to try to create the appropriate conditions for learning and then hope that something favorable will happen to the student as a consequence.

Whether the hope is fulfilled depends, of course, on whether the instructor hits upon the *right* conditions for each student. This in turn depends on two things: (1) the quality of the information about each student that a teacher has to start with—that is, the information supplied by the feedback from a previous occasion, and (2) the validity of the hypothesis that the instructor develops in light of this information about what will work and what will not work to produce learning. According to this scheme of things the teaching-learning process is a continuous experiment. Its effectiveness is conditioned absolutely by the amount and quality of the feedback available for generating and checking hypotheses about what to do next. In other words, good teaching depends on good testing.

There is nothing really new about this conception. As far back as 1895 John Dewey was preaching it (McLellan & Dewey, 1895). In his words:

> Education is precisely the work of supplying the conditions which will enable the psychical functions, as they successively arise, to mature and pass into higher functions in the freest and fullest manner, and this result can be secured only by knowledge of the process. . . .

CONCLUSION

The primary task of those of us who are persuaded of the ancient truth that good testing really is essential to good teaching is to get others to see it in the same light, for the impact of testing on education is a function of the perceptions of the consumers of tests. If tests are perceived as peripheral to the educational process, their impact will be peripheral. If they are perceived as devices for putting constraints on the curriculum, they will indeed put constraints on the curriculum. If they are perceived as instruments for sorting children into iron-bound categories, they will be used for that purpose. But if they are perceived as supplying basic data needed for helping children learn to cope more and more effectively with the world into which they are growing, then they will be used to provide that kind of help.

At present there is a certain woodenness about the use of test results that fails to take account of the fact that scores can point inward as well as outward. The main problem seems not to be that tests are having a bad impact on education, but that they are having *insufficient* impact.

What are the chances that this deficiency can be overcome? Perhaps the answer can be found in the history of testing. It has taken just about 50 years for standardized tests to win general acceptance as aids in assessing and predicting academic performance. If one holds with the late Paul Mort's 50–50 theory concerning the diffusion of new ideas about education (Mort, 1964), it will take another 50 years before the full possibilities of testing will be brought to bear as an aid in the educational process. These possibilities will be realized only as more and more people work at the notion that the use of tests as predictors is not enough, that tests have a very large role to play in helping us to see the student's mind in action *here and now* so that we can help him upset the predictions. On this point, the advice of Alfred North Whitehead in his famous essay on the aims of education (1949, p. 18) is still good:

> The mind is never passive; it is a perpetual activity, delicate, receptive, responsive to stimulus. You cannot postpone its life until you have sharpened it. Whatever interest attaches to your subject matter must be evoked here and now; whatever powers you are strengthening in the pupil, must be exercised here and now; whatever possibilities of mental life your teaching should impart, must be exhibited here and now. That is the golden rule of education, and a very difficult rule to follow.

The right use of tests should help make the rule a little easier to follow and thereby sweeten their impact on the school and the community.

REFERENCES
1. Connolly, J. A., & Wantman, M. J. "An Exploration of Oral Reasoning Processes in Responding to Objective Test Items." *Journal of Educational Measurement,* 1964, *1* (1), 59–64.
2. McLellan, J. A., & Dewey, J. *The Psychology of Number and Its Applications to Methods of Teaching Arithmetic.* New York: D. Appleton, 1895.
3. Mort, P. "Studies in Educational Innovation from the Institute of Administrative Research." In M. B. Miles (Ed.), *Innovation in Education.* New York: Bureau of Publications, Teachers College, Columbia Univ., 1964, p. 318.
4. Piaget, J. *Psychology of Intelligence.* Paterson, N.J.: Littlefield, Adams, 1963. 1963.
5. Whitehead, A. N. *The Aims of Education and Other Essays.* New York: New American Library, Mentor Books Edition, 1949.
6. Wiener, N. *Cybernetics, or Control and Communication in the Animal and the Machine.* Cambridge, Mass.: MIT Press, 1948.

49 Appraising Progress Toward the Achievement of Fixed Objectives

Robert M. W. Travers

The statement is commonly made that any program should have means built into it for determination of the extent to which the goals of the program are being achieved. Cohen (1970) has pointed out that many federally sponsored educational programs are supposed to meet such a requirement but that this has often resulted in the most superficial appraisal, involving little more than the judgment of those involved. Although the federal plan was to appraise each program in order to determine which ones should be developed further, the difficulties of appraising the extent to which an educational program has been effective were vastly underestimated.

Appraisal in terms of follow-up. It has often been said that, under ideal conditions, the effectiveness of educational programs should be judged in terms of the performance of the individual, in real-life situations, after he leaves school. Insofar as school is preparation for life, the effectiveness of schooling should be judged in terms of the extent to which it provides such preparation. Tests and examinations may indicate the extent to which the pupil has mastered particular aspects of the educational program, but they lack much in telling us whether the school can produce a person who can meet life's problems with competency. The argument is plausible, even persuasive, but the many attempts to evaluate schooling in terms of adult performance have shown up the many difficulties the procedure encounters. Consider, for example, the commonly professed goal that the school should prepare the individual to take advantage of the many cultural facilities offered by his community. One can quite easily find out how many go to concerts, listen to concerts on the radio in their homes, borrow books from the library, buy books and so forth, but such data tell little about the effects of schooling. There are times when a large section of the public may not be able to afford seats at concerts, has no money for books, is too busy moonlighting to listen to music on the radio, and so forth. Such data may tell one more about prevailing economic conditions than about the habits acquired in school. Furthermore, the cultural activity may also reflect the habits and ways of life that the students acquired in his home, and it is difficult to distinguish the effects of

Reprinted with permission of Macmillan Publishing Co., Inc., from *Educational Psychology* by Robert M. W. Travers. Copyright © 1973, Robert M. W. Travers.

schooling from the effects of family life. In addition, behavior that one might expect to occur as a result of the intensive efforts of the school to produce cultural development may be masked by other social conditions. In a period of rapid social change, individuals may be engaged to such a degree in activist movements that they have little time for conventional cultural activities. Others, who are part of an affluent society, may be so busy all weekend playing with their recreational vehicles that they have no time for reading or music or the other arts.

Now consider another case in which one might attempt to study the effectiveness of schooling. Most school systems devote some attention to the matter of health and diet. One should be able to determine the effectiveness of that program through the study of the health and dietary practices of those who have gone through the school system. The effect of what is taught in school may manifest itself in only a very weak form, because the effect of schooling has to compete with the effect of commercials that advise the individual to consume large quantities of "junk" foods. A one-semester course in health or biology can be expected to have only a small effect compared with the effect of a lifetime bombardment of television commercials imploring the viewer to buy relatively worthless forms of starch or poor-quality protein found in gelatin. One cannot expect that the school program will be able to override all the competing elements in society.

Follow-up studies designed to explore school-related behavior in real-life situations generally provide quite disappointing results. What such follow-up studies give is an overall appraisal of the total effects of all the influences designed to produce learning in our society, and many of these competing influences draw the individual in different directions. At the time of writing, the same television station will provide educational materials produced by the American Cancer Society on the hazards of smoking and also commercials for manufacturers of tobacco products designed to develop an addiction to tobacco. These two sets of influences are opposite, and it is doubtful whether studies could be made that would separate out and measure the relative influence of these two forces in our society.

Although follow-up studies designed to evaluate the effects of schooling generally yield little useful information, there are a few cases in which they can be fully justified, for instance, in driver training. Such studies have produced substantial evidence that school driver training does produce better drivers than the home-brand of driver training. There are excellent criteria of the extent to which a driver is proficient, and nearly all members of society have to drive. One might run into difficulties in evaluating driver education if good public transportation systems were evolved and most people drove cars only rarely (a situation analogous to teaching people to enjoy reading and then having them live in a society where there were alternatives to reading).

An interesting case of the follow-up technique is found in the numerous studies of compensatory education. Programs are developed for underprivileged children who have difficulties in school because of the limited opportunities for learning provided by their home environment. The obvious way to evaluate the effectiveness of such programs is to follow the children into the school that they enter after the program of compensatory education comes to an end. Such children have been followed through the lower elementary grades, but the data that have come out of such a follow-up are difficult to interpret. The findings are typically negative. The children who have been exposed to compensatory education show little, if any, advantage over those that have not been thus exposed. The difficulty with such studies is that short periods of compensatory education can hardly be expected to compensate fully for years of deprivation, and the tests and devices used to conduct the appraisal are inevitably quite crude. Most of the tests, rating scales, and other means of collecting data on such children are probably not sufficiently sensitive to show what compensatory education has accomplished. It is like trying to show slight changes in the temperature of the body with a thermometer calibrated in twenty-degree intervals.

Appraisal in simulated situations. There are real, and often insuperable, difficulties involved in obtaining information about how the individual performs in life situations. An investigator could probably never find out how well a physician performs in the secluded examination rooms of his private practice. One is equally unable to check on the plumber. The private lives of individuals are hidden to an even greater degree from the scientist's eye. Sometimes it is possible to study the behavior of those who have been trained or educated in some way, not in real-life situations, but in situations that simulate closely those of the natural world. If one cannot observe the behavior of the pupil in the real world, then perhaps one can stage for him some of the problems that life presents. Such staged situations are referred to as **simulated situations,** and they can approximate closely the situations that he has been prepared to handle.

Simulated situations for appraising pupil progress can be found at all levels of education. An elementary-school teacher may find out whether the children can apply the mathematics they have learned to such problems as determining the best buy in the supermarket. The testing situation may involve showing the children a set of cans of different sizes and contents and determining whether they can arrive at a correct decision. The appraisal of their achievement may be informal and involve no more than a class discussion of the problem, or it may involve a formal testing situation. Aspects of achievement in the language arts may be evaluated by having the children undertake such activities as preparing a letter on some school issue to be sent to the local newspaper. Pupils' speaking ability may be appraised by having them make speeches. The outcomes of health education can sometimes be evaluated in a real situation by observing what food choices the children make in designing a meal, and one can also have testing situations in which children have to state what food choices they would make when confronted with a particular variety of foods. Most education in the lower grades is designed to provide knowledge and skills useful in a great variety of situations, but all too often the teacher makes little attempt to discover whether the children can make any applications at all of what they have learned.

The more specialized education becomes, at higher levels, the more readily it lends itself to the development of simulated test situations. The teacher of business English has little difficulty in concocting practical situations in which the students can demonstrate the extent to which they can apply, in a simulated real-life situation, the skills they have supposedly been taught. The student trained in radio and television technology can be given troubleshooting problems to solve on equipment that has been deliberately made to malfunction. The medical student can be given recordings of human hearts to listen to, and a determination can be made of his skill in diagnosing heart ailments from heart sounds.

At all levels of education, there are some possibilities of making such simulated real-life test situations. An evaluation of education and an appraisal of the pupil's ability to come to grips with the realities of the world can be undertaken through such situations. All too often the tests given in school determine only whether a child can perform the skills exactly in the way in which he has learned them, but learning to pass such a school test is different from learning to pass the test of life. Many children learn skills in school in such a way that they can apply them only to school situations. Testing for the ability to transfer knowledge and skill to life situations is an essential feature of useful evaluation of the pupil.

Appraisal through the observation of pupils. Some teachers are very skilled in obtaining data on the progress of their pupils through information about how the children behave in school-related situations. Some aspects of the success of the language arts program in the school can be obtained by finding out what books children borrow from the library of their own free will. If the program of language development in the school is successful, one might expect pupils to become individuals who read on their own and who borrow library books to develop knowledge about matters of interest to them or for the enjoyment of reading literature. The extent to which children are absent from school is a strong indicator of the extent to which life in school has been made pleasant, for it is known that differences in absentee rates in different schools reflect far more what happens in the school than they reflect differences in actual sickness rates. The effectiveness of the school program in the area of ecology is seen, to some extent, in the degree to which the school grounds are cluttered with rubbish, the extent to which pupils participate in drives to control pollution, and the extent to which the spare-time activities of the pupils involve the preservation or destruction of wildlife. If the social studies program is designed to help the pupil become a concerned participant in local or national affairs, then it is relevant to determine whether he does or does not read a newspaper and what he reads in the paper. The role that the individual wants to play in the larger society is also seen in the role that he plays in the classroom.

Such methods of appraising pupil development have potential for providing highly important data on the extent to which the goals of the program are being achieved. The main difficulty in the use of these methods of appraisal is that they are time consuming. Many teachers claim they do not have the time, but sometimes administrative arrangements can be made to make the application of these methods possible. For example, the author is familiar with a school in which two first-grade classes are combined under the direction of two teachers. At certain times in the year, one of the teachers leaves the classroom and goes to visit in the homes of the children for the purpose of finding out something about their out-of-school behavior. The teacher can then find out, for instance, whether the uncommunicative child who is slowly beginning to communicate with other children shows a similar progress in out-of-school hours. Such contacts of parents and teachers can be extremely important in keeping the school program from becoming a meaningless routine, unrelated to life in the community. Another approach is that developed in North Dakota, in which parents participate in classroom activity and a close link is developed between the teacher, the parent, and the school program.

Appraisal in terms of teacher-made tests. Although one may exhort teachers to make observations on pupils, the fact remains that most teachers rely largely on classroom tests to determine the progress that pupils are making. Classroom tests appear to be an easy and quick way of collecting information. For this reason, a consideration of evaluation techniques has to include some discussion of paper-and-pencil tests. Books on this topic written twenty-five years ago offer much the same advice as those written today, but the advice given is useful and some of it will be summarized here. Readily available and readable books on this topic include those by Ebel (1965), Lindeman (1967), and Gronlund (1970). Several new books on the construction of classroom examinations are in the process of publication, but they are unlikely to show any new departures.

Classroom tests typically measure the aspects of behavior that can be translated into words or are essentially word skills. Many of the important skills taught in schools are word skills. The teacher of English is interested in developing the ability of students to communicate both orally and in writing. Such a teacher may appraise the ability of pupils in the latter respect by asking each to write a letter applying for a particular job and outlining the qualifications they may have for it. The test measures an actual sample of the behavior that the teaching is designed to develop. However, sometimes an examination may be designed to measure a skill that is not ordinarily considered a word skill but can be translated into words. For example, a chemistry teacher might ask his students to design an experiment to show whether a particular sample of orange juice contains vitamin C. The chemistry teacher could, of course, ask the students to conduct the experiment in the laboratory, but this might involve providing many sets of equipment, and perhaps more than were available. Most of the skills involved can be translated into words, but not all. A student might be able to give a flawless description of the experiment and yet be too clumsy to actually carry out the routine he can meticulously describe on paper. Nevertheless, the chemistry teacher may justify the written test by saying that if a student cannot describe how he would carry out the experiment, he almost certainly would not be able to undertake the task in the laboratory.

One can easily think of some cases in which a verbal, written test could not possibly measure the skill that had been taught. One may teach generosity and kindness, but no one would attempt to measure these attributes through a paper-and-pencil test. Nobody would attempt to measure the ability to play a musical instrument by giving a written test. One could, perhaps, devise a test that would indicate the person's familiarity with a particular musical instrument, but performance on the test has only a remote relationship to performance on the musical instrument itself. Although one can add many items to this list of skills that cannot be convincingly measured by means of a verbal test, one can also make a strong case for the position that most of the knowledge, skills, and perhaps even appreciations taught in schools can be measured adequately with paper and pencil. Let us consider some of the characteristics that should be found in an adequately constructed test.

Pupils voice many complaints about the tests given in school, and these inadequacies can be viewed, from a technical standpoint, as involving a lack of what are referred to as **validity** and **reliability.** Let us consider these two concepts from the point of view of constructing classroom examinations.

Suppose that a teacher had given a course in twentieth-century American history and followed a syllabus put out by the state education department. For the final examination the teacher asked the pupils to list six Supreme Court decisions of the present century that had had impact and to explain what that impact was. Because the course had barely touched on Supreme Court decisions, having been focused on foreign policy, the students had a right to complain that the examination lacked relevancy for measuring the outcomes of the course. The educational psychologist would prefer to say that the examination lacked validity, for a core concept in validity is relevancy. Valid examinations are highly relevant measurements of the outcomes of the particular course in which they are used for appraising pupil achievement.

A second implicit concept is that a valid test should include a representative sample of the achievement expected in the course. In the case of the course in twentieth-century American history, the valid achievement test should include problems representing each important area included. It is not enough that the test cover particular areas included in the course; the test must also present problems measuring the ability of the pupil to perform each of the skills supposedly developed.

Although it seems logical to say that examinations should have validity in terms of the stated objectives of the course, one may well ask what should be done when the course itself does not closely correspond to the objectives. For example, suppose that a college teacher designed a course in statistics for graduate students of education and prepared a valid examination that would measure the extent to which the outcomes were achieved. This same college teacher then had the task of teaching the course. After a few meetings with the students, he found that they had far less background in mathematics than typical graduate students of education and prepared a valid examination that would give them the examination based on the original set of objectives and show them their inadequacies in terms of the stated goals? Of course he should not. He should recognize that his modification of the course involved a modification of the objectives. The items in the test should match the new objectives if the test is to measure achievement in relation to realistic goals.

Reliability, the other test characteristic related to validity, may be discussed with respect to our teacher of twentieth-century American history. Suppose that he viewed the course as involving six main areas and prepared an examination covering one very specific point in each of the areas. Some students might complain that, although they had studied, the six points covered in the examination just happened to be points to which they had not given any special attention. The students might argue that, because of the nature of the test, luck played an important part in the scores they obtained. They point out that if the teacher had asked questions related to six other relevant points, they might have obtained excellent scores. The questions asked were valid enough, but the test lacked reliability. A test is always a sampling of the knowledge and skill that the student has supposedly acquired, but the sample should be large enough so that a fair appraisal can be made of the student's accomplishments. If two tests are given, each one of which provides an adequate sample, the performance of the student on one test should be very similar to his performance on the other. In such a case, the tests would be said to have satisfactory reliability.

Let us consider some of the down-to-earth ways in which teacher-made examinations are deficient in these respects. Essay examinations are often deficient in that the teacher thinks of some "clever" questions, which generally detract from the validity of the tests. Essay questions may also sometimes lack validity because the writing of the essay calls for skills that have nothing to do with the content of the course. An examination in history is quite often a moderately good test of skill in English composition, but a valid test of English composition is unlikely to be a valid test of knowledge of American history. A good test of the wrong subject is likely to be demoralizing to the student. Another reason for poor validity of a test is inappropriateness of the item form. Suppose a teacher gives a course in modern American history and the main objective is an understanding of the development of American democracy. At the end of the course, the teacher gives an examination consisting of matching items, in which events are to be matched with their dates. Matching test items are simply not appropriate for measuring the kind of understanding that the teacher hoped to develop. Essay tests are particularly useful for measuring the student's ability to organize his thoughts and his ability to present arguments for and against particular positions. Multiple-choice questions have excellent properties for measuring knowledge of facts, the ability to interpret data, and the ability to distinguish between relevant and irrelevant data and correct and incorrect statements, among other common objectives.

Lack of reliability of classroom tests derives from two main sources. The test itself may have inherent properties that make for low reliability, and the scoring procedures may be unreliable. Scoring procedures are particularly the problem in essay examinations. Two scorers, quite obviously, show much less agreement in scoring a set of essay papers than they do in scoring two objective examinations. Indeed, if the same person were to score and rescore the same set of essay examinations measuring writing skills, one would expect only very moderate agreement between the two sets of scores: Quite commonly, a paper given an *A* on one scoring would receive only a *C* on a second scoring and vice versa. The scoring procedure for teacher-made essay examinations typically has poor reliability. Unfortunately, scoring procedures are particularly unreliable for such worthwhile features as the style of writing, the degree of organization, the thoughtfulness of the material, and originality. Scoring procedures are relatively reliable for such features as the amount and correctness of the information given and the number of spelling errors and simple grammatical mistakes. It has sometimes been said that the greater the triviality of the outcome, the greater the reliability of scoring.

Objective examinations do not have the same problem with reliability of scoring procedures. In fact, objective examinations are called objective because judgment does not enter into the scoring procedure; two persons scoring a set of such examinations would agree almost perfectly on the scores to be assigned. Therefore, scoring procedures have high reliability in the case of objective examinations. A major source of unreliability in objective tests arises from the fact that, with a short test, the pupil may obtain a high score through lucky guessing. If a teacher gives a sixteen-item true-false test, pure guessing will produce an average score of 8, and pure guessing will sometimes produce a score as high as 12 or more. The chances are actually about one in twenty that sheer guessing will produce at least as high a score. The remedy for this source of unreliability is to provide quite long objective examinations, but most teachers do not do this. The reason, of course, is that a good examination, with potential for being thoroughly reliable, might involve the use of seventy-five items and several full days of work on the part of the teacher. Most teacher-made objective tests have very poor reliability because they are far too short.

One way of overcoming this difficulty is for groups of teachers to develop pools of items. This can be done within a department of a high school, and perhaps within a particular grade of an elementary school. This kind of operation has been referred to by some European writers as **item banking** (see Wood and Skurnik, 1969). Such pools of items may be informal assemblies of test questions produced by an interchange among teachers of their examination materials or may involve sophisticated and centralized files also containing information on how difficult or easy each item has been found to be. In schools run along the lines of the Individually Prescribed Instruction program, this problem is solved by incorporating short tests with each unit of subject matter. The tests may be nothing more than the exercises through which the unit is mastered, or the tests may be separate from the unit of work. Many teaching kits also provide similar built-in procedures for evaluation. For example, some of the kits developed by

Science Research Associates for the teaching of reading include tests of comprehension in order to measure the extent to which the pupil has understood what he has read.

Standardized tests and national testing programs. Attempts are made in most school systems to obtain some evidence concerning the progress made by pupils through the use of standardized tests. The use of such tests is based on the assumption that there are certain goals that children should achieve by a certain age and that the degree of achievement of these goals can be effectively measured by standardized instruments. Even if there is such unity of purpose among teachers, school administrators, and parents, there probably should not be. Consider the case of reading—an area where one would think there is considerable agreement on what should be achieved and by what age. What should the child have achieved in this respect by the end of the third grade? Some would say that the most important goal achieved by that time would be the ability to read simple material accurately. Others would have quite a different opinion, taking the position that by the end of the third grade the child should have discovered that reading is an exciting and worthwhile experience through which he can obtain information he needs and also enjoyment. The two sets of goals are not necessarily compatible. A child who has learned to read simple materials with precision may be much less enthused with reading than the child who has stumbled through materials that fascinate him and who has not been drilled with kinds of simple materials likely to appear on a standardized test. The teacher who works to develop a fascination for reading may take the position that speed and accuracy will come as the child becomes more and more engrossed in reading what he wants to read. Traditionally, the stress has been on accuracy rather than on developing enthusiasm, but this may well be the wrong approach. The fact is that not enough is known about the whole problem of developing reading skills to say who is right. It would be unfortunate if the makers of standardized tests forced teachers into developing the skills that the test makers had arbitrarily decided to be the most important.

Much greater controversy exists in such areas as social studies, in which there are many different views about the content to be covered and the particular age level at which particular objectives should be achieved. When, for example, should the concept of democracy be introduced? At what age should children learn that there are forms of government other than our own? When should children begin to understand the diverse origins of Americans? At what age are children mature enough to understand that just as a person is fallible, so too is the government of their country sometimes wrong in the decisions it makes? Are elementary-school children too young to begin to understand that governments have to make important moral decisions about such issues as whether the poor should be helped, whether the oppressed should be freed, and who should be free to say what? Issues such as these are of vastly more consequence than those involved in deciding which details of history shall be taught at each age.

Standardized tests tend to avoid the crucial issues related to curriculum design and to concentrate on the areas about which there is agreement. In the social studies area, they tend to include test questions related to simple facts of history that have played an important role in the building of the American tradition, and they avoid the social problems and issues that form the crux of controversy and dissent on the contemporary scene. Nevertheless, they will continue to be given for a number of reasons. One is that school boards and principals like to have data that appear to provide evidence that the school system is doing as well as any other school system. The possibility that the evidence may not show anything much at all does not seem to bother those who make the decisions to use standardized tests.

If a teacher is competent, the administration of standardized tests is not going to tell him much about each pupil that he did not know in the first place. He already knows much about Jimmy, who came to him from the previous grade three years behind most of the other children in reading skills. He has worked with Jimmy over the past year and knows that a little progress has been made, but not enough to remove the gap between him and the other children. He also knows that Doris and John come from homes that provide no intellectual encouragement whatsoever and his task has been to show these children that intellectual pursuits can be rewarding. He has tried to interest them in hobbies and find related reading materials for them. Then there is June, who has been diagnosed as having brain injury. She is never in her seat long enough to learn anything, but she is now under the care of a physician who seems to be helping her to some extent. June should be in a special class for such children, but the school system has no facilities of this kind. The teacher just does his best under the circumstances, but the best he can do is far from what could be done if a special classroom were available. Then there is Bill. His problem is that he is enormously overconcerned with obtaining good grades. He is bright and competent as a student and performs far above his age group, but good grades come before anything else in his life. Even when a game is introduced as a technique for learning a particular skill, Bill cannot enjoy the game, for he is far too intent on winning.

The point is that the teacher should know a great deal about the pupils in his class and far more than he can find out from a standardized battery of tests.

REFERENCES

1. Cohen, D. K., 1970. "Politics and Research: Evaluation of Social Action Programs in Education," *Review of Educational Research,* 40, 213–38.
2. Ebel, R. L., 1965. *Measuring Educational Achievement.* Englewood Cliffs, N.J.: Prentice-Hall.
3. Gronlund, N. E., 1970. *Stating Behavioral Objectives for Classroom Instruction.* New York: Macmillan.
4. Lindeman, R. H., 1967. *Educational Measurement.* Glenview, Ill.: Scott, Foresman.
5. Wood, R., and Skurnil, L. E., 1969. *Item Banking.* Slough, England: National Foundation for Educational Research in England.

50 Functional Types of Student Evaluation

Peter W. Airasian and George F. Madaus

From the mid-'30's until the early '60's, primarily as a result of the writings of Tyler (1934, 1950), the emphasis in evaluation has been concentrated on teachers and their unique instructional objectives. Two factors have been instrumental in shifting the focus in the evaluation literature away from the classroom teacher. The first was the advent, during the late '50's and early '60's, of large-scale curriculum development projects, especially in the physical sciences. The appearance of these projects generated concern about the role of evaluation in course development and improvement (Cronbach, 1963; Grobman, 1968; Scriven, 1967; Stake, 1967).

The second factor, while harder to pinpoint in time, is no less a reality. It is the growing recognition that the busy teacher, responsible for varied work of large and varied classes, seldom has the time to carry out individually the operations called for in the Tyler rationale (Bloom, Hastings, & Madaus, 1971; Eisner, 1967; Jackson, 1968; Madaus, 1969).

Despite this shift in perspective, student evaluation of some kind is a pervasive and crucial feature of all instruction. Some evaluation is spontaneous, unsystematic, and informal, for the most part based on such cues as momentary facial expressions, shifts in posture, tone of voice, etc. (Jackson, 1968). On the other hand, some student evaluation is based on more systematic and quantitative data, derived principally from paper-and-pencil tests. The purpose of this article is to define four types of student evaluation (placement, formative, diagnostic, and summative) by comparing these evaluation types across nine dimensions (function, time, characteristics of evidence, evidence-gathering techniques, sampling, scoring and reporting, standards, reliability, and validity). Interactions are also described.

Figure 1 contrasts the four types of evaluation across the nine dimensions to be discussed. The remainder of this article treats each dimension separately, referring the reader to the appropriate row of the figure.

Reprinted from *Measurement and Evaluation in Guidance*, 4 (4): 221–233 (January 1972), by permission of authors and publisher. Copyright © 1972 by the American Personnel and Guidance Association.

FIGURE 1. Comparison of Four Types of Classroom Evaluation

	Placement	Formative	Diagnostic	Summative

FUNCTION OF EVALUATION	to place students by
	a. determining the degree to which prerequisite entry behaviors or skills are present or absent
	b. determining entering mastery of the course objectives
	c. matching students to alternative teachers or instructional modes according to characteristics known or thought to optimize achievement
		Formative evaluation is contributory. Its functions are
		a. to provide on-going feedback to the teacher for the purposes of
		  1. choosing or modifying subsequent learning experiences
		  2. prescribing remediation of group or individual deficiencies
		b. to provide on-going feedback to the student for the purpose of directing advanced or remedial study
			to recognize psychological, physical, or environmental symptoms manifested by students with extraordinary or recurrent learning and/or classroom problems	to grade, certify, or attest to student learning or teacher effectiveness

TIME OF EVIDENCE GATHERING	prior to entry into an instructional unit	several times prior to the completion of instruction on a predefined segment (unit, chapter, etc.) of a course	While a teacher should always be sensitive to the manifestation of symptoms known to be related to learning difficulties he should be particularly attentive to students when classroom or learning difficulties cannot be explained in terms of cognitive or instructional variables.	at the conclusion of a unit, course, or year's instruction

FIGURE 1. (cont.)

BEHAVIORAL CHARACTERISTICS OF EVIDENCE GATHERED	dependent on the functions stated above: typically cognitive or psychomotor when the function is to determine whether or not prerequisite entry behaviors are present or to determine the student's prior mastery of course objectives; may also be affective when the purpose is to match students to alternative teachers or instructional modes.	cognitive or psychomotor	physical (vision, auditory perception, dominance and laterality, general health, etc.); psychological (intelligence, emotional maladjustment, social maladjustment, etc.); environmental (nutritional, parent-child relationships, peer influences, etc.).	depends on course objectives; higher or lower level cognitive behaviors, affective and/or psychomotor
EVIDENCE GATHERING TECHNIQUES	depend on type of placement sought, but could include: a. commercial tests (intelligence, achievement, diagnostic, etc.) b. teacher-made instruments (formative, summative, specially designed pre-tests, observation, interviews, checklists, video-tapes, etc.)	a series of teacher-made achievement measures; supply, essay, or selection tests, interviews, video-tapes, check-lists, etc.	primarily observational although for certain symptoms general screening techniques to confirm hypotheses may be available to the classroom teacher (e.g. vision). Generally, upon noting symptoms, the teacher forwards his observations to proper agencies, e.g. guidance counselor, nurse, school psychologist, etc.	primarily internally or externally constructed achievement tests
SAMPLING CONSIDERATIONS FOR EVIDENCE GATHERING	depend on the functions specified above; evidence must be gathered on a. each prerequisite entry behavior b. a representative sample of course objectives c. those behaviors related to a construct(s) which in turn are known or thought to be	a. where the objectives of an instructional segment are interrelated (cognitively or sequentially within cognitive levels) the sample should include all objectives in the segment. b. where the objectives of a predefined instructional segment are not interrelated,	Sampling in the psychometric sense is not applicable. An ad hoc observational process designed to construct and confirm hypotheses about suspected cause of disorders.	weighted sample of course objectives; weighting may be in terms of teaching emphasis, purpose of evaluation, time spent, transferability of objectives, perceived importance in society, etc.

	related to different types of teachers or to alternative modes of instruction	the determination may depend on such considerations as the use of an objective in subsequent learning; the extent to which an objective integrates or reinforces prior learning, etc.		
SCORING AND REPORTING	patterns, profiles, subscores, etc. for all functions except placing students out of a course (where total score may be utilized)	patterns of item responses, abilities mastered or not mastered, etc. All reporting must be free of any intimation of a mark, grade, or certification.	sum of total number of correct responses, either by objective or on total exam; reported as letter or number grade, percentile, etc.	an anecdotal report containing specific behavioral instances forwarded to the appropriate referral agency.
STANDARDS AGAINST WHICH SCORES ARE COMPARED	predetermined norm or criterion referenced standards	criterion referenced standards	almost exclusively norm referenced	compare manifested behavior against specified abnormal behaviors
RELIABILITY	dependent on the trait measured, and the consequences of the judgments	stability and/or consistency of item response patterns	internal consistency	recurrence of behavioral symptoms
VALIDITY	primarily content validity but also construct validity (where students are matched with teachers or instructional strategies)	primarily content validity but also construct validity (where hierarchies of objectives are involved)	content validity	face validity

COMPARISON OF THE FOUR EVALUATION TYPES

Function of Evaluation

The first distinction between the four types of evaluation resides in the teacher's purpose for determining, valuing, describing, or classifying aspects of student behavior. At different instructional junctures teachers need to judge student progress. While the intent of evaluation at each juncture is to judge students, the purposes and consequences of the judgments can vary widely. The first row of Figure 1 contrasts the different purposes of placement, formative, diagnostic, and summative evaluation. Each type described is, in the true sense of the word, an evaluation. However, evaluation performed for different purposes engenders varied procedures.

As the name implies, *placement evaluation* is used to place a student. In many individualized instructional programs, as well as in more traditional instructional arrangements, the concept of correct student placement is central. For example, some schools refuse to permit a student who fails French I to enroll in French II. Other schools use a more sophisticated form of placement by specifying a series of skills, which students must have mastered prior to admittance to particular courses. However, the concept of placement can be defined more broadly than these examples indicate. Thus, based on prior achievement or the presence of certain cognitive and affective characteristics, a student can be placed (a) at the most appropriate point in an instructional sequence, (b) in a particular instructional method, or (c) with an appropriate teacher.

The following analogy illustrates the concept of placing a student at the optimum point in an instructional sequence. Picture each of the necessary prerequisite skills, as well as anticipated objectives of a course, as units on a number line. Absence of prerequisite skills is analogous to the negative numbers, while the presence of these skills but the absence of student mastery of any of the anticipated course objectives is analogous to the zero point. The objectives of the course are analogous to the positive numbers along the line. A primary purpose of placement evaluation is to locate a student on this "instructional number line." In many schools, if not in most, students are in fact "placed" at our imaginary zero point without regard to their prerequisite skills or their prior mastery of certain course objectives.

Matching a student with an instructional method or with a particular teacher is still in its infancy. However, as research on the efficacy of such placement becomes more abundant, it may be possible to place students either with the most appropriate teacher (Thelen, 1967) or in the optimal instructional mode (Bracht, 1969). Strategies of Mastery Learning (Block, 1971) that call for different instructional modes for different learners and the widespread availability of the green, yellow, and blue versions of Biological Sciences Curriculum Study (BSCS) Biology represent steps in the direction of this form of student placement.

Formative evaluation is intended to provide both student and teacher with information about progress toward mastery of the general course objectives. It is not used to grade students, but instead provides information that directs subsequent teaching or study. While formal procedures for formative evaluation have been developed (Airasian, 1968, 1971), teachers who administer nongraded "spot" quizzes or who use various observational cues to assess the progress of instruction are carrying out a type of formative evaluation in the sense that they are gauging the ongoing success of instruction. Such information is used less to grade students than to make instruction responsive to identified student weaknesses and strengths.

Summative evaluation is used to certify or grade students at the completion of relatively large blocks of instruction—e.g., units, terms, or semesters. Summative evaluations produce the marks typically averaged into student grades. The result of a summative examination is in the most real sense "final" and is likely to follow the student throughout his academic career. It is this use of evaluation that is currently under attack by students and educational critics.

The final type of evaluation, *diagnostic evaluation*, is used to identify students whose learning or classroom behavior is being adversely affected by factors external to instructional practices. We define the domain of diagnostic evaluation to encompass physical, environmental, emotional, or psychological factors generated outside the classroom. Thus, many Headstart programs did not result in improved learning until someone realized that students who did not have an adequate breakfast prior to the start of school were more prone to concentrate on food than on their instruction. Similarly, recognition that a particular student has sight or hearing difficulties that inhibit his learning is diagnostic evaluation. Teachers must be able to recognize factors that are in a sense extra-classroom but that adversely affect a child's classroom performance.

It must be stated explicitly at this juncture that any system of student evaluation incorporating two or more of the types we propose should not operate as a set of independent subsystems. The four evaluation types, then, interact to provide the classroom teacher with a data base from which to make different types of judgments about student learning. The primary distinction we are striving to make relates to the purpose of performing an evaluation. The remaining categories in Figure 1 overlap and interact to a large extent.

Time of Evidence-Gathering

It is clear from the different purposes of the four evaluation types that evidence for each type is gathered at different times. Any complete student evaluation system provides for continual evidence-gathering of one form or another. The second row of Figure 1 contrasts the time points at which evidence is gathered for placement, formative, summative, and diagnostic evaluation.

Since the aim of placement is to facilitate learning by identifying the student's optimum starting point or by providing him with the most reinforcing environment (in terms of teacher and materials), placement considerations occur prior to the start of instruction. In many circumstances, however, students may be "replaced" (in the sense of placing them again or differently) if the original placement proves to be less than ideal. Usually, evidence from formative evaluations provides the basis for replacing students. Occasionally, however, identification and remediation of a physical deficit identified during diagnostic evaluation may call for "replacing" a student.

Formative evaluation takes place as instruction unfolds. Summative evaluation, because of its grading or certifying function, takes place at the conclusion of an instructional unit. Like formative evaluation, diagnostic evaluation is a continual act that admits to no definite time constraints. The teacher should always be sensitive to the manifestation of behavioral symptoms assumed to be related to extra-classroom causes of learning difficulties. The four types of evaluation emphasize that teachers ought to be continually gathering evidence about student learning.

Behavioral Characteristics of Evidence Gathered

One problem that must be faced by any evaluation system is the definition of the behavioral domains to which evaluation with different purposes must attend. Row 3 of Figure 1 contrasts the four evaluation types across the behavioral characteristics of evidence gathered.

When we place students in an instructional sequence, assess the ongoing progress of instruction, or grade student achievement, we evaluate vis-à-vis the anticipated outcomes or objectives of our course. It is only natural, then, that formative, summative, and two types of placement evaluation (determining attainment of prerequisite skills or prior mastery of course objectives), gather evidence from similar behavioral domains. Since the majority of objectives defined and fostered in our schools are cognitive or psychomotor, these are the behavioral characteristics evaluated. The objectives of instruction form a focal point around which evidence-gathering considerations for placement, formative, and summative evaluation overlap.

Under certain conditions, placement and summative evaluation may also be directed toward the gathering of affective data. Placement evaluation should involve gathering of affective data if its purpose is to match student characteristics with either a certain type of teacher or with a certain mode of instruction, since the basis for matching will likely have more to do with personality and style than with intellective capacity. Some schools permit teachers to select their next year's class on the basis of the consonance between the teacher's instructional style and expectations and the student's perceived learning style and motivation. The aim is to define and match teachers and students on noncognitive factors so as to produce a harmonious, unfrustrating, and efficient learning environment.

There are two occasions when summative evaluation should also involve gathering affective data. The first is when the course objectives include affective outcomes. The second is when it is deemed important to gather evidence about the unintended outcomes that always occur as a by-product of instruction. Evaluative evidence about student performance should not be limited to data about course objectives. When a particular set of objectives is chosen, a tradeoff is involved in the sense that certain other desirable objectives may have to be neglected or deemphasized. It is important to know the cost of such tradeoffs, especially in terms of student attitudes.

If summative affective data are gathered, a strong case can be made against grading individual students on the basis of the data. Given the moral considerations involved in grading students' interests, attitudes, or values, the authors feel that the proper focus is the degree to which the class as a whole manifests particular affects. Data should be gathered to preserve anonymity and to permit inferences to be made that will not harm the individual.

No reference to affective evidence is made under formative evaluation. The reason is that nothing is as yet known about either the methodology required by or the consequences resulting from such a practice. The guidelines for summative evaluation of affective behavior, however, would likely hold as well for formative evaluation. That is, the data should be gathered anonymously and used to make judgments about group rather than individual affects.

While the characteristics of the evidence gathered in placement, formative, and summative evaluation are all related more or less directly to the objectives of a course, diagnostic evaluation seeks different types of data. The behavioral characteristics of the evidence gathered during diagnostic evaluation do not fall in the usual categories of cognitive, affective, or psychomotor, but rather are classified as physical, psychological, or environmental. Diagnostic evaluation seeks to go beyond identifying objectives that students have not learned. It strives to provide hypotheses related to extra-classroom factors that explain *why* students have not learned. Physical or biological factors may include problems of vision, speech, or general health. Psychological factors involve emotional or social maladjustment. Environmental factors include such things as dietary problems or a disrupted or disadvantaged home life.

Evidence-Gathering Techniques

In the fourth row the techniques used to gather evidence for each of the four types of evaluation are compared. To place a student at the appropriate instructional starting point or out of a course entirely, and to evaluate student learning formatively or summatively, achievement data are needed. For each evaluative purpose, we need to determine what and how much students have learned. The use made of such information would vary according to the purpose of the evaluation.

Although commercially available intelligence, achievement, and readiness tests can provide useful data, particularly for placement and summative decisions, locally constructed achievement tests are probably more valuable. The use of standardized tests presents the very real danger that course objectives will be altered to coincide with the skills required to perform well on the standardized test. Since student achievement is evaluated relative to the objectives of a course, and since courses vary from locale to locale, standardized instruments are unlikely to provide specific enough information for decision-making. They are designed to sample objectives that cut across curricula and geographical regions and consequently, are not the most parsimonious means of gathering placement, formative, or summative data. Achievement measures constructed at the local level and directed toward the course objectives will provide more salient evidence.

Useful achievement measures need not be conceived of solely as paper-and-pencil tests. A great deal of useful data about students' skills and behaviors can be acquired by such techniques as observation, checklists, interviews, videotape recordings, and the like. There are many school subjects such as shop, art, physical education, and speech, where major emphasis in evaluation is on what a student does rather than what he knows. Observational-type evaluative procedures are more relevant evidence-gathering techniques for these courses than are paper-and-pencil instruments. In general, too little attention has been paid to the use of teacher observation and intuition as an appropriate evidence-gathering technique for evaluation. This is especially true of formative, placement, and diagnostic evaluation, where the consequences of incorrect judgments do not leave irreparable scars on students.

In diagnostic evaluation, many schools periodically employ general visual and auditory screening techniques to identify students with sight or hearing difficulty. The primary evidence-gathering technique utilized in diagnostic evaluation, however, is that of sensitive teacher observation. Elementary school teachers are usually in a better position than secondary teachers to carry out diagnostic evaluation, since most elementary schools are organized with a single teacher teaching a given class. Prolonged student contact makes it easier to identify symptoms indicative of physical, psychological, or environmental causes of learning disorders. Such observation, to be sure, presupposes teacher familiarity with symptoms related to these extra-classroom causes. Once a teacher observes the symptoms, the correct procedure generally is to refer the student to the nurse, social worker, or other individual within the school system who is best prepared to provide assistance.

Sampling Considerations for Evidence-Gathering

Although the two types of placement evaluation as well as formative and summative evaluation are primarily concerned with gathering cognitive or psychomotor achievement data, the differences in purposes and timing call for different approaches to determining the characteristics of the sample of items to be used in evidence-gathering.

If entry into a course is determined by the extent to which a student has mastered a series of prerequisite skills, the instrument used in placement evaluation must include items evaluating each skill. Suppose that entry into Algebra I is dependent on prior mastery of ability to add signed numbers, to multiply and divide fractions, and to translate word problems into equations. Each of these abilities is prerequisite to being able to function at even a minimal level of competency in Algebra I. It is not sufficient for a placement instrument to gather data about only one or two of these abilities, since success in algebra is predicated on all. Similarly, in formative evaluation, where the attempt is to identify unmastered course objectives early enough to permit remediation prior to grading, each objective must be tested in order to obtain usable feedback.

To elaborate, consider the objectives sampled in a formative versus a summative evaluation. An algebra course may have as one of its ultimate objectives "to solve unfamiliar word problems by means of simultaneous equations." Items that evaluate this general course aim are appropriate for summative evaluation. We expect various topics covered in the course to contribute to the student's ability to achieve the objective. At the end of the term or semester we would want to know, for purposes of grading, whether a student had mastered the objective. Mastery of this general objective, however, implies that the student has mastered a series of more specific objectives—for example, "to solve simultaneous equations," "to translate word problems into equations," and so on (Airasian, 1971). If grading is the aim of evaluation, data about performance on the more general objectives are sufficient; but if evaluation is intended to identify learning weaknesses prior to grading, evidence about the student's ability to perform each of the more specific behaviors implied by the general objective should be obtained. Formative evaluation cannot help the student to direct his study if items testing each relevant skill are not included. Formative evaluation must be capable of telling the student to "learn to solve simultaneous equations" or "learn to state word problems in terms of equations" rather than the more general, and less useful, "work harder," "study more," etc., type of evaluation.

Evaluation instruments built along formative and summative lines can be useful for placing students at a particular point in instruction or out of a course entirely. Some courses, primarily at the college level, permit students who can pass the final examination to place out of the course. The reasoning is that if a student can pass the summative examination on the first day of class, his time will be more beneficially spent in some other course. Formative evaluation instruments that test the more specific skills required by the general course objectives are useful for determining that point in the course continuum where a student should be placed. In general, one could administer formative tests until a student evidenced nonmastery of a skill important for learning later skills. He would be placed at that point in the course where the unmastered skill was taught.

Since observations are gathered in an ad hoc manner in diagnostic evaluation, sampling in the usual sense of the word is not meaningful. It may be that the tell-tale symptoms of extra-classroom difficulties do not regularly manifest themselves. Further, to wait for additional occurrences may retard remedial action. The best approach for a teacher who suspects extra-classroom causes to be at the root of learning disorders is to talk to the appropriate referral agency (nurse, social worker, etc.) about his observations and hypotheses. The expert could then either see the child or direct the teacher to look for additional behavioral symptoms.

Scoring and Reporting

Row 6 of Figure 1 distinguishes the scoring and reporting procedures employed by the four evaluations. The concern in this category is how to array and record most meaningfully the scores obtained from the varied evidence-gathering techniques.

In placement evaluation—except when a student places out of a course—evidence should be reported in terms of profiles, patterns, or subscores on the objectives or characteristics in question, so that student mastery of each prerequisite skill or course objective can be viewed. Since placement is concerned with the extent to which a student possesses particular skills, abilities, or characteristics vis-à-vis those needed for effective functioning in a course, scoring and reporting techniques that sum disparate pieces of data do not provide the specificity necessary for accurate placement, except when students are placed out of a course based on their performance on a summative examination.

Since the results of formative evaluation are used to direct teachers' and students' activities while instruction is in progress, feedback must be highly specific. Consequently, scoring and reporting should be based on response patterns on items testing skills taught in relatively short instructional blocks. In formative evaluation, as in placement evaluation, a total score hides more than it reveals.

Diagnostic evaluation is based on teacher observation. Clearly, it is difficult, if not impossible, to quantify such observations. As a result, the concept of a score per se is not applicable. The most appropriate form for diagnostic data is a written, anecdotal report that summarizes the teacher's observations.

Standards Against Which Scores Are Compared

Scores by themselves are often meaningless. A set of standards against which to compare scores is needed for proper interpretation. Row 7 of Figure 1 shows that the different types of evaluation employ different standards in keeping with varying functions or purposes.

Standards are of two types—norm-referenced and criterion-referenced. In the former type, performance is judged relative to some larger group, usually the class as a whole. In the latter type, performance is judged relative to some absolute definition of mastery or adequacy. When we use summative evaluations to grade students we usually employ norm-referenced standards. That is, whether a student receives an A or a B is determined by how he performs in comparison with other students in the class. At one time or another all of us have had the experience of scoring 85 out of 100 on a test but receiving a C grade because most other students achieved higher than 90 on the test. "Grading on a curve" is another way of indicating norm-referenced standards.

Most placement, formative, and diagnostic evaluation data are judged in terms of criterion-referenced standards. Criteria of satisfactory performance are established prior to the evaluation and the evaluation results are compared with these criteria. For example, one might decide that placement in a particular course is dependent on mastery of each of eight prerequisite skills, or of any six of the eight. Placement with a particular teacher might depend on finding any four characteristics of the student that are similar to the teacher's characteristics. Or, the criterion for advancement to a succeeding topic in a course might be set at 90 percent mastery on the formative evaluation instrument testing mastery of the prior topic. Finally, one might decide that if a student manifests at least three symptoms consonant with a particular environmental, physical, or psychological difficulty, he will be referred for treatment. In each of these instances, the decisions made about an individual student depend only on his performance relative to the defined criterion. The performance of other students in the class is irrelevant when criterion-referenced standards are used. Placement, formative, and diagnostic evaluation represent situations when we are less interested in comparing a student with his peers than in studying him against independent criteria deemed indicative of acceptable learning or functioning.

Reliability

The reliability considerations for the evidence gathered under each evaluation approach are shown in row 8. Rather than dwell on particular types of reliability amenable to the different types of evaluation, we shall consider those characteristics of the evidence gathered that must be shown to be reliable. Traditional approaches to the question of reliability stress the need for consistent, accurate data if judgments made on the basis of the data are to be valuable. While we subscribe to such a point of view, we see differences in the stringency with which it can be applied. Basically, the consequences of the judgments should determine, to a great extent, the degree of reliability required.

In placement evaluation, in which the intent is to place a student at his proper instructional starting point, after which there is little latitude to "replace" him, the consequence of the decision is great. Thus, a high reliability is required of the instruments used to gather placement data. When placement decisions can be readily modified and systematic "replacing" is possible, the reliability considerations can be less stringent.

In formative evaluation, item response patterns must be demonstrated to be reliable, i.e., consistent, if instructional decisions are to be made with any degree of confidence. The reliability sought in diagnostic evaluation involves the recurrence of observed behavioral symptoms. The realm of diagnostic evaluation being what it is, however, particular observed symptoms can either disappear or become more pronounced over time. Therefore, our use of the term *recurrence* does not necessarily connote stability over time.

As is often the case in placing students, formative decisions can usually be rectified with relative ease. In diagnostic evaluation there is usually less harm in making an incorrect referral than in failing to refer at all. Thus, reliability constraints are less important in these types of evaluation. Summative decisions, however, are generally final. The results often follow a student throughout his academic career. Further, summative decisions made at particular points in a student's schooling are likely to serve the function of systematically reducing future options. A student who fails ninth grade algebra is unlikely, given present school organization and selection practices, to be admitted to college as a mathematics major. Because of the gravity of decisions made on the basis of summative evaluations, such evaluations should provide highly reliable, consistent data.

Validity

The final comparison, validity, is detailed in row 9. Since placement, formative, and summative evaluation are tied closely to the objectives of a course, the principal consideration in determining the validity of their evidence-gathering techniques is content validity—that is, whether the technique appropriately evaluates the objectives of instruction.

Less central, yet important, is the construct validity of placement and formative instruments. Matching students either to teachers or to particular instructional modes involves a construct or constructs hypothesized to be related to optimum placement. We might, for example, start out with the hunch that authoritarian teachers are best for authoritarian students. Determining whether our initial hunch is in fact borne out is a problem of construct validity. Similarly, the construct validity of a formative instrument that purports to measure a hierarchy of skills leading to a more general objective can be tested by determining whether students who fail an item testing a particular objective fail all succeeding items testing more complex objectives. These validity considerations are more in the realm of research concerns than in the realm of classroom concerns.

To discuss validity in diagnostic evaluation we have resurrected the term "face validity," not because the term itself is important, but rather because it is familiar to most evaluators and because it briefly describes the characteristic of the validity involved. The symptoms observed by the teacher are valid if they appear to be symptoms of psychological, physical, or environmental causes of learning disability. Teachers are not trained psychologists, social workers, or nurses. Their primary function, in this context, is to recognize symptoms. It is the trained specialist, to whom the teacher refers particular cases, who must determine whether the teacher's observations are valid.

SUMMARY

We have attempted here to indicate the multiplicity of purposes evaluation can have in the classroom context, and to view evaluation as a system that collects a variety of data, at different times, to facilitate different types of judgments. In the explication of the four types across the nine dimensions it should have become apparent to the reader that the notion of an evaluative system is an appropriate one, since many of the considerations inherent in one type of evaluation are applicable in carrying out other types. The four types proposed overlap and interact to some extent on all dimensions with the exception of purpose.

To reiterate, our intent is not to suggest that the individual teacher be responsible for the development and implementation of such a complete evaluation system; however, neither is it our intent to suggest that the individual teacher disregard a formal system of evaluation in favor of the more spontaneous and informal evaluation practices that have been operative for so long. What is needed is a careful consideration of how the four types of evaluation can be made available to the individual teacher. In addition, we must conceive of evaluation as involving a much broader role than simply grading student achievement at the end of instruction. The interaction between various parts of the evaluation system proposed here are consciously designed and intended to enhance student learning so that in the future less emphasis need be placed on making fine, often meaningless, distinctions between individuals on the basis of final classroom achievement.

REFERENCES
1. Airasian, P. W. "Formative Evaluation Instruments." *Irish Journal of Education,* 1968, *2*, 127–135.
2. Airasian, P. W. "The Role of Evaluation in Mastery Learning." In J. Block (Ed.), *Mastery Learning: Theory and Practice.* New York: Holt, Rinehart & Winston, 1971. Pp. 77–88.
3. Block, J. H. (Ed.) *Mastery Learning: Theory and Practice.* New York: Holt, Rinehart & Winston, 1971.
4. Bloom, B. S., Hastings, J. T., & Madaus, G. G. *Handbook on Formative and Summative Evaluation of Student Learning.* New York: McGraw-Hill, 1971.
5. Bracht, G. H. "The Relationship of Treatment Tasks, Personological Variables, and Dependent Variables to Aptitude-Treatment-Interaction." Unpublished doctoral dissertation, University of Colorado, 1969.
6. Cronbach, L. J. "Course Improvement Through Evaluation." *Teachers College Record,* 1963, *64*, 672–683.

7. Eisner, E. W. "Educational Objectives—Help or Hindrance?" *The School Review,* 1967, *75*, 250–260.
8. Grobman, H. (Ed.) *Evaluation Activities of Curriculum Projects.* American Educational Research Association Monograph Series on Curriculum Evaluation, No. 2. Chicago: Rand McNally, 1968.
9. Jackson, P. W. *Life in Classrooms.* New York: Holt, Rinehart & Winston, 1968.
10. Madaus, G. F. "The Cooperative Development of Evaluation Systems for Individualized Instruction." Keynote address to the annual Southeast Invitational Conference on Measurement in Education, University of Tennessee, Knoxville, Tennessee, October 3, 1969. (mimeo)
11. Scriven, M. "The Methodology of Evaluation." In R. Stake (Ed.), *Perspectives of Curriculum Evaluation.* American Educational Research Association Monograph Series on Curriculum Evaluation, No. 1. Chicago: Rand McNally, 1967. 39–83.
12. Stake, R. E. "The Countenance of Educational Evaluation." *Teachers College Record,* 1967, *68*, 523–540.
13. Thelen, H. "Matching Teachers and Pupils." *National Education Association Journal,* 1967, *56*, 18–20.
14. Tyler, R. W. *Constructing Achievement Tests.* Columbus: Ohio State Press, 1934.
15. Tyler, R. W. *Basic Principles of Curriculum and Instruction: Syllabus for Education 305.* Chicago: University of Chicago Press, 1950.

51 Reporting Student Progress: A Case for a Criterion-Referenced Marking System

Jason Millman

Two major trends in education have been increased implementation of individualized instruction[1] and greater emphasis by test specialists on criterion-referenced measurements. My primary purpose in this paper is to indicate how these trends invite a completely different format than that presently used for the reporting of school progress to students and to their parents.

INDIVIDUALIZING INSTRUCTION

Instruction can be individualized in two ways: pacing and branching. Linear programming is an example of individualizing instruction by permitting each student to go through a set of instructional materials at his own rate. Use of self-teaching materials effects differential progress. When individuals are permitted to learn at their own rate, the more able students will complete the instruction and demonstrate competence *many* times more quickly than the less able students.[2]

Providing alternative instructional materials is a second way to individualize instruction. This method may be implemented on a macro level (e.g., students study different elective courses) or on a more micro level (e.g., the particular way a student is taught a unit of instruction depends on his interests and learning style).[3] Of course, individual pacing and providing alternative instructional materials can be combined.

Regardless of how the instruction is individualized, the usual procedures of assessing student progress seem inappropriate. When students in a class are proceeding at their own rate or "doing their own thing" or both, the practice of assigning grades on the basis of the administration of a common achievement test is inapplicable.[4] More appropriate would be a report of an individual's own progress. These points will be elaborated in this article.

Reprinted from *Phi Delta Kappan*, 52 (4): 226–230 (December 1970), by permission of author and publisher.

CRITERION-REFERENCED MEASUREMENT

Since the writings of Ebel and Glaser on the subject[5] there has been increased attention to criterion-referenced measurement, which relates test performance to absolute standards rather than to the performance of others.

Criterion-referenced measures are those which are used to ascertain an individual's status with respect to some criterion, i.e., performance standard. It is because the individual is compared with some established criterion, rather than other individuals, that these measures are described as criterion-referenced. The meaningfulness of an individual score is not dependent on comparison to others.

. . . Norm-referenced measures are those which are used to ascertain an individual's performance in relationship to the performance of other individuals on the same measuring device. The meaningfulness of the individual score emerges from the comparison. It is because the individual is compared with some normative group that such measures are described as norm-referenced. Most standardized tests of achievement or intellectual ability can be classified as norm-referenced measures.[6]

An example of a criterion-referenced test is presented in Figure 1. These items were chosen because they constitute a representative set of situations which a student should deal with correctly if he is to demonstrate proficiency in the desired skill. Regardless of how his classmates perform, the student passes the test only if he answers all (or, possibly, nearly all) of the questions correctly. These same items could be part of a norm-referenced test. In such a case, they would have been selected because of their usefulness in discriminating among the students. How well a student does on such a norm-referenced test would be determined by comparing his score with those of his classmates.

A, B, C GRADING IS NORM-REFERENCED

The grading systems which use number or letter scales, as found in the vast majority of schools,[7] are indicators of the comparative performance of students and are devices for *ranking*. Thus, this system is not useful for indicating an individual's progress against performance criteria. Some teachers may object, arguing that their grades *rate* their students' command of course content or degree of fulfillment of predetermined course objectives. Consider these four arguments against such a position:

1. Teachers who say, "The test scores speak," and "I do *not* grade on a

Objective: Given a set of objects, the student will be able to identify the longest and/or shortest. (Words to be read aloud to the student.).

1. Put a line through the *shortest* boy.

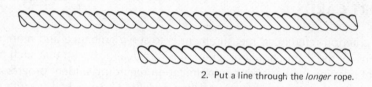

2. Put a line through the *longer* rope.

FIGURE 1.   Example of a Criterion-Referenced Measurement

curve," find themselves using adjustments to make the grade distributions more reasonable. These adjustments take such forms as giving another test, raising marks by some mysterious formula, making the next test easier, and altering grading standards. Naturally, a teacher's increased experience with what students in his school and in his course can do on his examinations reduces the extent of the adjustments necessary to insure that a reasonable curve will result.

2. There is a marked similarity between grade distributions found in high schools and those found in colleges having a different quality of students. If grades were assigned according to standards so that an A, in introductory physics for example, meant a certain proficiency, then the percentage of students earning an A should be substantially different at the different schools. This is not the case.

3. Perhaps the most convincing evidence to support the claim that A, B, C grading or one, two, three grading is norm-referenced grading is that as the quality of students entering any given college goes up over the years, as attested to by objective test data, the grade distributions of that college remain essentially unchanged.

4. Regardless of what the teacher feels the grade signifies, the students feel they are competing with each other, that is, that the grade is a measure of comparative achievement.

INSTRUCTIONAL GOALS AND MANAGEMENT

A key task of our schools is to maximize the amount of a subject each student has "mastered."[8] Indeed, a reason for having individualized instruction is to maximize achievement by appropriate pacing and provision of instructional materials. The rational management of such an individualized instructional system requires knowing whether each student can perform at some criterion level on measures of the component objectives of the system. Such criterion-referenced measurement characterizes the management of the well-known University of Pittsburgh Individually Prescribed Instruction system.[9]

REPORT CARDS

If criterion-referenced measurement is to serve guidance and monitoring functions for the instructional program, it is a logical next step that such measurement become the basis for communication regarding student progress. Not only could student records contain a listing of skills to be checked as proficiency is demonstrated, but so too could the reports going to the students and their parents.

The essential features of such a report card are: a listing of objectives (most likely abbreviated descriptions of tasks), space to indicate if proficiency has been demonstrated, and a checking system which identifies objectives achieved since the previous report. Since parents, quite reasonably, desire norm-referenced information, some grade designation *might* be included at the lower grades. For high school or junior college courses, skills for which proficiency is usually demonstrated may be differentiated from optional or supplementary skills. A sketch of the kind of report card being suggested is shown in Figure 2.

The number of skills shown on the report card will probably be less than the number used in the school record. For example, before the teacher would check "Understands dollar value of money," he may require identification of coins, converting coins to equivalent amounts of other coin values, counting dollar value of coin sets, and making change.

The report card should probably use objectives stated narrowly enough so that all students will have a chance during a marking period to demonstrate proficiency on tests relative to at least one objective.

The reporting system being suggested should not be confused with various self-marking plans which frequently have been advocated.[10] The mature student, however, may best be able to assess whether proficiency has been demonstrated on objectives covering hard-to-measure student qualities and skills.

MATHEMATICS
Grade Two

Skill	*Date*
Concepts	
Understands commutative property of addition (e.g., $4 + 3 = 3 + 4$)	*9/27*
Understands place value (e.g., $27 = 2$ tens $+ 7$ ones)	*10/3*
Addition	
Supplies missing addend under 10 (e.g., $3 + ? = 5$)	*10/8*
Adds three single-digit numbers	_____
Knows combinations 10 through 19	_____
*Adds two 2-digit numbers without carrying	_____
*Adds two 2-digit numbers with carrying	_____
Subtraction	
Knows combinations through 9	*10/4*
*Supplies missing subtrahend — under 10 (e.g., $6 - ? = 1$)	_____
*Supplies missing minuend — under 10 (e.g., $? - 3 = 4$)	_____
*Knows combinations 10 through 19	_____
*Subtracts two 2-digit numbers without borrowing	_____
Measurement	
Reads and draws clocks (up to quarter hour)	_____
Understands dollar value of money (coins up to $1.00 total)	_____
Geometry	
Understands symmetry	
Recognizes congruent plan figures — that is, figures which are identical except for orientation	_____
Graph Reading	
*Knows how to construct simple graphs	
*Knows how to read simple graphs	_____

*In Jefferson Elementary School, these skills are usually learned toward the end of grade two. Some children who need more than average time to learn mathematics may not show proficiency on tests of these skills until they are in grade three.

FIGURE 2. Report Card Based on a System of Criterion-Referenced Measurement.

IS THE PLAN FEASIBLE?

It is not reasonable to expect the typical school to itemize, from scratch, a comprehensive set of objectives and to construct related criterion-referenced measures. In the elementary school, students often use workbooks containing exercises which could serve as criterion-referenced tests. The tasks these students are expected to perform are isomorphic to the objectives.

Further, the objectives of many new curricula have already been identified and test items covering these objectives have been provided.[11] More frequently the staff in individual school systems is constructing "behaviorally stated" objectives in conjuction with learning packages covering these objectives.[12] Commercial firms are now including tests in their learning packages.[13]

The most ambitious effort in this regard is the Instructional Objectives Exchange, which was created to perform the following functions:

Serve as a clearinghouse through which the nation's schools can exchange instructional objectives, thereby capitalizing on the developmental efforts of other educators rather than being obliged to commence afresh the development of objectives. Collect and, when necessary, develop measuring techniques suitable for assessing the attainment of the objectives available through the Exchange. Develop properly formulated instructional objectives in important areas where none currently exists, that is, fill the gaps not covered by available objectives.[14]

In connection with an ESEA Title III project, 30,000 items have been produced, accompanied by the objectives they are measuring.[15] Thus, the availability of statements of objectives and criterion-referenced items permits the teacher or school staff to *select* those objectives or items most relevant to their situation rather than to *construct* them.

Even admitting the feasibility of selecting and preparing objectives and tests (a *relatively* fixed, one-time-only expenditure of time), the question of how to operate the system remains.

When instruction is individualized, students must assume an increased responsibility for their own activities. It is reasonable to expect that at least the older students can assume responsibility for self-administering the criterion-referenced tests and, in some cases, scoring them. The teacher need only place a single checkmark (or date) to record the fact that proficiency has been demonstrated. At reporting periods, the teacher merely transfers these checks to the cards.

When considering feasibility, it should be remembered that a school system need not convert to the criterion-referenced reporting system in all subject areas at once. A school system, or an individual school or teacher, may choose to utilize the criterion-referenced reporting system first in subject areas where the defining and measuring of objectives is easiest: These areas would include mathematics and those vocationally oriented courses in which a large segment of the objectives involves performance skills.

ADVANTAGES

The emphasis on proficiency forces the school staff to focus on both instructional process and outcomes rather than on process alone and to view formal education "as an enterprise which is designed to *change* human beings so that they are better, wiser, more efficient."[16] The instructional means are judged by the ends achieved. In these days when decentralization brings parents closer to the schools, when parents demand more information, when school bond issues are being rejected because of ignorance about the school's benefit as well as for financial reasons, and when accountability is in fashion, the staffs of our schools would be well advised to demonstrate that the modifications they wish to promote do occur.

The report card format suggested in this paper permits a degree of communication and accountability to the parent not possible with other systems of reporting. Every student will be shown to be learning, and both the parent and student will know better what has been learned and what can now be done.

Besides change of focus, other advantages of a criterion-referenced system have been listed elsewhere.[17] These include improved student attitudes where the less wholesome competition for grades gives way to competition (frequently within oneself) to acquire proficiencies in much the same way that a scout earns his badges.

NOTES

1. For example, the *Health, Education, and Welfare News* (November 9, 1969) reports that nearly 50,000 children are learning mathematics mostly on their own with the University of Pittsburgh Individually Prescribed Instruction materials.

2. Benjamin S. Bloom, "Learning for Mastery," *Evaluation Comment*, May, 1968, 12 pp. (published by the UCLA Center for the Study of Evaluation of Instructional Programs); and Robert Glaser, "Adapting the Elementary School Curriculum to Individual Performance," in *Proceedings of the 1967 Invitational Conference on Testing Problems*, Benjamin Bloom, chairman, Princeton, N.J.: Educational Testing Service, 1967, pp. 3–36.

3. See, for example, John C. Flanagan, "Functional Education for the Seventies," *Phi Delta Kappan*, September, 1967, pp. 27–32.

4. This point was made by Henry M. Brickell, who writes: " . . . If the innovation individualizes instruction in such a way that students begin to move through the same material at variable rates of speed controlled by their mastery of the material, report cards which tell parents about the student's *degree of success* in learning the content (usually expressed as letter grades indicating class standing) should have been replaced by new report cards which tell parents about the student's *rate of progress*." From "Appraising the Effects of Innovations in Local Schools," in Ralph W. Tyler, ed., *Educational Evaluation: New Roles, New Means*. Chicago: National Society for the Study of Education (68th Yearbook, Part II), 1969, pp. 301–302.

5. Robert L. Ebel, "Content Standard Test Scores," *Educational and Psychological Measurement*, Spring, 1962, pp. 15-25; and Robert Glaser, "Instructional Technology and the Measurement of Learning Outcomes: Some Questions," *American Psychologist*, August, 1963, pp. 519–21.

6. W. James Popham and T. R. Husek, "Implications of Criterion-Referenced Measurement," *Journal of Educational Measurement*, Spring, 1969, pp. 1–9.

7. "Reporting Pupil Progress," *NEA Research Bulletin*, October, 1969, pp. 75–76.

8. See, especially, Bloom, *op. cit.* The ungraded school, an administrative device to facilitate adapting the curriculum and modifying instruction to the individual learner, is said to be based on the assumptions that "up to a certain point a 'slow learner,' if taught appropriately and given more time, can learn the same things that more capable students do" (an assumption of the Carroll Model of School Learning which was followed in the Bloom article) and that "up to that certain point all students *should* learn the same things." Mauritz Johnson, Jr., *Grouping in Graded and Ungraded Schools*, Cornell University Curriculum and Instruction Series, No. 4, pp. 15–16.

9. William W. Cooley and Robert Glaser, "An Information and Management System for Individually Prescribed Instruction," technical report, University of Pittsburgh Learning Research and Development Center, 1968.

10. See, for example, Peter G. Filene, "Self-Grading: An Experiment in Learning," *Journal of Higher Education.* June, 1969, pp. 451–58; and Ronald J. Burke, "Some Preliminary Data on the Use of Self-Evaluations and Peer Ratings in Assigning University Course Grades," *Journal of Educational Research,* July/August, 1969, pp. 444–48.

11. For example, objectives of the Wisconsin Design for Reading Skill Development, an individualized reading system for the elementary school, are assessed through commercially available criterion-referenced tests. These objectives and tests were developed by the Wisconsin Research and Development Center for Cognitive Learning and are distributed by National Computer Systems, 4401 W. 76th Street, Minneapolis, Minnesota 55435.

12. See, for example, three articles on an educational system for the 70's, *Phi Delta Kappan,* December, 1969, pp. 199–210.

13. For example, Individual Mathematics Programme Kits, Rigby Ltd., Australian Council for Educational Research, Frederick St., Hawthorne, Victoria 3122 Australia; and Individual Mathematics: Drill and Practice Kits, L. W. Singer Company, Westminster, Md.

14. W. James Popham, *Instructional Objectives Exchange,* Los Angeles: UCLA Graduate School of Education, p. 1 (no date).

15. Evaluation for Individual Instruction, Downers Grove School District 99, 1400 West Maple Ave., Downers Grove, Ill. 60515.

16. W. James Popham, "Focus on Outcomes: A Guiding Theme of ES '70 Schools," *Phi Delta Kappan,* December, 1969, p. 208.

17. William Clark Trow, "On Marks, Norms, and Proficiency Scores," *Phi Delta Kappan,* December, 1966, pp. 171–73.

52 Promotional Policies

George J. Mouly

The oldest attempt at dealing with individual differences in the classroom revolved around what might be called rigid standards of grade placement. A child was retained in a given grade until he had mastered its content and, conversely, he could get a double promotion if he had already mastered enough of the content of the grade following that which he had just completed.

Acceleration was particularly common in the old one-room school where a gifted child could go through the first eight grades in perhaps four or five years. In fact, repeated double promotions could result in college graduation perhaps as early as age fifteen. It has been frowned upon in recent years on the argument that it overemphasizes the intellectual and the academic at the expense of the other phases of the child's all-round development and that the accelerated child may become a misfit from the standpoint of physical, social, and emotional adjustment.

At the other end of the continuum are those whose work is below par and who, according to the older view on the subject, needed to be retained lest they got hopelessly bogged down and interfered with the progress of students in the next grade. Before we proceed to a discussion of the validity of this position, let us consider the question: "Why fail students?" Whereas the specific answer to that question varies, the policy of failure "where warranted" is said by its advocates to serve three important functions:

(a) To motivate students who apparently will work only when the threat of failure is kept constantly before them. This is not true. Otto and Melby (1935), for example, found no difference in the achievement of children threatened with failure and those assured of promotion—and fortunately so, for it would be a sad commentary on the appropriateness of our curriculum and our methods if it were. Failure is a last-ditch attempt at motivation and it ought to be possible for the few teachers who still rely heavily on fear of failure as a motivational device to locate more positive measures.

(b) To maintain standards. Some people feel that the high school is losing its academic reputation by graduating students who have been carried along for years, and community groups have on occasions demanded a return to the "good old standards" where one did not graduate without a certain amount of knowledge. They overlook the fact that the solution in those days consisted of forcing the student to drop out, sometimes long before he got to high school.

(c) To reduce the variability within the classroom. It is argued that his increased mental development and the general overview of the work will enable the child who is retained to do much better as he repeats the grade. This has not been realized in practice. As early as 1911, Keyes showed that repeaters do worse, rather than better, than they did the first time. Cook (1941) and Klene and Branson (1929) likewise showed that potential repeaters profited more from being promoted to the next grade than from being retained. Thus, Cook, in his comparison of schools with rigid standards as represented by an average retardation of nearly two years in Grade 7 with a matched sample of schools having liberal promotional policies with a corresponding average retardation of only .17 of a year, found a significant difference in achievement favoring the schools with lenient promotions; but he found no difference in the range of individual differences in the two sets of schools. Coffield and Blommers (1956) found that children who reached Grade 7 in eight years (because of failure) knew less than comparable children who had been promoted. Evidently, the standards of the school cannot be raised by accumulating the dullards any more than the standards of a ball team can be raised by keeping the unfit for an extra year or two. Of course, emphasis in school must be on the individual child but, if our concern *has* to be for the standards of the school, let us at least be logical and eliminate, not retard.

Also to be considered, in view of the modern emphasis on the total child, are the effects of retention on his personality. Although the evidence is not entirely conclusive, the consensus supports the statement by Goodlad (1952, p. 449) that "throughout the body of evidence runs a consistent pattern: undesirable growth characteristics and unsatisfactory school progress are more closely associated with nonpromoted children than with promoted slow-learning children." In view of his need to maintain a consistent self-image, the child who is retained is likely to see himself as dumb, tough, or unconcerned, as many teachers who have repeaters in their class can readily attest. Having been separated from the group to which they belong and being out of step physically, socially, and emotionally with the new group, these children find it difficult to get accepted and often react to the whole situation with discouragement, hostility, and misbehavior.

Evidence points to the fact that retention is not effective in reducing the range of individual differences and that it tends to have negative effects on academic achievement and personality development. It does not follow, however, that children should never be retained; no doubt a child who is retarded physically, socially, and emotionally as well as mentally and academically, may profit from being put into a somewhat younger age group; each case must be evaluated on its own merits. The decision to promote or to retain should be made only after consideration of all the factors—not just the academic—and generally the teacher should have to show cause why the child should be retained in terms of how he can be helped more by retention than by promotion. The important thing is not to promote or to retain but rather what the teacher does after having made this decision, for the element of failure is not eliminated by universal promotion.

NOTES

Coffield, W. H. and P. Blommers. 1956. "Effects of Non-promotion on Educational Achievement in the Elementary School," *Journal of Educational Psychology,* 47:235–250.

Cook, Walter W. 1941. "Some Effects of the Maintenance of High Standards of Promotion," *Elementary School Journal,* 41:430–437.

Goodlad, John I. 1952. "Research and Theory Regarding Promotion and Non-promotion," *Elementary School Journal,* 53:150–155.

Klene, V. and E. P. Branson. 1929. "Trial Promotion Versus Failure," *Educational Research Bulletin* (Los Angeles City Schools), 8:6–11.

Otto, Henry J. and E. O. Melby. 1935. "An Attempt to Evaluate the Threat of Failure as a Factor in Achievement," *Elementary School Journal,* 35:588–596.

53 Accountability—The Next Deadly Nostrum in Education?

Robert J. Nash

As educators, we have had a history of applying pet nostrums to nagging problems. In the past, we have been piously intoxicated over such lofty educational ideals as adjusting the child to the society; recognizing individual differences; inquiry, exploration, and discovery; team teaching; and open classrooms. Presently, we are exhorting each other to adopt flexible modular scheduling and differentiated staffing. At this time, another potential nostrum is emerging in American education, and it has been the focus of no less than seven articles in a national journal.[1] The ideal—accountability—usually can be heard in hushed conversation among properly reverent educators, or in angry polemic among politicians, whenever each group feels the need to invoke an incontrovertible authority to support its latest educational proposals.

As a guiding ideal, the concept of accountability is rooted deeply in the American value configuration.[2] Few can challenge the necessity of holding institutions and their personnel responsible for what they purport to do. Americans always have believed that their institutions ought to exist for the benefit of their clients, and, until these institutions can prove themselves responsible to their clients, they are always suspect. Consequently, if schools function to teach children basic skills and knowledge, educators must be held accountable if these things are not learned.

However, in spite of the undeniable cogency of accountability, we are in danger of becoming uncritical devotees to an ideal which, at this time, cries out for more careful examination. If we are to avoid relegating accountability to the educational junkpile of quack remedies, we must begin to raise penetrating questions regarding its underlying assumptions and its implications for the practice of education. What follows is an attempt to raise four basic, interrelated questions about a concept which elementary and secondary educators are being asked to embrace as the operative norm of their professional activities.

First, who is accountable? According to the advocates of accountability, educators must be held responsible if children fail to learn. Students are to be perceived as clients who have an indisputable right to learn the skills and knowledge which educators have been promising for years.[3] Consequently, if learning fails to occur in the classroom, it is not the student who has failed—it is

Reprinted from *School & Society*, 99 (2337): 501–504 (December 1971), by permission of author and publisher.

the educational caretaker who has failed. The concept of accountability shifts the learning responsibility from student "input" to professional "output."

The basic fallacy in this line of reasoning is the assumption that educators can assess, with any kind of precision, where proximate, intermediate, and final responsibility is lodged whenever a child fails to learn the knowledge, skills, and behaviors which he has been promised. At this stage in the research on learning theory, educators know painfully little about the intricate and pervasive influence which external forces have on motivation and learning outcomes in conventional public school settings. Until we understand more about the learning process and the complex interrelationships which cohere among the home, the community, the peer group, the media, and the school, we can not fix accountability for learning failure exclusively on the teacher or the administrator.

However, this is not to say that educators never must be held accountable for other kinds of failures. Presently, we are thinking of accountability only when students have failed to learn how to read, write, and compute. But, if accountability is to mean anything, it must be stretched to indict educators whenever they make fallacious assumptions about what is important for students to learn, as well as what must be omitted from the curriculum in the name of accountability. Also, we must stretch accountability to include those learning failures which occur after students have left their classrooms. We are producing a public which increasingly refuses to read, write, or compute anything after it leaves the formal educational setting. If this is true, how do we sort out the precise degree of complicity in frustrating post-classroom learning which each educator in the teaching-learning nexus bears? How do we determine accountability in any meaningful way when so many cultural institutions—and their personnel—can be seen to be mis-educative, in the sense that they have helped to contribute to the deterioration of learning after students have escaped from the classroom?

Second, for what are we accountable? Perhaps the single most serious limitation of accountability, at the present time, resides in the kinds of learnings for which we are becoming responsible. Because it is easier for us to assess accountability for learnings which are most conducive to measurement, we are beginning to consider only certain kinds of knowledge and skills as worthy of being conveyed to learners. We are emphasizing only those learnings which are concrete, occupational, and capable of being programmed into objective, behavioral sequences. Those learnings which Paul Goodman and John Dewey have called "incidental" or "collateral" are being ignored, largely because of their lack of specificity and selectivity. In the language of systems analysis—one of the more influential modes currently being used to describe the procedures of accountability—we are looking only for those results in education which are identifiable and measurable.

The issue ranges far beyond the usual sneering reference to the cognitive-affective dichotomy in education. The principal failure of accountability-centered curricula is their quantitative predisposition to overlook or to depreciate those learnings which are the outgrowth of students' incidental experiences with such personal concerns as loneliness, anxiety, sexual and drug conflicts, and hostility.[4] Also, Haberman has implied that, in the name of behavioral objectives and the "notation of observable skills," teachers might tend to limit students' learnings to the technicalities of a subject such as mathematics, rather than to explore spontaneously the "basic and real" learnings implicit in subjects such as art, music, theatre, dance, and even experimentation in communal creation and living.[5] One only has to look at the current evangelical promotion of behavioral objectives and performance criteria in colleges of education to get a sense for the direction which accountability is taking. Potential learning experiences which might derive from the personal, emotional, or valuational dimensions of human life often are dismissed by enthusiasts for accountability because such experiences resist classification and prediction structures,[6] or because they frustrate efforts to be translated into the blank torpor of systems or behavioral jargon.

If we are to be held accountable for restricting learning experiences only to what can be measured, every person who advocates accountability bears some degree of blame. Goodlad has said that genuine educational innovation demands much more in the way of measurement than our usual, archaic criteria and our timeworn assessment instruments. In fact, Goodlad argues that, if educational innovations are truly radical, they will have objectives which conventional evaluative instruments are incapable of measuring.[7] Therefore, to the extent that accountability supporters ignore or devalue learnings which could emerge from radical experiments in painting, dancing, self- and social awareness, and communication with peers, in the name of "measurable" learnings, they are all equally guilty. As educators, we must be held accountable whenever we limit our curricula to the existing realities which can be measured, while we ignore those possibilities for learning which cannot be measured. The classroom teacher who assiduously has cleansed his curriculum of all non-measurable learnings by zealously applying performance criteria and behavioral objectives is as culpable as the administrator who has insisted intractably that his teachers translate their objectives into rigorously specified learning outcomes. Also, performance contracting firms which are providing the hardware for individualizing instruction are as much to blame for ignoring the value of non-measurable learnings as are colleges of education which are indoctrinating teacher-trainees with behavioral objectives and performance criteria as the exclusive indicators of learning and success.

Third, to whom are we accountable? As educators, we ought to be accountable primarily to those clients we directly serve—students, parents, and taxpayers. However, educators only can be held accountable if they have been instrumental in helping to determine educational policy. Rarely, if ever, have teachers been consulted about the issues and practices which concern them most vitally. Until teachers have been given a voice in those crucial decisions which determine educational policy, teacher accountability always will be an unfair procedure. It is simply unreasonable to ask classroom teachers to be accountable to their clients when educators for so long have been rendered impotent by politicians, school boards, administrators, and other external sources.[8]

Often, when external sources obtrude upon the formal educational procedure, the accountability begins to shift in subtle ways. External accountability often entails external standards, far removed from the purview of the educator. For example, in July, 1970, the Office of Economic Opportunity announced that it would fund six private firms to serve 16 states as performance contractors. The total cost to the government was $5,600,000.[9] Whenever the Federal government makes such a substantial capital investment in local educational matters, there is always the probability that the determination of accountability criteria will shift from the local community to a national office. The ever-present danger is that the educational needs of children and parents will be subordinated to what a national authority thinks a community's needs ought to be.

One alarming harbinger of the direction which the Federal government might like public school education to take was suggested recently in an obscure news release.[10] In his first major speech, the new U.S. Commissioner of Education, Sidney P. Marland, maintained that the country needs a revamped educational system premised on two objectives: training each student for "salable skills" and getting students into college. One unsettling implication of Marland's remarks is that, in the future, educators could be held accountable by the Federal government if the schools do not emphasize careerism or college preparation in their programs. In the event that children, parents, and educators were to resist the unilateral imposition—by any external force—of these kinds of learning foci, then it is possible that schools could be denied Federal funding if it were available.

Fourth, when are we accountable? There is always another meaning implied by accountability. We are accountable when we are the cause of something. In order to determine accountability in the causal sense, we must strive to be aware of the normative implications of our educational activities. Also, we must strive to understand as many of the unintended outcomes of those activities as it is humanly possible to determine.[11] Within this broader normative framework, then, we are accountable whenever we convey intended or unintended values which are not made explicit, and which are not the object of intensive critical scrutiny.

For example, it makes little sense to speak of responsibility to our clients solely because we are teaching them to read, write, and compute. If, as an unintended outcome, we also are producing what Herbert Marcuse has called "moronized, dehumanized, and one-dimensional" consumer-voters, or what C. Wright Mills has called "happy robots," we must bear the burden of accountability for cultivating a bourgeois mentality which is characterized by an excessive functionality and an excessive competitiveness.

An American sociologist, Philip Slater, has pointed out that we still are acting as if the core of the American culture is based on an assumption of scarcity. We are teaching students to compete with one another in order to develop "salable skills" so that they might accumulate scarce material resources. According to Slater, the flaw in this assumption is that scarcity is the spurious invention of an economic system content mainly on perpetuating itself. And so we continue to produce an "educated" public which is anxious and suspicious because it has been taught to pursue hysterically so-called "scarce" commodities—even though it occasionally finds itself in the position of having killed someone to avoid sharing a meal which turns out to be too large to eat alone.[12]

We must begin to insist on accountability, not only when the transmission of basic skills and knowledge is concerned, but whenever we are unwilling to examine critically the cultural assumptions upon which the scarcity ethic is based. So, too, must we be held accountable whenever we cause students to accept racist, militaristic, and acquisitive assumptions about the world in which they live. As educators, we must be held accountable whenever we foster the development of expansiveness, competitiveness, achievement, profit, and mobility drives in our students, to the exclusion of values such as gentleness, kindliness, generosity, reflectiveness, and simplicity.[13] In brief, we must begin to push accountability to its furthest moral limits.

At the present time, for example, nobody has asked that Commissioner Marland be held accountable for his reference to general education as "irrelevant pap," or his exhortation that, henceforth, all educators must teach students to develop "salable skills" and "the proper attitude toward work. . . ."[14] When perceived within the broader framework of moral accountability, such sentiments could contribute to a whole series of unintended consequences—the least of which might be to produce an acquisitive citizenry which eschews liberal or general education because of its "irrelevance" to the pursuit of material wealth. Marland's permutations of accountability exemplify perhaps the most deadly distortion to which this educational ideal can be subjected. What is most disturbing is not Marland's facile rejection of non-occupational or non-college preparatory studies as ornamental marginalia in public school education. What is most seriously distressing is his subtle use of accountability to maintain and to perpetuate education and the social system as they already exist. If educators ever are to overcome the mindlessness of their endeavors, they must cease issuing prescriptive dicta on the desirability of preparing people to assume the "proper" attitude toward work, or to increase college board scores so that students can gain access to the most prestigious colleges. Silberman has stressed the importance of thinking profoundly about education's basic purposes, and questioning relentlessly the most entrenched educational practices, if we ever are to create a more humanely responsive social order.[15] To the extent that accountability can be made to serve Silberman's vision for education, the concept is potentially valuable. But when accountability is used to maintain an economic and educational status quo which continues to flourish in spite of its inherent destructiveness of human potential, the concept is bankrupt.

In conclusion, if we continue to use accountability as a shallow catchword, it is destined to become but another educational nostrum—which will prove finally to be as evanescent and as perishable as all the nostrums which have preceded it. If, however, we begin to hold ourselves accountable for purposes which are always larger than skill and knowledge proficiencies, accountability could prove to be a fecund educational principle. Ultimately, the most conclusive test of accountability will be whether educators have helped to produce the humanely responsive people who are needed to create a humanely responsive social order.

NOTES

1. Myron Lieberman, ed., special section on accountability, *Phi Delta Kappan,* 52:193–239, December, 1970.
2. Francis L. K. Hsu, *The Study of Literate Civilizations* (New York: Holt, Rinehart and Winston, 1969), p. 79.
3. Fred M. Hechinger, "Accountability: A Way to Measure the Job Done by Schools," *The New York Times,* Feb. 14, 1971, p. 7.
4. See Martin Engel, "The Humanities and the Schools," *Teachers College Record,* 72:239–248, December, 1970.
5. Martin Haberman, "Behavioral Objectives: Bandwagon or Breakthrough?" *Journal of Teacher Education,* 19:91–94, Spring, 1968.
6. See Ian McNett, "Assessing College Effectiveness," *Change,* 3:13-14, January–February,1971.
7. John Goodlad, "Thought, Invention, and Research in the Advancement of Education," in Charles Silberman, *Crisis in the Classroom: The Remaking of American Education* (New York: Random House, 1970), p. 256.
8. See Helen Bain, "Some Misgivings About Teacher Accountability," *Parents' Magazine,* 46:40, March, 1971.
9. "Businesses as Teachers Are Paid for Results," in "Annual Educational Review," *The New York Times,* Jan. 11, 1971, p. 68.
10. "U. S. Education Chief Urges New Educational System," *Boston Sunday Globe,* Feb. 7, 1971, p. 10-A.
11. See James B. Macdonald and Bernice J. Wolfson, "A Case Against Behavioral Objectives," mimeographed, College of Education, University of Wisconsin—Milwaukee, 1970.
12. Philip Slater, *The Pursuit of Loneliness: American Culture at the Breaking Point* (Boston: Beacon Press, 1970), pp. 96–118.
13. See Jules Henry, *Culture Against Man* (New York: Vintage Books, 1965), pp. 13–15.
14. *Boston Sunday Globe, loc. cit.*
15. *Crisis in the Classroom, op. cit.,* pp. 1–49.

54 Interaction Analysis

Edmund J. Amidon

Interaction Analysis is a system for describing and analyzing teacher-pupil verbal interaction. Although this particular approach has been used for classroom research for nearly twenty years, its use has become widespread only during the last four years. It has found its way into many different kinds of educational programs—both research and developmental. Basically, Interaction Analysis has been used to help quantify teacher verbal behavior. The system can also be used to study the relationship between teaching style and pupil achievement.

A recent application of Interaction Analysis has been in teacher education. It has proven useful in educational psychology and education courses as a tool for analyzing teacher behavior. Research on teacher-pupil interaction patterns has also provided the basis for education or educational psychology courses concerned with the teacher's role and behavior in the classroom. It is also a valuable tool in courses concerned with observation skills. The greatest use of Interaction Analysis has probably been in student teaching or teaching internships. In such activities, the tool is used for several basic purposes: (1) developing skill in observation of teaching; (2) providing a tool for the analysis of teaching; (3) providing a tool for feedback about one's teaching; (4) setting a framework for practicing and learning specific teaching skills; and (5) providing a framework for conceptualizing and developing various teaching styles. Inservice teacher education projects employing Interaction Analysis are also geared toward these objectives.

Projects testing Interaction Analysis in teacher education have demonstrated that the use of Interaction Analysis as a teacher training tool results in specific changes in teacher behavior—teachers have usually become more accepting and less critical. Their classes are also characterized by a greater number of student initiated comments.

In Interaction Analysis observation, all teacher statements are classified as either indirect or direct. This classification gives central attention to the amount of freedom granted the student by the teacher. Therefore, in a given situation a teacher has a choice. He can be direct, minimizing the freedom of the student to respond, or he can be indirect, maximizing such freedom. His choice, conscious or unconscious, depends upon many factors, among which are his perceptions of the classroom interaction and the goals of the particular learning situation.

To make total classroom behavior or interaction meaningful, Interaction

Reprinted from *Theory into Practice*, 7 (5): 159–163 (December 1968), by permission of author and publisher.

Analysis also provides for the categorizing of student talk. A third major section, that of silence or confusion, is included to account for the time spent in behavior other than that which can be classified as either teacher or student talk.

All statements in the classroom, then, are categorized into one of three major sections: (1) teacher talk, (2) student talk, and (3) silence, confusion, or anything other than teacher or student talk. [See Figure 1.]

The larger sections of teacher and student verbal behavior are subdivided to

TEACHER TALK	INDIRECT INFLUENCE	1. *ACCEPTS FEELING:* accepts and clarifies the feeling tone of the students in a nonthreatening manner. Feelings may be positive or negative. Predicting or recalling feelings is included. 2. *PRAISES OR ENCOURAGES:* praises or encourages student action or behavior. Jokes that release tension, but not at the expense of another individual; nodding head, or saying "um hm?" or "go on" are included. 3. *ACCEPTS OR USES IDEAS OF STUDENTS:* clarifies, builds, or develops ideas suggested by a student. As teacher brings more of his own ideas into play, shift to Category 5.
	DIRECT INFLUENCE	4. *ASKS QUESTIONS:* asks a question about content or procedure with the intent that a student answer. 5. *LECTURING:* gives facts or opinions about content or procedures; expresses his own ideas; asks rhetorical questions. 6. *GIVING DIRECTIONS:* directions, commands, or orders with which a student is expected to comply. 7. *CRITICIZING OR JUSTIFYING AUTHORITY:* statements intended to change student behavior from nonacceptable to acceptable pattern; bawling someone out; stating why the teacher is doing what he is doing; extreme self–reference.
STUDENT TALK		8. *STUDENT TALK–RESPONSE:* talk by students in response to teacher. Teacher initiates the contact or solicits student statement. 9. *STUDENT TALK–INITIATION:* talk by students, which they initiate. If "calling on" student is only to indicate who may talk next, observer must decide whether student wanted to talk. If he did, use this category.
		10. *SILENCE OR CONFUSION:* pauses, short periods of silence, and periods of confusion in which communication cannot be understood by observer.

FIGURE 1. Summary of Categories for Interaction Analysis

make the total pattern of teacher-pupil interaction more meaningful. The two subdivisions for teacher verbal behavior, indirect and direct teacher talk, are further divided into categories: (1) accepting feeling, (2) praising or encouraging, (3) accepting ideas, and (4) asking questions. Direct influence is divided into three categories: (5) lecturing, (6) giving directions, and (7) criticizing or justifying authority. Student talk is divided into only two categories: (8) responding to teacher, and (9) initiating talk. All are mutually exclusive; yet together, are totally inclusive of all verbal interaction occurring in the classroom. A description of these categories is described in Figure 1.

There is no scale implied by the numbers. Each number is classificatory; it designates a particular kind of communication event. To write these numbers down during observation is to enumerate—not to judge a position on a scale.

Interaction Analysis, originally used as a research tool, is employed by a trained observer to collect reliable data regarding classroom behavior as a part of a research project.

The system is especially meaningful as an inservice training device for teachers. It may be employed by a teacher either as he observes someone else teach or as he categorizes a tape recording of his own classroom behavior. In either case, the method is the same.

Every three seconds the observer writes down the category number of the interaction he has just observed. He records these numbers in sequence in a column, usually about twenty numbers per minute; thus, at the end of a period of time, he will have several long columns of numbers. It is important to keep the tempo as steady as possible, but even more crucial is to be accurate. The observer may also make marginal notes from time to time to explain classroom happenings as analysis is developed.

The observer stops classifying whenever classroom activity is changed so that observing is inappropriate, when, for example, there are various groups working around the classroom or when children are working in workbooks or doing silent reading. He usually draws a line under the recorded numbers, makes a note of the new activity, and resumes categorizing when the total class discussion continues. The observer always identifies the kind of class activity he is observing—the reading group in the elementary school is obviously different from an informal discussion period, a review of subject matter, a period of supervised seat work, teacher-directed discussion, introduction of new material, or evaluation of a completed unit. Such diverse activities may be expected to show different types of teacher-pupil interaction, even when guided by the same teacher. A shift to a new activity should also be noted.

A thorough knowledge of the categories and much practice to achieve accuracy are basic to the use of this technique for analyzing teacher-pupil interaction.

There is a method of recording the sequence of classroom events so that certain facts become readily apparent. This consists of entering the sequence of numbers into a 10-row by 10-column table, called a matrix (see Table 1). The generalized sequence of the teacher-pupil interaction can be examined readily in this matrix. How an observer would classify and record in the matrix what occurs in a classroom is illustrated in the following example.

A fifth-grade teacher is beginning a social studies lesson. The observer has been sitting in the classroom for several minutes and has begun to get some idea of the general climate. The teacher begins, "Boys and girls, please open your social studies books to page 5." (Observer classifies this as a 6, followed by a 10 because of the period of silence and confusion as the children try to find the page.)

Then, the teacher says, "Jimmy, we are waiting for you. Will you please turn your book to page 5?" (Observer records a 7 and a 6.)

"I know now," continues the teacher, "that some of us had a little difficulty with, and were a little disturbed by, the study of this chapter yesterday; I think that today we are going to find it more exciting and interesting." (Observer records two 1's, reacting to feeling.)

"Now, has anyone had a chance to think about what we discussed yesterday?" (Observer records a 4 for a question.)

A student answers, "I thought about it, and it seems to me that the reason we are in so much trouble in Southeast Asia is that we really haven't had a chance to understand the ways of the people who live there." (Observer records three 9's.)

The teacher responds by saying, "Good, I am glad that you suggested that, John. Now let me see if I understand your idea completely. You have suggested that if we had known the people better in Southeast Asia, we might not be in the trouble we are in today." (This is classified as a 2, followed by two 3's.)

Second

First	1	2	3	4	5	6	7	8	9	10	
1	1			1							
2			1								
3			1							1	
4									1		
5											
6	1									1	
7						1					
8											
9		1							2		
10						1	1				Matrix Total
Total	2	1	2	1	0	2	1	0	3	2	14
%											

TABLE 1. Sample Interaction Matrix

The observer has now classified the following sequence of numbers in this fashion (the use of a 10 at the beginning and end of the sequence is explained in the discussion that follows):

$$
\begin{array}{ll}
& 10 \;)\; \text{1st pair} \\
\text{2nd pair } (& 6 \\
& 10 \;)\; \text{3rd pair} \\
\text{4th pair } (& 7 \\
& 6 \;) \\
(& 1 \\
& 1 \;) \\
(& 4 \\
& 9 \;) \\
(& 9 \\
& 9 \;) \\
(& 2 \\
& 3 \;) \\
(& 3 \\
& 10
\end{array}
$$

Tabulations are now made in the matrix to represent pairs of numbers. Notice in the above listing that the numbers have been marked off in pairs—the first pair is 10-6; the second is 6-10, etc. The particular cell in which tabulation of the pair of numbers is made is determined by using the first number in the pair to indicate the row and the second number in the pair for the column. Thus, 10-6 would be shown by a tally in the cell formed by row 10 and column 6. The second pair, 6-10, would be shown in the cell formed by row 6 and column 10. The third pair, 10-7, is entered into the cell, row 10 and column 7. Each pair of numbers overlaps with the previous pair, and each number, except the first and the last, is used twice. This is the reason that a 10 is entered as the first number and last number in the record. This number is chosen because it is convenient to assume that each record began and ended with silence. This procedure also permits the total of each column to equal the total of the corresponding row.

Checking the tabulations in the matrix for accuracy is easily done by noting that there should be one less tally in the matrix than there are numbers entered in the original observation record (N-1). In this example, there are 15 numbers and the total number of tallies in the matrix is 14. This tabulation is shown in Table 1.

Ordinarily a separate matrix is made for each specific lesson or major activity. If the observer is categorizing forty minutes of arithmetic and twenty minutes of social studies, he makes one matrix for the arithmetic and another for the social studies. If a secondary teacher has a thirty-minute discussion period, followed by a twenty-minute period of more structured lecture in another area, then the observer usually makes two separate matrices. Matrices are more meaningful when they represent a single type of activity or work.

After the observer tabulates a matrix, he then has to describe the classroom interaction. There are several ways of doing this, but he begins by reporting the different kinds of statements in terms of percentages. The first step is computing the percentage of tallies in each column to determine the proportion of the total interaction in the observed classroom situation found in each category. This is done by dividing each of the column totals, 1 through 10, by the total number of tallies in the matrix. A similar procedure is used to determine the percentage of total teacher talk in each category. This is done by dividing the total of each category, 1 through 7, by the sum of these seven categories. For example in Table 2 the teacher had 105 tallies in columns 1-7. If 10 of these tallies are in column 3, then 10 is divided by 105, and the amount of teacher talk that falls into category 3 is approximately 9½ per cent of the total amount of teacher talk. The pattern of interaction that the teacher has used with the class is now evident.

The total percentage of teacher talk that is of prime importance in interpreting the matrix is found by dividing the total number of tallies in columns 1 through 7 by the total number of tallies in the matrix. There are 150 tallies in the matrix, 105 of which are in columns 1–7 (Table 2). This teacher talked 70 per cent of the total observation time.

					Second						
		1	2	3	4	5	6	7	8	9	10
	1	1				1				1	
	2		4	1					2		
	3		1	6	1				2		
	4			1	14				5		
First	5	1				48			6		
	6						1		4		
	7							4	1		
	8		2	2	5	6	4		11		
	9	1						1		9	1
	10									1	2
	Total	3	7	10	20	55	5	5	30	12	3
	%	2	4½	9½	13½	36½	3½	3½	20	8	2

Matrix Total 150

TEACHER TALK

Columns 1-7 = 105
105 ÷ 150 = 70%

STUDENT TALK

Columns 8-9 = 42
42 ÷ 150 = 28%

Indirect (1-4) ÷ Direct (1-4) plus (5-7) = I/D Ratio

$$40 \div 40 \text{ plus } 65 = \frac{40}{105} = .38$$

Indirect (1-3) ÷ Direct (1-3) plus (6-7) = Revised I/D Ratio

$$20 \div 20 \text{ plus } 10 = \frac{20}{30} = .67$$

TABLE 2. A Typical Illustration

To find the percentage of student talk, the total number of tallies in columns 8 and 9 is divided by the total number of tallies in the matrix. Assuming that columns 8 and 9 contained 42 tallies, the students talked 28 per cent of the time. A total of three tallies in column 10, when divided by 150, shows that 2 per cent of the time was spent in silence or confusion.

Next the observer focuses on the relative number of indirect and direct teacher statements. The total number of tallies in columns 1, 2, 3, and 4 is divided by the total number of tallies in columns 5, 6, and 7, plus the total in columns 1, 2, 3, and 4, to find the I/D ratio or the ratio of indirect to direct teacher statements. An I/D ratio of .5 means that for every indirect statement there was one direct statement; and I/D ratio of .67 means that for every two indirect statements there was only one direct statement, etc.

A revised I/D ratio is used to find the kind of emphasis given to motivation and control in a particular classroom. The number of tallies in columns 1, 2, and 3 is divided by the number of tallies in columns 1, 2, 3, plus those in 6 and 7, to find this revised ratio. Categories 1, 2, 3, 6, and 7 are more concerned with motivation and control in the classroom and less concerned with the actual presentation of subject matter. This ratio eliminates the effects of categories 4 and 5, lecture and asking questions, and gives information about whether the teacher is direct or indirect in his approach.